purely postcolonial phenomenon, is dependent on great-power unity (or disunity), and is severely handicapped by lack of advance planning. The author finds these explanations wanting but suggests that each particular operation does depend to a large extent on the attitudes of the major powers. He concludes that peace-keeping, because it plays a significant role in maintaining international security, will probably continue to be carried on for some time. His book is essential reading for anyone interested in the problems of preserving the security and, indeed, ensuring the survival of the world's nations.

THE AUTHOR: Alan James is a senior lecturer in international relations at the London School of Economics. In 1968, he was a Rockefeller research fellow in international organization at the School of International Affairs, Columbia University. He has contributed articles to a variety of journals in the field of international relations.

STUDIES IN INTERNATIONAL SECURITY

*

I. Nato in the 1960s *by Alastair Buchan*

II. The Control of the Arms Race *by Hedley Bull*

III. Men in Uniform *by M. R. D. Foot*

IV. World Order and New States *by Peter Calvocoressi*

V. The Spread of Nuclear Weapons *by Leonard Beaton and John Maddox*

VI. Arms and Stability in Europe *by Alastair Buchan and Philip Windsor*

VII. Strategic Mobility *by Neville Brown*

VIII. The Security of Southern Asia *by D. E. Kennedy*

IX. China and the Peace of Asia *ed. Alastair Buchan*

X. Defeating Communist Insurgency *by Robert Thompson*

XI. The Sea in Modern Strategy *by L. W. Martin*

STUDIES IN INTERNATIONAL SECURITY: 12

THE POLITICS
OF PEACE-KEEPING

Alan James

Published for The Institute
for Strategic Studies

FREDERICK A. PRAEGER, Publishers

New York · Washington

BOOKS THAT MATTER

Published in the United States of America in 1969
by Frederick A. Praeger, Inc., Publishers
111 Fourth Avenue, New York, N.Y. 10003

Library of Congress Catalog Card Number: 68-19852

Printed in Great Britain

To My Mother and Father

ALAN JAMES is Senior Lecturer in International Relations at the London School of Economics. In 1968 he was a Rockefeller Research Fellow in International Organization at the Institute of War and Peace Studies, Columbia University, New York.

Contents

Chapter	page
1. Peace-keeping in International Politics	1

PART ONE: *PATCHING-UP*

2. Investigation	15
3. Mediation	36
4. Supervision	90
5. Administration	130

PART TWO: *PROPHYLAXIS*

6. Accusation	177
7. Sedation	260
8. Obstruction	294
9. Refrigeration	337

PART THREE: *PROSELYTISM*

10. Invalidation	371
11. Coercion	402

*   *   *

12. The Powers and Peace-keeping	424
Bibliography	441
Index	445

Acknowledgements

THIS study of the UN's peace-keeping operations up to mid-1968 has been written under the auspices of the Institute for Strategic Studies on the basis of a grant received by the Institute in 1965 from the Carnegie Endowment for International Peace. I would like to acknowledge my debt to the Endowment, and also to the Institute and its Director, Alastair Buchan, for inviting me to undertake the study. I am particularly grateful to Alastair Buchan for his generous encouragement, advice, and, not least, for his patience throughout the period of research and writing.

The Endowment's grant made it possible for me to visit North America and the Middle East during 1966, and my thanks are due to the many governmental and UN officials who willingly assisted my research. It also enabled me to take a term's leave from the London School of Economics and Political Science in the same year, for which I record my appreciation to the School and my colleagues in the International Relations Department. For the whole of 1968 I am visiting Columbia University, New York, as a Rockefeller Research Fellow in International Organization, and I wish to express my gratitude to the Director of this Research Programme, Professor Leland M. Goodrich, for having allowed me time to finish the book.

Although he has had no direct part in it, this work owes much to Professor C. A. W. Manning, to whom my intellectual debt is very great indeed. For having helped to launch me upon it, I thank Professors Hedley Bull and Geoffrey Goodwin. A number of typists have coped with the manuscript, the bulk of the task being performed, with great efficiency, by Miss Joan T. Breslin.

Above all, I am indebted to my wife for her cheerfulness, immense patience, and unfailing support.

Chapter 1

Peace-keeping in International Politics

'PEACE-KEEPING', as applied to the United Nations, is a term which has been given a variety of meanings. They range from the missions which have been undertaken by international armies down, ever more inclusively, to the activities of an individual who has been sent to the field on some political task. Not often, however, does the term denote the threat or use of force to deter or repel aggression, despite the fact that action of this kind is a traditional and important way of keeping peace. In part this reflects the practical consideration that the UN's assumption of such a role has not been a live issue since 'peace-keeping' came into general use. But it is also attributable to the fact that defensive military action by a universal or quasi-universal organization has for the past 50 years commonly been referred to as 'collective security'. And, while there is much argument as to what is properly brought within the category of peace-keeping, there is widespread agreement that collective security should be excluded.

This is not so much due to semantic conservatism as to the circumstances in which 'peace-keeping' entered the international vocabulary. For the term emerged from what amounted to a major alteration in the UN's objects and activities, giving the new situation distinctive verbal recognition. The UN had been set up principally as a further and better attempt to implement collective security. But within a few years it was evident that the deepening division between its two chief members put a very serious obstacle in the way of this goal. Each camp therefore began to make its own arrangements for defence, and the UN seemed to be faced with impotence, if not disintegration. However, the events which followed the invasion of South Korea by the Communist regime of the North in June 1950 raised hopes in some quarters that the UN might, after all, be able to play a significant role in the security field. For the Security Council immediately recommended that members should help the South to repel the Northern attack, and subsequently created an American-led UN Command for this purpose. It was able to take these decisions because the Soviet Union was boycotting its meetings at this time; had things been otherwise the Western initiative in the Council would undoubtedly have met with a veto.[1] Therefore the General Assembly, by a 'Uniting for Peace' resolution of November 1950, tried to clear the decks for future action by asserting its right (which some would not have regarded as being in question) to make recommendations for the maintenance of peace when the Council was blocked by a veto. But the exceedingly meagre response to the Assembly's enquiries concerning the forces which members were willing to place at its disposal, together with the renewed attention given by the rival blocs to the strengthening of their alliance systems, showed the true worth which was put on the UN as a source of security. Evidently the Organization's Korean experience was a false start, if, indeed, it was a start at all.

In 1956, however, the UN was given another shot in the arm, which proved to be very much more significant than the one it had received from the Korean episode. It arose out of the joint Anglo-French-Israeli attack on Egypt, which was launched at the end of October. That aspect of the enterprise which represented a rather belated attempt by two major Powers to discipline one of their lesser fellows was, by some standards, a milk-and-water affair, and evoked a fair measure of quiet sympathy. But, officially, the world was aghast at the sight of a non-aligned and relatively weak state being assaulted by two colonial Powers. Clearly something had to be done, but what could be done was less clear. The Afro-Asians were unable and the United States was unwilling to bring armed force to bear on the invaders, and, whatever she said in public, the Soviet Union was not prepared to make such a move on her own. However, there was a general readiness to use all other forms of pressure, and the United States, in particular, was anxious to bring the embarrassing affair to an early close. She therefore encouraged Mr Lester Pearson, of Canada, to go forward with his proposal for the establishment, with the consent of those concerned, of a UN force. The idea was eagerly endorsed by the General Assembly, and within a fortnight the first members of the UN Emergency Force (UNEF) had arrived in Egypt.

UNEF's immediate purpose was to supervise the cease-fire and provide face-saving cover for the malefactors, withdrawal. But what was to prove its major role only began when, the invaders eventually having left, it encamped at the Egyptian–Israeli border in the hope of keeping the erstwhile combatants apart. The method

[1] Two conditions must be satisfied for the Security Council to take a decision on a non-procedural matter. They are that the draft resolution must
    (a) obtain at least seven votes (nine after the Council's enlargement from 11 to 15 in 1965) and
    (b) not be voted against by any of the Council's five permanent members: Britain, China, France, the Soviet Union, and the United States. A permanent member's negative vote in respect of a draft resolution which satisfies condition (a) is popularly called a veto.

by which it planned to do this was very different from the one out-lined in the Charter, which envisaged aggressors being deterred or thrown back by the might of the major Powers. UNEF, by contrast, was made up of contingents from middle and small Powers, was neither designed nor equipped for fighting, except in self-defence, and relied upon its mere presence to produce a deterrent effect. The gambit seemed to be successful, for the border soon became quieter than it had ever been since Israel's creation in 1948, and as a result UNEF was widely hailed for its beneficial properties.

This gave rise to considerable discussion regarding the contribu-tion which non-fighting forces could make towards the maintenance of peace. Such activities were very congenial to the growing number of non-aligned states in the UN, who were repelled by collective security on account of its reliance on armed force and the cold war connotations which it had attracted during the UN's first decade. The Western Powers, too, were generally in favour of the UN's new course, for on the whole it promised to contribute to stability in areas which could not be covered by their private defensive arrange-ments. Thus, during the next 10 years, several other such forces were established. One was sent to the Congo in 1960 to assist that very new state with the maintenance of law and order, remaining until 1964. Another Force was sent to West New Guinea in October 1962 to maintain order while the territory was administered by the UN. This was part of an arrangement for its transfer from the Netherlands to Indonesia, and the period of international rule lasted for seven months. Finally, in 1964, a Force took up positions between the Greek and Turkish communities in Cyprus, and is still in being. Meanwhile, UNEF remained at the Egyptian–Israeli border until its abrupt withdrawal in May 1967.

At an early point these developments came to be spoken of as 'peace-keeping'. The term was used not just for its descriptive value but also as a means of differentiating the new procedures from those other, somewhat discredited aspirations which went by the name of collective security. The cardinal distinction between the two activities was seen to lie in their attitudes towards the associated issues of force and consent, collective security relying, ultimately, on the mandatory use of force, while peace-keeping eschewed force, except in self-defence, and required the consent of the host state for the admission of UN personnel.

So defined, the question arose as to why 'peace-keeping' should refer only to the new kind of UN force. The Organization had mounted a number of other non-violent operations which, while of lesser magnitude, could hardly be regarded as insignificant, and certainly had to do with keeping the peace. Some of these predated the events which were first referred to as peace-keeping. Since 1948, for example, the UN Truce Supervision Organization had been trying to maintain quiet along the Arab–Israeli borders, and from 1949 a UN Military Observer Group had been supervising the cease-fire between India and Pakistan in Kashmir. Both of these operations are still in progress, although in the Middle East there have been drastic changes in the lines which it is the UN's duty to watch. Also in the late 1940s, the UN set up a Special Committee on the Balkans which for a few years investigated the extent of foreign interference in Greece.

Activity of this order continued alongside the establishment of forces in the post-Suez period. In 1958, for example, a UN Observation Group spent some months in the Lebanon, endeavouring to check any infiltration into that country from the Syrian province of the United Arab Republic. In 1963 a UN mission began a year-long effort to observe the implementation by The UAR and Saudi Arabia of their undertakings to stop interfering in the Yemen. And in 1965 a UN team was established to supervise the withdrawal of Indian and Pakistan troops from each other's territory. From a number of viewpoints operations such as these seemed essentially similar to those larger enterprises which were being described as instances of peace-keeping, and many commentators used the term accordingly.

If, however, the category of peace-keeping is to be extended beyond international forces, there is no very obvious reason why it should not also include those smaller operations, chiefly of a fact-finding or conciliatory nature, which the UN has established on numerous occasions in the name of peace. From 1947 to 1949, for example, the UN was deeply involved in an effort to secure an agreement regarding the establishment of Indonesia. Twenty years later, the Organization's representative was conspicuously active in trying to bring peace to the Middle East following the Arab-Israeli war of June 1967. And throughout its life the UN has freely resorted to investigatory missions in connection with cold war and colonial disputes.

On colonial and allied issues the UN has not always played a passive role. In recent years it has sometimes turned its attention to the possibility of using force to remedy situations which, although they cannot be described in terms of actual or potential aggression, are nevertheless deemed to present a threat to peace. The UN force in the Congo provided the first instance of this, by taking action in 1961 and 1962 which had the effect of toppling Tshombe's secessionist regime in Katanga. In 1966 the Security Council authorized Britain to use force on the high seas to prevent oil from reaching Rhodesia, and later it ordered mandatory economic sanctions against this maverick territory. Many members would be only too pleased to see the UN taking similar, and stronger, measures against Portugal's colonies and South Africa, and may be relied upon to keep pressing the Council in this direction.

Clearly, such action cannot be spoken of as peace-keeping if the concept is to be limited to non-fighting forces and other operations of a non-violebt character. Accordingly, it is often described and distinguished by the word 'enforcement' (although the UN's operations in Katanga were not identified in this way). But the kind of enforcement which was envisaged in 1945 and which is mentioned in the Charter consists of measures taken in support of the principle of collective security. The use of force to secure change is something quite different, and also, moreover, is sometimes referred to as an instance of peace-keeping. In conjunction with what has already been said about the possible ambit of the term, this gives rise to a very broad definition.[2] In fact, on this meaning, so many and such a variety of cases are brought under the heading of peace-keeping as to attract the criticism that the category loses its point. There is force in this claim. But to restrict the concept in any of the various possible ways would create some rather insubstantial divisions, and obscure the wide range of missions which the UN has undertaken, formally, at least, in the cause of peace. And as the UN's activities in the field comprise an area of experience which is significant from the international society's viewpoint as well as from a narrower institutional perspetive, there is considerable merit in trying to see them as a whole. The most comprehensive definition of peace-keeping would to a very great extent permit such an approach, for of all the UN's political operations it would exclude only its part in the Korean war—the UN's single attempt at collective security.[3] It will, therefore, be adopted in this book.

The large number of cases which fall within the widest definition of peace-keeping could be divided on the basis of whether they have

[2] If, in future, the UN should find itself able to use force for defensive purposes—by way of action on behalf of one small Power against another, perhaps—it is not at all inconceivable that such measures will be spoken of as much in terms of a further extension of peace-keeping as of a revival of collective security. In one sense this would not be inappropriate, for although the UN's history and generally accepted usage have both drawn a sharp distinction between collective security and peace-keeping, which is followed here, this should not be allowed to obscure the fact that they are by no means without affinity. The object of collective security is to prevent physical breaches of the peace, and many peace-keeping operations have the same aim. The difference between them is that the use of force for this purpose is regarded as appropriate for collective security but not, at least as yet, for activity which attracts the term peace-keeping.

[3] On the UN and Korea, see Leland M. Goodrich: *Korea: A Study of United States Policy in the United Nations* (New York: Council on Foreign Relations, 1956).

involved the use of an international force. This has the advantage of bringing together those of the UN's operations which, by virtue of their size and composition, are usually regarded as the most significant, and which give rise to a number of common problems—of, for example, command, communications, supply, and techniques. Such an approach might attract the student who wishes to explore organizational questions of a narrower kind. UN forces, however, have not been given identical tasks, and the sorts which have been allotted to them have also been carried out by missions organized on different lines. Thus, someone who is chiefly interested in the variety of mandates which the UN has tried to execute might well base his analysis on categories such as fact finding, conciliation, observation, interposition, and international government. By contrast, a lawyer would probably wish to distinguish, for example, the different legal bases on which the UN has established its operations and the kinds of legal relationship with member states to which the Organization's activities have given rise.

Another possibility would be to concentrate on the nature of the disputes which attract UN operations. They could be classified with reference to the identity of the parties: Great Power relations, middle power adventures, small power quarrels, for example. Alternatively, the substance of the issue could provide the basic criterion, giving rise to categories such as border problems, intervention, internal disorder, and colonial and racial questions. Whichever angle is chosen, attention could be paid to the factors which condition the likelihood of the dispute and success of a UN mission. Yet another analysis could turn on the attitudes of the host or prospective host states towards having a UN group on their soil. There is a whole range of responses here, from great keenness at one end to undisguised hostility at the other. An endeavour could be made to account for these attitudes and to see if there is any correlation between them and the diverse types of operation which the UN may conduct. Both these approaches would be very relevant to the concerns of the student of international relations and organization. But for someone who is anxious to illuminate the politics of peace-keeping, a rather different focus may be more valuable.

To speak of the UN as a political body is a truism. Its members do not come to it humbly and submissively, as to an oracle, if only because they, collectively, are it, the Organization. Some members may have an open mind on some of the issues which are considered in its chambers. Policies may occasionally be changed as a result of the UN's debates or, more likely, of the diplomatic pressures which precede and follow its public activities. Over a period of years some viewpoints may undergo a radical alteration on account of the perseverance of a group of members. But on most of the items discussed at the UN, states will have broadly clear-cut views, and will try to ensure that they prevail. Thus the UN is the scene of a continuing discussion regarding policy, and the form of words which eventually receives endorsement, and will henceforth be the UN's position on the matter, is the product of this process. It represents success, in varying degrees, for a number of states; failure, maybe, for some others. This is perhaps less well-recognized with regard to peace-keeping than to other questions. But, just as UN resolutions are an attempt to exert influence in accordance with the majority's view, so also the decision to dispatch a mission to the field will be an effort to affect the international scene in a particular and often a partial way.

It would therefore seem advantageous to analyse peace-keeping operations by asking what, in each case, the UN is trying to do. That it is not always hoping to reach the same end has possibly been obscured by the mesmeric effect of frequent invocations of the 'peace and security' theme. Everything which the UN does officially in the political field is officially done towards these goals. However, they can be sought in rather different directions. They may be mutually contradictory. It is even conceivable that they might be used as a cover for activity which by no stretch of some observers' imagination could be regarded as falling within their ambit. Thus there is a good case for directing attention to the functions which the UN hopes its operations will fulfil. By doing so one is looking at some of the more important ways in which the Organization endeavours to play a role in international politics.

When the UN's peace-keeping operations are considered in this light, they fall into three categories. The first, which may be called 'patching-up', consists of activity which is intended to bring dis-putants to an agreement or to assist in the execution of a settlement. The UN's attempt in 1947–8 to ensure that Britain's impending departure from Palestine was followed by an orderly transfer of power is a case in point, as is its supervision of the withdrawal of troops from Egypt after the Suez war. As the second example sug-gests, an outward accommodation does not necessarily remove the source of hostility, which is why the term patching-up, with its rather tentative suggestion of optimism, is more appropriate than one which implies a deeper-seated reconciliation. Peace-keeping of this kind is, in fact, often in the nature of surgery the long-term success of which is in some doubt. Moreover, it may be that in offering its services or in pressing the parties to accept its help, the UN is moved by other than disinterested reasons, by, for example, a wish to assist the disputant who is likely to come off best in a non-violent settlement. This was very much its role in the later stages of the Indonesian struggle for independence. But for the present purpose the criterion is not the UN's motive but its goal. What brings an operation within the patching-up category is its encouragement of or association with an agreed resolution of tension.

Often, however, the UN is faced with conditions which are at least potentially threatening and which fail to offer a realistic prospect of a negotiated settlement. It may therefore adopt a second, prophylactic, approach, taking action which is designed to prevent the situation from deteriorating. It may hope that this will provide the basis for a subsequent improvement in relations between the parties, but the immediate aim in these circumstances is to maintain calm or prevent violence. In theory, such moves could be taken at a very early stage, when difficulties are no more than latent. This was the object of the 1967 proposal that upon South Arabia's independence the island of Perim, which lies at the mouth of the Red Sea, should be transferred to the UN. But the long-term is not the most persuasive view in politics, and it is very much more likely that the UN's prophylactic resources will be utilized to keep an already tense situation from getting worse. It was only, for example, after there had been fighting in Kashmir that the UN was called upon to help in preventing its recurrence by watching over the cease-fire line. Likewise in Cyprus, it was the crisis which erupted at the end of 1963 which led to the involvement of a UN Force charged with the task of preventing inter-communal violence.

Operations of this nature may not differ substantially in their make-up or activity from those which fall into the first category, for the distinction between the two is not based on the specific mandates which the UN gives to its missions, but on the wider purposes which their establishment is intended to serve. Both since 1949 and in the months following the Indo-Pakistan war of 1965, for example, the UN's main task in Kashmire has been supervision. But its long-term role has been the essentially prophylactic one of keeping a dangerous situation in check, whereas the group which was sent to the sub-continent in 1965 was designed to assist in the restoration of 'normal' conditions. Similarly, in Cyprus the UN Force is simply trying to hold the ring, whereas the Force which maintained order in West New Guinea in 1962–3 was playing a part in the winding-up of a long dispute. And the question of motive has no more bearing on the allocation of cases to this second category than it has to the first. It may be that a majority of members favours this or that action less out of an abstract concern for peace than because of their particular interest in keeping the disputants quiet or in preventing the weaker party from being overrun. But this does not affect the role of such operations as the means whereby the UN hopes to exert a quietening influence on a worrying or turbulent area.

The third and final peace-keeping category comprises those UN operations which are neither conciliatory nor preventive but which are instituted out of a desire to upset certain aspects of the established order of things. They are instances of UN proselytism, the Organization seeking to act as an instrument of change in order to rid the international society of situations which the majority regard as little better than sinful. In other contexts such action might be called, pejoratively, 'power politics', but here it is usually exempt from such criticism on the ground that the world community, in the shape of the UN, is going about its legitimate business of enforcing standards. It may be that a country gives offence only on account of a single strand of its foreign or domestic policy, but one so outrageous and so closely associated with the ruling group as to justify, in the UN's eye, the encouragement of the regime's overthrow. South Africa provides the major instance of this in its policy of apartheid. The same course may be favoured in respect of a country whose extreme unpopularity stems less from specific acts man from its general ideological character and outlook, in which case fairly minor cases of misbehaviour on its part may serve as pegs for a hostile UN campaign. At the height of the cold war the Western states sometimes tried to use this ploy against their Communist rivals, and the UN's approach to the Katangan problem would also fall in here. Or a Power's determined effort to retain its overseas possessions may stimulate the UN to adopt measures which are designed to produce a reassessment of that policy, as in the case of the Portuguese colonies.

The UN's various peace-keeping activities do not always slot neatly into this threefold framework. Sometimes the Organization has engaged, at the same time and in relation to the same situation, in both patching-up and prophylactic endeavours, as in Kashmir, Indonesia, and Cyprus. Occasionally a single mission has been given both tasks, one instance of this being the office of UN Mediator for Palestine which was established in 1948. Then, too, an operation may make an informal transfer from one function to another. For the first few months of its life the UN Emergency Force helped to patch-up the Middle Eastern crisis by supervising the withdrawal of the forces which had invaded Egypt. After its arrival at the Egyptian–Israeli border in March 1957 it took on a prophylactic role. Similarly, it became increasingly clear during 1961 that the UN's Congo Force was assuming a proselytizing mantle, having moved in this direction from a task which was chiefly prophylactic but which also, at the outset, had distinctive patching-up characteristics. In relation to such cases, therefore, it may be desirable to split up the discussion of the UN's involvement.

A more difficult problem can stem from the fact that the UN's purpose in setting up a 'presence' is not always clear. The mandate which is given to a mission is usually a good guide to the role which the UN, often meaning a majority of UN members, wishes it to play. But it is not invariably so. Sometimes, therefore, it is necessary to look behind the formal terms of reference to the Organization's debates and the attitudes of its members. This, however, is by no means calculated to produce a confident answer. In the case of the Observer Group which was sent to the Lebanon in 1958, for example, it is arguable that the UN's purpose was to patch-up the dispute between the host country and Syria by showing that there was no significant infiltration from the latter into the former. But it can also be argued, more convincingly, that most of the Security Council members who favoured the Group's dispatch did so in the hope and expectation that it would serve the prophylactic function of exposing and deterring a Nasserist plot to subvert the Lebanon's independence. Thus the allocation of an operation to one category rather than another is sometimes a very subjective matter.

These problems, however, do not substantially detract from the value, for the student of UN and international politics, of an analysis of peace-keeping operations on the basis of the purposes for which they are established. It will therefore form the framework for this book. Within each of the three categories which emerge in answer to the question 'what?', the UN's activities will be subdivided with reference to the question 'how?', this being designed to illustrate the different ways in which the same goal may be sought. It gives rise to four methods of patching-up, four of prophylaxis, and two of proselytism.

One possible route to an agreement lies through an impartial investigation into the facts of the case. The theory is that this course will not just reveal the true situation but will also point to an obvious solution, which the parties can hardly do other than accept. Especially during its early years, the League of Nations relied heavily, and successfully, on this device, and the UN has also tried to put it to good use.] In 1948, for example, the UN recommended the holding of a plebiscite in Kashmir, a goal which it has pursued ever since, though with decreasing energy. Similarly, in 1963, when Indonesia and, to a lesser extent, the Philippines were objecting to the creation of the federal state of Malaysia, a UN mission made a brief visit to North Borneo and Sarawak to ascertain whether the

---

4 While focusing on the UN, this book will also consider, briefly, the League's peace-keeping operations.

two territories really wished to join Malaya and Singapore. But conditions since 1945 have not favoured investigation as a means of settling disputes. The UN has found mediation a more suitable procedure and there have been a number of instances of its use, ranging from the dispatch of a Good Offices Committee to Indonesia in 1947 to the appointment of a representative of the Secretary-General to try to obtain a Middle Eastern peace settlement following the 1967 war.

As well as conducting operations which are intended to shepherd disputants towards an understanding, the UN can also help to repair quarrels by being prepared to assist in the implementation of an agreement. Thus, if the UN is willing to supervise the parties execution of their promises, this may do more than increase the likelihood of their actual fulfilment. It may also, where doubts exist as to the good faith of any of those who are involved, encourage the making of the agreement in the first place. The part which the UN was scheduled to play in connection with the UAR and Saudi Arabian undertakings of 1963 to stop interfering in the Yemen, for example, may well have helped to secure those undertakings. And the UN's anticipated role in relation to the winding-up of the Cuban missile crisis of 1962 may have had a similar significance. Certainly, when the Cuban arrangement fell through, other means of supervision had to be found. The UN may go beyond this activity, however, to the assumption of an administrative role. Its ability to do so may permit a peaceful and perhaps a face-saving solution to a territorial dispute by enabling the area in question to spend an interim period in international hands. The way in which the issue of West New Guinea was resolved is an example. Equally, the UN could take over permanent responsibility for a disputed area, along the lines of the plans which it approved in 1947 for the internationalization of Trieste and Jerusalem.

The forms of prophylactic activity which are open to the UN are no less varied. One is the device of accusation, by which is meant the garnering of facts on the assumption that they will expose, and so may check, unpopular behaviour. There are many examples of this procedure, an early case being the UN's Special Committee on the Balkans which was established in 1947. The UN Observer Group in the Lebanon was meant by many members to fulfil the same role, as was the Secretary-General's representative in Dominica during the period of American-led intervention from 1965 to 1966. Another and contrasting way of trying to reach the same end is for the UN to make private representations in favour of restraint, particularly to officers of the armed forces on each side of a tense frontier or demarcation line. Such activities may be termed sedation, the most notable case of it being the work of the Truce Supervision Organization along the Arab–Israeli borders since 1948.

A more ambitious task for the UN, at least in terms of the number of personnel involved, is that of obstruction: the placing of a UN force between two disputing states or communities in the hope that, while relatively small, it may serve as something of a barrier to the outbreak of violence. The UN Emergency Force fulfilled this role for 10 years, and the UN Force in Cyprus has played a similar part since 1964. It is also open to the UN to try its hand at the refrigeration of areas which give rise to tension by taking them over, formally or informally, until tempers have cooled or a settlement can be reached. Proposals to this effect may even be made with a view to removing no more than a possible source of trouble, as with Perim in 1967 and the former Italian colonies 20 years earlier. More usually, however, such ideas are likely to arise from an existing crisis, the 1948 suggestion that Palestine be placed under international trusteeship being a case in point. The single instance of UN action along these lines was the dispatch of a force to the Congo in 1960, the principal international object of which, in the early stages, was to insulate the country against the possibility of Great Power intervention.

There are only two types of proselytism. The first employs that familiar device—the fact-finding mission. Here, however, it is used in the expectation that its report will be so damaging as to suggest that the regime in question is morally unfit for continued rule. The aim, in short, is invalidation. It has been pursued in some cold war contexts and, most energetically, in respect of colonialism and racialism. However, the unresponsiveness of the criticized governments to the UN's hints that they should give up part of their domains or make way for more acceptable regimes, has turned some thoughts towards coercion as a more effective expression of the UN's proselytizing zeal. Two such operations, or something like them, have been seen to date: against Katanga and Rhodesia. But these were rather exceptional cases in that both the entities which felt the world's disfavour could be shown to be illegitimate in terms of another state's constitutional law. Moreover, the relatively drastic Katangan action grew out of the fact that a Force was already in the Congo for a different purpose. In respect of issues of a more squarely international character, the UN may find that the threat or use of force, or even of economic pressure, is less easily available. Nevertheless, it is unlikely that the last has been heard of coercive proselytism.

PART ONE

Patching-Up

Chapter 2

Investigation

ONE approach to the patching-up of international quarrels rests on the premise that many disputes are essentially accidental and non-contrived. It is further assumed that the parties find their hostile relationship basically distasteful but have difficulty in getting out of it on their own. In such circumstances it is often held that the path to an honourable settlement lies through an impartial investigation into the facts of the case. This procedure may simply provide time for the cooling of tempers. It may remove misunderstandings. It may open the way for a dignified and face-saving acceptance of responsibility for the dispute. Or it may be a means of obtaining acceptable terms for the resolution of a problem.

Generally, however, states do not warm to the thought of their activities, policies, or popularity being the object of an independent appraisal. If, therefore, this method of pacific settlement is to be employed, those concerned often have to be nudged, cajoled, or pushed into accepting the idea, and there are certain advantages in channelling such pressure through an international institution. For, on the one hand, states may be reluctant to press for this device individually, or even in concert. And, on the other, the parties may be more willing to give way to representations from an institutional source. This procedure also makes it more likely that the solution to which the investigation points will be put into effect, on account of the appointing body having a permanent existence and also, probably, an interest in bringing the matter to a successful conclusion.

If an institution is to play this role, it will usually need the backing of its more prominent members, or at least the keen support of some and the assent of the others. It is by no means the case that such conditions can be relied upon. Even if the most important members are on relatively good terms, joint enthusiasm may, for a variety of reasons, be difficult to secure in a specific case. To a remarkable degree, however, the years immediately following World War I were suitable for the settlement of quarrels by way of investigation. In the first place, there were a number of disputes between states who were favourably disposed towards agreement, some of them being of a basically conciliatory outlook while others, having recently been defeated, were not in a position to adopt any other attitude. Secondly, the newly established League of Nations was dominated by Britain and France, who, although having their differences, were broadly agreed on the need to keep the peace and were prepared to move with some energy in the service of that end. As they could make their writ run over most of Europe, where the majority of the period's disputes took place, their wishes commanded respect. Additionally, the League's Covenant reflected the theory that investigation is a very suitable means of pacific settlement. Thus, an independent enquiry into the facts was an important element in the resolution of several disputes.

The first such case concerned the Aaland Islands, which, lying across the entrance to the Gulf of Bothnia, were held by Finland but claimed by Sweden. There was some danger of war, but the situation was much improved by the League's appointment in 1920 of a Commission of Enquiry. In the following year the dispute was settled on the basis of the Commission's recommendations, which were in Finland's favour. The same device was used in 1923–4 with a view to settling a dispute over Memel, which was German in population, of considerable commercial importance to Poland, but held by Lithuania. Again the report was in favour of the sitting tenant, and after endorsement by the League was accepted, although unwillingly, by the other interested parties. (Fifteen years later, when power in the area was distributed very differently, Germany took her revenge.)

The League's attention during its early years was overwhelmingly focused on the European scene. But in 1924 its investigators were sent to Mosul, which had been allocated to the new state of Iraq but was claimed by Turkey. The Commission of Enquiry recommended that virtually all of the province should go to Iraq, as the lesser of the evils in the eyes of the local population, provided that Britain's mandate over Iraq continued for some considerable time. The condition was disliked by Britain, and circumvented by the provision that the mandate would terminate if and when Iraq was admitted to the League. Turkey had substantive objections to the recommendation, but in 1926 she made the best of a bad job by accepting it. However, the League was now in very bad odour with her, and she therefore halted the steps she had been taking towards membership. She did not join until 1932, just a few months before Iraq, by which time Mosul was not a serious issue.

A Commission of Enquiry was also used to settle a Greco–Bulgarian frontier skirmish which occurred in 1925, its recommendations being accepted without hesitation. The frequent description of this case as the League's greatest success, however, is due to the alacrity with which the parties accepted the League's demand for a cease-fire. London, Paris, and Rome were all agreed that the quarrel should be swiftly snuffed out, and with the Treaty of Locarno only a week behind them, were in just the right mood to assert themselves in the cause of European tranquillity. There was talk of sanctions and the League Secretariat made some unofficial enquiries about the problems involved in the organization of a naval demonstration. Greece, militarily the stronger of the disputants, was particularly susceptible to such pressure, and was also in dire economic straits and suffering from political unrest. Bulgaria had to a large extent been disarmed under the Treaty of Neuilly and was diplomatically isolated: a feeler which she put out towards Germany met with no response. Thus, neither party was in a position to defy the Powers. Moreover, their dispute was no more than an inflated border incident. It could therefore be abandoned with relative ease, and was also very suitable for patching-up through the medium of an impartial investigation into its immediate origins.

At this point the prospect for the League, Europe, and so for the world, looked bright. But the League's record was not unblemished. In 1920 it had decided to settle a dispute between Poland and Lithuania over Vilna on the basis of a plebiscite conducted by the League in the presence of an international supervisory force. The city was Lithuania's historic capital but the majority of its inhabitants were Poles, and as the League's arrangements took shape so Poland warmed to them, thinking no doubt, of her numerical superiority. By the same token Lithuania became increasingly disenchanted and began to speak, as Poland had done elsewhere, of the superiority of the historic over the democratic principle. Her prevarications accumulated, and to them was added a Soviet objection to the presence of an international force near its borders. As a result the nine states who were to make up a 1500-man force began to get nervous: most of them were in very much a post-war frame of mind and were not disposed to take any risks for an area which was, by contemporary means of communication, far away, and of which it could certainly be said that their people knew nothing. Thus in March 1921 the idea of a plebiscite was dropped, and Vilna remained in Poland's possession.

An awkward disputant and difficult circumstances also accounted for the League's failure to investigate the situation which gave rise to the case of Corfu, despite the fact that, in theory, investigation would have been a very suitable device. In August 1923 an Italian general and four subordinates had been murdered in Greece while

delimiting, on behalf of the Conference of Ambassadors, the boundary between that country and Albania. Some of Mussolini's humiliating demands having been refused, Italy bombarded and occupied
the Greek island of Corfu, and threatened to withdraw from the
League if it so much as discussed the matter. Effectively, the League
complied, and in a sense this was just as well as it was thus spared
even greater embarrassment. For Mussolini was in a very truculent
mood, and the other Powers were divided. France, being at this
time in occupation of the Ruhr, was not anxious to see Italy hauled
over the coals at Geneva for a like action in the Mediterranean, and
was certainly unwilling to consider joining Britain in a naval demonstration. Britain, for her part, was not prepared to go it alone against
Italy. Hence there was in any event no chance of the League taking
effective action.

Vilna and Corfu indicated the limitations of investigation as a
means of settlement. The 1930s did likewise. In December 1931
the League decided to send a high-powered Commission to Manchuria to investigate China's charge of Japanese aggression. It was
clear, however, that an agreed outcome to this issue was exceedingly
remote, and it is therefore very probable that the intent with which
the Commission was established was prophylactic.[1] In 1933 a Commission of Enquiry was set up in connection with the Chaco war
between Bolivia and Paraguay, but despite its title its activities
were of a mediatory character.[2] In fact, the only instance of the
League seeking an agreement by way of an investigation was its
conduct of a plebiscite in the Saar on 13 January 1935, in accordance
with the Treaty of Versailles. A three-man Plebiscite Commission
and a Supreme Plebiscite Tribunal were appointed, each of them
having an international staff. Order was guaranteed throughout
the period by an international force of 3,300 men which was hastily
assembled from four European countries when first Britain, and then
Germany, dropped their opposition to the idea just a month before
the plebiscite. And for the actual voting a large number of neutral
officials were brought in. As a result, the Saar, which had been
governed by the League since the end of the World War I[3], rejoined
Germany.

This did not effect a lasting improvement in Franco-German
relations. But it did remove a sure source of contention, which was
all the League was required to do and was probably more than anyone else could have done. However, while the League deserves
credit for its handling of the complexities of the plebiscite, the issue

[1] See below, p. 185–191.
[2] See below, p. 41–42.
[3] See below, p. 151–153.

was, in political terms, straightforward: the population was un-mixed, and so could be expected to give a clear-cut decision, as proved to be the case; the area was already in international hands; and once Germany had abandoned her campaign of propaganda and threats, the co-operation of all the interested parties was secured. Even so, it may be doubted whether the problem of the Saar could have been solved at this point by means of a plebiscite had not obligations to hold one been undertaken some 15 years earlier, at a time when Germany had no option but to accept them.[4]

The poverty of the League's later record in the field of patching-up by investigation is a reflection of the uncongenial spirit of the times, of the fact that the 1930s were marked by intransigence and growing division rather than by accommodation and Great Power unity. World War II recharged some of the earlier optimism, but the speedy break-up of the victorious coalition and the establishment of two hostile camps made conditions far less favourable for the use of investigating missions than at any time between the two World Wars. Three points may be noted. In the first place, direct inter-bloc quarrels were beyond amelioration by this means.

Secondly, there was no desire to settle intra-bloc disputes in this way as, quite apart from the unwelcome publicity which would be obtained, the involvement of the UN would be virtually certain also to involve a member of the opposing bloc in the investigating pro-cedure, which would be quite unacceptable. And thirdly, the development of the cold war meant that the Great Powers would hardly be likely to unite their efforts in an endeavour to persuade non-participants to accept international enquiries into their disputes.

As, therefore, it was improbable that those states who were not directly involved in the East-West struggle would be pressed to repair their quarrels by means of investigation, the use made of this procedure largely depended on whether they would turn to it of their own accord. This points to a further post-war circumstance which has militated against its employment, one which concerns the character of those who have remained outside the two major blocs. Most of them are new Afro-Asian states, having until recently been colonial territories, and are relatively small and weak. However, they have been anxious to make themselves heard in international society and are much attached to that part of the UN Charter which

---

[4] On the various League of Nations cases mentioned here, see further F. P. Walters: *A History of the League of Nations* (London: Oxford University Press, 1952) and G. M. Gathorne-Hardy: *A Short History of International Affairs 1920–1939* (London: Oxford University Press, 4th edn., 1950). On the Greco-Bulgarian dispute see also James Barros, 'The Greek-Bulgarian Incident of 1925', reprinted in Joel Larus (ed): *From Collective Security to Preventive Diplomacy* (New York: Wiley, 1965).

declares that the Organization is based on the sovereign equality
of its members. Very jealous of their new status, they have been and
are quick to resent suggestions which appear to threaten it in any
way, and this has led to a desire to keep their affairs wholly in their
own or at best in regional hands. Accordingly, the idea of the UN
investigating their disputes and making proposals for their solution
has appealed to them not at all, for it offends their concept of independence and smacks too much of a hierarchical and paternal
society.

There is another factor which has had a most significant bearing
on the use of this procedure. It relates to the ability of an international organization such as the League or UN to secure a group
of investigators in whom there is general confidence. Once their
report has been issued there may, of course, be a marked change in
the attitude of a party who feels that insufficient account has been
taken of his interests in the case. It would, perhaps, be surprising if
this was not so. But it is essential that prior to this point there should
be a very strong presumption on the part of the states immediately
concerned, and the instructing organization, that the investigating
team will act fairly and justly. If there was not, the outlook for an
agreed settlement would be very poor, for a disputant who distrusted
the fact-finders from the very beginning would not be disposed to
accept proposals which seemed only to confirm his suspicions. It
could also be said that an institution which put such a team into the
field hardly did so with the intention of obtaining an agreement.

The requirements for confidence in an investigating mission are
twofold. Clearly, in the first place, there must be a belief in the
integrity of its members. Whatever their manner of appointment, it
must be possible to rely on their addressing themselves only to the
facts of the dispute, putting on one side all preconceived views, both
national and individual, about the merits of the dispute and the
parties. But this is not enough. For, secondly, it must be possible to
assume that they will look at the dispute in the same way, having
similar ideas about what is important, about the interpretation to
be put on important phenomena, and about the criteria which will
provide the basis for a satisfactory settlement. Putting the point
differently, it is necessary that the investigators have a similar ideological framework, that they see the world through the same kind of
spectacles. If they do not, then it is highly unlikely that they will
be able to reach an agreed assessment of the issue which it is their
duty to investigate, and in those circumstances it is equally, if not
more, unlikely that those who sent them will be able to procure a
peaceful settlement.

This was a factor which was barely relevant to the inter-war period. Most League members would probably have been surprised to be told that there was even a potential obstacle here. After World War II, however, the picture altered considerably, for the growth of enmity between the victorious Powers was accompanied by a serious ideological division. The Soviet Union viewed many international events in a different light from that in which they appeared to Western countries; the content which each side gave to important concepts, such as democracy, freedom, intervention, and peace was far from the same; and Soviet hopes and expectations about the development of the international society differed fundamentally from the views which were common elsewhere. This had the effect not only of deepening the conflict between the Soviet Union and the United States, but also of making their fruitful co-operation in the patching-up of other disputes by means of investigation very much less likely.

The writing was early on the wall. In October 1946 two British destroyers passing through the Corfu Channel, running between Albania and the Greek island of Corfu, were damaged by mines, with the loss of 44 lives. Britain claimed that the mines had recently been laid by Albania and, having failed to obtain satisfaction in direct negotiations with her Communist Government, took the dispute to the Security Council in January 1947. Here conflicting accounts of the facts of the matter were put forward, and the Council therefore appointed a subcommittee to look more closely at the evidence which had been adduced and to come to a view regarding it.[5] The subcommittee was comprised of Australia, Colombia, and Poland, and it failed to agree as the Polish representative, whose Government was well on the way to being formally as well as actually controlled by Communists, could not accept that the facts suggested Albanian responsibility. This, however, was the interpretation which was adopted by most members of the Council, and it was subsequently shared by the International Court of Justice. But their consensus did not produce a settlement, for Albania has resolutely refused to act on it, illustrating the limitations of investigation as a means of ending cold war disputes. In fact such issues have not again attracted any fact-finding activity which could remotely be described as patching-up in character, those UN groups which have examined East-West questions being established with prophylactic or proselytizing intent.

All the other situations in which the UN has tried or proposed investigation as a patching-up device have arisen out of the

[5] The subcommittee did not travel. Nevertheless, it is mentioned here on account of its bearing on the UN's use of mobile missions of enquiry.

B

withdrawal of Western Powers from their overseas possessions. It
has, for example, often been used in connection with the winding-up
of trusteeship arrangements where there was some doubt about the
people's wishes regarding their political future, the UN taking
advantage of its supervisory responsibilities in respect of these
territories to urge and watch over elections or plebiscites.[6] Thus, as
a result of plebiscites held under UN supervision, British Togoland
joined the Gold Coast in 1957 to form the new independent state
of Ghana, and in 1961 the northern and southern parts of the
British Cameroons adhered to Nigeria and the Cameroun Republic
respectively. In French Togoland the administering authority
organized its own plebiscite, and announced that the territory
favoured autonomy within the French Union. The UN, however
not being happy about this, successfully pressed for elections under
its supervision, which returned a Government in favour of independence. The outcome was the emergence of the independent
Republic of Togo in 1960. Western Samoa, too, in what some
regarded as a superfluous plebiscite, opted for independence as from
1 January 1962 but, most unusually, chose to play a limited part
in international relations: she has joined certain international
organizations which are of special interest to her, but not the UN;
for the rest, New Zealand has undertaken to conduct her foreign
relations on an agency basis.

The case of Ruanda-Urundi was less straightforward. The internal
situation, particularly in Ruanda, was unstable, and relations
between Belgium, the administering authority, and the UN Commission which was supposed to be overseeing the movement towards
independence were very bad. But a change of government in
Brussels in April 1961 produced a marked improvement in this
respect, and the Commission was able to supervise elections held in
both territories in September of that year. They had been jointly
administered by Belgium, and the aim of the Commission was to
secure their independence as one unit. However, it failed to obtain an
agreement between their leaders, and so had to recommend that
each come to independence as a separate state. This was what
happened on 1 July 1962 amid considerable foreboding about the
likelihood of their being able to maintain law and order and to
establish good relations with each other.

[6] It is perhaps worth making the point that internationally-supervised or organized plebiscites (or the like), or even temporary international government for the
purpose of securing a free expression of opinion, are included in this Chapter and
not in those headed 'Supervision' or 'Administration' on the ground that they are
instances of settlement by way of investigation. The enquiry into what are regarded
as the relevant facts may entail supervisory or administrative activity on the part
of the UN, but such activity is ancillary to the process of investigation.

These questions were all on the margin of international politics.
By making it as clear as possible to the electorate, covetous neighbours, and to the world at large that the principle of self-determination had been fully complied with, the UN no doubt helped to
minimize any disputes regarding the territories' proper destiny.
But it was their special status and not the threat of international
tension which allowed the UN to play an investigating role. By
contrast, the four remaining cases in which the UN has tried or
proposed investigation as a method of settlement were ones in which
there was disagreement as to who should succeed the departing
colonial Power. In only one of them did the UN's activity or recommendations have any bearing at all on the outcome.

This was the case of Eritrea. The 1947 Peace Treaty with Italy
had stipulated that the final disposition of her colonies—Libya,
Italian Somaliland, and Eritrea—should be determined jointly by
Britain, France, the Soviet Union, and the United States within a
year of the Treaty coming into force. If they were unable to agree
regarding the future of any of the territories, the matter was to be
referred to the General Assembly for a recommendation, which, it
was understood, the Powers would treat as binding. They were
unable to agree and the question was therefore referred to the
Assembly, where, after much activity, a solution was reached in
respect of Libya and Italian Somaliland in November 1949.[7]
Eritrea, however, took some more time. There was general agreement that land-locked Ethiopia should obtain access to the sea
through Eritrea, but there the agreement ended. Ethiopia wanted
all the territory, Sudan—at that time an Anglo-Egyptian condo-
minium—had claims on its western province, and Italy fancied the
resumption of her rule in one form or another. The Soviet Union
was in favour of trusteeship with the administering authority being
guided by an advisory council. No doubt it saw in this suggestion
some possibility of a purchase for Soviet influence on the eastern
shore of the Red Sea. Some Eritrean political groups favoured
immediate independence. A generation or two earlier the obvious
course would have been to divide Eritrea between Ethiopia and the
Sudan, and this solution still had much appeal, but not enough to
obtain the approval of two-thirds of the Assembly.

It was therefore decided that in view of the disagreement, the
decision should be postponed while an investigation was held 'to
ascertain more fully the wishes and the best means of promoting
the welfare of the inhabitants of Eritrea'.[8] This was justified on the
ground that the four Powers themselves admitted that their earlier

[7] See below, pp. 339–341.
[8] General Assembly resolution 289A (IV).

investigations had not discovered the wishes of the inhabitants as
definitely as in the other two colonies, but a more immediate concern
of most members was the possibility that disagreement over Eritrea
would jeopardize the decision on Libya and Italian Somaliland,
which seemed to be coming just within reach. Postponement also
had the advantage of providing some more time for the emergence
of a consensus at the diplomatic level. The Commission of Investigation split three ways, Burma and South Africa recommending that
Eritrea become a self-governing unit in an Ethiopian-Eritrean
federation, Norway advocating its union with Ethiopia with the
western province being given the opportunity later to join the Sudan,
and Guatemala and Pakistan urging a ten year UN trusteeship
followed by independence. But this was less important than the fact
that by December 1950 the General Assembly was prepared to
recommend that Eritrea constitute an autonomous unit federated
with Ethiopia under the sovereignty of the Ethiopian crown, and
the Federation was established in 1952. Now Eritrea was beyond
the UN's reach and in firm Ethiopian control, with the result that
when, ten years later, it was incorporated as a province of Ethiopia,
there was no question of any international enquiry into the matter.

The other three territorial disputes in which the UN has advocated
or used investigation as a method of settlement all arose in anticipa-
tion or in consequence of Britain's reduction of her overseas responsibilities—in South Asia, the Middle East, and South East Asia. Upon
her withdrawal from India in 1947 it was open to each of the 500 or
so princely states of the sub-continent to accede either to Pakistan or
India. For the vast majority there was no real choice in the matter,
but this was not true in respect of the largest: Kashmir. It was about
the size of England and Wales, had a population in the region of
four million, possessed borders with both the successor states
and also with China and Afghanistan, and, although predominantly
Muslim in population, was ruled by a Hindu. While considering
her decision, however, Kashmir was subject to harassment from
armed tribesmen infiltrating from Pakistan, and by the end of
October 1947 this was reaching serious proportions. Turning to
India for help, the Maharajah was advised that it could only be
extended if Kashmir had first joined India, whereupon he executed
the appropriate document. It was accepted with equal promptitude,
but on the understanding that once tranquillity had been restored,
the question of its accession should be 'settled by a reference to the
people'.[9] India now sent her troops into Kashmir, and when they
found themselves fighting those who had come from Pakistan,

[9] Quoted in A. G. Noorani, *The Kashmir Question* (Bombay: Manaktalas, 1964), p. 33.

brought the matter to the Security Council on 1 January 1948. In April the Council recommended various measures to stop the hostilities, and India and Pakistan eventually ordered their forces (it had become clear during 1948 that regular Pakistani troops were in Kashmir) to cease fire as from 1 January 1949, the cease-fire line being agreed in the following July. It left the northern and western parts of the state under Pakistan's control, and the eastern and southern parts, including the Vale of Kashmir, which is the richest part of the state, and Srinagar, the capital, in Indian hands.

The cease-fire line was meant to be a temporary division pending a final decision by the Kashmiris regarding their future. In November 1947 Pakistan had suggested that the UN should administer the state while a free and unfettered plebiscite was organized and held. India was totally opposed to such a course, declaring that a plebiscite should be conducted by the Government of Kashmir with the UN's role being confined to observation. On this particular issue the Security Council leant in Pakistan's direction. In a resolution of 21 April 1948 it provided for a UN-appointed Plebiscite Administrator, who, for the purposes of his mandate, was to have such powers as he considered necessary including 'the direction and supervision of the State forces and police'.[10] However, this scheme was rejected by Pakistan as well as India, to the Council's considerable annoyance.

On 20 January 1948 the Council had established a UN Commission for India and Pakistan, composed of three member states, one to be chosen by each of the parties, and the third by the other two. India nominated Czechoslovakia, and Pakistan the Argentine. These two having failed to agree on the other member, the President of the Security Council designated the United States, by which time the Council had added Belgium and Colombia to the Commission. Its job was to investigate and mediate, and it suggested arrangements for a plebiscite which were markedly more favourable to the Indian point of view than to Pakistan's. It also accepted all the reservations with which India accompanied her acceptance of its terms. Not surprisingly, Pakistan was uncooperative, but at the end of 1948 she accepted a further set of proposals along similar lines, probably being chiefly influenced by her worsening military position in Kashmir.

However, this proved to be the beginning, rather than the end, of the attempt to settle the dispute on the basis of an impartial investigation into the wishes of the people. The Commission failed to make any progress towards securing the conditions which had been agreed to be necessary for the conduct of the plebiscite, the main stumbling

[10] Security Council resolution 47 (1948).

block being the question of the withdrawal of troops. It therefore recommended its own winding-up and replacement by an individual.[11] In March 1950 the Council followed the Commission's recommendation, its President having first failed in a mediatory attempt, and Sir Owen Dixon of Australia was appointed as UN Representative. His activities bore no fruit and in the following year he was replaced by Mr Frank P. Graham of the United States. For two years he was very busy and produced a number of reports, but since 1953 there has been relatively little activity by the UN on this front, although the office of UN Representative continues to exist, and is still held by Mr Graham. His last report was submitted in 1958.

By about this time the Kashmir dispute was looking even more intractable than at the beginning of the 1950s. Then India had accepted its international character. Now her position was hardening, and by the early 1960s she had come to the view that Kashmir's accession was irrevocable and that in consequence questions concerning the territory were essentially domestic. She was prepared, in the interests of peace and friendship, to engage in bilateral talks with Pakistan, but was anxious for it to be understood that Pakistan's status in the matter was that of an aggressor, who was unlawfully holding on to a part of India. Certainly, in the Indian view, there could be no question of the UN continuing to interest itself in the question, for mediation and the plebiscite it was designed to facilitate were unacceptable on an issue involving her sovereignty. When, therefore, in 1962, the Security Council discussed Kashmir, India took strong exception to a mild proposal urging talks and asking the acting Secretary-General to provide 'such services'[12] as might be required in order to secure them. The draft resolution obtained the necessary number of votes but was vetoed by the Soviet Union.

This discussion had been held on Pakistan's initiative, reflecting her constant endeavour to keep the matter before the UN and maintain its involvement. In her fervent view, India was in unjust possession of an area which, on a free vote, would choose to join

[11] There had been some complaints of American interference in the work of the Commission. In the minority report of the Czechoslovakian delegation appended to the Commission's Third Interim Report, reference was made to the fact the Commission decided on a cablegram, which was 'unanimously approved and voted upon by all members of the Commission', protesting at this. However, the cabled protest of the Commission's Chairman (at that time a Czechoslovakian) to the Chairman of the Security Council (at that time a Russian) was 'withheld' by an American member of the UN Secretariat, Mr Andrew Cordier, on the ground that the complaint was addressed to the Chairman of the Security Council personally. See UN Document S/1430 Add 3, p. 9. A UN document which is referred to in the Czech minority report as giving further information regarding this incident is classified.

[12] UN Document S/5134.

Pakistan. The likelihood of direct talks leading to a plebiscite seemed remote, to say the least, and she therefore turned to the UN, where she could invoke the earlier resolutions of the Organization and its Commission in favour of her case. The Soviet Union and her friends were supporting India, but apart from them there was a good deal of sympathy for Pakistan's claim that a plebiscite was a fair way of solving the dispute. Many members saw the idea as a means of giving expression to the principle of self-determination, and no doubt also obtained some satisfaction from putting India on the moral spot, so treating her with her own medicine. On account of these factors India naturally wanted to keep Kashmir away from the UN, especially as she was moving towards an acceptance of the *status quo* as the least unsatisfactory solution for the problem. A plebiscite would probably be to her disadvantage, would offend the secular principle on which India was based, and might illustrate the fragility of that basis by causing communal trouble. Mr Nehru's personal connections with Kashmir are also thought to have contributed to India's inflexibility. Thus she could do without the UN on this matter, needing only to sit tight in her part of Kashmir.

Later in 1962 it looked as though there might be a chance of breaking the deadlock, for China's attack on India made her keenly aware of the undesirability of having enemies on two fronts and so led to a reconsideration of her relations with Pakistan. Early in 1963 ministerial talks were held, and it appeared that India might agree to some form of mediation being tried again. For her part, Pakistan was moving away from her former insistence on a plebiscite throughout Kashmir. But she could not agree to India continuing to hold the Vale, and India refused to give it up. Thus the talks failed. The matter was discussed by the Security Council in 1964 but no progress was made. There was no hope of India accepting Pakistan's suggestion that a fact-finding body should be sent to Kashmir, and the very proposal perhaps indicated that Pakistan was abandoning any hope of an agreed settlement and was instead becoming more concerned to invalidate India's position. Certainly relations were deteriorating, and Pakistan began to increase her pressure on India, probably calculating that it was a case of now or never on account of the military aid which India was receiving from the West following the border war with China in 1962. In August 1965 armed infiltrators entered Indian Kashmir in increasing numbers, and full-scale hostilities quickly developed, spreading beyond Kashmir to envelop all of the border between India and West Pakistan. They were almost as speedily brought to a halt, and there were some hopes that they might have given an adequate impetus towards the settlement of the Kashmir dispute. For when the Security Council demanded a cease-

fire in a resolution of 20 September, it also promised to consider
what steps could be taken to assist 'towards a settlement of the
political problem underlying the present conflict'.[13] And at Tashkent
in January 1966, when the good offices of the Soviet Union led to an
agreement on the withdrawal of troops, it was declared that meetings
would be continued 'both at the highest and at other levels on
matters of direct concern to both countries'.[14] But, as was not
unsuspected at the time, these proved to be no more than convenient
formulas, and led to no basic improvement in the situation regarding
Kashmir. Pakistan called for a 'meaningful'[15] discussion of the
question, but India was not prepared to do more than explain why
she was not willing to reopen the issue. At home her Government
found it necessary to insist on several occasions that Kashmir was
not negotiable, and the weakened administration which emerged
from the 1967 elections made it even less likely that she would find
it possible to make concessions on the subject. Only with India in
critical circumstances could Pakistan now hope to obtain Indian
Kashmir, but as yet she shows no sign of being prepared to forget
the past and settle for the *status quo*. So it seems that the issue will
continue to poison relations between the two states. Whatever its
future, it is exceedingly unlikely that it will be resolved by way of a
plebiscite, whether or not conducted by the UN.

In this case the UN has recognized, implicitly, that it is not much
use trying to bring the parties together, not only because their
positions are both irreconcilable and deeply-rooted, but also
because one of them is strongly opposed to the Organization's
involvement. Even if the Great Powers united behind a UN proposal, it might still be rejected. But quite apart from this, such
unity is most unlikely, for the friendship of both parties is highly
prized in almost all quarters. Until recently each party has had a
special relationship with a Great Power. Pakistan has sought
American support by joining the Western system of alliances, and
India has had the Soviet Union firmly behind her on Kashmir.
But now there has been something of a diplomatic upheaval, with
Pakistan consolidating her relations with China, India increasingly
regarding the United States as her best friend, and the Soviet Union
gradually loosening her partisan ties—to assume the unlikely role
of honest broker at Tashkent. But however the diplomatic alignment
develops, as there are three major Powers closely interested in the
Indian sub-continent, to say nothing of the disengaging Britain and
the, as yet, reserved Japan, it is highly improbable that a firm and

---

[13] Security Council resolution 211 (1965).
[14] Quoted in *Annual Register for 1966* (London: Longmans, 1967), p. 519.
[15] Ibid., p. 75.

united front will be presented to the parties in order to obtain an agreed settlement.

The most likely eventuality is that some of the Powers, as in the case of the September 1965 war, will insist that the Kashmir problem is not settled by force of arms. The UN too has a particular interest in this, on account of its long-standing prophylactic activities along the cease-fire line.[16] This may help to account for its patching-up arrangements being left in mothballs rather than completely discarded. But a more influential factor is its reluctance formally to admit failure. This is not just collective pride, although that enters into it. It also reflects the thought that the situation may develop in such a way that, one day, the UN may once again be able to try its hand at a Kashmir settlement. If that did happen it might be helpful to be able to reactivate disused arrangements instead of having to start organizing from scratch. This consideration may reflect undue optimism, but optimism is a characteristic to which the UN as an institution is committed.

An even more difficult problem than that of Kashmir, and which, similarly, is still on the UN's agenda, is that of Palestine. At the end of World War I it had been detached from the defeated Ottoman Empire and included in the League of Nations Mandates system, with Britain as the administering Power. The agreement between Britain and the League included the principle that a national home should be established for the Jewish people in Palestine, which led to considerable immigration.

With it, however, tension rose between the growing number of Jews and the indigenous Arabs, who saw the possibility that they would become a minority in what they regarded as their own land. Terrorism and lawlessness increased, and were resumed on a substantial scale after the end of World War II. For some time Britain had been trying to bring both sides to an agreement on the future of the country, but a scheme acceptable to both seemed to be beyond reach. In 1947, therefore, she decided to wash her hands of the matter and drop the problem into the UN's lap, asking that the matter be considered by the General Assembly. As one of her delegates put it: 'We have tried for years to solve the problem of Palestine. Having failed so far, we now bring it to the United Nations in the hope that it can succeed where we have not'[17].

In Britain's estimation the facts of the matter were sufficiently well known as not to require an on the spot enquiry, but most UN

---

[16] See below, pp. 290–293.
[17] L. Larry Leonard: 'The United Nations and Palestine', *International Conciliation*, No. 454 (October 1949), p. 610.

members took a different view and called for an impartial international appraisal of the situation. Therefore in May 1947 the
General Assembly set up the United Nations Special Committee
on Palestine (UNSCOP), consisting of representatives of Australia,
Canada, Czechoslovakia, Guatemala, India, Iran, the Netherlands,
Peru, Sweden, Uruguay, and Yugoslavia. Its task was in keeping
with the role which had been allotted by the League to its investigating missions, for it was told to find the facts, investigate all relevant
questions, and make proposals for a solution. It spent six weeks in
the Middle East, and on the main issue, was unable to agree on the
settlement to which the facts pointed. The minority report urged an
independent federal state, made up of Arab and Jewish units, with
Jerusalem as its capital. The majority of the Committee's members
were in favour of partitioning the area into Arab and Jewish states,
with an international regime for Jerusalem, and their proposals won
the most support.

On 29 November 1947, 33 states voted in favour of the partition
plan, including the Soviet Union and the United States; 13 opposed
the proposal; and 10 abstained. Those voting against included all
the Arab members and they made it clear that they would do their
utmost to prevent the partition of Palestine. For her part Britain
said that she was not going to try to impose the UN's or anyone
else's solution. Guatemala therefore proposed that an international
force be set up to implement the Assembly's scheme, with the
permanent members of the Security Council paying for it but not
otherwise contributing, but this suggestion was ignored: the Palestinian potato was much too hot for anyone to want to handle.
Instead, a Commission was appointed to ensure that everything
went according to plan, and was supposed to arrange a progressive
transfer of administrative authority from the Mandatory to itself,
assume full power on 1 August 1948, and hand over to the successor
states two months later. It proved quite impossible to implement this
orderly proposal,[18] and when Britain withdrew on 15 May 1948,
war broke out between the Arabs and the Jews.

The Palestinian case could hardly have been a worse one to try
to patch-up by investigation. An agreement between the parties was
never in prospect, and although the dispute was not a part of the
emerging cold war, the Soviet Union and the United States were
not prepared to join forces to secure a pacific settlement—and in the
circumstances a quite literal joining of forces would have been
required. Nor were the other UN members prepared to get physically involved in support of the proposed settlement: the cost in
terms of men and money, domestic politics, and diplomatic repercus-

18 See further, below, pp. 170–171.

sions was far higher than anyone was ready to pay. It is therefore hardly surprising that the General Assembly's plan was ignored. It could be said that the passions and interests which it aroused made the case an extreme one, but even so it was not untypical of the disputes to which the post-war period was to give rise. The times were not conducive to peaceful settlement, especially by means of investigating missions.

The only other dispute which the UN has tried to patch-up by means of investigation concerned the creation of the Federation of Malaysia. In 1961 the Prime Minister of Malaya had put forward the idea of what became known as 'greater Malaysia'—a state comprising the already independent federation of Malaya, the British colonies of Singapore, North Borneo, and Sarawak, and the British Protected State of Brunei. The Sultan of Brunei declined to cooperate, but opinion in the other territories was agreeable to the scheme, and preparations were put in hand for proclamation of the new state on 31 August 1963. However, Indonesia became strongly hostile to the idea and she took a somewhat reluctant Philippines, who had a territorial claim on North Borneo, along with her in her opposition. In form they acted together, but it was clear beyond a doubt that Indonesia was making the running. She said she was not thinking of annexation, and was concerned only that the people of North Borneo (henceforward to be known as Sabah) and Sarawak had not had a chance to express what she perceived to be their unwillingness to join the new state.

Be that as it may, it was obvious that her immediate purpose was to put as many obstacles as possible in the way of Malaysia coming into being, and on the last day of July Malaya, at a summit meeting of Indonesia, the Philippines, and herself, yielded to pressure for a UN survey of opinion in North Borneo and Sarawak. The Secretary-General, U Thant, said that a plebiscite would take some months and would require the sanction of the General Assembly. Such a delay, indeed any delay, was acceptable neither to the territories who were to make up the new state nor to Britain, and the proposal was therefore watered down. An assessment of opinion, said U Thant, could be done more quickly and on his own authority. Indonesia agreed to this and in return Malaya was willing to countenance a postponement of Malaysia Day if that should prove necessary. Britain, however, was unhappy. She was opposed to enquiries being held by the UN in her colonial territories, and saw this proposal as possibly the thin end of a wedge. She was also anxious to be quite clear about the nature of the enquiries the Secretary-General intended to make (Sukarno was still reported to be

talking of a 'referendum') and the timetable he would establish.
Receiving satisfaction on these points, she agreed, as a matter of
courtesy, to a UN investigation, and emphasized that the three
Powers who had initially agreed to it had no standing whatsoever in
the matter. A point that received equal emphasis from both Britain
and Malaya was that U Thant was acting in a 'personal capacity'.
Quite clearly he was not, but their insistence to that effect was another way of saying that the General Assembly was not a party to
the arrangement and should not become concerned with it.

On 12 August the Secretary-General appointed the nine-man
team of Secretariat officials who were to conduct the enquiry. Their
job was to examine whether the recent elections in the two territories had resulted in the Malaysian issue being adequately venti-
lated, and also to receive the views of organizations and individuals.
No sooner had they arrived, however, than their work was held up
by a controversy over the number of observers who were to accompany the two groups into which the investigators split. The principle
of observation by the interested parties had formed a part of the
original plan, and Britain therefore agreed that Malaya, Indonesia,
and the Philippines should attach one observer to each group. Now,
under pressure, she doubled her offer, but it fell far short of Indonesia's demand for thirty. Thus it was that when, on 26 August, the
investigation got under way, only Malaysian observers were present.
Further haggling took place, but agreement looked unlikely. Then,
however, Indonesia capitulated, and for the last three days of the
ten-day investigation the UN officials were accompanied by
Indonesian and Philippine observers.

Possibly this was due to the announcement on 29 August that the
Federation of Malaysia would be proclaimed on 16 September. Until
then Indonesia may have been hoping that in the absence of her
observers there would be a general disposition to regard the investigation as invalid, with the result that the inauguration of Malaysia
would be postponed. Realizing that that was not going to happen,
she may well have calculated that the only hope now open to her
was to discredit the investigation, and this required the presence of
her observers. Certainly she protested at the facilities they were
given and at the general conduct of the operation, but to no avail.
The UN group reported that the participation of North Borneo
and Sarawak in Malaysia could be regarded as the result of 'the
freely expressed wishes of the territories peoples',[19] and their findings,
together with U Thant's endorsement, were published on 14
September. Two days later Malaysia came into being.

This dispute could be seen as one which turned on a lack of clarity

[19] *Yearbook of the United Nations, 1963*, pp. 42–43.

as to the views of the people of North Borneo and Sarawak regarding their membership in the proposed Malaysia, or at least an uncertainty on Indonesia's part as to their true view. If this was its nature, then a UN investigation should have served very well as a means of achieving a settlement. But this was not its nature, and so the UN's attempt to patch it up failed completely, and never had a chance of succeeding. For, on the one hand, Britain and Malaya had no intention of doing more than postpone the establishment of the new state for a brief period. The notion that as a result of the investigation they might not go ahead with their scheme was totally foreign to them. From their point of view the object of bringing in the UN was only to counter the criticism that had already been made and forestall the possibility of more. This was made quite evident by the fact that the new date for Malaysia's proclamation was announced while the investigators were less than half-way through their task. In their defence Britain and Malaya could argue that they knew full well that the investigators could not but report in their favour. Even so, such a blatant prejudgment of the investigators findings was in no way calculated to appease the Indonesians and pave the way towards an agreed settlement. It earned a rebuke from the Secretary-General, and Malaya's later explanation that an announcement was necessary to comply with a statutory obligation was not very compelling.

On the other hand, Indonesia's attitude hardly warranted a conciliatory approach. Just as Britain tried to use the UN presence to obtain moral support for the establishment of Malaysia, and hence deter Indonesia's campaign against it, so, it is clear enough, Indonesia valued the UN's investigation for the obstacles it might put in the way of the establishment of the new state. She was deeply suspicious of Britain and, as she later said, wanted observers not so much to keep an eye on the UN officials as on the activities of the colonial authorities, thinking they would rig the proceedings—this being the counterpart of the equally frank British statement that the activities of the observers had to be limited because the Indonesians couldn't be trusted. Thus Indonesia in no sense looked upon the UN's investigation as a prelude to patching-up her complaint regarding Malaysia's establishment, and was in no mood to heed the Earl of Home's imperious call either to deny the impartiality of the Secretary-General and his investigating teams 'or keep quiet and accept the findings with good grace'.[20] In the weeks following 16 September Indonesia cut all diplomatic, trade, and communications links with the new state of Malaysia and began her policy of confrontation in all spheres, which was only brought to a formal end in the

[20] General Assembly, *Official Records*, 1219th Plenary Meeting, para 181.

summer of 1966 after a change in the internal balance of power in Indonesia. In this case, therefore, although the UN may be supposed to have acted with patching-up intent, it could do nothing effective towards that end on account of the intransigence of the parties.

Had the Malaysian issue gone to the General Assembly it is quite possible that most members would have endorsed the spirit of the Secretary-General's action. For while Indonesia might have obtained a good deal of anti-colonialist sympathy, it might well have been less fervent than usual because of doubts about the merits of her claim. As a result, an impartial fact-finding mission might have had the most appeal, representing a concerned but middle of the road and non-partisan approach on the part of the Organization. This would have been a relatively unusual course for it to take, for in most disputes which have come before it the UN has had firm views about their rights and wrongs, and has acted accordingly. Hence, while it has engaged in many fact-finding operations, the majority of them have been meant to find facts of a certain kind, those which will advance the cause of the disputant favoured by the UN. Such missions therefore fall into the category of prophylactic or proselytizing rather than patching-up presences.

Patching-up by investigation is, in fact, something of a lost cause in the life of the UN. There is no reason why it need be, and if the conditions are appropriate it may well be successfully resorted to in future. Should the East-West *détente* develop, it could be that the Great Powers would in some cases have a joint interest in putting their weight behind proposals for this method of settlement. It is, for example, very suitable for the investigation of charges that a country's air space or territorial waters have been infringed, and so can lead towards the ending of such disputes—if the parties want to move in that direction. It is conceivable that the use of the UN for this purpose might sometimes be less easy if China is admitted to membership. But quite apart from this possibility, the value of investigation as a means of securing agreement rests on a condition which, in the world at large, seems increasingly to have been left behind since the 1920s: a readiness on the part of states to let others play an influential and independent role in the settlement of their disputes, whether those others are states, persons acting in their individual capacities, or, in the case of territorial problems, the people directly concerned.[21] Even a growing Great Power interest

[21] It may be that within certain regions conditions are more favourable for investigation. The inter-American system, for example, gives prominence to this device, cultural, historical, and geo-political factors all contributing to its doing so. It is not yet obvious that the African states are likely to follow suit, and it could be that their background and situation will lead them to give more weight to mediation as a method of pacific settlement.

in this method of settlement (for others if not for themselves) would not guarantee its effective use, on account of the general resistance to the attitude it requires. It must also be noted that contemporary disputes over the legitimacy of governments or the propriety of some of their internal policies are much less suitable for resolution by means of investigation than were the territorial and border questions which came before the League of Nations in its early days. Thus, while patching-up by investigation remains a valuable method of pacific settlement, neither the general character of the present international society nor the experience of the post 1945 years suggests that in the immediate future it will be a frequently encountered phenomenon.[22]

---

[22] But see below, pp. 164–167, for a discussion of Indonesia's undertaking to hold a UN-supervised plebiscite in West Irian not later than 1969.

Chapter 3

Mediation

A SECOND way of trying to patch-up international quarrels is through the device of mediation. The word is not used here in the narrow, technical sense of an activity which is distinct from good offices and conciliation, but refers to all attempts by intermediaries to draw disputing states together and so obtain an agreed settlement. The process takes the positions of the parties as its starting point, and tries to establish enough common ground to support a solution. This may involve no more than a third party offering to act as a medium of communication, so as to get the states concerned talking to each other. It may lead to proposals being put forward by the intermediary for the consideration of the parties. Or it may result in much toing and froing by the mediator as he tries to persuade one of them to agree to a formula which holds out some hope of acceptance by the other, at least as a basis for negotiations. The object, in any event, is to get the parties to reduce their claims to an extent which brings an agreement within reach. Normally the mediator would go about his business in private, although at the end of the day it may well be that his report is published in a last endeavour to bring the parties to accept his proposals. However, such a course is also likely to be a despairing one, representing in effect if not in intent, the failure of the mediatory mission, for publicity is usually inimical to this method of peaceful settlement.

It may be that the outcome of a successful mediatory process will not be very dissimilar to that which would have emerged from investigation. For, in framing their recommendations, those charged with making an independent enquiry may have an eye to what the parties are likely to accept. But, in principle, the tasks of mediatory and investigating missions are quite different. The object of mediation is to secure an acceptable compromise, and therefore it pays primary regard to the views and claims of the disputants. By contrast, the investigators' job is to make their own assessment of the contentious issues and so point, directly or indirectly, to the settlement which they regard as fair and just. Thus mediation may well take longer than investigation, but its chances of securing an agreement are perhaps greater. Certainly it is a process to which states assent more readily. In doing so they are unlikely to be risking more than allegations of undue obstinacy or bad faith, and states do not usually find it difficult to show, at least to their own satisfaction and that of their friends, that such charges are more appropriately made in respect of their opponents.

As the encouragement of pacific settlement is one of the UN's main functions, the Organization is particularly suitable for the conduct of mediatory activity. Its Charter sets out what it may do in this respect, and the Security Council and General Assembly may well take the initiative in suggesting that they be allowed to try their hand at mediation. It is also to be expected that the Secretary-General and other high-ranking members of the Secretariat will hold themselves available for service towards this end, quite apart from any instructions they may receive from the UN's political organs. There is no guarantee that disputing states will readily avail themselves of these procedures and facilities, but the likelihood of their doing so is somewhat enhanced by the fact that alternative sources of adequate help are in short supply.

A condition of mediation is a belief in the impartiality of the mediator, which, besides calling for the absence, on his part, of a direct interest in the dispute, also requires that each side assess his general preference for the other as not greater than that for itself. At one time the heads of uninvolved states often satisfied this condition, but since the end of the World War II ideological labels have been so freely assumed and assigned that it has become very difficult for disputing states to identify a third state which both believe would make a fair mediator.[1] It might be possible for them to agree on an individual, but the conduct of mediation is not commonly left in private hands. Accordingly, the obvious course for states seeking mediation is to turn to the UN, or to some other international body which is constitutionally inclined towards the idea.

[1] One interesting post-war example of a monarch being called upon to play a part, albeit a small one, in a mediatory process occurred in 1957 in connection with the border dispute between Ethiopia and the Trust Territory of former Italian Somaliland. The General Assembly recommended that an arbitration tribunal be established to delimit the frontier in accordance with terms of reference which were to be agreed between the two Governments with the assistance of an independent person appointed by them. In the following year the tribunal was appointed, but the parties failed to agree on its terms of reference or on the independent person who was to assist them in this respect. The matter therefore came back to the Assembly where, after some private activity on the part of the Secretary-General, a draft resolution was prepared which satisfied both parties. Its passage was then a formality. It provided that if they were unable to agree within three months on the appointment of an independent person, he should be nominated by the King of Norway. In the absence of agreement the King appointed Mr Trygve Lie, the first Secretary-General of the UN. But the story did not have a happy ending, for Lie was unable to bring the parties to an agreement on the terms of reference of the arbitration tribunal, and this approach was dropped. The dispute, however, was still very much alive.

This, however, does not dispose of the problem of suspected bias. If the UN, as it often did in its early years, appoints a committee of member states, their representatives cannot be regarded as free agents. The degree of direction which they receive from their governments may vary a good deal, and conflicting attitudes towards the dispute in question may cancel each other out. Nevertheless, and understandably, such groups are looked at with a calculating and easily jaundiced eye by the quarrelling states, which can have an important bearing on the success of the effort at mediation. The same is true of single states who might be appointed to act on the UN's behalf. In order, therefore, to obtain the greatest possible confidence in the mediators' impartiality, it is desirable to leave their appointment solely in the hands of the UN, so that the single mediator or those making up the mediatory group will be responsible only to the appointing UN organ or the Secretary-General, as the case may be. This, latterly, has been the practice in respect of mediation conducted by the UN, and with it has gone a marked tendency to appoint an individual rather than a group, so making it likely that the activity will be conducted with greater dispatch.

This does not obviate the need to pay attention to the nationality of the mediator. For the prevailing tendency is to assume an identity of views between nationals and their governments, or at least the possibility of a national being influenced by his government's position on any dispute. As a result, a mediator drawn from an interested country would in all probability be charged with partiality if his approach to the dispute seemed rather similar to that of his home state, and while there might be no ground for the charge, a belief in its substance would be enough to wreck the endeavour to obtain a settlement. This factor must equally be borne in mind in those cases where a member of the UN Secretariat is asked to perform a mediatory role, for service as an international official is not regarded as placing a man beyond the reach of national sympathies or even influence, as is made abundantly clear when the UN elects a Secretary-General. Thus a belief in the fairness of the mediator is by no means assured merely by involving the UN in the process. And early confidence in him may evaporate speedily, on one side at least, as the attempt at mediation proceeds, for it is not at all difficult for a disputant to feel that its position is not receiving proper consideration. But it remains that mediation conducted by the UN is more likely to be accepted by the parties than mediation placed in others' hands, especially if a member of the Secretariat or an outside individual acting on behalf of the Organization is to be the intermediary.

Acceptance of mediation, however, is a long way from successful mediation. The very fact that recourse has been had to the process suggests a measure of caution regarding the likelihood of a favourable outcome, for third-party assistance is usually sought only in situations of particular difficulty. Against this there is the argument that a readiness to accept mediation implies some desire, on one side at least, for an end to the dispute, but this is not a point of much substance. A desire to settle is not at all the same thing as a willingness to settle on terms which are acceptable to the other side. And it may well be that neither side is very keen on the idea of mediation, both having agreed to it in order to satisfy concerned spectators. Especially is this likely to be the case when the UN interests itself in a quarrel. If the Organization is already involved in some way, the parties would find it embarrassing to resist the suggestion that mediation be attempted. But apart from this, mediatory gestures are, one might say, in the UN's nature, and also appeal to the nature of its members, for states are often not at all slow to call on others to accept the help of a third party to settle their disputes. However, there is generally a considerable reluctance to follow this up with strong support for the mediator's activities, and in its absence they may very well be unsuccessful. For it is frequently the case that disputants, particularly if they were unenthusiastic about mediation in the first place, need to be offered inducements if they are to be brought to an agreement.[2]

A mediator, therefore, is usually very much on his own, in the sense that there is unlikely to be powerful backing for his endeavours to establish some common ground between the disputants. He may be skilful, and both parties may look on him as impartial, but skill and impartiality, while necessary, have a limited effectiveness so far as the securing of settlements is concerned. Virtually everything will depend on the attitude which the parties choose to adopt, on whether they are ready to be assisted towards an agreement. If they are, mediation may make a crucial contribution to the translation of pacific attitudes into a settlement. But if they are not, the mediatory role will be a frustrating one. The factors which make it so, however, are exactly those which explain, if not its appeal, its acceptability. Thus the UN and its predecessor have engaged in a good deal of mediation, but their overall rate of success has not been high.

I

The bulk of the League's mediatory work was conducted by its rapporteurs. In 1920, at its second session, the Council agreed to

[2] The conditions which bear upon the likelihood of mediation being supported by pressure are considered below at pp. 52–56.

a British proposal that each question on its agenda should be assigned to one of its member states who, through its representative, was to make a special examination of the matter, conduct such discussions and negotiations as were necessary, and suggest a course of action to the Council. The procedure was subsequently adopted by the Assembly. Thus the rapporteur often had to act as a mediator, and usually did so with success. In acute conflicts it might have been very difficult or even impossible to get a single member to perform the task, and in these circumstances a committee of several members was appointed, a device which both provided some protection for the rapporteurs and put rather more weight behind the proposals which eventually came to the Council. The system was used throughout the League's life, and the readiness of members to entrust such functions to one, or, occasionally, a few, of their fellows and, even more, their usual willingness to accept the rapporteur's suggestions, are a striking tribute to the character of the period. They also indicate the conditions which are necessary for the successful working of such an arrangement: a general commitment to peaceful settlement, and trust in the integrity of the mediator, conditions which have been noticeable by their absence since 1945.

The mediatory activities of the rapporteurs, however, do not fall within the ambit of this study, for virtually all of their work was done at Geneva. A rapporteur may occasionally, while in his capital city between Council meetings, have discussed the matter assigned to him with the diplomatic representatives of the states concerned. Hardly ever, if at all, did a rapporteur, in that capacity, visit any of the countries involved in the issue for which he had a League responsibility. Very possibly the need to do either of these things was rarely felt, but quite apart from this there was the consideration that it was desirable from all points of view—the League's, the disputants' and the rapporteur's own state's—that the rapporteur did not mix up his work in that role with his continuing responsibility as a member of his country's government or diplomatic service. Strictly speaking, the nominated member state *was* the rapporteur, but it was its representative who was usually spoken of in this way. Certainly, he could not be expected to act in a manner which was contrary to his country's interests, but equally it was assumed that as rapporteur he would put exclusively national considerations on one side. There was unlikely to be a serious problem here, otherwise a different country would have been chosen as rapporteur. But, even so there would be one fewer difficulty in the way of a settlement if as clear a distinction as possible was kept between the work of the rapporteur and the official views of his country. Thus the League's rapporteur system, including its important mediatory aspect, was

very much a sedentary affair, and does not provide any examples of
an international 'presence'.

It is also the case that the activities of the League's Secretaries-
General are barren from the point of view of a study focusing on the
role of international organizations in the field. Its first Secretary-
General, Sir Eric Drummond, was constantly at work behind the
scenes, and acquired a considerable reputation for his discretion and
impartiality. It would therefore be surprising if he did not, on occasion, act as a mediator. However, he eschewed publicity and did not
undertake any dramatic journeys. Mediation, in fact, is an activity
which does not require the presence of the intermediary in the area
of tension, nor even in the capitals of the disputing states. Direct
and face-to-face negotiations with their representatives will almost
certainly be conducted, but there is no reason why they should not
be held at the headquarters of an international organization or
wherever the mediator is to be found, as was the League of Nations'
usual practice.

There were, however, two notable cases in which the League
established mediatory presences: Danzig and Chaco. Danzig had
been detached from Germany at the end of World War I in order
to provide Poland with a seaport. But as it was purely German in
character, it was not handed over to Poland but established as a
Free City, subordinate to Poland in its foreign relations but internally
autonomous. The League was to act as guarantor for Danzig and
appoint a resident High Commissioner. Despite his title, this official
had no governmental functions. His chief task was to act as a mediator in disputes between Poland and the Free City, and although
many of their numerous quarrels in the 1920s had to be taken to
the League Council, the High Commissioner played a valuable role.
In the 1930s Poland and Danzig preferred to settle their problems by
direct negotiations or to leave them unsettled, but as this aspect of
the High Commissioner's work declined, so his help was increasingly
sought by citizens of Danzig against the actions of their Nazi
Government. From 1936 onwards there was no chance of his receiving
effective support from the League. Nevertheless, for as long as
Danzig remained formally independent of Germany, and it was not
annexed until 1 September 1939, the High Commissioner was able
to play a useful albeit a quiet role, for instance in dissuading Germany on several occasions from going ahead with plans to extend
its anti-Jewish laws to the Free City.

The Chaco dispute was over a huge, remote, and largely uninhabited plain of that name claimed by both Bolivia and Paraguay.
Fighting broke out in 1932 and, the efforts of an inter-American
body having been in vain, the League established a Commission

of Enquiry in July 1933. It was asked to report on the facts, but its
main duty was to negotiate with the parties, the object being to
secure an armistice and an agreement to submit the dispute to arbitration. It had no real success, and in November 1934 the League's
proposals for a settlement were rejected by Paraguay, then militarily
in the ascendant. But she was not strong enough to bring the war to
a clear-cut conclusion and fighting came to a stop in 1935 through
the exhaustion of both parties, a formal treaty of peace being
signed three years later.

There is not much strength in the argument that the League's
failure in the Chaco case is attributable to the fact that it did not
have the mediatory field to itself. From Geneva the conflict appeared
to be utterly senseless, and the League was anxious to do what it
could to bring it to an end. But the contestants were set on a fight
to the finish, or until they could continue no longer, and in view of
their mood it seems unlikely that more concentrated pleas for a
negotiated settlement would have caused their ears to be more
receptive. Even if active support for the League's mediatory efforts
had been received from those states who were in a position to speak
persuasively to the contestants, it is questionable whether it would
have resulted in a lessening of their intransigence. In short, this was
not a situation which was suitable for immediate patching-up,
whether by mediation or any other means. International activity
of a prophylactic kind may have offered greater prospects of success,
and had the League been able to organize an arms embargo earlier
than the middle of 1934, the war might have ended sooner, but not,
perhaps, with the finality to which it was eventually fought. The
League's Commission, however, aimed chiefly at an agreement, and
this was something which was precluded by the attitudes of the parties.

II

Since 1945 the procedure followed in the Chaco case of sending
mediators to the countries which they are trying to bring to an
agreement has for a variety of reasons been widely followed. The
speed of modern transport has permitted it. Democratic theory has
encouraged it, for much ground has been gained by the view that
a country's disputes should be handled by the chief representatives
of the people rather than by their diplomats at the headquarters
of the UN. Sometimes the situation has demanded it, inasmuch as
the regime involved in a conflict has not belonged to the UN and
has possessed few international contacts. It has also accorded with
the popularity of an on the spot approach to matters and has
satisfied the self-esteem of new states. Thus much of the UN's

mediatory work has taken the form of the dispatch of individuals or groups to disputing states.

One of the earliest and most successful examples of UN mediation was in the dispute which arose concerning the independence of Indonesia. When, shortly after the end of World War II, British troops arrived in the Dutch East Indies to take over from the defeated Japanese, they found the newly-proclaimed Republic of Indonesia in virtual control of two of the colony's largest islands, Java and Sumatra. Fighting soon broke out between the nationalists and the representatives of the allies, and in January 1946 the situation was brought to the Security Council's notice by the Ukraine. However, there was little support for her suggestion of an international enquiry, and eighteen months elapsed before the question again appeared on the UN's agenda. It was widely supposed that the episode reflected not so much a concern to pursue the matter as an endeavour to conduct a diversionary tactic in face of Iran's complaint that Soviet officials and troops were interfering in her internal affairs.

During the intervening period the Dutch regained control of much of their colony. But they were clearly going to have considerable difficulty over Java and Sumatra, and, with the assistance of British intermediaries, entered into negotiations with the nationalist leaders. A draft document was eventually initialled at Linggadjati on 15 November 1946, which recognized the Republic of Indonesia as exercising *de facto* authority over Java, Madura, and Sumatra, and provided for the early establishment of a United States of Indonesia—a federal entity comprising the Republic, Borneo, and East Indonesia. The new sovereign state was to join with the Netherlands in a Union which would have the function of organizing co-operation in matters of joint interest, notably foreign relations and defence. The Agreement was formally signed in the following March, but relations between the parties deteriorated, and in July 1947 the Netherlands repudiated it and launched a 'police action' against the Republic in order, she said, to create the orderly conditions which were necessary if the Linggadjati goals were to be reached. This resulted in Australia, then under a Labour Government, and India bringing the matter to the Security Council.

Here the Netherlands maintained, as she was to do throughout, that the UN had no right to intervene, as the dispute was an internal one, and therefore covered by Article 2.7 of the Charter. Her claim did not go without support, but the majority of Council members were unwilling to be obstructed on such grounds, and, in a manner which was to become characteristic of the Organization, brushed the question of their legal competence to one side; both then, and subsequently, any reference to specific articles of the Charter was studiously avoided in the resolutions which were adopted on the Indonesian issue. This course undoubtedly reflected the opinion of most other members of the UN. For the general feeling was that a conflict between a European colonial Power and the *de facto* authorities in what promised to be one of the world's most populous states should not be kept from the UN by what was regarded as a technicality. Strictly viewed, it might not be an international quarrel, but it had, and would have, international repercussions, possibly of a substantial order. Accordingly, the majority considered that the dispute should come before the body which had general responsibility for the maintenance of peace and security. Their attitude did not cause the Netherlands to modify her basic position regarding the UN's competence, but neither did it lead her to boycott the Organization's proceedings or shun the missions which it established. Instead, she tried to minimize its involvement and ensure that those field activities which could not be avoided were placed in favourable hands. In this endeavour she knew that she would not be without friends at court, notably France, who, through her power of veto would probably block any really obnoxious proposal. This might be a two-edged weapon, for if the Council was unable to proceed the matter might well be taken up by the less sympathetic and less controllable Assembly. But, equally, such an outcome would be unwelcome to the other members of the Council, and therefore the prospect of a French veto could be expected to have a moderating influence.

The following two and a half years saw a good deal of UN activity in relation to the Indonesian problem. Several presences were established covering a wide range of functions, from straightforward fact-finding to activity which could easily have assumed a proselytizing character. But throughout this period the Security Council's overriding concern was to help the Indonesians and the Dutch to patch up their quarrel by offering itself as a mediator. This attitude was not, perhaps, shared on all sides in the Council, for the Soviet Union lost no opportunity to denounce the Netherlands, and clearly would have liked to see the UN bundle her out of Indonesia in short order. As it was, proceeding on what later became the familiar basis that anything touched by capitalists could not be pure, she claimed that the action taken by the Council was designed only to allow the Dutch to regain control of their colony. In which case, one might have thought that the logical consequence for the Soviet Union would have been to prevent the Council from acting by the simple device of a veto. But here she met a difficulty, for those who would be most offended by such a course were precisely those whom she was least anxious to offend—the Arab and Asian states, who looked to the UN to balance the power of the Dutch. Most keen of all, in this respect, were the Indonesians themselves, who, while they regarded the UN's action as woefully inadequate, were painfully aware that in it lay their best hopes. They would therefore have been very displeased if it had been stopped or interrupted by the state who was claiming to be their only Great Power friend. Thus the Soviet Union was in a dilemma, which she tried to resolve by abstaining on the resolutions which, in the preceding debates, she had bitterly attacked. Only at the end of the day, and on an unimportant matter, did she indulge herself, vetoing a congratulatory resolution.

But the members of the Council other than the Soviet Union and Poland, while differing a good deal in their attitude towards the Republic of Indonesia and the Netherlands, were all in favour of an agreed settlement. At this time colonialists were not perceived to have quite the bad odour which was subsequently attributed to them, and hence the suggestion that negotiations be held with them did not seem dishonourable. Further, the dispute seemed eminently suitable for mediation, for the Netherlands had already indicated, in the Linggadjati Agreement, that she was not opposed to independence for the East Indies. The problem, therefore, appeared to be one of implementation, which, while not without difficulties, offered hope of success. And there was the additional consideration that most members of the Council had an interest in the restoration of order in Indonesia, an end which was most likely to be achieved if the contestants could be brought to a mutually acceptable arrangement. Thus throughout the various activities of the UN in this case the thread of mediation can be clearly traced. What the Organization was trying to do, basically, was to assist the parties to put an end to their conflict.

The question remained, however, of the kind of role which the UN could play in endeavouring to reach this goal. There were some, apart from the Soviet Union, who favoured a relatively strong line with the Dutch. But for some time the balance of opinion within the Council was against them, for France and Britain were not the only major Powers opposed to the UN taking such a course. The United States, too, was an advocate of moderation, and she played a central role in the UN's handling of the Indonesian affair. In accordance with her traditional attitude towards colonies seeking independence, she sympathized with Indonesian aspirations, but this did not lead her, in the summer of 1947, to bolster up their detailed hopes by putting pressure on the Dutch. She may have calculated that the Indonesians were more susceptible to Dutch pressure than the

Dutch would be to the pressure of third parties, and that given the fact that both parties seemed to be looking in the direction of an agreement, the best way to obtain an early settlement was to let events take very much their natural course. Much more certainly, one can say that the American attitude was influenced by the fact that at this time her attention was very much concentrated on Europe and the possibility that the defence of the western part of the continent might have to be organized on a collective basis. The Netherlands was not a large country, but in strategic terms she was by no means unimportant, and in any event the United States was not anxious to offer gratuitous or avoidable offence to anyone in the area. Thus, for some time, the Netherlands in Indonesia benefited from America's growing preoccupation with the Soviet threat in Europe.

This was evident as soon as the first police action was considered by the Security Council, which, on 1 August 1947, called for an immediate cease-fire and the peaceful settlement of the dispute. The United States had already, on the previous day, offered the parties its good offices and within a week both had accepted, but to no purpose: the Republic asked that the United States try to establish an arbitration commission, which was quite unacceptable to the Netherlands. During August the situation was clearly deteriorating, and the question therefore came back to the Council. Both Poland and Australia were urging what can best be described as a form of political arbitration, but the United States successfully argued that the Council ought not to press any particular form of settlement on the parties, but just offer its good offices. This was to be done through the medium of a three-member committee, each party choosing one and the two so chosen selecting a third, the resultant body being called the Committee of Good Offices. It was more than the Netherlands wanted, inasmuch as it kept the UN's finger in the pie, but given the Organization's participation, the form which it took could hardly have been less objectionable. For, as the Dutch were always quick to emphasize, the parties were under no obligation to accept the Committee's suggestion. Moreover, it had to operate in private, and so there was no possibility of support being whipped up for its proposals, which, if they were to carry much weight with the parties, would need to reflect the agreement of all three of its members. In view of its composition, it was improbable that unanimity would be forthcoming for suggestions which either party would regard as drastic, particularly the Netherlands. For, besides being able to feel happy about the soundness of her own nominee on the Committee, Belgium, she could also derive some confidence from the fact that the chairman chosen by Belgium and the other nominee, Australia, was the United States. Indeed, it may be supposed that when suggesting the structure of the Committee the United States had it in mind that she would be the obvious candidate for chairman, and so would be able to play a large part in the conduct of the UN's mediatory activities.

In the event, however, the composition of the Good Offices Committee boomeranged on the Netherlands. The Committee's initial discussions with the parties made little progress, but then on 17 January 1948, it succeeded in bringing them to sign a truce and also a list of twelve principles which concerned the negotiation of a political settlement. Together, these two documents were known as the *Renville* Agreements, taking their name from the American ship on which they were signed and which had played host for a good deal of the prior discussions. At the same time the parties were formally presented by the Committee with six additional political principles for their consideration, and accepted them two days later. They had first been put forward a week earlier, and both their origin and substance seemed to make their rejection by the Dutch a foregone conclusion. But they were accepted within 24 hours, due, it seems clear, to considerable American pressure.[3] However, the contestants were not agreed on the interpretation which was to be put on the *Renville* Agreements, and subsequent negotiations made it clear that they were indeed very far from a resolution of their disagreement regarding the future of the Indies. The Netherlands rejected proposals put forward, firstly, by the Australian and American members of the Committee, and then a plan advanced on the initiative of the American member alone. Meanwhile the position of the Republic of Indonesia was rapidly deteriorating. It had lost control of a good deal of territory, was in increasing economic difficulties, and was faced with the prospect of a Communist revolt. And to cap it all, the Netherlands was moving to a position which seemed to presage a *coup de grâce*, which would neutralize both the personalities and the policies which stood chiefly in the way of her scheme for Indonesia's future. And so it was, for on 19 December 1948 she terminated the truce and began a second 'police action'. The Republican capital and its leaders were taken without difficulty, and in re-establishing her control over Republican-held areas the Netherlands met no appreciable resistance. It looked as if all was over for the Republic.

But the Dutch had overreached themselves. Not for the last time a smooth and expeditious local action turned out to be self-defeating on account of the widespread opposition which its very success

[3] See Alastair M. Taylor, *Indonesian Independence and the United Nations* (London: 1960), p. 310,

aroused. Twice in quick succession the Security Council called for the release of the political prisoners taken by the Dutch and then, on 28 January 1949, without a dissenting vote, passed a crucial resolution. France, the Soviet Union, and the Ukraine abstained, but all the other members, including Britain and America, were now willing to support a call for negotiations with a view to the creation of a sovereign Indonesia not later than 1 July 1950. In this a UN Commission for Indonesia (a renamed Committee of Good Offices). In this process a reconstituted Good Offices Committee was to play a large part, acting as the 'representative of the Security Council',[4] and being entitled to make recommendations to the Council or the parties by majority vote. Clearly the UN was now getting tough with the Netherlands, and the factor which chiefly accounted for the new policy was the changed attitude of the United States. She had reacted very strongly against the second 'police action', immediately suspending aid to the Netherlands East Indies, and followed this up with threats to cut off assistance to the Netherlands herself. In part this was undoubtedly due to the drastic nature of the action which had been taken, but it is also the case that it came at a moment which found the United States ready to alter her approach to the Indonesian problem. She had not been pleased by the attitude of the Dutch during the negotiations of the previous 18 months and this was accompanied by a growing concern with the East Asian situation, for Communism was doing well in China and not at all badly in Indo-China and Malaya. The prospect of a Communist guerrilla movement in a Dutch-held Indonesia was not alluring, and it seemed as though the most profitable course for the United States would be to work for an independent Indonesia, in the hope that it would not look too badly upon the West. Accordingly, the United States found herself in keener sympathy with the nationalist leaders than before, and was anxious to demonstrate it. This did not mean that Europe was now a secondary theatre; far from it. But plans for the North Atlantic treaty were well-advanced, and Soviet policy was not such as would be likely to encourage the Dutch to withdraw from the scheme on account of an American-inspired reverse in the East. Thus some Dutch displeasure could be afforded.

Following the passage of the resolution of 28 January events moved quickly. International pressure was maintained, and within a few months discussions between the disputants at Batavia (soon to be known as Djakarta) had resulted in agreement on the discontinuance of hostilities, the return of the Republican Government to its capital, and the holding of a Round Table conference at the Hague to arrange for the withdrawal of the Netherlands from its

4 Security Council resolution 67 (1949).

colony and the constitutional establishment of the new Indonesian state. The UN Commission played a prominent role in these negotiations and also participated fully and influentially in the Hague Conference, which opened in August and was brought to a successful conclusion in November. Sovereignty over Indonesia (except New Guinea) was formally transferred from the Netherlands to the United States of Indonesia on 27 December 1949.

This was not the end of the UN Commission's activities in Indonesia, for it had been asked to observe the implementation of the Hague agreements. But it was now of far less importance. In part this was because many issues did not give rise to difficulties. The more important reason, however, was that neither the local sovereign nor the UN wanted the Commission to continue the role it had assumed in 1949. Several incidents made this clear. One was the South Moluccas revolt of April 1950, which the Indonesian Government, having failed to negotiate a settlement, proposed to quash by the use of its armed forces. The Commission, fearing for the safety of the civilian population, twice offered its good offices and also stated its readiness to go to the headquarters of the revolt to try to persuade the rebels to negotiate with the Government. But the Government would have none of it, saying that such action would encourage the rebels by creating the impression that their case was being raised to an international level. The Netherlands, fearing the repercussions of fighting on those members of the former Netherlands Indonesian Army who came from the area of the revolt and who, pending their return, were still under Dutch control, urged the Commission to try again. It did so, but without result. It therefore suggested to the Security Council that the Indonesian Government might be called upon to utilize the existing machinery in order to settle the dispute peacefully, but the Council took no action. The revolt was finally ended towards the end of the year.

A rather similar series of events took place regarding Indonesia's constitutional structure. It had come to birth as a federal entity, but within a matter of months the Government was preparing to establish a unitary state, which it did in August 1950. The Netherlands was concerned about the effect this would have on the right of self-determination of the various parts of Indonesia, and told the Commission so, hoping that it might take the initiative which was its prerogative. But in reply the Commission said that it was under no obligation to intervene, and was obviously not minded to make a move, knowing the hostility with which it would be received by the Indonesian Government. In view of this the Netherlands let the matter drop. Yet another instance of the same trend occurred when Indonesia rejected a Netherlands suggestion that discussions concerning West New Guinea be assisted by the UN Commission or some other body. The Commission therefore kept clear of the issue.

Clearly the boot was now on the other foot so far as the utilization of UN presences was concerned. The Netherlands, prior to Indonesian independence, had always tried to minimize the UN's role, for, being the stronger party, she wanted to keep the issues under her own control. The Indonesian nationalists, for their part, had been most anxious to increase the UN's participation, seeing it as a potential counterweight to the Netherlands. When, however, Indonesia became independent, she was keen to exert her right to be master in her own house, and did not take kindly to the proposition that a UN presence should interfere in her affairs. There was also the consideration that the Australian elections of 1949 had produced a government which was less sympathetic to the Indonesian cause than the previous administration, which meant that Indonesia's nominee on the UN Commission could no longer be regarded as safe.

The Dutch, however, in their suddenly changed and much weakened position, now looked on the Commission as a possible source of needed support. Had the UN continued to interest itself in the question, its Commission on the spot might have been able to satisfy the Dutch in this respect, but New York provided no such encouragement. The issues raised by the Netherlands seemed unimportant, and would surely be pursued without success. Even, however, if the situation had been more serious or less unpromising, or both, the UN might not have stirred. Those members who had been on Indonesia's side had no reason to embarrass her, and others, now anxious to cultivate this new and potentially important member of the international society, had perhaps even less. There was, too, much support for Indonesia's view about the undesirability of intervention in the affairs of an independent state, a matter which the majority distinguished from intervention in the colonial affairs of an independent state. And all had just combined to congratulate their collective self, the UN, on a very successful ending to a difficult case. Hence there was no disposition at all to reopen it. Unwanted locally, neglected centrally, the UN Commission decided that the time had come to withdraw, and on 13 April 1951 reported that it had adjourned *sine die*.

Throughout the UN's handling of the Indonesian case its mediatory endeavours were supplemented by operations of a rather different nature, partly designed to encourage the combatants to desist from fighting, and partly to help them implement their agreements. The prophylactic side of this activity was begun in August 1947 at the outset of the Security Council's consideration of the question. The Soviet Union proposed that a commission made up of all members of the Council should be sent to Indonesia to supervise a cease-fire,[5] but although the draft resolution to this effect received the necessary seven votes, including that of the United States (but not Britain's), it failed in adoption because of a French veto. There is some question as to whether France intended this result, for it has been said that she did not expect the resolution to obtain the number of votes which would turn the opposition of a permanent member of the Council into a veto.[6] More plausible, however, is the suggestion[7] that France was aware of the consequences of her negative vote, and cast it to prevent the Soviet Union's physical involvement in what, from one point of view, was still a colonial matter. Instead of the Soviet scheme the Council, on 25 August 1947, accepted a Netherlands suggestion that a Commission be made up of those Council members with career consuls in Batavia, overruling Indonesia's objection that the countries concerned—Australia, Belgium, Britain, China, and France—were predominantly sympathetic to the Netherlands' point of view.

The Consular Commission was asked to report on the situation, and in particular on the extent to which the Council's cease-fire order was being observed. Subsequently, it was requested to make its services available, firstly to the Good Offices Committee, and then to the UN Commission for Indonesia in connection with their mandate to assist the parties to maintain a cease-fire. This it did by reporting on compliance, by helping to settle incidents, and liaising between the military forces of the two sides. Each state involved in the Consular Commission supplied a small number of military observers to enable it to carry out its functions. By the end of September 1947, 27 officers were at its disposal, rising to 55 following the *Renville* Truce Agreement, and a maximum of 63 in August 1949 when the Cease-Hostilities Agreement was signed. Thereafter their numbers declined, and they finally withdrew at the same time as the UN Commission wound up its activities. All of China's observers departed earlier, in May 1949, owing to the internal situation in their country.

The Consular Commission's reports to the Security Council, both directly and via the other UN presences in the field, were valuable, particularly on the state of affairs which existed immediately after

[5] This was the first of several Soviet attempts to secure a place on the UN's Indonesian missions. Her subsequent efforts attracted less support, the Western Powers having by then agreed on the undesirability of such a development.
[6] David W. Wainhouse, *et al*: *International Peace Observation* (Baltimore: Johns Hopkins, 1966), p. 306.
[7] Taylor, *op cit.*, p. 380.

the second 'police action', but it cannot be said that the Commission
had a significant prophylactic influence. This was due not so much
to its small numbers as to the fact that the Netherlands, while not
contemptuous of the UN observers, was not in any sense deterred
by them, as is illustrated by the fact that shortly before the second
'police action' the Dutch required most of the observers to return
to Batavia, and refused to allow them to observe behind the Netherlands' lines until the following May. So far as their supervisory
activities were concerned, however, the observers were more successful, contributing to the smooth handling of a number of matters,
notably the evacuation of 35,000 Republican soldiers from behind
the Dutch forward positions in accordance with the *Renville* Truce
Agreement, the return of the Republicans to their capital, the
implementation of the final cease-fire, and the demobilization and
repatriation of Dutch forces following the transfer of sovereignty.
Given the suspicion which each side entertained for the other, they
might have found considerable difficulty in dealing with these
issues had they not had the assistance of neutral third parties who
possessed the necessary expertise.

The UN's main object in the Indonesian case, however, was to
bring the parties to an agreement. Its success points to five conditions
which increase the likelihood of mediation being advanced by the
activity of interested outsiders.[8] In the first place, it is probably
necessary that there is no hint at the outset that the process might
be used as a channel for pressure. If, for example, the Netherlands
had been able to foresee where her acceptance of the UN's good
offices was to lead, she might have refused her co-operation. Second,
it is highly desirable that there be a set of reasonable and relatively
specific proposals for the resolution of the conflict, for this provides
a clear means of identifying the recalcitrant party and an exact set
of demands which can be made of him. In the case of Indonesia
there was no problem here, for the goal was common ground and
the steps which led in its direction had been laid down at Linggadjati
and on the USS *Renville*.

Third, the plan must, at a pinch, be acceptable to the more
doubtful party if the framework of mediation and an agreed settlement is to be maintained. Whether a proposal measures up to this
requirement can be extraordinarily difficult to say in advance, and
often can only be answered on a trial and error basis. How much
a party is ready to concede is hardly ever revealed by his public
comment, and may not even be known to the state itself in advance

---

[8] For the sake of simplicity the discussion is based on the assumption that the
obstacles to an agreed settlement lie only in one quarter. The position is more
complex where both parties are obdurate, but is similar in its essentials.

of the time of decision. Here, therefore, is the point at which it may become evident that a negotiated solution is not within reach, not, at least, along the lines currently being pursued. In which case, if the obdurate party is generally out of favour the majority may move from patching-up to proselytizing action. During 1949 the UN was not far from crossing the line between the two in respect of the Netherlands, but the critical step was never quite taken. The UN was prepared to act despite the Netherlands, but had no desire to humiliate her. And events proved that, notwithstanding the conclusions which might have been drawn from her second 'police action', the Netherlands was prepared to climb down. Thus although she was essentially defeated, the outcome was a negotiated settlement rather than unconditional surrender.

In the fourth place there must also, be some Power or Powers who are able and willing to exert telling pressure on the obstinate state. This is a requirement which is likely to be obtained only rarely. States are usually ready to discuss their fellows' quarrels, and may have quite strong views about the desirability of their being peacefully settled, but it is not often that their views are so strong that they are prepared to back them up with sanctions. This could be due to the feeling that such action is out of keeping with the nature of mediation, but it is much more likely to reflect the considerable and costly problems which stand in the way of insisting on an agreement—and also the thought that such action could establish a precedent which might later be cited to one's disadvantage. Moreover, the states in the best position to act in this way are also likely to be the ones most preoccupied and, therefore, anxious to avoid further additions to their commitments. There is also the further point that as mediation usually takes place at a fairly low level of tension—the very fact that it is being conducted is generally indicative of that—there is unlikely to be much enthusiasm for vigorous intervention. Deadlock may be undesirable, but as long as it is a relatively quiescent deadlock it may not cause very deep concern. An outside initiative in these circumstances might be hard to justify, and the state concerned would lay itself open to the charge that it was unnecessarily increasing the level of tension. Only if the situation is clearly deteriorating, or if one of the parties has already resorted to drastic action, is a state with an interest in its pacific settlement likely to move.

This is what happened in the Indonesian case. The Netherlands, throwing mediation to one side and seemingly bent on cutting Indonesia's throat succeeded only in cutting her own, for at this point the United States decided that the time had come to insist on a negotiated settlement. But it was by no means the Netherlands'

action alone which brought this about. A state is unlikely to put
strong pressure on a friend just because it dislikes what he has done.
Some more specific interest in the case is needed before a state will
go to such lengths. This the United States had, for she had come to
the view that an early settlement in Indonesia's favour was necessary,
and that a failure to achieve it might damage her own position
quite severely. Thus the second 'police action' was the occasion or
catalyst rather than the cause of the United States' changed attitude.
She still favoured negotiations, for she did not want to offend the
Netherlands more than necessary, but she was prepared to exert
herself considerably to obtain the revised goal.

This leads to the fifth and final requirement for the successful
combination of mediation and pressure. It is that there should be
no balancing counter-pressure, that the state being urged to accept
the proposals which have emerged should be isolated. This condition
can by no means be relied upon. The candidate for the application
of pressure may have a powerful associate who is prepared to come
to its aid, or it may receive an offer of support from a state with
whom it has no ties but who is a rival of those who are pressing for a
settlement. Military assistance will hardly be forthcoming in these
circumstances—and it is most improbable that there would be any
question of its need. But the promise of other forms of help could be
very credible, for there is less to be lost and perhaps more to be
gained by giving economic, diplomatic, or psychological succour
to a state in distress than there is in embarking on the rather uncertain process of using these weapons in an effort to persuade
someone to accept a scheme he dislikes. In these circumstances
those proposing to back the mediator may think twice before doing
so, for their efforts may be embarrassingly unsuccessful.

The situations in which, on the other hand, it is most likely that
mediation will be furthered by outside pressure are where the
country concerned is heavily dependent on a Power who is very
keen on a negotiated settlement or where all the Great Powers are
agreed on its necessity—or at least where none of them are opposed
to it. Their unity could reflect a common desire for a quiet and
orderly international society, or simply a conjunction of interests in a
particular matter despite a general rivalry—as in the Indonesian
case. Its beginning coincided with a hardening in East-West relations, and as it could be depicted in terms of a colony struggling
for its freedom it seemed on the face of it as if the Soviet Union
would have a field day. But she not only failed to secure a place on
any of the UN's missions but also had difficulty in representing the
Western Powers as supporters of the Dutch. For the goal of Indonesian independence was agreed on all sides, and the most that could

plausibly be said about the Western-dominated UN was that it was moving with insufficient energy. And after the second 'police action' even this charge looked thin to the point of transparency, for the Indonesian cause was clearly receiving powerful support from the United States, and Britain and France were not at all prepared to oppose it. Thus the Soviet Union was unable to make any capital out of the situation. Her 'natural' friend, the Indonesian Republic, did not need her support, and she could hardly offer it to the Netherlands, who, increasingly isolated, was unable to resist the pressure for a speedy transfer of sovereignty.

A question arises regarding the significance of an institution's involvement in the mediatory process when pressure is needed to achieve a negotiated settlement. There are two ways in which it may have a positive impact. Firstly, if its principles and desires are flouted, the sense of outrage felt by interested states may be greater than if a private mediator was treated in the same way, perhaps making it more likely that they will put their weight behind the effort at mediation. Secondly, such states may be similarly encouraged by the opportunity which the situation affords for their support to be channelled through, or placed behind an institution, for in this way their action can be represented as serving a higher cause. But it is likely that these considerations will be of marginal importance, and that the states on whom the institution's effectiveness depends will be chiefly influenced by extra-institutional factors of a specific and acute character. The alteration in the United States' attitude towards the Netherlands at the end of 1948, for example, is mainly attributable to Communist successes in China and the consequential American concern to bolster up her position in South East Asia. Had it not been for this the Netherlands might well have been able to hang on in Indonesia, and would probably have done so. She would have found international life very uncomfortable on account of the strictures emanating from New York, which would certainly have become even sterner in tone in the absence of a withdrawal. She would also have run into difficulties in Indonesia for, while locally superior, her control over Java and Sumatra had not been easily restored, and in other parts of the East Indies, which had formerly been amenable to her wishes about Indonesia's future arrangements, the second 'police action' had led to a remarkably sharp fall in her popularity. But her position might not have been insupportable. In view of the United States' changed policy, however, the Netherlands found it very expedient to retreat. On the face of it, she did so in consequence of the UN's strong tone, and by focusing the widespread hostility which the Dutch action aroused, as well as by conducting the mediatory process throughout, the Organization played a not unimportant role in securing a conclusion in Indonesia's favour. But basically, this result was a consequence of factors which lay outside the UN.

The clearing of a mediatory blockage in the way which occurred in respect of Indonesia is very uncommon. It might therefore seem that its repetition more than ten years later in regard to one aspect of the matter left over from 1949 was an exceedingly unusual coincidence. But on closer examination this reveals itself less as a coincidence than a continuation of the circumstances of the main dispute: the parties, the issue, and the general manner of the resolution were all the same, for this was the final settlement of a long and unfinished piece of vestigial business. The Dutch East Indies extended to the western part of New Guinea, but it had been agreed in 1949 that this territory should not pass to Indonesia and that the *status quo* should be maintained pending an agreement concerning its future. This was supposed to be reached within a year after the formal establishment of the United States of Indonesia by negotiations between the new state and the Netherlands. However, they found themselves unable to agree: the Indonesians demanded its incorporation into Indonesia, while the Dutch declared that they proposed to retain it until the population was in a position to exercise its right of self-determination. They also proposed that negotiations be held under the auspices of the UN Commission for Indonesia, which did not appeal to the Indonesians, who were aware that Australia, particularly Australia under a right-wing Government, did not relish the prospect of having Indonesia as a neighbour in New Guinea. Equally, the Indonesians rejected a suggestion that the matter should go to the International Court of Justice. Instead, in 1954, they took it to a body which they thought would be much more favourably disposed, the General Assembly of the UN, but although draft resolutions urging negotiations were adopted in committee in that year and, twice in 1957, they were not endorsed by the Assembly. Then there was a four-year lapse until, in, 1961, the Netherlands herself raised the question, but her proposal found favour with neither Indonesia nor the Assembly.[9]

As was implied by the fact of the Dutch initiative matters were now coming to a head. Three years earlier Indonesia had already said that she was prepared to annex West New Guinea by force, and in December 1961 there was a clash between the Dutch and Indonesians. The following month saw an attempt by Indonesia to land her forces in the territory by both sea and air, and although they were repulsed, time was clearly running out for the Netherlands. The military balance of 13 years before had largely been reversed,

[9] See below, pp. 157–158.

and Indonesia's growing bellicosity increased the likelihood that Dutch rule in West New Guinea would come to a violent and ignominious end. The state of the diplomatic balance made such an outcome all the more probable, for it remained very much the same as in 1949, a point which was underlined by the fact that both the Acting Secretary-General of the UN and, more significantly, the United States now urged the disputants to enter into negotiations. The Netherlands had always rejected this idea in the past because of Indonesia's insistence that the only thing to talk about was the arrangement of a transfer of sovereignty, stating in reply that the wishes of the inhabitants must first be ascertained. Now, however, she decided that the time had come to abandon this position, and in consequence U Thant appointed a former (and subsequent) member of the American Foreign Service, Mr Ellsworth Bunker, as his mediator. By the summer of 1962 agreement was reached, providing, once more, for a Dutch retreat, but again without complete humiliation. On this occasion the face-saving device of an interim period of UN administration was adopted.[10]

A dispute which, while altogether different in scale and significance, raised issues very similar to those of the Indonesian case, was that between France and Tunisia concerning the French base at Bizerta. Yet, the way in which it was handled provides a sharp contrast to the UN's response to the problems which arose over the independence of Indonesia. Conflict broke out very unexpectedly in the summer of 1961 when, with an uncharacteristic lack of moderation, President Bourguiba of Tunisia demanded that France immediately begin a phased withdrawal from the base, which was occupied under a 1958 treaty. In its timing as well as its terms, the message invited rejection, for it was presented on the eve of the reopening of the Algerian negotiations, a moment when France could not afford the slightest impression of weakness. But, as well as rejecting it, France also began to extend the runway of her airfield at Bizerta, giving the impression that, far from going, she was planning a long stay. As a result, Tunisian volunteers began to blockade the base on 19 July, and fighting broke out between the regular forces of both sides. The Tunisians lost some 700 men (a revised and almost doubled figure was issued a month later) and the French 25 before hostilities were brought to a halt on 23 July, following a call from the Security Council. The Council also urged the return of all armed forces to their original positions, but the French remained in the town of Bizerta in order to maintain their lines of communication and the security of their base.

[10] See further, below, pp. 159–169.

Besides passing its cease-fire resolution, the Council had rejected a draft resolution which aimed at the withdrawal of all French forces from Tunisia, and also a milder one urging Franco-Tunisian negotiations. The latter proposal had little appeal for Tunisia and her friends, for they recognized that in bilateral negotiations the French would hold a marked advantage. Hence their policy was to keep the question before the UN in the hope that its sympathy for Tunisia's case would generate sufficient support to persuade France to evacuate Bizerta. The first move in this direction was a request from President Bourguiba for a direct and personal exchange of views with the Secretary-General, who, saying that he considered it his duty to do what he could to establish contact between the parties, left immediately for Tunisia. Thus Mr Hammarskjöld depicted his mission as one of minimal mediation, and it may be that he recognized that the most he would be able to do towards establishing contact would be to urge a moderate course on the Tunisians. For not only was France steadfastly opposed to the intervention of a third party, but was also very likely to look with particular disfavour on that role being conducted by an Organization for which President de Gaulle rarely bothered to hide his contempt. Not surprisingly, therefore, the Secretary-General's attempt to engage in direct mediation was a complete failure. His suggestion that he might visit Paris was turned down; the Commander of the Bizerta base was instructed not to see him; and when visiting Bizerta his car was held up and searched by French troops. The question now went back to the Security Council, which found itself unable to come either to a mild or a critical decision, so Tunisia turned to the Assembly. Within a short time a majority of members were persuaded to request a Special Session, which, after a five-day debate, passed a resolution calling for immediate negotiations for the withdrawal of all French forces from Tunisian territory.[11]

If the Indonesian precedent had been followed, key members of the UN would by now have been deciding that the time had come to put an end to French obstinacy, particularly as she had been so disrespectful of the Organization as to boycott the Assembly's Special Session. But putting effective pressure on France was a far more difficult proposition than it was in respect of the Netherlands. And those who, by virtue of their links with France, were in the best position to do so were the least willing. The United States, Britain, and other Western states had some sympathy for Tunisia, and a particular concern not to offend the Afro-Asians by seeming to con-

[11] The idea that a UN force might be sent to Bizerta was raised informally with the Secretary-General by the United States: see Joseph P. Lash, *Dag Hammarskjöld* (London: Cassell, 1962), page 295. However, the French attitude made any such scheme completely unrealistic.

done military action against one of their number by a colonial Power. But they were also most anxious not to oppose their ally for, quite apart from the fact that pressure would have been unlikely in the extreme to cause de Gaulle to withdraw and would only have given great offence to him, this was a time of crisis for the West. The Berlin Wall was started on 13 August, and the maintenance of Western unity was therefore an overriding consideration. Accordingly, the Western powers were exceedingly embarrassed by the Bizerta affair, and in the Assembly abstained on the ground that no useful purpose would be served by adopting a critical resolution.

It seems that the strength of this argument soon appealed to the realistically-minded Bourguiba. The dispute was hurting Tunisia more than it was her adversary, and the endeavour to use the UN to press France into an agreement was clearly a failure. Tunisia therefore wanted to cut her losses as soon as possible, and the measure of her desire to do so can be seen in the unlikely looking peg which she pressed into service. In Paris on 5 September, at one of his famous press conferences, de Gaulle maintained his country's stand regarding Bizerta. But in Tunisia some of his words were interpreted to mean that France was contemplating an eventual evacuation, and the local situation swiftly improved. At the end of the month France agreed to withdraw to the positions which she had held before the fighting occurred, her freedom of communication being guaranteed verbally. In October Tunisia asked for direct talks regarding the future of the base. These were begun towards the end of the year but broke down in January 1962 due to France's refusal to set a date for her withdrawal. However, Tunisia was still in a conciliatory mood and agreed to a French suggestion that talks be resumed in six months. This was done just after Algeria had become independent, and although no formal agreement was reached, France began to evacuate her forces, leaving the base finally in October 1963.

It could perhaps be argued that the outcome of the Bizerta dispute was expedited by the Assembly debate of August 1961, inasmuch as it may have encouraged France not to delay in coming to the decision that the base could safely be relinquished. But this is about all one can say regarding the UN's impact on the matter. The strange episode of July 1961 must have quickly brought it home to Tunisia (though it is surprising that it needed to be brought home) that she was not able to throw the French out of Bizerta by the threat or use of force. Therefore the most she could hope for was that the UN's endorsement of her case would lead to France being pressed into an agreement for withdrawal. But even this proved unrealistic, for the necessary pressure was never in sight. And, as the Secretary-General's undistinguished visit to Tunisia made clear, even a minor mediatory role was not open to the Organization, for France, upon whose co-operation it depended, would not permit it. She was not opposed to negotiations with the Tunisians, first about immediate problems and later regarding the future of the Bizerta base, but her distaste for the UN was such that she would not accept it as an intermediary.

III

As far as UN mediation is concerned, the Indonesian and Bizerta cases represent two extremes. In the one, mediation was eventually brought to a successful conclusion through the application of pressure by a concerned Great Power. In the other, it was abandoned virtually before it had started on account of the attitude of one of the parties. Of the two, the latter is the more typical because it is rare for mediation to be accompanied by effective pressure in favour of an agreed settlement, which has the consequence that the success of such activities is essentially dependent on the policies of the contestants. France's policy on the ending of the Bizerta crisis highlighted this basic fact in a particularly vivid way. It often happens, however, that a discouraging attitude, whether in the shape of a refusal to treat with the UN or an inflexible approach to negotiations, does not prevent the UN from attempting mediation. A number of cases bear witness to this point, one of them being Palestine.

Its own scheme for the solution of the Palestine problem having proved a dead letter,[12] the UN established the office of Mediator on 14 May 1948, which was the eve both of Britain's formal abandonment of authority in Palestine and of the outbreak of war between the Arabs and the Jews. The Mediator, Count Folke Bernadotte of Sweden, could hardly have begun his search for an agreement at a less propitious time, and it was not surprising that he made no headway on the basic issue. He also became deeply involved in the supervision of the truce which the Security Council had called for on 29 May and that which it ordered on 15 July.[13] On 11 December, therefore, provision was made for the transfer of the Mediator's patching-up responsibilities to a Palestine Conciliation Commission, although he was left with the final task of ensuring that, in accordance with a Council decision of 16 November, armistice agreements were established in all sectors of Palestine.[14]

By this time the military situation had made both sides think in

[12] See above, pp. 30–31 and below, pp. 141–144 and pp. 170–171.
[13] See below, pp. 272–276.
[14] In September Count Bernadotte had been assassinated in Jerusalem. A member of the UN Secretariat, Dr Ralph Bunche, was then appointed as Acting Mediator.

# MEDIATION 61

terms of the advantages of putting a halt to the fighting,[15] and following negotiations on the island of Rhodes, where the Acting Mediator had this headquarters, Armistice Agreements were signed between Israel and Egypt on 24 February 1949, and Israel and Jordan on 3 April. The Israel-Lebanon Agreement was negotiated at a former Palestinian frontier post, and concluded on 23 March. That between Israel and Syria, which gave rise to the most difficulty, was eventually signed on 20 July, having been negotiated in no-man's-land—territory which the General Assembly's partition plan had allotted to the proposed Jewish state but which had been captured by Syria. In all these negotiations the Acting Mediator and his personal representatives played an invaluable role, chairing the formal meetings and being extremely and fruitfully active in private discussions. Had it not been for their efforts, and in particular for Dr Bunche's diplomatic skill, it is very conceivable that the negotiations would have been unsuccessful.[16]

The Acting Mediator having completed his duties, he was relieved of them by the Council in August 1949, leaving the Conciliation Commission with the field to itself in its endeavour to assist the parties towards a final settlement of all outstanding questions between them. When the Commission was established in the preceding December it had been laid down that it should consist of three states appointed by the permanent members of the Security Council, which had led to a difference of opinion. Four of the five agreed that two of their number—the United States and France—should serve together with Turkey, but the Soviet Union objected to the Commission being made up mainly of Great Powers, and urged that in order to introduce a spirit of impartiality and objectivity smaller states, such as Poland, should be included. Poland herself appealed to the principle of equitable geographical distribution. Both these suggestions fell on stony ground, for the Western states were determined to keep the Soviet Union and her

---

[15] See below, pp. 277–278.
[16] Cease-fire and armistice agreements, inasmuch as they are usually meant to do no more than erect some interim bulwarks against the continuation or renewal of violence can be regarded as instances of prophylactic activity. Where, however, as is often the case, they are also envisaged as the precursors of a final settlement, they may equally well be seen as the first stage in a patching-up process. In 1949 it was at least hoped that the Arab-Israeli Armistice Agreements would soon give way to a treaty of peace, which justifies their mention in this Chapter. But if, as here, such hopes are disappointed, any arrangements for the supervision of the cease-fire or armistice fall into the category of prophylactic rather than patching-up operations: they are being continued with a different intention from that with which they were established, with a view to keeping the situation from getting worse instead of trying to ensure its betterment. Accordingly, the UN's attempt to maintain the 1949 Agreements is discussed in Part Two, in the Chapter on Sedation, and not in the next Chapter of Part One.

friends as far away as possible from the unsettled Middle Eastern
situation. In this the United States was to the fore: having lately
succeeded to Britain's role as the guardian of stability in the
eastern Mediterranean, she wanted to ensure that the UN's
field machinery would minimize trouble rather than be a source of
it.

More significant, perhaps, from the point of view of the Commission's chances of success, was the attitude to it of the parties.
Israel was not opposed to its establishment, but generally argued
that the most important question—the territorial one—could best
be settled by the parties themselves. The Arabs, on the other hand,
took exception to the idea of such a Commission, for to their mind
the suggestion that there was a problem to be discussed was half-way
towards recognition of the principle of partition. In their view Israel
was in illegal and immoral occupation of Arab territory. It may,
once, have been the home of the Jews, but since the seventh century,
with the relatively brief exception of the twelfth, it had been held
by Arabs, and so was the homeland of part of the Arab people.
In these circumstances there could be no question of a settlement on
the basis of Israel's existence. The only way in which the dispute
could be settled was for the state of Israel to go into liquidation.
This, however, was asking the politically impossible of the Israelis.
They were prepared to discuss border questions and to live at peace
with their neighbours. But they regarded the land which they now
held as their own, and were prepared to defend it vigorously, to the
last yard and the last man.

Here, then, was an irreconcilable dispute and the Conciliation
Commission soon found that it had been given an impossible task.
It got off to an illusory start, for in May 1949 the parties agreed
to take the 1947 partition plan as a starting-point and framework
for their discussion of territorial questions. All of the Armistice
Agreements had not then been signed, and the Arabs may well have
been anxious not to provoke the militarily superior Israelis. They
may also have calculated that Israel, in possession of a larger area
than had been assigned to her under the 1947 plan, would be unwilling to give up any of it, and could therefore equally well,
more profitably if not attacked on the lesser issue of her boundaries,
than on the greater one of her very existence. In any event, the Arabs
lost nothing by agreeing to negotiate on these terms, for it was
quickly evident that they would not have to meet an Israeli readiness
to settle on the basis of the boundaries suggested in 1947. Indeed, the
parties refused to do so much as talk to each other directly, for the
Arabs wanted to be treated as a single party, whereas Israel saw
greater possibilities in separate discussions with each Arab state. In

an endeavour to break the deadlock the Commission called a conference in Paris in the autumn of 1951 and presented proposals to each side, preceded by a preamble declaring the pacific intentions of the parties. Even the preamble led to disagreement, and on the substantive points the parties took up positions which seemed to be completely opposed. The Commission therefore terminated the conference and with it, in effect, the endeavour to settle the major problem.

In its report it criticized Israel for her refusal to accept those of the 600,000 refugees made homeless by the 1948–49 war who wished to return to their homes, and the Arab countries for their clear unwillingness to move towards a negotiated settlement with Israel, and stated that all the procedures open to it had been exhausted. The implication seemed to be that the time had come for the Assembly to wind up the Commission, and the Soviet Union proposed as much, not liking the United States' membership and her own exclusion. The large majority of members, however, were not prepared to do this and the Arab states themselves saw some value in continuing the Commission. They could be indicted by it for their unwillingness to accept Israel's existence, but equally the Commission could be used as a means of drawing attention to Israel's refusal to implement the Assembly's request, made when establishing the Commission, for the repatriation of refugees or the payment of compensation—an issue which was both specific and emotional. The Commission was therefore urged to continue its efforts to obtain an agreement. Its response was to concentrate on two issues which, in relation to the main problem were very unimportant: the release of Arab refugee bank accounts blocked in Israel, and the identification and valuation of refugee-owned land in Israel. By 1956 four-fifths of the blocked accounts had been released and in 1964 the Commission reported that it had completed its work on refugee-owned land. This might seem to open the way to a settlement of the refugee problem, for Israel has occasionally departed from her view that it is an integral part of the whole question of Arab-Israeli relations, and has indicated her preparedness to separate the two and pay compensation— provided she is helped to do so, and that the refugees are integrated in the Arab world. However, quite apart from the fact that the Arabs dispute the basis on which the Commission valued the refugees' land, they show no disposition at all to agree to the Israeli condition of integration, arguing that if the refugees wish to return to their homes, they must be permitted to do so. This Israel refuses to accept, because of the tremendous economic and security problems which such a course would involve.

Thus the Commission labours in the wilderness. In effect it has

been reduced to dealing with the refugee problem, and even here it
can make no progress. Each year it reports to the Assembly, which
in turn usually urges it to intensify its efforts and quickly passes
by. And so far as the wider issue is concerned, the UN had at an
early date apparently given up the effort to do anything positive
about it. There were some hopes that the Suez crisis might have
induced some flexibility, but they were soon disappointed. A
mutually acceptable solution seemed impossible, and the pressure
which would be required to change either side's mind was
immensely greater than the most which would conceivably be put
behind a UN plan. The UN would not formally admit failure,
not least for the reason that it was also maintaining a significant
prophylactic activity in relation to the problem, and wished to do
nothing to encourage the criticism that it was more interested
in keeping disputes quiet than in repairing them. But until
1967 it had to all intents and purposes abandoned its patching-up
role.

Then, however, the search for an agreed settlement was given a
considerable stimulus by the six-day Arab-Israeli war of June 1967,
in which Israel won a remarkable victory. It was generally thought
that Israel ought not to remain in occupation of the Arab territory
which she had captured, so that there was in any event a need for an
agreement between the parties. And it was widely hoped that the
opportunity could be taken to put Arab-Israeli relations on a much
more stable footing than they had been at any time since Israel's
creation. On 22 November 1967 the Security Council unanimously
affirmed that a just and lasting peace settlement must include an
Israeli withdrawal from the territories which she had recently
occupied, and the 'Termination of all claims or states of belligerency
and respect for and acknowledgement of the sovereignty, territorial
integrity and political independence of every State in the area and
their right to live in peace within secure and recognized boundaries
free from threats or acts of force.'[17] It also spoke of the necessity of a
just settlement of the refugee problem and of free navigation through
international waterways. To help in the achievement of these ends
the Secretary-General was requested to send a Special Representative to the Middle East, and he appointed Mr Gunnar Jarring,
Sweden's ambassador to the Soviet Union.

Mr Jarring set up his headquarters in Nicosia, Cyprus, and soon
broke the deadlock which was holding up a complete exchange of
prisoners. He also appeared to open the way to the extrication of
15 ships which were stranded in the blocked Suez Canal. But this
success was illusory for Israel refused to allow the Canal to be com-

[17] Security Council resolution 242 (1967).

pletely cleared until her right to use it had been firmly established, and the UAR would not agree to the opening of one end of the Canal only.

In pursuit of his main goal of a peaceful settlement Mr Jarring embarked on a series of visits to the relevant capitals, although not to Damascus as Syria refused to have anything to do with him. He found great difficulty in making progress. Led by the UAR the Arab states insisted that Israel must accept and promise to implement the Council's resolution, by which they meant that part of the resolution which called for her withdrawal, before they would agree even to indirect talks regarding a settlement. For her part, Israel was not willing to make such far-reaching concessions in advance of the negotiations, and also emphasized the necessity for direct talks and for a formal treaty of peace. She has, however, gone some way towards the Arab position, offering to 'respond affirmatively',[18] to and 'abide by'[19] the resolution, and saying that she is agreeable to the UN's involvement in her negotiations with the Arabs.

The Arab states, too, have not been wholly intransigent. The Lebanon presents no real problem: as Israelis have been reported as saying, whichever Arab state makes the first agreement with Israel, the Lebanon can be counted upon to be a very close second. Jordan has clearly shown her interest in the success of the Jarring mission—but also her inability, for reasons of domestic politics, to take a conciliatory initiative. And the UAR has indicated a willingness to negotiate through the UN mediator and, possibly, to make concessions to Israel in advance of her withdrawal from Arab territory. However, President Nasser has his domestic problems too and is very reluctant to take the plunge into talks in which his side would, essentially, be in the poorer position, its bilateral weakness not being counter-balanced by the diplomatic support it could expect to receive. Israel has also given him several excuses for stalling: the promulgation at the end of February of 1968 certain administrative measures which were widely interpreted as meaning that the occupied areas would no longer be regarded as 'enemy territory'; the conduct in March of what Israel called 'localized and limited preventive measures'[20] in Jordan which involved the use of tanks, jet aeroplanes, and paratroops in a thrust on a 200 mile front to within 25 miles of Amman; and the routing of a military parade through the Arab sector of Jerusalem at the beginning of May. Whether a less provocative policy would have secured the opening of talks is very problematical. But neither side is without blame for the fact that

[18] *New York Times*, 9 March 1968.
[19] Ibid., 2 May 1968.
[20] Ibid., 22 March 1968.

as of the end of June 1968 the discussion of a settlement has not even begun.

Five months of intensive travel and talks having failed to produce any progress on the main issue, Mr Jarring proposed, early in May, that the work of his mission should be transferred from the Middle East to the UN headquarters in New York. The parties agreed and there was some hope that the move would be followed by pressure in favour of a compromise. Both major Powers have an interest, although perhaps in varying degree, in Middle Eastern stability, of which the unanimous Security Council resolution of 22 November is evidence. And a settlement could be rather easier to obtain than prior to the 1967 war, for Israel is now in a better position to make concessions and the Arabs have been given cause to reassess the strength of their bargaining position. However, with the Soviet Union backing the Arabs and the United States being generally seen as Israel's ultimate protector, it is unlikely that the Powers will unite behind a really tough line in the Middle East, especially as toughness cannot, in this context, be guaranteed to produce an agreement.

The parties are still, in fact, far from the frame of mind which is likely to produce a settlement, whatever outside representations are made. Israel has from time to time indicated her readiness to withdraw in return for firm and final agreements with the Arab states, but it is as certain as anything can be in politics that she will not voluntarily relinquish the Old City of Jerusalem. And, given her deep suspicion of the Arabs and their continued verbal belligerence, she will undoubtedly be very demanding on the question of what constitutes a satisfactory peace.[21] So far as the Arabs are concerned, even if, contrary to their fundamental policy of the past 20 years, they could bring themselves not just to a formal recognition of Israel's existence but also to a public acceptance of her right to live in peace in the area, it is very difficult indeed to see them doing this for anything less than a complete return to the *status quo ante*—and perhaps not even for that. Thus the movement of Mr Jarring's mission from the Middle East to New York could be the first step away from substantive to ritual endeavours to settle this intractable problem.

In the Palestine case UN mediation was conducted alongside and in the shadow of the Organization's more important prophylactic activity. In the Congo the two roles were again pursued, but the disparity between them was very much greater. This was partly

---

[21] For a discussion of the position regarding the west bank of the River Jordan, see below, pp. 350–352.

because the UN Congo Force, by virtue of its size and functions, would in any event have been likely to steal the limelight from a small and generally unobtrusive mediatory presence. But it was also due to the fact that the situation presented fewer opportunities for mediation than many of the problems in which the UN had been involved. The former Belgian Congo achieved independence on 30 June 1960, and only a fortnight later, in consequence of the mutiny of the army and the breakdown of public order, the Security Council sent a force to the country. In its international aspect, it was largely designed to prevent outsiders from intervening, and so in this connection there were no immediate disputants whom the UN might have tried to bring to an agreement. The force was also designed to facilitate the withdrawal of the Belgian troops who had emerged from their bases in the Congo and neighbouring Ruanda-Urandi in order to protect lives and property. It was the Congolese Government's objection to their intervention which resulted in it taking the question to the UN, and so here was a dispute between two sovereign states in which the UN might have attempted mediation. But within a few months the Belgians had quietly withdrawn from most of the Congo. Some remained for a further year, seconded to Mr Tshombe's gendarmerie in secessionist Katanga, but they were involved in a dispute which was considered less in the framework of Belgian-Congo relations than in the context of the Congo's internal divisions. These were not confined to the question of Katanga, and they also, indirectly, had international consequences. Hence, in principle, there was scope for mediation. But not in practice. For the various groups and factions within the Congo were interested not so much in mediation as in victory or survival, according to their situation. In these circumstances the UN might have been hard put to induce a less extreme frame of mind, even if it had been agreed on its desirability. But in New York no less than in the Congo the prevailing mood in relation to the country's internal affairs was far from conciliatory.

Thus the UN's patching-up efforts in this case were very small affairs. Early in September 1960 the Soviet Union, her own clumsiness having been assisted by Western states, found herself in the position of having to veto an Afro-Asian draft resolution which was before the Security Council. The question was immediately transferred to the Assembly which, on 20 September, passed a resolution asking, *inter alia*, the Advisory Committee on the Congo to help the Congolese settle their political differences by appointing Afro-Asian conciliators. Accordingly, the Committee set up a Conciliation Commission comprising the representatives of all the African states who had troops in the Congo and the four major Asian contributors.

The Congolese Government objected strongly to its not having been consulted regarding the Commission, taking particular exception to the inclusion of governments who had 'publicly taken a stand on problems of Congolese internal policy',[22] meaning a stand which was contrary to that of the Government. This, added President Kasavubu, would be difficult for 'Congolese public opinion' to understand.[23] He insisted on the removal of unfriendly elements and instructed Leopoldville hoteliers not to accommodate the Commission. Fortunately for its members comfort, the main offenders—Guinea, Mali, and the United Arab Republic—withdrew before the Commission arrived in the Congo in January 1961, their ground being that the Commission, like the UN Force, from which they were also withdrawing, was weighted against the left-wing Gizenga regime in Stanleyville. However, this did not put the Congolese Government in a co-operative humour, and the other main factions were not very helpful. Thus the Commission was unsuccessful. The UN did make one further mediatory attempt, the General Assembly establishing a Commission of Conciliation of seven member states in April 1961. It was charged with the task of assisting the Congolese to achieve reconciliation and end their political crisis, but did not play an active role in subsequent events. In effect the UN's unenthusiastic attempt at mediation had come to an end. The ground was too stony for conciliatory seeds, and in any event there was a grave shortage of sowers. Britain was one of the few who were anxious that the activity be conducted, at least in relation to rightwing groups, but her motives were suspect.

The experience of the Congo Conciliation Commission draws vivid attention to the difficulties which can arise when the representatives of states are appointed as mediators. Awareness of them may help to account for the fact that since the middle of the 1950s UN mediation has generally been conducted by individuals responsible only to the Organization, and often by members of the Secretariat, most notably by the Secretary-General himself. This tendency can be traced back to 1950, when the Security Council appointed a Representative to try to get India and Pakistan to agree on the holding of a plebiscite in Kashmir.[24] Another development during the period has been that mediation has usually been conducted less formally, in the sense that the creation of a mediatory office in respect of a particular dispute has been rare. Instead the Assembly or Council,

[22] Quoted in Catherine Hoskyns: *The Congo since Independence* (London: Oxford University Press, 1965), p. 259.
[23] *Ibid.*
[24] See above, p. 26.

or the disputing parties, have simply asked the Secretary-General to mediate or appoint a mediator. And sometimes the Secretary-General has done so on his own initiative. Then, if circumstances become less propitious, the mediation can just stop: there is no question of having to wind up an office or, the more popular alternative, keep it in being although it has become superfluous. In these ways mediation has become more flexible, and, more important, the possibility of the mediator being suspected of partiality has lessened. However, as several cases have emphasized, belief in a mediator's good faith and objectivity, while a precondition of success, is not a guarantee of it.

One such issue was the dispute between Britain and Saudi Arabia over the Buraimi oasis. In eastern Arabia frontiers are undelimited over long distances, and an attempt made in 1935 to place them on a more certain basis had been unsuccessful. Among the reasons for this was the Saudi Arabian desire to obtain an outlet to the sea in this area through territory which Britain recognized as belonging to someone else and which she also had a legal obligation to protect. For almost twenty years the question lay dormant, but in 1952, shortly after the discovery of rich oil resources along the Persian Gulf and at a time when both King Ibn Saud's health and Britain's willingness to assert herself in the Middle East were declining markedly, Saudi nationalists seized the oasis. Within whose sovereignty it fell was not entirely clear, for both the Sultan of Muscat and Oman and the Sheikh of Abu Dhabi, the rulers of two independent states, could make out a claim, the Sheikh receiving the allegiance of six of the eight villages of the oasis and the Sultan that of the remainder. But it seemed evident that Saudi Arabia, despite the presence of some of her slave traders, was not entitled to it, and it was therefore with some confidence that Britain, who looked after Abu Dhabi's external affairs and had a treaty of friendship with Muscat and Oman, proposed that the dispute should go to arbitration. At the end of 1954 it was agreed that a tribunal consisting of one representative from Britain, Saudi Arabia, and three neutral states should adjudicate. However, the Saudis tried to improve their cause by means of bribery, both in the oasis and among the members of the Tribunal, and the arrangement broke down with the withdrawal of the British and one neutral member in the latter part of 1955. The oasis was immediately reoccupied by British-officered troops, an act which, so Britain discovered during the Suez crisis, was privately referred to by the United States as one of aggression. Not for the last time, Saudi Arabia threatened to complain to the Security Council, and received words of encouragement from an ideologically remote source, the Soviet Union, but nothing was done and for some years the dispute did no more than smoulder.

Diplomatic relations between Britain and Saudi Arabia were broken off over Suez, and when Egypt revived her official link with Britain in 1959 Saudi Arabia failed to follow suit on account of Buraimi. The two countries did, however, hold talks at the UN with the Secretary-General, and in 1960 Mr Hammarskjöld appointed a special representative, Mr Herbert de Ribbing, the Swedish ambassador to Spain, to study the problem and try to secure an agreement. In this cause he did a good deal of travelling and brought the parties together in bilateral talks, but without result as far as Buraimi was concerned. However, the 1962 republican revolution in the Yemen caused Saudi Arabia to reconsider her position. In 1963 full diplomatic relations with Britain were resumed, and it was agreed that discussions regarding the oasis should continue with Mr de Ribbing's assistance. The matter has not been settled, and the outlook for mediation is not bright. But relations between the two countries have become noticeably warmer, and Saudi Arabia has not prosecuted her claim to Buraimi with any vigour. No doubt she thinks that while Britain maintains her present relationship with the Trucial states of the Persian Gulf and with Muscat and Oman, the best she can do is to let the matter rest, especially as she is not likely to obtain much support if she reopened the matter in one way or another. The United States, despite her estimate of the 1955 reoccupation, would hardly encourage Saudi Arabia to precipitate a dispute with Britain. And the Soviet Union, for all her fine words at the same time, would probably find a close association with Saudi Arabia somewhat embarrassing, certainly in the context of the UN.

In fact, from the UN's point of view a significant part of the Buraimi problem lay in the fact that it did not fall neatly into any approved category. Britain could easily be condemned for continued imperialism in the area and her support for reactionary regimes. But the claimant state is perhaps even less attractive to the anti-colonialists, a factor which helps to account for Saudi Arabia's reluctance to go ahead with her threats to take the matter to the UN. If, however, her monarchical regime was overturned and replaced by a republic no doubt the question would then attract a good deal of the UN's attention. Or, when Britain withdraws her forces from the Persian Gulf—and they are due to go by the end of 1971—the issue might become alive again. But in either event there would probably be even less likelihood of an amicable settlement than there has been up to now.

A dispute which could easily have caused the UN infinitely more embarrassment than that over Buraimi was one which arose between Rwanda and Burundi at the very end of 1963. The power of the tall aristocratic Tutsis in Rwanda had been broken in 1959 by their former subjects, the Hutus, and more than 100,000 Tutsis thereupon fled the country. In December 1963 some of these refugees invaded Rwanda from neighbouring Burundi, and almost succeeded in taking its capital. They were driven back, but the panic with which the Rwanda Government was seized resulted in drastic action being taken against its remaining Tutsi subjects, who numbered about 250,000. No less than 35,000 were estimated to have been killed, and some observers thought that the situation could properly be spoken of in terms of genocide.

These events exacerbated the already strained relations between Rwanda and Burundi, and it might have been thought that there was a strong case for UN intervention, both to resolve the immediate tension and to prevent its repetition. However, with the Secretary-General trying to get the UN's Congo Force out of that country as quickly as possible, this was no time for substantial UN action. More to the point, even a mild role for the Organization would probably have been unpopular with most members. For they had no wish to publicize, let alone denounce, the massacre of Africans by Africans, not even when, as here, it had a marked international aspect. The UN was not completely inactive, for in January 1964 and again in February the Secretary-General sent a special representative, Mr M. Dorsinville, on a peace mission to the two countries. But there was no demand by the parties for the UN's involvement (Rwanda was reported also to have made a representative of the International Committee of the Red Cross unwelcome) and no pressure for it from the Organization's membership. The matter was therefore quietly dropped, and, except in relation to its impact on the refugee problem, finds no place in the UN's public records.

An internal dispute with strong international connections and repercussions in which the UN has attempted mediation is that of Cyprus. At the end of the 1950s Britain's impending departure raised the question of what protection was to be afforded to the Turkish Cypriot minority against the Greek majority. The Turks formed about one-fifth of the island's population of about 600,000, and in the Zürich and London Agreements of February 1959, which were subsequently embodied in a series of treaties and in the Cyprus Constitution, they were provided with a variety of seemingly powerful safeguards. They were given 30 per cent of the legislature, civil service, and police, and 40 per cent of the army. Fiscal legislation required the concurrence of a majority of the Turkish deputies

in the legislature, and the Turkish Vice-President was given a veto
in matters of defence and foreign policy. Turkey was entitled to
maintain an army contingent in Cyprus, as was Greece, and both
these Powers and Britain were to join on guaranteeing the independence and territorial integrity of Cyprus and the basic articles of the
Constitution. Both union with Greece (*enosis*) and partition were
forbidden. Should concerted action prove impossible each of the
guarantors had the right to act separately.

In 1960 Cyprus came to independence on this basis and soon
found that the provisions of the Constitution which protected the
Turks were often difficult to work. There was also mounting
resentment on the part of the Greeks at the disproportionate influence wielded by the Turkish Cypriots, and from time to time each
community took pleasure in obstructing the other. The unitary
taxation system broke down at the end of 1961 when the Turks
refused to vote for the budget, and a year later there was a serious
dispute over whether they should have their own municipalities.
The crisis came to a head in the latter part of 1963. In August President Makarios announced that he intended to put forward certain
constitutional amendments, which produced increasing belligerence
on both sides. In November his proposed changes were made public,
which, while not uniformly hostile to Turkish interests, would have
removed some of their most important internal safeguards. On 21
December 1963 fighting broke out in Nicosia and quickly spread
throughout the island.

The immediate reaction of Britain, Greece, and Turkey was to
offer their good offices and a peace-keeping force which would help
to keep the communities apart. The Cyprus Government, fearing
Turkish intervention, accepted this proposal, and on 27 December
the first British patrol became operational, being able to do so with
much speed on account of the presence of British forces in two
bases which had been retained under British sovereignty when
Cyprus became independent. Discussions took place regarding a
more permanent arrangement for keeping the peace, for Britain,
who was bearing the brunt of the operation, was anxious at least to
spread the responsibility. However, neither of the suggestions which
she made was acceptable to President Makarios. It looked as if the
question would have to go back to the UN (it had come briefly
before the Security Council at the end of December), and on 15
February both Britain and Cyprus asked for an early meeting of the
Security Council, Britain just getting in first.[25] The Council's main

---

[25] The procedural advantage which a disputant obtains by instituting international
proceedings had already been vividly exemplified by Britain in a dispute which
arose with Persia in 1932 following the cancellation of the Anglo-Persian Oil Com-

business was to discuss the establishment of an international force, and on 4 March it recommended that one be created.[26] But it also took account of the problem which gave rise to the need for a force, and recommended that, in agreement with the four countries concerned, the Secretary-General designate a mediator who was to use his best efforts with the representatives of the two communities and the Four Governments to promote a peaceful and agreed settlement. The Secretary-General suggested Mr J. Rolz-Bennett of Guatemala, a member of his own Executive Office, but Turkey rejected him on the ground that he lacked the necessary stature and competence. Subsequently their agreement was obtained to the appointment of Mr S. S. Tuomioja, the Finnish ambassador to Sweden. Upon his death in September, ex-President Galo Plaza of Ecuador, who had been in Cyprus for some months as the Secretary-General's special political representative, was appointed.

In this case it seems likely that a mediatory presence was established more in the hope than in the expectation that an agreed settlement could be obtained, for this was, and is, a particularly difficult dispute. On the one hand the Greeks had by 1963 fairly clearly come to the view that in 1959 and 1960 they had made too many concessions to the Turks, and that the time had now come to rectify the earlier mistakes. The Turkish position, on the other hand, had hardened in the opposite direction. They had come to realize that whatever the Constitution might say, the physical fact of their being a minority meant that they were in a weak and exposed position for as long as Cyprus was governed as a single unit. Accordingly, as they were not prepared to accept the role of strangers in a foreign land, they urged that if Cyprus was to survive as a sovereign entity, power must be handed down from the centre and not gathered to it. Short of partition, the only solution was for Cyprus to become a federal state.

If there had been no more to the situation than this, the Cyprus Government would probably have won the day. The Turks were a sizeable and martial minority, but it is unlikely that they could have held out against the Government's forces. However, in the 1960 arrangements Turkey had been proclaimed as and had willingly accepted the role of protector of the Turkish Cypriots. As against this the Greek Cypriots could look to Greece for help, and undoubtedly

[26] For the discussion of the UN Force, see below, pp. 320–333.

pany's concession. For, when Sir John Simon, in Geneva, heard that Persia proposed to complain to the League Council, he, not wanting to appear as a defendant 'hurried in person to the Secretary-General—Geneva gossip had it that he actually ran in order to be sure of getting there first—with a formal demand that the question should be placed on the agenda of the Council'. F. P. Walters, *op cit.*, p. 572.

would be glad to do so in a crisis. But Greece was 500 miles away, more than ten times as far as Turkey, and was also generally thought to be by far the weaker of the two. The local Turks were not, therefore, in the position of weakness which an island-oriented view would suggest, for the Greek Cypriots were held in check by the mainland Turks. When, therefore, on Christmas Day 1963, Turkish fighters flew low over Nicosia in response to Greek excesses in the capital and the threat of terror beyond, it was recognized on all sides that this was no empty show of strength.

At first sight this situation presented some promising opportunities, for if Greece and Turkey wanted to persuade the Cypriot communities to move towards a settlement it looked as if they would have some telling advantages in such an exercise. Nor was the threat of Greek displeasure any less real to the Cyprus Government than that of Turkey's to the Turks. For although Greece might not inspire great confidence as a protector, she effectively controlled the armed forces which were at the Greek Cypriots' disposal and on which they depended for their supremacy over the local Turks. This was because the plan for a Cyprus army, with community representation on a 60–40 basis, had failed. Subsequently the Cyprus National Guard was built up, but it was largely officered by mainland Greeks and in effect was controlled by Greece. Numerous Greek troops were also introduced into Cyprus over and above the contingent permitted under the 1960 arrangements. In fact, the only armed force in the sure control of the Cyprus Government was the Greek Cypriot police, which was small and of generally poor quality.

It was also very conceivable that Greece and Turkey, besides being in a strong position in relation to the island communities, would be inclined to favour an agreed settlement. For they were involved in the dispute *ex officio*, as it were, rather than for what could be got out of it. And from most points of view it was a considerable liability to them both. Thus, for all that they might say in public, it was possible that they would actively support proposals for an agreement which involved concessions on both sides and which could be expressed in a suitably face-saving formula. It is probable, however, that the weight which such moves would carry with Cypriot communities would be less than they might, on the face of it, seem to demand. For the very involvement of Greece and Turkey meant that threats to abandon their protégés would, short of grave provocation or outrageous behaviour, be less than completely credible. To leave them in the lurch would not do much good to the international standing of the supposed protectors, nor to their domestic positions: the kith and kin argument is powerful in all contexts. Even, therefore, if Greece and Turkey, whether severally or jointly, were minded to press the Cypriots towards a settlement, it was probable that they would move very cautiously.

One remaining possibility was that effective pressure might come from beyond the eastern Mediterranean. An obvious source would be the United States, for the Cyprus dispute already causes her considerable embarrassment and, by introducing the risk of war between two of her NATO allies in a politically sensitive area, threatens much more. Thus she has a close interest in an agreed solution, and in the normal course Greece and Turkey might be receptive to urgent American representations. But this is not a normal situation for either of them, and there was little chance of their adopting a tough policy towards their cultural compatriots just at the behest of their powerful ally. To a large extent this exhausts the opportunities open to the United States for she finds it difficult to bring a direct influence to bear on the disputants. The Turkish Cypriots have no international standing and so there is no means of getting a grip on them. Formal dealings with the Greek Cypriots are possible, for they make up the Cyprus Government. But the position is complicated by Cyprus's non-alignment policy, which means that any attempt to make life awkward for Makarios might cause him to incline his face towards the Soviet Union. He is unlikely to go far in that direction, for too active a Soviet role would complicate his relations with Greece and endanger his own concern for his country's independence. But, even so, the United States would not welcome any increase of Soviet influence in this area, which puts limits on the amount of pressure which it is expedient for her to put on the Greek Cypriots.

There is one further, and perhaps very appropriate source from which pressure in support of mediation might come: the UN itself. This is not to suggest that the UN Force in Cyprus might be instructed to hold one or other of the communities to ransom, a course which would surely lead to the very early withdrawal of the contingents making up the Force, and an increased reluctance on the part of potential host states to accept UN forces in future. But it is open to the UN to withdraw its Force, and, in theory, the threat to do so could be a potent form of pressure on the contestants. The most immediate consequence of its presence is to protect the Turkish minority against the Greeks, which gives the Turks a lively concern for its continuance. For although they may be able to count on Turkey's help in a crisis, they have no ground for thinking that her intervention would be soon enough to prevent the killing of many of their number. At one stage removed, however, the Force helps to protect the Greeks from the possibility of Turkish intervention, and so they, too, would be reluctant to see it go, for the kind of incidents which might provoke an invasion would be much more likely in its absence. The Greeks may also calculate that, as the party in the saddle of power in Cyprus, time is on their side, and so the continued presence of the Force serves their interests by keeping the internal situation relatively quiet. Thus both sides find that the Force is in some respects an annoying factor, an obstacle in the way of their goals, but on balance both would prefer to have it there.

It might seem, therefore, that the UN has an ace up its sleeve which could be a powerful inducement to the parties to listen attentively to what the UN Mediator suggests. But, once more, a doubt arises as to the credibility of the suggested threat, and serves to neutralize it. For, while it may be assumed that most UN members, including most members of the Security Council—the body which established and periodically continues the Cyprus force—want to see a settlement in Cyprus, it is also quite clear that they want even more to avoid a resumption of civil war. They are therefore not willing to take the risk of withdrawing the Force. It is true that sometimes, on renewing the mandate of the Force, the Council has grimly hinted that unless some progress is made towards a settlement, it will not be renewed again. But this has been recognized as bluff. The UN does not want to get blood on its hands—not here, at least —and so the idea that the undoubted desire of the parties to keep the Force could be used as a way of bringing them to an agreed settlement has proved to be empty of substance.

Thus there was little chance of the UN's endeavour to mediate being supported by the significant pressure on either of the Cypriot communities. And even if it had been, a conciliatory disposition would not necessarily have resulted. For, while both Greeks and Turks were, and remain, very vulnerable, they were also very intransigent, perhaps with good reason: the Turks were fearful of exposing themselves once more to the possibility of discrimination, and worse, at the hands of the Greeks; and the Greeks were unwilling to accord the Turks the kind of privileged position which they enjoyed under the 1960 arrangements. The two sides were therefore far apart on what they regarded as essential points, and in consequence it could not be assumed that pressure would be able to bridge the gap. Both parties might have preferred to insist on their positions, taking the chance that this might result in a heavy defeat.

Another stumbling block in the way of an agreed settlement was that it could not but have moved Cyprus away from *enosis*, to the chance of which the Greeks were still deeply committed. But this was perhaps not a major problem, for, whatever might be said in public, it is quite conceivable that in private its attractions were diminishing on account of an increasing liking for the fruits of independence. However, the other issues were very real ones, and the tough attitude taken by the parties with regard to them must have helped to discourage outsiders from attempting to secure their modification. The resolution of the dispute, therefore, lay very much in the hands of the two island communities. Neither was able to impose its will on the other, nor were interested third parties able to produce a willingness to negotiate a settlement. They could pull such minor strings as were safely available, and the Mediator could advise, encourage, and possibly warn. But the stalemate which existed on all fronts could probably be broken only if both parties, largely of their own accord, came to the view that a settlement was so desirable as to warrant major concessions. The question remained whether the events of 1960 to 1963 had excluded, for some considerable time, the possibility of such an outcome.

Some hope of an agreement perhaps lay in the possibility of the Cypriot people tiring of the costs and inconveniences of living in a *de facto* partitioned country, so causing their leaders to make a serious effort to end the dispute. And it may be that there were some who were prepared to pay a good deal for the resumption of normal life on the island. But the continuation of the division doubtless had the opposite effect on others, deepening their distrust of the other community and making them more determined to insist on a foolproof settlement, which was a recipe for no settlement. And, as always in such situations, the zealots had it: they were the ones who laid down the patriotic line, from which it was very dangerous for anyone minded to make a career in communal politics to depart. Thus, during 1964 the positions of both Greece and Turkey seemed to harden and it also seemed that there was much deep-rooted support in each community for their leaders. Early in 1965, however, there arose at least the theoretical possibility of a breakthrough. For on 26 March the Mediator submitted a major report to the Secretary-General, who transmitted it to the parties and Council members, and subsequently to all other members of the UN. In it he set forth his ideas as to the lines along which the parties might reasonably be expected to try to reach an agreement, suggesting that the Greeks should agree to put the question of *enosis* on one side for as long as there was a risk of it inflaming the Turks, and that the Turks should reconsider their insistence on the geographical separation of the two communities under a federal system of government. Rigorous guarantees of human rights and safeguards against discrimination were proposed, with the UN itself acting as the guarantor of the settlement and establishing a Commissioner in Cyprus to supervise its observance. If the parties had been at all interested in a settlement here was an opportunity for them to begin

talks without loss of face, but Turkey would have none of it, rejecting
the report within 24 hours and claiming that it went beyond both
the Mediator's term of reference and the assurance he had given
them as to its nature. The Turkish Cypriots followed with a comment to the same effect, whereas both Greece and the Greek Cypriots
reacted much more mildly, the Government of Cyprus making some
reservations but speaking of the Mediator's constructive approach.

This episode raises a number of questions. By taking the lead in
rejecting the report, Turkey reversed the usual order of instransi-
gence, and it has been suggested that had she not been so speedy in
her condemnation the Turkish Cypriots might have adopted a more
conciliatory approach. However, even if there is something in this
supposition, one wonders how much progress would have been
made if talks had in fact begun. For the abandonment by the Turks of
their federal claims would have represented a remarkably big concession, especially as it was linked with the suggestion of a UN
guarantee: the promise of discussion at New York in the event of
Greek misbehaviour was just about worthless from the Turkish
point of view. Indeed, it was less than that, for it would have meant
the loss of Turkey's right to intervene, so reducing the actual
prospect of physical support from Turkey in their hour of need.

There was, of course, no obligation to follow the Mediator's proposals, but as they had been made public it was unlikely that the
Greeks would easily agree to less. It was true that their reaction was
very conciliatory, but this was in the light of the Turks' hostile
response. It was already clear that nothing would come of the
Mediator's report, and therefore it could be that the Greeks phrased
their comment in the way which would bring them the maximum
diplomatic benefits. Had they responded first, or had the Turks
taken less objection to Mr Galo Plaza's suggestion, the Greeks
might have well taken a rather tougher line. This, however, should
not obscure what was probably a genuine element in their reactions.
Given the fact that the Greek Cypriots were probably losing some of
their enthusiasm for *enosis*, and given the fact too that the Government of Greece may have had some reservations about incorporating
Cyprus within their constitutional structure and her elusive President
within their politics, the Mediator's report did not look at all bad
from their point of view, satisfying, as it did, their demand for a
unitary state. Thus the Mediator's suggestions, while not entirely
pleasing the Greeks, did offer them an important part of their case,
whereas the Turks were being asked to give up their basic claim
without getting anything of substance in return. This might have
seemed just to many eyes, but it was unlikely to appear so to the
Turks.

In these circumstances a question arises as to the reason for the report being made public. Under the resolution of 4 March 1964 the Mediator was to 'report periodically to the Secretary-General on his efforts'.[27] It may usually have followed from such an instruction that his reports would be published, but it does not follow that they must be, nor that they must be written reports. Or, if some difficulty was felt about this, there was no obligation on him to report at this juncture, or if it was thought that one was called for in view of the imminent need for an extension of the Force's mandate (although in the event the mandate was extended four days before the Mediator's report was received), it need not have given the Mediator's ideas about a satisfactory settlement. In short, one way or another, there was no necessity for a report of this nature to be published at this time, and the fact that it appeared suggests that a conscious decision was taken to try to stir things up, although it may be assumed that there was no intention to provoke Turkey to the length to which she went. The thought may have been that as the two Mediators' intensive discussions had borne no fruit, the time had come to give the matter a public airing by putting forward a possible solution, hoping in this way to bring some pressure on the parties to move towards a settlement. It could also be the case that UN circles put more weight than Turkey on the proposal for a UN guarantee and Commissioner, and in this way underestimated the degree of Turkish hostility which the report would arouse. For the Turks now refused to have anything more to do with Mr Galo Plaza and at the end of the year he resigned. It was now clear that they were hostile to the reactivation of the kind of role he had played, and since that time the UN's 'mediation function' (to use the Organization's phraseology) has been in abeyance. Instead, on 2 March 1966 the Secretary-General asked his Special Representative in Cyprus, Mr C. A. Bernardes of Brazil (who dealt with the political issues which were ancillary to the operation of the UN Force), to employ his good offices and make such approaches to the parties, both inside and beyond Cyprus, as might help to get the discussions going once more. This, it was emphasized, was not the activity of mediation as it had been carried on earlier. Then the Mediator had had, or at least had claimed, an independent standing in relation to the parties. The conduct of good offices, on the other hand, was to be a subordinate activity, operating wholly in private, and making suggestions only with considerable diffidence. Its aim was to get the parties to agree among themselves and not to get their agreement to a plan which was the work of a third party.

[27] Security Council resolution 186 (1964).

It may be that Turkey welcomed the opportunity to reject the Mediator's report on the ground that it enabled her to put an end to the activity of mediation. It is even conceivable that the misunderstanding which she had with Mr Galo Plaza regarding the nature of his role was engineered, for the same reason. For Turkey had never welcomed the UN's involvement in the Cyprus dispute, and the passage of time had done nothing to alter her views regarding its desirability. The UN is generally unsympathetic to the claims of minorities, for they are too numerous for the comfort of many of the UN members. And when the minority concerned comes from a NATO nation, and lives in a new, small, and non-aligned state, whose President had the distinction of being exiled by the British for a number of years before his country became independent, the Organization is likely to be particularly lacking in a deep concern for its welfare, and certainly to look with grave disfavour on any attempt to intervene on its behalf. The General Assembly's resolution of 18 December 1965, which gave great satisfaction to Greece by calling upon members to refrain from any intervention directed against the 'sovereignty, unity, independence and territorial integrity'[28] of Cyprus, was indicative of this, even though the number of states abstaining exceeded those who voted in its favour. Turkey may therefore have been very anxious, while continuing to pay lip service to the idea of the UN's participation in the search for a settlement, to lower the level of that participation, and the Mediator's report was just the peg she was looking for.

Since then no successor has been appointed to Mr Galo Plaza, nor have the efforts of Mr Bernades, or those of Mr Osorio-Tafall of Mexico, who succeeded him in January 1967, borne any fruit. The same is true of the mediatory activities which have been conducted outside the UN, including the secret dialogue between Greece and Turkey, which was resumed in May 1966. A meeting of the two countries' Premiers in September 1967 ended in failure, and the crisis which occurred in Cyprus two months later brought Turkey to the brink of intervention.[29] However, private negotiations were resumed early in 1968. And at about the same time President Makarios made some conciliatory gestures towards the Turkish Cypriots, lifting restrictions on their trade and travel in almost all parts of the island, and expressing a willingness to enter into talks with them, which were begun at the beginning of June. Superficially, at least, the prospect was brighter than it had been for some time. But it is difficult to see either side making the concessions which an agreement will require, and it may be that no amount of paper

[28] General Assembly resolution 2077 (xx).
[29] See below, pp. 264–264.

guarantees would satisfy the Turks.[30] Events can move suddenly and strangely in politics, but this dispute's course so far does nothing to suggest that it is likely to be removed from the international agenda at an early date. As yet, and so far as its main object is concerned, success has completely eluded the UN's mediatory effort.

Another case in which the same thing has to be said is the Vietnam war. No initiative has been taken in respect of this conflict by the Security Council, or by the General Assembly,[31] but on numerous occasions since 1963 the Secretary-General has tried to bring the parties together, and has put suggestions to them regarding the ways and means whereby a solution might be sought. However, the United States, while officially welcoming his efforts, is no doubt often privately annoyed, for it is clear that there are fundamental differences in the analysis and attitude of America and the Secretary-General in respect of the conflict. In fact U Thant's approach is closer to Hanoi's than Washington's, which helps to explain why his suggestions have so often failed to commend themselves to the United States, but it is not so close as to enable North Vietnam to accept his proposals.[32] This, in short, is a war in which both parties have seemed overwhelmingly interested in victory rather than compromise, and neither of them have shown any inclination to be deflected from this aim, whether by domestic and foreign opposition or by the adversary's bombs. In these circumstances a mediator labours in vain, and the prospects for the peace talks which opened in Paris in May 1968 (which were neither attributable to nor involved the UN) were not very favourable.

In none of these instances of unsuccessful mediation could any of the parties have had doubts about the independence and integrity of the proposed or actual mediator. The United States probably has reservations about U Thant's judgment in respect of Vietnam, and after the publication of Galo Plaza's report Turkey looked upon him with a very jaundiced eye: but prior to that point she had given no indication of doubting his impartiality. In all these situations, therefore, the failure of the UN's attempt to mediate cannot be attributed to the person of the Mediator or the manner of his appointment. All were free and fair-minded agents, and the reasons for their lack of success lay elsewhere, in the character of the disputes

[30] As of the end of June 1968, for example, the Turks are maintaining the defences around their enclaves, and refusing to admit Greek Cypriots to them.
[31] See further, Lincoln P. Bloomfield, *The U.N. and Vietnam* (New York: Carnegie Endowment for International Peace, 1968).
[32] North Vietnam might in any event have difficulty in doing this, on account of its assertion that the UN has no competence to deal with the Vietnam problem.

with which they were called upon to deal. This underlines the crucial point it is on the policies and attitudes of the parties, on their willingness to modify them if pressed to do so, and on the availability of such pressure, that the chances of a negotiated settlement depend. The point is emphasized in a positive way by those cases where the UN's mediatory presences have been more successful.

IV

One such was Mr Hammarskjöld's first major involvement, as UN Secretary-General, in international disputes. In January 1953, six months before the Korean Armistice, eleven American airmen had been shot down while flying a war mission on behalf of the UN Command. China alleged that they had infringed her air space, and in the autumn of 1954 they were sentenced to imprisonment for espionage. This aroused very strong protests in the United States, as did the revelation that four more American airmen were in Chinese custody, and there were demands for decisive action. Wishing to avoid further complications with her allies over China, the United States brought the question to the General Assembly which, in December, asked the Secretary-General to try to secure their release. To do this he proposed to travel to Peking, and the Chinese Government said it would welcome such a visit but also made the point that the UN was not entitled to interfere in China's internal affairs. To get over this difficulty, and for honour to be preserved on all sides, Hammarskjöld conducted his discussions by virtue of the authority which lay in his office rather than on the basis of the Assembly's resolution, and after his visit to China in January 1955 he was said to be expecting the release of the airmen after some delay. This is what happened. The group of four were freed at the end of May, and the eleven others early in August.

Such a move was in accord with the way in which China's policy was developing at this time. At the end of March she announced the withdrawal of six divisions from North Korea, and at the Bandung Conference of the following month her line became noticeably more pacific. The question of Taiwan was still very much a live issue, but it was becoming clear that no one wanted it to precipitate a war, and at the end of April China proposed negotiations with the United States with a view to relaxing tension in the Far East. It has been suggested[33] that before agreeing to talks the United States required the release of the airmen as a conciliatory gesture and that the group which was returned at the end of May served this purpose.

[33] Geoffrey Barraclough and Rachel F. Wall, *Survey of International Affairs 1955–1956* (London: Oxford University Press, 1960).

The release of the eleven convicted as spies may also have been linked with this question, for it was announced on 1 August, the day on which the Sino-American ambassadorial talks began in Geneva. Chou En-lai was subsequently reported as having said that the object of releasing them was to create a favourable atmosphere for the talks. Thus an argument could be developed to the effect that Hammarskjöld's mediatory efforts had no bearing on the outcome. But this would be to go too far. Especially as considerations of face were so important to her, China probably found that Hammarskjöld's involvement eased the freeing of the prisoners very considerably. The time was ripe, but that was not enough. A satisfactory reason had to be found for the act of clemency, and it was to hand in the shape of consideration for the Secretary-General. The release of the group of eleven was in fact announced in a message to Hammarskjöld which spoke of China's desire to strengthen and maintain friendship with him. In this way the Secretary-General's activities as an intermediary helped to patch-up what could have been a nasty quarrel. He had fulfilled the desire which he had expressed when taking up the office of Secretary-General, to be 'active as an instrument, a catalyst, perhaps an inspirer'.[34]

Another dispute in which a UN mediatory presence played a helpful role was that between Cambodia and Thailand. It would be possible to analyse the intermittent quarrels between these two countries in terms of the cold war, for Thailand is a member of SEATO and on very good terms with the United States, whereas Cambodia professes neutralism and practices it with a bias in favour of China. However, the dispute is really both narrower and deeper than such an approach would suggest, for it has roots which go back to the days of Khmer (Cambodian) dominance in the area from the ninth to the thirteenth century. Thereafter the Khmer empire went into decline, and first the Thais and later the Vietnamese were active in furthering the process, giving rise to much hostility and unfinished business. In July 1958 relations took a turn for the worse when Cambodia recognized Communist China, and within a few months border talks being held with Thailand had broken down. In November Cambodia cut off diplomatic relations with Thailand, who replied by closing the border. This was followed by a Cambodian complaint to the UN Secretary-General that Thailand was concentrating troops and military equipment on her border, which brought forth a Thai riposte in the shape of a suggestion that the border be observed by a representative of the UN. Nothing came of this, but the exchange led to private discussions being held at the

UN, from which it emerged that both sides seemed ready to restore diplomatic relations and would be willing to use the services of a third party in an endeavour to patch-up their quarrel. Therefore, on 22 December, after informal consultation with the Security Council, the Secretary-General announced that at the invitation of the two Governments, he was sending a Special Representative to help them settle their differences, and named Mr J. Beck-Friis, a retired Swedish diplomat, to fill this role. He visited the area during the first two months of 1959 and the improvement in the situation which he facilitated was marked by the restoration of diplomatic relations, for his part in which both Governments were publicly appreciative.

The success of this episode was basically due to the willingness of both Cambodia and Thailand to put an end to their quarrel. It was relatively unimportant and lacking in complexity, but even so the implementation of their pacific disposition might not have been straightforward had they not had the assistance of an impartial intermediary. His intervention enabled them to move towards a solution without loss of face, and eased its actual negotiation. The wider situation was also favourable inasmuch as the Great Powers were happy to see the dispute settled quietly. However, the basic rivalry of the two states had not been reduced, and within a few years was manifest on the surface once more. In 1961 the pattern of 1958 was repeated, with Cambodia breaking off diplomatic relations with Thailand, and Thailand retaliating by closing her Cambodian border. Much of the recent border trouble had centred on the ancient Temple of Preah Vihear, which at that time was in Thai hands. The question had been taken to the International Court of Justice by Cambodia in 1958, and now in June 1962 the Court ruled that it belonged to her. It was surrendered, most reluctantly, by Thailand, but the outcome of the case led to a worsening of relations. Discussions were held in New York, with the result that on 19 October the Secretary-General formally reported to the Security Council that both parties had asked him to send a personal representative to enquire into their difficulties. He appointed Mr N. S. Gussing, a Swedish member of the Secretariat, to conduct this mission, which was continued throughout 1963 and 1964 under the rather more formal title of the Secretary-General's Special Representative. Mr Gussing was assisted by a small staff, and the costs of the operation were borne equally by the two states concerned.

Shortly after Mr Gussing's arrival in the area, the Secretary-General noted that his activities had coincided with a lessening of tension between the disputants. He was now instructed to hold himself at the disposal of the parties with a view to helping them solve their difficulties, but was not able to make any lasting progress in this direction during the following two years. Evidently the parties were content to have him there, and his presence mitigated the inconvenience which followed from the absence of diplomatic relations. It has also been suggested that the Gussing mission had some prophylactic significance, in that it 'helped to prevent [relations] from worsening'.[35] But so far as its patching-up role was concerned it can hardly be accounted a success, and at the end of 1964 Thailand indicated that she was not in favour of its continuation. Thus the mission was withdrawn, leaving Thai-Cambodian relations in their familiar grumbling condition with occasional outbreaks of hostility.

They continued in that state during 1965 and 1966, and in July of the latter year it was reported[36] that Cambodia had rejected U Thant's proposal that the UN, now through Mr. J. Rolz-Bennett, a senior member of the Secretariat, should make a third attempt at mediation. In the next month, however, a Swedish diplomat, Mr H. de Ribbing, was appointed as the Secretary-General's Special Representative in an endeavour to reduce tension between the two countries and resolve their mutual problems. With the parties agreement his assignment was extended for two succeeding periods of six months, but they were unable to agree on a further extension. Thus the de Ribbing mission came to an end in February 1968, accompanied by Cambodian charges of Thai acts of aggression.

Three other cases of successful UN mediation should be noted. The first of these was the activity during 1962 of Mr Ellsworth Bunker who, acting on behalf of the UN Secretary-General, succeeded in bringing Indonesia and the Netherlands to an agreement, signed on 15 August, regarding West New Guinea. As has been suggested,[37] the Netherlands was by that time anxious to dispose of the problem, but even so the participation in the negotiations of a representative of the UN was a very valuable, perhaps an essential, factor in the events which led up to a settlement. Relations between the parties had deteriorated considerably, and so an impartial go-between was of great procedural importance. He was also able to add some urgency to the negotiations, especially in view of the fact that his own country, the United States, was closely interested in an early and pacific settlement. Thus, through being able to supply an independent and authoritative mediator, the UN played a

---

[35] Wainhouse, *op. cit.*, p. 404.
[36] *The Times*, 8 July 1966.
[37] See above, pp. 56–57, and also below, pp. 155–159.

D

subordinate but nevertheless a very significant role in bringing this dispute to an agreed end. No doubt mediation could have been conducted under different auspices, but the UN was not only the most appropriate body to act in this way but also the one which was most acceptable to both the parties. In this further way, therefore, through just being available the UN facilitated a settlement.

Two months after the signing of the West New Guinea agreement the world suddenly found itself faced with its most serious crisis since 1945, that which arose over the installation of Soviet missiles in Cuba. In the events leading to the Soviet-American agreement which brought it to an end, the UN played some part. Its exact role is not fully known, and in consequence any attempt to assess the significance of the UN's mediatory effort must be even more conjectural than usual. But, at the least, it can be said that the UN acted as a convenient post-box, as a passive intermediary, for until the last 48 hours of the crisis all exchanges between the two superpowers were being made through the UN. Further, it was the case that U Thant made a number of appeals to the parties in an attempt to prepare the way for the speedy settlement which was essential. And, to refer to the highest possibility, it can be noted that it is not difficult to cite assertions, by those who claim to be informed, that the acting Secretary-General played an important mediatory role. Whether the moves towards a settlement would have been significantly hampered by the absence of such efforts is perhaps improbable. But it does seem plausible to suggest that the UN facilitated a solution. And at the end of October 1962 any contribution towards that end was very valuable.

In the Cuban case there may have been more to the UN's mediation than met the eye. In the case of the Yemen there was, effectively, a good deal less. The royalist regime in the Yemen had been overthrown in a republican *coup* at the end of September 1962, but its following in the country had by no means been destroyed, and civil war ensued. Very soon it had become more than just an internal conflict, for the United Arab Republic began sending troops to support the new Government, while the Royalists received arms and supplies from the neighbouring state of Saudi Arabia. From the Western point of view the intrusion of disturbing elements into the oil-rich and reactionary Arabian peninsula was most unwelcome, and for Britain it had a particularly disturbing twist in that it involved the presence of her bogey-man, President Nasser, immediately to the north of the important colony of Aden. There was, therefore, a keen desire to get the UAR out of the Yemen, even if this involved accepting a republican regime there, and, happily, this coincided with the UN's principled objection to most forms of international armed conflict. Since late 1962 the Secretary-General had been consulting with the three countries chiefly involved and also with other Middle Eastern states regarding the international aspects of the war, and the Yemen eventually agreed to a short visit from Dr Ralph Bunche, the UN Under-Secretary for Special Political Affairs—the Secretary-General's right-hand man. This took place early in March 1963, and from the Yemen he went on to Cairo. Another visitor to the Middle East was the negotiator of the recent West New Guinea agreement, Mr Ellsworth Bunker of the United States, who had now been asked by his Government to try to patch-up the international side of the Yemen affair. Out of these activities came an agreed formula for UAR and Saudi Arabian disengagement from the Yemen, which U Thant reported to the Security Council on 29 April. Thus the UN had once more demonstrated the fruitful possibilities which lay in the involvement of its mediators in international disputes. However, in this case the fruit turned sour, for the promised disengagement of the UAR forces did not occur. Instead they increased within a few years from about 15,000 to 50,000 or more, before being withdrawn in 1967.[38] Thus the affair demonstrated the strength and weakness of the UN in the mediatory field. By providing mediation, a settlement was reached. But the execution of settlements, like their conclusion, depends on the will, whether free or aided, of the parties.

By virtue of the UN's nature it can offer states first-class facilities for mediation, being able to provide them with intermediaries whose ability and integrity is unquestioned. If, therefore, disputants are of a conciliatory frame of mind, or can be persuaded into one, their search for a settlement need never fail for want of help from an impartial third party. Here, if the UN acts as a mediator, it is playing possibly an essential but certainly a subordinate role. It has not influenced the decision to seek a settlement, but may be a vital instrument for the achievement of that end. Sometimes, however, the situation may be less clear-cut than this, with the disputing states being hesitant about the desirability or expediency of resorting to mediation. They may think that they have more to gain by less pacific action, or judge that the likely consequences of resisting the pressure to mediate are just worth risking. In these circumstances it may be that the ability and experience of the UN in the conduct of mediation tips the balance in favour of trying it, perhaps because of the difficulty of refusing. In which case, if it is successful, the UN will have had rather more than just a secondary hand in the outcome. But if one or both of the parties have quite definitely set their

---

[38] For the UN's attempt to supervise the observance of the Yemen agreement, see below pp. 108–117.

faces against a negotiated settlement, or if the necessary pressure
is not available to turn obstinate states in this direction, then the
availability of appropriate procedures and skills will count for
nothing, and the UN can play no positive mediatory role. Its success
at mediation, therefore, will chiefly depend on factors which lie
outside the Organization, on the disposition of disputants and the
attitude and persuasiveness of other interested states. It is for others
to use it or to encourage its use. Sometimes this has been done, with
success, and there is no reason why it should not continue to happen,
for, inevitably, from time to time the international society will
resort to mediation.

The UN, however, is by no means the only body capable of
playing a mediatory role, and in certain circumstances states will
positively wish to avoid utilizing this aspect of its services. Particularly will this be the case when a dispute arises between two members
of a regional organization which is committed to the idea of pacific
settlement. The inter-American system has always been very jealous
of its prerogatives, and in the mediatory sphere, as distinct from that
of investigation, its activities have been conducted by the Inter-
American Peace Committee. This body, which was set up in 1948,
eight years after provision had been made for its establishment,
'extends a rudimentary form of good offices to parties in conflict
when they choose to avail themselves of it',[39] and during the first
16 years of its life considered 14 disputes, making 'a major contribution to the peaceful solution of controversies among the American
states'.[40]

The attitude of the Organization of African Unity towards the
handling of disputes between its members is identical to that of the
inter-American system. Shortly after its establishment in May
1963 a border conflict broke out between Algeria and Morocco.
The Moroccan Government showed signs of wishing to take the
matter to the UN, thinking that it would not do very well in the
new African organization, on account of the popularity both of
Algeria and the Algerian case. However, after several false starts,
both parties were prevailed upon to accept the mediation of two
African heads of state, out of which came a request for an extraordinary meeting of the OAU's Council of Ministers. This was duly
held, and the resolution which emerged spoke of 'the imperative
necessity' of settling intra-African disputes not only by peaceful
means but also in 'a strictly African framework'.[41] A special com-

---

[39] Wainhouse, *op. cit.*, p. 190.
[40] Ibid., p. 88.
[41] Quoted in Patricia Berko Wild, 'The Organization of African Unity and the
Algerian–Moroccan Border Conflict', xx *International Organization*, No. 1 (Winter
1966), p. 30.

mittee was set up in order to obtain an agreed settlement, but as yet it has not been able to disband. By contrast, the long standing territorial dispute between Somalia and Kenya has been greatly eased under OAU auspices. In June 1967 a new Prime Minister took office in Somalia and he was quick to accept an OAU offer of mediation by the President of Zambia. By the end of October an agreement had been signed which promised peace along what had been a very threatening border.

It is perhaps more likely that the Algerian-Moroccan experience will be more typical than the Somali-Kenyan. A number of factors suggest this: the divisions which exist in Africa's ranks, the numerous disputes which lie not far below its surface, and the absence from the scene of a dominant state which might put its authority and weight behind the OAU's mediatory efforts. But whatever the prospect, one factor will probably remain constant—the desire to keep African quarrels within an African forum. It may not be easy to implement this wish where a dispute causes sharp divisions among the African states themselves, or where there is extra-African pressure for mediation in a dispute in which most Africans do not want to get involved. An example of the latter kind concerns the breakaway Nigerian state of Biafra, the fate of which has aroused much international concern. An OAU mission made up of a number of heads of state visited Nigeria in November 1967 to consult regarding the matter, but the caution of its members together with their bias in favour of the Nigerian Government resulted in no progress being made. However, this did not lead to the involvement of the UN. Instead, it was the Commonwealth Secretariat which secured the agreement of the parties to the holding of preliminary talks in London in May 1968, out of which came a plan for substantive discussions in Uganda (which suffered an early breakdown). Thus it seems likely that even where the OAU does not make headway in respect of intra-African disputes, the UN cannot be assumed to be the second best choice. Nevertheless, it remains probable that, as in the past, the UN will from time to time and in varying contexts be regarded as the most acceptable source of mediation.

Chapter 4
Supervision

WHERE an agreement for the settlement of a dispute requires some specific acts of commission or omission, whether at the international or internal levels, the possibility arises that the UN might watch over the parties' execution of their promises. Such operations, therefore, unlike those concerned with investigation or mediation, are post-agreement phenomena, their object being to ensure that a paper settlement really does lead to the patching-up of the preceding conflict. This aim can be sought in a variety of ways. A supervisory team may be able to help in arranging the actual implementation of an agreement. It provides a speedy means of settling any incidents which arise in this connection, and could be associated with formal procedures for dealing with complaints. And its mere presence should discourage any deliberate breach of the obligations which the parties have assumed.

UN help with the fulfilment of an agreement's positive terms is most likely to be sought where uninvited troops are to be withdrawn from foreign territory. Incidents between erstwhile enemies can easily occur before and during the process of disengagement, especially if the line of advance has been irregular or, even more, if isolated pockets of territory are held by the invading forces. Friction can also arise over the mechanics of handing back occupied territory to the civilian authorities. And should the situation be one which involves a mutual withdrawal, it will be necessary to ensure that it is conducted at a rate which, in relation to the amount of foreign territory held, is equal, so preventing the possibility of one side being able to obtain an advantage by going back on its promise. In themselves these are not serious problems, and given the appropriate disposition on the part of the disputants, it should not be hard for them to make arrangements for the rapid and satisfactory handling of any difficulties which occur. It might be thought that in these circumstances the disposition of the parties would be conciliatory, on the ground that they have an interest in the smooth execution of their own agreement. But, while this may be so at the governmental level, armies which have but recently been fighting each other may have some difficulty in suddenly evincing a co-operative spirit.

Thus the disengagement of hostile forces could itself give rise to fresh sores and at the same time reopen the old ones, a process which takes place all the more easily and quickly in an area where resistance to conflict is already low. In these circumstances a neutral third party, such as a UN supervisory mission, can provide valuable antiseptic qualities, and so assist the healing process. It should have a good chance of securing the confidence and co-operation of both parties, and therefore be able to arrange a relatively untroubled withdrawal. It should also be able to contribute to the same end simply by watching what goes on, and by being on hand to settle any problems which occur. Provided always, of course, that those directly concerned are prepared to maintain a conciliatory frame of mind.

The exercise of a quietening influence is also likely to be important in respect of agreements which aim at the restoration of calm. A border which has been giving rise to serious difficulty, for example, whether by way of exchanges of fire or on account of it being crossed by hostile infiltrators, is unlikely to become trouble-free overnight just by virtue of the disputants agreeing to put their relations on a better footing. Incidents may well continue to occur during a transitional period and could jeopardize the improvement which has been promised. If, however, a UN mission is watching the situation, its members will be in a good position to work for an early end to any such trouble, with a view to allowing the situation to develop in accordance with the expressed intentions of the parties.[1]

The circumstances so far discussed point to temporary UN operations. Clearly, where the UN has to supervise the withdrawal of foreign troops, their departure brings its task to an end. And where its job is to help in the stabilization of a border, there is unlikely to be a call for supervision to be continued once its object has been achieved. Agreements of a different kind, however, may give rise to supervision on a long-term or indefinite basis, especially if they relate to matters which would not usually come under international notice, such as the treatment of a minority, an area's demilitarization, or the level of a country's armaments.

An international agreement regarding the rights which a state will accord to a minority is almost certain to give rise to domestic disputes regarding its application and observance. In the absence of an established means of adjudication it is very possible that they would be taken up by the minority's international sponsor, which would negate the two main objects of the agreement. For it would

[1] The UN's supervisory activities may continue even if the situation does not improve and shows little sign of doing so. But in that event, with the original patching-up decision having, in effect, been abandoned, the UN's role acquires a prophylactic character. See further, below, Chapter 7.

both put the question back in the international arena and, as it is unlikely that a government would look benevolently on those of its subjects who were the cause of its international embarrassment, it would probably diminish the chance of the minority receiving the treatment to which it was entitled. Accordingly, supervisory arrangements which embraced a system for hearing and passing upon complaints might well go some way towards ensuring the success of an attempt to settle a minority problem.

Such a scheme might also help to prevent disputes arising in the first place, as it may cause the government concerned to be more careful about honouring its promises. In fact, international supervision has the aspect of a deterrent in relation to all kinds of agreements, as the presence of observers may help to discourage not just calculated wrongdoing but also thoughtless or only doubtfully correct behaviour. Too much should not be made of this, for if a state is determined to disregard its obligations it is not going to be checked by the fact that it will immediately be the subject of an adverse report. But at the margin such a consideration could be important. This is especially so of agreements providing for demilitarization or arms control, for it is most unlikely that their infringement would be compatible with the continuation of the good relationship which they were meant to support. Thus, the supervision of such arrangements could have a particularly significant bearing upon their maintenance.

The importance of UN supervision, however, is not confined to the post-settlement period, for its prospect may play a valuable part in securing a settlement. States are generally anxious that any agreements which they make should be effective, in the sense of affecting behaviour in the intended way. Inasmuch as supervision increases the likelihood of this it may be an additional factor encouraging the parties to bring their negotiations to a successful conclusion. Moreover, it may have an influence in this respect over and above the ways which have already been noted. It is quite conceivable that disputants who are considering whether to come to an agreement may have some doubts about each other's good faith. And if there is some possibility of one party breaking its promises to the other's detriment, the disadvantages of being double-crossed may be thought to outweigh the advantages of a settlement. However, states are particularly cautious when it comes to giving hostages to fortune, almost always exhibiting a lively concern to avoid, if at all possible, action which might result in their later embarrassment. Thus if, during the negotiation of an agreement, one of the parties was giving thought to its evasion, it would hardly agree to an independent group being set up to watch over its observance. Nor would it do so if it had any inkling that its interests might subsequently require the unilateral abrogation of the agreement. Contrariwise, a readiness to accept supervision can generally be taken as an indication that the parties are moving towards an agreement in good faith, and are not thinking of anything other than the execution of its terms. The establishment of a supervisory presence, therefore, by providing evidence of the conciliatory disposition of the parties, can play a notable part in reducing suspicion and so can help to obtain an agreed settlement.

In two kinds of situation the significance of this type of presence goes beyond facilitating a settlement, inasmuch as it is a prerequisite of such an outcome that the parties agree on a supervisory scheme. This is so, firstly, in respect of agreements on issues of great importance and the execution of which, in the normal course, cannot be thoroughly checked by the parties. Arms control and disarmament treaties are examples, as might be a state's promise to withdraw arms or men from a country friendly to itself. It might be possible for those concerned to make private enquiries regarding the honouring of the agreement, whether by way of espionage on the ground, aerial surveillance, or even monitoring devices abroad. But evidence obtained in this way might not carry great conviction with the world at large and, more importantly, might not be reliable. This would be a matter of considerable concern to a suspicious party, on account, on the one hand, of the disadvantage in which he would find himself if he carried out his obligations while the other side defaulted, and, on the other, of the disadvantages of an unnecessary abrogation of the arrangement on his part. The latter course would not only bear on his relations with the other party but would also attract general obloquy in the event of the breach being on less than abundantly justifiable grounds. In these circumstances it becomes vital for the conclusion and smooth working of the proposed arrangement that its execution be efficiently supervised on an international basis.

The second kind of situation where supervision is necessary for the conclusion of an agreement is where it is required as a face-saver. If, for example, one party has consistently depicted the other as untrustworthy or aggressive, a sudden change of policy which makes an accommodation with him most desirable can cause the first party considerable embarrassment. One way of resolving this problem would be to make arrangements for an international watch on the execution of the agreement. This could carry the suggestion that the other state, while now a necessary treaty partner, could not be safely let out of sight, and also that the international community shared this view of his reliability. Of course, this could lead to a problem with the second party, but if he could be persuaded to accept supervision, the device, although strictly superfluous, might play the important role of making an agreement palatable.

It could have something of the same effect where a state was being strongly pressed to abandon a position on foreign territory but was unwilling to make an obviously ignominious retreat. For if the UN could become involved in a way which would allow the state concerned to claim that it was handing over its burden to the Organization, this might permit it to withdraw without undue loss of face. The first stage in such a process might well be a supervisory operation, which would provide physical evidence for the argument that the UN was intending to carry on from where the departing state was leaving off. This could raise very delicate issues between the UN and the host state. If the guest had been present by invitation the UN might be pressed for an undertaking that it would indeed carry on its role, which would hardly suit an Organization whose objection to what was going on had led it to take action. But if the guest's unpopularity was shared by the local sovereign, that state would probably require an assurance that supervision, besides being the first of the UN's tasks on its soil, would also be its last, which might endanger the intervener's willingness to withdraw. However, there might be a tendency to leave questions regarding the UN's future role in some obscurity in order to deal with the immediate matter in hand. And in this respect the UN might be able to resolve the dispute by providing a supervisory mission, seemingly as the beginning of an international substitute for unilateral action but in reality as a means of saving the dignity of a delinquent state who needs to be handled with some care.

In various ways, therefore, supervisory presences may be able to play a helpful, and possibly an essential, role in the patching-up of international disputes. It may be that the result so achieved is some way removed from a final resolution of the matters at issue between parties. The withdrawal of troops, for example, is in no way a settlement of a quarrel which led to their occupation of foreign territory, nor can it be taken as an indication that the basic dispute will now be concluded at an early date or allowed to wither away. But this does not deprive such operations of their value as a way of settling immediate problems. Moreover, as UN supervision is conducted in the light of an agreement which has already been reached, there would seem to be no question of it giving rise to an endeavour to press a particular kind of settlement on the parties: unlike the two previous categories, it would not appear to be capable of representing the thin end of a wedge. From the point of view of conciliatory-minded disputants, therefore, a supervisory mission might be an attractive device. Nor should the UN find it too difficult to mount such operations. Skilled and impartial personnel should be fairly readily available. Their costs should usually be manageable, if not by the UN then by the parties themselves. And those of a once for all nature, such as the supervision of the withdrawal of troops, should not be politically oversensitive. Nevertheless, they have been conducted by the UN on only three occasions.[2]

I

The first such presence was set up as part of the endeavour to resolve the conflict which was set in train by the withdrawal, on 19 July 1956, of the American offer of financial aid for the building of the Aswan Dam. In reply, President Nasser announced, exactly a week later, the nationalization of the Suez Canal Company, which had a lease to run the Canal until 1968. The Company was registered under Egyptian law, and had part of its headquarters in Egypt, but its owners were foreign, the most notable being the British Government, with 44 per cent of the shares. They were promised compensation, but as Nasser had also declared that the revenues received from the running of the Canal would be used to finance the Aswan Dam, there was some scepticism about his ability to make the necessary payments. More disturbing, however, from the British point of view, was the fact that she was the largest single user of the Canal, relying heavily on it for trading purposes, in particular for the import of oil. The Canal also had considerable strategic significance for her, inasmuch as it was a very important link between the United Kingdom and her forces in the Indian Ocean and South East Asia. Egypt had affirmed her intention to continue to honour her obligations under the 1888 Constantinople Convention, which provided for free passage through the Canal at all times, but Britain did not savour the prospect of the Canal being in the hands of someone whom she increasingly regarded as basically hostile to her interests in the Middle East and beyond. In Sir Anthony Eden's graphic phrase, Nasser could not be allowed 'to have his thumb on our windpipe'.[3] Distrust of and hostility to Nasser was also shared by the French, chiefly on account of the support he was giving to the Algerian rebels. But what was probably the most important factor of all in the situation produced by the taking over of the Suez Canal was the severe blow it delivered to Anglo-French prestige. For years

[2] But see also the UN's supervisory activity in Indonesia from 1947–51 and in West New Guinea in 1962, the first (see above, p. 52) being ancillary to a mediatory and the second (see below, p. 161) to an administrative operation. For similar activity of a prophylactic rather than a patching-up character, see below, Chapter 7.
[3] Sir Anthony Eden: *Full Circle* (London: Cassell, 1960), p. 426.

these two Powers had ruled the Middle Eastern roost, and now they suddenly found themselves being treated as of no account by an upstart Egyptian colonel. Their status in the world at large might have declined, but this, it was widely felt, was too much. Nasser had over-reached himself and must be cut down to size, or, better, toppled.

Thus the negotiations regarding the future of the Canal which took place during the next few months were doomed to failure, for the British and French conditions were unacceptable to the Egyptians. It was also the case that the two aggrieved Western states were not sorry to see them fail, for this provided an opportunity to settle accounts with Nasser in a more direct and drastic fashion. With the willing co-operation of Israel a plot was hatched which, at the very least, called for their occupation of key points along the Canal. On 29 October Israel invaded Egypt, and on the following day both the attacker and the attacked were presented with an Anglo-French ultimatum which required them to stop all warlike action, withdraw their forces to within 10 miles of the Canal, and, in the case of Egypt, to accept the 'temporary'[4] occupation of Port Said, Ismailia and Suez, which lay at the Canal's northern, middle, and southern entrances respectively. If it was not accepted within 12 hours, British and French forces would intervene in order to ensure compliance. Israel, at that time not within 100 miles of the Canal, agreed to accept the ultimatum if Egypt did likewise, a condition which, as might have been and was anticipated, was unfulfilled. On 31 October and the following few days, therefore, bombs were dropped on Egyptian aerodromes, effectively disabling her air force, and leaflets, calling for Nasser's overthrow, on her towns. Paratroops landed outside Port Said on 5 November and were supplemented the next day by the arrival of the main invasion force, which had been steaming eastwards from Malta as hard as it could go for the best part of the previous week, However, on the same day, Britain and France decided to call off their assault. The cease-fire came into operation at midnight on 6/7 November, by which time Port Said had fallen and the leading allied forces had progressed along the Canal to a distance of some 23 miles.

The decision to halt the Anglo-French expedition was Britain's, France agreeing only with considerable reluctance. In coming to it Britain was influenced by considerations other than those which related to the military side of the operation, for there was little doubt that the remaining 75 miles or so to Suez could have been covered without much difficulty in a matter of days. That they were not

[4] Noble Frankland (ed.), *Documents on International Affairs 1956* (London: Oxford University Press, 1957), p. 261.

covered was justified, in part, by the argument that, Israel and Egypt both having accepted the UN's call for an immediate cease-fire, there was no longer any need for action to separate the combatants. However, as their ultimatum had indicated, the two Powers were interested in more than mere interposition; they also intended to seize, or, as they would put it, safeguard the Canal. If, therefore, they had been so disposed, they could have proceeded with their advance to Suez on the ground that it was still necessary to ensure that the Canal was in responsible hands. If anything, the case for such action had by this time been strengthened, for, before the invasion was begun, Egypt had blocked the Canal by sinking numerous vessels in it, so creating a problem with which Britain was best fitted to deal. Her experienced and well-equipped salvage fleet could have begun work on it immediately if she and her ally were in control of the Canal, so reopening it for the world's shipping at the earliest opportunity. This might have been regarded as an appropriate exercise of its responsibility by a Great Power, and therefore as providing a further justification for the completion of the stated programme.

However, Britain rightly judged that to go ahead in this way would have but little appeal on any of her various non-military fronts. At home, the country was divided. Possibly the exceptionally hostile attitude of the Parliamentary Labour Party was not a fair reflection of the views of all those who gave it their votes, but as against this account had to be taken of the fact that the Conservative Party was not completely united in support of the operation. Abroad, there was very strong opposition to the venture in most parts of the Commonwealth, and at the UN Britain found herself in virtual isolation, the crisis having produced unity, at the voting level, between the United States and the Soviet Union. Encouraged by this unusual phenomenon, the Soviet Union, on the day of the Anglo-French landings, mischievously suggested to the United States that in order to provide the necessary support for the UN, their two countries should execute a joint military intervention in Egypt, a proposal which, by the brusque response it received, illustrated the limits of their agreement.

The Soviet Union was also active in other ways. On the day that she communicated with America she also addressed the invaders in sombre terms, speaking of the dangers of a third world war and of the Soviet determination to stop their aggression. In this connection she referred to the destructive character of modern weapons and to the ability of certain unspecified countries to deliver them by means of rockets. Moscow radio was also at this point calling for volunteers and arms for Egypt. It is, however, doubtful whether these verbal

demonstrations carried much weight in London. It was inconceivable
that the Soviet Union would have risked finding herself in a state
of armed conflict with Britain and France, and also the United
States, for the sake of stopping their movement along the Canal.
It also seems very unlikely, contrary to what Britain's ambassador
in Moscow thought might happen,[5] that she would have gone so
far as to interfere, if possible without being identified, with allied
ships in the Mediterranean, rather in the manner adopted by
Mussolini at the time of the Spanish Civil War. What seems much
more likely is that the Soviet Union was simply engaged on a
campaign to draw attention away from her activities in Hungary,
and was also trying, not surprisingly, to get what diplomatic benefit
she could from the situation by posing as the Arabs' protector. The
fact that her belligerent tone did not come until the eve of the
Anglo-French capitulation, which might well have been thought to
be imminent, adds cogency to this argument, for it made it unlikely
that she would have to explain a failure to support words with deeds.

The Soviet Union's activities may, however, have had an important indirect effect on Britain, inasmuch as they may well have
made the United States even more anxious to end the attack on
Egypt, not just in case the Soviet Union did something silly but also,
and more significantly, because of the rich diplomatic harvest she
was reaping from it. This draws attention to the factor which had far
and away the most important bearing on Britain's decision to alter
course: the very strong pressure which was put on her by the United
States, who was exceedingly angry at the whole affair and whose
anger was heightened by the fact that she had not been consulted
or informed beforehand. The major weapon which she used against
Britain was economic. There had been some speculation against
sterling since September, and during the first week of November it
reached critical proportions, largely due to American selling.
Within a few days the pound would have faced devaluation. The
United States also promised to oppose a British move to seek support
from the International Monetary Fund unless there was an immediate cease-fire, and there was the possibility of further economic
sanctions, which was particularly ominous in view of the fact that,
because the Canal was blocked, Britain was now having to turn to
dollar areas for oil. Faced with a situation of such gravity, Britain
called for a cease-fire.

It is, however, perhaps just conceivable that she might have
resisted had not the UN established an Emergency Force (UNEF)
Certainly, at the very least, the UN's action made the decision

[5] See Sir William Hayter, *The Kremlin and the Embassy* (London: Hodder and
Stoughton, 1966), p. 147.

somewhat easier than it would otherwise have been. At the request
of the United States, the crisis had first been considered by the
Security Council, where, on 30 October, Britain and France vetoed
a resolution calling on Israel to withdraw and on all members to
refrain from the use or threat of force. It was Britain's first veto. On
the following day the Council decided to convene an Emergency
Special Session of the Assembly which, on 2 November, adopted an
American-sponsored resolution urging an immediate cease-fire and
a halt to the movement of military forces and arms into the area.
Two days later, in the early hours of 4 November, the Assembly
endorsed a Canadian suggestion that the Secretary-General be
asked to submit, within 48 hours, a plan for the establishment, 'with
the consent of the nations concerned', of a force to 'secure and
supervise the cessation of hostilities'.[6] Hammarskjöld's first report
was ready on the same day, and as a result the Assembly, early on
5 November, decided to establish 'a United Nations Command
for an emergency international Force'.[7] On 7 November it approved
the Secretary-General's second report, which concerned its organization and functioning. By this time offers of assistance had already
been received, and so it was possible to inform Egypt that the first
members of the Force were ready to enter her territory. However,
they did not do so until 15 November, on account of some questions
raised by Egypt concerning UNEF's character and composition.[8]
Thereafter the Force expanded rapidly. By the end of November
2,500 men were on duty and little more than two months later it had
been brought to virtually its full strength of some 6,000 officers and
men drawn from 10 of the 24 members who had said they were
willing to supply contingents: Brazil,[9] Canada, Colombia, Denmark,
Finland, India, Indonesia, Norway, Sweden, and Yugoslavia.
Early in March it took up its position on the Egyptian side of the
Egyptian-Israeli international frontier and Armistice Demarcation
Line, and remained there until May 1967. The emergency with which
it was sent to deal seemed to acquire a permanent character, and
the withdrawal of the force did not signify that it had passed.

[6] General Assembly resolution 998 (ES-1).
[7] Ibid., 1000 (ES-1).
[8] It is widely supposed that the discussions between Egypt and the UN resulted in
Pakistan not being represented in the Force, in New Zealand's offer being declined,
and in a Canadian infantry unit being held back. Pakistan had recently been critical of Egypt, as had New Zealand, and Egypt apparently had doubts about the
desirability of accepting a Canadian battalion which in dress and name (the Queen's
Own) was not obviously distinguishable from the British forces then in Egypt.
(The battalion was already embarked in Canada on Her Majesty's Ship *Magnifi-
cent*.) Canada did, however, provide some supporting units, and a Canadian reconnaissance squadron joined the Force in March 1957.
[9] The United States, anxious that a 'sound' Latin-American state should be
represented in UNEF, pressed hard for Brazil's inclusion.

The interpository role which UNEF played for ten years is the one which has attracted the most attention and by which, therefore, it chiefly became known. From one point of view this is wholly appropriate, inasmuch as it is arguable that this is the part for which it was cast at the outset. One of the six states abstaining on the Assembly's resolution of 2 November was Canada, who did so on the ground that it did not provide for any measures to deal with the problems which lay at the root of the crisis. Explaining this, her representative, Mr Lester Pearson, spoke of the desirability of the UN sending a force to maintain quiet between Israel and Egypt while a political settlement was being worked out. His assumption seemed to be that the lack of quiet was a major obstacle in the way of an agreement, which was very questionable. However, he was encouraged by the United States and others to go ahead with his proposal, and the result was the establishment of UNEF. The resolution of 4 November asking the Secretary-General to report on the idea, and also that of the next day which established a UN Command for the Force, referred to the cessation of hostilities in accordance with the Assembly's earlier resolution of 2 November which, among other things, urged Israel and Egypt 'to withdraw all forces behind the armistice lines, to desist from raids across the armistice lines into neighbouring territory, and to observe scrupulously the provisions of the armistice agreements'.[10] On this basis it could be argued that the Assembly was looking to the establishment of a force which could act as a kind of barrier between the two local contestants.

The Secretary-General's comments could be read in the same light. In answer to a question he said that UNEF would have to function at the dividing line between Egyptian and Israeli forces, wherever that might be, and that it was therefore to be anticipated that while the Force would have to start close to the Canal, it would end up at the Armistice Demarcation Line. Evidently he did not consider that its role would be over once it had reached that point, for, in his second report, he said that its function would be to help maintain quiet during and after the withdrawal of non-Egyptian troops and to secure compliance with the terms of the resolution of 2 November. How long UNEF would remain was a point on which he was understandably imprecise, but, while emphasizing that it was a temporary force, he saw it as staying beyond the 'immediate crisis' for a period which would be 'determined by the needs arising out of the present conflict'.[11]

This was also the view of Britain and France. On the request to

[10] General Assembly resolution 997 (ES-I).
[11] UN Document A/3302, paras 17 and 8.

the Secretary-General to report on the feasibility of the idea of a
UN force, Britain's representative prevaricated, complained about
the lack of time for study and consultations, and abstained; he
took the same course on the proposal to set up a UN Command for
the Force, saying that he had not had an adequate opportunity to
obtain instructions. However, at the very beginning of the Assembly's
Emergency Special Session he had already indicated how pleased
his Government would be if the UN could take over the physical
task of maintaining peace in the area, a responsibility which, as he
later put it, his country had 'felt bound to shoulder'.[12] This would
involve, the Secretary-General was told by the two Western Powers,
the establishment and maintenance of a force until an Arab-Israel
peace settlement was reached, and also, they added, until satisfactory arrangements had been agreed concerning the Canal. These
points were repeated in the Assembly prior to their voting in
favour of a resolution which approved Hammarskjöld's second report.
There was, therefore, a basis for the argument that UNEF was set
up as an interpository force, in the hope that it would bring stability
to a border which, in recent years, had been particularly troublesome, and which had provided the occasion for the Suez crisis. In
this view its role prior to reaching the Egyptian–Israeli border was
incidental rather than primary.

However, it was clear from the outset of the discussions regarding a UN force that most members were not thinking about
what it might do once foreign troops had left Egypt. Their immediate and overriding concern was to prevent Britain and France
from landing in Egypt and, when they had done so, to secure
their withdrawal at the earliest possible moment. Accordingly, they
were interested in UNEF mainly for the part which it could play
in achieving this end and in this respect its supervisory role held very
considerable promise. It provided a safeguard against incidents
sparking off a resumption of hostilities or marring and perhaps
holding up the invaders' departure. The presence of large numbers
of UN personnel who could supply immediate information regarding
the situation in Egypt might also have been expected to discourage
any delaying tendencies at the political level. But so far as speeding
the Anglo-French withdrawal was concerned, UNEF was chiefly
and overwhelmingly significant as a face-saver. For the supervisory
operation meant that a sizeable UN mission would be present on
Egyptian soil after the invaders had left.[13] And as Britain and France

---

[12] General Assembly, *Official Records*, 567th Plenary Meeting, para. 99.
[13] Looked at purely as a supervisory body, UNEF's size was excessive. However,
the establishment of a force of 6,000 men was influenced by the need to make it
look as if a substantial operation was called for so as to assuage Anglo-French
feelings, and also to provide a force which, when it got to the Egyptian–Israeli

had proclaimed that their policy arose out of the necessity of separating the combatants, it could be understood by those for whom such an expectation was important that UNEF would serve as an alternative means of securing the Anglo-French goal. Obviously, it was not a perfect substitute, for, quite apart from the fact that its arrival was conditional, in law, on the permission of the territorial sovereign and, in effect, on the willingness of her three adversaries to call off their attack, it was not equipped to hold the Egyptians and Israelis apart. It was a non-fighting force, one which possessed arms only for the purpose of self-defence. In consequence, its success in keeping the two local belligerents from each other's throats depended chiefly on their readiness to maintain a cease-fire. UNEF was not therefore, the formidable proposition which might have been thought necessary for keeping the peace, but a policeman who was publicly committed to passivity. It might have seemed odd on the face of it, that an operation of this character could be regarded as anything like an adequate substitute for the uninvited and powerful Anglo-French force. But the oddity of this aspect of the situation was counter-balanced by the fact that the Anglo-French action which UNEF was supposed to be replacing was equally unable to stand up to scrutiny as a move chiefly inspired by the desire to keep the Egyptian and Israeli forces apart.

However, UNEF provided some superficial evidence for the British and French claim that they had been honourably engaged from the start, having acted in the international interest and always with a willingness, nay, a desire, to leave the moment the UN was able to discharge its responsibilities. Before long this reasoning was extended to include the suggestion that they had always hoped to galvanize the UN into just the kind of life which it was to display: honest citizens had risked denigration in order to arouse the dormant police. This might, to most ears, sound spurious, but that was not the point. The point was that the decision of Britain and France to withdraw was at the very least facilitated by the fact that they were enabled to explain themselves in this way. By allowing them to do so UNEF supplied, for many members, its chief *raison d'être* which doubtless explains, in part, why the Soviet Union and her friends were noticeably unenthusiastic about it. They would have preferred a straightforward demand for a humiliating withdrawal, and would not have been totally displeased had the invaders decided not to comply. For others, however, the prime need was to get Britain and

---

border, would be big enough to make a significant contribution to its pacification. It may also have reflected some uncertainty at headquarters about the number of men who would be required and by the fact that they were not at all in short supply.

France out, and in order to ensure this they were willing to make arrangements which would allow the aggressors to depart without a complete loss of dignity.

The emphasis placed by many UN members on the early withdrawal of hostile troops from Egypt doubtless explains why the resolution which Canada presented to the Assembly suggesting the idea of a UN force was much less broad in character than might have been expected, having regard to Mr Pearson's earlier remarks about the role which a force could play in paving the way for a settlement of the Arab-Israel problem. Apart from its reference to the observance of the Armistice Agreements, it was strictly contemporary in tone, reflecting the fact that the Organization's chief concern at that moment was the restoration of the *status quo ante*—so far as the question of foreign troops was concerned. This led to some difficulty between the UN and Britain and France. In agreeing to make way for UNEF they had spoken of the necessity for a generally acceptable solution to the Canal question, and this was a matter which concerned them acutely. In relation to this issue, however, the *status quo ante* nationalization was something to which most UN members had no real desire to return; nor were they anxious to see some new international arrangement which would give Britain and France a measure of satisfaction. There had been some sympathy for this line of argument prior to November, but now the opposition to it had hardened and extended, for the invaders were widely felt to have forfeited any moral right which they may have had to a compromise settlement. On the face of it, however, they had not given up their hopes, for they began to give the impression that they might not go quietly unless they were assured that some pressure would be brought upon the Egyptian Government to allow an international voice in the control of the Canal.

As a first move in this direction, Britain pressed the UN to act as if it already possessed some rights in respect of the Canal, urging it to begin clearance work at once, irrespective of Egypt's refusal to permit it until the Western Powers had left, and to station part of UNEF on the Canal after their withdrawal. Failing to receive satisfaction on either of these points, Britain ignored the Assembly's resolution of 7 November calling for the departure of non-Egyptian troops, save for the announcement a fortnight later of a token withdrawal as a sign of her good faith. Many members, however, refused to regard it as such, and were unimpressed by her assurance that she would leave once UNEF was in a position to carry out its functions effectively: it was the question of what, exactly, UNEF's functions were which was at issue. The difference of opinion was reflected in the debate on a resolution put to the Assembly calling

for the invaders' withdrawal 'forthwith'.[14] Britain attempted to get
this phrase struck out, and obtained a fair amount of support,
noticeably among West European and white Commonwealth
members, but was unsuccessful. Sir Anthony Eden attributed this
to the United States failure to give the amendment her support,
and commented bitterly on the failure to foresee that 'the United
States Government would harden against us on almost every point
and become harsher after the cease fire than before'.[15] She was one
of the 63 states who, on 24 November, called for immediate compliance with the Assembly's earlier resolutions, and Britain soon
realized that the game was up. On 3 December, together with France,
she notified the Secretary-General that her troops would be withdrawn without delay, and the operation was completed by 22
December. Only then did the work of clearing the Canal begin, and
subsequent efforts to obtain an agreement regarding its future
operation came to nought.

Sir Anthony Eden has implied that had Britain realized what
the outcome would be, she would not have agreed to call off her
attack on Egypt: 'We would have taken a second, and maybe a
third, look at the problem had we understood what was to come'.[16]
But, leaving on one side the question of her ability to have done so
in the crisis situation of the first week of November, this argument is
rather disingenuous. Certainly Britain hoped to salvage something
from the wreckage of the Anglo-French campaign, and she did not
fail through want of trying. But there could hardly have been many
illusions, on 6 November, about the final result. Few could have
seriously thought it possible that Britain was going to be allowed,
either by the direct pressure of her forces in Egypt or indirectly
through UNEF, to obtain the kind of settlement she wanted. If
there had been support for it, there would not have been quite
such an outcry at the Anglo-French action, or at least the two
attackers would have been allowed their request to act as the UN's
agents in Egypt. True, it was open to Britain to pretend that she
had called off the expedition under a misapprehension: that could
be part of the face-saving process. But it would have been a remarkable thing if she was really taken in by the escape hatch which was
offered her, conceiving it to be a way into a multilateral negotiating
group which was proceeding along essentially the same lines as
herself. The only possible hope for Britain and France, after they
had agreed to cease-fire, was to sit tight until their demands were
met. But that would have meant having the worst of both worlds,

---

[14] General Assembly resolution 1120 (XI).
[15] Eden, *op. cit.*, p. 561.
[16] Ibid., p. 558.

for they would have been in possession of only part of the Canal, and would have been sitting targets for powerful and virulent criticism. It was, therefore, a politically inconceivable course. Having stopped with the job of seizing the Canal only a quarter done, the invaders had no effective option but to carry through the logic of their decision of 6 November, and withdraw.

During the period which preceded their departure UNEF played a very useful role. It took up its position between the Anglo-French and Egyptian forces and so reduced the possibility of incidents and a resumption of fighting. Its contribution in this respect was said to be particularly valuable during the days immediately following its arrival, when tension was high. Complaints that the cease-fire had been violated were investigated by UNEF, which also exchanged prisoners and made enquiries regarding missing personnel. In part of the Port Said area it took over the responsibility for maintaining order, in co-operation with the local authorities, so as to lessen the chances of incidents between the local population and the Anglo-French forces, and in the final stage of their withdrawal UNEF prevented parting clashes by positioning itself around the grouping area. As the invaders departed, smooth continuity was maintained in respect of security and public services by their handing over the functions they had assumed in these fields to UNEF, which in turn passed them on to the Egyptian authorities.

In these ways UNEF helped to ensure an uneventful Anglo-French withdrawal. It performed very similar functions as the Israeli forces retraced their steps across the Sinai Peninsula, and with regard to them this was UNEF's main function, for Israel had far less need to save her face than had Britain and France. From their point of view the chief aims of the Suez venture were to remove the Canal from Egypt's sole control and, hopefully, to topple Nasser, and they failed ignominiously in both respects. Israel, on the other hand, while certainly having an interest in the Canal question, on account of the blockade which Egypt maintained on Israeli ships and cargoes, was mainly concerned, firstly, to administer a striking punishment to Egypt for the harassment she had been suffering at Egyptian hands, especially during the previous year, and, secondly, to try to put obstacles in the way of Egypt resuming her previous policy. This did not require that she make difficulties about withdrawing from most of the territory she had seized, nor did she need to be furnished with an excuse for withdrawal. She had occupied Sinai without difficulty, assisted by Egypt having concentrated her forces to meet the British and French, and although, early in November, she indicated that she would only withdraw in return for guarantees regarding Egypt's future behaviour, this position was quickly abandoned. American pressure materially assisted this retraction, but no doubt Israel also realized that to try to bargain about such a large slice of territory would cause needless offence and would also leave her in an exposed position in the event of the gambit not succeeding. She began her withdrawal early in December and by 22 January 1957 retained only the Gaza and Sharm-el-Sheikh areas. Here, however, she dug in her heels, for both were of great importance to her.

The Gaza Strip, about 25 miles long and 4 to 7 miles wide was the only part of the former mandated territory of Palestine controlled by Egypt, it having been left under her jurisdiction by the 1949 Armistice Agreement with Israel. It is fertile and heavily populated, containing (in 1956) about 300,000 people, two-thirds of whom were Palestine refugees. In these respects it was in marked contrast to the rest of the Egyptian–Israeli border, which ran southwards across the Sinai Desert to the Gulf of Aqaba. Accordingly, by far the greatest number of incidents between the two countries since 1949 had taken place across the Armistice Demarcation Line between the Strip and Israel, and it had been the main centre for the organization of the officially unofficial commando (*fedayeen*) raids into Israel which had recently become an increasingly serious source of tension. Thus Israel was most anxious that her withdrawal from the Strip should be accompanied by some scheme for its administration which would deny its use to Egypt for such aggravating purposes.

The case of Sharm-el-Sheikh was different, but illustrated the same concern. On account of Egypt's denial of passage through the Suez Canal to ships going to and from Israel, the only direct sea route between Israel and points east and south was via the port of Eilat, which lies on a very small strip of Israeli territory at the head of the Gulf of Aqaba. However, the Straits of Tiran, which form the narrow entrance to the Gulf from the Red Sea, can be controlled from Sharm-el-Sheik, and since 1950 Egypt had used her position there to close the Gulf to Israeli trade. In consequence, sea communications with Israel from East Africa and South Asia and beyond had to be via the extravagantly wasteful route of the Cape and the Mediterranean. Besides intending to put the Gaza Strip out of action as a terrorist base, Israel was also determined to break Egypt's blockade of Eilat. She therefore proposed that UNEF should take over from her at Sharm-el-Sheikh and guarantee freedom of navigation through the Straits of Tiran. With regard to Gaza, Israel's suggestion was that no military forces should remain in the Strip and that she should undertake administrative and economic responsibility for it, with security matters being dealt with by her police.

The Secretary-General, however, very properly insisted that both these matters would require Egypt's consent, and although there was a good deal of sympathy in the Assembly for Israel's point of view there was little support for her proposals. Hence there was no chance of even a start being made on an attempt to get Egypt to accept them: to have moved in that direction would have been regarded by many members as an outrage to the principle of national sovereignty and, more to the point, as a very dangerous precedent. Thus, on 19 January 1957, Israel's failure to comply with previous calls for withdrawal was regretted by a large majority, only France siding with Israel in opposition to the resolution. On 2 February this lonely alignment was repeated when the Assembly deplored Israel's non-compliance and demanded it immediately. On the same day, after a debate in which a variety of viewpoints were expressed about UNEF's future the Assembly resolved that it should be placed 'on the Egyptian–Israel armistice demarcation line'[17] once Israel had withdrawn, which may have given her some comfort, but not much. Failing her own administration of the Strip, the next best thing for her was that it should be controlled by the UN, but this, too, was not a popular cause. The position of the United States was crucial and she would have nothing to do with the idea, urging Israel, in effect, to get out and hope for the best. She did, however approve of the proposal that UNEF should be on the Gaza boundary and also in the Sharm-el-Sheikh area, saying that in her view the Straits of Tiran were international waters and that all states should therefore be permitted free and innocent passage. This was not enough for Israel, who wanted further guarantees, but instead she got a public threat from President Eisenhower that the United States would support UN sanctions unless Israel complied with the Organization's demands. In view of this Israel decided that she could hold out no longer, and on 1 March announced her impending withdrawal, which was begun on 6 March and completed within two days.

When announcing her departure, Israel had also stated that she was leaving in the confidence that freedom of navigation would be maintained through the Straits of Tiran and on the assumption that the UN would take over in the Gaza Strip and continue to exercise exclusive military and civilian control there until an agreement was reached on the area's future. This was an attempt to force the UN's hand, and in the general obscurity as to what exactly was meant to happen, it looked as though it might succeed. UNEF

[17] General Assembly resolution 1125 (xi).

relieved Israeli forces at Sharm-el-Sheikh and in the Strip in what had become the usual manner, and in Gaza town General Burns, UNEF's Commander, established his headquarters in the old Police Station, which was the recognized seat of the local authority. Experts were speedily assembled to administer the Strip.

But Israel's ruse had to be accepted not only by the UN but also by Egypt, and here it came unstuck. Egypt did not object to a small UN camp in the desert at Sharm-el-Sheikh, but the control of the Gaza Strip was another matter altogether. Not only was it populous and strategically important; the re-establishment of Egypt's authority was also demanded on grounds of prestige, to make it clear that it was not Egypt who had lost in this most recent Israeli war. Demonstrations were quickly organized demanding a prompt return to Egyptian rule, and the situation grew more tense when a ricocheting bullet killed a rioter. On 11 March Egypt named her Administrative Governor for the Strip, and there was no question of the UN preventing his entry. He arrived three days later and immediately invited General Burns to move out of the Police Station, which he did. Thus the UN's administration of the Strip was called off virtually before it had been begun: a refrigerative presence, covertly brought to birth, proved to be still-born. For a while these developments threatened to lead to a renewed crisis as, on the one hand, Egypt was reported to be thinking of sending troops to Gaza, and, on the other, Israel considered the possibility of a military riposte. But Egypt withheld her troops, and Israel realized that to retake what has once been given up is a much more difficult operation, diplomatically as well as militarily, than staying put. As it happened, things could have turned out worse for her. For UNEF now entered a second and much longer phase, moving from supervision to obstruction. During the next ten years it patrolled the Armistice Demarcation Line in Gaza and the international frontier across Sinai, and retained an outpost at Sharm-el-Sheikh. Whether or not on account of this activity, quiet was maintained along the Egyptian–Israeli border throughout the period and there was no attempt to interfere with Israeli commerce passing through the Straits of Tiran.[18]

II

The second supervisory presence established by the UN was also in the Middle East, in the Yemen. The republican regime which had seized power in September 1962 had immediately been supported by the United Arab Republic (UAR), both diplomatically

[18] See below, pp. 295–306.

and militarily, but had been unable to establish its authority throughout the country. Broadly speaking, the new Government controlled
the towns, ports, and roads, whereas the deposed Royalists dominated the intervening countryside, including the parts which adjoined
Saudi Arabia. From this sympathetic neighbour the Royalists
received support, chiefly in the shape of arms, supplies, and money.
Thus, the civil war threatened to involve two outside Powers with
each other, and conceivably could have had wider repercussions.
However, in April 1963 Saudi Arabia and the UAR agreed[19] to
end their participation in the Yemen's internal affairs, Saudi Arabia
promising to stop aiding the Royalists and the UAR undertaking
to withdraw her sizeable force, which was variously estimated at
between 15,000 and 30,000 men. It was also agreed that a demilitarized zone should be established to a depth of 20 kilometres, on each
side of the Saudi Arabian–Yemen border and that the disengagement process should be verified by UN or other impartial observers.
Discussion then took place regarding the implementation of these
terms, and at the end of May the Secretary-General reported to the
Security Council that the size of the observation team which would
be needed would not be more than 200 and that it should be
required for no more than four months. In his judgment, such a
presence was essential for the smooth execution of the agreement,
and he reported that he was therefore going ahead with its establishment as soon as possible. He was hopeful that the two states most
closely involved would divide its cost between them, and early in
June he was able to announce that they had agreed to do so for a
period of two months.

In this U Thant had the strong backing of the United States,
who found herself in a delicate position. She was anxious that an
early end should be put to the civil war in the Yemen lest it should
encourage instability in neighbouring Saudi Arabia and possibly
also in Jordan, both of whom might be regarded as susceptible to
revolutionary activity. But the diplomatic situation was such that
she found it difficult to move effectively in any direction. To the one
side lay her oil interests in Saudi Arabia, which made her reluctant
to annoy that country. On the other was her desire to maintain and
develop her standing in the eyes of the non-monarchical Arab
countries, which required that she avoid giving offence to President
Nasser—a concern which was exemplified in the early American
recognition of the Yemen's new regime. Her best course, therefore,
was to try to dampen down the Yemen trouble, and to do so in a
manner which involved her as little as possible. Thus she played a
significant role in obtaining the disengagement agreement, and

[19] See above, pp. 86–87.

gave her whole-hearted support to the idea that the UN should supervise its execution, hoping in this way to increase the likelihood of it actually being observed.

Britain, too, with her responsibilities in and around neighbouring Aden, was much in favour of the scheme. Indeed, it was one which aroused little opposition, as might have been expected of a plan which had to do with the ending of intervention in a country's domestic affairs. But the Soviet Union was known to have doubts about it, and to be trying to decide whether they were sufficient to justify the unpopular move of calling a meeting of the Security Council to consider the matter. She concluded that some unpopularity was worth while in order to prevent the establishment of an undesirable precedent, and so the Council was convened as the UN's advance party was about to travel to the Yemen. It was presented with the Soviet Union's well-known view that measures relating to international peace and security, such as those now being arranged by the Secretary-General, could only be taken under the express authority of the Security Council, and her representative referred to an important reason for this position when he complained that most of the UN's peace-keeping operations were taken in the Western interest. He said that his country preferred 'the resolute curbing of the aggressor [rather than] the stationing of UN troops or observers on the frontier between a foreign aggressor and his victim'.[20] As, however, in this case, the victim of aggression and her gallant supporter were in favour of a UN observation mission, the Soviet Union merely abstained on the Council's request to the Secretary-General, supported by the other ten members, to establish the mission in accordance with the plans he had already made.

From the point of view of the states immediately concerned, the UN Yemen Observation Mission (UNYOM) was, in principle, a very important part of the scheme for disengagement. Neither side was prepared to trust the word of the other regarding its execution of the agreement, and neither was in a position to check for itself, for the Saudi Arabians were not in direct contact with the Egyptians and the Yemenis were not in control of much of their border. It would no doubt have been possible for each to have made private enquiries about the other's activities, and the Saudi Arabians might have been able to feel that this procedure gave them a satisfactory answer, for the UAR troops were conspicuous. But ascertaining the state of Saudi Arabian-Royalist traffic would not have been so easy for the Egyptians, and they might not have felt much confidence in such answers as they were able to obtain. In any event, it was much better from a number of angles that information on these

[20] Security Council, *Official Records*, 1038th Meeting, para. 17.

matters should come from an impartial third party: its assessment was likely to be fair and in most quarters would carry more weight than *ex parte* announcements.

UNYOM began its activity on 4 July 1963. It consisted of a Yugoslav reconnaissance unit of just over 100 officers and men (transferred from UNEF), and a Canadian air unit of about half that size, each of them being deployed on both sides of the South Arabia–Yemeni border. Unusually for such UN missions, the observers carried arms for self-defence when on ground patrol. Additionally there were six military observers stationed in Hodeida, the main port, and Sana, the chief town and site of a military airfield. UNYOM also had its headquarters in Sana. UAR troops moving into or out of the country were likely to pass through one of these centres: from them, therefore, UNYOM should have been able to keep something of an eye on the UAR's execution of her promise to withdraw. However, there was a good deal of scepticism as to the mission's ability to function satisfactorily on the Saudi Arabian–Yemeni border. The frontier itself was difficult to observe, as it was about 400 miles long, lay through very rugged country, and for much of its length was not demarcated with any clarity. There was also the problem that it was crossed by numerous tracks and routes which, so the Saudi Arabians said, were utilized for normal commercial activity, and that Saudi Arabian assistance to the Royalists was relatively small and spasmodic. Moreover, the support being extended to them was not the most noticeable form of traffic nor the easiest to identify as having an anti-Republican destination. And even if that could be established, the possibility remained that either on a Saudi or a Royalist initiative, the material was coming from a private source: Saudi Arabia did not deny that the Royalists were receiving some aid in this way.

Doubt as to the capacity of a body of UNYOM's size and equipment to execute its mandate efficiently was said to be one of the reasons which produced, in August 1963, the resignation of its Commander, General von Horn, of Sweden. However, as it happened, the major problem in the Yemen arose not from the lack of thorough observation but from the fact that the agreement which UNYOM was supposed to supervise was not being executed. Following the Mission's arrival there appeared to be a net reduction of Egyptian troops and a lessening of Saudi Arabian support for the Royalists, but this development was not maintained and the Egyptians, in particular, soon began to act in a manner which was directly contrary to their undertaking to withdraw. It seemed that, in view of this, Saudi Arabia was going to refuse to repeat her earlier agreement to pay for an extension of UNYOM's life for a further two months, and the Secretary-General began to make plans for its disbandment. But under American pressure, Saudi Arabia changed her mind and so UNYOM was retained. It was, however, much changed in size and character. P. P. Spinelli, a civilian Secretariat member, was appointed as its head and also as the Secretary-General's Special Representative, and in December the Yugoslav unit was withdrawn. In partial compensation for this the number of military observers was increased to 21 (drawn from a variety of countries) and they were deployed in both Saudi Arabia and the Yemen. The form and a little of the already tenuous substance of observation, was to give the UN presence in the Yemen a marked diplomatic twist, in the hope that it would be able to assume a mediatory role. For, as the earlier agreement was not being implemented, supervision had lost its point and a new agreement was necessary, or at least a new and firmer decision to honour the old one. But it was not forthcoming, and by April 1964 the number of UAR troops in the Yemen was estimated by some at about 40,000. UNYOM's life was extended for several more two monthly periods after informal consultation with the members of the Security Council, but it was serving no useful purposes and in September 1964 no one stood in the way when the Secretary-General indicated that in his view the time had come for its termination.

It was implied by the Secretary-General and others that this unhappy ending might have been averted had UNYOM's mandate been stronger or wider, had it been able to observe the implementation of the disengagement agreement more thoroughly, investigate allegations regarding its breach, or establish itself as an interpository force. But this line of reasoning, which would have involved a larger presence, possibly a much larger one, is unconvincing. It assumes that the lack of compliance was essentially a marginal affair, and that a somewhat more searching or imposing presence would have been enough to tip the scales the other way, convincing the parties that they would be unable to commit unnoticed breaches, or giving each of them an obviously well-founded assurance that the other was honouring its promise. But the problem in the Yemen was not all of this order, for it reflected something much more than insufficient vigilance on the part of the international community.

The failure of the disengagement agreement cannot be ascribed wholly to one side, but at first Saudi Arabia did seem to show some willingness to act on its basis. The UAR on the other hand while apparently making a net reduction in the number of troops in the months immediately following UNYOM's establishment, did not give the impression of being seriously interested in the execution of its terms, and soon she was clearly making the pace so far as their breach was concerned. She justified her failure to withdraw by complaining of the continued Royalist activity in the Yemen, and no doubt this represented the truth of the matter, but it makes her original understanding to withdraw look very strange. There was no reason to expect, when the agreement was signed, that its implementation would be accompanied by a decline in the Royalist opposition to the Republican regime, for the Royalists were not a party to it. Nor was there any basis for the supposition that they would be called off by Saudi Arabia, for even if the latter had been able to secure such a result, which is very questionable, she had not said she would do so; the agreement had done no more than commit her to stop assisting the Royalists. In view of this, and of the fact that since the September 1962 *coup* there had been a big build-up of arms in the Yemen, it would have been very odd had the Egyptians thought that by obtaining Saudi Arabia's promise to disengage, she was thereby securing the collapse of the Royalist movement. Another line pursued by the UAR to account for her lack of compliance was that once she had left the Yemen supplies to the Royalists from Saudi Arabia would be resumed. Again, this was, for the Egyptians, a valid consideration, for once she had withdrawn her troops a thousand miles and more up the Red Sea, getting them back would have presented a sizeable logistic and political problem, whereas it would be a very easy thing for Saudi Arabia to recommence slipping supplies across the border. But, as with her previous point, this possibility could hardly have been unclear to the UAR when she signed the disengagement agreement.

It could be argued, therefore, that from the outset the UAR had no intention of observing it, perhaps relying on a lack of compliance on Saudi Arabia's part to justify her own refusal to withdraw. But this is not the most obvious explanation. It would have been very rash for the UAR to assume that she would be supplied with such a pretext, especially when Saudi Arabia had such a strong interest in getting the Egyptians out of the Yemen and was also in a good position to resume her intervention once they had gone. And states are by no means in the habit of signing agreements if they do not intend to observe them and where their lack of compliance would be obvious for all to see. Such a course would have simply invited some trouble without gaining any advantages for the Yemeni Republicans or discommoding the Saudi Arabians. Another factor which suggests that the UAR did not agree to disengage without any expectation of actually doing so is that at the time of signature she was probably already counting the cost of her expedition and wanting to leave before getting more deeply and inextricably involved. It therefore seems more plausible to suggest that for one reason or another the UAR's policy changed after she had undertaken to disengage.

This may have been due to a reassessment of her own interest in the matter. A Republican defeat would be a blow to her prestige, and would lose her a strategically valuable friend. She may therefore have calculated that, contrary to her original view, it would be unwise to risk it, even though the cost or precautionary measures, in the shape of maintaining the UAR presence in the Yemen, was high. But perhaps the most likely explanation of a somewhat improbable situation is that the UAR had misjudged the internal situation in the Yemen. She may have underestimated the extent of tribal support for the Royalists, and also have thought that by dragging out her own withdrawal she would be able to defeat them before she departed. Additionally, she may have overestimated the strength of the Republican regime, assuming that by the time her troops were withdrawn it would have acquired sufficient popularity and effectiveness to be able to stand on its own feet, and even cope with Saudi Arabian attempts to stir up trouble. It would not have taken the UAR long to realize such a mistake, but it could well have been her bad luck that she appreciated it only after having promised to disengage. This would account both for her signing the agreement and for her subsequent deliberate refusal to execute it.

If this was the case, schemes for a stronger UN presence were largely irrelevant. A UN force on the Saudi Arabian border would not have increased the Republican regime's ability to cope with the internal problem, nor, therefore, the UAR's willingness to leave. Nor was it practical to espouse the idea of a buffer between the Republican and Royalist forces, on account both of the difficulty of demarcating the division between them and of the response which such a suggestion would surely have elicited from the two parties immediately concerned. Proposals which would have enabled UNYOM to observe more completely, or to investigate claims that the agreement was being broken were even less to the point, for the UAR's reluctance to leave reflected neither a lack of clarity about what Saudi Arabia was doing nor the belief that she was covertly continuing to assist the Royalists. Similarly, the suggestion that what was really needed was a mediatory presence was equally wide of the mark, as was shown by the fact that UNYOM did partly assume this character at the end of 1963, but without positive result. The only expansion of UNYOM's role which might have made a significant impact on the situation in the Yemen would have been its conversion into an armed force which was prepared to use its strength in order to attain its object. But there was never any question of throwing the Egyptians out of the Yemen, and it was therefore a mistake to expect that a lesser amendment of the operation would produce the required result. Like all non-violent operations UNYOM was basically dependent on the co-operation of the interested parties.

The best hope for the solution of the Yemen problem, therefore, lay in a changed attitude towards the disengagement agreement on the part of the UAR. It might have been thought that the UN would itself have had an interest in making representations towards this end in order to support the arrangement which gave rise to its own operation. But in this case the UN was not minded to assert itself, for the UAR was a favoured state at the UN. Colonialists could be expected to be brought to book should they act in contempt of a UN presence, but the Afro-Asians are wont to indulge their own kind. Furthermore, the cause which the UAR was supporting in the Yemen was high on the approved list: a progressive Republican movement was being defended against reactionary monarchical forces. And her immunity was completed by virtue of the fact that she was a leader of the neutralists, and therefore a state which Western, no less than Eastern, members were not anxious to offend. Had the picture been reversed, were Saudi Arabian troops in the Yemen defending a Royalist regime against a Republican revolt, and refusing to honour their promise to leave, much would have been heard on the theme of the iniquity of the defaulting state. But in the case of the Yemen the UN was not disposed to condemn the UAR for remaining, nor were any of its influential members prepared to act outside the Organization to secure the UAR's withdrawal. She was able, therefore, to change her policy and sit tight without incurring undue international embarrassment. Economically, it was costing her a good deal, but in diplomatic terms she did not feel the pinch.

The UAR remained in the Yemen for three years after UNYOM's withdrawal. A cease-fire was announced in November 1963, and after some much-delayed meetings the UAR and Saudi Arabia reached an agreement on 24 August 1965 for their disengagement, it also being stated that the Yemenis would decide their own future by a plebiscite which was to be held not later than 23 November 1966. However, the conference which was to decide on the form of government during the transitional period and prepare for the plebiscite broke down. By now the number of UAR troops in the Yemen was commonly being estimated as in the region of at least 50,000 and it looked as though she was preparing for a long stay, encouraged perhaps, by the prospect of Britain's withdrawal from Aden in 1968. For the powerful UAR presence in neighbouring Yemen might have been thought to promise President Nasser an

important influence on events within an independent and relatively
weak Aden. Indeed, it was supposed in some quarters that it was
Britain's decision to leave Aden, announced in February 1966,
which led the UAR to cancel the plans which she had reportedly
made for her withdrawal from the Yemen in accordance with the
agreement of August 1965.

However, the crushing defeat which the UAR suffered in the
Arab-Israeli war of June 1967 brought about a drastic change in her
Yemen policy. For the cost of re-equipping her armed forces together
with the loss of revenue from the Suez Canal meant that she could
hardly afford to maintain large numbers of troops at a considerable
distance from her own country. Moreover, the fact that the war had
resulted in the closure of the Canal perhaps reduced the UAR's
strategic interest in the mouth of the Red Sea. Thus on 31 August
1967 the UAR and Saudi Arabia agreed once again to stop interfering in the Yemen. The UAR troops were to be evacuated within
three months, and it was proposed that a settlement should be
negotiated between the Republicans and Royalists with the assistance of a committee of three Arab states: Iraq (the UAR's choice),
Morocco (Saudi Arabia's), and the Sudan (who had played the key
mediatory role).

This time the UAR honoured her disengagement promise, the
last of her troops leaving the Yemen early in December. However,
the Yemen Government regarded the setting up of the tripartite
committee as an attempt to intervene in its domestic affairs, and
refused to have anything to do with it. Nor did the replacement of
President Sallal in November 1967 improve matters greatly in this
respect. In fact the Yemen seemed to be as far as ever from a solution
of its internal problem as the Government and its Royalist challengers
prepared for further military action. During the period of UAR
dominanace the Republican regime had been prevented from taking
delivery of a consignment of Soviet arms for which it had contracted,
but now the matter could be and was reopened, an agreement being
reached in November 1967. In February 1968 Soviet aid, together
with the help which the Yemen Government was alleged to be
receiving from Syria and the new state of the Southern Yemen which
had emerged in Aden, was cited by Saudi Arabia as a ground for
the immediate resumption of her aid to the Royalists—a development which some regarded as already having been in progress for
a couple of months.

Clearly the last has not been heard of the events which began
with the Yemen *coup* of 1962, and it could be that at some future
date the UN might be asked to watch over another arrangement for
the ending of intervention in the Yemen's affairs. In that case the

Organization may heed the call with less alacrity than in 1963, but if impartial supervision is a vital element in the disengagement formula it is probable that the UN would allow itself to be pressed into service, and so play a potentially valuable but essentially secondary role.

III

The third supervisory presence established by the UN arose out of the September 1965 war between India and Pakistan. During the previous month armed men had begun to cross from the Pakistan to the Indian side of the cease-fire line in Kashmir in an attempt to spark off a revolt. To prevent further infiltration India occupied a number of points on the Pakistani side of the line, whereupon the Pakistan army launched an offensive against Indian-held Kashmir, threatening to cut communications between it and India. This attack began on 1 September, and within a week India had replied by invading West Pakistan at several points. In fact, if not in form, the two countries were at war.

From its outset the crisis had aroused a good deal of anxious attention. Britain, the UAR, Yugoslavia, Canada, and the Soviet Union all offered to help the parties bring it to an end. The UN, too, was active, as was to be expected in view of its particular interest in the Kashmir problem and the presence of its observers along the cease-fire line.[21] During August the Secretary-General, U Thant, tried to exert a calming influence, but with no greater success than others were having, and on 1 September he appealed in vain for the cease-fire line to be respected. On the initiative of its American President, the Security Council met on 4 September and unanimously called for a cease-fire and the withdrawal of troops. Two days later it did so once again, also asking the Secretary-General to try to give effect to its call and to strengthen the UN's Military Observer Group in India and Pakistan (UNMOGIP), the body which had been in Kashmir for 16 years. U Thant then visited the two countries, but had to report to the Council that his efforts had been unsuccessful. He suggested that the Council might take a strong line in an endeavour to bring the conflict to an end, and on 20 September 10 of its 11 members, including all the Great Powers, 'demand[ed]'[22] that a cease-fire should take effect on 22 September, and called for the subsequent withdrawal of all armed personnel to the positions which they held before 5 August.

In deciding whether to comply with the resolution the contestants

---

[21] See above, pp. 24–29. and below pp. 290–294.
[22] Security Council resolution 211 (1965).

E

doubtless took into consideration the amount of world opinion which it represented. But a much more important factor was that world opinion was being led by the United States and the Soviet Union, both of whom, in a rare show of agreement, were keenly interested in the restoration of peace on the Indian sub-continent. One important reason for this was that each of them had links with both contestants. Pakistan, through her membership of SEATO and CENTO, was a part of the American-led alliance system, and although the United States had made it clear that she was not thereby obliged to support Pakistan against India, nevertheless it was not surprising that Pakistan should claim an entitlement to special American consideration. The fact that of late Pakistan-American relations had shown a marked degree of coolness, on account of Pakistan's *rapprochement* with China, did not make the situation easier for the United States, unless she was ready to cut her links with Pakistan, which she was not. On the other hand, America's relations with India had improved a good deal since China's attack on India in 1962, and as India could claim with some plausibility that Pakistan bore prime responsibility for the September war, she too looked to the United States for support.

The Soviet Union was in a similar dilemma. From the time of Stalin's death in 1953 she had cultivated her relations with India assiduously, and wished to remain on good terms with her. But since Khrushchev's downfall in 1964 she had also shown signs of wanting to change her policy of hostility towards Pakistan. Both major Powers, therefore, were anxious to maintain an impartial attitude to the war, and were aware that this could become difficult if it was allowed to continue, on account of the possibility of one side clearly gaining the upper hand. Having to take sides could also endanger the East-West *détente* which had been developing over the previous two or three years, but so far as this was concerned a more immediate threat was represented by the policy of China. On 7 September she had charged India with naked aggression against Pakistan, and then began to behave in a belligerent fashion. On 17 September she demanded that India dismantle all military installations on the Indian side of the Sikkim–Chinese border within three days, or face grave consequences, and it seemed as though war was imminent. At the least this would have threatened the improved relations between the United States and the Soviet Union, and could have had wider and more serious results. In the event, the ultimatum expired without incident, but the opportunity to make trouble which war between India and Pakistan offered to China reinforced the Great Powers' desire to bring the fighting to an early end, and to take measures to prevent its resumption.

There was, therefore, appreciable diplomatic pressure on India and Pakistan to agree on a cease-fire, and they could not discount the possibility of sanctions being organized, either through the UN or independently. As a sign of her displeasure the United States had already suspended arms shipments to both countries. But it could not be assumed that they would be susceptible to the views and efforts of third parties, especially as the war had aroused much chauvinistic feeling on both sides. However, in official circles there was a good deal less enthusiasm for the continuation of the war. It was proving a costly affair, and Pakistan, who had made the pace, was doing less well than she might have anticipated. It had been widely supposed that the Pakistanis, with their martial qualities and American equipment, would be able to cut deeply into India without too much difficulty. But this had not proved to be so, and the Pakistan Army had been badly mauled. This had been one of India's major aims, and she could therefore look with some satisfaction on the way the campaign had gone since her attack on West Pakistan on 6 September. She, too, had suffered considerable losses, but was in a better position to make them good than Pakistan. She had also, contrary to some expectations, been able to engage Pakistan without communal troubles at home. However, having made one or two valuable points, she was ready to put an end to the conflict, particularly as she was the contestant who was content with the Kashmir *status quo*. She therefore immediately agreed to comply with the Security Council's demand, and Pakistan did so two days later. The cease-fire was jeopardized by a series of violations on both sides, and on 27 September the Council required of the parties that they honour their commitments to it. But, effectively, the war was over.

In its resolution of 20 September the Council had asked the Secretary-General to arrange for the supervision of the cease-fire and the subsequent withdrawal, and this request led to the creation of the United Nations India-Pakistan Observation Mission (UNIPOM). General B. F. Macdonald of Canada was appointed Chief Officer and the group consisted of 90 unarmed military observers drawn from 10 countries plus 25 on loan from other UN operations. Its mandate was to observe, investigate complaints, and report on compliance with the Security Council's demands concerning the 1,000 mile long international frontier. Along the 500 mile cease-fire line in Kashmir the same tasks were to be conducted by UNMOGIP which was already on the spot, and which the Council had already, on 6 September, asked the Secretary-General to strengthen. At that date 43 observers were attached to UNMOGIP; while the crisis lasted their number was brought up to 102 (13 of whom, however were loaned to UNIPOM), eleven nationalities being represented. Each group had the use of three aircraft, which were flown, serviced, and maintained by a joint air transport unit of 80 men.

UNIPOM's creation led to some difficulties with India. Her relations with the UN had got off to a bad start during August, when the Secretary-General had sent both sides a report regarding the cease-fire violations in Kashmir, saying he proposed to publish it. Subject to certain modifications, India agreed, for it confirmed her account of the origin of the latest fighting. Pakistan, however, took a different view, and the Secretary-General decided not to proceed with his original proposal. India's response was to make it plain that Dr Ralph Bunche, who U Thant intended to send to the two countries to try to prevent a further deterioration in their relations, would not be welcome in Delhi, and so this plan, too, was abandoned. Then, in September, when the idea of a peace-keeping force of about 1,000 men was being canvassed, the Indian Prime Minister said he had told the UN that his Government would not allow such a force in Indian territory. He emphasized that the additional observers being sent to the subcontinent were to do no more than observe, and complained about the establishment of UNIPOM as a separate body. He argued that events since the beginning of August formed a single sequence of happenings, and that therefore the cease-fire and withdrawal should be supervised by a single body—a temporarily expanded UNMOGIP. The Secretary-General, however, said that he could not attach observers outside Kashmir to UNMOGIP, unless Pakistan agreed, which she decidedly did not. India's reply was to tell the UN, which already had enough financial troubles, that as the victim of aggression she could not be expected to help pay for UNIPOM; she therefore reserved her position in this respect.[23] Nor was this the end of the UN's problems over its new observer group, for France and the Soviet Union began to complain that in its establishment and control the Secretary-General had taken too much upon himself, and so had usurped the proper functions of the Security Council. A meeting of the Council for 1 November was postponed four times largely on account of disagreement over this issue. When it did meet the matter was successfully passed over in silence prior to a vote being taken on a draft resolution regarding the Indo-Pakistan question. But the Soviet Union raised the matter afterwards, said that it explained her abstention on the resolution, and hinted that the next time she might take more drastic action.

[23] India later witheld from her payments for 1965 and 1966 sums which represented her proportionate share of the cost of UNIPOM and of the extra expenditure incurred by UNMOGIP.

India's awkwardness over the creation of UNIPOM, and her parting financial shot, may have had something about it of injured dignity. She had not done too badly in the war, but she had not won a victory either, and on the morrow of the cease-fire she found the UN Secretariat going ahead with supervisory arrangements with what she might have conceived to be insufficient regard for her views. She may, therefore, have found it necessary to assert herself a little, to keep the international community in its place, so correcting any faulty impressions to which previous events might have given rise. The violated state was making it clear that she must be shown a proper respect, and in this India's attitude could be likened to that of Egypt when she held up UNEF's arrival in November 1956.

But other factors probably entered into the situation. India may possibly have felt that there might be a tendency to prolong the life of a separate mission, and largely for reasons connected with Kashmir, India was more than commonly touchy on the subject of international organizations trying to assert themselves against sovereign states. She may also have wanted to ensure that the overall control of the supervisory operation should be with General Nimmo, UNMOGIP's Chief Observer. The report which U Thant refused to publish in August, and which he subsequently issued in September, was based on Nimmo's evidence. India may therefore have taken the view that he knew the problem and, more specifically, how she had been wronged in Kashmir. But possibly the most important consideration for India was that separate withdrawal arrangements might obscure her argument that the events of August and September were all of a piece. She may have been the first to attack across an international frontier, but was anxious to make it clear that this was in response to Pakistan's aggression in Kashmir. Pakistan, on the other hand, distinguished between the two fronts, implying that trouble was to be expected along a cease-fire line but that the breach of a recognized boundary was indeed a grave crime. Her strong assertion that it would be illegal and arbitrary for UNMOGIP to operate outside Kashmir was intended to bolster her position on this matter, and also made India suspect that she might be trying to form a basis for an attempt to hold on to the important gains which she had made in Kashmir. However, the UN emphasized that the process of withdrawal from Kashmir and India and Pakistan proper would be treated as a single operation, and that the use of two bodies, which were to act in close co-operation, was only an administrative concession to propriety. In the light of this, India decided not to pursue her objections.

Pakistan certainly hoped to make some progress in Kashmir. This,

for her, had been the whole object of the initial exercise, which had
led to the war, and she showed a marked reluctance to withdraw
until she had won a concession. Her objection to U Thant's report on
the cease-fire violations related to its failure to give an account of the
political background to the crisis, and when Pakistan was visited by
the Secretary-General during the course of the war, she made her
acceptance of a cease-fire conditional on a plebiscite being held in
Kashmir within three months. She had to climb down from this
position, but her attitude was reflected in that part of the resolution
of 20 September which spoke of the future consideration of steps to
assist 'a settlement of the political problem underlying the present
conflict'.[24] In accepting it, Pakistan warned that if the Security
Council failed to settle the issue within a limited time, she would
withdraw from the UN. As a move towards her goal she proposed
that upon the withdrawal of forces from Kashmir they should be
replaced by a UN force drawn from Africa, Asia, and Latin America
with a view to the holding of a plebiscite, a proposal which India
rejected out of hand, saying the wishes of the Kashmiri people had
already been ascertained. Pakistan then gave enthusiastic endorsement to a Western proposal for a Great Power commission to discuss
measures to give effect to the resolution of 20 September. What the
Western states had in mind was the expediting of a mutual withdrawal, but Pakistan observed that as well as this the Commission
could undertake negotiations for a settlement of the Kashmir
problem. India, however, would have none of it, nor would she
accept Pakistan's next proposal, for a fact-finding mission to go to
Indian Kashmir to suggest measures to end what Pakistan regarded
as an intolerable situation. By now time was running out for Pakistan, as the earlier pressure for an end to the war was building up
again in favour of a speedy withdrawal. Therefore, referring to the
need for a discussion of the total relationship between the two
countries, she accepted a Soviet proposal for a meeting at Tashkent.
India also agreed, but emphasized that there would be no negotiations over Kashmir. The meeting began on 4 January and was
brought to an end six days later, the Soviet Union having played
the unaccustomed role of honest broker. In return for her promise
to withdraw Pakistan obtained no more than an anodyne agreement
to continue meetings on matters of direct concern. It proved
worthless.

The analogy here with the Suez affair is very striking. In both
cases the initiative was taken by states who claimed to be righting
a wrong which had been done to them. In both cases the method

[24] Security Council resolution 21: (1965).

they adopted met with relatively little sympathy, and with such hostility by certain key Powers that the principle of withdrawal had to be accepted. In both cases the aggrieved states postponed their withdrawal in an endeavour to extract a concession, but had eventually to go away empty handed. There were significant differences between the two situations, but both of them exemplify the contemporary opposition to the use of force to settle economic or territorial disputes, an opposition which is channelled through and encouraged by the UN.

During the period between the cease-fire and the withdrawal of forces, UNIPOM made an important pacifying contribution. For the cease-fire was at times a very tenuous state of affairs, with some units seeming not to be fully under control and some local commanders trying to improve their positions by edging forward. As a result clashes often occurred, occasionally of a serious character. On bad days each side submitted hundreds of complaints regarding the other's violation of the cease-fire. This was the situation with which a couple of hundred observers had to try to deal. They had no authority to order an end to fighting, but could and did try to persuade local commanders to restore the cease-fire where it had broken down. They also tried to make such clashes less likely by negotiating agreements for tactical readjustments where the two sides were confronting each other from particularly inflammable positions. They engaged both sides in negotiations for a no-firing agreement, a limitation on observation from the air, and a ban on test firing in the vicinity of the front lines, with eventual success in each case, although by the time it came tension had already subsided a good deal. However, the fact that negotiations had previously been in progress may well have helped to put a check on provocative activity, and certainly in other more limited ways UNIPOM, and also UNMOGIP, undoubtedly exercised a valuable cooling influence, clearing the way for the parties to move on to the winding up of the conflict.

In an effort to get the withdrawal of forces under way, U Thant announced on 22 October that he had asked General Sarmento of Brazil, then Commander of UNEF, to visit the sub-continent with a view to arranging a meeting between India and Pakistan which would have as its object the negotiation of plans for withdrawal. It might have been thought that this was a sufficiently technical matter to be entrusted to one of the two Generals which the UN already had on the spot. But, presumably in an attempt to separate even remotely political from military matters, a third General was asked to do the job. Pakistan accepted the idea, but it appeared that Indian susceptibilities had once again been inadequately catered for. Evidently she took objection to the General, or to the method of his appointment, or both, for it was only after it had been discovered that he had pressing business in Gaza that U Thant's idea could be put into operation—by a different general. After consultation with both parties, General Marambio of Chile was named as the right man. By now it was the end of November, but the delay was unimportant, for it was not the lack of facilities for agreeing on a withdrawal schedule which was holding matters up. On the eve of the opening of the Tashkent conference, General Marambio was able to begin a series of meetings with military representatives of both sides, and five days after the agreement at Tashkent the General was able to announce that agreement had been reached at his meetings also. It was confirmed at the highest military level on 22 January, and a week later the detailed ground rules for withdrawal were agreed at a meeting under Marambio's chairmanship. Everything went smoothly and according to plan, and by 25 February the withdrawal had been completed. The actual process was facilitated by the presence of UN observers, who were also able to assist in the exchange of prisoners of war. But at this stage, with the military leaders on both sides anxious to disengage as soon as possible and without incident, UNIPOM played a very subordinate role. It was still a useful one, but it is unlikely that its absence would have given rise to grave difficulty or serious clashes. It ceased to function on 1 March and disbanded within three weeks. At the same time UNMOGIP was gradually reduced to its former level.

IV

As was demonstrated by Egypt in 1956 and India in 1965, a UN supervisory mission does not always receive an unqualified welcome from the state on whose territory it is to operate. But where it is established in connection with the winding up of one state's activity on the soil of another, the territorial sovereign may not make insurmountable difficulties for fear of jeopardizing the arrangement for the departure of its guest. If, however, the two are on good terms and the foreign elements are only leaving on account of outside pressure, there may be a marked reluctance to co-operate with the mission. Or, if a supervisory scheme has been reached over the head of the state whose permission is legally necessary for its functioning, that state may well take umbrage. A wide range of promises and threats may be made by interested member states in an endeavour to launch the operation, but if the state who is being called upon to admit international supervisors is determined to erect a keep-out notice, the UN will be stymied.

A striking instance of non-cooperation with the UN occurred towards the end of 1962, during the liquidation of the Cuban missile crisis. On 27 October President Kennedy agreed to call off America's quarantine measures provided the Soviet missiles were removed under UN supervision, and on the following day Khrushchev said he was prepared for representatives of the UN to verify the dismantling of the bases. This news was received with enthusiasm at the UN, and plans were set in motion for the establishment of an observer team of between 40 and 50 drawn from neutral nations. On 20 October U Thant and a party of 18 officials flew to Cuba, and, at his request, the United States agreed to lift her blockade and stop her aerial surveillance of the island for the period of his visit. On the following day 12 further Secretariat officials were flown to Cuba, only to return later on the same day with all of the earlier party. The Secretary-General assured reporters that his discussions had been fruitful and that there had been agreement for the UN's continued participation in the peaceful settlement of the problem. However, the fact that, contrary to expectations, no official had been left behind, suggested that the agreement was not in the form which had been originally agreed upon by the United States and the Soviet Union. And so it proved.

The Secretary-General would still not admit failure, but it became clear that President Castro had flatly refused to have a UN supervisory team on his territory. This also meant the end of another and less publicized idea, which would have led to the UN conducting an aerial inspection of Cuba during the period when the missiles were being withdrawn. The United States and the Secretary-General had agreed on such an arrangement and the United States had made the necessary planes available, even to the extent of having their American markings painted over with those of the UN. But the scheme was said to be held up by the fact that the Secretary-General had difficulty in finding politically-acceptable pilots, and then Castro's attitude towards UN inspection led to its abandonment.

In an effort to change President Castro's mind, Mr Mikoyan, one of the Soviet Union's first deputy prime ministers, called at Havana on his way to and from the United States, but to no avail. Castro would have nothing to do with the agreement which had been reached without his participation. He took the line that if the Soviet Union wanted to withdraw her missiles, then that was her affair. But neither she nor anyone else was entitled to decide that international inspectors should operate on Cuban soil. Like Egypt before, and not entirely unlike India later, he was making up for the blow which his country had suffered by being awkward with the UN. And here, as Cuba felt she had been dealt a particularly humiliating

blow, so she was being particularly awkward. Further, in view of
the nature of the original proposal, her awkwardness was extended
to the whole principle of inspection in Cuba. Thus she rejected a
Soviet proposal that the International Committee of the Red Cross[25]
should undertake the necessary inspection of the missile sites. As a
substitute measure, the United States indicated that she would
accept the inspection of departing Soviet ships on the high seas by
the UN or the International Red Cross, but the political obstacles
which either of these courses would have presented were side-
stepped by an agreement with the Soviet Union for inspection by
United States officials. This was done by American warships drawing
alongside the Soviet ships, and by observation from helicopters.

There still remained a possible role for the Red Cross, for the
United States had said she was prepared, while the quarantine of
Cuba continued, for inspection of Cuban-bound ships to be conducted by that body. President Castro agreed to the idea, as did
the Soviet Union, to the considerable embarrassment of the Red
Cross, which was unsure whether such a task would be within its
humanitarian mandate. Eventually, and on conditions, the Red
Cross agreed to provide some 30 inspectors, who would probably
have been recruited from among Swiss Army officers, but it was
clearly unhappy about the scheme and the offer was not taken up.[26]
The United States continued its inspection at sea and also engaged
in aerial reconnaissance in order to satisfy itself about the withdrawal of missiles and the destruction of their bases. It announced
the ending of quarantine on 20 November, immediately following
Mr Khrushchev's statement that the Soviet Union's Ilyushin
bombers were to be withdrawn from Cuba.

One of the difficulties about international supervision is that, quite
apart from the way in which it is arranged, it can easily be regarded
by the supervised state as an offence to its dignity, particularly by
larger states, who like to feel that they can manage their affairs
without assistance from international bodies. India's attitude to
UNIPOM may have had something of this about it, an indication,
possibly, of a developing Great Power mentality. Smaller states
will probably also feel much the same way, but they may be more
concerned about the visible limit which supervision places on their
perhaps already restricted measure of independence and freedom.
They will, too, be more keenly aware than most that an international

---

[25] The International Committee of the Red Cross, while solely Swiss in composition, is international in function and also, it is generally thought, in outlook.
[26] The question of its involvement in the liquidation of the Cuban crisis led the
International Committee of the Red Cross to examine the propriety of its use in
such situations and to establish firm criteria for its future guidance.

presence could conceivably be used, whether on the initiative of its individual members or, much more significantly, of its parent body, for purposes other than those for which it was established.

Considerations of this nature are likely to be particularly telling when it is proposed that supervision should be conducted on a permanent or at least a long-term basis, in respect, for example, of schemes for the protection of human rights or the establishment of demilitarized areas. With regard to such matters it is unlikely that the UN will be encouraged by the record of the inter-war years. For a Mixed Commission[27] which sat in Upper Silesia for 15 years following its partition between Poland and Germany in 1922 did not have a very satisfactory record so far as the protection of minorities was concerned, being partly notable for the opportunity it offered to nourish the traditional hostility between the two peoples.[28] But the main difficulties would undoubtedly lie with the states who were being invited to accept inspection. If, for example, it was suggested that as part of a Cyprus settlement the rights of the Turkish minority should be guaranteed by giving the UN powers of supervision and adjudication, it is very likely that President Makarios would do less than enthuse. And, even if he was willing to accept such arrangements, the Turks might well regard them, on their own, as insufficient. Equally, proposals for Israel's withdrawal from most of the Arab areas which she overran in the 1967 war in return for their demilitarization[29] and supervision by the UN would probably be considered by her only if she also obtained direct Arab recognition of her existence and boundaries. Conceivably some of the Arabs might accept the demilitarization of the territory which Israel now occupies as a way of securing its return—Jordan in respect of the west bank, for example. But whether they would agree to any other Israeli terms is at least problematical.[30]

Even, however, where the need for supervision is agreed on all sides, it does not follow that the UN is the body to whom the parties will turn. Early in 1964, for example, the Philippines, Malaysia, and Indonesia proposed that as a step towards ending the confrontation between the last two the UN should supervise a cease-fire in Borneo through the medium of Siamese observers appointed by the Secretary-General. But then Indonesia quickly changed her mind

[27] The Commission's chairman was appointed by the League.
[28] Under the post-World War I treaties the Council of the League of Nations was given responsibility for the protection of minorities in a number of countries. But this work was conducted at the League's Geneva headquarters, and did not involve it in activity within any of the states concerned.
[29] In its resolution of 22 November 1967 the Security Council spoke of 'the establishment of demilitarized zones' as one way of 'guaranteeing the territorial inviolability and political independence of every State in the area' (Resolution 242 (1967).
[30] See further, above, pp. 64–66.

about the idea, suggesting instead that the observers should be appointed by Siam itself at the request of the three interested states, with the Secretary-General of the UN merely being informed of the decision.[31] Possibly this reflected her unfortunate experience at the hands of the UN team which the previous year had enquired into the wishes of the people of North Borneo and Sarawak with regard to their joining Malaysia. Another state whose attitude to the UN might limit its use in a supervisory (or any other) capacity is France. For in view of General de Gaulle's aesthetic distaste for the Organization (or, as he might put it, for its latter-day pretensions), it is difficult to see him agreeing to UN inspection of any of his country's activities.

There is even less chance of the UN being asked to assist in supervisory arrangements where one of the parties is not only hostile to the Organization but has also been excluded from it. Thus in 1954, when the International Control Commissions for Cambodia, Laos, and Vietnam were set up, they had to be outside the framework of the UN on account of Communist China's participation in the conference at Geneva which brought them to birth. Likewise, in the event of a negotiated settlement of the Vietnam war, any international supervision which is required would surely need, on account of North Vietnam as well as China, to be unconnected with the UN. And, to take the extreme case, there is no chance at all of the UN being given a supervisory role within the territory of a state to which it is avowedly opposed. The Korean Armistice Agreement, which was signed on 27 July 1953 after two years of negotiations, illustrates this point. It set up a Military Armistice Commission composed of representatives of both sides—the UN on the one hand and North Korea and the Chinese People's Volunteers on the other. Its job was to supervise the implementation of the Armistice, particularly within the Demilitarized Zone which divided the parties, and settle any violations. But the supervision of troop withdrawal and weapon replacement in North and South Korea was entrusted to a Neutral Nations Supervisory Commission of four: Sweden and Switzerland appointed by the UN, and Czechoslovakia and Poland appointed by the Communists. (It had a relatively brief history. Not a year had passed before South Korea was complaining that there was no effective supervision of North Korea, and in 1956 the UN Command suspended the Commission's activity because of Communist violations of the Armistice, and the obstruction of the Commission by its Communist members and by North Korea.)

A final reason for not using the UN for supervisory purposes,

[31] Nothing came of this proposal, and the confrontation continued.

however, is that for some issues a body of its size and wide membership is quite unsuitable. Or, putting it differently, there are some
matters which are simply too important to be handed over to the
UN, on account of their bearing on national security or, possibly,
prosperity. In these circumstances, the risk that information might
get into the wrong hands, or that the supervisors might allow themselves to be influenced by political considerations, or might just be
incompetent, is regarded as too great to run, and, accordingly,
supervision is kept firmly in the hands of the parties. Thus the restrictions which the continental signatories to the Western European
Union agreement of 1954 accepted on their armaments were to be
verified by the Union's own inspection system, and, in principle, still
are. The same situation holds in relation to Euratom in that it has
established what, viewed from outside, is a system of self-inspection.
Likewise, when, early in the 1960s, it was thought that the nuclear
test ban treaty then being negotiated would require international
inspection arrangements, it was intended that a separate control
organization should be established.

Thus, for a variety of reasons, states needing international supervision may prefer to turn to a body other than the UN, or to set
one up for the specific purpose. But it remains that the UN has
sometimes been a very suitable source of supervisory groups and
that the international society can be expected to continue to make
use of it from time to time. Its employment will not, in itself, ensure
that the parties remain in a conciliatory frame of mind. But if they
want to resolve their dispute, the UN may be able to help in the
achievement of that end by providing the impartial supervision
which, on substantive or face-saving grounds, is needed. So far as
continuing obligations in connection with matters such as arms control are concerned, it is unlikely that the UN will be utilized. But on
issues of a less crucial character it can play a valuable role. Its
supervisory facilities have not been much used, and they may not
grow any more popular in future. But that does not detract from the
fact that from the point of view of securing settlements, it is very
advantageous to have available an institution which can put
independent observers into the field at short notice. They also
serve . . .

Chapter 5

Administration

THE fourth and final way in which the UN can help to patch-up disputes is by engaging in administrative activity. It may assume, on a permanent basis, the government of a utility or region about which there is deep-seated disagreement, and in which, perhaps, the international community can show an interest of its own. Alternatively, the settlement of a territorial quarrel might be greatly eased by a limited period of international administration. A disputed area may, for example, be handed over to the UN to permit the opening of negotiations regarding its future. Or the parties may agree that the question at issue should be decided at a later date by the inhabitants of the region concerned, with the UN acting as their government meanwhile. A further possibility is that international rule may be the means of transferring an area from one authority to another.

I

To place the object of a dispute under indefinite UN control is, on the face of it, an attractive procedure. As no one is to have the prize, everyone has lost; but, equally, in the negative sense that the prize has not been obtained by anyone's rival, everyone has won. The outcome can thus be presented to all sides as one which, while not giving complete comfort in any quarter, is not the most unsatisfactory solution for any party. Further, international government can be pictured as particularly appropriate if the area in question can also be shown to have a general international significance, for example, on historical or religious grounds, or by virtue of its importance for communications. In any event, it can be argued that this solution is a victory for the international community, an example of how the UN can facilitate sensible compromises. All parties, therefore, by abandoning their initial demands, can be said to share a superior kind of prize. They have set an example which others would do well to follow, and may do so now that a precedent for enlightened behaviour has been established. Every cloud has its silver lining.

The attitude of the states most closely involved, however, is unlikely to be promising. The sitting tenant, in particular, will generally look very sourly on the suggestion that, in order to settle a dispute regarding its future, part of its territory should be handed over to the permanent keeping of the UN. Nor is its reaction likely to be much more promising even if it is proposed that, at the same time, a neighbouring state should make a similar sacrifice. Exceptions to this generalization may be found in respect of territory to which a state has no geographical or historical claim, and which it is not interested in retaining on other grounds. It may, for example, look favourably on an international solution in respect of an area which, having been occupied in war, has not been easy to dispose of in peace on account of a local quarrel as to the appropriate beneficiary, although if one of the claimants was a friendly country there would no doubt be a preference for placing the region in its hands. But in other, more usual, circumstances, states are exceedingly unlikely to be impressed by the somewhat high-minded reasons which can be advanced for surrendering disputed territory to an international organization, nor by the prospect of the diplomatic and psychological return which virtuous behaviour might bring. Some lack of enthusiasm might be expected in relation to areas of strategic or economic importance, or where it is psychologically desirable to continue showing the flag, but it is not confined to such cases. The proposal that a state should be relieved of a costly and troublesome responsibility, for example, is unlikely to elicit a more co-operative response. For suggestions that any part of the national soil should be relinquished touch an extremely sensitive nerve, and, in the normal way their acceptability is not affected by the identity of the proposed recipient. To whomsoever the territory goes, whether to another state or an international organization, it counts, from the point of view of the owner, as loss, and it is the kind of loss which states will only contemplate in the direst circumstances, and perhaps not even then.

The only situation in which a state is likely to see some merit in handing over part of its territory to international government is where, on account of the consequences of a refusal, it sees no alternative but to surrender the area in question. To do so to an international body avoids a more damaging outcome, puts something of an acceptable face on the transaction, and increases the hope that the loss is not irrevocable. For, whatever may be suggested by the formal documentation concerning the matter, it is unlikely to be regarded as a permanent measure by the state now being diminished. Once its strength has been recovered, it will probably take a keen interest in ways and means of restoring the lost land to the national bosom, and may well find that the collective will of an international organization provides much less formidable opposition than the undiluted determination of a single state.

These, however, are exactly the circumstances in which a willingness to place an area under international government is least likely to result in the device being adopted. For a conciliatory disposition would in all probability have been induced by a powerful claimant, who would hardly be satisfied by the proposed solution. Conceivably he might accept it as a way of avoiding the burden and uncertainty of a direct clash while also leaving open the possibility of the main objective being achieved later. But the greater likelihood is that, encouraged by his victim's weakness, a state bent on annexation would be content with nothing less, and would threaten to make such trouble if thwarted as to discourage the UN from accepting the area in question. In fact, when advanced in the course of a straightforward territorial dispute, the argument for international government is usually an argument from weakness: a possible half-way house for the party seeking change who is unable to obtain its goal outright, or the least undesirable way of losing. As a result, the occasions when there is agreement on its desirability are likely to be few. And when internationalization is widely urged as the best possible arrangement for areas in which many states are interested, it is doubtful whether its advocates will usually feel so strongly about it as to be able to procure the desired result.

Quite apart from the attitude of the parties immediately concerned, however, the practicality of schemes for UN administration of disputed areas also depends on the Organization's readiness to play a governmental role. Certainly it would be capable of doing so. From the ranks of the Secretariat and by means of requests for secondment from the public services of member states, it should be able to obtain administrators who can not only be relied upon to govern in good faith but will also be regarded as impartial by those who were formerly competing for the territory. It should also be able to make successful claims on those who can provide the technical expertise which the UN may need for the execution of its new responsibilities. Moreover, this is the kind of operation which, although it will usually be quite expensive, may not give rise to considerable financial difficulties. For, in the manner of governments, the UN will be able to tap the resources of its territory by means of taxation. But it cannot be taken for granted that the UN would wish to set up and maintain a system of government, and a number of considerations suggest that a wide variety of members might have considerable doubts about such a course.

One difficulty might arise from the reluctance of many states to encourage anything that can be regarded as a breach of the principle of territorial integrity and national sovereignty. Especially on the part of the newer, and on the whole, smaller states who form a large part of the UN's membership, there is a strong feeling that original boundaries should not be disturbed, and, therefore, that it is improper to press a state to give up any part of its territorial endowment. Their hostility to this course is not lessened by the prospect of a transfer to the UN rather than to another state, not even if the proposed transaction is spoken of in terms of a long lease or the maintenance of ultimate sovereignty, nor even if it relates to an area in which it is possible to demonstrate a considerable international interest. Indeed, the involvement of the UN in this way could be seen as even more dangerous than a direct demand from another state. For, while there is now less danger of old-fashioned territorial adjustments being made at the expense of smaller states, the idea of an international body administering disputed territory is, on the face of it, so much less objectionable to those not closely implicated as to be capable of attracting a good deal of support. Hence, a suggestion along these lines could increase the potency of territorial demands without making them less materially offensive. Accordingly, those who would not like to be urged to surrender any part of their own state to an international body, and who are apprehensive about the possibility and also their own ability to cope with it, could well discover an interest in avoiding a precedent. For, if one was set, it would probably encourage similar proposals and make their rejection all the more embarrassing.

This attitude is likely to be reinforced by the feeling that there is something improper about the UN dabbling in government, that it is in some way a reflection on sovereign states if an international organization has to be asked to exercise prerogatives which are normally theirs alone. This argument can be supported by a more specific complaint: that the idea of international administration is also out of date on account of its anti-democratic implications. By definition, an area which is governed by the UN can neither elect nor dismiss its governors, who receive their authority from and are responsible for its exercise to the world body. Representative institutions may be established, and consulted on a wide variety of domestic issues. But there can be no guarantee that the advice so received will be acted upon, for it may not be acceptable to an important section of the UN's membership. And on external matters, the area will almost certainly be without a real voice, for it could say very little which would satisfy all the significant voices in the Assembly or the Council. Thus in many respects an internationally governed territory will, for practical purposes, be in the position of a colony. So far as some areas are concerned, this would seem to matter less than others: should the UN be asked to take over the Sinai Peninsula, for example, or the island of Perim, which lies at the southern end of the Red Sea, the lack of democratic procedures and the withholding of the right of self-determination would be of less consequence than in the case of say, Berlin. But, even so, by giving overt offence to certain latter day idols, by failing to offer the territory the opportunity to espouse Democratic Socialism, Controlled Democracy, or whatever, and by preventing it from joining states which enjoy such freedom, the device of international government is likely to be looked upon by many UN members with a jaundiced eye.

It can therefore be argued that to hand territory over to the UN for an indefinite period runs counter to the spirit of the age, inasmuch as it violates several principles which, on all sides, are habitually said to be of fundamental importance. Not everybody, however, will feel equally strongly about this consideration and not all of those who profess to be much moved by it will be heard with equal respect. But there are two other points which will certainly be in the forefront of some states' minds when the question of international government is raised. The first is that, while an excellent way of keeping disputed territory out of a single pair of hands, it gives all UN members the right to have something of a finger in the new international pie. The exact extent to which each of them will be able to interfere in the affairs of the internationally-controlled region will depend on the nature of the arrangements which are made for its government and oversight. But a number of members, if not all, will be able to have some say regarding the manner in which the international community's representatives discharge their responsibilities. And, in the nature of things, it is likely that the ones with the greatest say would be the Great Powers, particularly the permanent members of the Security Council. They could be expected to play a large part in the appointment and dismissal of governors, in the supervision of their activities, and in the hearing of complaints. This will almost certainly produce a measure of reserve in some influential quarters when schemes for international administration are proposed, for each Power or group of Powers would have to consider whether the advantages to be gained therefrom would be outweighed by rival Powers receiving the same benefits. It is quite likely that, as a result, one group, the one which already exercises the most influence in the part of the world where it is proposed to establish an international regime, will discover serious objections to the idea, which may very well result in it not being implemented. In this way its rival will be prevented from obtaining something of a foothold, or a firmer foothold, in an area where it presently finds little opportunity for making itself felt.

The second objection stems not from the benefit which individual states might draw from an internationally-administered area, but from the effect it might have on the ability of the administering organization to play an increasing role on the international scene. Some members of the UN clearly look on such a possibility with deep suspicion, not to say hostility. This may be for a reason which has already been mentioned: that there is thought to be a certain incongruity in an international organization hob-nobbing with states, acting more as an independent equal than as a respectful servant. But a much more important factor for some is their estimate that the purposes to which the UN will be put by a majority of its members, perhaps aided and abetted by its permanent officials, will probably not be in the minority's interests, or, if they are, will be so by accident. In consequence, they will be hostile to any move which may increase the capability of the Organization to act at the majority's behest.

Conceivably, an improved capability for such action could result from allowing the UN to take over, on a permanent basis, the government of a part of the earth's surface. There will not be lacking those who will urge it to build up a reserve fund from the revenues derived from the territory, to be used for the Organization's general purposes. It will also surely be pressed to take advantage of the opportunity offered by a physical base under its exclusive control to establish a standing peace force. Such developments would allow the UN to intervene with greater freedom in the world's trouble spots, and it is therefore to be expected that those with doubts about the correctitude of its general approach to those matters, i.e. those who are not able to control the Organization, will not wish to give it a chance to secure a measure of independence from its members. Even those who generally have a sympathetic hearing at the UN and can usually persuade it to endorse their policies, may have some reservation about the wisdom of such a course. For one can never be sure that one's policies will always be favourably received, and in that event a UN with its own land and money could present a much more serious problem than a UN whose only immediate resource was a hostile vote.

Thus the idea that intractable territorial quarrels should be settled by placing the area in question in the UN's indefinite keeping is one which has little appeal to the disputants, and especially to the state being called upon to relinquish territory. It also evokes a good deal less sympathy among other UN members than might, at first sight, be expected. In consequence it is not too surprising that the UN has not been entrusted with such responsibilities, and that in this respect its record is identical with the League's. There have, however, been two situations in respect of which detailed moves were made in the direction of establishing permanent international government, but without success.

The first such proposal was in respect of Trieste, a city and port of about a quarter of a million people which lies on the Istrian peninsula at the north-eastern end of the Adriatic Sea. At the close of World War I Italy, in return for her entry into the war, had obtained the city and the surrounding region (which was known as Venezia Giulia), to the great chagrin of the new state of Yugoslavia. For, while the coastal towns were chiefly Italian in population, the hinterland was largely made up of Croats and Slovenes, about half a million of whom now came under Italian rule and found it very unsatisfactory. When therefore, towards the end of World War II, Yugoslav troops were the first of the victors to enter the region, it was only with difficulty that they were persuaded to withdraw from Trieste itself in favour of British and American forces, retiring behind a demarcation line, the 'Morgan line', which reached the coast to the south of the city. The Powers then tried to agree among themselves regarding the region's division between Yugoslavia and Italy, but were unable to do so. The chief problem was the future of the city of Trieste and the immediately surrounding area, and they eventually decided that the solution lay in a compromise which would involve the UN in governmental duties. Their suggestion was that most of the region should go to Yugoslavia but that the area which was particularly difficult should be designated as the Free Territory of Trieste. A Permanent Statute was drawn up for it, under which the Security Council was responsible for the maintenance of public order and the observance of the Statute, and in particular for the protection of the inhabitants' basic human rights. Provision was made for the demilitarization and neutrality of the Territory, and the Council was given the duty of ensuring its independence and integrity. No armed forces were to be allowed in the Territory, except under the Council's direction. After consultation with Yugoslavia and Italy, a Governor was to be appointed by and responsible to the Security Council, to whom he was to submit an annual report. His salary and allowances were to be borne by the UN.

When this matter was put to the Security Council in January 1947, Australia argued that the Charter did not permit it to accept such responsibilities. The other members, however, had no hesitations on this or any other score, and the Council therefore agreed to play the role allotted to it. The arrangement was confirmed in the Italian Peace Treaty which was signed in the following month, and so the way was clear for the Statute of the Free Territory to come into force. It was to do so on the appointment of a Governor, until which time the northern part of the Territory was to remain under Anglo-American military occupation and the southern part under Yugoslav, the border between the two being the Morgan line. This had been thought of as a purely interim arrangement, a state of affairs which would last only for a period of weeks, or at most months, while the necessary consultations were taking place. But, in the manner of other post-war divisions, this temporary measure displayed an exceptionally durable character.

The immediate reason for this was the failure to appoint a Governor. The West's candidates were turned down by the Soviet Union, and the Soviet Union's nominees found no favour in the West. The Security Council appointed a subcommittee to consider the matter, but there was no progress to be had in this direction. The Italian and Yugoslav Governments were asked to consult with a view to recommending a candidate, but they too failed to agree. All the interested parties were anxious to see the position filled by someone who might be expected to be, if not sympathetic to their own point of view, at least beyond the influence of the other side. This was a recipe for deadlock, and an indication of the difficulty of organizing international government when the governors are divided and mutually suspicious.

But even states who entertain some doubts about each other's intentions may find it possible to agree on limited measures which are in their joint interest. The Free Territory of Trieste might have been thought to be such a case, for the idea had been endorsed in the Peace Treaty with Italy. But it became clear that, on a number of sides, that endorsement was either less than whole-hearted or was speedily reconsidered and found wanting. Yugoslavia, for example, although she had not done too badly out of the Italian Treaty, nevertheless felt that the Free Territory should have been hers also. She had found it prudent not to press this view, for the Soviet Union, in return for a major voice in the settlement with Germany's Balkan allies, was one of the backers of the Trieste compromise. But it seemed from the outset that Yugoslavia was more interested in consolidating her hold on the southern part of the Free Territory than in facilitating its establishment and operation as a unit on the basis of its Statute. Half a loaf was better than no bread.

Italy's approach was not basically dissimilar. She, too, had been anxious to emerge from the post-war negotiations holding the city of Trieste and the coastal areas immediately to the north and south, but had failed to do so. For, although she ended the war as a 'co-belligerent' on the victorious side, she had originally entered it on the other, and was now having to pay for her faulty choice. She was therefore in no position to resist the arrangements which the Allied

Powers had agreed for Trieste. However, she could at least take heart
from the fact that she was not called upon to relinquish her sovereignty over the Free Territory, but only had to agree to it being held
in abeyance. No doubt this gave her the hope that the Peace Treaty's
clauses regarding Trieste would be less permanent than their wording
suggested, and that the scheme for the international administration of
the area would prove to be but a stage on the road to its return to
Italian jurisdiction. The failure to implement the compromise set
out in the Treaty, and Yugoslavia's activities to the south of the
Morgan line, greatly reduced the likelihood of Italy ever succeeding
to the whole area. But there was a compensating advantage in that
she could now hope to secure the early agreement of Britain and the
United States to her return to the northern zone, from which they
would probably be glad to withdraw their troops as soon as was consistent with safety and public propriety.

This aspiration received almost precipitate encouragement. By
the beginning of 1948 the development of the cold war was causing
the Western Powers to show a keen interest in the attitude which
Italy might adopt towards it. And, more particularly and most
urgently, they were getting very worried about the possibility that
the Italian Communist Party might come out on top in the general
election which was due to be held in April. The Party was, however,
under the disadvantage of not being able to take a national line on
Trieste, on account of the support which had to be given to their
ideological brethren in Yugoslavia and beyond, and the West decided that, in the circumstances, it could do much worse than to
rub this point in. Accordingly, in March, France joined Britain and
the United States in the proposal that the Peace Treaty should be
revised to give the whole of the Free Territory, including the zone
now under Yugoslavia's military occupation, to Italy. The stock of
the Christian Democrats duly rose, and in April they triumphed at
the polls.

For three of the four major signatories to an important treaty to
propose, only a year after its conclusion, an alternative which would
obviously be unacceptable to the fourth seems, on the face of it, an
unusual and costly way of seeking an electoral benefit in a friendly
country, even when account is taken of the importance to them of the
result of that election. But the point about the Western gambit is
that it reflected the view that the plan for a Free Territory was no
longer practical, or, if practical, was now undesirable. The difficulties which had arisen over the appointment of a Governor had provided a clear warning of the problems which would lie ahead if the
Trieste district was placed under international control. The exercise of
the Security Council's responsibilities in the matter would provide the

Soviet Union with an opportunity to encourage trouble in the Territory
if she so wished. It would also surely give rise to numerous disputes
between East and West, in which the latter's case might not always
sound the most convincing. And it was not impossible that such disputes could jeopardize the continued administration of the Territory
on the basis of its Statute, so precipitating a serious international
crisis. On these grounds, therefore there was a case for discarding
the scheme, and taking as much profit as possible from the public
announcement of its abandonment.

This course also had some other benefits. It was beginning to look
as if Soviet troops might be in Austria for some time yet, and Yugoslavia's attitude towards the West was shown by the support she was
giving to the Communist guerrillas in northern Greece. Hence there
was some reason, both from the point of view of Trieste's security and
on other grounds, for continuing to show the Western flag in the
area. The Italian domestic scene underlined this conclusion. For,
should the Communists come to power, a Free Territory of Trieste
would be very shakily placed. And if they were soundly defeated,
there was the possibility of handing the northern zone over to Italy
at some future date, which would be a very useful card to play in
Western relations with her, and would also produce a safe result. As
against all this, the major benefit which would accrue to the West
from the international administration of the Free Territory, if it was
still possible to establish it, would be the withdrawal of the Yugoslavs from its southern section: in effect this would involve their
movement from one side of its border to the other. It is not surprising that, in 1948, Britain and the United States were unable to muster much enthusiasm for the scheme and saw much more virtue in the
maintenance, for the moment, of the *status quo*.

The apprehensions of the Western Powers regarding the profit
which the Soviet Union might draw from the operation of the Free
Territory must have added to its attraction for that country. But it
was not something for which she showed great zeal. For, on the one
hand, she could not rely on benefiting from the deliberations and
activities of the Security Council in respect of Trieste, especially in
view of her minority position in the Council. And, as she already had,
in Yugoslavia, a faithful ally with a long Adriatic coastline, the Free
Territory was not going to give her some access to an area where she
was devoid of influence. On the other hand, the maintenance of the
status quo was not without its compensations. It avoided possible
difficulties with Yugoslavia over the withdrawal of her troops from
the southern part of the Free Territory, and gave the Soviet Union a
chance to extract political capital from the continued presence of the
Anglo-American force in the northern zone. Moreover, as that force

was only in the region of 10,000 men, it hardly constituted a threat to Soviet interests. She was, therefore, in no hurry to get the scheme started by agreeing on a Governor. She could afford to wait until the West was prepared to accept a candidate on whom she looked favourably, content in the knowledge that should an agreement fail to materialize, she was not going to be much, if any, worse off.

But then, in June 1948, the situation was suddenly changed by the Soviet Union's expulsion of President Tito's regime from the Cominform. This meant that she no longer had a direct land link with the Adriatic through her satellites, and gave rise to the danger, accentuated by the failure of ideological denunciation and economic sanctions to topple Tito, of a *rapprochement* between Yugoslavia and the West. Thus the Soviet Union suddenly discovered a keen interest in the early implementation of the international arrangements for the Free Territory, from which she now had a good deal to gain. Yugoslavia's withdrawal from the southern zone would be a blow to her prestige, or, if she refused to withdraw, could result in her international life being made even more uncomfortable. Either way, it should bring home to her the unwisdom of failing to heed Soviet wishes. The new situation also made an Anglo-American withdrawal from the northern zone much to be desired from the Soviet Union's point of view, for the presence of Western troops at the backdoor of an independently-minded Yugoslavia was at least an embarrassment to the Soviet Union, and possibly more. For it might well increase Tito's confidence and could even provide him with a source of support. Finally, the operation of the Free Territory, by giving the Soviet Union a say regarding its affairs, would offer an additional point from which trouble might be made for the heretical regime.

Such was the Soviet Union's new enthusiasm for international government in Trieste that early in 1949 she nominated as Governor a Swiss, who, eighteen months earlier, she had rejected when his name had been put forward by Britain. But it was too late. The Western Powers were no longer interested in the 1947 scheme. It was, however, also the case that recent events in the Communist world had led them to change their view regarding the question of their unilateral withdrawal from the northern zone in favour of Italy. This was a potentially attractive course so long as there was no reason to avoid giving offence to Yugoslavia and the Soviet Union. But now Yugoslavia was someone to be cultivated, cautiously, perhaps, and with domestic qualifications, but cultivated nevertheless. Even if she was unlikely to become a recruit on the Western side in the cold war, her attitude to Moscow was to be encouraged, both for its own sake and for the example it offered to others in eastern Europe. It would, therefore, be most undesirable to hand over part of the Free Territory to Italy without Yugoslavia's approval, for that would give her grave offence. What was needed was an agreement between Yugoslavia and Italy regarding the area, and the most obvious solution was for each to take a part with the zonal demarcation line being established as the frontier.

Some time had to elapse, however, before Italy and Yugoslavia could bring themselves, under pressure, to accept a settlement along those lines. The final process was begun in October 1953 when Britain and the United States precipitated matters by announcing their intention to withdraw and hand over the administration of their zone to Italy. This produced a minor crisis, but led, early in 1954, to direct talks between those two countries together with Italy and Yugoslavia. These continued in secrecy for eight months, agreement being reached in October. With one minor frontier rectification, Italy was to take the northern zone and Yugoslavia the southern. Italy agreed to maintain Trieste as a free port. This was announced to the world as an 'understanding', for these states could not, on their own, make a formal amendment to the Italian Peace Treaty. For this the agreement of the other signatories was necessary and, in particular, on account of her importance and interest in the matter, the assent of the Soviet Union. It had been thought that there might be some difficulty here, but it was not so, for, in the improving international climate, the Soviet Union raised no objection, and even took official cognizance of the new arrangement. The idea of international government for Trieste and its immediate hinterland had died a quiet death. There were no mourners.

The failure of a scheme for a Free Territory was due to the fact that those chiefly concerned, while all agreeing to its establishment, were none of them very keen on it, and found themselves less so with the passage of time. It was a convenient paper compromise, and as such served a purpose. But it had no life in it. And when one of the major parties subsequently perceived that it was, after all, a very good arrangement, it was too late for its resuscitation, especially as this late fervour came from the state which, not having any troops in the Free Territory or adjacent to it, was least able to do anything about it.

The other proposal for the international administration, in perpetuity, of a disputed region concerned Jerusalem. It was made in 1947 by the majority of the UN's Special Committee which had been appointed to make recommendations for Palestine's future following the announcement by the Mandatory Power, Britain, that she was going to withdraw.[1] In view of the Committee's suggestion that the country should be partitioned, placing Jerusalem in neutral hands was the obvious course. For as the city was holy to both Arabs and Jews, neither would consent to it being within the other's jurisdiction. It was also a recommendation which had very considerable appeal to Christians, and on 29 November 1947 it was adopted by the General Assembly, which asked the Trusteeship Council to prepare and approve a detailed Statute for an internationally-administered Jerusalem.

The difficulties which had recently been experienced over the appointment of a Governor for the Free Territory of Trieste possibly influenced the choice of the Trusteeship Council, where there was no veto, rather than the Security Council. Within a matter of months the Statute was completed, and approved on 21 April 1948. It provided for the appointment of a Governor by the Trusteeship Council, who was to be responsible to it and to administer Jerusalem on behalf of the UN. The city was to be demilitarized, and internal law and order was to be maintained by a special police force organized by the Governor and recruited outside Palestine. The Statute was referred to the General Assembly, but the growing violence in Palestine and the likelihood of a vast increase in its scale upon Britain's departure on 15 May left the Assembly with no time to consider a scheme which presupposed an orderly transfer of power from the Mandatory to its successor.

The Jews had accepted the UN's proposals for Palestine only with apparent reluctance, their complaint being that they were awarded less of the country than they had claimed. But it may be questioned whether they were as hesitant about the partition plan as they made out, for it brought with it the UN's blessing for the principle of a Jewish state, which was their overriding international aim. In return for this, a less than totally satisfactory set of boundaries was a price which was very well worth paying. Undoubtedly one of the plan's most galling aspects for them was that, while being given access to their holy places in Jerusalem, they would be unable to make their capital there. But they could hardly have expected the UN to give them Jerusalem in preference to the Arabs, and could hope that the future might permit some territorial rectification. They could also take comfort from the knowledge that, although they were not being given control of the city, neither were the Arabs. Even in respect of Jerusalem, therefore, the UN's plan had some merit from the Jewish point of view. And, as the party striving for international recognition, they were in no position to reject a scheme for its

[1] See above, pp. 29–30.

international government, especially as it seemed, from afar, so reasonable, and was a part of a still remarkably attractive proposal.

The Arabs, however, saw it in a very different light. To them the whole principle of the partition of Palestine was anathema, and the proposal that they should be denied Jerusalem was but a particularly objectionable feature of a wholly unacceptable scheme. Their brethren in Syria, Lebanon, Transjordan, and Iraq who, after World War I had been placed under British and French rule, had since become independent on the basis of the boundaries of the old Mandates. The Palestinian Arabs, it was argued, had no less a claim to Palestine, which should be established as a unitary state with Jerusalem as its capital. Any attempt to establish a separate Jewish state in the area, it was made clear, would be resisted by force. Thus with the departure of Britain and the proclamation of Israel, fighting broke out between the new state and her Arab neighbours. The result so far as Jerusalem was concerned, was division, its newer parts ending up in Israel's hands, and the old city, which contained virtually all of the places in Jerusalem which are holy to Christianity, Islam, and Judaism, in Jordan's.

Throughout the fighting and during its immediate aftermath the UN maintained its concern for the internationalization of the city. At the Assembly's request, Britain, immediately prior to her departure, appointed a Municipal Commissioner for Jerusalem, but he did not feel that the situation permitted him to assume his functions.[2] In December 1948 the Assembly instructed its Conciliation Commission to present proposals for a permanent international regime for the Jerusalem area, and the Commission later reported on the subject. The Jordan–Israeli Armistice Agreement of April 1949, which was reached with UN assistance, provided for a joint committee to consider issues regarding Jerusalem. And in December 1949 the General Assembly restated its view that Jerusalem should be placed under an international regime administered by the UN, and accordingly asked the Trusteeship Council to prepare a new Statute for the city.

But all this was to no avail. Israel had gone back on her earlier preparedness to see Jerusalem administered by an international authority, for she was determined to retain the part of it which she had won by force of arms. Jordan, now in possession of far and away the most important area of the city, the section which all tourists

[2] Britain had appointed Mr Harold Evans, an American citizen. Mr Evans was also, however, a Quaker, and as such felt that he could not accept the military protection which his position in Jerusalem would have involved. He therefore remained in Cairo, waiting for peace to be restored in Jerusalem. Meanwhile, he was attached to the staff of the UN Mediator, Count Bernadotte, and in this way did pay a short visit to Jerusalem. He returned to the United States shortly thereafter.

would want to see, was equally resolved to keep her part for herself. In view of this, it mattered not at all that the other Arab states, formerly so fervent in their opposition to the idea of internationalization, were now reduced to pressing for it very strongly. Having lost the war, and with it the hope of a unitary state in Palestine, the most they could hope for, and the least they could demand, was that the UN should take over Jerusalem. If successful, it would result in Israel's withdrawal from the city; if not, they no doubt hoped that Israel's obstinacy and repudiation of her former position would lead to her embarrassment. That their tactic might also be awkward for their brother Arab, Jordan, was probably not too distressing a consideration. Apart from Egypt's seizure of the Gaza Strip, Jordan had been the only Arab state to benefit territorially from the Palestinian war, obtaining a large area on the west bank of the river from which the country's name was taken. No doubt this was not a matter for unqualified joy in other Arab states, and made it easy for them to call on Jordan to make a sacrifice for the sake of an international Jerusalem and the discomforting of Israel. But Jordan was no more moved than Israel by these suggestions, and neither state seemed to find their lack of co-operation a source of embarrassment. Both made it plain that they were not to be shifted by fair words or foul, no matter whether they came from Arab states, other groupings, or the world at large.

There the matter rested. In 1950 the area on the west bank was formally incorporated in Jordan, which produced, abroad, some reservations regarding Jerusalem. In the same year Jerusalem was proclaimed as Israel's capital, which some states refused to recognize in view of the fact that the UN was committed to its internationalization. But the realization of this goal was clearly out of the question and Jerusalem remained a divided city until 1967. Then, in June of that year, Israel, by driving the Jordanians out of Jerusalem and back to the east bank, raised hopes in some quarters that an international regime might at last be established for the city. This, however, would require that Israel give up not only a conquest of enormous emotional significance, but also that part of Jerusalem which she had governed for 18 years. No talk of the interests of the international community in the Holy City, or the impropriety of annexation, is likely to cause her to do either of those things, not even if it was backed by considerable diplomatic and economic pressure. A united Jerusalem administered by the UN might be acceptable as a second or third best solution, as it was prior to her proclamation in 1948. But such a solution is not chosen when a better one is available, and is certainly not exchanged for the most desirable one of all. With Jerusalem restored to the Jews after the passage of 2,000 years, it is inconceivable that their grasp will be loosened, whether for the sake of world opinion or whatever. For them to let go of Jerusalem, their hands would have to be wrenched apart.[3]

It is also quite conceivable that strategic considerations will lead Israel to insist on retaining some of the other territory which she acquired in the 1967 war: the Gaza Strip is the most obvious candidate for annexation, with the Golan Heights above Lake Tiberias running the Strip a close second. However, she is less clearly committed to the rest of the Arab territory which she overran, and it was suggested immediately following the war that one such area, the Sinai Peninsula, should be entrusted to the UN's permanent keeping. The very suggestion was sufficient to ensure that it would win no support from either the UAR, the territorial sovereign, or Israel, who showed every sign of being willing to give up her conquests only in return for a general peace settlement which met all her requirements. But, further, the proposal was specifically intended not just to secure an early settlement of this aspect of the Arab-Israeli territorial issue, but also to do so in a way which would provide a base for a permanent UN force. This guaranteed the opposition both of those states who are openly opposed to encouraging the UN to become independent of its members, and of those others, perhaps numerous and probably influential, who might well discover a number of reservations and obstacles should the question of territory for the UN ever become a live issue. And, in any event, with the UN's reputation at a low ebb, this was hardly the moment to secure widespread support for a proposal which was meant to give the Organization a bigger role in the world. It won no official backing, and was very much a damp squib.

Sometimes it has been urged that the UN should control, on an indefinite basis, not a whole territory but that part of it which, while presently under the jurisdiction of the local sovereign, is in the nature of an international utility on account of the number of states who have an interest in it, and which, in consequence, has given rise to international controversy. Proposals to this effect have been made

[3] Within a few weeks of the June 1967 war Israel enacted what she referred to as 'administrative legislation' in respect of the Jordanian sector of Jerusalem. However it was widely interpreted as amounting to or at least presaging annexation. The General Assembly called upon Israel to rescind these measures, and Mr E. A. Thalmann of Switzerland was sent to investigate the situation as the Secretary-General's Personal Representative. In his talks with Israeli leaders 'it was made clear that Israel was taking every step to place under its sovereignty those parts of the city not under its control before June 1967 . . . The Israeli authorities stated unequivocally that integration was irreversible and not negotiable.' *U.N. Monthly Chronicle*, October 1967, pp 11–12. In the *New York Times* of 28 June 1968, Israel's Prime Minister was reported as saying, 'Israel will never surrender her absolute rule of Jerusalem as her united capital.'

in respect of, for example, the Suez Canal and the land access routes between West Germany and West Berlin. But such schemes, although they relate to geographically limited areas, elicit, often in heightened form, all the objections which are made to less specialized designs for permanent international government. For the country through whose territory the utility runs will be particularly anxious to retain a bargaining counter which will probably be very valuable in not only political but also financial terms. And the prospect of UN control will please neither those who, on general grounds, do not wish to see the UN in possession of a revenue-producing asset, nor, more importantly, those who have a particular interest in the manner in which the asset is administered. Thus, after the nationalization of the Suez Canal in 1956 and before the Anglo-French attack on Egypt, what the Western Powers proposed was not UN control but, variously, an international 'Board' or 'Authority' which would be constituted, or chiefly constituted, by those states whose pattern of seaborne trade or other maritime interests gave them a close concern in the running of the Canal. Likewise, in respect of access to Berlin, the Western Powers have never shown much enthusiasm for ideas for a 'UN Motorway' or the like. What they have preferred is an international authority established by themselves in conjunction with the Soviet Union.

Another kind of limited but permanent administrative role which, in theory, is open to the UN is the maintenance of an area's security. It has been said, for example, that Mr Khrushchev proposed to President Kennedy at their June 1961 Vienna meeting that as part of a settlement of the West Berlin problem neutral troops under the UN might be stationed in the city as a means of guaranteeing its freedom.[4] Likewise, in respect of Cyprus, it is conceivable that a settlement might include provision for the UN to be entrusted with the maintenance of the island's internal security which would also provide an indirect safeguard against outside intervention. Such schemes however, run into the difficulty that they easily offend the dignity of those whom it is proposed the UN should guard: states do not usually enthuse over the presence of foreign troops on their soil, especially if they carry the suggestion that the host cannot look after itself. And additionally, if the area concerned has a real security problem, it is exceedingly doubtful whether it, or those within it who are fearful of the future, would regard the UN as an adequate guarantee.[5]

Distance, in short, is what often lends enchantment to schemes for

[4] See Alexander Dallin, *The Soviet Union at the United Nations* (New York: Praeger, 1962) p. 180. The same idea has sometimes been suggested as a temporary arrangement.
[5] See further on Berlin, below, p. 208, and on Cyprus, above, p. 127. The present role of the UN Force in Cyprus is discussed below at pp. 320–333.

international government, or, and no less promisingly, the opportunity to thwart a rival. The higher a state's chances of controlling the area in question, the less enthusiastic it is likely to be about its internationalization. And those who would have to make the necessary territorial sacrifice are especially likely to see little merit in such arrangements. However, these matters do not detract from the feasibility of systems of permanent international administration, and the device remains available for those who wish or can be persuaded to make use of it. In theory it offers an excellent way of settling territorial disputes, and it may yet be used in this way. But in view of its unpopularity such occasions will probably be rare. And when it is resorted to, it is not to be expected that it will necessarily be as permanent as is officially intended.

II

In some circumstances it may be possible to settle disputes by asking the UN to engage in administrative activity for a temporary period. If, firstly, something prevents the beginning of negotiations for the settlement of a territorial quarrel, it may be possible to remove the difficulty by putting the area in question under international control until an agreement is reached. This arrangement could satisfy the doubts which may be held regarding the good faith of the party in principal possession of the disputed region, who may be suspected of having no intention of making any concessions. Or, where the object of a dispute is more or less equally divided between two or more states, reservations about the value of talks could be quelled by each handing over its portion to the UN. In such circumstances this arrangement also has the merit of increasing the likelihood that, where it is appropriate, the territory which has given rise to tension will be treated as a unit, and so avoid the fate of permanent division. It could also be that, quite apart from considerations of good faith, it is impossible to get negotiations started while one state is in possession of another's territory, a position which could well obtain at the end of hostilities. Here, too, resort to temporary international government could surmount the immediate obstacle and so, perhaps, play an important role in reaching a settlement.[6]

In the second place, a limited period of UN rule may itself con-

[6] This kind of case is distinguishable from those where the UN plays an administrative role to prevent a situation getting worse or to avert a crisis: see Part Two, Chapter 9, for a discussion of this possibility. It may be, of course, that the UN's assumption of governmental tasks in order to facilitate a settlement turns into prophylactic activity in consequence of its initial goal proving beyond reach. But where administration is immediately and directly associated with the hope of a settlement and is conducted in the expectation that it will allow one to emerge, it is properly regarded as an instance of patching-up.

stitute a settlement of an international dispute over territory. It could do so where the interested states agree on the area in question being handed over to the UN pending a final decision as to its future by its inhabitants. It may be that this will require no more than a brief UN intermission,[7] but sometimes circumstances may demand a relatively long stay for the Organization. This could be so on account of a need to educate the people to a standard which will enable them to make an informed and responsible choice. Or it may be that the dispute is so highly charged, politically, that it is necessary to postpone a decision as to the territory's ultimate disposition for some considerable time, the hope being that by then passions will have cooled sufficiently to allow the matter to be dealt with in peace. In this way the UN may be able to help in the buying of time.

Finally, as well as holding the ring to permit a settlement or to confine contention regarding a territory's future to the domestic level, the UN may also play a temporary administrative role in order to implement an agreement for the transfer of an area from one set of hands to another[8] In this kind of situation there is no doubt regarding the area's ultimate destination or status, but there may be some difficulty about getting it there. It may be that its direct conveyance would threaten peace on account of bad relations between the present and prospective holders of power, as in the case of the ending of an invasion or a revolt, or of a state being forced, in effect, to give up some of its territory, or of hostility and disagreement between those claiming the succession. A period of international government may also be desirable or even necessary in order to fit the territory out with the constitutional apparatus which it will require for its future role. And, over and above these considerations, the state in control may insist, and be in a position to do so successfully, on a transfer in stages in order to sweeten the pill of its departure.

The UN's ability to play a temporary administrative role in order to serve any of these three purposes could have a significant bearing on the readiness of the parties to put an end to their dispute. And if they are agreeable to this kind of UN participation in their affairs, it is unlikely that the Organization would find that the task was, technically speaking, beyond it. Nor, in the third kind of case, where the UN acts solely as a transfer agency, is it likely that the members

---

[7] In which case the governmental process could perhaps be regarded as ancillary to the UN's task of investigating the wishes of the inhabitants, making it an instance of patching-up by investigation rather than by administration.
[8] The UN might play a basically similar role by, for example, demarcating a boundary on the basis of principles and directions which have been agreed by the parties.

would disapprove of its playing such a role, except in the improbable circumstance of the UN being asked to help in the execution of a territorial settlement which it regards as unacceptable. In the second and first cases, however, the objections which may arise in respect of proposals for permanent international government may also be made when it is suggested that the UN should administer a disputed area for only a limited time. Especially if a fairly long period of international rule is envisaged, the necessary withholding of full democratic rights from the inhabitants will probably cause concern in some quarters, and in others there may well be reservations on the ground that the proposed scheme will give undesirable scope to mischief makers. But such doubts are likely to have markedly less force than when the design is to place an area in the UN's permanent keeping.

It may also be the case that the idea of temporary UN rule may not elicit too hostile a reaction from the occupant. Should the region in question have been taken in war, he may in any event be planning to leave. Or he may have a similar intention in respect of a colonial territory to which another nation has laid claim. In these circumstances handing the area over to international government may have some appeal in that withdrawal would not be to the immediate benefit of the enemy or claimant state. However, this procedure would also deny the departing state the advantages which he might otherwise expect to obtain in return for giving up territory. On balance, therefore, it is likely to be acceptable only as a face-saver, when the state concerned is negotiating from weakness. But a strong claimant may be impatient of suggestions that the territory it seeks should spend a while in UN hands, especially if there is a chance of this reducing the amount it may secure, which may make the UN very cautious about embarking on a governmental role. Claimants, in fact, generally favour temporary UN rule only when there is no better way open to them of detaching what they want from its present holder, which does not augur well for the procedure being adopted. Thus, while a limited period of international government can make an important contribution towards the patching-up of disputes, it is unlikely that all the interested parties will often agree on its use.

The use of temporary international rule to facilitate negotiations for a settlement is likely to be particularly uncommon, for this kind of incentive would probably be unnecessary if there was a real chance of agreement, and worthless (as a patching-up device) if the disputants were far apart. And in fact there has only been one instance of it to date, and that is a marginal case, arguably being an example of a

F

post-agreement transfer of territory rather than of a pre-settlement procedure. It concerned the South American district of Leticia, which, about 4,000 square miles in extent, undeveloped, and virtually uninhabited, had been ceded to Colombia by Peru in a treaty which was signed in 1922, but which took Colombia three and Peru six years to ratify. For Colombia it was an important acquisition, as it gave her direct access to the main stream of the Amazon, but this was the element in the situation which led to trouble. Upstream from Leticia lay a Peruvian district which resented the arrival of Colombians on the river, and in September 1932 some of its inhabitants drove out the Colombian officials. At first this move was disavowed by Peru, but as Colombia prepared to reoccupy Leticia the Peruvian Government felt obliged to come to the assistance of its free-lance citizens. Brazil, supported by the United States, endeavoured to mediate, but she was unsuccessful, and therefore withdrew from the scene in February 1933. This left the way clear for the League Council to try its hand at patching-up. It had already, in January, debated the matter and now, in March, it proposed that Leticia should be handed over by Peru to a League Commission which, with Colombian forces at its disposal to maintain order, should administer the territory while the parties negotiated a settlement. Colombia was agreeable to this course, but Peru was in no mood to back down. Tension rose, some fighting took place, and it very much looked as though the two states would soon be involved in a full-scale war.

At the end of April, however, the Peruvian President was assassinated, and his successor was of a much more conciliatory frame of mind. This resulted in the Council putting forward a further version of its earlier proposals, suggesting that a League Commission, using forces of its own selection and paid for by Colombia, should take charge of Leticia in Colombia's name for not more than a year. They were accepted by the parties on 25 May, and in June Peru evacuated Leticia in favour of a three-man League Commission, comprising an American, a Brazilian, and a Spaniard. For a year it governed the district without incident, being assisted by a garrison of 75 Colombian officers and men who had been seconded for duty as an international force. Negotiations between the disputants went less smoothly, however, and broke down in April 1934. Preparations for war were recommenced, but on 24 May 1934, only a few weeks before the Commission was due to leave, an agreement was reached which recognized that Leticia was a part of Colombia. It was not ratified until 1935, but no difficulties arose when, upon the League Commission's departure in June 1934, Leticia was returned to Colombia.

Clearly, it had been anticipated from the outset that this would be the eventual result. At one stage in the dispute the League had declared that Peru should not stand in the way of a Colombian reoccupation of Leticia, and although the method of settlement which was later agreed did not formally prejudge the issue, the resumption of Colombia's authority was expected. The fact that her sovereignty over Leticia had, in effect, been confirmed in the arrangement for temporary League government and that she was to pay the Commissions' expenses was sufficient evidence of that. Thus, even if the disputants had not reached an understanding before the year of international rule was up, Colombia would have been in a position to claim Leticia, would surely have done so, and, equally surely, would have received the League's moral support. But in all probability the agreement of May 1934 made this process much smoother than it would otherwise have been, and that agreement may well have been dependent on the device of temporary international government which was adopted. With the assassination of her President, Peru evidently decided that Leticia was not worth a war with Colombia and unpopularity in the wider world, and was therefore prepared to give it up. It was, however, much easier for her to withdraw in favour of the League pending a final arrangement with Colombia regarding Leticia than it would have been for her to hand the area over directly to her recent foe. Especially as the final result was still, theoretically, in doubt, this was a respectable and face-saving procedure, and one which made it easier for her to agree to and accept its subsequent transfer to Colombia. By acting as a temporary go-between while negotiations were held, the League thus made a significant contribution to the peaceful solution of this dispute. It could not bring Peru to a willingness to withdraw. But, given that willingness, the League was able to facilitate a settlement along those lines.

The only example of the second kind of temporary international rule, which settles a territorial dispute by making provision for the inhabitants of the area concerned to decide on their own future at a later date, also comes from the inter-war period. It concerned the Saar. Until 1919 this region was a part of Germany, and its population of about three-quarters of a million was wholly German. But it possessed rich coal and iron ore deposits, and at the end of World War I neighbouring France was most anxious to take advantage of Germany's defeat to secure the Saar for herself. Germany was in no position to prevent this, but it would have been quite contrary to the principles in accordance with which the victorious Powers claimed to be conducting themselves. Accordingly, they felt obliged to restrain their ally from behaving in such an outdated manner. Hence,

France had to put her annexationist ambitions on one side and accept
the expedient of League rule for 15 years, at the end of which the
Saarlanders were to decide whether their territory should rejoin
Germany, pass to France, or remain under the League.

During this interim period the Saar was governed by a five-man
Commission appointed by the League Council, to which it reported
quarterly. It was laid down that one Commission member was always to be drawn from the Saar, and another from France, and the
first French member, Mr V. Rault, was also appointed the Commission's first Chairman. He soon built up a commanding position for
himself, and the way in which the Commission, under his influence,
exercised its responsibilities was not always free of controversy. The
special voice which France claimed in the Saar was also typified by
the presence of a French garrison. However, in the improved international atmosphere of 1925, the Council decided that the Commission's chairmanship should rotate, and thereafter it was held, first, by
the Canadian member, and then by the British. In 1927 the situation
was still further improved by the withdrawal of the French troops, although the Commission retained the right to recall them in case of a
serious threat to public order. From that point until 1934 the government of the Saar gave the League no serious trouble, and Germany
did not use the opportunity which her Council membership gave her
to complain about its administration.

Before changing the law or levying their taxes the Commission
was required to consult the elected representatives of the population,
and in order to facilitate this procedure a local Council was established
in 1922. However, it was a purely advisory body, and, not surprisingly, the Saarlanders were not satisfied by these arrangements. Nor,
quite apart from this, was the Commission a popular body. Thus it
was widely expected that, when its chance came, the Saar would
decisively reject its option to continue the *status quo*. It was also
assumed that its German population would overwhelmingly vote for
a return to the Fatherland. However, the advent of the Nazi regime in
January 1933 and the excesses which followed could conceivably
have given the situation a different complexion. From some quarters the League was urged to make itself more attractive to the Saarlanders, offering more democratic procedures and another plebiscite
at a later date. The Council, however, would have nothing to do with
such ideas. Hitler was, relatively speaking, conducting himself in a
reasonable fashion, but the League Powers were well aware of the
kind of reaction which propaganda in favour of a continuation of
international government might produce, especially if it was successful. Britain and Italy, in particular, had no desire to be saddled, in
their capacity as permanent Council members, with what would

doubtless have been a disproportionate share of the responsibility for ruling, and therefore defending, a region to which an increasingly powerful state would surely lay virulent claim. France, too, who might have been expected to have had the closest interest in such a solution, was reluctant to press it on the League. Probably she calculated that, in the circumstances, the return of the Saar to Germany was inevitable at some point, and that it would be best for her if the transfer was made in a peaceful and outwardly amicable manner, an attitude which was in keeping with her general policy towards Germany. The other source from which a strong lead might have come for a continuation of the League's rule was the Catholic Church. But the local bishops threw their weight on the side of Germany, and so the campaign prior to the plebiscite, which was held on 13 January 1935, was conducted in the absence of a clear or convincing opposition movement. In the event, with 97.9 per cent of the electorate voting, only 8.87 per cent of the total opted for the maintenance of the *status quo*. A very high proportion, 90·8 per cent, voted for union with Germany, and less than 1 per cent expressed a desire to join France. The Saar was reunited with Germany on 1 March.[9]

Thus it could be argued that this experiment in international government served its purpose. In 1919 Germany had no choice but to relinquish control over the Saar, but the views of most of the other interested parties prevented its annexation by France and led to the compromise of long term but temporary international government. During the following 15 years France had adequate opportunity to accustom herself to the idea that the attitude of the inhabitants pointed to the Saar's eventual return to Germany, and to the fact that Germany's growing power precluded any French attempt to secure a different result. Hence, this particular territorial dispute was liquidated to Germany's satisfaction and in a way to which France had become resigned. That its solution had no bearing on the wider issues of the Franco–German relationship was not a matter which could be laid at the League's door.

The 1935 settlement, however, proved to be short-lived, for Germany's defeat in World War II led to the reopening of the whole issue. Once again, France wished to annex the Saar, and once again her allies prevented her from doing so. But this time there was no recourse to the device which had been employed in 1919. Having already had one unsatisfactory experience of it, France may well have been unwilling to agree to its use. This could have led to difficulties, but did not. For, on account of their growing suspicion of the Soviet Union, the Western countries were not at all inclined to involve the

[9] See above, pp. 18–19.

UN, and hence the Communist states, in the government of an area on the French border. Instead, they recognized the interests of their ally by agreeing, in 1947, that the Saar should be treated differently from the rest of Germany, becoming an autonomous region but subject to French influence and control in the political and economic spheres. With the growing strength and importance of West Germany, the Saarlanders became increasingly dissatisfied with this position, and when, in 1954, it was decided to establish the Western European Union, which included both France and West Germany, the opportunity was taken to prepare for the Saar's Europeanization. The Union was to have general responsibility for the region, which, until the signing of a German peace treaty, was to be governed in accordance with a European statute. But when, in the following year, this idea was put to the Saarlanders, they rejected it. Pro-German parties had been allowed to campaign for a three-month period prior to the referendum, and had succeeded in winning wide support for their opposition to the proposed solution. They were against any form of international control and in favour of the Saar's immediate return to Germany, and a Franco-German agreement to this effect was reached in 1956. Accordingly, at midnight on the last day of that year, the Saar was once more reunited with Germany.

It might be thought that in the post-1945 period there would have been some scope for temporary international government in respect of colonial areas which, in the UN's view, were being prepared for self-determination with insufficient speed. In the inter-war years there would have been no question of this, for then it was thought that the way in which colonial Powers managed their dependent territories was their own affair. It was assumed that they were acting in good faith and out of a regard for the best interests of their subjects, and in respect of most colonial areas there was no expectation, on either side, that independence was only two or three decades away. Since the end of World War II, however, the prevalent attitude has undergone a fundamental change. Colonial affairs have become everyone's business, and those who have administrative responsibilities in this field have been called upon to furnish an account of their stewardship, and in particular to show how they are getting their colonies ready to stand on their own feet. Their inquisitors have rarely been satisfied, and have required metropolitan states to show greater energy and enthusiasm in the liquidation of their empires. This would seem to open the way for the suggestion that the UN should take over from tardy colonialists, providing them with an honourable retreat from situations which were likely to attract increasing criticism. The Charter permits such operations, for Article 77 (c) makes provision for states to place their colonies under the Trusteeship System, and Article 81 allows the Organization itself to act as the administering authority. But this possibility has not been utilized, and the reasons are not hard to find.

Such is the contemporary commitment to independence at the earliest possible date, and also, it might be added, the shaky condition of many members of the international society, that only in the most extreme circumstances would the UN be prepared to allow that a territory was not in a position to exercise the right of self-determination. Indeed, it is hard to conceive a situation where the UN would favour the continuation of a dependent status for a colony. Even self-determination has been suspect if it has not led to the severance of links with the metropolitan power, as the case of Gibraltar has shown. On the other hand, it is only in circumstances of a different but equally extreme character that a state is prepared to hand over one of its colonies to the UN. Such an admission of inadequacy does not come easily, and in the event of pressure to withdraw becoming irresistible, the usual response has been to grant independence, whatever the political condition of the territory concerned. The two situations in respect of which it has been suggested that international government should bridge the gap between the departure of the colonial power and the full political development of their former subjects illustrate the exceptional character of such proposals. One concerned the disposition of Italy's colonies after her semi-defeat in World War II. The idea of temporary international rule, however, was put forward less as a means of patching up an existing dispute as to the colonies' future than as a means of preventing any disputes regarding a matter with which, somehow, the international society had to deal.[10] The other case arose not out of the claim that the dependent territory was being brought to political maturity too slowly, but from the assertion that it should be handed over to the state that had already inherited the rest of the colonial Power's possessions in the region. The territory in question was West New Guinea, 160,000 square miles in extent with a population which is usually estimated to be in the region of 700,000, most of them Papuans. In 1949 it had not been possible to agree on whether it should be transferred to Indonesia along with the rest of the Netherlands East Indies, so it had been decided that Dutch control should continue pending negotiations regarding its future, which were to be brought to a positive conclusion within a year.[11] However, an agreement to agree, while an easy way around a difficult problem, is often a recipe for the indefinite maintenance of the

[10] See below, pp. 339–341.
[11] See above, pp. 43–49.

status quo, and so it was here. No progress was made, and relations between Indonesia and the Netherlands deteriorated. In 1956 Indonesia unilaterally repudiated her debts to the Netherlands; in 1957 Dutch property was expropriated and Dutch nationals expelled; and in 1960 Indonesia broke off all diplomatic relations.

It appears that at about this time the Netherlands was beginning to realize that time was not on her side. Now that she had withdrawn from the rest of the region, and did not aspire, in the manner of some, to an independent peace-keeping role in the area, the maintenance of her rule in West New Guinea had no strategic advantage. Nor did it bring any economic benefits: quite the contrary, for it was costing her about £10 million per annum. More importantly, it was clearly going to become an increasing political liability. In an endeavour to put pressure on the Netherlands, Indonesia urged the opening of negotiations in the 1954, 1956, and 1957 sessions of the General Assembly, proposing or supporting suggestions that a UN good offices commission or the Secretary-General should assist in the process. On each of these occasions the pro-Indonesian draft resolutions, while approved by a simple majority in the relevant committee, were rejected in the Assembly's plenary session on account of their inability to obtain a two-thirds majority. They were opposed by the Netherlands on the grounds, firstly, that Indonesia was only interested in negotiations on a basis which prejudged the issue—that West New Guinea must be transferred to her immediately and unconditionally; and, secondly, that it would be wrong to negotiate about the territory's future status until the inhabitants were in a position to express their own view on the matter. In some quarters this response met with much sympathy, expecially on account of Indonesia's intransigent attitude and her manifest inability to make a success of governing the area she already controlled. But such considerations as these did not appear in the canon of the anti-colonialist movement. With 16 new African states on the verge of UN membership, and with the prospect of more to come, the Netherlands could not be sure that her position would be upheld in future. In itself this might not have troubled her very much, but she also had to take account of the fact that some of her Western friends might think it more important to trim their sails to the wind of change, and press her to do likewise, than to support her stand.

Thus, several factors induced the Netherlands to take another look at her policy in respect of West New Guinea. She was not led to alter it, but did introduce some significant modifications. On the one hand, the process of political development in the colony was speeded up, it being announced in April 1960 that a central representative body was to be established. And, on the other, she began actively to seek the world's understanding and support for her position in New Guinea. She twice asked the UN Secretary-General to send an impartial observer to the territory, and in October 1960 proposed at the General Assembly that a UN commission be sent to investigate conditions there. As her Foreign Minister put it in the Dutch Parliament: 'What the Government has in mind is to lure to New Guinea the presence of the United Nations'.[12] But both the political and secretarial organs of the UN were unresponsive to these requests. They took their cue from Indonesia, who, being alive to the risk that a UN enquiry or the like might serve to legitimize the Netherlands policy in West New Guinea, was opposed to the Organization becoming involved in the colony in any capacity save that of liquidator. Support for this doctrinal approach came not only from the confirmed anti-colonialists, but also from the new Kennedy administration in the United States. For when, in April 1961, the New Guinea Council was officially inaugurated, that country ostentatiously absented herself from the ceremony.

Already, in 1960, Indonesia had begun to land groups of infiltrators in West New Guinea, and she repeated the process in September 1961. They did not present the Dutch authorities with much of a problem, but were an indication that Indonesia's policy of confrontation would now be physical as well as diplomatic. This, together with the other factors which have been mentioned, produced some further rethinking on the part of the Netherlands, and led to what *The Times* called 'a handsome and unprecedented offer'.[13] At the 1961 General Assembly, her Foreign Minister stated that his country was prepared to withdraw from West New Guinea and place it under the UN's rule until its people were able to decide their own future. Meanwhile, the Netherlands would continue her present level of financial support for the territory and would urge the 2,800 Dutch civil servants to remain as employees of the UN governing body so long as they were needed. It was suggested that instead of being given the status of a trust territory, the UN should establish and operate a special international development authority for West New Guinea. The whole scheme was justified with reference to the Declaration on the Granting of Independence to Colonial Countries and Peoples which the Assembly had passed in the previous December: the famous, or infamous, resolution 1514 (xv), which was to become the point of reference for all subsequent anti-colonialist campaigns.

The anti-colonialists, however, refused to be played at their own

---

[12] Justus M. van der Kroef, 'The West New Guinea Problem', 17 *The World Today*, No. 11 (November 1961), p. 497.
[13] *The Times*, 29 September 1961.

game. Indonesia said that the Netherlands proposal was a tactic to
strike at her, and a misuse of the Assembly's Declaration. In support
of this argument she advanced the interesting theory that the people
of West New Guinea, although they had never come under Indonesian rule, must be deemed to have exercised their right of self-
determination: they were a part of the Indonesian nation; Indonesia
had determined her own future; therefore the Papuans must have
done so. Others, while not going as far as this, agreed that West New
Guinea was a part of Indonesia, and therefore concluded that the
principle of self-determination must not be applied there without
Indonesia's consent. Accordingly, nine of the Afro-Asian group of
states, including India, Guinea, and the United Arab Republic,
countered the Netherlands proposal by introducing a draft resolution urging further negotiations, but failed to secure its passage.
Thirteen others of a more moderate disposition—the ex-French
African states—proposed a resumption of negotiations with the good
offices of the Secretary-General, but added that if agreement was
not reached by 1 March 1962, a five-man commission should consider the possibility of an interim period of international administration. The Netherlands was prepared to accept this draft, but not
Indonesia, and she and her supporters were sufficiently numerous
to prevent it obtaining a two-thirds majority.

Thus, despite the willingness of the administering power, the UN
did not take advantage of the opportunity to establish temporary
international government as a means of settling this colonial dispute.
It would not have been an untroubled arrangement, for Indonesia
would have transferred her hostility from the Netherlands to the
UN, and at this time the Organization had sufficient problems to
cope with in the Congo. But nevertheless, 53 members voted for the
13 power draft resolution, and so expressed their support for the
idea, despite the difficulties it would have involved. And the large
and important bloc of members who opposed it undoubtedly did so
not out of practical considerations but because they supported Indonesia's contention that, as part of the former Netherlands East
Indies, West New Guinea should pass directly to her.

If the New Guinea Council is regarded as representative, it is
clear that the Papuans themselves did not relish a transfer to Indonesia, either immediately or at a later date. What they wanted was a
continuation of Dutch rule until they were able to stand on their
own feet, and in April 1961 the Council sought an assurance from
the Netherlands to this effect. In June the Dutch Government replied saying that it would safeguard the Papuan right of self-determination, but the ambiguity of this position was soon made evident.
President Sukarno had celebrated the Netherlands' failure to get the

UN to take West New Guinea off her hands by ordering the total mobilization of Indonesia's armed services and reiterating his preparedness to seize West New Guinea by force. Spurred on by these events, and by the pressure of the United States and other Western Powers, the Netherlands quickly took her policy a further and final stage, in effect capitulating to Indonesia's demands. On 2 January 1962 the Netherlands Prime Minister said that his country was ready for talks with Indonesia without prior conditions about the rights of the Papuans to self-determination. He also indicated that there would be no objection to the involvement of a third party or power in the talks, and in consequence a mediator was subsequently appointed by the UN Secretary-General.[14] Again, Indonesia's response was hostile, as if to indicate the strength of her position: West New Guinea was declared an Indonesian province, paratroops were dropped, and some infiltrators landed. But the Netherlands was in no position to take umbrage, for she had decided to cut her losses and withdraw, and was most anxious to do so on agreed terms. They were not easy to obtain, but eventually, on 15 August 1962, immediately in the wake of the dropping of more Indonesian paratroops, the long dispute was brought to an end, an agreement being signed in the Security Council chamber in the presence of U Thant.

This ceremony was held under UN auspices not just because of the part which the Secretary-General and his representative had played in the final series of negotiations, but also on account of the terms of the agreement. For it provided for the UN's assumption of governmental powers in West New Guinea, the first time that the Organization had been entrusted with such responsibilities. However, this was neither a case of permanent international rule nor of the UN being asked to administer an area until a settlement could be reached or pending a decision by the inhabitants as to their future political status. Instead it was the third type of temporary administration, an instance of the UN being asked to act in this capacity in order to implement an agreed decision regarding the territory in question. Usually the use of the UN in this way will relate to a transfer of ownership, the UN filling a gap which, for one reason or another, is deliberately being left between the departure of one state and the arrival of its chosen successor. Thus the duration of this kind of governmental operation is strictly limited, and there is no doubt, not even a theoretical doubt, as to the ultimate destination of the area concerned. That has been agreed beforehand, and the period of international government is only a means, albeit an unusual means, of executing the agreement, providing an uninvolved and impartial

[14] See above, pp. 85–86.

pair of hands through which the territory's governmental apparatus can be passed. Hence, in these circumstances international government is used as a procedural device. As such its part is subsidiary, only coming into existence once a settlement has been reached. But that is not to say that it is also unimportant. For the ability of the UN to offer this service may have a significant bearing on the readiness of the parties to put an end to their dispute. Its employment may also contribute notably to the smooth execution of an agreement which might otherwise be put in serious jeopardy.

In the case of West New Guinea, the agreement of 15 August provided for the transfer of authority from the Netherlands to a UN Temporary Executive Authority (UNTEA), which, headed by a UN Administrator and assisted by UN security forces, was to rule the territory until at least 1 May 1963. This date marked the end of what was referred to as the 'first phase' of UN administration.[15] At a time thereafter which was to be determined by the Administrator, UNTEA's responsibilities were to be handed over, by stages or all at once, to Indonesia. Such Netherlands armed forces as remained in West New Guinea when the UN took it over were to be repatriated as soon as possible, and, meanwhile, were to come under UNTEA's authority. Likewise, the Papuan police and the Papuan Volunteer Corps were to be at its disposal, as were those members of the Indonesian Army who had illicitly entered the territory. But after the end of the first phase of UNTEA's rule Indonesia was to replace the UN's security forces with her own. The question of the location of sovereignty during the interregnum was studiously avoided, refuge being taken in the colourless and unemotional term 'administration'. The almost equally tricky matter of flags was surmounted by declaring that it lay with the Governments concerned and the Secretary-General to agree on which, if any, should be flown alongside that of the UN.

The agreement having been ratified by the two signatories, the General Assembly, on 21 September 1962, adopted a resolution authorizing the Secretary-General to carry out the tasks which had been assigned to him on behalf of the Organization. No members voted against this course. The Western Powers were heartily glad to see the back of the West New Guinea dispute, and the Soviet Union did not make any difficulties. She had not taken much interest in the matter other than to give general support to Indonesia, and as her friend was pleased with the outcome there was no call on her to introduce a note of dissent into the widespread approval which was being accorded to the plan for the UN's temporary assumption of a governmental role. The generally benevolent attitude which it eli-

[15] UN Document A/5170, Annex, Article IX.

cited was doubtless in no small measure due to the fact that the parties had agreed to meet all the UN's costs, each paying half. There was one minor flaw in this picture, inasmuch as France and 13 other members, almost all of them former French colonies, abstained when the scheme was put to the Assembly.[16] Of these Dahomey argued, very reasonably, that the agreement infringed the absolute right of self determination, and Togo complained that the matter was being dealt with too hastily. The others kept silent. Probably the French position was a reflection of the view that the exercise of governmental responsibilities was not the kind of activity in which the UN should engage. However, at the diplomatic level, the way was now clear for the UN to play the part for which it had been cast.

Prior to this point, the Organization had already been active in West New Guinea in a different capacity. The formal ending of the dispute had necessarily been followed by the calling of a cease-fire, and the parties had asked the Acting Secretary-General to supervise it. Accordingly a 21-man military observer team drawn from six countries was set up and led by U Thant's Military Adviser, General Rikhye. There were about 1,500 Indonesian troops scattered throughout the territory, and a large part of the observers' task was to ensure that the news of the official ending of hostilities was transmitted to these forces and to secure their concentration in selected places. With the co-operation of both the Indonesian and the Dutch authorities this was soon done, and General Rikhye was able to report on 1 September that the cease-fire was fully operative. Thus there was no danger of UNTEA being faced with guerrilla activity, and, as the territory was now quiet, the Dutch could withdraw without too much local loss of face.

But before the UN could assume its governmental role it had to acquire a military force, not just to guarantee law and order but also to give some substance to the arrangement which had been reached regarding West New Guinea. For if UNTEA had had to rely solely on Papuan and Indonesian forces the claim that the UN was governing the territory would seem rather hollow, not least to the Dutch. It was expected that a contingent of about 1,000 men would be required from an uninvolved Power, and that they would probably be drawn from Malaya. But that country, already having a unit on duty with the UN Force in the Congo, indicated that it could not spare another. The Secretary-General therefore turned to Pakistan. Despite the fact that she had a large and well-trained army, her

---

[16] Senegal, evidently having failed to receive the message, voted in favour of the draft resolution. Three days later she handsomely compensated for her error by asking that her vote should be regarded as negative.

troops had not hitherto served with the UN. They had been available for inclusion in the United Nations Emergency Force which
was sent to Egypt in 1956, but the UN had decided not to accept
Pakistan's offer. Her Government had been critical of Egypt's behaviour, with the result that it had been made clear that Pakistanis
would not be welcome on Egyptian soil, and the UN saw no reason
to make an issue of the matter. For the West New Guinea operation,
however, Pakistan troops were politically acceptable. Their country
was a member of the Western alliance system, which satisfied the
Dutch, and yet was also, like Indonesia, Asian and Muslim. Nor
had the Pakistan Government offended either disputant. And, in
any event, their role was expected to be short and non-contentious.
For her part, Pakistan was happy to supply the UN with troops, and
thus it was that the ground forces of the UN Security Force (UNSF)
were entirely constituted by a Pakistan unit of about 1500 men.
Additionally, 110 members of the Pakistan Navy manned nine
vessels which had been transferred to the UN by the Netherlands to
provide transport for the Security Force and to carry out patrol duties.[17] The Force was completed by two small Canadian and American
air units, and was commanded by Brigadier General Said Uddin
Khan of the Pakistan Army.

A large advance party of Pakistan troops landed in West New
Guinea towards the end of September, the remainder arriving early
in October. Thus UNTEA was equipped for its assumption of
authority, which had been fixed for 1 October. On that day the
UN flag was raised in the main square of Hollandia, the capital,
soon to be renamed Kotabaru, and until the end of December the
Netherlands flag flew alongside. The way in which that had been
agreed was rather strange. President Sukarno had been insistent that
Indonesia's flag should fly over the territory before the dawning of
New Year's Day, 1963, and in order to satisfy him the Acting Secretary-General had agreed to this, without, however, involving or in-
forming the Netherlands. This was subsequently ascribed to 'an ad-

[17] The *UN Review* for December 1962 states that this was the first time that the
UN had had its own navy. This may have been so in the sense that the UN apparently became the temporary owner of the boats which it employed in West
New Guinea. But it was not the first occasion on which the UN had had the use of
naval elements. During the latter part of the first Palestinian truce, which lasted
from 11 June–9 July 1948, the UN had had one French naval corvette and three
American destroyers at its disposal, and was thus able to patrol the coastal waters
of Palestine and the neighbouring Arab states. The UN Mediator spoke highly of
this aspect of the Organization's operation.

There are also two cases of the UN controlling ships solely for logistical purposes.
At an early stage of the UNEF operation the UN purchased a landing ship tank
in order to land supplies at Gaza, but this was not a success and was soon discon-
tinued. And for most of the Congo operation an American transport ship was at
the UN's disposal.

ministrative oversight'.[18] When she was informed, her request that the Netherlands flag should fly alongside the UN's from 1 October until the end of the year could hardly be refused.

In order to ensure continuity of administration the Secretary-General sent Mr J. Rolz-Bennett, a high-ranking member of the UN Secretariat, as his personal representative to consult with the departing Dutch authorities, and on 1 October he was appointed Temporary Administrator. Subsequently, Dr D. Abdoh of Iran was named as UNTEA's head, and he arrived in West New Guinea in November. It had been provided that top Netherlands officials were to be replaced as soon as possible, and that during the first phase of UNTEA's rule the posts they had filled were to be held neither by Dutchmen nor by Indonesians, although it was open to the UN to employ less exalted Dutch officials. Most of them, however, were not anxious to stay, which made UNTEA's already complex task all the more difficult. What it had to do, on virtually no notice and in a short space of time, was to adapt the territory's institutions from the Dutch to an Indonesian pattern, arrange a smooth administrative take-over, and prepare the people for the change. Not surprisingly, its performance did not always reach the highest standards, although the fact that it was operating in one of the world's most primitive areas—it was estimated that more than one third of the territory's inhabitants were not yet subject to any central control—no doubt made its task easier in some respects as well as more difficult in others. However, UNTEA, in which 32 nationalities were represented, fulfilled its main task, which was to pass West New Guinea from Dutch to Indonesian hands, and there is little doubt that the transfer was greatly eased by the fact that it was indirect and conducted by a sympathetic intermediary. Throughout this period public order was maintained, only a few incidents being reported and none of them very serious.

The agreement of 15 August had not stated when UNTEA was to hand over West New Guinea to Indonesia. All it had done was to fix a date on which the 'second phase' of UNTEA's administration was to begin, and to leave its ending to the discretion of the Administrator. But as the agreement anticipated that during the second phase Indonesia would take over top posts in the administration of the territory and would replace the UN's security forces with her own, it was unlikely that the Administrator would feel able to prolong this stage. The import of the arrangement was obvious, and Indonesia was not slow to press it on the UN. Further, when the agreement was signed, it was accompanied by an *aide-mémoire* stating

[18] Paul W. van der Veur: 'The United Nations in West Irian', xviii, *International Organization*, No. 1 (Winter 1964), p. 55, n.7.

that the transfer of authority to Indonesia was to be effected as soon
as possible after 1 May. In the event it was announced on 9 February 1963 that UNTEA would withdraw on 1 May. There had been
some Indonesian pressure for an even earlier departure, and Indonesian officials were already influential in UNTEA and were not
deaf to the voice of Djakarta. In the circumstances there must
have seemed little point in staying beyond the end of the first phase,
for the beneficial effect of further preparations for the change might
have been outweighed by the Indonesian hostility which UNTEA's
continuing presence would probably have attracted. Hence the
second phase of its administration was omitted, or, in the view favoured by the UN, was reduced to a matter of hours. This interpretation was possible because it had not been specified at what
time on 1 May the first phase was to end, and the actual handing over
of authority was to take place at 12.30 pm on that day. Thus honour
was satisfied on both sides, and the UN's first experience of government was brought to a harmonious conclusion.

But the UN's role in respect of West New Guinea was not yet
over. At least, not in theory. For the agreement of 15 August provided for the Organization's involvement in what was variously referred to as 'the act of free choice' and 'the act of self-determination'.[19]
This, it was laid down, was to be completed before the end of 1969
and was to give the inhabitants the opportunity to say whether they
wanted to remain a part of Indonesia or to sever their ties with her.
The arrangements for the act were to be made by Indonesia, but
during the preceding year she was to have the advice and assistance
of a representative of the Secretary-General and supporting staff.
And, from the time of Indonesia's assumption of authority in West
New Guinea to the appointment of the representative, a number of
UN experts were to help in the preparations for carrying out the
provisions for self-determination. In the perhaps deliberately obscure
words of Article XVI, they were 'to remain, wherever their duties
require their presence'. Indonesia undertook to honour the decision
of the Papuans regarding their future.

When the agreement of 15 August came before the General Assembly the representative of the Netherlands said that his country
had reluctantly resigned itself to transferring West New Guinea to
Indonesia without a previous expression of the will of the population
in order to avoid involving the Papuans in war. But he added that,
undesirable though this alternative was, it would have been faced
had not Indonesia agreed to the participation of the UN in the exercise of the right of self-determination. However, the mere existence
of a supervisory scheme, such as was envisaged in the agreement, is

[19] UN Document A/5170, Annex, Articles xvii and xx.

not sufficient to ensure that the activity to which it relates will in fact take place. And in this case some doubt was clearly justified.

Only two days after the agreement was signed President Sukarno spoke of the principle it embodied as 'internal' and not 'external' self-determination.[20] The concept is not entirely self-explanatory, but there is no uncertainty as to what it does not mean, and the President made the matter quite clear by adding that there was no doubt that all the inhabitants of West Irian would reveal themselves as pro-Indonesian. In January 1963 the Deputy Chief of Indonesia's liaison mission to UNTEA referred to the possibility that the people might decide that the plebiscite was unnecessary, and some agitation to this effect was begun while UNTEA was still in West New Guinea. Upon its departure some UN representatives remained, but left before very long. It could have been argued that at this point, with 1969 some years away, there was no good reason for their presence, but the situation could also be interpreted more pessimistically. Indonesia's withdrawal from the UN in January 1965 in protest against Malaysia's election to the Security Council, decreased still further the likelihood of the Organization being involved in a plebiscite in West Irian, as the territory was now called, if indeed a plebiscite was held at all. In the next year she resumed her participation in the Organization, but this was not accompanied by any sign that the 1962 agreement was going to be honoured. Quite the contrary. For, on 7 December 1966, the Indonesian Home Affairs Minister renounced his country's undertaking to hold a plebiscite not later than 1969. This, he said, was not because it was the policy of his Government but because 'the Irianese people do not want such a plebiscite'.[21] This produced some critical comment abroad, with the result that a week later the Foreign Minister offered an amended version of the position. It was Indonesia's object to do no more than 'carry out the wish of the West Irian people'. Accordingly, said Mr Malik, 'if they want a plebiscite we will hold a plebiscite'.[22] Apparently Djakarta did not anticipate that discerning the true voice of West Irian would present any substantial difficulties. What was no doubt a greater problem was to explain how the procedure was consistent with Indonesia's international obligations. On this subject, therefore, nothing was said.

However, Indonesia's new regime must have realized that this sort of line was not going to do them any good in the world at large, and also that it was probably quite unnecessary.[23] Towards the end of the period of Dutch rule the Papuans were displaying a mea-

[20] van der Veur, *op. cit.*, p. 63.
[21] *The Times*, 8 December 1966.
[22] *The Times*, 15 December 1966.
[23] President Sukarno's power had been eroded during 1966.

sure of national self-awareness and indicating that they might, eventually, wish to think in terms of independence for their territory. But although, at the more sophisticated level, this attitude may not have disappeared by 1969, the electorate is, on the whole, unlikely to display a notable resistance to suggestion, and Indonesia can be counted upon to present the issue in a way which suggests an answer favourable to herself. In this she is most unlikely to be at all deterred by the possibility of a critical reaction from the UN observers, either because she may rely on their being sympathetic towards her case, or because, even if Indonesia did get a bad report, the UN's political organs are unlikely to pay much heed to it. Thus, in the Introduction to his *Report* for the year 1966–7, the Secretary-General was able to say that he had been assured by Indonesia that she would comply fully with her responsibilities under the August 1962 agreement. So it looks as if the 'act of self-determination' will, after all, be held. Indonesia is not risking much by agreeing to it, for, as her change of tune indicates, she must think it almost impossible that the Papuans will do other than confirm the existing situation. And even in the event of an unfavourable result, it is exceedingly doubtful whether the UN's interest in the matter would result in Indonesia being strongly pressed to relinquish West Irian. For the anti-colonialists treat the question as closed, and the Western Powers are not looking for trouble. Thus the statement of Indonesia's Home Affairs Minister on 7 December 1966, which was evidence both of Indonesia's determination to retain West Irian and of her disregard for the UN's and her own remaining responsibilities under the 1962 agreement, produced not a ripple on the surface of the Organization. If, say, South Africa was proposing to default on an obligation to hold a plebiscite on South West Africa, that would be a different matter. But new, non-white states are not regarded as eligible for dismemberment on the basis of the principle of self-determination. There are too many insecure limbs around for that.

It is inconceivable tha the Netherlands was unmindful of considerations such as these. More than any other state, she had good reason for being aware that Indonesia's attitude towards international law was not always such as to satisfy those to whom she owed legal obligations. And the course of the West New Guinea dispute had fully revealed the tenor of the times on such issues. The Dutch must therefore have known that their endeavour to safeguard the rights of their West New Guinea subjects was a very fragile edifice. It was better than nothing, and by stressing the importance of the agreement's self-determination provisions, she could hope that they would be held in somewhat greater respect by Indonesia and others. At the least, such a policy meant that they could not be deliberately forgotten. But she could not have been blind to the point that her withdrawal was viewed by Indonesia as a sign that the Papuans were being handed over once and for all, whatever paper qualifications may have been attached to the operation. Anything less, in Indonesian eyes, and those of the other anti-colonialists, would have been undignified and unjust.

In view of this, some criticisms which have been levelled at UNTEA are perhaps out of place. Van der Veur has complained that it did not support those Papuans who emphasised their rights or who displayed some hesitation over the prospect of Indonesian rule,[24] and it can indeed be argued that as UNTEA was part of an exercise which involved self-determination for the Papuans, and was obliged to defend their right of free speech, it should have taken a stand on their behalf although this would have offended Indonesia. But even if such charges could be upheld, possibly they neglect the point that UNTEA was simply a means of passing West New Guinea to Indonesia. Its life, like its function, was limited, and it would have done neither itself nor the Papuans concerned any good to have disregarded the fact that Indonesia would soon be in its shoes. Effectively, it was in no position to take an independent line in West New Guinea, despite the agreement's ritual reference to the maintenance of human rights.

It may be that some of UNTEA's difficulties stemmed from its being in West New Guinea for too long. It could do very useful work in preparing the territory for Indonesia, but as that result was al-already agreed there was a case for cutting its rule to the very minimum length of time which was necessary to arrange a smooth administrative transfer. For the longer UNTEA stayed, the more impatient Indonesia was likely to become, and the greater was the scope afforded to Papuan dissidents. Mr Bunker is said to have begun his mediatory activities with the idea of UN rule for between one and two years. In the event, even the very minimum period of seven months which the agreement allowed was almost too long for the state whose claim was at last being met.

It is very doubtful whether this period was the result of a considered assessment of the time UNTEA would need to carry out its tasks. Rather, it represented a compromise between Indonesia's urgent acquisitive impulse and the Netherlands' desire to deny her the fruits of victory for as long as possible. However, this in no way lessened the value of the arrangement, especially as here the need for it arose less out of the requirements of the local situation than of the approach of one of the parties. For the direct transfer of West New

[24] *Op. cit.*, especially, pp. 67–71.
[25] *Op. cit.*, p. 55.

Guinea from the Netherlands to Indonesia would not have been an impractical proposition, especially if the UN had first assisted with the concentration of Indonesian forces already in the territory. It would have carried the risk of incidents, and would have been an untidy operation. But it could have been done. However, it would have been a most humiliating course for the Netherlands, and she was unwilling to follow it. If, therefore, she was to agree to withdraw, it was necessary that she should not herself have to hand over her colony to her adversary.

The use of the UN in a temporary governmental capacity was an admirable solution for this problem. The parties might have found it difficult to agree on anyone else, and if they had agreed the state so chosen might have been reluctant to co-operate, for the task in West New Guinea, though not politically onerous, promised to be formidable in other ways. The UN, however, was acceptable to both disputants, and was willing to play a governmental role. Thus the Netherlands was able to leave in a manner which preserved her dignity, and this, together with the provisions of the agreement regarding self-determination, allowed her to capitulate to Indonesia and yet maintain a sufficient measure of self-esteem. Had she not been able to do so, it is conceivable that she would not have agreed to go. The peaceful settlement of the dispute, therefore, was not only facilitated by UNTEA and its Security Force. It may also have been partly dependent upon the possibility of their presence in West New Guinea.

In the events leading to a settlement, however, the opportunity of using the UN as a temporary government for the territory was not a decisive factor. The Organization would probably have been prepared to assist in this way at any time during the dispute. But its involvement depended on the agreement of the parties, for the permission of the Netherlands was necessary before the UN could enter West New Guinea, and, at least during the latter part of the dispute, the UN would have been most unlikely to agree to take over the territory without the consent of Indonesia. Hence the Netherlands proposal of 1961 that the UN should govern West New Guinea until its inhabitants were able to decide upon their own future came to nothing because it was not acceptable to Indonesia and her supporters. An accord between the parties was reached only when the worsening diplomatic and military situation of the Netherlands on the one hand and Indonesia's growing bellicosity on the other made it increasingly likely that the dispute would be brought to a violent and, from the point of view of the Dutch, an inglorious end. This led the Netherlands to decide that, provided it could be done in not too mortifying a manner, she would cede the territory to Indonesia. The

UN, by its willingness to provide a temporary government for West New Guinea, was then able to render significant assistance, but that stage was not reached as a result of its existence or activities.

As well as allowing the Netherlands to withdraw without too much loss of face, the UN's temporary rule in West New Guinea made an important contribution towards the orderliness with which the territory was transferred to Indonesia. No love was lost on either side, and direct contact between them would have afforded plenty of scope for trouble. But as one existing governmental apparatus was being exchanged for another in an adequately administered territory, the maintenance of basic public order was not an important issue in the settlement of this territorial dispute. In others, however, it could be a serious problem, and here, too, the UN could contribute towards a peaceful solution by conducting a brief governmental operation. If, for example, the metropolitan Power was withdrawing from a territory which was destined for independence but which completely lacked a governmental framework, it would clearly be necessary, if chaos was to be avoided, for an outside body to assume authority for an interim period. For such a role the UN would be widely regarded as the most suitable agency. At the popular level, this would be due to the assumption that the Organization could be relied upon to act impartially. In diplomatic circles the same conclusion would reflect one of two considerations: either, that, being collectively controlled, the UN would be least likely to give any one state or group of states the opportunity to draw undue benefit from the situation; or that the UN was the best vehicle for implementing the policy favoured by a majority of members.

It would, however, be exceedingly unusual for a dispute to end with the territory concerned being abandoned in a condition which was totally unsuitable for the role which it was intended to play. There have certainly been instances of colonies being given their independence when, in the opinion of some observers, they were hardly ready for it. But in those situations appearances, at least were satisfied, the territory being equipped with all the institutional apparatus which an entity needs for membership in the international society. In the normal course no self-respecting state would leave it to the UN to do this job. If, therefore, a territory was relinquished without the governmental arrangements which were necessary for its future, this would probably be due to the sovereign already having lost effective control. In which case the UN would hardly welcome the opportunity to try its hand at restoring order. Hence, it is not surprising that the Organization has never assumed a governmental role in order to make good a territory's inadequate institutional endowment, so allowing it to make a somewhat delayed but peaceful international debut. There have, however, been two occasions on which the UN has made plans to operate in this manner, and they illustrate why such schemes are unlikely to be brought to fruition, at least not in the context of pacific settlement.

The first such case arose out of the dispute regarding the future of Palestine. On 29 November 1947 the General Assembly voted for the partition of the territory, and set up a UN Commission for Palestine to arrange for a smooth transition of power. It consisted of the representatives of five states: Bolivia, Czechoslovakia, Denmark, Panama, and the Philippines. The Commission's task was to take over the administration of Palestine while Britain was winding up her responsibilities there, establish Provisional Councils of Government in the areas which had been allocated to the Arabs and the Jews, delimit the frontiers of those areas, assume full governmental authority in Palestine on the formal termination of the mandate, and hand it over to the Successor Governments on 1 October 1948. This plan, however, was a total failure. It presupposed the co-operation of the three parties and received it from none. The Arabs rejected the idea of partition and therefore would have nothing at all to do with a scheme which assumed that they would succeed to only a part of Palestine. The Jews got on with the business of establishing a skeleton government on their own and evidently did not regard the Palestine Commission as a body which would be of any value to them. Britain, already faced with enough difficulties in Palestine, refused to add to them by endeavouring to operate arrangements which were rejected by one of her local adversaries and ignored by the other. Accordingly she decided the date for the termination of the Mandate without consulting the UN, settling for 15 May 1948, which was two and a half months earlier than the UN had expected; she would not allow the Commission into Palestine earlier than two weeks before her own withdrawal,[26] although she did permit the entry of a small group from the Commission's secretariat early in March; and she prohibited any attempt to delimit frontiers within Palestine while she was still unhappily trying to hold the ring.

It had been anticipated that the projected Arab and Jewish states would each establish militia to maintain order, and the resolution of 29 November 1947 provided for their control by the Palestine Commission. When the unrealism of this and other aspects of the Assembly's plan became evident, the Commission reported to the

[26] A member of the Commission's secretariat has noted, however, that 'in spite of their declarations about the convenience of the Commission functioning in or near Palestine, most of its members were firmly resolved not to stir from New York': Pablo de Azcárate: *Mission in Palestine 1948–1952* (Washington D.C. Middle East Institute, 1966), p. 6.

Security Council that on the termination of the Mandate it would need to have a non-Palestinian armed force at its disposal if it was to carry out its allotted tasks. The Council, however, did not pursue this matter, nor an American suggestion that Palestine might temporarily be given the status of a trust territory. Instead it called a Special Session of the Assembly where the Commission repeated the point it had made to the Council. But the assured hostility of the parties made the Assembly unwilling to support its own resolution with armed force, and on the last day before the Mandate was due to end the Palestine Commission was wound up.[27]

The second scheme for a brief governmental role for the UN in order to facilitate an agreed transfer of power looks like being no more successful than the first, for once again it is part of an arrangement which is totally unacceptable to a party whose assent is crucial. It concerns South West Africa.[28] In September 1966 the General Assembly considered the matter in the light of the situation which had arisen following the International Court's rejection, two months earlier, of the claims which Ethiopia and Liberia had brought against South Africa. Undeterred by this set-back, the Assembly resolved on 27 October that South Africa had failed to fulfil her obligations in respect of the territory and that her mandate was 'therefore terminated'. It further decided that 'henceforth South West Africa comes under the direct responsibility of the United Nations', and appointed a committee to consider how the Organization should deal with this new responsibility.[29] This resolution was opposed by only two states, Portugal and South Africa; three abstained: France, Malawi, and Britain; and 114 states voted in favour, not including, however, either Botswana or Lesotho, who were not present when the vote was taken. No doubt they judged that even abstention was an insufficiently discreet course for states so weak and exposed as themselves.

A Special Session of the Assembly was convened in April 1967 to consider the committee's report, and now it was decided, on 19 May, to establish an eleven-member UN Council for South West Africa, to administer the territory until its independence, which the Council was to endeavour to establish by June 1968. The Council was charged with the task of establishing a legislative assembly on the basis of universal adult suffrage, was to be based in South West Africa, and was to entrust all executive and administrative tasks to a UN Commissioner. It was requested to enter immediately into

---

[27] See further, above pp. 29–31 and below, pp. 272–273.
[28] See also below, pp. 256–258.
[29] General Assembly resolution 2145 (xxi).

contact with South Africa in order 'to lay down procedures' for the transfer of the territory, and South Africa was called upon to be co-operative.[30] An earlier draft, sponsored by 58 Afro-Asian states, had been even more imperious in tone, declaring that South Africa's continued presence in South West Africa, and any action of hers which frustrated or obstructed the task of the UN Council, was an act of aggression which should attract enforcement action by the Security Council. However, it was thought wise to water down these sentiments in the interests of a larger supporting vote, and in the event 85 states voted in favour of the resolution. Portugal and South Africa once more voted against, but now the abstaining ranks swelled to 30, including Britain, France, the Soviet Union, and the United States. Botswana also felt able to join this company, but the representative of Lesotho was once more detained on pressing business elsewhere.

Clearly, there is virtually no likelihood of South Africa agreeing to a scheme such as that proposed by the UN. She shows every intention of retaining South West Africa, and even if she could be persuaded into setting up all or part of it as an independent state, she would certainly not allow the necessary arrangements to be made by a transitional UN regime. It is perhaps possible that international government might be established in consequence of a successful assault on South West Africa, which would be evidence of the UN's proselytizing and not its patching-up abilities. But that day is likely to be a long way off: the abstention of the Great Powers on the resolution of 19 May is significant, and until then the UN will have to content itself with being a government-in-exile.[31]

Thus, where a territorial dispute is settled by a transfer of power, it is unlikely that the UN will be called upon to play a temporary governmental role to ensure the maintenance of law and order. For, if this is a straightforward task, it will almost surely be performed by the departing Power; and if it is not, it will probably be beyond the capacity of the Organization. Conceivably, however, a territorial dispute which ends in favour of the incumbent could involve the UN in an administrative capacity while order was being restored, where, for example, large scale guerrilla warfare has been waged. It may be that the forces of the state abandoning its claims and endeavours cannot be relied upon to act in a pacific spirit if the arrangements for their withdrawal are made by their former enemies. Also, not all of them may have been notified of the order to leave, which would be another sure source of trouble. In the normal way, international assistance given in such circumstances would take the form of a supervisory presence, perhaps a large one. But it could be that,

[30] General Assembly resolution 2248 (s-v).
[31] For subsequent developments, see below, p. 400–401.

on account of the size of the problem, it would seem more appropriate for the UN to take over the government of the country for a short while. The case for this would have added strength if it had been agreed that, concurrently with the departure of the foreign forces, political changes should take place in the 'host' state. There might also be scope for an international scheme for the development of a country ravaged by war. An obvious candidate for such an arrangement is South Vietnam. Should a settlement be reached which involved the withdrawal of the Northern elements and a return of the indigenous Viet Cong to full-time civilian life, the magnitude of the operation and the possibility of seriously upsetting incidents might suggest a period of international government for the South. But the example also illustrates the difficulty, for, even assuming a settlement, it is almost impossible to see the South Vietnamese Government, or any government, agreeing to the temporary assumption of its powers by the UN, in this or any other circumstances.

It may be, however, that a government in dire domestic straits may accept a quasi-governmental presence to get it back on its feet again. There would be no question, in form, of the UN taking over the country with a view to handing it back when it was in a better condition. The theory of the case would be that the UN was merely helping the sovereign government to maintain law and order and perform certain other essential tasks. But in practice the situation might not be so very different from straightforward international government. The operation could probably be justified on the ground that in its absence other states would be tempted to intervene and so might provoke a serious international crisis. It would thus have a prophylactic rather than a patching-up character. But it might also be of the latter type in a situation where the presence of the UN was necessary in order to secure the withdrawal of a state who had already intervened in defence of its property or its nationals, and whose action was unwelcome to the host state. Such, in part, were the circumstances of the UN's action in the Congo in July 1960.[32]

But despite the fact that many new states start their international life in a relatively unprepared condition, and often have grave internal problems, this is a far cry from degeneration into such chaos that it becomes necessary for an outside body to take over the reins of government. States may sometimes have trouble with rebellious subjects, and may frequently welcome technical assistance in order to develop their public services. But what is and will probably remain rare is the kind of situation which occurred in the Congo: the disintegration of the armed forces, the breakdown of the government's authority, and the absence of any indigenous body or bodies

[32] See below, pp. 354–357.

laying a relatively effective claim to its place. The typical consequence, when a government is in serious trouble, is either its quick
replacement by the forces capable of preserving order or by a group
acceptable to them, or a situation which takes on the aspect of a civil
war. In neither event would there be any question of the UN being
called upon to administer the country for a while.

There is not, therefore, much greater likelihood of the UN being
employed in a temporary administrative role than there is of it
governing a disputed region indefinitely. Nevertheless, from time
to time the international society may be glad to take advantage of
the UN's ability to do either of these things. But the very lack of
controversy which is likely to surround the actual conduct of such
operations, as distinct from the disagreement to which their suggestion is likely to give rise, is indicative of their role. They may assist
either the conclusion or execution of a settlement, but they are essentially adjunctive to it, of significance only when, for one reason
or another, the parties are disposed to put an end to their quarrel.
Then, administrative presences may have an important place in the
conciliatory scheme, but prior to that point they have no part.

PART TWO

Prophylaxis

Chapter 6

Accusation

THE growth of international institutions in the twentieth century has both reflected and increased the attention which has been given to the idea of world public opinion. Just as within the state foreign policy is no longer regarded as a matter for experts alone, so at the international level disputes are not treated as the sole concern of those who are directly involved and affected by them. Rather, it is commonly held that the international community as a whole is entitled to express a view on all situations which threaten or disturb any part of its peace, and that its opinion should be paid a decent respect by those who profess a belief in democracy, a category from which no state is willing to exclude itself. The identification of the community's authentic voice could present a difficulty, but it has been surmounted. For although, domestically, the official organs of government are not always thought to provide a wholly accurate representation of the views of the people, in international society the collective deliberations of states are widely taken to indicate not just the balance of diplomatic thinking on the matter in hand but also the opinions of mankind. In consequence, it becomes more than a matter of common prudence for states to take some account of what goes on in a body such as the General Assembly of the United Nations.

However shaky the reasoning on which it rests, this argument provides international institutions with a way of trying to act prophylactically in respect of actual or imminent quarrels. Opinion can be mobilized in favour of a cessation of fighting or the adoption of pacific procedures, and special attention can be paid to the more belligerent party. But it may be that the exact nature of the conflict is, or is deemed to be, less than entirely clear. Such claims are particularly plausible in relation to many of the troubled issues of the post-1945 years. For, during this period, straightforward attacks by one state on another have been relatively rare, and it has become unheard of for hostilities to be initiated by a formal declaration of war. Instead, conflict has often been informal and fragmented: guerrilla warfare; frontier skirmishes; internal disputes concerning legitimacy linked with charges of external interference; allegations regarding inflammatory conduct—all these have been common. In such situations, and especially when, as has regularly been the case, they have involved ideological differences, competing accounts of what is going on and different judgments as to the party who is responsible for its continuation are likely to be advanced, and not only by the states directly concerned. In these circumstances, a majority of an institution's members may favour the dispatch of observers to the area in question to secure an independent report, which will enable the institution to make an informed judgment on the situation. Such a decision may also be encouraged by the fact that when states are not in direct and open conflict, the circumstances may not seem to be sufficiently urgent or appropriate for the issue of a simple demand that aggression should stop. An enquiry may appear to be much the more obvious first step. It may even be thought desirable to establish observers in an area where no overt conflict presently exists but where it is considered likely to occur, so enabling the institution to receive an immediate report should the situation in fact deteriorate.

The establishment of such a presence is unlikely to run into difficulties on technical grounds. All that the operation requires is the temporary service of a small number of individuals, for which both the personnel and the finance should be easily forthcoming. Moreover, their mission would be less demanding than an investigation which was conducted with a view to repairing a quarrel, for they would not be asked to propose terms of settlement or to furnish a report which pointed to such terms. They would be required to do no more than state the facts of the troubled situation, or to place themselves in the position of being able to make such a report should a crisis occur.

In another sense, however, a reporting operation plays an ambitious role. For, while it is not embarked upon in the immediate hope of putting an end to the dispute, it is intended to produce a quietening effect. Fact-finding is to be put to a prophylactic purpose. This end may be served by the mere decision to obtain a first-hand account of the situation, for, by signifying the concern of the international community, it could have a sobering effect on the disputants. More particularly, they may deem it wise to exercise some restraint on account of a desire not to be depicted in an unfavourable light. Once a report has been made, the parent body will be in a position to make an authoritative call for the cessation of hostile acts, taking into account any finding as to the degree of belligerence shown by the parties. The assumption is that any such decision emanating from a world institution will carry a good deal of weight, by virtue both of its authorship and of the fact that it is the product of an independent enquiry, thus causing the states directly involved to reconsider their policies and the other members of the institution to bring pressure on them to do so. In these ways it may be possible for a body such as the UN to place some obstacles in the way of the beginning or continuation of aggressive policies, and so contribute towards the reduction of international tension.

For this to happen it is desirable that the parties should display a respectful and co-operative attitude, permitting an enquiry to be held on their territory, giving it the facilities it requires, and accepting any recommendations which are made in consequence of its report. It is also desirable that the other members of the institution should be keenly interested in the lowering of tension, whoever is involved and for whatever purpose. The ideal picture is of an impartial and high-minded group of states who, intending to take steps to prevent the continuation of disturbing behaviour but unclear as to its source, call for a report on the facts in order to clear up this preliminary point. The truth must be obtained so that their overriding concern for a peaceful world can be given just expression. In reality, however, the situation is likely to be different in a number of important respects.

In the first place, a reporting presence is rarely dispatched in ignorance of the facts of the case. More often, a report will be called for by those who are already clear in their own minds as to the fundamental character of the dispute. Its details may be obscure, but the evidence regarding the broad lines of what is going on may well seem to be heavily balanced in one direction. It may even be that the nature of the situation is all too obvious to those who care to look. Nevertheless, the states who are of this opinion may think it prudent for their formal judgment on the merits of the case to be based on the report of an internationally-organized enquiry. They will thus be provided with a defence to the charges of undue haste and partiality, and so may hope, on the one hand, to minimize the offence given to those who see events in a different light, and, on the other, to increase the likelihood of their view being accepted by those who are not committed to any of the rival analyses. But although this procedure has the appearance of putting the institution in the position of being able to make an independent and balanced judgment, the reality is that a report which has been called for with a prophylactic intent frequently serves less to throw light on dark places than to provide confirmation and support for a pre-existing view.

This leads to the second point: that the state which anticipates censure is most unlikely to welcome the idea of a report being made on its activities. It may not go so far as to refuse entry to the investigators, as it may feel that the conclusions which could be drawn from such a course would be more damaging than a critical first-hand report. It may even agree with apparent willingness to the proposal that an enquiry should be made. This could be due to the calculation that a show of innocence is the best foundation for subsequent anger at the suggestion of guilt. Alternatively, it might reflect the hope that the report would not be entirely a black and white affair. Or it could simply be a device to gain some valuable time. But it will be much more usual for a state to do what it can to prevent an institution from taking a path which is all too likely to lead to a public reproof and a call for reform. This is not because a critical report is a necessary or even a likely preliminary to stronger action: it takes a lot to bring an international organization to the point of applying sanctions; and if it wishes to apply them it will not be in a mood to hold matters up because its representatives have not made an on the spot survey of the position. But the state which expects to be identified as the offender will nevertheless heartily dislike the prospect, particularly as such a judgment may appear to be all the more cogent by virtue of being based on an international investigation. It will face him with an additional element of uncertainty, make his international life more awkward and complicated, and sully his supposedly good name. If at all possible, therefore, it is something to be avoided.

The concomitant of this is that the state which expects to be shown in a favourable light will be very anxious to obtain a report which accuses its adversary of bad behaviour. Again, there will be exceptions to this general proposition. If there is any doubt regarding the outcome, a state may prefer to do without a probable benefit, for a report which gave less than full support might be worse than no report at all. Likewise it has to be borne in mind that it is always open to a presence to misbehave which, here, would mean that its version of events was quite different from that which had been expected by those responsible for its dispatch. Quite apart from these considerations, a state may think it beneath its dignity to allow an enquiry to be held on its soil, or to have international representatives sitting there waiting for trouble to arise. Or, even if it had no objections to this course, it may have an influential friend who is strongly opposed to the institution's involvement in the dispute. For any of these reasons, therefore, a reporting presence could be unwelcome even though the host is likely to benefit from its activities. But states are not in the habit of rejecting possible sources of support, and will therefore usually value an operation which should result in a UN declaration in their favour. For, by legitimizing its cause, it would not only bring the defensive state personal satisfaction but might also lead to it receiving additional assistance, a possibility which would be especially attractive if it was in a position of weakness, even though that circumstance would decrease the likelihood of it obtaining much help. It is not only drowning men who clutch at straws.

The third point concerns the attitude not of the parties but of the institution which is called upon to secure a report. There will, however, be a close connection between the two. For in coming to a decision the institution will be influenced not just by its estimate of whether the situation warrants such action, but also by the support which each of the parties can muster for their view of what should be done. The state whom the proposal is aimed is likely to be the key factor here, and with the help of its friends it may be able to discourage an accusatory move. For while the institution may be enjoined by its foundation document to prevent the contravention of certain stated principles, in executing this mandate its members will show a lively concern about the effect of collective decisions on their individual relations with other states. Politics, unlike law, is respectful of persons. If, therefore, a proposal for an enquiry arouses the displeasure of someone who is not, on other grounds, irretrievably hostile, those who favour such a move may develop second thoughts. They will be all the more likely to do so if the dissenting state is able to wield considerable influence. And should his friendship be particularly valued, or, more important, sought, the idea of a report will arouse grave misgivings. In short, an institution will take into consideration not only the charge that peace is being threatened or broken, but also the identity of those who promise to take offence should the situation be investigated.

Should a report nevertheless be made, notice must, finally, be taken of the fact that the state whom it accuses is most unlikely to fall meekly into line. States are certainly sensitive to criticism, but it does not follow that they will alter their policies just to accommodate world opinion, for they also tend to show a reasonable measure of resolution. Having begun a course of action, governments generally do not regard it as consonant with their dignity, or, perhaps, with their domestic stability, to abandon it on account of the say-so of an international body. Its demands may even increase a state's determination to stand firm, and in this it may well receive comfort and support from its friends. This draws attention once again to the importance of a dispute's diplomatic context. For, in the probable event of a state failing, of its own volition, to do what is required of it, the likelihood of it being induced to do so will depend on the policies of its fellow members of the international society, and on two factors in particular.

The first concerns the extent to which the badly-behaved state is acting in isolation. If an international report is to have a maximum effect, it is necessary that, at least for the purposes of the issue in question, the accused party should be largely dependent on its own devices. It may, and almost certainly will, have special links and associations with other states, but it should not be able to rely on outside assistance to influence the result of the dispute. For, if it knows that certain powerful friends will stand by it whatever decision is taken by the organized international community, it can afford to take little notice of those decisions. However, it is not enough for the criticized disputant to be relatively isolated, for that may mean no more than that, for all effective purposes, its quarrel is ignored by other states, either out of a lack of interest in the outcome or because of a desire to avoid the embarrassment which taking sides would involve.

If, therefore, a reporting presence is going to contribute towards checking an assertive or provocative policy, it is necessary, in the second place, that those who are opposed to what is going on, and, more particularly, the states who are able to speak persuasively to the aggressive disputant, should be prepared to go to some trouble to see that the international admonitions to which a report gives rise are respected. Here, therefore, as elsewhere, the efficacy of international action will largely turn on the attitude of the major Powers. If they are agreed on the desirability of preventing violent change and maintaining a peaceful international atmosphere, willing to put some effort behind their desires, and need to do so only in relation to smaller states, then it will be possible for international reports on troubled situations to have a prophylactic effect.

I

An early League of Nations case is a good example of this. In 1913 the European Powers had declared Albania to be an independent sovereign state, but her independence was far from secure. Parts of her territory were eyed covetously by Montenegro and Serbia to the north, and Greece to the south. Italy, too, had designs on the country, not least on account of the fact that the 50 mile wide entrance to the Adriatic could be controlled from the Albanian town of Valona, which possessed a fine harbour. The end of the World War I found troops from three foreign countries within Albania's 1913 boundaries (Yugoslavia having inherited both the Montenegrin and Serbian claims) and in 1919 the Supreme Allied Council entrusted the settlement of the country's frontiers to the Conference of Ambassadors. Italy withdrew her forces in 1920, but Greek and Yugoslav soldiers remained. This, however, did not prevent Albania's admission to the League in December 1920, and in the following year she appealed to the Council to settle the uncertainty regarding her borders and to rid her of foreign troops. In reply, Greece and Yugoslavia claimed that this was entirely a matter for the Conference of Ambassadors, and the Great Powers on the Council, being also members of the Conference of Ambassadors, supported this view. Accordingly, the Council did no more than urge the Conference to bring its task to an early conclusion.

Dissatisfied with this, and also with the failure of the Conference to make any evident progress, Albania took her grievance to the Assembly in September 1921. Here she found much sympathy for her plight and, although the Great Powers clearly wished to be left to themselves, the Assembly asked the Council to send a Commission of Enquiry to Albania, which it did. The Commission's task, in part, was to supervise the execution of the Ambassadors' decision once it was made. However, it was also asked to report on the disturbances which Albania was regularly reporting to the Assembly, the hope of most League members clearly being that the presence of an international body would not only expedite a decision but would also help to check the aggressive activities of foreign troops in Albania, particularly the Yugoslavs. Such an enquiry would certainly have focused and reinforced the League's concern about the situation, but it is unlikely that, of itself, it would have been able to have had a significant deterrent effect. However, before it arrived, the Conference of Ambassadors had at last, on 9 November, announced their decision, declaring Albania's frontiers to be those of 1913 apart from a few rectifications in favour of Yugoslavia. That Britain, for one, was now determined to put an end to fighting in the area was made plain by the fact that on the previous day her Prime Minister, Lloyd George, called for an immediate Council meeting and the application of economic sanctions against Yugoslavia if she continued to misbehave. Yugoslavia took the hint, and announced her acceptance of the Ambassadors' decision, as did Albania and Greece. The concomitant of Britain's warning was a Great Power agreement that Albania was to be regarded as within Italy's sphere of influence. Should Albania ever require help in order to preserve her territorial integrity, said the Powers, they would favour entrusting the task to Italy.

Had trouble continued in and around Albania, there is good reason for thinking that the League's Commission would have been able to play the prophylactic role for which it had hopefully been cast by the Assembly. For now, in the changed situation which accompanied the Ambassadors' decision, the Powers seemed to be willing as well as able to exert themselves in favour of the withdrawal of foreign elements from Albania. Under the new dispensation, only Italy was entitled to take the close interest in Albania's affairs which

Yugoslavia was then exhibiting. Thus the Yugoslavs were told to leave, and if, as was likely, Britain spoke for her fellows, the Powers were ready to make use of the League to implement their will. In that event, the reports of the Commission of Enquiry would have provided a basis for telling international pressure. But the prospect of this was enough to make it unnecessary. In consequence the Commission's supervisory functions became predominant. It observed the withdrawal of Yugoslav troops and Albania's reoccupation of the areas they had held, and also kept in touch with the Delimitation Commission which had been dispatched by the Conference of Ambassadors to mark out Albania's frontiers. However, the Commission did engage in what could be spoken of as long-term prophylactic measures. For it had been asked by the Council to recommend measures to prevent the recurrence of disturbances, and under this part of its mandate it played a valuable part in helping Albania to establish herself as a viable member of the international society, so hoping to make outside interference in her affairs less likely. It concluded its activities in April 1923, having provided an early instance of the opportunities open to international institutions to assist in nation building. But this could not alter the geopolitical realities of the situation, and in 1939 Albania was annexed by Italy.

This case helps to show why the League did not make more use of fact-finding as a deterrent measure. The decision to send a Commission of Enquiry to Albania was, in effect, an attempt by the smaller states to do just that, and reflected their dissatisfaction with the apparent lack of concern on the part of the major Powers. But once these influential states became anxious to maintain Albania's integrity, prophylaxis became irrelevant, for now it was possible to put an end to the existing threats to the country's independence, so settling and not merely quietening the dispute. Likewise in most of the other issues which arose at this period, the Great Powers presented a united front, with the result that when, as frequently happened, international enquiries were held, they were not confined to reporting on the facts of the situation, but were to investigate it with a view to the production of a suitable formula for its final settlement.[1] Prophylactic fact-finding is thus in the nature of a second best measure, a device which is utilized when there is little likelihood of an investigation providing a basis for the settlement of a dispute, but where at least one party is willing or anxious to permit a more limited international operation. The inability of an institution such as the League or UN to play a more positive role in these circumstances may reflect the intractable character of the dispute. It may also,

[1] See above, pp. 16-17.

however be indicative of divided councils within the institution itself
as to the merits of the dispute and the desirable course of action. A
division of opinion between the senior members of the Organization
is likely to have the most far-reaching consequences in this respect
and, *a fortiori*, the opportunities which are open to an institution
when one of these states is itself involved in a dispute are severely
curtailed.

This was vividly illustrated ten years later in the Manchurian
crisis. Since the end of the nineteenth century Japan had shown a
close interest in this large Chinese province, which was of considerable strategic importance to her, forming a possible wedge between
China and Russia. It had also become valuable on economic grounds,
constituting a secure market and a source of some essential raw
materials. Much Japanese capital had been invested there, and the
conjunction of her economic and strategic interests was exemplified
in her leasehold ownership of the South Manchurian Railway and
her right to maintain 15,000 troops within the Railway Zone. It
was therefore to be expected that she would be keenly concerned regarding the maintenance of order in Manchuria and that she might
be tempted to make up for some of the local deficiencies in this respect, or make her presence even more forcibly felt. Only as recently
as 1928, at the end of the Chinese Civil War, Japan had opposed the
reincorporation of Manchuria in China, but had not pressed her
objections in view of Britain's support for the move. However, this
did nothing to improve relations between Japan and the Manchurian
authorities, and there were many opportunities for friction, the situation not being improved by the presence of Japanese consular police
as well as her railway guards. Numerous incidents took place, and on
18 September 1931 one occurred at Mukden which had far-reaching
consequences.

It was alleged by the Japanese Army command in Manchuria that
some of its soldiers who were on manœuvres had been fired upon by
a group who were blowing up a section of the South Manchurian
Railway. The army's response was to occupy Mukden overnight and
two other Manchurian towns, one of which lay some 65 miles beyond
the Railway Zone, within the next few days. China immediately
brought the situation to the notice of the League Council under
Article 11, and there the statements of the Japanese representative
suggested that his Government intended to limit the scope of the
operation and make an early withdrawal to the Zone. It was far
from clear at Geneva, however, as to what exactly was happening
in Manchuria and it was therefore expected that the Council would
call for an early report from a group made up of diplomats already
in the Far East. But no such action was taken, for it was opposed by

Japan and also by the United States who, although not a member of the League, was closely interested in the area and whose views therefore needed to be taken into account. Shortly afterwards the Council, Japan dissenting, invited the United States to appoint a representative to attend its meetings, and as a result her Consul at Geneva did so for a short while. But his instructions required him to act only as an observer save in any discussions which concerned the Briand-Kellogg Pact, and in fact he played no substantive part in the Council's deliberations. Meanwhile, the situation in Manchuria was worsening as Japan, contrary to the assurances of her representative at Geneva, steadily widened her control over the province. This led to a resolution coming before the Council on 24 October calling on her to withdraw immediately. However, Japan, taking advantage of the understanding which now governed the voting procedure under Article 11, prevented its passage by casting a negative vote.

In order to avoid the Japanese veto it was necessary to hold proceedings under Article 15 of the Covenant. This Article required the Council, if it failed to effect an agreed settlement, to publish its recommendations regarding the dispute, and in its decision the votes of the parties were to be ignored. It also laid on League members an obligation not to go to war with the party complying with the Council's recommendations, and from there it was but a short step to enforcement action. For Article 16 provided that any member resorting to war in disregard of its obligations under the previous Article should be deemed to have committed an act of war against all other members of the League, who were thereby committed to the imposition of economic and diplomatic sanctions, and might find themselves faced with the question of whether force should be used to persuade the erring state to behave in accordance with her undertakings.

The burden of such action in respect of Japan would have fallen on the other major League Powers, Britain and France in particular, and neither of them were at all disposed to make a move which would take them any way towards a confrontation with Japan. For some time, in common with other members, they were reluctant to question her protestations of good faith, and although, by early November, it was becoming all too clear that, whatever the part of the Japanese Government in the matter, Manchuria was being systematically overrun, the League was still unwilling to act in accordance with its own precepts. On the one hand there was some sympathy for Japan on account of the hazards to which her interests had been exposed: she was, after all, engaged upon an action which would have been unremarkable in pre-1919 terms. And on the other hand there were some telling considerations which told against sanctions. For the economic troubles then affecting western Europe had put Britain and France in no mood to make further problems for themselves in that field, and Manchuria's geographical remoteness not only failed to give the issue the urgency which might have attended aggression nearer home, but also put substantial difficulties in the way of physical action against Japan. This lack of zeal was not counterbalanced by keenness in other quarters. China herself was most reluctant to resort to Article 15 for fear of Japan's reaction. And the two great absentees from the League, the Soviet Union and the United States, both of whose interests were closely involved in the situation, were neither of them spoiling for a head-on collision with Japan.

When, therefore, the Council reconvened in the middle of November there was much uncertainty as to its next step. However, the Japanese representative came forward with the proposal that the whole situation should be investigated by a League commission of enquiry and this suggestion, which was strongly endorsed by the United States, was accepted. It took three further weeks to negotiate the Commission's terms of reference, as Japan was in no hurry to complete the task, and on 10 December the Council formally established a Commission to study and report on all circumstances of an international character which threatened peace and good relations between China and Japan. It was not explicitly asked or empowered to make recommendations, but clearly its report would provide a possible basis for a settlement of the Manchurian dispute. It thus appeared to be another instance of the League moving towards the ending of a quarrel through the conduct of an international investigation into the facts of the case.

However, in this particular situation it would be incorrect to view the League's Commission, which, after the name of its chairman, became known as the Lytton Commission, in this light. It was reasonably clear, at the time when it was established, that the only kind of settlement which Japan would accept was the one which the League would be quite unable to countenance: the *de facto* annexation of Manchuria. There was virtually no hope, therefore, of the Commission introducing a conciliatory element into the situation, so resulting in an agreement which would be freely acceptable on all sides. Nor could there be any expectation that an impartial report would lead to sufficient diplomatic pressure being put behind the League's proposals as to induce Japan to settle on its terms. Neither the League Powers nor Japan were in a mood for that. In consequence the Lytton Commission cannot be regarded as a patching-up presence. The League's Council may have had some hopes that it might play such a role, but those hopes must have been extremely slender. Indeed, in some quarters there was very probably a private tendency to view the Commission chiefly as a device to gain time, giving the appearance of League activity while avoiding the necessity for a show down.

To the extent to which it was regarded as having a real part to play, the Lytton Commission was doubtless thought of as a possible means of exerting a moderating influence on Japan. It was not intended that it should provide a justification for the exertion of considerable pressure towards that end: the members were not prepared to go that far. Instead, the Commission was valued for its ability to mobilize international opinion. Whatever may have been thought about the inefficiencies of the Manchurian administration, and the difficulties this posed for Japan, there was widespread sympathy for China and criticism of Japan, especially among smaller states and interested publics. Japan was seen as acting in blatant disregard of her obligations under the Covenant, not to mention the Washington Treaty of 1922 and the Briand-Kellogg Pact of 1928. Less technically, she was simply viewed as a bully, taking advantage of the weakness of a neighbour to behave aggressively. There was therefore a general feeling that something should be done in support of China, but this met the unwillingness of those who counted most to do anything substantial. A reporting presence was therefore an excellent scheme, representing the least the League could do and the most that it would do. It could be conducted in the hope that a searching enquiry might cause Japan to curb her activities in Manchuria in order to avoid being portrayed in an unfavourable light and appease international opinion. Fact-finding might have a prophylactic effect.

Even this, however, was a very optimistic appraisal of the situation, as the members of the Council must have been aware at the time. And so it proved. The Commission was constituted in January 1932, its five members being selected by the President of the Council and approved by the parties. They were to act not as representatives of their governments but in their individual capacities. Early in February they left for the Far East, but not by the quickest, overland route. Instead they travelled via the United States and the Pacific, arriving in Tokyo at the end of the month and subsequently proceeding to Manchuria through other parts of China. By the time they got there the province had been formally detached from China and declared to be the new independent state of Manchukuo. Few were taken in by this, and in its authoritative report which was published in October 1932 the Lytton Commission declared Manchukuo to be Japan's puppet. The Report substantially vindicated China's claim that she had been unjustifiably attacked, but said that a solution should be found which satisfied the interests of both China and Japan. It set out ten principles which it thought could form the basis of a satisfactory arrangement, their essence being that Manchuria, while remaining a part of China, should have an autonomous and stable government, able to maintain order on its own.

At the end of the previous January China, evidently having decided that things could not get much worse, had asked the League to consider her dispute with Japan under Article 15 of the Covenant. She also exercized her right to have the question dealt with by the Assembly rather than the Council, presumably calculating that her case would be more likely to be viewed sympathetically by the membership as a whole than by a body which was heavily weighted in favour of the major Powers. Thus the Lytton Commission's Report was considered by the Assembly, first in a general debate and then by a special committee. An agreed settlement being beyond reach, the committee submitted a statement to the Assembly asserting that Manchuria was under the sovereignty of China and that the members of the League would not recognize Manchukuo. On 24 February 1933, with Japan in sole opposition and Siam in a lonely abstention, the statement was adopted. The Japanese delegation thereupon walked out of the Assembly, and in the following month Japan gave notice of her intention to withdraw from the League. Manchuria remained in her hands until she was defeated in World War II.

Thus the Manchurian case provided a notable example of the failure of a reporting presence to have any deterrent effect whatsoever. In this connection both the League and the Lytton Commission have been criticized for moving at a relatively leisurely pace, the argument being that if the League's opinion was to have any impact it was necessary for it to be brought to bear before Japan fastened her hold on Manchuria. But there is little ground for the view that the outcome would have been materially different had the League acted with greater dispatch. Even a speedier enquiry accompanied by a preparedness to take a tough line in support of its recommendations would probably not have caused Japan to change her course. Certainly a quicker investigation on its own would hardly have affected the issue. This is not to say that Japan cared nothing for the League's disapproval: her delaying tactics were evidence of her desire to postpone a League decision for as long as possible, and the earlier it came the more embarrassing it was likely to be. But however early her condemnation, it is hardly conceivable that it would have resulted in a change of policy. The Army was largely in control in Manchuria and was gaining the upper hand in Japan, and received much popular support for its forward policy.

Clearly Japan was set upon gaining complete domination over Manchuria and was not going to be deflected by the reproof of the League.

In these circumstances, an international enquiry into the facts of the case could neither produce a settlement nor prevent the situation from worsening. Their realization of this may help to account for the Council members' lack of zeal in pursuing Japan. It also, however, reflected their attitude towards her, quite apart from the difficulty of doing anything effective about her misbehaviour. Until this affair she had been a loyal and respected member of the League. The other major members had no quarrel with her on general grounds, and even a Japanese annexation of Manchuria would not present a significant threat to their interests. It could even be seen as of value to them by placing a friendly country in a favourable position *vis-à-vis* the possibly hostile Soviet Union. Thus the League Powers could not easily think the worst of Japan and were not at all inclined to treat her as a criminal in the dock; their natural reaction was to proceed in a way which gave her the least offence. This could be rationalized as the approach which would be most likely to induce a moderate response, so permitting, maybe, a solution which would be compatible with the doctrine of the League and would not seriously or permanently jeopardize their relations with Japan. But to walk cautiously and hope for the best was not a suitable formula in this case. A compromise is always particularly difficult to arrange over disputed territory, and in any event Japan would not countenance one. Thus, having set the League machinery in motion, it eventually produced the almost inevitable result of a breach with Japan, and the fact that it came later rather than sooner made no difference so far as the fate of Manchuria was concerned.

The League's response to this affair provides support for the argument that its approach to the question of peace and war was unrelated to the realities of international politics. The scheme of the Covenant called for resistance to anti-social behaviour as such, irrespective of the identity of the wrongdoers or the effects of their wrongdoing, and in the case of Manchuria the Powers clearly showed that they were unwilling to act on this basis. It may have been a particularly difficult problem arising at a particularly difficult time but, on the ground that the strength of an arrangement is properly tested only when it is put under strain, it could be said that the fragility of the League system had been comprehensively exposed. Japan was undoubtedly engaged upon an enterprise which was contrary to her obligations, and an obligation lay on her fellow League members to try to stop her. But nothing effective was done. It could, however, be argued that, from the post-1945 as well as the pre-1914 perspective, what is largely significant about the Manchurian case is not that the League moved ineffectively but that it moved at all. For the League Powers would have found it much more satisfactory to have ignored the whole affair, or to have arranged matters so that the Commission of Enquiry produced an equivocal report. However, reluctantly and hesitantly, they proceeded on a course which gave fair promise of making some trouble for themselves. They may have done so in a muddled or optimistic way, and under some pressure from their fellow members and their publics. But it could be said in their favour that at least they were not prepared to act in total disregard of their obligations, or to interpret them dishonestly. International relations had not been altered in a fundamental way by the League system, but, for better or worse, they were not entirely unchanged.

This was shown, albeit somewhat belatedly, in 1935, when Italy attacked Ethiopia. She had eyed it covetously since the latter part of the nineteenth century, and during 1935 it became increasingly apparent that she was determined to expand at Ethiopia's expense. This threatened the most important members of the League with even greater embarrassments than those which had arisen over Manchuria. For the question of sanctions would be less easy for Britain and France to avoid, and, if applied, would ruin the friendship with Italy which, worried about Germany's European ambitions, they were intent on cultivating. They therefore formally averted their eyes.

This was the situation when, in June 1935, Ethiopia asked the Council to send observers to report on Italy's allegations that her colonies were being threatened by Ethiopia. An undertaking was given that the authorities would co-operate fully with the League's representatives, and Ethiopia also offered to meet all their expenses. But no member of the Council thought fit to do so much as mention the proposal. Designed, on the face of it, to clear up a disputed matter of fact, it was obviously intended to have some deterrent effect, Ethiopia's hope probably being that an overt attack would not take place while the observers were in her border areas, and that their favourable report might bring her a little support and take some of the wind out of Italy's sails. But this meant that Italy would regard the move as an unfriendly act, and so nothing was done. Even when, early in September, Italy presented the Council with a long memorandum setting out the justification for her claim that she was forced to treat Ethiopia as a barbarous enemy, the members were still not prepared to burn their boats, and did no more than appoint a committee to seek a peaceful settlement.

Within a fortnight the committee had proposed that Ethiopia should be given top-level administrative assistance in order to reform and reorganize her public services. Each branch of the service would be headed by a principal adviser appointed by the Council with the Emperor of Ethiopia's approval, and these advisers were to form a commission which would report from time to time to the Council and the Emperor. At the end of five years the plan was to be reviewed. In form it was to make no difference to Ethiopia's international status, but it looked as if what was being proposed would amount, in practice, to not very much short of international government.

Even in the more paternalistic atmosphere of the 1930s, the prospect of being virtually administered by an international body must have had very little appeal for Ethiopia. But her situation was desperate, and she therefore agreed to accept the scheme as a basis for negotiations. Italy, however, rejected it: it may have met her complaints against Ethiopia, but it would have gone no way at all towards supplying her with the public triumph which she sought. Ethiopia therefore once again requested that observers be sent to report on any incident which might arise, and, at the same time, to emphasize her pacific intentions, announced that her troops were being withdrawn 30 kilometres from the frontier. The Council now agreed to consider her request, and worked out a plan for an air patrol, but before any decision could be taken Italy had, on 3 October, begun her invasion.

The League now moved speedily. The Council condemned Italy and the 50 out of the Assembly's 54 members who did likewise set up a committee for the purpose of arranging co-ordinated pressure against her. This was a significant step, for most of those concerned did not see Italy's designs on Ethiopia as a direct or even an indirect threat to their own security or well-being, and for some there were marked disadvantages in picking a quarrel with Italy. It can therefore be said that the League's attempts to do something about Italy's aggressive and unlawful behaviour was motivated less by immediate self-interest than by principle alone, which is generally accounted a virtue. However, this also explains why the economic and diplomatic sanctions which, in the circumstances, were mandatory upon those who had condemned Italy, were applied haltingly and half-heartedly. Italy was not seriously inconvenienced by them, and by May 1936 she was in a position to proclaim the annexation of Ethiopia.[2]

---

[2] On Ethiopia and also Manchuria see further, Walters, *op. cit.*, Gathorne-Hardy, *op. cit.*, and Alfred Zimmern, *The League of Nations and the Rule of Law 1918–1935* (London: Macmillan, 2nd edn. 1939).

II

In both the Manchurian and Ethiopian cases, therefore, the League, while greatly influenced by the identity of the wrongdoer, was not guilty of turning a totally or permanently blind eye towards wrongdoing. Its refusal to do so was undoubtedly facilitated by, although it was not just a reflection of, the fact that at this period the international society was without any deep or relatively permanent divisions. The major Powers did not, on the whole, feel gravely threatened, and there was some fluidity in their relations. In consequence, when one of them misbehaved, there was no automatic move on the part of the others either to give the offender support or to capitalize upon his delinquency. The lines of political allegiance were not that tightly drawn. Since 1945, however, the situation has been very different. The two super-powers have entertained the most serious suspicions of each other, and have gathered camp followers around them. On this East–West division another, that between North and South, has been superimposed, making itself most controversially felt in the colonial and racial fields. Together, they have had some very important effects on the use of reporting presences.

In the first place, decisions regarding their establishment have turned overwhelmingly on the identity of the states involved, little attention being given to the action complained of, everything to the actors. For, generally speaking, states have felt an overriding concern, on the grounds of both duty and interest, to sustain their friends and discomfort their enemies. If, therefore, a friend proposes that a tense situation should be the subject of a report, this has been taken as a sure sign that one's own associates will be exonerated and one's rivals embarrassed; it is therefore something to be supported. But if a member of the other camp is pressing for an enquiry, this has immediately suggested that the move will have the opposite effect; accordingly, steps must be taken to prevent it. Thus, the very real tension which the members of the League felt between their obligation to try to prevent certain sorts of behaviour, and their desire not to make trouble for themselves has largely been removed. Instead, whenever a call has been made for the investigation of allegedly aggressive or troublesome behaviour, the clear-cut ideological divisions of the post-war period have offered a simple guide to the appropriate response, along the lines of 'my side right or wrong'. This has required a readiness to overlook or even defend the misdemeanours of one's friends, which some have found easier than others. But reservations on this score have to a considerable extent been allayed by the consideration that action which has an adverse effect on the common enemy can hardly be condemned, or even, perhaps, regarded as a bad thing. Contentious issues have not, of course, been discussed in these terms, but this is the way in which they have usually been approached.

Secondly, the composition of reporting presences is of much greater importance than formerly. In the inter-war period the procedure was to nominate one person of high standing from each of a number of Powers. The members of the Lytton Commission, for example, were drawn from Britain, France, Italy, Germany, and the United States. This was thought to provide a guarantee of both the impartiality and the accuracy of its report: there might be some differences among its members, but it was assumed that such a group would have no great difficulty in identifying the true facts of the case. Putting it differently, it was thought, and there was then no reason to doubt it, that men of integrity would all see more or less the same thing. But for them to do so it was necessary that they should have a common understanding of what it is they are about and hold a broadly similar value-system, thus enabling them to put the same interpretation on a particular phenomenon.

Between the two World Wars these conditions were largely met, but, on account of political and ideological developments, they have not obtained since 1945, although in respect of some matters they are perhaps closer now than they have been for the past twenty years. Thus a UN presence representing the whole spectrum of its members would be made up of persons of different sympathies and outlooks, with the result that they might well disagree as to the nature of the situation which they were sent to examine. Guerrilla warfare, for example, might be seen as a sign of indirect aggression by one member, of straightforward disorder by another, and of governmental oppression by a third. And it could be that one or more of those three observers went already knowing what it was he would find, perhaps in the sincere belief that the situation was of a certain kind, perhaps in a conscious attempt to bring aid and comfort to one of the disputants or to deny it to the other. In these circumstances, those who favour a report being made will need to secure not just a decision to that effect but also a mission which is composed in such a way as to promise the right result. Hence they will try to exclude nationals of states which are hostile to the promoters' purposes, or at least to keep them in a minority. It may be expected that they will try to do this even if the members of the reporting team are not acting as the representatives of their governments but in their individual capacities, for such persons will nevertheless be suspected of sharing their governments' views on the merits of the case, perhaps entirely of their own volition, perhaps not.

To pay such close attention to the make-up of a reporting presence has, on the face of it, the serious disadvantage of inviting a vigorous challenge to its findings by the state who is found wanting. It could argue that the membership of the group was rigged in the first place, making the tenor of its report a foregone conclusion. A critical statement was commissioned, has been produced, and should receive the contempt which such a partisan document deserves. The state concerned would no doubt propose to set an example itself in this respect. But this is merely to put a convenient dress on what would in any event be its reaction, and in itself is unlikely to detract from the utility of the procedure. For, even under favourable conditions, the effectiveness of international reports does not depend on the response of the criticized state but on that of third parties, on their willingness to act in accordance with what has been found. In an ideologically divided society, however, those who have any intention of involving themselves in a dispute may already be firmly entrenched behind one or other of the parties. They will not change their loyalties or be moved to action which they would not otherwise have taken by virtue of the publication, under an international *imprimatur*, of a new account of the case. Thus the third consequence of post-1945 developments on this kind of activity is that there has been little real expectation of it having an immediate influence or bearing on the situation. One side will look forward to justification and the other will prepare to meet its critics, but both will in all probability carry on exactly as before.

As an immediate prophylactic measure, therefore, fact finding enquiries have become largely irrelevant. In the longer term, however, they may serve this end through their usefulness as a means of influencing opinion, both unofficial and official. Undoubtedly the state at whom the procedure is aimed will try to obstruct it by alleging that the report on which it is based is inaccurate or inadequate. But it is perhaps unlikely that these endeavours will be very successful. It may indeed be the case that the reporters found what they were expected to find, but it does not follow, nor will it universally be taken to follow, that in doing so they have misrepresented the facts. Many, besides the favoured party, are likely to prefer the opinion that it was desirable to exclude or limit the influence of those who could be relied upon to take a perverse view of events. It is therefore probable that a UN report will be widely regarded as presenting a fair picture, and, as such, while not having any immediately obvious effect, may in several ways, work to the detriment of the state whom it takes to task.

The least likely, but still possible, consequence of a critical report is that it may give rise to some questioning and doubts among the public of the state concerned, should they have the opportunity to consider it, that is. Then, too, it may perhaps have a similar effect, at both the popular and governmental levels, on his associates and friends. They are most unlikely to fall away from the party line on the issue in question, but the report could have a bearing on their general attitude towards the criticized state, a point which is likely to have rather greater validity so far as the uncommitted states are concerned. The members of the rival camp will undoubtedly do what they can to encourage such reappraisals, and towards this end will make full use of the propaganda potentiality of the report itself. But from their point of view, it might be most valuable on their own home fronts. Here it will surely boost the morale of the state on the defensive, for states, no less than people, like to think that they are in the right and like others to think so too, preferably in public. International recognition of the propriety of a state's cause may therefore significantly encourage its resistance. It may also, by providing an international and domestic justification for less than wholly popular action, make it easier for the friends of the defensive party to continue their support, and may conceivably allow them to increase it.

Thus although, since 1945, reporting presences have marshalled world opinion in vain, if one is looking for immediate prophylactic results, they have by no means fallen out of fashion. For their propaganda value is high in struggles which, after all, are to a significant extent conducted by this means. The powerful, in many contexts are too powerful to wage war, and the weak are too weak. Hence both groups have seized upon the possibility of using UN reports as a means of furthering their policies. No longer is it generally the case that an investigation is favoured as the course which is least likely to give offence to the misbehaving state, or perhaps for fear of causing any offence at all. Rather, the device is often turned to in order to give the maximum possible offence which circumstances permit. Thus those who sympathize with a state on the defensive, provided they are also hostile to the aggressive or provocative state and not too much in awe of him, may well try to secure an international catalogue of the wrongs which are being done to their friend. Contrariwise, the troublesome state, and those who have no wish to see his activities given additional and apparently convincing advertisement, will do their best to obstruct such a move. In consequence the question of whether a report should be sought has itself become a matter of acute controversy, and an ability to manipulate the UN's procedures in order to secure the desired result has become an important political weapon.

III

The cold war provides a number of examples of this. Here the West has generally been on the defensive, and has also found that the sympathies of the new, uncommitted states have often inclined in the Soviet direction rather than its own. Accordingly, it has been particularly anxious that the world should be in as little doubt as possible regarding the nature of the conflict, and one of the ways in which it has tried to ensure this has been to urge the international investigation of some of the disputes in which it has been involved. In this manner it has hoped to discredit the Soviet Union by establishing the iniquity of her behaviour or the baselessness of her charges. The Soviet Union, however, not wishing to suffer the embarrassment of an adverse report, has tried to obstruct such moves, and has frequently been successful. However, this has not been entirely satisfactory from her point of view for it has clearly suggested that she has something to hide. By the same token, even when it has failed on the main issue, such episodes have not been all loss for the West.

An instance of this occurred during the Korean war, when, in August 1950, Communist China complained that her side of the Yalu river had been attacked by American aircraft. In the following month the matter came before the Security Council, where the Soviet Union would have had the United States condemned. However, she not only failed to win any support for her proposal but also met an awkward American riposte. The United States allowed that one of her aircraft might have mistakenly strafed a Chinese air-strip, and suggested that the matter should be investigated on the spot, by a two man commission, one member being appointed by India and the other by Sweden. She also stated that she was willing to leave the question of damages to the commission. To this proposal the Soviet Union found it desirable to advance a wide variety of objections. Not unreasonably she suggested that the matter should first be discussed with a representative of Communist China. Less convincingly, she argued that in view of America's admission of guilt an enquiry was unnecessary. However, although the facts were clear, they evidently required detailed consideration by the Council, for the proposed commission was declared to be an attempt to prevent the Council from giving the matter the degree of attention which it demanded. It was also alleged that the United States was pursuing hidden and hostile objectives regarding China, and would use the commission's secretariat for espionage purposes. For all these reasons the Soviet Union felt obliged to vote against the American proposal, and by so doing prevented its adoption. This was something to which the

United States did not fail to draw attention when, in February 1951, the Soviet Union tried, with an equal lack of success, to persuade the General Assembly to censure the United States for her misdeeds in relation to China.

At a later stage of the Korean war the United States did its best to capitalize even further on some much publicized but rather improbable Communist charges. It had been alleged that the UN forces in Korea were engaging in bacterial warfare, and in reply the American-dominated UN Command had asked the International Committee of the Red Cross to investigate the matter. The Committee was willing to do so provided that the parties were agreeable, and in July 1952 the United States requested the Security Council to call upon all concerned to co-operate. This proposal was vetoed by the Soviet Union, as was a second which would have had the Council take note of the Soviet action and conclude that the charges must be false. In justification the Soviet Union complained about the Council's refusal to invite China and North Korea to its meetings, and alleged, firstly, that the International Committee of the Red Cross was an American tool, and, secondly, that the American initiative was an attempt to divert public attention from the question. Determined to clear her name and also to make the most of the Soviet predicament the United States took the matter to the General Assembly where, in April 1953, it was decided, in face of Soviet opposition, to establish a commission of five states to investigate the charges if the Assembly's President received assurances of co-operation from all concerned. Nothing came of this on account of the failure of North Korea and Communist China to reply to the UN's communications, and so the United States did the next best thing by transmitting to the UN the repudiation by certain of her officers of the confessions which they had made regarding bacterial warfare when prisoners of war. The Soviet Union tried to counteract this by raising, not for the first time, the fact that the United States was not a party to the Geneva Protocol of 1925 prohibiting the use of bacterial weapons. But she was out-manœuvred by the Assembly's decision to refer the Soviet draft resolution to the Disarmament Commission.

With the signing of an armistice in Korea on 27 July 1953, Indo-China became the principal Far Eastern scene of East–West conflict. Ever since her return at the end of World War II, the sovereign power, France, had not been able to re-establish full authority over the area, largely on account of the activities of the Communist-led nationalist movement, the Viet Minh. This organization was at its strongest in Vietnam, but it was also influential in the other two Indo-Chinese states, Cambodia and Laos, where there were separate insurgencies. During the 1950s the struggle in Indo-China increasingly assumed cold war overtones, largely on account of the rising American concern at the possibility of a nationalist and therefore a Communist victory, which led her to give very considerable diplomatic and financial support to the French campaign. But, at the end of March 1954, it was suddenly realized that, on its own, this was going to be insufficient. France had opted for a major battle with the Viet Minh at Dien Bien Phu, but instead of a decisive victory found herself faced with defeat. For a short while there seemed to be a real likelihood of armed American intervention. But this idea was rejected and, at the end of April, as previously arranged, the Foreign Ministers Conference on Indo-China and Korea opened at Geneva. The discussions on Indo-China were subject to an initial delay, and when they were begun, on 8 May, it was the very day following the announcement of the fall of Dien Bien Phu. This was a tremendous strategic and psychological blow for France, and underlined the point that this was one situation where the West would not be negotiating from strength.

This was the position when an attempt was made at the UN to send a group of observers to Thailand, a country which was markedly sympathetic towards the West and a prospective member of the South East Asian security organization which the United States was now hastily trying to erect. Thailand shared a long border with Laos and Cambodia, and she complained to the Security Council that the activities of the Viet Minh in those countries threatened to spill over into her territory. She also referred to false charges being made against the Thai government and said that there had been some attempt to subvert it. She therefore asked that a sub-commission of the Peace Observation Commission be sent to report on the situation.[3]

From the point of view of the Western members of the Council, this proposal could do no harm and, by holding out the possibility of a report critical of the Viet Minh, might do some good. They therefore agreed that the situation described by Thailand warranted the UN's concern, and that an observation mission would enable the Organization to decide what further measures were called for. The Soviet Union, however, took strong exception to the idea. She claimed that it was an America attempt to deepen the conflict in Indo-China and prepare the way for Western intervention under

[3] The Peace Observation Commission had been established by the Assembly's 'Uniting for Peace' resolutions of 3 November 1950. It was made up of the representatives of 14 states, including the five permanent members of the Security Council, and was intended to facilitate the obtaining of reports on situations which appeared to endanger international peace and security. The Commission acts by majority vote on the basis of requests from the General Assembly or the Security Council.

the UN flag, as in Korea, and nullified the positive votes of nine members of the Council by exercising her veto. This was on 18 June. Almost three weeks later, Thailand, hardly behaving like a seriously threatened state, let it be known that she was proposing to find out whether a majority of General Assembly members would agree to that body being reconvened to consider her request. Soon afterwards, however, on 21 July, the Geneva Conference reached agreement on Indo-China which, at least on paper, removed the grounds of Thailand's apprehension, and, indeed, was more favourable to Western interests than might have been expected. Viet Minh troops were to be withdrawn from Laos and Cambodia, and plans were made for the reintegration of the indigenous rebels with their national communities. In the atmosphere of *détente* which was thus engendered, Thailand informed the Secretary-General that she was not pressing for a resumed session of the Assembly, and at its next regular meeting, which opened in September, the matter was not raised.

The Geneva Agreements settled the immediate crisis. But they proved to be very far from having settled the problem which restemmed from the French decline and fall in Indo-China. An instance of this was the failure of the attempt to bring the Laotian insurgents into their state's political and military life. Meanwhile, the government moved to the right, and by about the middle of 1959 had lost much of its already tenuous control of the north-east of the country and also the area along the border with Vietnam. It alleged that the rebels had been armed and equipped by North Vietnam, and in August informed the UN Secretary-General of its appreciation of the situation. Additional aid was being received from the United States to deal with the problem, but suddenly, on 4 September, Laos sought assistance from the UN requesting the early dispatch of an emergency force to halt North Vietnamese aggression. The Secretary-General asked the President of the Security Council to convene the Council as a matter of urgency, and it met on 7 September.

The Laotian request did not please the Western members of the Security Council. For, in the first place, if they gave it their support, it was far from clear that the UN would take the required action. There was clearly no hope of the Security Council agreeing to it, for the Soviet Union could be relied upon to veto what was undisguisedly an anti-Communist move. The matter would therefore need to go to the Assembly, and here, too, there could well be obstacles. The difficult nature of the terrain in Laos and the fact that the country possessed only primitive communications were hardly encouraging factors. Further, the political situation there seemed to be neither entirely clear-cut, nor particularly serious, and therefore might not be thought to justify the trouble and expense of establishing a force. Even if the necessary majority of members were prepared to accept the Laotian Government's version of events, this did not mean that they would wish to come to its assistance. It was quite possible that a good number would hesitate, either because their political sympathies did not cause them to look with favour on right-wing regimes, or because of the widespread view that it was highly expedient for a UN force to avoid getting involved in anything that looked like a cold war conflict. In this particular case, the fact that two of Laos' six neighbours, North Vietnam and China, were Communist, could only have underlined the applicability of the general consideration. There were, therefore, ample grounds for thinking that the UN might not agree to the Laotian proposal, and this must have suggested to the Western states that they would do well to react cautiously to it, so as to avoid committing themselves to an unsuccessful course. For that would not only be a blow to their prestige but might also, subsequently, put them in the invidious position of having to do on their own something which the UN had already considered and rejected.

Secondly, however, they themselves were not in favour of the Laotian request. They certainly wished to see the rebels defeated but, for rather different reasons, did not think that this necessitated a UN force. Britain seemed rather sceptical about the gravity of the situation, and was thought to have been toying with the idea of a UN fact-finding mission, which would have been amply justified by the obscurity with which the supposed crisis was surrounded. The United States, however, saw the situation very much in cold war terms. She therefore took a very much less relaxed view than Britain and, in general, the Western camp was willing to take its cue from her. She wanted to support and strengthen the right-wing regime which had emerged in Laos, and was not willing to take any chances regarding its survival. Hence, on the one hand, she was most reluctant to see the UN wielding much influence in Laos, for fear that it might not be used towards the desired goal or with an appropriate degree of zeal. And this consideration was all the more important in view of the fluid nature of Laotian politics, for a change in its regime might lead to a UN force being used, with the co-operation of the General Assembly, for purposes quite other than those which were originally intended. On the other hand, the United States was anxious to ensure that such help as the Government of Laos needed was received from states or bodies who were fully in sympathy with its aims. In other words, the United States wanted to keep the field to herself. This would both leave her free to step up the level of her non-military assistance and keep the way clear for her troops. As of September 1959 the situation was not thought sufficiently serious to warrant a deeper American involvement, but it was quite conceivable that at some later point it might become so. In that case the presence of a UN force would be a considerable embarrassment. If one was not sent, all the options would be kept open.

Thus the Western attitude to the question of Laos was significantly influenced by its concern not to have its cold war policies impeded by the UN. But, equally, its cold-war role meant that it could not allow the UN to ignore, or easily cast aside, a request for help from a Government which professed to be the object of Communist aggression. To do that would both damage its prestige and invite the transfer of the request from the UN to one or more of its own number. The West therefore came up with the suggestion that the situation should be investigated. Hitherto the United States had regarded that idea as more of a hindrance than a help, but now that Laos herself, no doubt most unwisely in the American view, had brought the UN into the picture, a fact-finding mission seemed to be the least undesirable course. It would give the appearance of action and hold out the promise of some useful propaganda material, but would neither stand in the way of continued American assistance nor carry any commitment as to the UN's future action. If stronger moves proved necessary, the idea of a UN force could probably be put on one side on the ground of Soviet obstruction, and Western action could be justified in the light of the UN's report. Thus honour would be satisfied and nothing lost. Possibly something might even be gained.

Britain, France, and the United States therefore proposed that the Council should appoint a subcommittee of Argentina, Italy, Japan, and Tunisia 'to examine the statements made before the Security Council concerning Laos, to receive further statements and documents, and to conduct such enquiries as it might determine necessary and to report to the Council as soon as possible'.[4] In support of this move Britain spoke of the gravity of the despatch of a UN force to a troubled area, and of the necessity for the facts to be fully known before such a decision was taken. The United States did not appear to share Britain's inadequate information, for she roundly declared that aggression had clearly been committed and that it was the Council's duty to take action. However, while her representative's tone implied that large and important measures were required, he went on to explain that what was suggested was a mere matter of procedure, no more than the establishment by the Council of a subsidiary organ to assist its deliberations. Accordingly, the

[4] UN Document S/4214. Adopted as Security Council resolution 132 (1959).

decision regarding it would be a procedural one, to which the veto provisions would not apply.

The Western arguments were opposed by the Soviet Union on two counts. In the first place, she said that what the situation required was not a UN body but a return to the agreements reached at the Geneva Conference in 1954, and, particularly, the revival of the tripartite International Control Commission which had adjourned *sine die* in 1958.[5] This was a shrewd move for, when mooted earlier in 1959, it had been condemned by the Laotian Government as threatening an intolerable interference in its affairs. In this it had been immediately supported by the United States, who apprehended that the sympathies of the Indian chairman of the Commission might be much nearer those of the Polish than the Canadian member. Britain, too, had fallen into line on this point, producing the interesting argument that the Commission's revival would be inconsistent with that part of the Conference's Final Declaration which had undertaken to respect the sovereignty of Laos. Now, in a more favourable context, the Soviet Union took this further opportunity to exploit Western and Laotian unease about the Control Commission, and at the same time was able to avoid an entirely negative position on the subject of international action concerning Laos.

Quite apart from this argument, however, the Soviet Union, secondly, took strong exception to the Western view regarding the status of the proposed fact-finding body and the procedure which, in consequence, would govern its establishment. Her representative referred to an agreement reached by the major Powers in 1945 at San Francisco which had laid down that a decision which might have major political consequences, such as the appointment of an investigating body, was a substantive issue. In reply the Western Powers denied that the proposed body was to investigate: its duty was to enquire, which meant, apparently, that it was passively to receive such facts as were presented to it rather than look for them on its own initiative. All members of the Council except the Soviet Union were satisfied with this nice distinction, and with the conclusion which was drawn regarding the appropriate voting procedure. The Soviet Union, however, could and did rely on another argument. It had also been agreed at San Francisco that in the event of a disagreement as to whether a particular vote was procedural, that matter was itself to be voted on, and under the rules which applied to substantive

[5] At Geneva in 1954 it had been decided that each of the Armistice Agreements regarding Cambodia, Laos, and Vietnam should be watched over by an International Commission for Supervision and Control. They later became known as the International Control Commissions. Each one was made up of an Indian chairman, who was also head of the Indian-composed secretariat, and representatives of Poland and Canada.

questions. Thus a permanent member of the Council could, on such occasions, exercise a double veto, first by negativing the majority's opinion that a vote was procedural, and then by vetoing the decision on the main issue. This procedure was in fact used a few times early in the UN's life, and now the Soviet Union sought to resort to it once more. But the President, the representative of Italy, refused to allow it, and out-manœuvred the Soviet Union, as well as the San Francisco agreement, by declaring, on his own authority, that the draft resolution concerned a procedural matter. His ruling was challenged by the Soviet Union, but upheld in what was an admittedly procedural vote. The subcommittee was then established by ten votes to one.

In the event, however, the Soviet Union had the last laugh. The Council's subcommittee spent the best part of a month in Laos, and its mere presence was said to have had a notable effect: Viet Minh 'columns' were reported to have brought a successful offensive to a sudden halt in order to create a misleadingly peaceful atmosphere for the international investigation.[6] If this was in fact so, it was a remarkably successful gambit, for from the Western point of view, the subcommittee came back more or less empty handed. It reported, on 3 November, that there had been action in Laos of a guerrilla character and that varying degrees and kinds of support had been given to the dissidents by North Vietnam. But it concluded that it had not been clearly established whether the frontier had been crossed by regular North Vietnamese troops, which was another way of saying that it did not accept the Laotian claim that it had been subject to foreign aggression. This was not at all the kind of report the United States wanted. The finding that the insurgents had received some help from a Communist source was valuable, but on balance the report did not serve American interests. It more than justified her initial opposition to the involvement of the UN at all, and, accordingly, her policy now was to encourage it to forget the whole affair.

This, however, was not easy and one of the difficulties came from a rather embarrassing quarter. For the Secretary-General of the UN seemed determined to maintain the Organization's interest in Laos. There were indications that, earlier in the year, he had been considering the possibility of establishing a UN presence there, and now, immediately following the report to the Council, he announced that in consultation with the Government of Laos, he had been considering whether he might visit the country. Two days later on 8 November, he announced his acceptance of an invitation, saying that it would enable him to acquire an independent and full knowledge of the problem. In view of the fact that, only a matter of days

[6] S. M. Champassak, *Storm over Laos*, quoted in Wainhouse, *op. cit.*, p. 392.

before, the Security Council subcommittee had purported to supply such an account, Mr Hammarskjöld's decision seemed, on the face of it, a little strange. It seemed even stranger in view of the committee's finding that Laos was in no obvious danger. However, the Secretary-General paid his visit and during its course Mr S. Tuomioja, Executive Secretary of the UN Economic Commission for Europe, was summoned to Laos to review the economic situation and see how the UN could best help promote growth and stability. His report was received in December, and among its recommendations was one for the appointment of a high level official to co-ordinate the various activities of the UN in Laos. In February 1960 an experienced Swiss diplomat, Dr E. Zellweger, was appointed as the Secretary-General's special consultant for this purpose.

It seems that these rather extravagant moves represented an attempt by Hammarskjöld to keep Laos out of the cold war and nudge her into a policy of neutrality. This, it was widely believed, was the advice he gave during his visit of November 1959, and his subsequent appointments, while formally having to do with economic matters, may plausibly be seen as the establishment of a reporting presence, a small standing body which would be able to report on developments as they occurred and so might exercise some deterrent effect. It may be that his policy was conducted in the expectation that it would not be opposed by, and might even secure the co-operation of, the two major Powers. He may well have calculated that if the Soviet Union reacted in a hostile manner it would be chiefly for the record, and that in private account would be taken of the fact that this initiative involved a set-back for the United States as well as the left-wing groups in Laos, which in any case had little chance of seizing power at that time. If he did, he was apparently proved right. For when Hammarskjöld's visit to Laos was announced he was publicly taken to task by the Soviet Union, but the matter was not pursued. The United States seemed to present a more difficult problem, for she was supporting the right-wing regime in Laos and showed no sign of wanting to see it adopt a less committed posture. But there is some evidence for thinking that American policy was believed by Hammarskjöld to be on the point of change. If this was so, however, he was wrong, for it was not until the Kennedy administration of 1961 that the United States veered towards a neutralist solution for Laos. Some further time was to elapse before the various factions in Laos were to agree on it, but in July 1962 a declaration was signed at Geneva proclaiming the country's neutrality. Meanwhile, the UN presence was left to observe the intricacies of Laotian politics, valued by the various Governments which appeared for the knowledge it brought that threats to the country's integrity would not go unnoticed, but having little visible impact on the course of events.

So far as their effect on national unity was concerned, the 1954 Geneva Agreements were even less of a success in respect to Vietnam than they were with regard to Laos, the goal of a united Vietnam within two years never coming in sight. This was perhaps not surprising as two of the principal parties, the United States and South Vietnam, had refused to sign the Agreements. Subsequently, the United States became increasingly involved in support of the South Vietnamese Government, and as its action was by no means seen on all sides as a clear case of resistance to aggression, there was a marked American reluctance to have any aspect of the situation investigated by the UN. However, when Cambodia complained to the Security Council in 1964 about violations of her territory by American and South Vietnamese forces, the United States saw an opportunity both to demonstrate her good faith, and to make it more difficult for the Viet Cong to use Cambodia as a refuge. She therefore accepted and developed the Cambodian proposal for UN inspection of her border with South Vietnam, suggesting that it be patrolled by a joint Cambodian-North Vietnamese force, with or without UN observers, or by a UN force. She also proposed that the UN should assist the two countries to define their frontier more clearly.

Meanwhile, however, Cambodia had been having second thoughts and now her doubts seemed to be strengthened. She did not oppose the idea of using the UN (although she did say that she wouldn't help to pay for it) but she did speak in favour of the reconvening of the Geneva Conference and the use of the International Control Commission machinery for the supervision of her frontier. In this she received support from both France and the Soviet Union. The United States, on the other hand, thought that the task was not suitable for the Commission, no doubt thinking that, even taking account of India's growing hostility to China, the Commission could not be relied upon to report in a manner which was agreeable to American interests. Britain supported the United States position, saying that the Cambodian and Vietnam Commissions were already sufficiently occupied with their 1954 tasks. This argument lost such cogency as it might have possessed when account was taken of the fact that as long ago as 1955 the Cambodian Commission had been reduced to symbolic size on account of a lack of work, and that in Vietnam there was no armistice to speak of for the Commission to supervise. South Vietnam, too, opposed the suggestion that the Control Commission's terms of reference should be extended.

In the event, a compromise was reached, and the Security Council was able, on 4 June, to agree unanimously that three of its members should be sent to the two countries concerned to consider what measures should be taken to prevent a recurrence of incidents. But nothing came of it. Brazil, Ivory Coast, and Morocco made up the Council's team, and reported that both Governments wanted concrete, even if limited, agreements. In accordance with what they thought to be Cambodia's view, they recommended that civilian observers be placed on the border, but Cambodia now declared that this would be unacceptable. It appears that she considered the report to be unduly favourable to South Vietnam, and from this point onwards she veered increasingly in China's direction, a movement which was accompanied by a worsening of her relations with both the United States and the Soviet Union. She continued to complain from time to time about the accusations which were made by various Western states that she was helping the Viet Cong, and repeated her willingness for the matter to be checked by international inspectors, saying that she would agree to their distribution, in fixed and mobile posts, throughout her territory. But the supervision which she was prepared to accept was supervision by the existing Control Commission, and her initiatives met with a negative Western response. Probably this was not so much on account of the merits or demerits of the proposal as of the repercussions it might have on the situation in South Vietnam.

Cambodia's liking for the use of the International Control Commission no doubt reflects China's hostility towards the UN, a fact which places strict limits on the role which the Organization can play in relation to any aspect of the Vietnam war. In Europe there has been no such obstacle, yet the UN has been very little involved in the East–West confrontation on that continent. In part this has been due to the fact that Great Powers generally dislike an international organization having a hand in their mutual conflicts: they do not need help from such a source and are aware that, if accepted, it could be something of an irritant by widening the circle of those who feel entitled to a say in the making and execution of policy. There has also, in Europe, been another factor inhibiting the participation of the UN, and that is the generally direct, clear-cut, and static character of the conflict, so well conveyed by the phrase 'iron curtain'. Both sides have, on the whole, kept strictly within their own domains, and so there has been little call for the UN to expose the interference of one in the affairs of the other. In fact, in respect of only two European situations has there been any question of the West trying to obstruct the Soviet Union and its friends through the establishment of an accusatory.

One issue which has attracted such proposals, but very half-heartedly, is that of Berlin. Lying 100 miles or so within East Germany, and yet divided, in effect, between East and West Germany, the Soviet Union has from time to time proposed that West Berlin should become a free city. This would involve the departure of the American, British, and French troops who are there in consequence of the inter-allied arrangements which were made at the end of the war. Therefore the proposal has usually been accompanied by the suggestion that, perhaps in order to reassure the West, the UN should station token contingents of non-NATO troops in the city. The Western Powers have shown no more interest in this idea than has West Germany and the West Berliners themselves, but it has sometimes led to the counter-suggestion that, without in any way impairing Western rights, some UN agencies might be transferred to Berlin, possibly in conjunction with a small UN force.

If the last mentioned scheme was implemented, a kind of standing reporting presence would be created, a body which, while not designed for that purpose, would be on hand to give an impartial account of the situation should trouble occur and which, by being there, might possibly help to deter such trouble. But none of the Western countries have shown more than a perfunctory interest in the idea. It is not really expected to add to the security of West Berlin, and essentially it has been a means of demonstrating that the West is not hostile to the UN idea and is prepared to see if it can find a suitable role for it. From the Soviet point of view, however, this would not be at all suitable, for, while it would be most unlikely to have any bearing on her policy towards West Berlin, it would have the undesirable effect of giving an additional aura of legitimacy to the West's presence there. Nothing, therefore, has come of such proposals, nor does it seem likely that anything will should they make a further appearance. They arise out of an attempt by the Soviet Union to deal with West Berlin in isolation and, in particular, to get the Western Powers out of the city. For its part, the West is prepared to do neither of these things and, while willing to accept the UN as a supplement to its own presence, does not regard it as an adequate substitute. The UN alone would, as the West sees it, be no guarantee at all of the integrity of West Berlin, which would then be at the mercy of the East. Thus the Western garrisons in Berlin are negotiable only in the context of an attempt to settle the German problem overall, and that, as a realistic proposition, seems no more likely than at any time since 1945, despite the East–West *détente*.

The other European dispute in which the West suggested the establishment of a reporting presence was very different. It concerned the

fluid internal situation which arose in Greece immediately following
the end of World War II, in which both the West and its Communist
rivals were working for the establishment of a regime favourable to
themselves. The Athens Government was pro-Western, but was subject to heavy pressure from Communist insurgents, which made the
West most anxious that the situation should be examined and publicized by the UN. Moreover, this was one of the few occasions on
which such a Western move was successful.

The dispute had its origin in the course of events in Greece during
the war. In 1941 the country had been occupied and the unpopular
right-wing government had gone into exile. At first the British-sup-
ported underground movement was led by Communists, but subsequently a non-Communist resistance group emerged, and in 1943
Britain switched her support to it. She then endeavoured to reconcile
the two sides, and an agreement was reached in 1944, but proved
very fragile. By the end of the year Greek Communists were fighting
British troops and, having been defeated, retired to the north of the
country to engage in guerrilla warfare against the Government and
its foreign supporters. Here they soon received a substantial fillip
in the shape of assistance from sympathetic regimes which had been
indigenously established in two neighbouring countries, Albania and
Yugoslavia, and installed by the Soviet Union in a third, Bulgaria.
In August 1946 the Soviet Union tried to give the Communist cause
a different kind of support by getting the Ukraine to complain to the
Security Council that, chiefly on account of the presence of British
troops, Greece was following a dangerously provocative policy.
The Council rejected a Soviet resolution critical of Greece, but that
was not the end of the matter, for the United States took the opportunity to propose that a small commission be asked to investigate
border incidents between Greece and the surrounding Communist
countries. This was not at all to the Soviet Union's liking and, accordingly, she exercised her veto.

A few months later, however, in December 1946, when Greece
protested to the Security Council about the outside help which was
being given to the guerrillas, and the United States again proposed a
fact-finding mission, the suggestion was unanimously accepted. The
most plausible explanation of this is that both sides hoped to use the
mission's report to good advantage. Like its earlier proposal, the
West no doubt saw this one as a means, on the one hand, of providing some moral support for the Greek Government and its allies
and, on the other, of embarrassing the Communist states at the UN
and, conceivably, of causing them to move more circumspectly in and
around Greece. For its part, the Soviet Union can had have little confidence the mission agreeing with its interpretation of the situation.

But it did afford her with an opportunity to air her views regarding the political situation in Greece, possibly securing some sympathy for them among the other Council members and beyond. For, whereas the first American proposal would have established a three man group chosen 'on the basis of their competence and impartiality',[7] the second proposal envisaged a body made up of one representative of each member of the Council, giving the Soviet Union a direct finger in the pie. Under this arrangement she was assured of a favourable minority report, and this was doubtless the factor which led her to give it support.

The Commission of Investigation was quickly established and made on-the-spot enquiries early in 1947, out of which emerged a three volume report. The majority concluded that Yugoslavia and, to a lesser extent, Albania and Bulgaria, had supported guerrilla warfare in Greece, and recommended that a small body be set up to investigate incidents and try to improve the situation on the frontiers concerned.[8] The Soviet Union and Poland, on the other hand, reported that Greece's allegations were totally unfounded, and that the trouble in and around Greece was due to its Government's antidemocratic and expansionist policies. They objected to the proposed frontier body on the ground, among others, that it would infringe Greece's sovereignty, and then proceeded in the Council to express themselves in favour of a commission to ensure that the foreign economic aid which Greece was receiving was used only in the interests of the Greek people! As was becoming the custom, the Soviet proposal failed to secure any non-Communist support, and the Soviet Union used her veto to defeat a draft resolution based on the Commission's recommendations, and also two others which called for the cessation of foreign intervention and the establishment of an observer group to report compliance. Having got what she could out of the Commission, and also, perhaps, realizing that there was not much in it for her, she was anxious to wind up the UN's actitivies in Greece.

The Western states, however, realized that they were on to a good thing. Earlier in 1947, on 12 March, the Truman Doctrine had been enunciated, under which the United States declared its intention 'to support free peoples who are resisting attempted subjugation by armed minorities or by outside pressures', and Greece and Turkey were declared to be its first beneficiaries.[9] This was in response to

---

[7] *Yearbook of the United Nations, 1946–7*, p. 358.
[8] Yugoslavia alleged that the Belgian member of the Commission had switched his views after receiving a telegram from his Government, and that another small Power had done likewise. See John Maclaurin, The *United Nations and Power Politics* (London: Allen and Unwin, 1951), p. 205.
[9] Margaret Carlyle (ed.): *Documents on International Affairs 1947–1948* (London: Oxford University Press, 1952), p. 6.

Britain's inability to maintain her support of the Greek Government: in effect, the major Western Power was taking over from one of its weakened allies. But it gave the Communist states a new opportunity to disparage Western policy. Clearly, therefore, it would be most useful for the West if the UN could, from time to time, confirm that the Greek troubles were not an internal affair but fell squarely within the terms of the Truman Doctrine. Thus, although it involved winding up the subsidiary group of UN investigators who had remained in Greece, about whose standing there had been controversy in the Council, the United States proposed that the matter should be taken off the Council's agenda. This was with a view to having it considered by the General Assembly, to which the Soviet Union was strongly opposed. But she could not deny that the composition of the agenda was a procedural matter, and so was unable to veto the Western move.

The General Assembly, at this time, was dominated by the West. It therefore willingly agreed to discuss the question of Greece, and threw out another Soviet attempt to set up a body to supervise the administration of foreign aid in Greece. Now, however, without a veto and in a small minority, the Soviet Union was unable to reply in kind, and on 21 October 1947 the Assembly adopted an American draft resolution which called on Albania, Bulgaria, and Yugoslavia to stop aiding the guerrillas and normalize their relations with Greece. The core of the resolution, however, lay in its establishment of a UN Special Committee on the Balkans (UNSCOB) to observe compliance and help in the implementation of the Assembly's recommendations.

UNSCOB was to consist of the representatives of the five permanent members of the Security Council and of six other states: Australia, Brazil, Mexico, the Netherlands, Pakistan, and Poland. The Soviet Union and Poland, however, would not take up their membership, and Albania, Bulgaria, and Yugoslavia refused to provide any facilities for the preparation of a report which was obviously going to censure their conduct—although Bulgaria did on one occasion admit UNSCOB so that it could investigate an incident which was at least as damaging to Greece as to herself. UNSCOB had, therefore, to operate solely on the Greek side of the border. Besides trying, unsuccessfully, to improve relations between the disputants, it conducted surveys and made enquiries regarding guerrilla activities, frontier incidents, and related matters. From these it concluded that Greece's three Communist neighbours had provided her insurgents with material and moral assistance, and so had endangered peace and security in the Balkans. Its mandate was renewed by the Assembly in November 1948, but with greater emphasis on its conciliatory functions, and the Assembly also set up its own Conciliation Committee. However, the situation was such that UNSCOB made no headway with this side of its work, and, essentially, its role continued to be that of a chronicler of Communist iniquity. In 1949, 1950, and 1951, it filed critical reports, stating, in 1949, that the guerrillas had been principally assisted by Albania, and, in 1950, that Bulgaria was the chief potential threat to the independence and integrity of Greece. In reply, annually, came a variety of Soviet charges, popular among which were UNSCOB's illegality, its bias in favour of Greece, its character as a tool of American and British ruling circles, and their endeavour to use it for espionage.

By the 1950s, however, the situation had altered in a number of important respects. Yugoslavia's expulsion from the Cominform in June 1948 had led, over the following 12 months, to a marked reduction in her aid to the guerrillas, so that UNSCOB was able to report, as of July 1949, that it might even have ceased. Certainly Yugoslavia announced in that month that her frontier with Greece was closed, and shortly afterwards the two countries began to move towards the re-establishment of normal relations. Then, too, as well as being deprived of a source of assistance and place of refuge, the guerrillas were having a much tougher time in Greece itself. For, on the one hand, the economic situation had improved considerably, so reducing their appeal, and in the other, the Greek military forces had been much strengthened and were operating with notable effect. Thus UNSCOB reported that by mid-1950, while the leaders had not abandoned their aims and the remnants of the movement within Greece had not been dissolved, all large-scale guerrilla activity along Greece's northern frontiers had been eliminated. Clearly a question was now arising as to the continued necessity for UNSCOB and in December 1951, on a Greek initiative, the General Assembly decided to wind it up. However, as a reminder that Communists could not be trusted, it was also decided, with Greek support, to keep an eye on the situation through the recently-created Peace Observation Commission.[10] It was asked to establish a Balkans sub-Commission, situated at the UN's headquarters, but with authority to dispatch observers, upon request and with the consent of the proposed host, to any area of tension in the Balkans. The sub-Commission, consisting of Colombia, France, Pakistan, Sweden, and the United States, was set up in January 1952. At the request of Greece a team of observers, one from each member and a Chief Observer from Britain, was sent to its frontier areas and made periodic reports. It was reduced in size at the end of 1953 and withdrawn in 1954.

[10] See above, p. 199 (n) 3.

In UNSCOB's own estimation, the UN's vigilance regarding Greece was a significant factor in preventing a Communist takeover. This view should be treated with caution. There seems little doubt that the principal reason for the withering of the Communist campaign was the opposition which it met in Greece itself, which in turn was due chiefly to American military and economic assistance and Greek resolution. Secondarily, the defection of Yugoslavia was a considerable blow to the Communists and, combined with the first factor, must have induced a reconsideration of policy on the part of the Greek guerrillas and their Albanian and Bulgarian supporters. An obviously failing cause, like its opposite, has its own momentum, and Communist states are more ruthless than some when it comes to cutting losses. In this context, UNSCOB's strictures may have been an irritant to Albania and Bulgaria, but, especially in view of their very poor relations with the non-Communist world at this time, hardly more.

Nor was UNSCOB of great importance for the Western countries, but, although subsidiary, it did play a useful role so far as they were concerned. For, besides boosting Greek morale, it put the seal of UN approval on the Western analysis of the situation, and so provided a good-looking justification for supporting the Government, which could be used at both the domestic and international levels. More generally, it also provided some valuable material for anti-Communist propaganda. Possibly UNSCOB's findings may have lost something in some eyes on account of the fact that, of the nine countries whose representatives signed its reports, six were committed Westerners, two were Latin American, and the other was a well-disposed Asian. But certainly in the area where it counted most—outside the Communist bloc—UNSCOB's reports were on the whole accepted at their face value, as fair and impartial accounts of the situation, and the fact that they bore the UN's name added to their weight. They therefore served to legitimize the West's arguments and actions, and were valued accordingly.

IV

Most states in the Middle East have displayed marked sympathies towards one or other of the sides in the cold war. But on the whole they have remained formally uncommitted, and this has been largely responsible for the fact that questions regarding the use of accusatory missions in the area have given rise to less clear-cut divisions than when the move has been discussed in relation to the Far East or Europe. Thus one proposal to this effect petered out. Another was approved without a dissenting vote in the Security Council,

H

although the members entertained rather different hopes about the group they were establishing. And a third was brought to fruition without controversy but only with the very cautious assent of the state that it was designed to benefit.

The first of these three cases arose out of a complaint which Syria made in 1957 regarding what she described in the General Assembly as a provocative and threatening concentration of Turkish troops close to her border. At this time Syria was moving sharply to the left, and she received the support of the Soviet Union both for her general claim and for her proposal that the matter should be investigated by a commission of seven members—each side designating two with the remaining three being chosen by agreement. Turkey and her American ally, on the other hand, and also Britain, while stating their willingness to discuss what they referred to as Soviet trouble-making in the Middle East, showed a marked reluctance to agree to the idea of a commission, preferring the mediatory initiative which had been taken by Saudi Arabia. Thus there was considerable doubt whether Syria would get the commission she sought, and even if she did it was unlikely that she would profit much from it, if only because the matter was not of great importance. She therefore agreed to withdraw her proposal and the issue was dropped.

It was Syria's leftward momentum however, which helped to precipitate a vastly more serious crisis in the following year. It concerned the Lebanon. Political life in that country, and also its international activity, is dominated by the religious complexion of the country. About half the population is Muslim, but the rest is made up of a number of Christian groups, by far the most important being the Maronite Church, which entered into full union with Rome in the eighteenth century. Very conscious of their isolation among the Muslim Arabs of the Near East, the Christians had traditionally looked to Western countries, and particularly to France, for protection. With the coming of independence, however, it was recognized that the continuance of this practice, even if it was feasible, would be both inappropriate and a source of much trouble. Therefore, in the National Covenant of 1943 it was agreed that in return for putting it on one side the Muslim element in the population would not attempt to unite the Lebanon with Syria or any other Arab country. Lebanon was to regard itself as a special part of the Arab world—a co-operative member of the Arab family but one who would not take sides in any family quarrels. And the internal religious situation was to be reflected in the distribution of public offices, it being decreed that the President, who holds office for six years and cannot be re-elected, must be a Maronite, the President of the Chamber of

Deputies a *Shia* Muslim, and the Prime Minister a *Sunni* Muslim. By these means it was hoped that the delicate balance of forces which existed within the country would remain at a point of equilibrium, so providing a sufficient basis for a stable and prosperous existence.

For the first 10 years or so of its independence the Lebanon trod carefully in its international relations, observing the principles of the National Covenant. But in the mid 1950s, under President Chamoun, it began to take a rather different path. In 1955 Chamoun exchanged state visits with President Bayar of Turkey, and this led to speculation that the Lebanon might join the most recent addition to the Western alliance system, the Baghdad Pact, which had been hotly denounced by a number of Arab countries. She did not do so, but seemed clearly to be aligning herself with the anti-Nasserist group which was emerging in the Arab world under the impact of the thrusting and controversial line being taken by the Egyptian President. When that country was attacked in the following year by Israel, Britain, and France, the Lebanon gave the appearance of being even further to the right by refusing to do more than express her verbal solidarity with Egypt. A few months later her government eagerly accepted the Eisenhower Doctrine, by which the United States indicated its increased willingness to support freedom-loving countries in the Near East against the advance of international Communism, which, during 1957, appeared to be making ominous strides in Syria. Then on 1 February 1958, to Chamoun's great alarm, Syria joined Egypt in the United Arab Republic (UAR). In the eyes of his Muslim subjects, however, Nasserism, far from being a threat, was something to be joyfully applauded, and they thus took a very poor view of their country's policy. If the Lebanon was to diverge from neutrality, they would have preferred it to incline in the direction of the 'progressive' Arab forces. The Lebanese Christians, on the other hand, tended to share Chamoun's apprehension about militant Arab nationalism, but not all of them were equally happy with his internal activity. He had succeeded in falling out with most of their leaders, despite the fact that he was vigorously charged by the Muslims with glaring discrimination in favour of Christians, and he was thought in many quarters to be practicing corruption on a wide scale. When, therefore, early in 1958 rumours began to spread that he was planning to amend the Constitution to open the way to his re-election, dissatisfaction with both his internal and external policies combined to produce a dangerous situation.

The event which sparked off the crisis was the murder on 8 May 1958 of the Christian editor of a Beirut newspaper which was severely critical of the Chamoun regime. Violence broke out in Tripoli, in the north, and quickly spread to the capital and other parts of the country, and just as quickly was attributed by the Government to interference in the Lebanon's affairs by the UAR. Within a fortnight it had complained to both the Arab League and the Security Council, the latter postponing discussion in order that the regional organization should first have an opportunity to solve the problem. In the Arab League the omens looked good, for a draft resolution of a conciliatory character was acceptable to the Lebanese delegation and was not opposed by the UAR. However, it was rejected by the Lebanese Government, which seemed intent on getting the matter dealt with by the UN. Accordingly, on 6 June the Security Council opened its substantive debate on the subject, and heard the Lebanese Foreign Minister, Charles Malik, claim at some length that there had been and still was 'massive, illegal, and unprovoked intervention'[11] in Lebanese politics by the UAR, which threatened both her independence and international security. Arms and men of a considerable order of magnitude were alleged to be passing from Syria into the Lebanon, which therefore sought the protection of the UN. After a four-day adjournment for consultations, Sweden proposed that the Council should send an 'observation group' to the Lebanon 'to ensure that there is no illegal infiltration of personnel or supply of arms or other *matériel* across the Lebanese borders'.[12] This suggestion appealed to all members of the Council except the Soviet Union, but as the Lebanon and the UAR were not opposed to it she did not veto the draft resolution but only abstained. Thus on 11 June the Security Council authorized the establishment of the United Nations Observation Group in the Lebanon (UNOGIL).

The resolution left unexplained the process whereby an 'observation group' was to 'ensure' that there was no illegal infiltration, and no doubt this lack of clarity reflected a division of opinion in the Council regarding UNOGIL's role. At the one extreme was the Soviet Union, who rejected the Lebanon's allegations and was opposed to the UN having anything to do with what she asserted was a purely internal matter. She clearly suspected the West of wanting to use the UN for its own purposes, and also spoke darkly of the way in which the ground was being prepared for American intervention. This reflected her dilemma, for if she obstructed action in the Council she might find herself going down to defeat in the Assembly, which would also mean that her control over subsequent UN activities in the Lebanon would be substantially diminished. Alternatively and more unfortunately, a veto in the Council might precipitate the landing of United States troops which, for all its propaganda value, was something which the Soviet Union certainly wished

[11] Security Council, *Official Records*, 823rd Meeting, para. 11.
[12] UN Document S/4022. Adopted as Security Council resolution 128 (1958).

to avoid. For her, therefore, the UNOGIL resolution was probably
the least of all evils. It would discourage Western intervention, but
also looked relatively innocuous. And its general acceptability
made it easy for the Soviet Union to avoid a veto, which ensured
that the Security Council's control over the matter would be
maintained.

Sweden represented the middle of the road, as she so often does,
and on this occasion was joined by Panama. The fact that Japan
and Colombia limited themselves to expressions of support for peace
and the Charter suggests that they shared this position. The line
taken here was that the situation was unclear, and that the UN should
therefore not jump to judgment but should first of all send an international and impartial body to ascertain what was really going on.
In all probability this was another way of expressing scepticism
about the Lebanon's allegations, and indicating the belief that while
the Lebanon's troubles might be aggravated by the UAR, the basic
cause of the crisis was internal. In their view, there was no call for
the UN to play a prominent role. But on the other hand serious allegations had been made and there was the danger of Western intervention: undoubtedly a crisis was on hand. Thus in the eyes of these
states, who in principle favoured a significant peace-keeping role
for the UN, the situation demanded that the Organization assert
itself by taking some action. UNOGIL was the answer, for it was
hoped that by watching the frontier it would put a check on such
infiltration as was taking place and assure the Lebanon that there
was no substantial outside interference in its concerns, so encouraging
the Government to concentrate on quietly putting its own political
affairs in order, assisted, possibly, by some unofficial help from the
Observer Group. Further, by advising the world that the Lebanese
problem was essentially domestic in origin, UNOGIL would serve
to calm the jittery nerves of some outside Powers who might otherwise be tempted to worsen the situation by intervening. Thus by
clearing up misapprehension, international tension would be reduced.

But President Chamoun and his external backers took a somewhat
less olympian view of the scene, and in consequence had a conception of the UN's role which was at the other extreme. Chamoun's
reluctance to leave the matter in the hands of the Arab League was
probably due not only to the fact that the UN was a much more
suitable forum for the denunciation of President Nasser, but also
because there was no hope of the League providing him with tangible
assistance: a conciliatory committee chosen from among the members
of its Council fell far short of what he wanted in terms of both composition and strength. For, clearly, he was a worried man, fearing

for the continuance of his regime. Whether or not he believed that his difficuties were mainly due to the action of the UAR, it seems that he certainly thought that he would be helped by a strong international presence which, whatever it did on the border, would ensure that the country did not disintegrate into anarchy and might deter the rebels from further action. The Lebanese Army could be relied upon for neither of these things, certainly not the second, for it chose to view the conflict largely from the sidelines—an extreme case, a *reductio ad absurdum* in the eyes of the Government, no doubt, of the principle that the armed forces should be above politics. Thus Chamoun looked to the UN for a show of strength in support of his regime.

In this it is unlikely that his position was fundamentally different from that of the United States and his other Western friends. They may well have had reservations about some of the government's actions which had preceded the crisis and about some of the claims which it was making concerning its origin. It could also be the case that already the United States was reappraising the markedly unsuccessful Eisenhower Doctrine and coming to the conclusion that a new approach was called for in the Middle East, one which did not lay such stress on public commitments to the Western cause. But even so, this was no time for allowing a Middle Eastern regime which was friendly to the West to go down in disorder, with the loss of prestige and invitation to troublemaking which that would entail. Indeed, such an outcome could have checked the implementation of new ideas about America's proper role in the area, for fear of giving rise to the impression that the change was made out of weakness. Hence there was a strong American interest in supporting Chamoun. It was known that she was supplying the Lebanon with small arms and anti-riot weapons, and she also quietly doubled the size of her Mediterranean amphibious force. But at this point the United States, who was setting the Western line, did not think that the situation warranted the hostile Arab and Soviet reactions which would assuredly follow a landing of the marines. Far better, therefore, to hold back for the moment and take advantage of the lack of urgency to see whether the UN could pull Chamoun's chestnuts out of the fire. Britain, France and Canada were also in favour of the argument that, friends, especially Middle Eastern friends, should be helped in their hour of need, as were two other members of the Security Council, Iraq and Nationalist China less, probably, for the argument's general merits than on account of two of its possible applications.

Thus the third group would have preferred a stronger resolution than that proposed by Sweden. But like the Soviet Union, they too were in a dilemma. If they pressed for more than observation, they might not even obtain the necessary seven votes in the Security Council, which would be a considerable blow to their prestige and would make action outside the U N extremely embarrassing. On the other hand, if sufficient votes could be obtained by the exercise of persuasion on any one of Japan, Colombia, or Panama, the West would almost certainly run into a Soviet veto. They could transfer the matter to the General Assembly, but it was unlikely that that body would look with much sympathy on their proposals, and so this too might well be a dead end. An observation group therefore presented a way out, for it would be less likely to attract a Soviet veto, and if it did would probably be approved by the Assembly. It was not as robust a move as they would have liked, but the ambiguity introduced by the word 'ensure', which probably appeared in the Council's resolution as a result of Western pressure or at least as a concession to known Western views, held out the possibility of an interpretation which would result in Chamoun's regime receiving tangible assistance from the U N. In any event the resolution meant that the U N would obtain a foothold in the area, which held out several possible advantages. By being able to report on the border situation U N O G I L would, it was hoped, deter Syria from taking, or continuing to take, large scale advantage of the Lebanese unrest. It was expected that its reports, by supplying impartial evidence of Syrian infiltration, would provide useful anti-Nasser and by implication, anti-Communist propaganda. And if the worst came to the worst this material could be used to justify Western intervention. From the Western point of view, in short, (and of the three groups into which the Security Council divided on this move the Western was the strongest), U N O G I L's significance was chiefly prophylactic, and was to serve this aim by levelling an accusing finger at Syria and her supporters.

The Council's resolution of 11 June had left it to the Secretary-General 'to take the necessary steps' to establish the Observation Group, and he moved very quickly.[13] As had happened before, the U N was able to take advantage of the presence in the area of its Truce Supervision Organization and the first observers arrived in Beirut on the day following the passage of the resolution, beginning their operational activities on the next. A three-man committee was appointed to head the Group: Galo Plaza, a former president of Ecuador; Rajeshwar Dayal, an Indian diplomat; and Major-General Odd Bull of Norway. Galo Plaza was subsequently made Chairman and General Bull put in charge of the military observers, who patrolled roads, established some permanently-manned observation posts and, towards the end of June, when they numbered about

[13] Security Council resolution 128 (1958).

100, had their efforts supplemented by the start of aerial reconais-sance. The value of this activity, however, was limited by physical and political difficulties. The first of these arose from the fact that the long eastern frontier with Syria ran along very rugged and moun-tainous country and, with the exception of the Beirut–Damascus road, all the main lines of communication ran parallel with the border and not across it. Hence it would in any event have been ex-ceptionally difficult to keep under effective observation. But for some time UNOGIL was not in a position even to try to cope with this problem for, with the exception of a few miles on each side of the Damascus road, the whole of the 175-mile-long frontier with Syria was controlled by rebel elements, who prevented UNOGIL teams from entering their areas or controlled their entry in such a way as to minimize the usefulness of the subsequent observation. It was also the case that local conditions were such that the Group decided against night patrols in any area. These problems were referred to in its first report, made at the beginning of July, which also said that it had not been possible to establish whether the rebels who had been observed had come from Syria. Nevertheless the Group felt justified in asserting that there was very little doubt that the majority of those actively opposing the government were Lebanese.

This brought a very strong reaction from the Government, who described the Group's conclusion as 'misleading and unwarranted'.[14] Nor was it alone in thinking that UNOGIL had hardly had sufficient opportunities to come to so firm a view of the situation. But the real trouble with UNOGIL, from President Chamoun's point of view, was not so much that it was too hasty in coming to judgment, em-barrassing as that was, nor even that it was as yet unable to keep the frontier under effective observation. The basic objection to it was that its careful impartiality and endeavour to build up confi-dence with the rebel leaders so that they might let it inspect the areas under their control, was not what he was looking for. He wanted an international military force which could be seen to be supporting his regime, and he made no effort to hide his disappointment with hav-ing received mere observers. However, the United States had pri-vately informed him that if the UN was unable to protect his regime, she would do so, and on several occasions he was on the brink of declaring that the time had come for her to honour her promise.[15] However, the American Ambassador successfully counselled pa-tience, and this was maintained until 14 July, when the monarchy was overthrown in Iraq and the right-wing Prime Minister, Nuri-es-

[14] UN Document S/4043, p. 2.
[15] See Charles W. Thayer: *Diplomat* (London: M. Joseph, 1960), p. 76.

Said, and the Crown Prince were killed. The revolution, in which
Chamoun, like others, saw the hand of Nasser, produced an emergency atmosphere in both Washington and Beirut, and the United
States was now very willing to respond to Chamoun's urgent plea
for assistance. All was ready for such an eventuality, and on the
afternoon of 15 July about several thousand marines landed outside
Beirut, to be met by Coca-Cola vendors. Not for nothing do the
Lebanese have a reputation for commercial instincts. Within a few
days further marines and army detachments arrived, bringing the
total number of American forces in the country up to about 14,300.
To complete the picture the entire Sixth Fleet, comprising about 70
ships, was moved to the eastern Mediterranean.

The purpose of the landings, like the almost simultaneous dispatch
of British troops to Jordan,[16] was to prevent a disintegration of the
Western position in the Middle East. The revolutionary momentum
which the Iraqi *coup* had engendered was surely going to encourage
the opposition in the Lebanon to make a further effort to topple
Chamoun. If that happened, and perhaps even if it didn't, King
Hussein's seemingly shaky regime in Jordan might be defeated,
which, besides being a considerable blow in itself, could precipitate
an Arab-Israeli conflict. Thus the prospect conjured up in Washington, and London, was of a possible loss of the friendship and goodwill of two Middle Eastern countries, and the further possibility of
widespread disorder, from which the Soviet Union would be likely
to lose far less than the West. There was also the consideration that
American reactions to the crisis would be closely watched by those
other states in the Middle East and elsewhere who looked to her for
protection against direct and indirect aggression. If she failed the
Lebanon they might begin to reconsider their relationship with her,
and with the Soviet Union. Thus the United States was determined
to make it plain that she was not going to allow the Lebanese opposition to overthrow Chamoun.

At a hurriedly summoned meeting of the Security Council she
once again referred members to Syria's alleged part in the Lebanon's
troubles, and already, only a day after the Iraqi *coup*, was able to
inform the Council that on account of it 'the infiltration of arms and
personnel into Lebanon from the United Arab Republic in an effort
to subvert the legally constituted Government has suddenly become
much more alarming'.[17] She explained that her action should be
seen as in keeping with the spirit of the Council's resolution of 11
June, and expressed her willingness to withdraw once the UN was
able to take on the extension of its task which the United States,

[16] See below, pp. 229–233.
[17] Security Council, *Official Records*, 827th Meeting, para. 40.

faced with an emergency, had initiated. But in some quarters these remarks were not much better received than the Anglo-French suggestions two years earlier that in going into Egypt they were about the UN's proper business, and were only trying to get the Organization moving. Those members who had previously taken the view that the Lebanese problem was an internal one, the UN's job being to certify that it was so, saw no reason to change their opinion on account of the Iraqi *coup*. It might be that UNOGIL would require strengthening, but that would be in line with the UN's endeavour to help the Lebanon settle her affairs free from real or imagined outside interference. The introduction of the forces of a keenly-interested Great Power was not obviously in accord with this policy. America's move could perhaps find some justification, in UN terms, in the argument that the Observer Group was not doing its job. But it happened that on the very day of the American landings UNOGIL reported that, by agreement with the rebels, it would now have full and free access to all parts of the Lebanese frontier with Syria, and would be entitled to establish permanent observation posts in the areas they controlled. This news was followed on 17 July with a proposal for the rapid expansion of the Group to enable it to take full advantage of the new situation by maintaining a 24-hour watch on the frontier from the air and on the ground.

The Secretary-General, in a critical statement, rightly foresaw that the development of UNOGIL's work along the lines just reported to the Council would be jeopardized by America's action. Sweden thought that, in the circumstances, the proper course would be for UNOGIL to suspend its activities, but the American representative, Mr Cabot Lodge, deplored this proposal, saying that 'if ever there was a time when the United Nations should be active, it is a time like this'.[18] He therefore proposed that 'additional measures, including the contribution and use of contingents',[19] be taken to protect the Lebanon. Predictably, the Soviet Union called for an immediate American withdrawal. This proposal, when it and the two others came to a vote on 18 July, found no other support. The American proposal, on the other hand, probably on the ground that, whether one liked what the United States had done or not, it would be better to have a UN force in the Lebanon than a Western one, obtained nine votes in its favour, but was defeated by a Soviet veto. For this the Russians probably earned the silent thanks of the Secretariat. Sweden's suggestion, which presumably reflected pique over America's seeming contempt for the UN, obtained only the Soviet vote. Japan therefore proposed a way forward in the shape of a draft

[18] Security Council, *Official Records*, 830th Meeting, para. 50.
[19] UN Document S/4050, Rev. 1.

resolution empowering the Secretary-General to take such action 'as he may consider necessary'[20] to implement the purposes of the resolution of 11 June, but the representative of the Soviet Union was implacable: he could not persuade the Security Council to call for America's withdrawal and he therefore, on 22 July, vetoed the new proposal.

Meanwhile, UNOGIL continued to favour the view that the Lebanese crisis was essentially internal, so that its strained relations with the Chamoun regime were not improved. Allegations were heard to the effect that, besides not being in a physical position to make an adequate judgment, UNOGIL did not go about its business with sufficient zeal and dispatch, and it was also murmured that there was some bias at the head of the UNOGIL in favour of the rebels. The United States, too, was embarrassed by UNOGIL's early reports and frequently felt obliged to emphasize that much damage had been done before it had arrived, and that the amount of infiltration which the UN mission was able to find was a good deal less than that suggested by the information available to her.

However, the situation within the Lebanon seemed to be getting better. The American landings were widely deplored, tending to focus the hostility of the opposition on the foreign troops rather than on the Government. This small movement in the direction of a closing of the national ranks was also encouraged by the fact that the time for the election of a new president was approaching, which necessitated consultations among the various political leaders. The Government had announced at the end of May that there would be no attempt on its part to amend the Constitution in Chamoun's favour, but until a successor had been chosen his ambitions could not be discounted. It seems that he entertained hopes that the Americans would help him to crush the opposition,[21] thus at least ensuring the election of one of his supporters. But it was immediately clear that, provided the internal situation did not deteriorate, they had no intention of playing such a role. A small number of them were given duties in Beirut, chiefly of a protective nature, and the marines also tapped the telephone line between the rebel headquarters and Damascus,[22] but the bulk of the American force remained within its camp outside the city. It was their mere presence which was thought to be important. On the other hand, an American Under-Secretary of State, Robert Murphy, who was now spending all his time in the Lebanon, was active in the negotiations for a new president, trying to

[20] UN, Document S/4055, Rev. 1.
[21] See Fahim I. Qubain, *Crisis in Lebanon* (Washington: Middle East Institute, 1961), p. 119.
[22] See Robert Murphy, *Diplomat among Warriors* (Garden City, N.Y: Doubleday, 1964, p. 402.

obtain a candidate who would be widely acceptable. The obvious man was the Maronite commander of the Army, General Chehab, but he was most reluctant to stand and Chamoun was not at all keen on him doing so. Eventually, however, Chehab was prevailed upon to let his name go forward and Chamoun to support him. The election, already postponed for a week, was held on 31 July by the Lebanese Parliament acting as an electoral college, and Chehab was successful.

This did not lead to an immediate restoration of calm for clashes continued until his installation on 23 September, which was followed by a three week crisis over the composition of his cabinet. But outbreaks of disorder became fewer and the country was clearly returning to normal. In its internal aspect, the Lebanese crisis was effectively over by the end of July. Equally, the international scene was much improved by that date, although at this level the clearing up of the crisis and its consequences could not be dealt with so speedily. In Iraq it seemed that there was no likelihood of a counter-revolution, for the new regime had quickly consolidated itself and returned the country to normal. It also seemed that the revolt was going to be an isolated affair, for whether or not on account of the United States' and Britain's actions, the situation appeared to be very much more stable than a fortnight before in both Lebanon and Jordan and also on the Persian Gulf. On the wider stage negotiations were in progress to liquidate the crisis. Mr Khrushchev had proposed on 19 July that an immediate summit conference be held 'to put an end to the conflict which has broken out'.[23] This seemed to be a serious proposal, and not one which was just meant to cause embarrassment in the West. But this was its effect, particularly on President Eisenhower, whose endeavour to evade the urgent and relatively conciliatory Khrushchev was not very distinguished. But he received help from an unexpected quarter, Communist China, for in pursuit of the summit idea Khrushchev had run into trouble with his ally by agreeing to a Western proposal that the meeting be held in the framework of the Security Council, where China would be represented by Chiang Kai-shek's Taiwan regime. Early in August, therefore, he abandoned his proposal, and turned directly to the Security Council, which on 7 August unanimously decided to convoke a special session of the General Assembly.

The UN's role in the Lebanese crisis now moved into its final, and bizarre, stage. Debate in the Assembly was unhurried and far-reaching, the members addressing themselves to a variety of issues which bore on the question of the Middle East stability. But the

[23] Quoted in G. Barraclough, *Survey of International Affairs, 1956–1958* (London: Oxford University Press, 1962), p. 178.

matter which underlay the discussion, and was, indeed, its *raison d'être* was how to get the American troops out of the Lebanon, and the British out of Jordan. It was widely held, for more than one reason, that this was desirable, and both countries were willing to go, but they were not prepared to give the appearance of being pushed out, or to go in a manner which would suggest that their journeys had been unnecessary. The Assembly therefore adopted the assumption that there was a problem in the Middle East which required international treatment, and the remedy which was almost universally popular was that the UN should replace Britain and America as physical guarantors of the situation. Even the Soviet Union agreed that a UN presence would be necessary, and put forward a relatively mild resolution which, as well as recommending the withdrawal of the two Western nations, would have led to the strengthening of UNOGIL. It met with a number of objections however, as did a vague resolution proposed by Norway and other states asking the Secretary-General to take measures to uphold the independence of Lebanon and Jordan. Thus it looked as if the improving situation might suffer a setback on account of the General Assembly's inability to reach a formula which could satisfy honour on all sides. Then, however, the Arab members, including Lebanon, Jordan, and the UAR, came up with a verbal accord which called upon all UN members to refrain from interference in each others internal affairs, and asked the Secretary-General to make 'such practical arrangements as would adequately help in upholding the purpose and principles of the Charter in relation to Lebanon and Jordan in the present circumstances, and thereby facilitate the early withdrawal of the foreign troops from the two countries'.[24] It was unanimously adopted on 21 August.

When, almost a month earlier, the Security Council had found itself deadlocked over the Middle East, the Secretary-General had taken the initiative, saying that in the circumstances it was 'in keeping with the philosophy of the Charter' that he take action 'to help prevent a further deterioration of the situation . . . and to assist in finding a road away from the dangerous point at which we now find ourselves.'[25] As a result, UNOGIL was expanded by almost half, to 190 members, within a space of a few weeks, and on the basis of further negotiations with the rebel leaders was able, early in August, to make good use of its increased personnel. On 12 August it reported that the main possible infiltration routes were now under direct observation and that in the very near future further observation posts would be established and air patrols would be carried out on a

[24] UN Document A/3893, Rev.1. Adopted as resolution 1237 (ES–III).
[25] Security Council, *Official Records*, 837th Meeting, paras. 12–14.

24-hour basis. It also said that the political situation had much improved since the election of General Chehab and that the previously limited importation of arms across the Syrian frontier had markedly diminished. In view of this it might be thought that little more remained to be done in the way of expanding UNOGIL's size and activities, and while the General Assembly was considering the question its development was slowed down. But then there was a remarkable spurt of activity. The Secretary-General had greeted the resolution of 21 August with a degree of enthusiasm which on the surface seemed disproportionate, saying it was one of the strongest resolutions ever passed by the UN, and demonstrated the invaluable contribution which the UN was able to make to international life. He went about its implementation with dispatch, visiting a number of Middle Eastern capitals, and although some differences of interpretation emerged he reported that in the case of the Lebanon there was no difficulty, as an enlargement of UNOGIL would meet the resolution's requirements. By 20 September, therefore, the number of observers had risen to 287 and UNOGIL reported that 'if any infiltration is still taking place, its extent must be regarded as insignificant'.[26] Nevertheless UNOGIL's development proceeded apace, and on 14 November it had a total of 591 observers.

If UNOGIL had been meant to stay in the Lebanon to keep a close long-term watch on its Syrian border, acting as a kind of international watchdog whose job was to alert far-flung police at the first sign of danger, both its expansion and the speed with which it was executed would have been explicable. For the United States, now finding some value in UNOGIL's presence, had already withdrawn one battalion of troops in August. Others followed in the second half of September, and on 8 October an agreement was reached with the new Lebanese Government for a total withdrawal, which was completed without loss of face on 25 October. Thus it might have been thought necessary for UNOGIL's point of maximum efficiency to be reached as soon as possible after the American departure. Such a role might not, on the face of it, have seemed out of keeping with the resolution of 21 August, and certainly not with the preceding debate, which included in a good deal of discussion regarding a UN peace force. But quite apart from the fact that a strengthened UNOGIL might not have been desired by the Lebanon and would hardly have suggested the warm fraternal relationship which was now supposed to exist between the Arab states, such an analysis misconceives the significance of the Special Session of the Assembly.

The Assembly's resolution of 21 August had spoken of 'practical

26 UN Document S/4100, para. 54.

arrangements'[27] to support the Lebanon's independence once the
foreign troops had left, and the continuation of UNOGIL could be
and was regarded as such an arrangement. Hence it could not be
withdrawn until after the Americans had gone, and in any event the
UN would probably not have wished to withdraw it earlier for reasons relating to its prestige: it would not have welcomed the implication that its job had been taken over by the United States. While it
was waiting for this to happen, a modest increase in UNOGIL's
size might have been appropriate, to make it clear that the UN was
taking its new mandate seriously. But it is extremely unlikely that the
members of the Assembly envisaged a very much larger UNOGIL
settling down for a long watch on the Lebanese–Syrian border. In
fact it is unlikely that they gave very much thought at all to the
arrangement they were authorizing. For this was something which
did not really interest the Assembly. The crisis had, in essence, already subsided, and could therefore be put on one side. The General
Assembly's job was just to bring it to a formal close and tie up its
loose ends. For this purpose a formula was needed which would
clear the diplomatic air and pave the way for an Anglo-American
withdrawal, and it was found in a public gesture of reconciliation
from all concerned and by a vague suggestion that the security of
Lebanon and Jordan could safely be left to the UN. But it may be
assumed that this last point was not thought to involve an ambitious
peace-keeping enterprise, only some undertakings and relatively
minor dispositions, which could safely be left to the Secretary-
General while the international society moved on to much more
pressing issues.

It is true that the Secretary-General was, on the face of it, given a
free hand, but he must have known that the Organization would
not have countenanced the expense of maintaining an intensive
watch on an established and calm international frontier. Things
might have been 'left to Dag', but he had not been left a blank
cheque. It might therefore have been in the mind of the Assembly
that once the American forces had left, once, as it were, the coast was
clear, UNOGIL would leave too. The fact of the United States'
departure would mean that there was no real threat to the Lebanon,
for its Government would hardly treat even an expanded observer
group as an adequate substitute for 14,000 marines and troops. And,
there being no threat, and UNOGIL having served the purpose of
facilitating the American withdrawal, there would no longer be any
object in its staying. This is what happened.

No sooner had UNOGIL reached its peak than it was withdrawn.
In its mid-November report, by which time all foreign troops had

[27] General Assembly resolution 1237 (ES–III).

left the Lebanon, UNOGIL said that no cases of infiltration of men or arms had been so much as suspected by the Group during the previous two months, and this, combined with the improvement in the internal situation and in relations between the Lebanon and the UAR, led it to believe that its task had been completed. At the same time the Lebanese Government requested the deletion of its complaint from the Security Council's agenda. The Secretary-General, his decision being noted by the Council a week later, immediately ordered the withdrawal of the Group, and the last of its personnel left the Lebanon on 9 December, 1958. The question remains as to why, when neither the local situation, nor the requirements of the General Assembly, nor the wider international scene demanded it, UNOGIL was so hurriedly and so hugely increased in size during the final two months of its existence. It would have been most unlike the Secretary-General to have misjudged any of the relevant factors, and any suggestion that he was hoping by this means to establish the nucleus of a permanent force can be discounted, for, quite apart from his awareness of the political difficulties in the way of such a course and the unsuitability of UNOGIL for the purpose, he had just completed a report which advised against any such scheme.[28] Perhaps the least unlikely explanation for this strange course of events is that the Secretary-General was anxious to demonstrate the UN's ability to organize a large observer group speedily and efficiently, both as a reproach to the United States for not having relied on the expansion of UNOGIL when the July crisis arose, and as an indication of the kind of operation which could be launched in future.

If this was indeed the case, the Secretary-General's calculations may have been partly misconceived, for it is unlikely that the UNOGIL operation had a great deal of bearing on American policy towards the Lebanon. It may be that during its early weeks UNOGIL had the effect of checking Syria's assistance to the Lebanese dissidents or at least stopped her from increasing it, although whether it did so is largely a matter of conjecture. But the basic problem in the Lebanon seemed to stem from internal factors. Hence, even an operation of the size and efficiency which UNOGIL eventually attained would not have had a significant impact on the development of the crisis, nor on the American attitude towards it. For what the United States was primarily concerned about was the fact of Chamoun's troubles and not their origin. Whether they were largely inspired from abroad was irrelevant to the American determination that the Chamoun regime must not be overthrown. As UNOGIL was not suitable for the shoring-up process, and had

[28] UN Document A/3943.

no chance of having its mandate extended to enable it to fulfil that purpose, the United States had to act outside the UN. It happened that UNOGIL was able to play a part in the winding-up of the situation which the crisis had produced. But during the earlier stages it was very much on the sidelines. And as it was unable to discover any significant intervention it even failed to live up to the marginal accusatory role for which, in the eyes of the West, it had been cast.

Besides deepening the existing Lebanese crisis, the Iraqi *coup* of 14 July 1958 also raised an international alarm regarding Jordan. On 16 July, the day following President Eisenhower's announcement that American forces would immediately be stationed in the Lebanon 'to protect American lives and by their presence there to encourage the Lebanese Government in defence of Lebanese sovereignty and integrity',[29] King Hussein of Jordan appealed to Britain for similar encouragement. He cited a number of subversive activities which the UAR had organized against his country over the previous year and which, in sum, were said to menace its independence. Britain responded with no less alacrity than the United States, and on 17 July her forces landed near Amman. At their maximum they numbered about 3,000. Like the American action, this was intended to calm jittery nerves in a conservative sector of the Arab world, and warn the progressive forces that any attempt to repeat their Iraqi success would be sternly resisted.[30]

Unilateral action of this character is out of keeping with modern ideas about proper international behaviour, and, accordingly, its practitioners generally find it prudent to emphasize its temporary character and their preference for a multilateral solution. Britain did not supply an exception to this rule. On the very day of the landings in Jordan her representative at the UN declared in their defence that 'Aggression by fomenting civil strife in the interest of a foreign Power is one of the gravest offences against peace and security', and went on to assert that, 'Not for the first time in our long history we are actuated in what we have done by a sense of responsibility and a desire to see truly peaceful and stable conditions in the world'. But he prefaced all these remarks with the undertaking that 'If arrangements can be made by the Security Council to protect the lawful Government of Jordan from external threat and so maintain peace

[29] Paul E. Zinner (ed.) *Documents on American Foreign Relations, 1958* (New York: Harper, 1960), p. 303.
[30] Britain was also said [to have] made 'a precautionary landing in Libya (without invitation) and (to have) alerted other contingents for possible dispatch to the Sudan': Richard P. Stebbins: *The United States in World Affairs, 1958* (New York: Harper, 1959) p. 203. '

and security, the action we have felt obliged to take will be brought to an end'.[31] The last theme was frequently repeated, and a few days later Britain announced that as there was no prospect of the Security Council agreeing on the necessary measures, she proposed, in conjunction with the Government of Jordan, 'to explore urgently with the Secretary-General the possibility of devising some form of effective action by the United Nations'.[32]

In the event, the situation quickly lost its urgency. By the end of July, whether or not on account of Britain's move, there seemed little danger of an upheaval in Jordan, and the chief remaining problem was the formal liquidation of the crisis. The favoured idea—that the UN should appear to replace the Western Powers—was not easy to implement in respect of Jordan, for she was not all at keen to play host to a UN presence. It was, her representative said, the UN's responsibility to prevent both direct and indirect aggression against Jordan, but this must not involve 'the dispatch of [UN] forces or [UN] observers to be stationed on Jordan territory or to guard the Jordanian frontiers'.[33] He went on to say that his country would continue to rely for security on her own forces although towards that end she would value assistance in the shape of arms and money. He also seemed to imply that, as a means of trying to stop provocative propaganda, Jordan would not object to the establishment of a UN listening post in her country, but clearly this was near the limit of what she would accept. Subsequently he thought it desirable to emphasize that this did not mean that Jordan was opposed to co-operation with the UN, and he recalled her attitude towards the Secretary-General and the UN Truce Supervision Organization. But he stressed that his Government had definite views about the type of UN presence which it would welcome, and that they did not include one based on the pattern of the UN Emergency Force which was stationed at the Egyptian–Israeli border or even one along the lines of the Observation Group then in the Lebanon.

Jordan's sensitivity on this point was probably not abnormal, for no state likes the idea of having a sizeable UN presence on its soil. It means not being in complete control of one's own country, and so far as that is concerned it does not greatly matter who the international body represents: the fact that it is under alien authority is what goes against the grain. Then, too, in most circumstances such a presence provides tangible and cogent evidence for the claim that the host is unable to look after itself, which could have domestic as well

---

[31] Security Council, *Official Records*, 831st Meeting, paras. 32, 33, and 30.
[32] *Ibid.*, 835th Meeting, para. 17.
[33] General Assembly, *Official Records*, 735th Plenary Meeting, para 51.

as international repercussions. However, states who are, or anticipate, bargaining from weakness cannot afford to have too many
scruples of this kind, and it might therefore have been thought that,
given the intended departure of British troops, Jordan would be glad,
on balance, to have a UN presence inasmuch as it would be a sign
of the Organization's concern about her integrity. But in all probability Jordan entertained a serious doubt as to whether a presence
would in fact reflect such a concern.

In August 1958 the Arab states were displaying mutual forbear-
ance and fraternal regard in a notable degree, but Jordan could have
been under no illusions as to the durability of that state of affairs.
On account of her conservative and monarchical regime, she was
unpopular in progressive Arab circles, and it was they who called
the tune in the Arab world and who were in harmony with majority
opinion in the UN. Jordan could not, therefore, exclude the possibility that a UN presence might be less than totally vigilant on her
behalf, whether on account of instructions received from headquarters or because of the political sympathies of its members: in this
respect the Lebanon's criticism of the UN Observation Group to
which it was then playing host could hardly have been reassuring.
Thus, by accepting a substantial UN presence, Jordan would be
risking an argument with it, and perhaps worse. Moreover, her
account of such a situation would be unlikely to find much favour
at the UN. Hence, from Jordan's point of view, the issue of whether
the UN should take the place which Britain was being pressed to
vacate did not present itself in the simple form of half a loaf as
against no bread, for it raised a question as to the wholesomeness of
the popular solution.

In this Jordan was not looking to the immediate but to the more
distant future. As of August 1958 her position seemed secure, and all
members of the UN, particularly the Arabs, were primarily concerned about removing the signs of the previous month's crisis. Thus,
although it took some time to reach, an acceptable way forward was
eventually found,[34] and led to an agreement with Jordan regarding
a UN presence. It was to consist of a Special Representative of the
Secretary-General, stationed in Amman and assisted by such staff
as were found to be required, whose particular task would be to report privately on the question of foreign intervention. Jordan indicated that she would like to see similar arrangements made in
respect of other Arab countries, notably Iraq and the UAR, clearly
hoping that this would have an additional restraining effect. But
they refused to entertain the idea, and would do no more than
agree to the designation of a high-level representative at the UN's

[34] See above, pp. 224–225.

headquarters, whose function would be to make such visits to their capitals as were, from time to time, deemed to be necessary by the Secretary-General.

In this way a small UN diplomatic representation, a kind of embassy, was established in Jordan, and is still in existence. Moreover, it continues to be led by its original chief. In September 1958 the Secretary-General dispatched P. P. Spinelli, the Under-Secretary in charge of the UN's European Office in Geneva, to find out what in practical terms, would be required, and to act as his representative for the time being, with the rank of ambassador. It was anticipated that he would soon need to be replaced, on account of the UN's other claims on his time, but this proved not to be so. Mr Spinelli's duties have not required more than an occasional visit to Amman, which has resulted in his being dubbed 'the absent presence', and thus he and his mission continue to symbolize the UN's official concern for Jordan's integrity.

This was a popular outcome. Hammarskjöld would probably have preferred something more ambitious, but at least he had obtained acceptance for his idea of a UN presence at this potential trouble spot. It met the requirements of the general membership of the UN, inasmuch as it led to the departure of the British troops from Jordan, the operation being completed by 2 November 1958. And it also suited Jordan, who, indeed, successfully urged its continuation when, after six months, Mr Spinelli suggested that the situation was sufficiently quiet to warrant the mission's withdrawal.[35] The presence did not obtrude physically, nor was it politically offensive. Its head was an international civil servant in whom the Jordanian authorities had confidence, and with whom good relations were developed; and as its reports to the Secretary-General are not public documents, unless he decides to make them so, Jordan's affairs have not been subject to regular debate at the UN. More positively, the presence ensured that, should any externally inspired subversion occur, the UN would immediately be supplied with a report from a senior member of its own Secretariat, which could not easily be disregarded. This would not stand in the way of any who were set upon the overthrow of the regime, nor would it, of itself, result in international support being given to Jordan, which helps to explain why those at the UN who have little sympathy for Jordan have not thought it worth their while to try to get the presence removed. But it does not follow that it is equally insignificant in Jordan's eyes. It may have virtually no material effect, but it brings her the knowledge that should there be internal trouble the UN might well have good

[35] See Leon Gordenker, *The UN Secretary-General and the Maintenance of Peace* (New York: Columbia University Press, 1967), p. 244.

grounds for favouring an interpretation of events different to the one which would be speedily advanced by her enemies. That must be a satisfying thought, and no doubt largely accounts for Jordan's continued willingness to have the presence on her soil. For the same reason the presence is of some value to those other states who have an interest in the maintenance of the present Jordanian regime, or at least in the prevention of instability in the area. In this way therefore the cause for which British troops entered Jordan is still being served, in a very small way, by the device which was used to facilitate their removal.

V

It was, perhaps, not wholly inappropriate that the UN operations in Lebanon and Laos should backfire on their Western supporters. For, quite apart from the point that the Laotian mission was established only by procedural manœuvring of a very doubtful kind, it may be regarded as some recompense for the very poor record of Communist states in this field, their attempts to use reporting presences as a means of making propaganda against the West having been completely unsuccessful in a purely cold war context. And in fact such operations have been set up to the embarrassment of the West on no more than one occasion. Chiefly this is because an accusatory operation is a defensive weapon, and on the whole it is the West which, since 1945, has needed to defend itself rather than the Communist bloc and its friends. But when the Communists have tried to use the UN to mobilize opinion against Western initiatives, they have found that their minority position in the Organization is a severe and usually an overwhelming handicap.

This was evident right at the outset of the UN's life. In February 1946 a Ukrainian proposal that the fighting in the Dutch East Indies should be investigated was put to the Security Council, and was supported only by Poland and the Soviet Union.[36] In 1947, when the Indonesian problem was again before the UN, the Soviet Union urged that the Council's recent call for a cease-fire should be supervised by a commission made up of all its members. The appeal of this idea to the Soviet Union doubtless lay as much in the opportunity it offered to give the nationalists moral support against the Dutch as in the bearing it might have on the resolution of the conflict. But at the time it seemed innocuous enough and, quite exceptionally, it obtained the necessary seven votes, only to be defeated by a French veto.[37] Much more typical was the hostile reception given,

[36] See above, p. 43.
[37] See above, p. 51.

in the same year, by both the Council and the Assembly to the Soviet proposal that the administration of foreign aid in Greece should be supervised by the U N.[38]

These were relatively minor set-backs for the Soviet Union, for although success would have given her opportunities for making trouble, especially in the case of Greece, it is unlikely that the West would have been embarrassed on account of its basic policy: it had nothing to hide in respect of either question. In 1954, however, a situation arose which was much more promising from the Soviet point of view, but she was unable to exploit it fully on account of the weakness of her position as regards the initiation of UN action. It concerned political developments in the central American republic of Guatemala, which, under the presidency of Colonel J. Arbenz, had for some time been moving towards the left. Large tracts of land belonging to the powerful United Fruit Company, of Boston, had been expropriated, Communist influence was said to be growing in the Government, and it was alleged that Guatemala was being used as a base for subversion in other parts of the area. Due warnings emerged from Washington regarding the menace of a Soviet bridgehead in the Americas, and in March 1954 the American Secretary of State, Mr John Foster Dulles, persuaded the tenth inter-American Conference, meeting at Caracas, to pass a resolution which both gave expression to the American view and paved the way for action. It declared that 'the domination or control of the political institutions of any American state by the international Communist movement, extending to this hemisphere the political system of an extra-continental power, would constitute a threat to the sovereignty and political independence of the American states, endangering the peace of America, and would call for a Meeting of Consultation to consider the adoption of appropriate action in accordance with existing treaties'.[39]

Thus prepared, the United States stepped up her propaganda campaign against Guatemala and entered into special military agreements with two other central American states: Honduras, who shared a border with Guatemala, and Nicaragua. In Honduras an exiled Guatemalan officer, Colonel Armas, was openly plotting to 'liberate' his country from the Arbenz regime and was widely assumed to be receiving considerable assistance from the United States Central Intelligence Agency. In news conferences Mr Dulles indicated that an Organization of American States (OAS) Foreign Ministers meeting would soon be held to deal with the threat which Guatemala was deemed to pose, and on 10 June he publicly stated

[38] See above, pp. 210–211.
[39] Wainhouse, *op. cit.*, p. 126.

his hope that the OAS 'will be able to help the people of Guatemala to rid themselves of the malignant force which has seized on
them'.[40]

However, on 18 June, before the OAS could be brought into
action, Colonel Armas had crossed the frontier with a small band of
a few hundred men, supported, it was said, by aeroplanes coming
from the same direction. Guatemala immediately appealed to the
Security Council to put a stop to the aggression which was in progress, claiming that it had been perpetrated by Honduras and
Nicaragua 'at the instigation of certain foreign monopolies'.[41] She
also made a similar request to the Inter-American Peace Committee,
which, strictly speaking, was not a part of the OAS machinery.
Nevertheless, this latter move was probably mistaken, for it enabled
the United States to argue with greater conviction than would
otherwise have been possible that the matter should be left in the
hands of regional agencies, in which she was the predominant figure.
Guatemala appeared to realize this, for her second appeal was suspended and then, on 21 June, withdrawn. But by this time the
Security Council had already taken its first decisions on the matter.

At the Council, which met on 20 June, Guatemala asked that
Honduras and Nicaragua should be called upon to apprehend the
exiles and mercenaries who were responsible for the invasion, and
that an observation mission should be dispatched to Guatemala, and
to other countries if necessary, to report on the situation. There was
no evidence to indicate that such a body would check her adversaries,
although she could always hope that it might have some effect of
that kind. But her willingness to receive it was at least a way of proclaiming her innocence to the world, and there was also the consideration that if her request was met it would probably be something of
an embarrassment to those who were working for her Governments'
downfall. They, however, no doubt for that very reason, were
strongly opposed to Guatemala's suggestion. They therefore, in the
first place, claimed that there was no basis for the charges of aggression: it was, said the United States representative, 'an unspeakable
libel', and 'flatly untrue'.[42] And, secondly, they argued that the
matter should be dealt with by the OAS, saying that it was precisely
the kind of problem which, in the first instance, should be dealt with
by that Organization. A draft resolution which would have had the
Council refer the case to the OAS was introduced by Brazil and
Colombia and supported by 10 members, but vetoed by the eleventh,

---

[40] Inis L. Claude, Jr. 'The OAS, the UN, and the United States', *International
Conciliation*, No. 547 (March 1964) p. 29.
[41] Wainhouse, *op. cit.*, p. 127.
[42] Wainhouse, *op. cit.*, p. 129.

the Soviet Union. The Council was, however, able to agree unanimously to a French call for the immediate termination of any action likely to cause further bloodshed.

Interest now shifted to the Inter-American Peace Committee. Guatemala had withdrawn her complaint to this body, but Honduras and Nicaragua were anxious that it should send a fact-finding mission to the three countries. From their point of view such an enquiry promised to be much safer than one organized by the UN. For this same reason Guatemala refused to co-operate and once again turned to the Security Council in the company of the Soviet Union. But the Council did not even discuss the substantive issue, for on 25 June Brazil and Colombia opposed the motion for the adoption of the agenda, and were supported by China, Turkey and the United States, which was sufficient to block this preliminary procedural requirement. In desperation, Guatemala agreed, on the following day, to receive and co-operate with an Inter-American commission of investigation, but it was too late, for within 48 hours the Arbenz regime had been ousted by Colonel Armas forces. The new government requested the Peace Committee not to intervene, and there was now no pressure for it to do so. The desired end had been accomplished, and the OAS meeting which had been called to guard the peace of the continent was postponed *sine die*. Guatemala's policy swung back into line with that of the United States, and the United Fruit Company was reunited with its land.

The Guatemalan case seemed to illustrate that the Soviet Union would find it even more than ordinarily difficult to defend her friends with a UN reporting presence should they be Latin Americans. For any such attempt would encounter not only the usual Western opposition but also the traditional concern of the United States to keep foreigners, especially hostile foreigners, out of Latin American affairs, an attitude which, naturally enough, had been intensified by the cold war. Moreover, at the time of the Guatemalan crisis, Senator McCarthy was still a power in the land, and the hysteria which he had generated could plausibly be seen in the presentation of the American case. In a statement issued on 22 June, the United States Ambassador to the UN, Henry Cabot Lodge, Jr., claimed that by endeavouring to involve the Security Council, Guatemala appeared to be 'a cat's paw of the Soviet conspiracy to meddle in the Western Hemisphere'[43], and when at the Council next meeting on 25 June, the question arose as to whether the provisional agenda containing Guatemala's complaint should be adopted, Mr Lodge warned that if the Council failed 'to respect the right of the Organization of American States to achieve a pacific settlement of the dispute

[43] Claude, *op. cit.*, p. 25.

between Guatemala and its neighbours' it would produce 'a catastrophe of such dimensions as will gravely impair the future effectiveness of both the United Nations itself and of regional organizations such as the Organization of American states'.[44] Such remarks seemed only to support the claims of those who urged that essentially, the OAS was a means whereby American power could be channelled and legitimized, and the role of the Organization at this time together with the outcome of the crisis did nothing to weaken this point of view.

However, a channel is capable of allowing movement in two directions, and the OAS does offer the Latin American states some opportunities to put pressure on the United States. For they are not her puppets, and the need which, from time to time, she feels to obtain their support does put certain limits on her effective freedom of action. Moreover, the existence of the UN strengthens the bargaining power of the Latin Americans, for it provides them with an alternative forum in the event of their being completely dissatisfied with American behaviour. Thus if the United States is anxious to keep a matter away from the world body, the ability of the Latin Americans to raise it there, and the support they would be sure to get from a number of other UN members, can only cause her to move with an added measure of caution and solicitude. Of course, there are many devices short of force which the United States can use in an effort to win Latin American acceptance of her view. And there are some issues on which she will do as she thinks fit, whatever the OAS or the UN may say. But she does like to have the Latin Americans behind her in hemispheric crises, and does not wish this to be obviously the result of intensive arm twisting. Which means that the OAS is of value not only to the United States and is far from being the passive instrument of her will.

In the case of Guatemala, the issue which arose was the sort which most easily offends Latin American susceptibilities, for, in effect, it concerned the intervention of the dominant continental power in the internal affairs of one of its weakest states. However, this was largely counterbalanced by the anti-Communist banner under which the United States acted, which was very popular at the time, and by the zeal which she was demonstrating. Clearly, it would have been most unwise to fall out of line at this point. Nevertheless, the United States' path was not entirely smooth. Mexico and Argentina abstained on the OAS resolution of March 1954; Brazil, while helping to put the American case in the Security Council, at the same time indicated her belief that the Council was competent to deal with the matter; and at the subsequent meeting of the

[44] *Ibid.*, pp. 26–27.

General Assembly several Latin American states emphasized that their OAS membership did not prevent them from taking a matter straight to the UN if they so wished. The outlook for the Soviet Union so far as Latin American issues was concerned was not, therefore, quite as black as it might have seemed. And eleven years later a breakthrough was achieved, when another Central American crisis involving the intervention of the United States saw the establishment of a UN reporting mission, despite the fact that the United States was receiving the formal support of the OAS.

It occurred in Dominica. In 1961 the dictator Trujillo had been assassinated after a long and corrupt rule, and two years later, following a number of governmental changes, the left-wing Juan Bosch became the republic's first democratically elected president for over a generation. He had won a decisive victory but, within a matter of months had been overthrown by the military, who, in September 1963, installed a civilian triumvirate. However, its policies were resented both within and beyond the armed forces, and on 25 April 1965 it was overthrown by Colonel Caamano acting with left-wing support and with the intention of securing the return of ex-President Bosch. This provoked an immediate reaction on the right led by General Wessin, a staunch Catholic and fierce anti-Communist. Fighting broke out between the two factions, the challengers to Caamano's regime staking their claim to legitimacy on 28 April by setting up a three man military junta at the vital San Isidro base which Wessin commanded. On 4 May Caamano was sworn in as the 'Constitutional President' to which his opponents replied, four days later, with a new junta under General Imbert, which took the name of the Government of National Reconstruction.

Into this anarchical situation, on 28 April, came United States marines and parachute troops, the first time that they had moved in this way since President Franklin Roosevelt had inaugurated the Good Neighbour policy in 1933. Their landing was also a departure from the popular inter-American doctrine of non-intervention, which, as laid down in the OAS Charter, declares that save for 'measures adopted for the maintenance of peace and security in accordance with existing treaties', the territory of an American state 'may not be the object, even temporarily, of military occupation or of other measures of force taken by another state, directly or indirectly, on any grounds whatever.'[45] However, President Johnson explained that the collapse of governmental authority in Dominica put the lives of American and other foreign nationals in jeopardy, and therefore demanded this humanitarian measure. By 30 April

[45] Articles 19 and 17.

2,500 out of the 3,000 Americans in Dominica had been evacuated, but strong United States forces continued to arrive, reaching 9,500 by 2 May, on which date it was announced that another 4,500 were on their way. This might have seemed a somewhat disproportionate measure, but at the same time President Johnson stated that, as had not been unsuspected, the exercise was also intended to prevent the emergence of another Communist state in the hemisphere. It had emerged, he said, that what had begun as a popular democratic revolution, was being taken over by a band of Communist conspirators, and on 5 May his Government published to a somewhat sceptical world the names of 58 'Communist and Castroist' leaders who were alleged to be involved. The list was then found to contain some duplication, which reduced the number to 54. By this time they were pinning down about 19,000 American troops.

In Dominica's capital, Santo Domingo, the United States forces had established a 'safety zone', which included the American and a number of other embassies and the hotel where many foreign nationals had gathered. They had also thrown a defensive perimeter around the San Isidro base, which was the headquarters of the right-wing contenders and was much used by the United States in connection with her troop movements. Additionally, on 3 May the United States established a corridor linking the safety zone and the San Isidro base. Its object was said to be to ensure the flow of food and medicines to the population of Santo Domingo, but it was also noticed that, besides running through, and thus splitting, territory controlled by Caamano, it also had the effect of encircling that part of the city in which he had his headquarters and his greatest strength.

The containment of the Caamano regime was clearly within the power of the United States. But, while she was willing to bear the burden of resisting a Communist conspiracy in Dominica, she was anxious that the honour of doing so should be shared by her fellow American states, who, in 1962, with the exception of Cuba, were persuaded to declare 'that adherence by any member of the Organization of American states to Marxism-Leninism is uncompatible with the inter-American system'.[46] However, the American republics varied considerably in their zeal for the ideas which this declaration represented, and there was also a great deal of doubt in some inter-American quarters as to whether the Dominican situation fell within its terms. Thus, while, on 1 May, the OAS agreed to the dispatch of a five member committee to Dominica with a view to obtaining a cease-fire, it responded much less keenly to the American suggestion that order should be restored there through the medium of an

[46] Gordon Connell-Smith: 'The OAS and the Dominican Crisis', 21 *The World Today* No. 6 (June 1965) p. 232.

inter-American force operating under the authority of the OAS. The vote on the proposal was deferred more than once, and when, finally, on 6 May, it was taken, the American scheme was approved by only 14 votes to 5, the bare two-thirds majority which was necessary for its adoption. Venezuela abstained, and Chile, Ecuador, Mexico, Peru, and Uruguay voted against it. One of those in favour was the Dominican representative who, very conveniently, was speaking for the right and not the left-wing faction. In the absence of this vote, the resolution would have failed.

Its passage, however, made little difference on the ground. The inter-American force came into formal existence on 24 May, and consisted of 250 troops from Honduras and 164 from Nicaragua, together with 25 Costa Rican policemen and the American contingent, which now numbered 22,000. With the confidence that came from her superiority, both generally and in Dominica, the United States was able to take a magnaminous view of the question of command, and on 25 May General Alvim of Brazil was appointed Commander of the force, which was shortly to be strengthened by the addition of 1,250 troops from his country's army. General Palmer, who headed the American forces in Dominica, became the deputy commander, but rather spoiled the effect of this democratic gesture by saying that he would retain tactical command of the force and that if there was a policy conflict between the OAS and the United States he would follow the guidance of his own Government. Which, a week later, brought the unhappy comment from Washington that the General was not authorized to say that he maintained a direct responsibility to his own Government and that if he had said it he would have been mistaken.

Meanwhile, the whole question of Dominica had been vigorously discussed in the Security Council on the initiative of the Soviet Union, who wished the Council to condemn the United States and call for her withdrawal. Without going this far, Uruguay, France, and Jordan were also critical of the American action, whereas Britain said she understood what had prompted it and, like the other members of the Council, agreed with the United States that it was best left in the hands of the OAS. Whereupon Uruguay indicated her dissent from this point of view by proposing that the Secretary-General be invited to follow closely the events in Dominica and take such measures as he might deem appropriate for the purpose of reporting to the Council on all aspects of the situation. To have the UN meddling in Dominica, even in the mild shape of enquiries being made on behalf of the Secretary-General, was just what the United States did not want, and her representative therefore regretted that he could not agree that Uruguay's suggestion would be helpful at the current point; indeed, he judged that it would only complicate the situation. That seemed to put an end to any possibility that the Council might be able to establish a presence in Dominica. The United States, with whom, effectively, the matter rested, was making it quite clear that the U N must keep out of her central American concerns, and was also successfully prolonging the Council's consideration of the matter to avoid it being taken to the less sympathetic Assembly. It would be a mistake, she urged, to interpose the Security Council into the situation just when the regional organization seemed to be coping with it effectively.

Then, however, an event occurred which, though of small importance in itself, enabled the U N to get its foot in the Dominican door. As a result of the efforts of the O A S mission, a cease-fire had been signed on 5 May. But, on 14 May it was reported to the Security Council that U Thant had received a telegram from the Ministry of Foreign Affairs in the Constitutionalist Government claiming that as the result of an air attack on the Caamano radio station Santo Domingo was threatened with destruction, that United States forces were moving into his Government's territory, and that the O A S was no longer capable of handling the situation. In vain did Mr Stevenson of the United States endeavour to show that this was another way of saying that the O A S was proving too effective for the Caamano rebels. Nor was attention paid to his argument that occasional clashes in Dominica no more pointed to the failure of the O A S than clashes in Cyprus indicated the failure of the U N Force there. Equally fruitless were his denials that the United States had either permitted or ordered the attack and his explanation that the extent of American penetration into the rebel zone consisted of a vehicle being driven into it by mistake. The fact was that the incidents now complained of, in which it was reported that at least two people had been killed, had a numbing effect on those who were opposed to the involvement of the U N, and crystallized the restlessness which had been growing within and beyond the Council at the U N's inaction and apparent helplessness. Sudan, the Ivory Coast, and Malaysia quickly put a draft resolution together calling for a strict cease-fire and inviting the Secretary-General to send a representative to Dominica 'for the purpose of reporting to the Security Council on the present situation',[47] and it was put to the Council on the same day. None of those who did not like the proposal felt able to oppose it, not even the United States, and they all made the best of a bad job by voting in its favour, so passing it unanimously.

The Secretary-General immediately dispatched an advance party to Dominica under the leadership of his Military Adviser, General

[47] UN Document S/6355. Adopted as Security Council resolution 203 (1965).

Rikhye. Three days later, on 17 May, he appointed Mr J. A. Mayobre, the Executive Secretary of the UN Economic Commission for Latin America, as his personal representative in Dominica, and he arrived there on the following day, setting up a small mission.[48] He was said to have played an important part in bringing about a suspension of hostilities on 21 May, which, two days later, by informal agreement, was extended indefinitely. However, the UN presence in Dominica was chiefly significant, both in intention and in actuality, for its reporting activities. The states who keenly supported its establishment saw such a move as a way of expressing their opposition to the action of the United States and of placing some obstacles in her path. And, although those of this persuasion were in a minority in the Council, it seems clear that they reflected the wishes of most members of the UN. Their thinking probably also had much in common with that of the Secretary-General. The role of the presence, therefore, was to keep an independent eye on what was going on, and particularly on the United States and the Government of National Reconstruction, who were thought to be most deserving of critical attention. It was also intended to be available as an amplifier to those in Dominica who wished to ventilate a grievance, especially to the Constitutionalist regime, which was generally regarded as having most reason to complain. In both these respects it was hoped that through the mission's reports to the Secretary-General wide publicity would be given to its accounts of the situation, and that in turn this would have some deterrent effect on the actions of the right-wing and its American supporters. In short, in accordance with the balance of sympathies at the UN, the presence was conceived as a moral counterweight to the physical strength of the United States, as something of a safeguard for the weaker side.

The Secretary-General's representative fulfilled these expectations in his very first report, which made it clear that, in effect, the United States was aiding the Imbert faction. This could only have underlined American feelings about the UN's intervention in the Caribbean. She had not felt able to oppose the resolution of 14 May, which, after all, was a relatively mild affair, but even so there is no doubt that she was exceedingly annoyed at the circumstances which permitted its passage, and was anxious that it should be of as little consequence as possible. Thus, at the UN, she tried to minimize both

---

[48] Mr Mayobre, a Venezuelan, experienced some difficulty in gaining admission to Dominica, for when he arrived it emerged that, under a decree dating from Trujillo's days, he was officially *persona non grata*. Fortunately, the United States, although not at all keen on his presence, was willing to lend its good offices, with the result that Mr Mayobre was able to proceed with his task. However, certain formalities had to be observed each time he re-entered Dominica.

This incident perhaps helps to explain why inter-American bodies generally find it convenient to establish their headquarters in Washington.

the importance and the role of the UN mission. On 19 May the Council unaminously agreed to ask Mayobre to concentrate his efforts on the immediate securing of a suspension of hostilities, but this was not put in a formal resolution because of the insistence of the United States that the role of the OAS should be upheld. Subsequently she introduced a draft resolution which would have requested the Secretary-General's representative to co-ordinate his activities with the OAS Secretary-General, but it was later withdrawn. On the other hand, an amended Uruguayan resolution, which would have invited the OAS to co-operate with the UN's Secretary-General, was found wanting by the United States on the ground that it neither gave sufficient recognition to the role of the OAS nor reflected the proper balance between the UN and the regional organization. She must also have taken objection to it on account of its call to all states not to give direct or indirect help to either of the factions. However, not much was required of the United States and her friends in order to defeat the resolution, both because only five states were in favour of it and because it was opposed by the Soviet Union on the ground that it was insufficiently direct in its condemnation of the United States: hence they needed to do no more than abstain.

By contrast with Uruguay, Britain earned a favourable mark by introducing a resolution which would have welcomed recent OAS decisions, but, like its American counterpart, it was not voted upon. France, however, in a manner which was becoming familiar, caused pain by publicly taking note of the divisions within the Council and proposing that it should merely express its serious concern over the Dominican situation, recall its resolution of 14 May and request that the truce at Santo Domingo should be transformed into a permanent cease-fire. This draft resolution, observed Mr Stevenson, omitted any reference at all to the OAS. When, therefore, it came to the vote on 22 May, the United States abstained, but the other 10 members of the Council gave it their approval. Subsequently there were some moves to get the size of the UN mission increased and to give it the additional task of investigating complaints and acts of violence. However, in view of the American attitude there was no chance of extending Mayobre's mandate, and the Secretary-General assured the Council that his representative had sufficient staff to carry out his existing functions of observation and report.

The Soviet Union therefore tried another tack. On 16 June the United States complained in the Council that the inter-American force had been subject to a deliberate and premeditated attack by Colonel Caamano's forces on the previous day, and, in an endeavour to take some of the wind out of her opponents sails, she added that its primary purpose was to incite the Council to action in support of Caamano. Whatever the calculations in Dominica, this, as the United States had rightly anticipated, was certainly the Council's response. Caamano's spokesman declared that the incident had been provoked by the United States, and demonstrated the need for a strengthened UN mission. The Soviet Union, however, was more imaginative, and, relying on Article 28 of the Charter, proposed that a visiting mission of the Council should continue its consideration of the question of Santo Domingo. This was not at all pleasing to the United States, whose representative spoke ominously of how it would cause great confusion and exacerbate an already difficult situation. As a result, nothing came of the idea.

Clearly the United States wanted to be left alone in Dominica, and, after her initial humbug, let the world know what, in general terms, she was trying to achieve. But there was very much less clarity as to the way in which her intervention was expected to reach the stated goal. There was no doubt that her immediate intention was to contain the Caamano faction, and so prevent them taking over the Government of Dominica. It is also probable that, at the outset, she looked on Caamano's rivals as at least the lesser of two evils, and would therefore have favoured a regime led, if not by one of their number, then by someone who was distinctly in sympathy with them. Certainly the disposition of United States troops assisted General Imbert's forces. The Latin American Correspondent of *The Times*, for example, reported on 21 May that 'Nobody supposes that General Imbert could control the capital if the Americans were not there'. However, it was also the case that the American forces were not allowed to take the offensive against Caamano, and stood in the way of Imbert doing so. As between the factions they were supposed to observe strict neutrality. In one sense this merely confirmed, in a new setting, the old adage that non-intervention is a form of intervention, but it did leave the problem of what to do about Caamano. He might not be able to take over Dominica, but, equally, he was firmly entrenched in downtown Santo Domingo. Possibly the United States thought that once he realized that his cause could not succeed he would call off his 'revolt' if he was presented with a presidential candidate who was not drawn from the ranks of the Imbert junta or its immediate supporters. An alternative possibility, however, was that the United States had not intervened on the basis of a clearly thought-out plan regarding the future, but rather out of the jitteryness which anything at all resembling the Cuban precedent tended to produce.

Whether or not this was so, it did seem to be the case that even before her build-up of troops was complete, the United States was having second thoughts about its necessity. It was reported that as early as the middle of May she was reassessing the situation on the basis of evidence that Caamano's faction was not, after all, in the hands of Communists, and, indeed, had wide support in Dominica. On 16 May a small high-level group, led by Mr McGeorge Bundy, the special Presidential Assistant for National Security Affairs, visited Dominica on a secret mission and these were signs that 'the restoration of order' was now beginning to mean not so much a defeat for Caamano as a genuine compromise between the factions. The United States was said to be backing the establishment of a national coalition under a minister in the 1963 Bosch regime. At the end of May, the OAS announced that, out of a sum made available by the United States, it would pay the salaries of all Dominican civil servants, irrespective of which side they supported. And the inter-American force had no sooner reached its peak than it began to suffer drastic reductions. With the arrival of the Brazilian unit of 1,250 troops, the United States withdrew 6,000 marines, and further cuts brought the size of the force down to 12,700 by the beginning of July.

No doubt all this had something to do with the generally critical international reaction to the American intervention, which found some reflection in the Security Council. But in all probability it was chiefly a consequence of the realization by the United States that she had misjudged the situation in Dominica. For talk of a Communist threat was now played down, a process which must have been helped by the awkwardness of the Imbert faction, which showed no disposition to do as it was told by the United States, and, indeed, sometimes caused her much embarrassment. However, the United States could not simply withdraw, for that would surely lead to more fighting between the factions, and so make a mockery of her but recently completed efforts to get an inter-American arrangement for keeping order in Dominica. It might also raise the bogey of Communism and Castroism once again. Thus the achievement of an agreed political settlement became the chief aim of American policy.

Such a solution, however, was not at all easy to achieve. A three-man OAS committee consisting of the representatives of Brazil, El Salvador, and the United States, began negotiations with the two Dominican groups in June, and also had discussions on the matter with the Secretary-General's representative. But it was distrusted by Caamano, who would have preferred to deal with the UN, and was also falling out of favour with Imbert, whose attitude towards the OAS was seen in his request on 21 July to the Security Council to use its influence to secure the withdrawal of the inter-American force. A similar request was made to the same meeting by Colonel Caamano's spokesman: evidently both sides now felt, or professed to feel, that they were being impeded by the force. But the United States was unmoved. Her troops, and those of her friends, were now ful-filling an interpository role, keeping the potential combatants apart, and she was determined that they should not leave until a settlement was reached. Perhaps this knowledge acted as a spur to the contend-ing factions. In any event, after long negotiations with the OAS committee, they agreed, on 31 August, to an 'Act of Dominican Re-conciliation', and on 4 September Dr H. Garcia Godoy, the Foreign Minister in the Bosch regime, was installed as provisional President for nine months pending general elections at the end of the period. No doubt as part of the bargain the power behind the Dominican right wing, General Wessin, left the country on 9 September in an American aircraft, bound for Miami, where he was supposed to become Consul-General. But he complained that he had been exiled literally at the point of an American bayonet, and refused the post.

The inter-American force now assumed the role of guarantor of the provisional Government, and the need for such an arrangement was soon evident. The Godoy regime was assailed by assassinations, riots, and plots from both political wings, and in January 1966 the leaders of both sides, including Colonel Caamano, were ordered into virtual exile. In accordance with a growing international practice the diplomatic corps was deemed to provide suitable employment for some of the troublemakers, 12 of them being appointed as military attaches in various parts of the world. The remaining group of 22 were appointed to an extended study and training mission in Israel. This almost provoked a right-wing *coup*, but it was realized that the United States was behind Godoy, and so the officers concerned went quietly. On 1 June, elections were held for a new president, and saw the defeat of Bosch and a decisive victory for the right of centre Dr S. Balaguer, whose party also won the Congressional elections. He was not anxious for the immediate withdrawal of the inter-American force, now down to 6,500, including 5,000 Americans and a small Paraguayan contingent. But he accepted a phased withdrawal which was to begin in July and be completed by 20 September 1966. The deadline was met.

In the year which had passed since the installation of the provis-ional Government the UN's presence had not played a significant role. The Security Council had adjourned its meetings on Dominica on 26 July 1965, and did not discuss the subject again. It was, how-ever, the Council's wish that the Secretary-General should continue to submit reports on the situation, based on those of his representa-tive, and this was done. It was a sign of the Organization's continued interest in the situation and was something of a safeguard against the possibility of further unilateral American action. The UN's presence was not, therefore, much to the liking of the United States, but in practice, and by contrast with the earlier period, it did not give rise to any tension after September 1965, for the mission did not now present a threat to American interests. Both it and the United States were anxious for the same result: an agreed and stable Dominican government which would permit the departure of the inter-American force. Thus the UN's presence, while not without significance, became essentially symbolic, and did not serve an active political function. The Secretary-General's representative found that it was not necessary for him to be in Dominica all the time, and therefore, while maintaining a small office in order to gather and submit reports to headquarters, was able to fulfil his duties by periodic visits. Once the inter-American force had finally left, the Secretary-General also withdrew the UN mission.

On more than one occasion U Thant commented on the fact that the Dominican case was the first occasion on which a UN presence had found itself having to coexist with the activity of a regional organization, and he usually implied that he would not have been unhappy to think that it might also be the last. This was not another way of encouraging regional bodies to assert themselves in the peace-keeping field; rather the Secretary-General was expressing his concern that the action of the OAS might possibly be a dangerous precedent for the UN. To think in these terms, however, could be misleading.

In the first place, while the UN may not hitherto have had to work in conjunction with a regional organization, it had frequently operated in the presence of armed forces, and it had not been uncommon for some, at least, of those forces to be foreign to the host country. Too much should not be made in this connection, therefore, of the fact that the United States got the OAS to legitimize her presence in Dominica. The second points flows from this. It is that the Dominican question did not so much illustrate a conflict between a universal and a regional organization as between the UN and the United States. And, seen in this light, the UN really was breaking new ground, but of a kind rather different from that identified by U Thant. For, however much the UN may feel it desirable to play a part in the world's troubles, it usually finds the way firmly barred when a conflict occurs within the geographical sphere of influence of a major Power and is already being handled by that Power. In this case, therefore, the remarkable thing about the UN's action was not that it was relatively minor but that it was able to make any physical move at all. Some have lamented the fact that the financial crisis over peace-keeping which the UN was going through at this time prevented the Organization from replacing the United States and the OAS with its own force. But there would have been no realistic possibility of that even if the UN's own arrangements had been in tip-top shape, for clearly the United States would have stood in its way. Even a small reporting mission was almost too much for her to swallow, and it was only established on account of the situation which was created on 14 May 1965 by the misbehaviour of the faction which was receiving American support, and by the reluctance of the United States to cast her first veto. Thus the UN was not only able to establish its first Latin American presence. It was also, for the first time in the peace-keeping field, acting in a manner which was contrary to the wishes and interests of the United States, and that in an area which she had long claimed as solely her preserve. This, from the regional point of view, was the true significance of the Dominican case.

VI

Thus the Soviet Union scored her first, albeit minor, peace-keeping success against the United States. But although the United States depicted her action in Dominica in an East–West context, the criticism which she met in the Security Council stemmed not from Communist sympathies but from the fact that the American action had about it an unmistakably colonialist air. For, by 1965, the UN contained many new, weak, and potentially unstable states who were understandably touchy about a large state sending its troops into the territory of a small neighbour on the grounds that it was about to undergo some undesirable political developments. Such action smacked too much of the paternalism which many UN members rejoiced to have but recently overthrown. However, the Dominican operation was and remains the only case of a fact-finding mission being established for a clearly prophylactic purpose in other than cold war circumstances. This has been chiefly due to two reasons. First, in such situations the Great Powers have moved very cautiously in their relationships with smaller states and the colonial Powers have been overwhelmingly concerned with the conduct of orderly and face-saving retreats rather than with asserting themselves in the world. And second, the countries who have tried to use reporting presences as a means of defence have been the colonial Powers themselves, which has meant that their appeals have met with a stony response from the UN. For most members, far from having sympathy with them, have been working for their downfall. Accordingly they have vigorously opposed any fact-finding activities which might conceivably show the colonialists in less than a totally unfavourable light.

This has resulted in Britain being twice rebuffed in respect of

South Arabian problems. In 1959 six territories in the hinterland of Aden came together as the Federation of South Arabia, and, continuing her defence obligations to the component sheikhdoms, amirates, and sultanates, which dated back to the 1880s, Britain undertook to protect the new entity. Subsequently it was joined by most of those other territories in the area who were in some kind of dependent relationship with Britain. The Federation was seen by Britain as a way of establishing a viable state in the area, which would permit her ultimate withdrawal. The anti-colonialists, however, saw it as a device to secure the landward defences of Britain's base at Aden. The Yemenis, in particular, were irate, as they conceived themselves to be the rightful owners of the area, and apprehended that the realization of their claim would now be a more difficult task. However, they did not lose heart, and by subversion and intervention notably added to the problems of the Federal Government.

One base for their activities was a fort near Harib, just on the Yemeni side of the border with South Arabia. On 28 March 1964, following the Federation's invocation of its treaty with Britain, this fort was the object of a punitive air raid, the inhabitants having first been warned by the dropping of leaflets. This was meat and drink to the anti-colonialists, whose doctrine permitted attacks on the Federation but not its defence, and the Security Council was called into session to hear the Yemen's charges of British aggression. Here Britain made it clear that, for her part, she would welcome the withdrawal of military forces from both sides of the border and the stationing of UN observers along its whole length. This, however, was attacked by the Arab states as a diversionary manœuvre and an effort to further Britain's policy of balkanizing the area. In short, it would, as intended, assist the defensive party, and in this context such action was deemed to be wholly improper by those who, backed by the Soviet Union in the Council and by a majority of the Assembly's members, were in the stronger procedural position. Thus the suggestion was quietly forgotten, although the draft resolution which condemned reprisals and deplored Britain's action did call on both parties to exercise restraint and ask the Secretary-General to try his hand at settling the problem. In consequence when, on 9 April, the resolution was put to a vote, Britain, with the United States keeping her company, did no more than abstain, so allowing its passage. She still professed to hope that it might be possible to get UN observers on the frontier, or at least to secure its demarcation by the UN. The Yemen, however, would not co-operate, and even refused to take official note of the existence of a border, this being based on her assertion that South Arabia was a part of southern Yemen. In face of this attitude nothing came of Britain's ideas, and the wider mediatory mandate which the Council had entrusted to the Secretary-General met an identical fate.

A similar series of events occurred two years later. Air attacks on the South Arabian Federation continued, and on 4 August 1966 Britain asked the Security Council to deplore them, and repeated her willingness to explore the possibility of some form of UN observation in the area. The representatives of the UAR and the Yemen replied by asserting that Britain's claims were a complete fabrication, and the Soviet Union made the debate an occasion for merriment, comparing Britain's complaint to the flying saucers and other unidentified flying objects which, her representative said, people in the West sometimes thought they discerned. Later New Zealand suggested that the Secretary-General should arrange for a qualified and impartial team of observers to carry out an on the spot enquiry into the particular incident which Britain had complained about, and this proposal obtained a fair measure of support, including Britain's. It looked as if it might obtain the necessary nine votes (the Council had now been increased from 11 to 15 members), but the Yemen and the UAR were strongly opposed to it, and it seemed certain that the Soviet Union would cast a negative vote, so defeating the proposal even if it obtained the support of nine members. As a result it was not pressed to a division, and instead, on 16 August, the Council accepted, without objection, a formula which merely asked the Secretary-General to continue to use his good offices to settle outstanding differences. Nothing came of this, in any shape or form.

A country which, much more than Britain, would have valued the help of the UN but which has repeatedly failed in its efforts to obtain sympathetic reports, is Portugal. She has set her face against the prevalent view as to the proper treatment of colonies, and instead of offering independence to her overseas possessions, has declared them to be a part of a unitary Portuguese state, putting before them the goal of a racially integrated society to be reached through the civilizing influence of the Lisbon Government. This has enraged the swelling ranks of the new, ex-colonial states, which, together with her relative weakness, has caused Portugal to look to the UN as a means of certifying the sincerity and beneficence of her intentions and their harmlessness to other states. However, as the UN, for these purposes, is simply the ex-colonial states writ large, there has been no question of a presence being established which, on account either of its composition or the circumstances of the case, might conceivably bring in a report which gave Portugal's policies some justification or support.

The most notable instance of this occurred in 1961 in connection with India's threat to Goa. This small territory, with a population of some 600,000, had been a Portuguese possession for four centuries, but—surrounded on three sides by India and with the western Indian Ocean on the fourth—some uncertainty had hung over its future since Britain's departure from the sub-continent in 1947. Portugal had made it clear that she had no intention of handing it over to India in the manner in which Pondicherry and four other French settlements had been transferred in 1956, and thus over the years the issue had given rise to sporadic tension. Towards the end of 1961, spurred on by an Afro-Asian 'seminar' on Portuguese colonialism held in Delhi in October, by the embarrassment caused by China's Himalayan incursions, and by the approach of general elections, the Indian administration began to take a tougher line. In November shots fired at Indian boats from a Portuguese island sparked off a series of incidents along the Goa frontier, and was followed by the movement of large numbers of Indian troops to the immediate vicinity. On 11 December, in a phrase which was unhappily reminiscent of the 1930s, Mr Nehru declared that India's patience was exhausted.

Already, in September, Portugal had announced that Goa was open to all impartial observers, and had expressed the hope that the territory might be visited by world personalities. Now, on 8 December, she suggested to India that independent international observers should be placed on the frontier, and emphasized that, contrary to what was being alleged, India was in no way threatened by Portugal. However, as the Indian representative said later in the Security Council, that was not the point. 'The point is that this is a colonial territory which is part of India in an inseparable part of India—and it must come back to India.' In his country's judgment Portugal was in illegal and immoral occupation of her territory, having obtained it through the infliction of force and trickery on the people of India 450 years ago, and 'there can be no question of aggression against your own frontier'.[49] Equally there could be no question of placing international observers on what was but an artificial internal boundary, and one, moreover, which India proposed to rectify. Hence Portugal's suggestion came to nought. On the night of 17–18 December Goa was invaded, and was taken within two days. Portugal had been refused the use of the British air bases for the transfer of reinforcements, and she was also denied any comfort in the Security Council. The United States, Britain, France, and Turkey introduced a resolution calling for a cease-fire, an Indian withdrawal, and a solution by peaceful means, but although it received the necessary seven votes it was not passed on account of a Soviet veto. A counter-resolution, calling on Portugal to terminate her hostile action and

[49] Security Council, *Official Records*, 987th Meeting, paras 43 and 46.

co-operate with India in the liquidation of her colonial possessions in India received only four votes. The outcome was represented by Mr Stevenson of the United States as possibly the first act in a drama which could end in the death of the Organization. The Soviet Union, however, declared that the rejection of a proposal aimed at supporting a colonial Power was to the Council's credit. There is no doubt where the sympathies of the Assembly would have lain had the matter been taken there.

One significant aspect of the Goan affair was Portugal's emphasis that any outside appraisals of the situation must be made by persons of an impartial and independent frame of mind. Even at a time of crisis she was insistent on that. She must have realized that any such international action would in all probability be of no practical avail, but it would have held out the promise that Goa's death would be officially recorded in terms of murder. If, however, she paid no attention to the composition of the team of observers which she sought, she ran the risk of Goa's demise being accompanied by a certificate declaring that it was an instance of justifiable homicide, which would have been appreciably worse for her than an unobserved killing. In other words, Portugal was most anxious that the UN, or whoever else was involved, should pay attention only to the immediate facts. What she wanted to avoid was an insistence that the facts must be placed in the appropriate framework, or a tendency to ignore the facts altogether in favour of the application of relevant first principles. For, having regard to the attitude of most UN members, this meant that, in either case, the episode would be judged in the light of the proposition that colonialism is among the deadlier of sins.

This concern has expressed itself in all of Portugal's attempts to secure the dispatch of reporting presences to her overseas possessions. It has done so in several forms, the most constant of which has been an attempt to obtain visits by individuals rather than groups, her hope being that, free from the pressures of an ideologically-oriented committee, the persons concerned would be content simply to report what they saw. But the UN has made a similar calculation, and has therefore been extremely reluctant to allow this procedure. On the very morrow of the invasion of Goa, the General Assembly established a Special Committee to examine information regarding Portuguese territories. Not receiving any such information from Portugal, it sought to visit the areas concerned, but was refused permission. A short while before the Goan affair, however, Portugal had invited the Chairman of a UN subcommittee on Angola to Lisbon, but found that his visit brought her little profit. Subsequently, under American pressure, the furthest that she would agree to go was to consent to the appointment by the President of the General Assembly of two representatives, one for the purpose of gathering information on political, economic, and social conditions in Angola and the other in Mozambique. The United States then, on 18 December 1962, introduced a resolution to this effect into the Assembly, and Portugal gave it her support. However, the Afro-Asians spoke darkly of important omissions, and they were clearly apprehensive that they might not get the right sort of report. Ostensibly they were seeking information, but really they wanted grounds for Portugal's condemnation. Seeing the way the wind was blowing, the United States agreed that her proposal, which, she had said earlier, was the result of a very high-level understanding with Portugal, should not go to a vote.

In the following year, Senegal complained to the Security Council that her air space had been violated by aircraft coming from neighbouring Portuguese Guinea. Replying, Portugal suggested that a small commission, consisting of equal numbers of technicians named by each party and presided over by a neutral, should be set up to carry out an on the spot investigation. But this had insufficient appeal for those who wished to make political capital out of the complaint. As an alternative Ghana suggested a Security Council committee, but then took fright in realising that this too might, in effect, result in Portugal's vindication. She therefore joined Morocco in proposing a formula which just asked the Secretary-General to keep the situation under review. Predictably it was adopted by a unanimous vote.

In 1965, Senegal made further complaints, and Portugal replied with a suggestion which was not dissimilar to that which had been spurned in 1963, but it, too, was not taken up. Instead the Security Council, of Senegal's sovereignty and territorial integrity. In the same year Portugal responded to a call for her suspension from UNESCO pending an enquiry into educational conditions in Angola, Portuguese Guinea, and Mozambique by saying that she would raise no objection to it, and would even call for it, if India and her African co-sponsors agreed to similar enquiries being made in their own countries. Her offer was not taken up. On a number of occasions, Portugal has invited U Thant to visit Angola and Mozambique to verify her own claims about conditions there and see for himself whether they constituted a threat to international peace. The Secretary-General, however, has never been able to find the time for such a visit, and, in his most recent refusal, on 9 September 1967, said that if he did make one it would have to be in the context of the Security Council's 1965 call to Portugal to recognize the rights of the peoples of her territories to self determination and independence.

There has, however, been one small incident in which Portugal has, as it were, got her own back on the UN. It was alleged during the Congo crisis, very plausibly, that Tshombe's secessionist regime in Katanga was receiving assistance from the neighbouring territories of Rhodesia and Angola. At the very end of 1961, therefore, the Acting Secretary-General suggested to Britain and Portugal that UN observers should be stationed at a few selected airports and roads leading from Rhodesia and Angola into Katanga in an endeavour to check any help which Tshombe was receiving along these routes. The suggestion that a watch for misbehaviour should be kept within the territory of the supposedly misbehaving states was in any event unlikely to make much progress. But as not two weeks had gone by since the UN had ostentatiously stood aside during the Indian assault on Goa, it was hardly the moment to suggest to Portugal that she should assist the UN. Her reply was negative. Britain was also unable to agree to U Thant's proposal. She would have been prepared to consent, for, although critical of the UN's recent activities in the Congo, she was anxious to demonstrate her basic good faith. But on this matter she did not have the last word (which may go some way towards explaining her readiness to accept the UN's suggestion), for the area concerned, while British for international purposes, was part of the internally self-governing Federation of Rhodesia and Nyasaland. And as its Government was even more hostile to the UN's anti-Tshombe campaign than Britain's, there was little hope of its co-operation. Indeed, when Britain urged the acceptance of UN observers on the Federation, its Prime Minister, Sir Roy Welensky, characterized the proposal as 'one of the most objectionable . . . that has ever been made to me'.[50] Welensky was, however, prepared to invite the International Red Cross, which was then watching over rail traffic between Rhodesia and Katanga, to extend its observation to road and air communications. After consulting the Congo Advisory Committee, U Thant rejected this counter-suggestion. Evidently the UN wanted its own accusatory arrangements, or nothing.

The country which, together with Portugal, has been in most serious trouble at the UN has been South Africa, on account of her policies of racial segregation and separate development, or apartheid. She has, as it were, been viewed as an internal colonialist, or, more simply, as a racialist. This has meant that she has hardly ever tried to employ a UN reporting presence as a means of defence. For she has not only realized that she would be unlikely to get very far in that direction, and, if she did, might do herself more harm than

50 Sir Roy Welensky: *Welensky's 4000 Days* (London: Collins, 1964), p. 251.

good, but has also been most anxious at all times to emphasize the domestic character of her racial policies. In her estimation the UN has no right to concern itself with what goes on inside her borders, and, accordingly she has not, generally speaking, been willing to give rise to any doubts on this score or to strengthen her opponent's case by herself inviting the UN to survey her internal scene. This, she has always claimed, is not due to a desire to cast a shroud over her racial policies. They are, she asserts, nothing to be ashamed of, and, indeed, exemplify her solicitude for the best interests of her inhabitants. But, conscious that virtually all other members of the UN see the situation in a fundamentally different light, at least officially, South Africa has adhered very rigidly to the position that apartheid is entirely her own business.

She did, however, make a small exception to this principle in 1961. In the previous year she had been called upon by the Security Council to abandon racial discrimination, and in that connection the Council asked the Secretary-General, in consultation with the Union, to take adequate measures to uphold the purposes and principles of the Charter. This led, in January 1961, to Mr Hammarskjöld making a six-day visit to South Africa. No progress was made with the execution of his mandate, but he expressed the opinion that the lack of agreement with South Africa was not conclusive, and he looked forward to further consultations. For its part, South Africa declared that the talks had been useful and constructive, and announced her intention of inviting Hammarskjöld again at an appropriate time. She must have felt that in view of the Secretary-General's background and his cautious and realistic temperament, he was hardly the man to engage in a sweeping condemnation of South Africa's policies, and, therefore, that his first-hand information would not be used to increase the plausibility of such an assault. Indeed, she probably calculated that if his visit had any influence on the UN, it would be in the direction of moderation, and this was a development to be encouraged. However, it was cut short by Hammarskjöld's death in September 1961, and by the fact that his successor was an Asian who did not conceal his antipathy towards South Africa's racial policies. But even if Hammarskjöld had not been killed, a question-mark hung over the continuation of his contact with the South African Government. For it is most likely that many UN members would have become increasingly restive at the sight of their chief executive officer engaging in discussions with their arch-enemy which did not obviously further the cause which they so fervently espoused, and which might even have redounded to South Africa's credit.

South Africa has also given offence because of her refusal to place the mandated territory of South West Africa under the trusteeship system, which makes it possible for her to be regarded as tarred with the brush of colonialism. But here too, as in respect of the metropolitan territory of the former Union and now Republic, the gravamen of the charge against her has concerned her policy of apartheid. In general, she has been rather more flexible on the subject of South West Africa, as she has allowed that, in certain circumstances, it might properly give rise to international discussions, although she has vigorously denied that the UN has any rights in the matter. She has also been very aware that the UN's major concern in this matter is to get her out of the territory. Thus, for the same reasons which applied to the question of apartheid, she has usually been quite unwilling to let the UN send a fact-finding mission to South West Africa. However, as on the issue of apartheid, she has not been completely unbending in this respect, and on a few occasions has modified her stand when it seemed that to do so would not adversely affect her interests.

The first occasion when this happened was in connection with the UN's establishment, in October 1957, of a Good Offices Committee, which from South Africa's point of view, held out some promise in respect of both its mandate and its membership. Its terms of reference were unusually wide and open, requiring the Committee to do no more than find 'a basis for an agreement which would continue to accord to the Territory of South West Africa an international status'.[51] And it was made up of Brazil, Britain, and the United States, the last two of whom South Africa could, at that date, legitimately regard as sympathetic. Both of them had also been members of the group of Principal Allied and Associated Powers which had allocated the mandates at the end of World War I and it was South Africa's view that those states had a far better claim to raise the question of South West Africa than any others. She therefore consented to enter into negotiations with the Committee, and invited it to visit South Africa, as a result of which two of its members did so. But nothing came of this, as the idea of partition, which the Committee urged should be considered, and which South Africa, too, was willing to discuss, found no favour at all with the other members of the UN.

Since 1953 the UN had been endeavouring to supervise the administration of South West Africa through a committee which had been set up solely for that purpose. In 1961, at the General Assembly's request, it endeavoured to visit the territory, but was unsuccessful: South Africa would not allow it, and the immediately adjacent Powers, Britain and Portugal, would not facilitate an attempt at an

[51] General Assembly resolution 1143 (XII).

illegal entry. However, South Africa, now having been pushed out of the Commonwealth, expressed her willingness, in November 1961, to receive three former Presidents of the General Assembly, with a view to their examining the truth of allegations about conditions in South West Africa. They were to be selected by South Africa in agreement with the President of the General Assembly, were to act in their personal capacities, and were to submit their report to South Africa, who, however, undertook to publish it in full. The Assembly, however, did not like this idea, and proceeded, instead, to replace its existing committee with a Special Committee on South West Africa, giving it provocative terms of reference. However, when, as its first task, it sought to visit the territory, it met with a conciliatory South African response, its chairman and vice-chairman, Mr V. Carpio of the Philippines, and Dr M. de Alva of Mexico, being invited to do so.

This gambit paid off handsomely. The visit took place in May 1962, amid conditions of maximum secrecy, and on 27 May resulted in a communique issued by South Africa and the two representatives of the UN. It made no mention of apartheid, found charges that the territory was being militarized unproven, recorded the Government's aim to speed up development, and rejected allegations that conditions in South West Africa constituted a threat to international peace. In the words of one commentator, this statement was greeted with 'baffled astonishment'[52]: it was not at all what had been expected. Retribution followed. Mr Carpio, who was the Philippines' permanent representative to the UN, had declared, ten days after the communiqué was issued, that he had not agreed to the final text, owing to illness. But in vain. He was 'effectively refuted'[53] by the South African Prime Minister, and was quickly dispatched by his Government from New York to Cairo, to become the Philippines Ambassador to the UAR. Dr de Alva, it was reported, was ordered to withdraw from the Committee by his Government. However, before they departed the two miscreants put the record 'straight' by officially reporting to the Special Committee in terms which were highly critical of South Africa, and urging that if she would not give up South West Africa she should be forced to do so. The Committee adopted this report as apt and timely, ignoring the earlier communique. But the damage had been done. In an attempt to cover it up the Assembly, in December 1962, wound up its but recently established Special Committee and transferred its functions to a body which was less likely to deviate from the orthodox line, the Special Committee of 17 on colonialism.

[52] 18 *The World Today*, No. 8 (August 1962), p. 315.
[53] *Ibid.*

Since this episode South Africa has not thought it prudent to invite any UN bodies or representatives to visit South West Africa. It is interesting to note, however, that during the proceedings in the case brought against her by Liberia and Ethiopia in respect of her conduct in South West Africa, she invited the International Court of Justice to inspect the territory. Evidently she felt that enough of its members would be sufficiently free from ideological preconceptions as to make a visit worthwhile. But the Court announced in November 1965 that it did not accept the invitation, possibly because by this time the applicants had dropped their claims of oppression in South West Africa and were relying solely on a point of law.

Just as beleaguered or threatened states are sometimes anxious to obtain a reporting presence, providing its composition is satisfactory, so also dissatisfied minorities within a state sometimes think of appealing to the UN against their sovereign masters. And there may well be sympathy for their plight, perhaps chiefly in consequence of hostility towards the government whose actions have given rise to internal complaint. But, even so, unless the situation can be conceived in racial or colonial terms,[54] it is exceedingly unlikely that such appeals will lead to any UN action. For there are relatively few states who possess overseas territories, and only one who overtly distinguishes between its subjects on the basis of the colour of their skin. But there are many who include within their metropolitan territory groups which might easily discover that they were being discriminated against by their government. Accordingly, that part of international law which declares that what goes on within a sovereign state's boundaries is, generally speaking, its own affair, has a sound basis in reality, and there is no tendency at all, on the part of the UN, to encourage disaffected minorities to seek its help. A complainant from Fiji or South West Africa can expect a sympathetic hearing, but not someone who speaks for the Nagas of north-east India, or the Ibos of Eastern Nigeria. Even if the criticized state is not over popular, its fellows would be reluctant to put it in the dock on account of the precedent-setting effect of such action. Thus, even if, in August 1967, the Manx Parliament had agreed to the proposal that the UN be asked to conduct an urgent investigation into the situation caused by Britain's intention to close down a 'pirate' radio station which was bringing pleasure and, more important, publicity to the Isle of Man, it is virtually certain that nothing would have come of it.

---

[54] In which case the UN's action would probably be more appropriately described as invalidation rather than accusation, inasmuch as it would be trying to weaken the government's authority and not simply recall it to a higher standard of behaviour. See further, below, Chapter 10.

And the result would hardly have been different had the issue been of greater substance. For, welcome though Britain's embarrassment is in many quarters, the members of the UN are not prepared to achieve it at the cost of possibly helping to undermine their own domestic authority.

This last example accidentally exemplifies the trend in the UN's use of accusation as a prophylactic device. The heat has gone out of the East–West conflict, so the Western states are less likely to feel the need to supplement their defences in this way. They themselves rarely take the kind of initiative which could lead to a demand for an enquiry, and, even if such a call is made, might well be able to block it. In the colonial field there is not much left to defend, and, in any event, little sympathy for that activity. On the racial issue, it will only be by accident that South Africa gets any succour from the UN, and this is one field where accidents can be discounted. However, it remains that a reporting presence can be very useful as a means of demonstrating one's good faith, deflating one's critics, and possibly winning some support. Accordingly, states under pressure, and there will certainly continue to be plenty of instances of that phenomenon, may still be glad to appeal to the UN for support in the shape of a fact-finding mission. Whether they get it will depend on their popularity, or that of their cause.

Chapter 7

Sedation

SEDATION consists of direct endeavours to exert a calming influence on inflammable situations. Hence, in contrast with the accusatory procedure, it requires that the UN's representatives have substantive dealings with officials of the involved states, the main hope being that on-the-spot exhortations in the name of the world organization will prevent the dispute from getting out of hand. Such operations may take place in two ways: firstly, by negotiations with the governments concerned; and secondly, where hostile forces confront each other along a frontier or demarcation line, through cooling activity at the military level.

I

Only in exceptional circumstances is a desire for measures of the first kind likely to be frustrated by political difficulties. If the initiative comes from the UN and the Organization is in very bad standing with one of the parties, that state may well, as a matter of principle refuse to engage in talks. And it is probable that the UN's suggestion will be rejected if it entails a damaging postponement of an offensive campaign. But in less extreme situations, the inconvenience and annoyance of having to explain one's position to a representative of the UN will almost certainly be outweighed by the opportunity it offers to justify oneself and by the incriminating implications of a refusal to do so. Peace may, in fact, be divisible, but the concern for peace is not, with the result that it is no longer respectable, and is therefore generally regarded as inexpedient, to argue that a conflict is exclusively one's own affair.

Another consequence of the twentieth-century attitude that any war or threat of war, anywhere, is everybody's business, is that an appeal to the UN to play a moderating diplomatic role is unlikely to fall on deaf ears. It could do so if the defensive party was very unpopular, but that apart, it is to be expected that the UN will respond positively. The urging of restraint, after all, is a very mild form of intervention. It can hardly cause grave offence or seriously threaten anyone's interests, and, accordingly, is not a worrying precedent.

Moreover, it raises no problems of personnel or finance: it is essentially a one-man exercise and it should not be at all hard to find a candidate of suitable nationality and standing, beyond if not within the Secretariat; in turn this means that its call on the UN's finances will be minimal. In fact, so politically innocuous is the operation that, while the Secretary-General may wish to strengthen his hand by first securing a mandate from the Council or the Assembly, it may well be possible for him to make the necessary arrangements on his own responsibility, and without much danger of incurring criticism for not having sought permission from one of these bodies.

Nevertheless, it is not often that the UN has sent a representative to disputing states solely with a view to persuading them to adopt a less belligerent posture. Partly this is because such efforts are frequently combined with, and sometimes overshadowed by, attempts at mediation, it being the UN's object not just to stop a difficult situation from getting worse but also to put it on a new and more secure footing. There are a number of examples of this, from the work of the UN Mediator in Palestine in 1948 to the endeavours of the Secretary-General in respect of the Vietnam war. Partly, too, it is a consequence of the fact that sedation at the diplomatic level does not necessarily require that an agent of the UN should visit the countries concerned. It can also be attempted, and often is, by means of resolutions of the UN political organs, or through the Secretary-General making private representations to the heads of the disputants' UN missions.

Sometimes, however, prophylactic measures of this kind may be conducted in the relevant capitals rather than at the UN's headquarters. This is, perhaps, most likely to happen at periods of considerable tension, inasmuch as the procedure not only avoids a loss of time but is also designed to maximize the effect of the UN's intervention. For the dispatch of a special emissary both underlines the gravity with which the situation is viewed and focuses attention upon it. Moreover, it ensures that the key decision-makers in the states concerned are left in no doubt as to the UN's opinion. It is, therefore, the most effective diplomatic instrument which the UN can deploy at a moment of crisis, especially when, as will often be the case, it is accompanied by a public call for restraint.

An important instance of this procedure occurred in 1956, in respect of the Arab–Israeli borders. In the early months of the year the situation was deteriorating badly along the Syrian and Egyptian fronts, and there was a growing apprehension that it might culminate in a full-scale war. Nor was the position eased by the sudden dismissal, on 1 March, of the British Chief of Staff of the Jordanian

Army, General Glubb. Britain and the United States were particularly worried, and came to the conclusion that the Secretary-General's personal intervention might help to keep the peace. Mr Hammarskjöld was very willing to try to act as a cooling agent, and had already visited the area in January. But for any further venture he was anxious to have the backing of the Security Council. Accordingly, it met on 4 April, and unanimously requested him, as a matter of urgency, to report on the situation, especially on the question of compliance with the Armistice Agreements of 1949 and the Council's own resolutions. He thereupon embarked upon an intensive round of visits to the capitals of the region, and succeeded in obtaining from all the parties a written undertaking to observe the cease-fire provisions of the Agreements, subject only to a qualification regarding the right of self-defence. Officially, at least, he was optimistic, and in commending him the Council asked, again unanimously, that he continue his good offices with the parties with a view to ensuring that the agreements were fully observed. But he had not long left the area before serious incidents began to recur, and the announcement, on 26 July, of the nationalization of the Suez Canal opened a series of events which led to the complete collapse of the Egyptian–Israeli armistice.

Even if there had been no Suez crisis, it hardly seems likely that Mr Hammarskjöld's visit would have resulted in a less hostile stalemate, let alone have marked a turning point in Arab–Israeli relations. For they were so deeply steeped in distrust and enmity that it was less than realistic to expect that a formal reiteration of existing obligations, on its own, would have a significant pacifying influence. The outcome might well have been different had the Great Powers, or some of them, made it known that they were determined to uphold the renewed commitment to a cease-fire. For this purpose a ready-made instrument was to hand, in the shape of the Tripartite Declaration of May 1950. By it, Britain, France, and the United States had stated their 'unalterable opposition to the use of force or threat of force between [Israel and her Arab neighbours], and that, consistently with their obligations as members of the United Nations, they would immediately take action, within and outside the United Nations, to prevent any attempt by either side to violate frontiers'.[1] Had this resolve now been firmly underlined by its signatories, the states concerned would have had very good reason to reconsider the collision course on which they were increasingly set. That is not to say that they would have altered it: a Western *démarche* might have lacked credibility, or, even if it was not deficient

---

[1] George Kirk: *The Middle East 1945–1950* (London: Oxford University Press, 1954), p. 313.

in this respect, it might have had no impact on policies which were so rooted in emotion. But it was the measure which, in conjunction with the Secretary-General's efforts, held the greatest prophylactic possibilities.

In the event, however, there was no question of the Western Powers taking a strong line. They continued to have a keen interest in Middle Eastern stability, but not to the extent of being prepared to guarantee it. Such an undertaking, honestly given, implies a degree of singlemindedness and strength which is rare in international relations, and which the authors of the 1950 Declaration certainly failed to exhibit at this time. Their concern, rather, was with a typically wide and conflicting range of interests, and with their interpretation in the light of particular situations. Thus they were reluctant to tie themselves down to a specific course of action irrespective of the circumstances, especially at a moment when one of the local parties, Egypt, was fast losing Western favour on account of the growing warmth of her relations with the Communist bloc, which had been vividly exemplified by her 1955 arms deal with Czechoslovakia. It was, therefore, not too surprising that the Secretary-General's cooling activities had no real effect.

The UN's experience in this episode is of general relevance to its attempts to tranquillize agitated or bellicose governments. For the success of such operations usually depends on the inducements, positive and negative, which accompany them, and the UN has very few resources of this kind. It may be expected that if its calming words are heeded, the disputants will be acclaimed for their statesmanship and commitment to peace. Contrariwise, if the UN's endeavours meet with no response, the Organization may well record its disapproval. But beyond these probably inadequate devices of honour and disgrace, it has little with which to cajole or threaten, and must therefore rely upon its members, acting independently, for persuasive support. More particularly, the UN's representations will generally need the wholehearted endorsement of some of those who are able to speak to the parties in a telling way, and at least the acquiescence of the others. It cannot be assumed, however, that the willingness of members to let the UN call for restraint indicates that they are ready to go to some trouble, outside the UN, to ensure that its appeal is respected. When war looms, most states, in most cases, like the preacher in respect of sin, will be against it. But its prevention by third parties will commonly involve risks of various kinds, and the ranks of those who are prepared to run them will probably be thin and possibly non-existent. Accordingly, UN sedatives, when administered to governments, will often be lacking in potency.

The Cyprus crisis of late 1967[2] illustrates this argument. Earlier in the year the Greek Government had been taken over by the military, and during the following months it looked as if the new regime might find it possible to reach an agreement with Turkey regarding Cyprus. But talks broke down in September. Even had they produced a solution, however, its implementation would in all probability have met with considerable opposition on the part of the Government of Cyprus, which would doubtless have set its face against far reaching restrictions on its legal freedom, and would have been no less hostile to the idea of partition. At other times, such attitudes would not have been unwelcome in Greece, but in the context of a preparedness to engage in serious negotiations with Turkey, they were less attractive. Greece might also have been none too pleased at the fact that, while the union of Cyprus with Greece continued to be held in high formal regard in Cyprus, the Makarios Government seemed to be becoming increasingly attached to the country's status as an independent sovereign state. Besides being unflattering to herself, this added to the obstacles in the way of an international settlement.

Accordingly, there is some ground for thinking that Greece was not averse to a move which, while not giving anything away to the Turks, would remind the Greek Cypriots of their dependence on the mother country. For this purpose an instrument was readily available in the Cypriot National Guard. There was no Cypriot army to speak of, and the National Guard was officered by Greeks, with the result that, while nominally under the control of President Makarios, it was at least as attentive to the voice of Athens. Thus a display of strength on its part was a way of drawing indirect attention to the fact that the local Greeks were effectively without any forces of their own. It was not likely that the Guard's Commander, General Grivas, would have much hesitation about rubbing this in, for he was a fervent advocate of *enosis* and had had a number of previous encounters with Makarios. Moreover, at this time he had another reason for dissatisfaction with the Cypriot Government. At about the end of October the exiled Turkish Cypriot leader, Mr Rauf Denktash, who favoured partition, had made a clandestine arrival in Cyprus. He had quickly been captured by the Government's forces and then, under pressure from Turkey, was returned to the mainland. To Grivas this must have seemed an abject course, and there is evidence that he planned a show of force to demonstrate to Makarios the realities of power on the island. Equally, it was to be a means of making the same point to the Turkish Cypriots and to Turkey. As such it had some appeal to both the Greek and Cypriot Govern-

2 For its background, see above, pp. 71–81.

ments, both of whom were thought to have given advance approval to Grivas's scheme.

On 15 November, therefore, on an insubstantial pretext, a Turkish Cypriot village and a Turkish Cypriot section of a mixed village, both of them astride the important Nicosia–Limassol road, were attacked by the National Guard. Before the Turks succumbed more than two dozen of their number were killed. The operation also involved the forcible disarming of UN soldiers and the establishment of National Guard positions alongside the UN's observation posts, which were supposed to stand between the two communities.[3] However, this attempt to publicize the local pecking order misfired, for Turkey, inflamed by atrocity stories, responded very strongly, and it began to look as if she was going to take the opportunity to make a final settlement of the Cypriot account. This would have alarmed Greece at any time, but particularly when it had a Government which was inclined towards a negotiated settlement of the Cyprus problem. Thus it made a number of conciliatory gestures. The National Guard was withdrawn from the two occupied areas; Grivas was recalled to Athens and his dismissal was rumoured; Mr Pipinelis, who was on excellent terms with the Turks, was appointed Foreign Minister; and Greece made it clear that she was willing to negotiate. Turkey, however, was evidently preparing for war.

This resulted in the hasty mounting of a variety of sedative operations. Canada fulfilled her accustomed role by putting forward a set of peace proposals, which, characteristically, relied to a large extent on the involvement of the UN. On 22 November the UN Secretary-General dispatched Mr J. Rolz-Bennett, his Under-Secretary for Special Political Affairs, to the area, and, two days later, made a strong appeal for restraint. Mr Rolz–Bennett was immediately followed by a special representative of President Johnson, Mr Cyrus Vance. On 24 November it was made known that Signor Brosio, Nato's Secretary-General, was to visit Greece and Turkey. And on the next day the Security Council announced that it was agreed on the need for moderation and peace.

This intensive bout of activity produced the required result. Within a matter of days reports began to emerge indicating that a pacifying formula had been reached. It was said to concentrate, as a first step, on the withdrawal from Cyprus of those Greek and Turkish troops who were in excess of the permitted figures of 950 and 650 respectively. These limits had been agreed prior to Cyprus becoming independent, and had been infringed by both states, but particularly by Greece, who was variously estimated to have between 5,000 and

---

[3] A week later both the Cyprus Government and the National Guard apologized to the UN Force for interfering with its personnel and equipment.

15,000 troops in Cyprus. She, therefore, would be making the biggest immediate sacrifice; in return Turkey was to call off her threat of invasion. A plan for the complete demilitarization of Cyprus, except for the UN troops, was also under discussion, but led to difficulties with President Makarios who was unwilling to agree to the disbandment of the National Guard in advance of a complete Turkish withdrawal, and without a guarantee against an external attack on Cyprus. In the event this matter was left on one side, and on 3 December, in accordance with the agreement, U Thant appealed to Greece and Turkey to end any threat to each other's security and to that of Cyprus, and, in particular, to reduce their forces in Cyprus to the lawful level. They immediately accepted his appeal.

On 8 December the first Greek troops left Cyprus, and all were due to go by 5 January 1968, with a 15-day period of grace in case of logistic difficulties. Their departure was not without some ill omens, for Turkey's Prime Minister announced that his country was under no obligation to remove her illegal troops from Cyprus simultaneously with the evacuation of the Greeks, and Greece refused a UN offer to supervise her withdrawal. Even, however, if the operation was scrupulously observed by the UN this would have been no guarantee against subsequent contention, on account of there being no firm knowledge as to the number of Greek troops on the island in the first place. But, as it happened, it was clear that a large number of Greek troops were repatriated within the period laid down by the agreement. They did not include the officers and men serving individually with the National Guard (whose position under the published accounts of the agreement was obscure), but it seemed that neither side had much to hide for both asked that the UN Force should check that the remaining Greek and Turkish forces were not in excess of the permitted contingents. The Secretary-General was hesitant about undertaking such a difficult and sensitive task, but in March 1968, after a further request from the parties and a promise of co-operation from Cyprus, he agreed to do so. At least for the moment, calm had been restored.

The question arises, how significant was the UN's role in producing this state of affairs? It was valuable that the agreement between Greece and Turkey could be established by way of individual replies to an identical appeal from the UN Secretary-General, for this avoided the difficulties which might well have arisen had a more formal arrangement been sought. But this was hardly of great importance, and so far as the actual cooling process was concerned, both *a priori* considerations and the balance of contemporary comment suggest that the key figure was Mr Vance. For he was speaking for one of the world's two Major Powers, and symbolized its keen interest in the prevention of a war between two of its NATO allies. His words must, therefore, have carried a great deal of weight. Mr Rolz-Bennett, on the other hand, was representing an Organization which, in physical terms, was powerless. Even the threat to withdraw the small UN Force was not available to it here, for that would surely have precipitated the very event which the UN was trying to avert. Thus all it could offer was verbal inducements and the general sentiment of its members in favour of peace. Mr Rolz-Bennett's activities were useful, no doubt, as another voice urging restraint, and as an additional channel of communication. But there is no reason to suppose that his impact on the disputants was nearly so effective as that of the personal representative of the President of the United States.

It could be argued that this in no way detracts from the claim that the prevention of war was a victory for the UN. Mr Vance's role could be seen as supplementary to that of the UN rather than as separate from it, as indicative of the support which the United States was giving to the policy of the Organization to which she belonged. To show that she acted less out of loyalty to the UN than out of a keen concern to prevent a conflict in the eastern Mediterranean would not affect the validity of this argument: why states act as they do is a different question from that which concerns the most realistic description of what they do. However, in this particular case, the United States did not give the impression of supporting a UN initiative, of being the backer, albeit a crucial one, of another's move. If, indeed, the question of who was supporting whom, so reminiscent of relations between Makarios and Grivas, had to be answered decisively, the balance would clearly tip in favour of the United States as the principal external actor. However, it is probably more realistic to see the UN and the United States as moving on parallel but independent courses, with the latter being able to act with altogether more purpose and effect. In part the United States' decision to conduct her own cooling operation may have been due to the need to lose no time, but it probably also reflected the consideration that the matter was, from her point of view, too important to be left to the UN. In consequence, the UN's attempts to administer a sedative to the involved governments, while not without importance, cannot be regarded as having a very significant bearing on the resolution of the crisis.

In this case questions of face were relatively unimportant. Turkey had little need to be troubled by them, for it was obvious that she was bargaining from strength; and Greece, being only too anxious to extricate herself from what was an exceedingly embarrassing situation, could not afford to pay them much attention. Thus, the fact that it was the UN which called for restraint did not materially assist the parties to adopt a conciliatory posture. In other circumstances, however, this factor could well be of greater moment. For as the UN stands for an elevated level of behaviour, acceptance of its cooling appeal can be easily and honourably justified. Thus it is quite conceivable that the UN's verbal intervention could result in a halt being put to what might otherwise be a collision course, even though its call is without powerful backing. But for this to happen it is probably necessary that the parties should already be disposed towards moderation, for it is most unlikely that the UN's words will alone be sufficient to induce such an attitude. Which serves to emphasize the limits of the Organization's own ability to calm agitated governments.

II

Where tension finds expression in the ranging of armed forces along an inflammable frontier or demarcation line, it may also be open to the UN to attempt a different sedative procedure. Instead of operating from, as it were, above, it may try to act prophylactically from below, through cooling activity at the border itself. This may be done by stationing a relatively small group between the disputants, equipped with the right to communicate on substantive matters with the forces of both sides. So placed, such a group has a number of opportunities to exert a moderating influence. By acting as a point of contact, it may be able to prevent misunderstandings and hasty reactions, and so avert incidents. It can urge restraint in face of provocation. And it will be able to work for measures which should reduce the likelihood of friction, such as the demarcation of the border, the withdrawal of forces to a certain distance from it, and the agreement of procedures which are to be followed in the event of trouble. Further, should shooting occur, a UN team which is on the spot will be able to try to prevent its spread and bring it to an early halt. In the event of these efforts being unsuccessful, an appeal may be made to the governments concerned, and, if necessary, the mission can bring the issue to the attention of the UN's political organs. But this last possibility is not only indistinguishable from the role of a group whose sole task is to report on a troubled situation; additionally it is a sign that the sedative mission has failed in its immediate task. For the essential feature of this kind of operation is its emphasis on the local, the strictly local, situation. Its first and primary job is to prevent or snuff out trouble at its principal source, to check any infectious symptoms at birth rather than deal with a full-blooded illness. Its object is not to put pressure on the parties to take a more pacific line but, by keeping the military temperature low, to minimise the pressures on them in favour of belligerent action.

On the face of it such groups might seem to be of relatively minor importance. Operating in a context of admitted enmity, it is just possible that they may be able to prevent the escalation of incidents which are deliberately contrived by one of the involved governments. But their main sphere of activity relates only to those problems which are inherent in the physical confrontation of hostile forces. Nevertheless, such matters could very quickly assume a wider significance. Incidents involving civilians, or a local bout of shooting, could well produce a situation in which the area commanders or their political superiors might find it inexpedient to take the first conciliatory step. Such a move can be very much easier if it is made in response to an appeal from an impartial third party who is on the spot and able to hold out the offer of a fair investigation into the origin of the affair. Once tension has been lowered, that investigation may become quite unimportant, except as a possible means of increasing the evidence of the other side's iniquity, but its promise will serve the purpose of increasing the acceptability of the UN's appeal for restraint. It is the case that such appeals will almost certainly be useless where one or other of the governments concerned is set upon a demonstration of strength, or even upon war. Short of this position, however, a small group intent upon sedation may be able to do a lot of work which, while not of great importance in itself, could prevent grave consequences. In this way it can help to keep a border as quiet as is compatible with the overall political situation, which may be much quieter than it would be in the absence of such an operation. Hence it holds out a greater prospect of success than the type of sedative activity which was previously discussed. This is because it is a less ambitious affair, in that it is usually trying not to alter but to maintain governmental policies. But it is not on that account necessarily of lesser significance.

This prophylactic device is more costly, in terms of both men and money, than the accusatory process. But its demands would normally be well within the UN's resources. The military personnel, usually of officer rank, which it requires would probably be counted in dozens rather than hundreds, and especially as they would generally be drawn from a variety of countries, it should not be difficult to secure them. Nor should the UN Secretariat find it hard to equip them with the necessary supporting services. The operation might well continue for a fairly long period, giving rise to recurring expenses. But they are not likely to be so large, nor to relate to such a controversial activity, as to prevent their inclusion in the UN's regular budget.

It does not follow, however, that operations of this nature are established with great freedom whenever circumstances arise which, to an uninvolved observer, seem appropriate for their use. States are generally antipathetic to having their affairs supervised by foreigners, both on emotional grounds and on account of the critical implications of the activity. It is likely to be all the more firmly resisted if, as in this type of case, the supervision is for an unspecified term. But over and above these considerations is the point that this kind of operation touches a particularly sensitive nerve: that of security. To have one's border forces surveyed by military observers who are free to cross to the enemy's side of the line presents a hazard which states will usually be most anxious to avoid. Thus disputants are unlikely to propose to the UN, either openly or covertly, that it should conduct a sedative operation along their common border. And even if one party is willing to do so, it is not at all inconceivable that the other will object, with the result that no progress will be made in this direction. Reporters can be stationed on one side of the border only, as can a force which is designed to act as a physical barrier to infiltration. But, by contrast, sedation requires that the group in the middle be able to communicate with both sides. If, therefore, it is not acceptable to one, the exercise cannot be underaken.

For these reasons the UN is likely to be most hesitant about initiating the suggestion that it be allowed to act as a cooling agent on a tense border. In circumstances, that would only invite a rebuff. If, however, it is already seized of the issue, and especially if, for one reason or another, it is able to claim a special responsibility for it, the Organization may be much more willing to make such a move. But, even so, there are some further conditions which will probably need to be met before it acts in this way. Particularly if one of the Great Powers is involved in the dispute, the UN will want to be quite sure, in advance, that the Power will not be offended by its suggestion— and, Great Powers being what they are, it is quite likely that such an assurance will not be forthcoming. The omens for UN intervention will be much better if none of the Powers are directly involved and if all of them, plus a large percentage of the other members, have the prevention of physical conflict as their chief immediate interest in the matter. Further, the UN is likely to find its way to the border eased if the parties, whether under pressure or otherwise, have come, or are in the process of coming, to an agreement regarding their frontier relations. The absence of a cease-fire, truce, armistice or the like is not fatal to the UN's chances of involving itself in the situation. It can still put it to the parties that it would be helpful if it was allowed to watch over their border, address cooling observations to the opposing forces, and investigate incidents. But such a suggestion may not be too well received. If, on the other hand, the parties are just agreeing to certain restrictions upon their legal freedom, they will find it more difficult to resist the proposal that their observation of these new undertakings should be supervised by the UN. And besides assisting its passage into the field, such an agreement will also strengthen the UN's hand *vis-à-vis* the parties once it has got there.

It should be emphasized that this kind of activity, while it may be described in terms of observation or supervision is not passive in character. It is precisely its active involvement in the situation, its right to make representations to the forces of the parties, both in advance of and during physical conflict, which distinguishes it from a group whose job is merely to report what it sees. Moreover, it must be remembered that supervision in these circumstances is not designed to achieve a settlement of the dispute. The UN may hope that, if things can be kept quiet for long enough, the basic political situation will also improve. But a sedative operation is essentially prophylactic rather than patching-up in character. Its very mounting is indicative of an intractable problem. Indeed, it will probably be easiest to arrange where there has already been one round of fighting which has been brought to an inconclusive halt, which may have all the appearance of being only temporary. In these circumstances the UN's object in organizing sedation will be to do what it can to extend the lull, and, more specifically, to ensure that any further large-scale fighting which does occur is not, from the governments' point of view, accidental.

Such an operation could last for a considerable time, especially where the parties, in military terms, are in a position of stalemate. Moreover, short of a new war or a marked improvement in relations, it is unlikely that the cooling group will be withdrawn. Unless there is a military imbalance, and the weaker side becomes very unpopular at the UN, on account, for example, of a change in its ideological outlook, the Organization will probably find no reason for putting an end to a going concern. As with other matters, and perhaps more so, peace-keeping operations are much harder to start than to stop, so there is little enthusiasm at the UN for bringing them to a formal end. From the point of view of the parties, a withdrawal of consent to the group's presence is equally unlikely, for that would incur some diplomatic unpopularity, and would result in the loss of a means of indicting the other side. Even the laying of aggressive plans is unlikely to lead to a request for the group's departure. For, on the one hand, it would cause the opponent to be even more vigilant, and, on the other, it would not facilitate aggression, for such a small group would be no physical obstacle to an attack on the other side. Thus it is not surprising that the two border operations of a sedative character which the UN has mounted[4] have a history which is not much shorter than that of the Organization itself. Both can trace their origin back to 1948 and were still in existence in mid-1968, at least in an attenuated form. They also have in common the fact that both arose out of disputes which accompanied the beginning of Britain's withdrawal from her imperial role, on the one hand in the Middle East and on the other on the Indian sub-continent.

III

In November 1947 the General Assembly recommended that the mandated territory of Palestine, which Britain intended to leave in the following year, should be partitioned between the Arab and Jewish claimants. This was completely unacceptable to the Arabs, and the following months were marked by widespread and serious disorder. The Security Council, having refused a suggestion that it should implement partition by force, attempted to negotiate a truce, but without success. Its next step, on 17 April 1948, was to call for a cease-fire, but this, too, was of no avail. Therefore, on 23 April, it established a Truce Commission for Palestine, in what seemed to be the hope of putting pressure on the parties to agree to a truce which the Commission could then observe. The Council also looked to this new organ for impartial information regarding an increasingly confused situation. The Commission was made up of those Council members, other than Syria, with career consuls in Jerusalem: Belgium, France, and the United States, a method of composition which served a triple purpose. It facilitated the speedy organization of the Commission, for the intention was that the states concerned should appoint their consular representatives in Jerusalem. It ensured that its members would have knowledge of the local situation. And it prevented the participation of the Soviet Union, a result which was especially desired by the United States. In reply the Soviet Union charged the United States with using the UN to further her own growing interests in Palestine, and therefore refused to vote for the Commission's establishment.

As it happened, however, the Truce Commission was of relatively little direct importance. It tried to obtain a cease-fire in Jerusalem, but without success, and the smallness of its staff meant that it was unable to give the Security Council authoritative information

[4] Excluding the UN's sedative activity in Indonesia for which see above, pp. 50–52.

regarding the continuing conflict. It was even less well placed to play a significant role when, in the middle of May, immediately following the proclamation of the state of Israel and the expiration of the British mandate, the internal Palestinian war was enlarged by the entry of forces from five Arab states. Moreover, it was overtaken by events in a second sense, for many of its functions were soon assumed by another UN organ.

On 14 May 1948 the General Assembly, bowing to events, wound up the Palestine Commission which it had established in the previous November to implement its partition plan.[5] At the same time, with a view to the peaceful resolution of the conflict regarding the future of Palestine, it established the office of UN Mediator. The appointment was placed in the hands of the five permanent members of the Security Council, and on 20 May it was announced that they had chosen Count Folke Bernadotte, President of the Swedish Red Cross. He served for only four months, being assassinated in September, and was succeeded, as Acting Mediator, by Dr Ralph Bunche, a member of the UN Secretariat. Not surprisingly, neither individual was able to make any headway with the basic problem, and in December 1948 most of the Mediator's patching-up responsibilities were transferred to the new Palestine Conciliation Commission.[6] In the meantime, however, the Mediator had been given prophylactic tasks by the Security Council, and these assumed considerable importance. On 29 May the Council called on the parties to order a four-week truce, decreeing that it should be supervised by the Mediator in conjunction with the Truce Commission and that the two organs should be assisted by a sufficient number of military observers. Previous requests to this effect by the Truce Commission had gone unheeded, and its lack of weight was further indicated by the way in which the Mediator quickly assumed a position of leadership in respect of truce supervision, the Commission's responsibilities being largely confined to Jerusalem where it became, in effect, the Mediator's agent. It ceased to operate in January 1949, but has never been formally wound up.[7]

The Truce Commission did, however, have a wider and longer-lasting significance in that it had an important bearing on the national composition of the truce supervision team. Count Bernadotte had arrived in the Middle East towards the end of May and,

---

[5] See above, pp. 170–171.
[6] See above, pp. 60–62.
[7] The UN's failure to bring the Truce Commission to a formal end and thank it for its labours was, according to its Secretary, but the last of a series of indignities which the Commission suffered at the UN's hands. See P. de Azcarate, *Mission in Palestine 1948–1952* (Washington D.C.: Middle East Institute, 1966), ch. VII.

immediately following the Council's resolution of 29 May, had made informal approaches to the American, British, French, and Soviet diplomatic missions in Cairo regarding the possible need for observers.[8] This suggests that he was thinking of drawing his team from the Great Powers. The United States, however, had other ideas, suggesting that only those countries on the Truce Commission should be represented.[9] It is unclear whether this argument simply seemed convincing to Bernadotte, or whether he had no option in the matter: in his diary[10] he suggests the former; in his report of 12 July he implies the latter.[11] But in any event he adopted it, and requested Belgium, France, and the United States to let him have 21 officers each. The Soviet Union did not let this pass. It made no mention of the Mediator's enquiry of its Cairo mission, but argued that the Security Council must decide on the composition of the supervisory team, and proposed that each member of the Council, other than Syria, should be entitled to send observers. It announced its own willingness to do so, indicating that it had it in mind to appoint no more than five. But the United States was not at all impressed by such modesty, and, asserting the right of the Mediator and the Truce Commission to make whatever arrangements they thought fit, secured the defeat of this Soviet attempt to get a foot in the Palestinian door.

Thus the four-week truce, which, following negotiations by the Mediator, came into effect on 11 June, was supervised by 63 observers drawn from three Western countries. They were supplemented by 51 guards from UN headquarters and about 70 auxiliary technical personnel from the United States, and were subsequently joined by 10 more officers from each of the Truce Commission states. Count Bernadotte also secured five Swedish officers to act as his personal representatives and appointed one of them as his Chief of Staff for truce supervision. The job of the observers, which was conducted in the air and at sea as well as on land, was to engage in routine observation, investigate incidents and complaints, which over the four-week period numbered about 500, and endeavour to settle them. They had no power to prevent violations or enforce their decisions, but, nevertheless, on the whole the truce worked well. In Jerusalem its observance was facilitated by the success of the Truce Commission and the military observers in negotiating agreements establishing a no man's land and the demilitarization of an island of Jewish occupation on Mount Scopus.

Towards the end of the truce the Mediator tried to obtain the

---

[8] See UN Document S/888, para. 13.
[9] Folke Bernadotte: *To Jerusalem* (London: Hodder and Stoughton, 1951), p. 45.
[10] *Ibid.*
[11] See UN Document S/888, para. 13.

agreement of the parties to its extension, but without success. On the whole the truce could not but favour the defensive party, Israel, and she was therefore willing for it to be continued. But the Arabs were not prepared to give the Jews any more time to entrench themselves, and on 8 July hostilities broke out once more, the UN observers, save for a few in Jerusalem, having been evacuated together with their equipment when it became clear that there was no hope of prolonging the truce. In his report on the situation the Mediator in effect told the Security Council that it should now forbid the use of force in Palestine, and this is what it did, finding, on 15 July, that the situation threatened international peace and security and ordering the combatants to cease-fire within three days, and within 24 hours in Jerusalem. The resolution obtained the support of only seven members, the minimum number necessary for its passage, and the Soviet Union was not among them. But she did not defeat it by casting a negative vote, for her objections related not to its substance but to the extent of the role being given to the Mediator. This, indeed, was one of those rare post-war occasions when the Great Powers were broadly agreed, all of them being chiefly interested in the restoration of peace in the Middle East rather than in espousing the cause of one side or the other. In consequence the Council's threat that further action would be considered if its order was disobeyed could not easily be ignored, and a cease-fire was instituted within the stated time limit.

The resolution of 15 July had instructed the Mediator to supervise the observance of the new truce, no mention being made of the Truce Commission. Thus Count Bernadotte set about bringing his previous organization back to life, and this time on a larger scale in view of the indefinite nature of the truce. He turned once again to the Truce Commission countries, and they agreed to provide 300 officer observers, 50 from Belgium and 125 each from France and the United States. As before he obtained a small personal staff of Swedish officers and appointed one of them as his Chief of Staff, and secured 78 auxiliary technical personnel, almost entirely from the United States. It shortly became clear to the Mediator that his supervisory arrangements were inadequate, and he therefore asked the constituting countries to supplement their officers with the same number of enlisted men. They agreed to do so.[12]

---

[12] In his diary, (Bernadotte, *op. cit.*, pp. 190–95), Count Bernadotte complained with some bitterness about the contrast between the United States, zeal for a truce and the slowness with which she fulfilled her promises to supply a large proportion of the necessary observers. He says that a reliable source attributed this to a fear of seriously complicating relations with the Soviet Union, and of the American public being deeply offended if United States personnel were endangered, which in turn might influence the November Presidential election. The latter point is more convincing than the former. The United States may also have been influenced by the

The role of the observers during the second truce was similar to that which they had played during the first. They kept a watch on opposing front lines and also tried to observe the vast hinterland in order to check whether men and material were being moved in a way which, contrary to the terms of the truce, would alter the military balance. The Truce Commission again collaborated in supervising the truce in Jerusalem, although with less success than before. In fact, this was a generally more precarious truce. There were fewer complaints and incidents than formerly, and many of the smaller ones were settled on the spot by UN observers; their presence and prompt action probably avoided a number of others. But on the whole those breaches of the peace which did occur were more serious than during the four-week truce, some of them particularly so. A Central Truce Supervision Board, under the chairmanship of the Mediator's Chief of Staff, was set up to deal with such questions, and major violations were reported to the Security Council. But the use of such devices, especially resort to the Council, was a sign that the situation was getting beyond the UN's sedative capabilities. Moreover, although the Soviet Union and the United States were still agreed on the undesirability of a further round of fighting in the Middle East, it was highly unlikely that either of them, or France or Britain, would be willing to use arms to prevent it. For, quite apart from the cost and trouble of such an enterprise, both East and West wanted to prevent the other's physical presence in Palestine. This stood in the way of joint as well as unilateral action (whether inside or outside the UN), the latter for fear that one's rival might follow suit, and the former on account of the danger that one's partner might fall out of step. A tacit understanding that the Council would confine itself to verbal exhortations was much more acceptable.

Such considerations help to account for the fact that the situation soon began to deteriorate. Both sides were restless, each feeling, or professing to feel, that they would have been victorious had it not been for the truce ordered by the Security Council. On this matter the Arabs may to some extent have been victims of their own propaganda, but there was substance to the growing Israeli confidence in their position and capabilities. In this context the thought that the Security Council might have been bluffing in July, or that, if it wasn't

---

fact that at this time there was a strong feeling that American troops should be brought home from their various foreign stations as soon as possible. Bernadotte adds that the United States was much slower at providing observers than Belgium and France, but this is not the picture one gets from the Mediator's report to the UN—certainly not so far as the enlisted men were concerned and not obviously with regard to the officers. See UN Document A/648, Part 2, para. 4.

then, it would now be unlikely to take a very strong line, hardly contributed to stability. Violations of the truce increased in frequency, and in the middle of October full-scale hostilities broke out again, the Israelis making a southwards thrust to safeguard some of their settlements in the Negev desert. At the end of the month they swept through upper Galilee. If the parties, and Israel in particular, had calculated that the Council's bark was worse than its bite, they were proved right. For it responded with nothing more than calls for a cease-fire and the withdrawal of forces to their previous positions.

Nevertheless the fighting had an important bearing on the Council's next step. For, by underlining the precariousness of the truce, which had already been emphasized by Count Bernadotte in what proved to be his final report, it put the Council in a frame of mind to accept the proposal of the Acting Mediator that, as an intermediate step to a final settlement, the truce should be replaced by an armistice. The Soviet Union urged that the Council should be bolder and require an immediate peace treaty, but his idea was rejected by most other members (a course which they may later have regretted). Hence, on 16 November 1948, with the Soviet Union abstaining, the Council 'Decide[d] that . . . an armistice shall be established in all sectors of Palestine', and called upon the parties to conduct negotiations to-towards this end.[13]

The wording of this resolution suggested that the Council intended to impose a legal obligation on the parties to reach an armistice. Such an obligation is neither easy to enforce, nor, if the parties make a show of negotiating, is its infraction easy to pinpoint. It may be, therefore, that the Council's decision, on its own, would not have made a big impression on those concerned. However, another consequence of the October fighting was that there was now a greater prospect of an agreement. For the Israelis, by definitely coming out on top, and capturing a good deal of ground in the process, had demonstrated that the Arabs no longer held the initiative, and so encouraged them to think in terms of negotiation. On the other hand, the Israeli successes were not so great as to drive the idea of negotiation completely out of their heads. Thus Israel announced its readiness to move towards an armistice, and Jordan, Egypt, and the Lebanon also accepted the Council's resolution, but only in principle.

Their hesitation was costly, for it gave Israel an opportunity to consolidate some of her newly-won ground by making a further assault on Egyptian positions in southern Palestine. She even went so far as to enter Egypt, which produced some sharp international

[13] Security Council resolution 62 (1948).

K

reactions. The United States deprecated this course, and as she had been very sympathetic towards Israel her views must have carried a good deal of weight. Britain also protested, but no doubt with less effect as her sympathies lay in the other direction, and if anything must have been confirmed when Israel shot down four of her planes which had gone out to survey the fighting in Egypt, and of another which was dispatched to look for them. But by threatening that unless the Israelis withdrew she would invoke her rights under the Anglo-Egyptian Treaty of 1936 and intervene, a move which reflected her concern about the security of the Suez Canal and her adjacent base, Britain certainly influenced Israel's victim. For Egypt had no desire to be assisted on this basis, having vainly tried as recently as 1947 to get the Security Council to agree with her claim that the 1936 Treaty was invalid. Hence, on 6 January 1949, threatened, as she saw it, by both Britain and Israel, she announced her willingness to enter into immediate armistice negotiations. Israel was now equally willing to call a halt, and a cease-fire came into effect on the next day. Negotiations began almost at once, and, with the valuable assistance of the Acting Mediator, an agreement was reached in February. Armistices with the Lebanon and Jordan were signed in March and April respectively. Syria was a much more difficult case. It was only in March that she expressed her willingness to talk, and the actual negotiations were long and difficult, an armistice not being signed until 20 July 1949.

The office of Mediator had originally been established to seek a solution to the basic Palestinian problem. Already, however, in December 1948 the General Assembly had transferred this responsibility to a Conciliation Commission,[14] and with the conclusion of the Armistice Agreements the Security Council relieved the Acting Mediator of the rest of his duties.

However, the prophylactic role which had also been assigned to him, and which he had taken over from the Truce Commission, did not disappear with the Mediator, for the organization which he had built up to supervise the truce now received recognition as an independent body. This arose out of the fact that all the Armistice Agreements referred to the UN 'Truce Supervision Organization' (UNTSO) as if it was already in existence as a separate entity, and relied upon it for some aspects of their functioning. Thus in each case it was provided that the execution of the terms of the Armistice was to be supervised by a Mixed Armistice Commission (MAC), composed of an equal number of members from both sides under the chairmanship of the Chief of Staff of UNTSO or of one of its senior

14 See above, pp. 60–62.

officers. Additionally, each MAC was empowered to employ observers either from the armed forces of the parties or from UNTSO's military personnel, the UN observers remaining under the command of the Chief of Staff during such employment. Further, in the case of three Armistices, the deployment of UN observers from UNTSO was specifically provided for in connection with the administration of demilitarized zones.

When, therefore, in August 1949, the Security Council considered the situation which had been produced by the Armistice Agreements, it found itself pressed by the Acting Mediator to continue the existence of a body which had not been formally created, and the name of which referred to a state of affairs which had now been superseded. The Soviet Union took exception to this, but not on logical grounds. She had never been happy about the degree of independence which had been accorded to the Mediator, nor about the national composition of the truce supervisors, and her unease on this latter point must have increased when the changes which followed Count Bernadotte's assassination resulted not only in the appointment of an American as Acting Mediator but also of others of the same nationality to the top civilian and military posts on his staff. She therefore proposed that all UN personnel should be withdrawn from Palestine. Other members, however, while showing no great enthusiasm for a large UN representation there, felt that the Council should not refuse to do those things which were necessary in order to implement the provisions of the Armistices for which it had itself called. They were also reassured by Dr Bunche's reminder that it was the parties and not the UN which had general responsibility for the supervision of the Agreements, and by his estimate that no more than 30 or 40 observers would be required if the UN was to fulfil the role which the parties had devised for it. Accordingly, on 11 August, with the Soviet Union and the Ukraine abstaining, the Security Council asked the Secretary-General to arrange for the continued service of such of UNTSO's personnel as were necessary to assist the parties to supervise the Armistice Agreements in accordance with their terms.

In view of the parties having agreed upon an armistice regime, the Council accepted the Acting Mediator's recommendation that it should withdraw the various restrictive provisions of the July 1948 truce, which had been designed to maintain the military *status quo*. But although each Armistice prohibited any hostile or warlike acts the Council decided to reaffirm that part of its truce resolution which had ordered a cease-fire. It added nothing to the parties legal obligations under the armistice, but it did maintain the Council's involvement in the situation. And the Council took the opportunity to instruct UNTSO to observe and maintain the cease-fire and report back to it from time to time. In this way UNTSO, which would hardly have been continued had it not been for the provisions of the armistice, also obtained a basis for its operations which was independent of the parties.

It had been envisaged that the armistice regime would be a brief interlude between the suspension of hostilities and a treaty of peace. In the event it proved to be an often precarious state of affairs which lasted, in most of its aspects, for 18 years. And the hostility which accounted for the parties failure to move beyond an armistice also found reflection in the widespread breakdown of the scheme for its supervision.

As early as 1951 regular meetings of the Israeli–Syrian MAC were suspended on account of Israel's refusal to allow that the MAC had any right to place on its agenda, let alone discuss, any matters relating to the demilitarized zone, which lay almost entirely on the Israeli side of the Armistice Demarcation Line. Informal meetings were sometimes held, as were occasional emergency meetings, but in 1961 even the latter ceased. A brief series of extraordinary meetings were held in January–February 1967 in an endeavour to seek a solution to what had become the perennial problem of Israel's activities in the demilitarized zone, but they made no progress.

The situation in respect of the Israel–Jordan MAC was not a great deal better. In March 1954 Israel withdrew from the Commission, alleging that the Chairman, Commander Hutchison, was biased in favour of the Arabs.[15] Following his departure from UNTSO at the end of the year Israel returned to the Commission. A large number of complaints had accumulated and the Chief of Staff, General Burns, proposed that they would all be put on one side. Israel, however, by insisting on the discussion of one of them, blocked an agreement. Two years later, all formal meetings of the MAC were brought to what proved to be a long halt as a result of Israel's objection to a decision of the Chairman. In 1961 she endeavoured to rectify this situation by proposing a resumption of meetings combined with the removal from the MAC agenda of all outstanding complaints, which numbered about 3,800. Now, however, it was Jordan who stood in the way by insisting on the discussion of a couple of dozen cases. However, this did lead to a resumption of emergency meetings, which tended increasingly to be called to deal with relatively minor matters. Informal meetings also continued, as before, and also the meeting of a routine subcommittee.

The border between Israel and Jordan was about 300 miles long,

---

[15] For the chairman's own account of his experiences with UNTSO, see, E. H. Hutchison, *Violent Truce* (New York: Devin Adair, 1956).

which helps to account for the large number of incidents which occurred, most of them of a comparatively unimportant character. That between Israel and Syria was only about 20 miles, but although there were many fewer incidents, they were often very much more serious in nature. The frontier with the Lebanon presented a contrast with both these two, for throughout the period of the armistice it remained very quiet. This was facilitated by the fact that it ran along the old international frontier between Palestine and the Lebanon, and included no demilitarized zones. But chiefly it was due to the fact that the Lebanese, for both economic and confessional reasons, were very anxious indeed to have no trouble with Israel. For her part Israel had no unfinished business here, and so the MAC was able to function harmoniously. Regular meetings were held, and no votes were taken, such problems as arose being solved by mutual agreement. It was not, perhaps, a case of the MAC operating smoothly because it was really unnecessary, but the situation did not fall far short of that state of affairs.

The case of the Israel–Egyptian MAC presented another contrast. It met for seven years, and was the scene of bitter disputes: there were many violations of the border and casualties on both sides were higher than elsewhere. Then, in 1956, Israel declared that her invasion of Egypt and the events which preceded it had put an end to the armistice. As it happened, the establishment of the UN Emergency Force and the 10-year calm which followed its arrival at the border, meant that there was little need for the MAC. But, very properly, the UN refused to accept that one party could unilaterally abrogate an agreement, and continued to play its part in maintaining the MAC machinery. There was no reason why this, or any other, Commission should not meet with only one side present, and the Israel–Egypt MAC occasionally did so at Egypt's request. Egypt, and the UN, also insisted that border incidents and other issues which arose between Egypt and Israel were the proper concern of the MAC and its UNTSO personnel. However, as Israel now refused to have any dealings with them, but was willing to talk (although not to play host) to UNEF, all communications between the two countries on frontier matters were channelled through the Emergency Force.

The MACs' frequent failure to meet did not result in the breakdown of the supervisory machinery. Each Commission remained formally in existence and received and investigated many complaints, and the Chief of Staff, chairmen, and observers continued to be in touch with both sides. However, the kind of joint supervision by the parties which had been envisaged in 1949 failed, on the whole, to materialize, which meant that the UN became the sole sedative agent. And the troubled situation on three of the four borders led the UN Secretariat, with the general support of the Security Council, to emphasize that UNTSO was not simply the handmaiden of the MAC but also, in accordance with the Council's decisions of 15 July 1948 and 11 August 1949, had an independent responsibility for the maintenance of peace. In consequence, UNTSO grew in size. During the first half-dozen years the number of military observers was usually in the region of 35. Then in 1956, following the Secretary-General's visit to the Middle East, they increased to about 60, and over the next three years doubled in number. They remained at about 120 until 1964, when UNTSO asked for and after some delay reserved a further 15 observers. During the next three years its strength remained more or less constant. Its original practice of looking only to the three Truce Commission countries for military personnel was quietly dropped in 1953, and in 1966 the observers were drawn from 12 countries. At this date they were backed by a civilian staff of about 160 Secretariat members plus some locally recruited people.

UNTSO's attempt to play a wider role than that of the MAC's investigation branch was often hampered by its observers being prevented from moving freely along the Armistice Demarcation Line and in the demilitarized zones and defensive areas.[16] This was done in various ways besides the most obvious. The parties insisted, for example, that the UN's observers should be accompanied on their investigations by liaison officers, which was reasonable enough. But it frequently happened that when observers wanted to move quickly a liaison officer was not immediately available, sometimes giving rise to the suspicion that the opportunity was being taken, or made, to cover tracks or brief 'witnesses'. Restrictions were placed on the air corridors and airfields which could be used by UNTSO's aircraft, which interfered with the observers' ability to move with the maximum speed. Proposals for the establishment of a small number of fixed observation posts in areas of particular tension were by no means always welcomed. And where they were established it was sometimes the case that their occupants were virtually incarcerated within them.

No doubt all this was partly a reflection of the feeling that, as the Egyptian delegate put it in the debate on the proposal to keep observers in the area after the armistice, 'No one wants outside supervision if it can be helped'.[17] Moreover, as most of the parties had but recently obtained their independence, they might in this instance

---

[16] Areas to the rear of the Armistice Demarcation Line in which restrictions were placed on the deployment of military forces.
[17] Security Council, *Official Records*, 435th Meeting, p. 10.

have felt particularly strongly that supervision was inconsistent with
their sovereign dignity. It is also very likely that they were apprehensive about the possible repercussions of unimpeded freedom for
UNTSO personnel on the secrecy of their defensive arrangements,
and also, perhaps of any less reputable preparations. Israel was
particularly obstructive in this matter. She repeatedly emphasized
that UNTSO's proper role was to speak when it was spoken to,
which meant that it could only move about in Israel at Israel's
request. This line was not inflexibly applied, and the UN's observers
were often able, in time, to argue their way into the areas to which
they wanted to go. Israel also agreed, in May 1956, that for an ex-
perimental period of six months an equal number of fixed observation posts should be established on each side of the Gaza Armistice
Demarcation Line. And, beginning in 1957, after previous hesitation, she agreed to the placing of some posts along the Syrian border,
four being set up on her side and six on Syria's during the next five
years. But, during the same period, she would not match Jordan's
willingness to have some posts established along that border.[18]
And she also steadfastly refused to agree on the proposal, to which the
UN periodically returned, that UNTSO should be allowed to have
a boat on Lake Tiberias (Galilee) which, while wholly within Israeli
territory, was not wholly under her control, on account of the fact
that in one area the Syrian frontier was only 10 metres from the
shore. This, plus a dispute over Syrian fishing rights in the lake, often
gave rise to tension.

Israel's attitude to UNTSO, in short, reflected the tough and unyielding line which she took in respect of her interpretation of the
Armistice Agreements and also the touch of brashness and arrogance
with which that line tended to be expressed. This did not mean,
however, that she was insensitive to UNTSO's criticism, which
may partly explain why she had very serious differences with two of
UNTSO's Chiefs of Staff, General Bennike of Denmark and General
von Horn of Sweden. The office they held was bound to be very exposed and it would have been surprising if the incumbent had not
sometimes incurred the criticism of one or both sides. It was, for
example, rumoured that the replacement in 1953 of the first holder,
General Riley of the United States, was explained by his poor relations with the Arabs, and it could be that his tenure gave the Israelis
the wrong idea of what to expect. Be that as it may, his successor,
General Bennike lasted for little more than a year. He soon incurred

---

[18] Nevertheless, from 1958 onwards, one post was established on the Jordanian side
of a very sensitive border area, and several others were set up within Jordanian
territory. The latter, however, which were the departure-points for UNTSO
patrols along agreed routes, seemed to be as much designed to exercise a calming
influence within Jordan as to watch for international incidents.

Israel's hostility, being publicly charged with onesidedness in his reports to the UN and it being indicated to him at one point that Israel would not be responsible for his safety when he was on her soil, an ominous warning in view of Count Bernadotte's fate at the hands of Israeli terrorists. He was followed by General Burns of Canada who, while criticized by both sides from time to time, succeeded in retaining their respect.[29] His appointment in 1956 as Commander of the UN Emergency Force led to Colonel Leary of the United States taking over as Acting Chief of Staff. Towards the end of 1957 he fell out with the Jordanian Government, but this was as nothing compared with the hostility shown by Israel towards his successor, General von Horn, in the last year of a period of office which began in March 1958.[20] Neither he nor the UN Secretary-General immediately gave way under the bitter Israeli campaign, but his usefulness as UNTSO's Chief of Staff had been much diminished. In June 1963 he was replaced by a fellow Scandinavian, General Odd Bull of Norway, a quieter individual, who has succeeded in retaining the confidence of both sides.

The antipathy which the parties developed towards some of UNTSO's Chiefs of Staff, together with the restrictions on its members' freedom of movement and the breakdown of much of the MAC machinery, must have hampered the Organization's ability to maintain quiet. But it ought not to be assumed that in the absence of these difficulties UNTSO would have been a much more effective deterrent. Such MAC's as met seemed to be looked to chiefly for propaganda material rather than for guidelines as to proper behaviour. Firing often broke out in full view of observation posts. And good relations between the parties and the Chief of Staff were no guarantee that his advice or exhortations would be heeded. UNTSO, in short, was never meant to be in anything other than a position of weakness. It had no legal right to give orders to the parties, or forcibly to prevent their wrongdoing, and the situation was so highly charged that there was little disposition to attribute any moral authority to its calls. Moreover, while it spoke for the UN, the parties were well aware that the parent body was most unlikely to give it any tangible support. In 1948 the Security Council's menacing words had commanded respect, but the growth of the cold war made a repetition of that episode increasingly improbable. And when, towards the middle of the 1950s, the Soviet Union began to espouse the Arab cause, the chances of UNTSO being able to secure compliance by threatening to go to the Council became ever more remote.

[19] For General Burns's account of his experiences with UNTSO, and later with UNEF, see E. L. M. Burns: *Between Arab and Israeli* (New York: Obolensky, 1963).
[20] See Carl von Horn: *Soldiering for Peace*, (London: Cassell, 1966) Chapters 22 and 23.

In these circumstances there could be no question of UNTSO standing in the way of calculated acts of aggression, still less of war. But for as long as there was a desire to avoid war, UNTSO was able to play an exceedingly valuable sedative role. One way in which it did this was to encourage the parties to take measures, or to allow it to take measures, which would reduce the likelihood of incidents. For example, it urged the conclusion of local commanders agreements, and between 1951 and 1954 three agreements were in successive operation on the Israeli–Jordan front with the object of controlling infiltration (by cattle[21] as well as men) and settling minor disputes. In 1955 another agreement was reached regarding the maintenance of the cease-fire in Jerusalem, and lasted for a year. UNTSO had less success on the Egyptian front, its proposals for such agreements and also for joint patrols and the construction of a fence along part of the demarcation line being turned down. It made a little progress in its endeavours to get the Israeli–Syrian border demarcated and secured mutually satisfactory arrangements in part of the demilitarized zone regarding the division of land between Israeli and Arab cultivators. Sometimes it was also able to ensure that the cultivation of such land was carried out in safety. Where the parties were agreeable it could despatch observers to areas of tension, and, in the event of prisoners being taken, effect their exchange.

Although all these arrangements were relatively minor and fragile, they were not unimportant. But undoubtedly UNTSO's most significant sedative activity related not to the prevention of incidents but to the prevention of their escalation. For this was an area in which shooting could easily break out, and could almost as easily get out of hand. The overall situation was tense; infiltration was encouraged by Egypt, until 1956, and was not discouraged by Jordan; and the demilitarized zone on the Syrian border and the area between the lines on Jordan's gave rise to numerous disputes. Thus there were ample opportunities for outbreaks of firing, and once it had begun neither side was likely, of its own accord, to take the initiative in bringing it to a definite end. This, however, was just what the UN's representatives could do. On the basis of the authority given to UNTSO by the Security Council's resolutions of July 1948 and August 1949, the chairman of the relevant MAC could propose a cease-fire to each side's delegates,[22] or conceivably to the local commanders if they were easily available. Indeed, it became almost a matter of routine, in such circumstances, for UNTSO to suggest a time for it. And by getting observers to the scene of the trouble as

[21] See Burns, *op. cit.*, pp. 41–43 for 'Operation Bo-Peep'—or the Case of the Missing Prize Ram.
[22] It was not unknown, however, when fighting broke out, for an MAC delegate to disappear until his side's purposes had been accomplished.

quickly as possible, UNTSO could try both to encourage the conclusion of a cease-fire and the honouring of one which had already been agreed. In the event of a repeated failure to obtain a cease-fire, or in a particularly serious case, it was possible for the Chief of Staff to intervene at the governmental level. In these ways fighting was brought to an early conclusion in 'countless instances'.[23] Had it not been for UNTSO's action it is very probable that such fighting would often have been prolonged, with a real danger of spreading, and it is not inconceivable that some of these encounters might have resulted in full-scale war.

As the Arab states were the weaker side, UNTSO was probably of greater value to them than to the Israelis. It also served what, from the Arab point of view, was the very valuable function of emphasizing the temporary character of the situation, as evidenced by the fact that at least a part of UNTSO's role arose out of a series of Armistice Agreements. By taking note of them the UN itself had recognized that there was still a question as to Israel's boundaries, or, as the Arabs would say, as to her existence, and for as long as UNTSO remained on the scene Israel was to some extent prevented from arguing that these matters had been settled by the passage of time. It was partly for these reasons that Israel was always anxious to emphasize her sovereign rights *vis-à-vis* UNTSO. She stressed that she had not invited it on to her soil but had merely accepted it on account of the UN's interest in the circumstances of her birth. She insisted that UNTSO's role was very limited, her attitude to the question of a UNTSO boat on Lake Tiberias, for example, being largely determined by the apprehension that her agreement would allow Syria to argue that the lake enjoyed a special status, which might be the thin end of a wedge. And from time to time she said she would be happy to see UNTSO go, this being in connection with the theme that the quickest way to Arab–Israeli peace would be for the parties to be left to settle their problems without an intermediary. However, as the Arabs have been steadfast in their refusal to talk directly with Israel, she was probably glad to have UNTSO as a point of contact. Further, for as long as Israel was unwilling to precipitate another full-scale war with the Arabs, UNTSO was probably an essential means of maintaining the *status quo*.

However, the Suez war underlined the point that all UNTSO could do was to help the parties hold the situation, and that when one of them chose war sedation became irrelevant. Moreover, Israel claimed that the war had brought her Armistice Agreement with Egypt to an end and that henceforth UNTSO had no *locus standi* on that frontier. This meant that, despite the UN's insistence that

[23] UN Document S/7603, p. 2.

Israel alone could not abrogate the Agreement, UNTSO was no longer able to operate as a sedative agency along this border. Eleven years later Israel claimed that the six days war had destroyed the other Armistice Agreements. Again the UN refused to accept this, and, so far as is compatible with the new demarcation lines, maintains the MAC machinery. In the case of the Lebanon, for example, that country still makes complaints to the Israel–Lebanon MAC, which, as before, has its headquarters in Beirut. But Israel refuses to recognize it, makes no complaints to it, nor allows it to investigate Lebanese complaints on her side of the border. Hence this MAC now functions more as a means of channelling accusations against Israel than as a device which is designed to cool the tempers of both sides.

The old type of UNTSO activity, however, has not disappeared. On 6 and 7 June 1967 the Security Council called for an immediate cease-fire in the new Arab–Israeli war, in which Israel was winning such striking successes. Of the combatants only Syria said she would refuse to accept the Council's call, and she quickly changed her mind as Israel engaged in a vigorous assault on her positions. This led the Council, on 9 June, to demand that hostilities cease forthwith, and to ask the Secretary-General not just to report on the situation but also to make contact with the parties in order to arrange immediate compliance. On the basis of this resolution, supported by another on 12 June, a sedative operation was established with the agreement of the parties, UNTSO personnel being used to supervise and maintain the new cease-fire, which was established on 10 June. By 27 June 110 UN observers were deployed on both sides of the ceast-fire line, manning a total of 16 observation posts and a control centre.

In July this activity was extended to the Suez Canal, the new demarcation line between Israel and Egypt. There had been a good deal of firing across the Canal, and on 10 July the Council authorized the Secretary-General to deploy observers in an endeavour to make the cease-fire more secure. Israel and Egypt had agreed in principle to this, and a week later, after UNTSO's Chief of Staff, General Bull, had made the necessary practical arrangements with both sides, the observers took up their positions. General Bull had at first estimated that he would need 25 observers for this task, but in August found it necessary to request that this number be doubled, which was done following the Secretary-General's report to this effect to the Security Council. At the end of October the Secretary-General reported that it would be necessary to increase this figure to 90, enabling the mission to double the number of its observation posts from 9 to 18, to be divided equally between both sides of the

Canal. This led to some mild expressions of discontent on the part of the Soviet Union, to the effect that the Secretary-General was taking too much on himself at the expense of the Security Council. This was also France's view, and early in December, after U Thant had reported that he had been recruiting 47 additional observers from countries, acceptable to the parties, the Soviet Union called for the matter to be discussed by the Security Council. Private consultations followed and as neither France nor the Soviet Union objected to the expansion of the observer corps, but only to the way in which it was being accomplished, a compromise was not hard to reach, the President announcing on 8 December that the members 'recognize the necessity of the enlargement by the Secretary-General of the number of observers in the Suez Canal zone and the provision of additional technical material and means of transportation'.[24]

Thus on two of the former Arab–Israel borders UNTSO observers have re-acquired a sedative mission, although, as Israel emphasizes, their operations relate not to the 1949 Armistices but to the 1967 cease-fire. As before, General Bull and his staff have their headquarters in Government House in Jerusalem, which instead of being on one of the demarcation lines is now well within territory controlled by Israel.[25] The Secretary-General suggested that observers should also be placed on the troublesome Jordan cease-fire line, but Jordan was unwilling to agree to their presence. Her reluctance probably stemmed from a desire to do nothing which would give the new demarcation line any semblance of permanence, for in terms of the value of the territory which was lost and the likelihood of getting it back, Jordan's position is probably the worst of all of Israel's neighbours. However she is in no position to attack Israel, can hardly expect to come off best in the border exchanges which were becoming increasingly common in 1968, and has a considerable interest in a quiet frontier. It therefore looked as if King Hussein's call, on 16 February 1968, for an end to the use of Jordanian territory for provocative anti-Israel activity might be a straw in the wind, and that Jordan might follow the example of her more militant Arab neighbours and agree to the posting of UN observers.

If Jordan had done so, Israel might not have raised any objections to their presence on her side of the cease-fire line, for, obviously strong and secure, she can now afford to take a more relaxed view of UN operations on territory under her control, as she had already

24 UN Document S/8289.
25 During the June war Government House was occupied by Israel, and when, in August 1967, she agreed to hand it back to the UN, she was unwilling to return more than a third of its grounds. Part of the area which Israel insisted on retaining included UNTSO's communication facilities, although Israel agreed that UNTSO should have access to them.

done in respect of two other borders. However, in the nine months following the end of the war there were many more incidents across the Jordan cease-fire line than across those with Syria and the UAR, with the large number of refugees in Jordan providing a ready supply of guerrillas, and the 600,000 Arabs on the west bank of the Jordan river affording them cover and support. Hence Israel found the need for retaliation much greater on this front than elsewhere, which might have made her less responsive to the idea that UN personnel should be in a position to report on the situation. But as against this, King Hussein's possible willingness to clamp down on the Jordanian-based terrorists was a promising sign.

However, the chance of extending UNTSO's activity suffered a serious set-back when the mounting incidents between Jordan and Israel culminated, on 21 March 1968, in a massive Israeli assault on terrorist bases in Jordan. This led to the United States suggesting in the Security Council that observers should be posted between the two countries, and support for the idea came from Canada, Britain, and France (sic). But the Arabs' friend, the Soviet Union, was not among this company. And even if all the Great Powers had been agreed, it is unlikely that anything would have come of the proposal. For Jordan was firmly opposed to it, her attitude being in considerable measure a reflection of the fact that the Israeli attack had made heroes of the guerrillas. There would in any event have been a serious problem for Jordan here, for the support which the terrorists received from the population at large might well have put a severe limit on the Government's effective ability to curtail their activities. But in the changed atmosphere following the Israeli raid, it was not open to King Hussein to put difficulties in the way of those who were to the fore in what was ever more fervently regarded as the Jordanian national cause: the harassment of Israel and her expulsion from the west bank. Thus, for the time being the 'necessity' for a UN sedative operation in this sector also ensures that there is little chance of the Organization being able to play such a role.

It may be that UNTSO's job on the Syrian and Egyptian demarcation lines will be somewhat less exacting than it was in the 18-year period which followed the 1949 Armistices. For it is argued by some that the 1967 war, by clarifying the power relationship between the Arabs and the Israelis, will have provided a firmer foundation for Middle Eastern stability, putting the Syrians in their place, recalling the Egyptians to theirs, and so relieving the Israelis of the need to engage on these fronts in any further large-scale demonstrations of their power and resolve.[25] Those of this persuasion also tend to argue that it would have been no bad thing if the 1967 war had come

[25] But on this point see further, below, pp. 333–336.

earlier, and therefore, by implication, that UNTSO stood in the way of stability. Be that as it may, UNTSO's job was to keep the situation quiet, and within the limits of its resources it conducted this prophylactic task in a very creditable manner. In so doing it provided, and continues to provide, an admirable instance of the sedative opportunities which are open to the UN where border tension is high but where neither party is anxious to precipitate a war.

IV

The UN's second frontier operation of a sedative character has been in progress along the cease-fire line in Kashmir since January 1949, and is still in being. It has some striking parallels with UNTSO. Both arose out of the cutting back of Britain's imperial role and followed the UN's initial involvement in a conciliatory capacity. Neither was begun as a separate activity but, in an ill-defined or even obscure way, became divorced from the patching-up endeavour to which it had originally been linked. And in both cases the failure to solve the basic issue has meant the prolongation of the sedative operation far beyond the time which was at first envisaged, and into what sometimes seems like an infinite future. Moreover, both have survived a war.

The dispute over the future of Kashmir was brought to the UN's attention on 1 January 1948 when India lodged a complaint with the Security Council regarding Pakistan's activity in the state.[26] Pakistan counter-complained, and on 17 January both parties were urged to calm down. Three days later the Council appointed a Commission to investigate and mediate, and followed this up on 21 April with a statement of the measures which, in its view, were necessary in order to bring about a cease-fire and a free and impartial plebiscite. At first the Commission's efforts were unsuccessful, but then it obtained the parties' agreement to a cease-fire, which came into operation on 1 January 1949. Meanwhile, the Commission had felt the need for an independent source of information on the military situation, and as a result General Delvoie, of Belgium, was appointed as its military adviser. He arrived in the sub-continent on 2 January 1949, and was immediately called upon to report to the Commission on the observance of the cease-fire, the Secretary-General being asked to furnish a sufficient number of military observers to enable him to do so.

This, therefore, was the beginning of what later became known as the UN Military Observer Group for India and Pakistan (UNMOGIP). A few dozen officers from Belgium, Canada, Mexico,

26 See above, pp. 24-29.

Norway, and the United States were quickly dispatched to Kashmir and, headed by the Commission's Military Adviser and in close co-operation with the military authorities on both sides, watched over the cease-fire and prevented minor incidents from getting out of hand. The cease-fire line was formally established in an agreement which was signed on 27 July 1949, and subsequently demarcated on the ground with the assistance of the UN's military observers. However, the hope that this would be followed by the demilitariza-tion of Kashmir, which was the condition for a plebiscite, proved false. At the end of 1949 the Commission reported that its mediatory efforts were exhausted, and suggested that it should be replaced by a single person, and on the 14 March 1950 the Security Council transferred its responsibilities to a UN Representative. At some later, unspecified point, the Representative and the Secretary-General agreed that the military adviser should report directly to the Secre-tary-General, and in March 1951 the Security Council, when ap-pointing a new Representative, also 'Decide[d] that the military observer group shall continue to supervise the cease-fire',[27] which appears to be the first occasion on which the military adviser and his observers were formally recognized as having at least a semi-autonomous existence.

UNMOGIP started off with about 30 observers. The cease-fire line which they had to watch was in the region of 500 miles long and much of it was over difficult terrain. It is, therefore, not surprising that by the middle of 1952 the Secretary-General had found it necessary to double UNMOGIP's observer strength, widening its geographical basis as he did so. Thereafter it was generally between three and five dozen strong, being led by the Australian General Nimmo from 1950 until his death in January 1966. He was succeeded by General Tassara-Gonzalez of Chile.

The terms of the cease-fire gave plenty of opportunity for argu-ment and recrimination, for besides the prohibition on a renewal of hostilities, it had been agreed that the troops of both sides should not advance within 500 yards of the cease-fire line, and that there should be no increase in forces or defences to the rear of the line. The whole question of Kashmir also gave rise to frequent tension between the two capitals. Nevertheless, the situation at the front has, on the whole, been relatively quiet, certainly when judged in the light of the position on most of Israel's borders. In part this has been due to the fact that the cease-fire line has not been nearly so provocative as that which was drawn in Palestine in 1949. Both sides have felt that their honour is involved in Kashmir, but not their national existence. The quarrel has run deep, but it has not completely

[27] Security Council resolution 91 (1951).

dominated their relations. And, distressing though the division of Kashmir has been for many of its inhabitants, the dispute has not been such as to arouse local passions of the kind which have flowed from the creation of Israel.

Despite these relatively favourable conditions, the cease-fire would still have been precarious but for the conjunction of two other factors: the existence of UNMOGIP and the attitude of the military authorities on both sides. UNMOGIP has been able to deal with civilian infringements of the line, to investigate complaints, and to prevent minor incidents from escalating into large-scale warfare, this last being its most important function. It has also been a means of giving each side the valuable assurance that the other is observing the terms of the cease-fire. In all these respects its task has been made much easier and it has been able to act with greater efficiency on account of the fact that both the Indian and Pakistan armed forces have been anxious that quiet should be maintained in Kashmir. This has found expression in the fact that UNMOGIP's field observer teams are attached to specific army units on either side of the cease-fire line, the teams being moved from one side of the line to the other from time to time in order to prevent the development of too close an emotional attachment to one party. (UNMOGIP's headquarters is also rotated, at six-monthly intervals, between Indian-held Kashmir and Pakistan.) The observers are allowed access to top secret information regarding the identity and disposition of each side's forces, thus enabling them to confirm that the 1949 cease-fire undertakings are being honoured, and UNMOGIP's possession of its own communications network increases the likelihood that this information will remain confidential.

Clearly, this arrangement, which is such a marked contrast to the suspicious and sometimes hostile environment in which UNTSO has had to work, is dependent on the parties having confidence in the integrity of UNMOGIP's personnel. If some doubt should arise on this score, UNMOGIP's access to secret information would doubtless be curtailed, which in turn would reduce its sedative powers. This means that here it is more than usually the case that its personnel should be of nationalities which are acceptable to the parties, a point which was highlighted by the phasing out of the American observers at India's request following Pakistan's entry into SEATO in 1954.

All of UNMOGIP's activity, however, is basically dependent on the desire of the Indian and Pakistan Governments to avoid a war. For as long as they are willing to do this, UNMOGIP can help them to maintain a relatively quiet cease-fire line in Kashmir. Thus, although there were many incidents during the latter part of the

1950s, the period of Krishna Menon's incumbency of the Indian Foreign Ministry, the situation was contained. But it threatened to get out of hand towards the middle of the 1960s when Pakistan began to step up the pressure on India, and UNMOGIP could do nothing to check the entry of armed infiltrators into Indian-held Kashmir in August 1965, which led to the outbreak of full-scale hostilities in September. Once peace had been restored UNMOGIP helped to supervise the withdrawal of troops to their proper side of the cease-fire line,[28] and then reverted to its previous task of keeping the situation cool. In June 1968 this was still its role, and, short of a major Indo-Pakistan war, which seems unlikely, the end of the road is not in sight for UNMOGIP. Like UNTSO, it stands as an instance of the sedative possibilities which are sometimes open to the UN where hostile neighbours are anxious to avoid a resort to arms.

[28] See above, pp. 117–124.

Chapter 8

Obstruction

As a way of keeping peace, the mobilization of world opinion or the issue of cooling injunctions has obvious limitations. Where, however, a dispute finds expression in a dangerous frontier or demarcation line, there is a third prophylactic possibility which may be open to the UN: the placing, with the consent of the host state(s), of a non-fighting force between the contestants in the hope of preventing them from coming to blows. Thus the deterrent effect of such a force would lie not in its physical strength but in its vicarious character, in the assumed reluctance of states to brush aside a force which represents the UN's desire for peace. As such, its violation would probably incur the world's displeasure, conceivably in a tangible form. But quite apart from its ability to stand directly in the way of violence, an interpository force might be able to exert an important indirect effect by guarding against the kind of border incidents which could give rise to an accidental war. Its presence also provides some *prima facie* testimony as to the peaceful intentions at least of the host, and so may have a valuable calming influence. Moreover, in the event of rising tension a UN force on the spot can provide a first-hand and impartial account of the threatening situation. And, although this could give rise to delicate issues of protocol, it is not out of the question that at the local military and even, perhaps, at the political level, the representatives of the force might take it upon themselves, or be instructed by the Secretary-General, to do what they can to induce restraint.

This obstructive device has a number of attractions from the UN's point of view. It has the appearance, or at least the sound, of solidity and dependability, giving rise to the image of a concrete and significant obstacle to aggression. Yet, inasmuch as it does not involve fighting, either to get to its position or to throw back a would-be invader, it should be vastly easier to arrange, in both military and political terms, than the collective security operations which were envisaged in Chapter VII of the Charter. It does, however, place far greater demands on the UN than most of the Organization's other peace-keeping activities. And even if the necessary ships (or, nowadays, transport planes) and men are forthcoming, the UN cannot boldly say, with nineteenth-century Englishmen, 'we've got the money too'. Nevertheless, if the UN is really anxious to erect a human barrier in the cause of peace, it should be able to cope with these essentially subsidiary problems.

Accordingly, the idea of obstruction is one which, at first sight, might be expected to form an important part of the UN's prophylactic armoury. However, the Charter, written under wartime influences, makes no specific mention of any substantial intermediate phase between the threat and actuality of full-blooded defensive measures. Further, during the Organization's first decade, the stalemate which the cold war had produced in the Security Council meant not just that planning for collective security was put on one side; all other forms of military activity were also assumed to be beyond the UN. It was not until 1956, when the East-West conflict was easing just a little, that the UN's part in ending the Suez crisis resulted in the speedy revision of this view.

I

The catalyst was the creation of the UN Emergency Force (UNEF).[1] This was the device which allowed Britain and France to leave Egypt without too much loss of face, and which supervised Israel's more reluctant withdrawal. It is open to doubt whether, in November 1956, all its creators anticipated that, once the invaders had departed, the Force would settle down at the Egyptian–Israeli border. However, as the pressure built up for Israel's complete withdrawal, a draft resolution was put forward which would have had the UN declare that 'the scrupulous maintenance of the Armistice Agreement requires the placing of the United Nations Emergency Force on the Egyptian–Israeli armistice demarcation line'.[2,3] It was co-sponsored by six small states, all of whom had troops in UNEF, and the United States, and on 2 February 1957 it was passed by the Assembly, 56 votes being cast in its favour. No one voted against it, but 22 members abstained.

The reasons which led the United States to support this move are not hard to find. Fighting between the Arabs and Israel could hardly fail to cause her severe embarrassment, on account of her desire to maintain good relations with both sides and because of the

---

[1] See above, pp. 98–99.

[2] UN Document A/3518. Adopted as General Assembly resolution 1125 (XI).

[3] The dividing line between Israel and Egypt, as set out in the 1949 Armistice Agreement, ran for most of its length along the international frontier between Palestine and Egypt. Accordingly, that part of the line is usually referred to as the international frontier, only the line dividing the Gaza Strip from Israel being spoken of as the Armistice Demarcation Line. However, it seems that in the resolution of 2 February 1957 the phrase Armistice Demarcation Line was meant to refer to the whole of the line dividing Israel from Egypt.

general threat which it presented to the stability of the Middle East. The Soviet Union, on the other hand, had come down decisively in favour of the Arabs, and could well profit from unrest in the area. Thus the United States was anxious that tension should be kept low, but was much less well placed to influence this situation than she was in respect of some other areas of the world. Accordingly, she welcomed the possibility that the UN might be able to keep things quiet along the troublesome Egyptian-Israeli border. Further, by making this proposal, she was going as far as she could towards providing Israel with a positive inducement to complete her withdrawal from Egyptian territory. Britain, too, had a keen interest in the maintenance of Middle Eastern stability, and, having vividly demonstrated that the era of her own dominance in the region had come to an end, was very willing to see the UN assume a prophylactic role. The fact that it would extend the Organization's opportunity to cut something of a figure in the world must have appealed to many of the smaller members who had no stake in the Middle Eastern situation other than a general desire to prevent fighting.

The Soviet Union and her friends, however, took a different view. With virtually no chance of being able to win the support of a majority in the Assembly on a contentious issue, they were most reluctant to do anything which would enhance its standing so far as the establishment or extension of armed forces was concerned. Moreover, with a force in being, the Assembly might have a freer hand in future cases, whether in the Middle East or, conceivably, elsewhere. For the extension of UNEF's terms of reference, or even its transfer, would be much easier than the establishment of a new force from scratch. In either event, the Communist states were in little doubt that the chosen course would not be the one for which they had opted. Accordingly they reiterated their argument of the previous November that, because it was the child of the Assembly and not of the Council, UNEF had been illegally constituted. Further, they claimed that in any event its job was to do no more than see the aggressors off Egypt's soil. Once Israel had gone, therefore, so must UNEF. If it remained in being, they argued, it would be used by the Western Powers for their own ends, and would be a vehicle for further pressures on the part of the original aggressors against their intended victim, which, apart from anything else, would be a gross infringement of Egypt's sovereignty.

Egypt, however, was unconcerned by this prospect. She professed her confidence that the Assembly would keep UNEF within the bounds of legality, and abstained on the draft resolution—which resulted in the Communist bloc doing likewise. Evidently she was coming to see that she could reap some not inconsiderable advantages

from the presence of UNEF along the border between herself and
Israel. The 1956 war had demonstrated for the second time in
eight years that, even allowing for the participation of Britain and
France, her forces were in no shape to meet those of Israel. Hence
she had everything to gain from a policy of non-provocation, and
had already announced her willingness to observe the terms of the
1949 Armistice Agreement. Israel, however, on the morrow of the
war, had declared that the Agreement was violated beyond repair,
and the implication of this was that she would no longer co-operate
with the Mixed Armistice Commission and the UN's military
observers. Thus, while this machinery would still be able to
operate on Egypt's side of the border, and so might be able to provide some anti-Israeli propaganda, its value for Egypt as a sedative
arrangement had come to an end. In consequence there was some
additional reason for welcoming a new and possibly more effective
UN presence in the area, one which would still not be able to communicate with Israel in the absence of her consent, but which might
stand in the way of any further aggressive designs which she might
entertain.

Egypt, therefore, while not giving the resolution her formal
support, was without much doubt in favour of what it proposed.
Israel, on the other hand, while also abstaining, took a very different
view. However, at the time of the Assembly's debate, with her
forces still on Egyptian territory, she said nothing of substance
regarding the resolution's terms. Only later did she make it known
that under no circumstances would UNEF be allowed on her side
of the border, and, both then and subsequently, the UN's representatives argued in vain that the resolution's use of the word 'on'
required that the Force should straddle the frontier.

This attitude should not be taken as a sign of Israel's hostility
towards the idea of the Force being placed between the two countries.
Having been pushed out of Gaza and Sharm-el-Sheikh, and with no
intention, for the moment at least, of retaking them by force,
Israel's interests clearly pointed towards the support of all measures
which would make Egypt a less troublesome thorn in her side.
Hence she had good reason for favouring UNEF's use as a barrier
in Gaza and as the guardian of freedom of navigation through the
mouth of the Gulf of Aqaba, and her subsequent behaviour indicated
her goodwill towards the UN Force. Unlike Egypt, she did not withhold her share of its cost. She was prepared to communicate with its
representatives, complaining to them about border incidents and
being anxious to hand back Egyptian infiltrators to them rather than
to the representatives of the Egyptian-Israeli Mixed Armistice
Commission. She was willing to allow UNEF personnel to use

Israel for leave purposes and invited its Commander to social occasions. All of which brought no response from the UN, in whose eyes Israel was in bad standing on account both of her unilateral denunciation of the Armistice Agreement and because of her refusal to allow UNEF to operate on her soil.

On this latter point, however, Israel was adamant. It has been suggested that this is partly due to a UNEF-type force being more effective in deterring the large-scale reprisals in which Israel occasionally engages than in preventing the small border crossings which are the standard Arab practice.[4] But, assuming this is a correct assessment of the efficacy of the Force, the conclusion does not follow. For as there was no question about UNEF's establishment at the border, it was hardly very material, from Israel's point of view, whether it was on the Egyptian side only or on both—unless, as was exceedingly unlikely, Israel was expecting, by her refusal, to induce Egypt to withdraw her consent to UNEF's presence. The same writer has also suggested that Israel might have feared UNEF's use as a means of imposing a settlement of the Palestine question on her, so that, for example, if she was ordered to give up some of her territory, the UN Force already on her territory could close in to the newly determined limits.[5] But in this context, that was a highly unrealistic suggestion, from the point of view both of the UN's willingness to engage in such an enterprise and of the suitability of UNEF as an enforcement agency. And in any event, if that object was sought, it would make little odds whether the UN's men started out from one side of the frontier or the other.

A more plausible explanation of Israel's policy can be drawn, in part, from her general sensitivity regarding her sovereign prerogatives and the integrity of her soil. She has always been strongly opposed to the idea of a third party exercising jurisdiction on her territory and to restrictions being placed on the use which she is allowed to make of it, characteristics which probably reflect her newness, smallness, and, most important of all, her keen concern with the question of security. Additionally, however, Israel's unwillingness to play host to the UN Force can be related to the circumstances of its creation. Having been gradually forced to withdraw from the Suez Canal across Sinai, and then made to leave the desirable prizes of Gaza and Sharm-el-Sheikh, it would have been very humiliating for her to agree that her troops should be followed across the border by those of the UN, and that the foreigners should then take up their positions inside the Israeli state. It would have

---

[4] See William R. Frye: *A United Nations Peace Force* (New York: Oceana, 1957), pp. 43–44.
[5] *Ibid.*

given additional emphasis to her diplomatic defeat, and might even have looked as if she had been militarily defeated as well. Altogether, it would have been too far for the Israeli Government to go, causing deep injury not only to its self-respect, but also, possibly, to its domestic position.

Thus when UNEF entered Gaza on the night of 6–7 March 1957, it followed the departing Israelis only up to the Armistice Demarcation Line, which ran for a distance of about 35 miles around the perimeter of the Strip. UNEF also took up positions along the Egyptian side of the international frontier, which extends from the south-eastern corner of the Gaza Strip to the head of the Gulf of Aqaba and measures about 117 miles. Further, in accordance with the Secretary-General's report of 24 January 1957, which had been approved by the Assembly in its resolution of 2 February, the Force took over at Sharm-el-Sheikh from the Israeli unit which had been commanding the navigable channel—the Straits of Tiran—at the entrance to the 100-mile-long Gulf of Aqaba.

The way in which UNEF was subsequently deployed depended on the terrain. Along the boundary of the heavily populated and agricultural Gaza Strip, which prior to the Suez war had been the scene of many incidents, 76 observation posts were soon established, each of them visible from at least the next. During the hours of daylight they were permanently manned. At night the Armistice Demarcation Line was kept under observation by ground patrols. Towards the end of UNEF's life, its precarious financial position together with the quiet which prevailed resulted in a reduction in the degree to which the line was observed, not all the posts being occupied every day or for the whole of each day. However, the principle that the whole of the line be under constant watch was not abandoned, and to ensure that the efficiency of the operation was not reduced a number of watchtowers were constructed, which were always manned from sunrise to sunset. Along the international frontier, which ran along the eastern edge of the Sinai desert, the rugged physical conditions and the absence of a settled population produced a different form of activity. Some field observation posts were established but UNEF's watch was chiefly based on ground patrols in conjunction with aerial observation. The most sensitive areas were patrolled daily, while other parts of the frontier were checked between one and three times a week. At first, UN planes kept watch on the frontier every day, but after a few months the prevailing quiet led to the reduction of this form of reconnaissance to three days a week. Mobile reserves were maintained in readiness for dispatch to any spots where trouble developed. A small detachment was placed on static guard duty at Sharm-el-Sheikh, opposite the Straits of Tiran, and the coastline of the Sinai peninsula from this point up to the head of the Gulf of Aqaba was watched from the air.

UNEF was only very lightly armed. In dealing with infiltrators or other border incidents its personnel were instructed to use only the minimum amount of force which the circumstances required and not to fire except in self-defence. They were authorized to take into custody those who were trying to cross the border or who were approaching it (from the Egyptian side) in suspicious circumstances. Those who were apprehended, including those who crossed from the Israeli side, were, after interrogation, to be handed over to the local Egyptian or Gaza authorities, and the latter co-operated by prohibiting movement at night within a zone extending to a depth of 500 metres from the Demarcation Line. Local inhabitants were also forbidden to go right up to the line by day unless they were working in the fields. Prior to UNEF's arrival, there would have been no question of workers coming into the open near the Line, but the quiet which accompanied its presence led to the fields being cultivated, on both sides, to the maximum extent. So much so that the planting of orchards threatened to hamper the process of observation, which was another reason for the construction of watchtowers.

When UNEF first took up its duties along the Armistice Demarcation Line and the international frontier it was composed of approximately 6,000 officers and men drawn from 10 countries: Brazil, Canada, Columbia, Denmark, Finland, India, Indonesia, Norway, Sweden, and Yugoslavia. After six months, however, Indonesia withdrew her contingent. She had made it clear, prior to UNEF's entry into Gaza, that while she recognized the need for it to remain in the area for a while in order to secure stability, it should not settle down for an indefinite stay. She had participated in the Force on the understanding that it was a temporary, emergency affair, and warned that if this concept was altered she would want to reconsider her position. Whether or not the concept was altered, it soon became clear that it was not the one held by Indonesia, and that UNEF was in fact likely to stay on the Egyptian–Israeli border for as long as it was welcome. She therefore acted accordingly. Three months later, in December 1957, the Finnish contingent was also withdrawn, very likely in deference to the Soviet Union's view regarding the illegality of the operation. And in October 1958 Colombia withdrew her troops. This resulted in the expansion of the Indian and Scandinavian contingents, but UNEF was not brought up to its former level, and in fact sporadically declined in size over the years. By 1962 it numbered not much more than 5,000, and at the end of 1963 a reduction in its strength to about 4,600 was recom-

mended, and endorsed by the General Assembly. Early in 1966 its
size went down to about 4,000, and before that year was out yet
another reduction was in process, bringing the Force to a figure of
about 3,400, which was its approximate size at the date of its withdrawal in May 1967.

While this process was clearly influenced by financial considerations, it was also a reflection of the fact that for virtually the whole
of UNEF's incumbency the Egyptian–Israeli border was remarkably
quiet. Incidents occurred fairly frequently during the few months
immediately following its arrival, but in August 1957 there was a
marked drop, only five being reported, and thereafter the number
remained at about this level, none of them being very serious. The
chief responsibility for this state of affairs is often ascribed to UNEF.
In his report on the Force to the seventeenth session of the General
Assembly, the Secretary-General declared that in the maintenance
of peace in the area UNEF is 'the decisive influence'.[6] Four years
later, in what proved to be the penultimate account of UNEF's
activities, he stated that it was 'a major stabilizing influence'.[7] And
his final assessment of UNEF's efficacy was in similar terms, the
quiet which had prevailed in Gaza and Sinai since UNEF's arrival
being declared to be 'very largely, if not entirely', due to its presence.[8] Nor were such remarks confined to the ranks of those who
might be regarded as having a professional interest in optimism
regarding the UN's capabilities. Journalists, politicians, and
academics have all made similar observations, on numerous occasions.

There is no doubt that UNEF made a very important contribution towards peaceful relations between Egypt and Israel. It did so
in several ways. In the first place its presence on the border, and
particularly in the Gaza Strip, meant that the armed forces of the
two sides were no longer in sight of each other. As UNEF did not
operate on the Israeli side of the Demarcation Line, Israel was still
able to patrol right up to it, and exercised her right to do so, although
usually only with small numbers of men. However, UNEF's responsibilities on the other side resulted in Egypt's forces being kept away
from the Line, with the consequence that the two sides did not come
into visual let alone physical contact. This was a great improvement
on the situation which previously existed. Then, with no third party
between them, incidents could arise only too easily between hostile
and trigger-happy troops, and although none of them developed to
the extent of precipitating an immediate war, it is clear that they

[6] UN Document A/5172, para 1.
[7] UN Document A/6406, para 3.
[8] UN Document A/6672, para. 7.

exacerbated already tense relations and contributed towards the build up of the situation which produced the Israeli attack of October 1956.

UNEF's desire to do nothing to jeopardize this relatively auspicious state of affairs can be seen in its policy towards the question of the use of its arms at night. It sought the right to fire at those who, being within the prohibited 500 metre zone during the hours of darkness, refused to halt when challenged. Egypt was agreeable, provided UNEF also received the right to fire into Israeli territory, a condition which had no chance of being accepted. Alternatively, Egypt was willing to allow UNEF to fire provided members of the Palestinian police were allowed to join its patrols. This, however, was not acceptable to UNEF, for her Commander feared that it would encourage firing across the Line, and so lead to the deterioration of an improving situation.

It was not, however, only the regular forces of each side which had caused trouble prior to 1956. Much of the difficulty had arisen from the small, commando-type raids which the Egyptians were in the habit of making under the cover of darkness. The *fedayeen*, as they were called, were not officially acting on behalf of Egypt, but there is no doubt about the support which they received from the Government. The relative ease with which they had been able to cross the border—another sign of governmental benevolence—had greatly assisted their task, and the arrival of UNEF, therefore, made a significant impact on the situation. Now, right at the Line, was a third party who was able to keep it under constant watch, and who could be relied upon to try to apprehend anyone who was trying to slip across it. Moreover, UNEF's presence could be taken, correctly, as implying that the former policy of hit-and-run raids was now out of favour, so that anyone who was caught crossing to or from Israel would be uncertain of his reception when handed over to the Egyptian authorities. Thus it seems very plausible to see a direct correlation between UNEF's role from March 1957 and the reduction in infiltration which ensued. This drastic lessening in the provocation which was given to Israel was important, for it had given rise to occasional large-scale acts of retaliation which only underlined and, if anything, deepened the hostility between the two countries. The culminating invasion of October 1956 may be regarded, in part, as a response to the mounting irritation which had been caused by the Egyptian guerrillas. Hence, by acting as a physical obstruction to such incidents, UNEF helped very materially to maintain the peace.

Over and above these two points, UNEF may well have helped to maintain quiet in a third way. Whatever might have been said about the legal relationship between Egypt and the Force, there could have been little doubt that in the event of it no longer being welcome on Egyptian soil, it would leave.[9] Even if the UN stood out against this course, those states whose contingents made it up, not having a vital interest in its maintenance in Egypt, would in all probability have withdrawn their men. Not to do so would have invited the possibility of a loss of life, which would be very unpopular with their publics. It would also have incurred the wrath of Egypt and her sympathizers, who would probably not have been a small company, on account of the favour in which the idea of territorial integrity is held. Thus the maintenance of UNEF at the Egyptian–Israeli border, and, even more importantly, the absence of a question as to its continuance there, was indicative of Egypt's willingness to keep tension low. In turn, this may well have helped Israel to adopt a similar attitude, for in the event of minor problems, she had, *prima facie*, no reason to believe that they were the harbingers of more serious trouble. Thus, such issues would be dealt with in a relaxed manner, and on the assumption that Egypt was not spoiling for a fight. Equally, UNEF's presence meant that interested outsiders had less cause to get jittery whenever the scene was disturbed. This had no necessary bearing on the fundamental antipathy of the two sides, but inasmuch as UNEF was a kind of pledge of good Egyptian behaviour, it may, by virtue of this quality, have helped to introduce a little additional surface calm into the situation.

There is a fourth way in which UNEF may have made a prophylactic contribution to the Egyptian-Israeli relationship: through preventing the full-scale invasion of one side by the other. This is a point which had more relevance to Israel's position than Egypt's. For, as has been suggested, Egypt would not have found it too difficult to get rid of UNEF, had she wished. Alternatively, she might have tried to use it as a cover, both physical and diplomatic, for the preparation of an all out attack on Israel—although it is exceedingly unlikely that this would have escaped notice by the Israeli intelligence service. But invasion was a weapon which was much more suited to Israel than Egypt, on both temperamental and practical grounds, and she could by no means rely on being able to get UNEF out of the way. Having refused to have it on her side of the border, she was in no position to tell it to leave Egypt. At least, she had no legal right to do so. She could still have hinted at the wisdom of its withdrawal, and if she was clearly planning an invasion, some, if not all, of the contributing states, may have taken the hint.

[9] For an earlier expression of this view, see the author's 'UN Action for Peace. I. Barrier Forces', 18 *The World Today*, No. 11 (November 1962), p. 480.

But it is very likely that there would have been a good deal of opposition at the UN, and outside, to such a move. It was, as a result arguable that there was a considerable obstacle in the way of a further invasion of Egypt, and some commentators have claimed that had UNEF been in existence prior to the Suez crisis, the attack of October 1956 would probably not have taken place.[10]

The argument to this effect usually rested on the symbolic rather than the physical strength of UNEF. It was recognized that it was not designed, and therefore not equipped, as a fighting force, and that hence there was never any question of it trying to prevent the passage of an aggressor, from whatever direction he might come. It was there, as someone once put it, to be shot at, and not to shoot. However, a good deal was made of UNEF's representative quality, of the fact that it stood for the world Organization. This was judged to give it a certain moral standing, which might well inhibit someone who was minded to remove or scale it. But beyond this, the point was made that it also had a somewhat less intangible deterrent power, inasmuch as its violation might well have unwelcome repercussions, all the more ominous because of their uncertain nature. It was suggested that condemnatory resolutions and the breaking off of diplomatic relations would very probably follow such behaviour; that economic sanctions might be imposed; and that some might even give military assistance to the attacked state. Thus UNEF has been pictured as a trip wire, as an alarm mechanism, or as a plate-glass window, the point being in each case that a state who acted as if UNEF was not there was taking a chance. Physically, UNEF could be discounted, but to do so was to take serious risks.

While the details of this argument are valid, as a whole it is insubstantial. For a decision regarding invasion would hardly have turned on the anticipated response of those states who would feel badly about an indignity suffered by UNEF, and by the UN. However strong their feelings, their reactions were most unlikely to include a readiness to wage war on the offending state, and it is considerations of that order which are significant when invasion is being discussed. In this light, the consequences of offending the UN do not appear as reckless living, but as a relatively small element to weigh in the negative side of the balance. Thus it is most unlikely that UNEF served to deter Israel from invading Egypt. The more plausible claim is that during UNEF's 10 years on the frontier, Israel was not minded to attack Egypt. She could probably have done so successfully at any time during this period. But, as well as having to do without Anglo-French assistance, she would

[10] See Frye, *op. cit.*, p. 93, and Gabriella Rosner, *The United Nations Emergency Force* (New York: Columbia University Press, 1963), p. 201.

have found such a move very disadvantageous in diplomatic terms. She could expect to obtain very little support, and to meet much opposition at the UN, and outside, to such a move. It was, as a result Union. Thus, she would have needed compelling reasons for attacking Egypt again and, until the crisis of 1967, they were not forthcoming. Nevertheless, had she decided to do so, UNEF's presence would, from her point of view, have been hardly more than regrettable.

This conclusion has a wider relevance, for it is equally applicable to Egypt. Following the 1956 defeat, President Nasser decided that the policy of provoking Israel was mistaken. Egypt's chosen task was to build up her strength until she was able to meet Israel face to face. Meanwhile, Israel was not to be given another opportunity to attack while Egypt was insufficiently strong to cope with it. Hence UNEF served Nasser's purposes very well. It prevented the risk of escalating incidents, stood in the way of infiltration and gave Egypt a good excuse for discouraging it, reassured Israel as to Egypt's current intentions, and may have given Egypt some protection if Israel became more belligerent. But all this was predicated on the assumption that Egypt did not want a war with Israel. So long as that held good, UNEF could play a very valuable role. But only for that long.

This points to UNEF's real significance. What it did during its 10 years in the Middle East was not to keep the peace. Rather it helped Israel and Egypt to implement their temporary disposition to live in peace. It was a derivative rather than a primary obstruction to the worsening of the situation. However, it may well be that as such it was an essential aid. Without such a force, tension would almost certainly have been very much higher on account of border incidents, and it is very conceivable that, as a result, the parties would, willy-nilly, have found themselves at war.

It is clear from their attitudes towards UNEF that Egypt and Israel appreciated this. Israel would not have it on her side of the border but, while she would not say so openly, was very glad to see it on Egypt's. Not being desirous of another conflict with Egypt, UNEF helped her by standing in the way of the kind of build-up of tension which had preceded the 1956 war. Thus, whenever the UN proposed to reduce UNEF, Israel's concern was, in private, very evident. And any hint that UNEF might be withdrawn was calculated to produce alarm. Egypt was likewise concerned for the maintenance of UNEF. In public her position was that she was no more than a gracious host. The UN, in its wisdom, had sought to place a force along her border with Israel. She had not asked for it, nor did she seek its continuance, but had no objection to its presence.

There is every reason for believing, however, that privately Egypt was very glad indeed to have UNEF on her soil and did not favour its reduction, despite her refusal to help pay for it. Certainly she would not have welcomed a UN proposal to withdraw the Force.

Thus UNEF remained on the frontier between Egypt and Israel for 16 years. The maintenance of quiet throughout that period may have slightly increased their willingness to continue living in peace. But, no more in international than in personal relations is time occasionally necessarily a healer. It may have this effect, but not always. And in this case the basic attitude of Egypt towards Israel did not improve. For some time Egypt, like Israel, was prepared to accept a physically peaceful relationship, and many observers concluded that, assisted by UNEF, this could continue indefinitely. Quips were heard about the Emergency Force having become the everlasting force. But the peaceful situation which had existed since 1957 was the product of calculations which had little to do with the presence of a UN force; nor did UNEF have a fundamental bearing on the factors which accounted for its continuance. When, therefore, one of those factors changed, UNEF suddenly found that the situation excluded the only role which it was capable of playing.

After the Suez war, the Arab state which gave Israel the most formidable trouble was Syria. Egypt was now holding back.[11] The Lebanon, as always, was most anxious to keep her border quiet. On the long Jordanian border numerous incidents occurred, but usually they were not of great significance. Syria, however, was another matter altogether, more unstable and extreme than any of Israel's other neighbours, and during the early months of 1967 tension between the two countries reached a high level. Raids and assaults from both sides increased in number, and it began to look as if Israel's next response might be more formidable than usual, although it is most questionable whether, as Egypt was to claim, she was planning a full-scale invasion of Syria. However, the situation produced a military agreement between Syria and Egypt, and gave rise to a dramatic and far-reaching series of events.

The first sign of this occurred on 16 May, when UNEF's Commander, General Rikhye, received a communication from the Chief of Staff of the Egyptian armed forces telling him that Egypt's troops were already concentrated in eastern Sinai and asking that orders be issued for UNEF's immediate withdrawal from the border. General Rikhye properly referred this demand to New York,

[11] Following the union of Egypt and Syria in 1958 the new state took the name of the United Arab Republic (UAR). On its breakdown three years later Egypt retained the name of the UAR for herself. However, for convenience, she will throughout this Chapter be referred to by her pre-1958 name.

where the Secretary-General sought clarification from Egypt's permanent representative, who turned out to know nothing about the matter. He was warned by U Thant that there could be no question of UNEF standing aside just for the duration of the crisis, and that any such request would be treated as one for UNEF's complete withdrawal. On the following day UNEF's troops in Sinai, numbering only a few hundred, found Egyptian units deployed in their vicinity, and in two cases between their camps and the international frontier. And on 18 May, by which time there were some 20,000–30,000 Egyptian troops at the border,[12] UN troops were forced out of two of their observation posts in Sinai. The same day brought Egypt's formal request to the Secretary-General for UNEF's withdrawal.

When UNEF was set up the General Assembly had also established a Committee to advise the Secretary-General on matters concerning the operation of the Force, composed of the representatives of Brazil, Canada, Ceylon, Colombia, India, Norway, and Pakistan. It was given the right to request the convening of the Assembly whenever the situation seemed to require it, but UNEF's affairs were so smooth that the Advisory Committee itself had not had occasion to meet since 1958. Now, however, it was convened by U Thant before he replied to Egypt's letter of 18 May, and was joined by the representatives of those states who had troops in UNEF but were not members of the Committee. This meeting did not give rise to a request that the Assembly be convened. Instead it was immediately followed by the Secretary-General's reply to Egypt in which he agreed, reluctantly, to withdraw the Force. Thus UNEF ceased all operations on 19 May, along both the international frontier and the Armistice Demarcation Line around the Gaza Strip, and arrangements were straightaway put in hand for its withdrawal. That of the Canadian contingent was accelerated as a result of a demand to that effect by Egypt, who alleged that the Canadian Government was taking an unduly pro-Israel stand. More to the point may have been the fact that Canada had been particularly loud in her lament at the UN's speedy acceptance of the demand for UNEF's withdrawal. The departure of some other sections of the Force, however, was delayed and disorganized by the six-day war which occurred between Israel and the Arabs early in June, so that it was only on 17 June that the last elements of UNEF left Egypt.

[12] Quite apart from being contrary to the whole idea of UNEF, this was also a breach of a commander's agreement by which UNEF was entitled to the sole use of an area five kilometres in depth from the international frontier. This averted the possibility of troop clashes between Egypt and UNEF, as well as between Egypt and Israel.

For agreeing so readily to Egypt's request, and for not giving a lead in the matter of convening the General Assembly or the Security Council, U Thant received a good deal of criticism. In reply, he placed great emphasis on his understanding that the principle of consent was at the basis of all peace-keeping operations. He distinguished between enforcement measures under Chapter VII of the Charter, which did not depend upon consent, and an operation such as the one conducted by UNEF. He referred to the fact that UNEF's entry into Egypt had been conditional upon her consent, reminded members that it was a lack of Israeli consent which had prevented the force from entering Israel, and drew the conclusion that Egypt had the unilateral right to withdraw her consent to UNEF's continued presence on her soil, in which case the UN had no option but to recall its force.

On the basis of the understanding which had been reached between the UN and Egypt regarding the execution of UNEF's mandate, a different, and probably a more compelling, legal argument could doubtless have been constructed, which would not have required the UN's immediate acceptance of Egypt's request. But, be that as it may, U Thant also emphasized that his decision was grounded in practical considerations. He argued that the effective functioning of a body such as UNEF depended on the co-operation of the host state, and that in the absence of such co-operation it would find it very difficult, if not impossible, to do its job, and might also place itself in danger. More particularly he claimed that in this case UNEF had really ceased to have any operational significance from the moment that Egypt advanced its troops to the frontier. It was designed to act as a buffer, as a body which stood between the disputants. If, however, one of them pushed it away and stood directly opposite the other side, then the whole object of the exercise was nullified. Hence, in the light of developments on 16–18 May, UNEF's 'continued presence was . . . rendered useless and its position untenable, and its withdrawal became virtually inevitable'.[13] Moreover, the Secretary-General argued, if Egypt's request had not been complied with, UNEF would have quickly disintegrated due to the withdrawal of individual contingents.[14]

There can be no doubt that, on 18 May, U Thant was faced with a critical situation. It was not open to him to order UNEF across the frontier into Israel, for that country, while claiming that

[13] Annual Report of the Secretary-General for 1966/7, General Assembly, *Official Records*, 22nd session, Supplement No. 1, p. 1.
[14] The Secretary-General justified his decision along these lines in a number of documents, notably S/7896, S/7906, A/6672, and A/6730, Add. 3. See also A/6669 for the events of 16–18 May.

the question of UNEF's withdrawal did not lie solely with Egypt and that she had a right to be heard on the matter, also reiterated her total opposition to UNEF's deployment on her side of the border. Yugoslavia and India had already made it clear that, in the event of a formal request for UNEF's withdrawal, they, at least, would remove their contingents, whatever the General Assembly or any other body might decide.[15] This would have been a serious matter for the Force, especially as it was the Yugoslavs who were on duty in Sinai. UNEF was also in some danger, for in the event of further Egyptian interference with its positions the lives of UN troops could easily be jeopardized, particularly, perhaps, if they received no firm order either to resist or retire. Hence time was very short. Moreover, there is no doubt that the Secretary-General was right to stress UNEF's dependence on the co-operation of Egypt. Quite apart from the situation on the border, the host state could have made life very difficult for UNEF in other ways, for example, by obstructing its freedom of movement behind the frontier and by restricting its supply. And any attempt to reinforce it, or to replace contingents which had been withdrawn—assuming such were forthcoming—could have been prevented. However, the question remains whether, had the UN not agreed so readily to Egypt's request for UNEF's withdrawal, war might have been averted.

It was certainly the case that the withdrawal of UNEF, at this or any other time, was likely to increase tension, a point which was emphasized by the Secretary-General. In agreeing to Egypt's request he spoke of his misgiving that the action which he felt compelled to take might have grave implications for peace. And in his final report on UNEF, following the June war, he referred to the 'disastrous shattering of peace . . . which soon followed the withdrawal of UNEF', and went on: 'What would probably happen whenever UNEF might be withdrawn had been pointed out by the Secretary-General in his reports on UNEF in preceding years'.[16] But it does not follow that it was UNEF's departure which created the subsequent trouble. As U Thant himself pointed out, Egypt's request was an expression of the underlying Arab-Israeli conflict, and also, he might have added, of the tense situation which had been building up during the early months of 1967. From the point of view of the UN's responsibility for the June war, therefore, the major question is whether, by refusing to withdraw UNEF, it was within the Organization's power to block the immediate crisis.

It is arguable that it may have been. It was quite widely thought

[15] At the very outset of the UNEF operation Yugoslavia and India, together with Indonesia, had stated that they would withdraw their troops whenever Egypt asked them to do so.
[16] UN Document A/6672, para 5.

that Egypt's request was more of a ploy in the war of nerves against Israel and at the same time an instance of Arab one-upmanship than indicative of a real desire to see UNEF leave. Egypt was not directly threatened, and therefore had no reason to, as it were, clear the decks for a pre-emptive blow. Nor, at that moment, had Israel made a move against Syria, and there were many who doubted whether she was likely to make a full-scale attack on that country. Moreover, there had been no indication at all to suggest that, on her own initiative, Egypt was spoiling for a fight with Israel. She might, at this time, have been able to rely on Israel's engagement on at least two fronts, on account of Syria's belligerent attitude, but that was hardly sufficient to bring her great comfort regarding the outcome of a war. In this light, it seemed only folly for Egypt to get rid of UNEF, for its departure would only invite her, encouraged by the more extreme of her Arab brethren, to close the Straits of Tiran and engage in a more actively hostile policy towards Israel. Moreover, such interference as UNEF had suffered had taken place in the area where it was most thinly deployed, and where there was plenty of room for the Egyptian troops to stand off. And by addressing the first request for UNEF's withdrawal to its Commander rather than to the Secretary-General, Egypt invited some delay. Thus there were a number of indications which suggested that possibly Egypt's request was not as urgent as it sounded and that she might not have been too unhappy to have had the opportunity of giving the matter further consideration. In which case an alternative response for U Thant would have been to ask Egypt to call a halt to her pressure on UNEF while he obtained a speedy decision on her request from one of the UN's political organs. He could have emphasized that this was in no sense a reflection of hostility towards Egypt but just a constitutional requirement.

If this course had been followed, it can by no means be assumed, as many seemed to do, that the UN would have been prepared to take issue with Egypt over UNEF's presence. Had the matter gone to the Security Council, the Soviet Union could have been relied upon to stand behind Egypt, and to have worked for the rejection of her request. And while there were many in the Assembly who would have regretted a cutting down of the UN's peace-keeping activities, this would probably not have been so strongly felt as to have caused a majority to do violence to the principle of territorial integrity. The idea that the UN, by a recommendation of the Assembly, could, in effect, occupy part of a country against its will would have been anathema to the smaller members, and not to them alone. What a referral of the question to a political organ would have secured was some time for President Nasser to have second thoughts and an opportunity for UN members to test his resolution. Combined with pressure on Israel to give some guarantee of her intentions regarding Syria, such a move may possibly have resulted in the cancellation of Egypt's request for UNEF's withdrawal. In which case the next fateful step—the closure of the Straits of Tiran to Israeli shipping and to vessels carrying strategic material to Eilat—could hardly have taken place, which, in turn, might well have ended the crisis before it had properly begun.

But this looks an unlikely unfolding of events. The Powers were divided in their Middle Eastern allegiances, rather than prepared to bring joint pressure on both disputants in the cause of peace. Israel was not at all in the frame of mind to offer any kind of guarantee regarding Syria which Egypt would have been able to treat as satisfactory. And Egypt would have found it very difficult indeed to go back on her request for UNEF's withdrawal. Some of her fellow Arabs had from time to time caused her mild embarrassment by their critical references to UNEF's presence. Now, having herself publicly indicated that UNEF stood in the way of Egyptian succour for Syria, and by implication, for any other Arab state in distress at Israel's hand, she would have been in very considerable trouble, domestic, possibly, as well as diplomatic, if she agreed that, after all, UNEF could remain on her soil. Moreover, difficult though it is to explain, it does look as if Egypt was in earnest when she presented her formal request for UNEF's withdrawal. For it did not come completely out of the blue. The first request to this effect, to General Rikhye, had been made on 16 May. It was on the following day that his troops began to be harassed by Egyptian forces, and not until noon on the 18th that the Secretary-General was officially informed of Egypt's 'decision' to terminate UNEF's presence. Thus there was an interval of 48 hours for Egypt to think further about the matter, and while it would have been awkward it would have been by no means impossible for her to disown the communication to General Rikhye and the behaviour of her troops in Sinai. But she did not take the chance. Nor does it seem that she was counting on the UN to reject her move, and prepared, in those circumstances, to back down. For, when U Thant said that he would appeal to President Nasser to reconsider Egypt's formal request for UNEF's withdrawal, he was pressed, on the authority of the Egyptian Foreign Minister, not to do so. Such a request, he was told, would be 'sternly rebuffed'.[17]

It would still have been open to the UN, despite the absence of a conciliatory word from Egypt, to have insisted that UNEF's withdrawal required its consent, and to have refused it. But, even in the

[17] UN Document A/6730, Add. 3, para. 22.

unlikely event of one of the political organs taking this course, this would not have created a future for UNEF as a barrier force between Israel and the UAR. It would have been subject to further humiliations along the lines of those it had already suffered, which would have eroded its ability to keep the border under surveillance. Moreover, it would have been no obstacle in the event of a physical conflict, for it was not designed to keep the disputants from fighting through the threat or use of force; nor, therefore, was it the kind of body which could secure and maintain a position in the 'host' state by force of arms. Hence, if the UN had tried to maintain UNEF in its place contrary to Egypt's express will, it would not have been making an effective contribution towards pacification, would thereby have damaged its own reputation, and might also have reduced the likelihood of it being asked to engage in peace-keeping operations in respect of other disputes.

Thus the charge that the UN, by so speedily withdrawing UNEF bears a large responsibility for the subsequent war is unconvincing. Had UNEF remained in its place, it may be that events would have been different and less dramatic—but only on the assumption that Egypt would not have pursued a more belligerent policy towards Israel in UNEF's presence. However, while the evidence is not conclusive, it provides weighty support for the view that Egypt had committed herself to such a policy, a very important consideration here being her apparently clear determination to get UNEF out of the way. The UN could have tried to resist this move, hoping that success would lead to a modification of Egypt's new anti-Israeli line. But, given that line, the UN's prospects were very poor, on both counts. It could still be argued that the Secretary-General should have insisted on obtaining a decision from the Assembly, but it must also be noted that he had to take account of the fact that even the smallest delay might have been dangerous for the Force, without increasing the likelihood of altering the final outcome.

The facts of the matter were that UNEF could only operate effectively if Egypt was willing to let it do so, and, more importantly, that its operations were only relevant for as long as Egypt and Israel wanted a quiet border. UNEF's own ability to influence these conditions was minimal, and once any of them changed there was no longer any real place for a force of its type. In May 1967 it seemed that, for whatever reasons, a decisive change had taken place in Egypt's policy towards both UNEF and Israel, in which case UNEF's usefulness was at an end. So viewed, its withdrawal neither precipitated the crisis nor failed to take an opportunity to stand in its way. The existence of the crisis was manifested in the demand for its withdrawal, and UNEF had no real chance of averting it.

Egypt may not have been calculating on a war with Israel, and may not have been chiefly responsible for it. But, manifestly, the first major step towards it was hers, and in face of her decision, after a ten-year interval, to live dangerously once again, the UN was powerless.

II

UNEF's experience provides an excellent example of the obstructive possibilities which are open to the UN, and also of the limitations which attend its activities in this field. Through the use of a relatively small and lightly-armed force, it can make a very valuable contribution towards keeping a potentially troublesome frontier quiet—if both of the disputants want it that way, and provided also, of course, that at least one of them is prepared to play host. But as soon as the mutually pacific disposition founders, even if the restless party has none of the force on its territory, the force has lost its *raison d'être*. For what it obstructs is only an accidental war, or a war which might be sparked off by unofficial border incidents. It bars conflict only for as long as the parties want peace to continue. It is stronger than a sedative operation, but is not designed to take an effective independent stand against either side, and functions best when its presence is welcomed and its purposes supported by both of them. Thus, so far as major issues are concerned, a UN border force cannot create peaceful conditions but can only reflect and assist a mutual desire to live in peace.

This is why a UN force of this type is of no substantial value to a state which feels itself to be physically threatened. Accordingly, if a state in this situation needs outside help it will look towards its friends, and first of all towards its Great Power friends, rather than to the UN. In 1958, for example, when the Lebanon felt that its independence had been endangered by the Iraqi *coup*, she did not ask that the UN Observer Group, then establishing itself along her borders, should be turned into a force. Instead she sought, and received, assistance from the United States. Likewise, Iraq's demands on the newly independent Kuwait in June 1961 produced an appeal not to the UN but to Britain; and when the British force withdrew in the following October, it was an Arab, and not a UN force which took its place.[18] Similarly in 1962 it was American and

[18] Within six months the Arab force had collapsed on account of the gradual withdrawal, for domestic reasons, of the national units of which it was composed. See, David Holden, *Farewell to Arabia* (London: Faber, 1966), p. 156. However, his was not important, for the Arab force was more a way of trying to show that the Arabs could look after their own problems than of providing a guarantee for Kuwait. As far as Kuwait's security was concerned, the important thing was that Britain had shown her readiness to come to her aid.

not UN troops who were successfully sought by Thailand when Pathet Lao forces had advanced close to her frontiers. What was wanted in each of these cases was not a non-combatant force, symbolic though it might be of the UN, but one prepared to fight, if necessary, in defence of the host country. And this concern was typical. Hence, for as long as the UN's prophylactic activities do not rely on armed strength to achieve their ends, they are not likely to appeal to states in distress. Quite apart from other considerations, therefore, the idea that the UN might be able to assist in a solution of the Vietnam problem by guarding the dividing line between North and South is unrealistic.

There are also other factors, relating to the nature of the UN, which account for UNEF not having begun a fashion. States generally dislike having to ask for help in the maintenance of their security, and they will usually be particularly reluctant to turn to the UN. Firstly, when one state sends troops to another, this takes place within the context of the theory of sovereign equality. One member of society is helping a friend, and although the assisting state is likely to be much more powerful than the assisted, for some purposes they are regarded as equals. Moreover, it will be recognized on all sides that the help is most unlikely to be the product of nothing more than a generous spirit, but will probably be serving an interest of the state giving aid as well as of the one receiving it. Thus the dignity of the recipient need not be too deeply offended. To go to the UN, on the other hand, as well as involving the public discussion of one's affairs, is akin to a request for international charity. Thus it can easily seem an especially degrading thing to do.

In the second place, there is the consideration that a UN force is, in political terms, a much more uncertain quantity than one which comes from a friend. It is not inconceivable that the UN itself may come to entertain a different conception of the force's role than that of the host state, a situation which is unlikely to arise when help is given by a well-disposed Power. Further, the force is likely to be made up of contingents drawn from a variety of countries, some of whom might possibly try to take advantage of the situation to further their own ends in relation to the host state. In short, a UN force may be much less satisfactorily controlled, from the host's point of view, than one which comes from a politically sympathetic state. Of course, friends can change their tune, and in that case the host state could be in real trouble, on account of the greater strength and firmer control of a force which represents a single state. But that is a most unlikely event.

Thus, while all circumstances are exceptional, they have perhaps to be very exceptional for a state to ask the UN for a border force. Only two such instances have occurred since UNEF's establishment, both of them rather bizarre, and in neither case did the request bear the required fruit. The first arose out of the political affairs of San Marino, a mini-state with an area of 23 square miles and a population of about 1,700, and which, unlike others of its kind, is both land-locked and possesses only one neighbour: Italy. Since the end of World War II this state within a state had caused Italy some irritation by expressing a preference for a socialist-communist government; she had also offended the Vatican for the same reason, and had added to her sins by permitting divorce. In September 1957, however, the Government lost its majority through defections, and the opposition parties, led by the Christian Democrats, looked forward to taking office. But half an hour before the six-monthly election of two Captains-Regent (who, jointly, were the head of state) was due to be held, the Council, in whose hands the election lay, was dissolved by the outgoing Captains-Regent and a general election was called.

The opposition immediately charged that this was tantamount to a *coup*, and responded by establishing a provisional Government with its headquarters in an abandoned factory just inside the San Marino border. It was immediately recognized by Italy, who proceeded to further its claims by blockading the mini-state. In reply the Government appealed to the UN on 2 October, asking that an international police force be sent to San Marino. On the following day they tried another tactic, appealing to the Italian President to set up an arbitration commission to investigate the conflicting claims of their two countries. However, the President was unforthcoming. Nor did any word come from the UN. In view of this, and of the fact that the provisional Government was threatening to march on San Marino, the left-wing regime soon capitulated, the provisional Government assuming control on 14 October. It arraigned all its parliamentary opponents on charges of high treason and called an election, but not before it had enfranchised those of San Marino's citizens who were living in the United States. It also promised to reimburse the travelling expenses of those San Mariensi who returned from Italy to cast their vote. The outcome, for whatever reasons, was a victory for the new order, which enabled the Government to display leniency towards its convicted opponents, although in a manner which ensured that they would not threaten the rightward path on which San Marino had now been set.

It may well be that the San Marino Government was itself less than clear as to what, exactly, it wanted of the UN. But, in general terms, it is evident that it felt the need of a body which would provide it with some defence against the Italian-backed provisional Government. It may therefore be doubted whether it would have received any satisfaction from the UN, for the prerequisites for the dispatch of an interpository force had not been met. But, in any event, the matter never came up for decision. San Marino was not a member of the UN, and, further, was so insignificant that her communication could safely be ignored: it does not appear in the Organization's official records. It may be wondered why the matter was not taken up by a state which might have been expected to show some sympathy for the Government's plight, such as the Soviet Union. Italy's behaviour certainly offered some useful propaganda material. But, on the other hand, the issue was of little intrinsic importance and, what must have been a much weightier consideration, had arisen at an inconvenient moment for the Communist bloc, when the Soviet Union and her friends were still stoutly resisting the UN's competence to involve itself in the Hungarian affair of the previous year. The two cases could be distinguished, but the exercise would, to many ears, have sounded pedantic and unreal, and would only have served to invite further critical attention to the Soviet Union's recent role in Hungary. This must have suggested, very forcibly, that this was an occasion when it would be wise to keep silent.

The second occasion on which a state has sought a UN interpository force was in 1959, when Laos suddenly asked that one be sent to her country in order to halt North Vietnamese aggression. This was not at all to the liking of the Western Powers, particularly the United States. As, at this time, they were giving the Laotian Government a good deal of support, they could hardly oppose their friend's request, and would have been embarrassed if the UN had turned it down. But they would have suffered even greater embarrassment had the UN agreed to it. A solution to the problem was found in the proposal that the matter should be investigated, and the Security Council, after stretching its procedural rules to circumvent the Soviet Union's opposition, adopted it.[19] No more was heard from Laos about its need for a UN force.

As the Laotian case showed, it cannot be assumed that the UN will always grant a request for a border force. Its response will depend, primarily, on the interaction of two factors. The first concerns the attitude of interested third parties. If the proposal that the UN should intervene meets with the opposition of influential members, they may, in one way or another, be able to forestall a vote on the issue, as in the case of Laos. Or, if they cannot do that,

[19] See above, pp. 200–206.

they will probably be able to convince enough other members of the unwisdom of the suggestion so as to ensure that it is not adopted. Even if the opponents include a permanent member of the Security Council, and the matter is before that organ, they will much prefer to have the proposal blocked on account of a lack of votes than through the exercise of a veto. The member which is best placed to conduct such an operation is the United States. If, for example, at the time of the 1954 Guatemalan crisis it had been proposed that a UN force be sent to Guatemala's borders, there is little doubt that the United States would have been no less anxious and able to prevent that happening, than she was in relation to the proposal that the UN should discuss the issue. Similarly, if Castro's Cuba was anxious to have some kind of UN surveillance around its shores at a time when an invasion was rumoured, the United States would doubtless use all her resources to obstruct the proposal, although this would probably not be as easy for her as it would have been in respect of Guatemala in 1954.

Even if the opponents of the establishment of a UN force were not influential in the UN, they might still be able to block such a course if they included a very powerful state and if the proposal related to an area which is within that state's geographical sphere of influence. Should the matter be handled by the Security Council, and the chief opponent has a veto, there could be no doubt about the outcome. Nor would it necessarily be different if the issue was taken or transferred to the General Assembly. For, to go ahead in these circumstances might put the UN force in some danger. And, quite apart from this consideration, a number of members might be most reluctant to give serious offence to one of their powerful fellows, on account both of the possible diplomatic repercussions on their own relations with it, and of the impact which it might have on that member's future attitude to the UN. The opposition of the Soviet Union, for example, would probably stand in the way of the UN agreeing to send a force to the borders of two of the smaller East European countries. A similar result might also attend the opposition of a powerful non-member, such as Communist China. If, for example it was proposed that a UN force be established along a South East Asian border, and China took strong objection to the idea, the UN might think hard and long before agreeing to it.

An alternative reason which might account for the UN's denial of a request for an interpository force relates not so much to the influence, or power of the opponents, as to the unpopularity of the appellant. If he is in bad standing at the UN, there is unlikely to be much disposition to help him in his hour of need. If, for example, in 1961 Portugal had asked the UN for the dispatch of a force to the border between Goa and India, there is no doubt that the UN would have treated it with as much disdain as it did Portugal's request for observers. What most members favoured was the liquidation of Goa by India, and not its defence. Likewise if, as is highly improbable, South Africa asked that her borders be policed by the UN in order to discourage infiltration, it is inconceivable that the UN would agree, at least not in good faith.

The second factor which bears upon the UN's willingness to create an interpository force has to do with the relationship of the parties and their attitude towards the UN's intervention. There would, for example, be no question of the UN trying to place a force between two combatant states. As in the case of the establishment of UNEF, the UN would insist on a cease-fire before it moved its troops to the field. Then, too, if there was a likelihood of war, it is improbable that the UN would agree to establish a force, even if it was generally sympathetic towards the weaker state. For a prophylactic force is neither designed to fight its way into a situation, nor intended to be a physical deterrent. Hence, to place it in a likely line of fire is to invite its failure. Many members would probably see no point in this, even if there was only some danger of the enterprise being unsuccessful. In such circumstances a refusal could be justified not only on the grounds of short-term prudence, but also as the course which best served the UN's long-term interests; the argument being that if the UN wished to gain a reputation as a peace-keeper, it would be wise not to incur a reverse, particularly one which might involve a loss of life.

Quite apart from the likelihood of war, the UN would also be influenced by the views of the parties as to the placing of a force along their common border. For if one of them was not agreeable, the establishment of a force would not be a straightforward matter. The difference of opinion would inevitably be reflected in the UN, and the objecting state might well be able to obtain sufficient support to ensure that the proposal was defeated. This would not necessarily reflect either power or popularity on the part of the objector. Rather, it might be due to the sympathy of a number of members for the argument that to establish a force contrary to the wishes of one of the disputants would be an unfortunate precedent. It is all very well for the UN, in effect, to support a disputant whom one favours. But not if by doing so one increases the likelihood that at some future date the same ploy might be used against oneself.

There is a third, but essentially subsidiary, factor which is relevant to a consideration of the UN's response to requests for interpository forces: the availability of the necessary men and money. Obtaining the requisite number of troops who have the required skills, and are politically acceptable to the host state would not always be easy. And even if any difficulties of this kind can be overcome, the force still has to be transported to its destination and paid for. The financial problem, in particular, is not likely to be easily disposed of. However, while considerations such as these could furnish a good excuse for the UN not acting when it was not keen to do so, it is most unlikely that the UN would be held back on these grounds alone. If the Organization is willing to establish a force, those in favour of it will in all probability include enough states with both the enthusiasm, and resources to ensure that the scheme does not founder on account of technical problems.

But requests for interpository forces have been rare, and their fulfilment even rarer. The UN's first experience in this field undoubtedly produced an awareness of the Organization's potentialities in spheres which were less ambitious than collective security, and without UNEF it is unlikely that the UN would have been asked, or have felt able to assist in the handling of later crises, such as those in the Congo and West New Guinea. It is also probable that in other and lesser ways, the UN played a more important role as a result of having proved itself at Suez. But, contrary to some expectations, the use of UN forces along troubled borders did not increase. This was because, by their very nature, such forces cannot inspire much confidence as a deterrent to aggression, so they will usually only be asked for when a more substantial barrier cannot be obtained—second-best expedients sought by states who are disputing, usually, from second-best positions. However, the strength of the other party is likely to be demonstrated not only in its not needing such a force on its side of the frontier, but also in its ability to dissuade the UN from agreeing to its rival's request. And it is in any event likely that the preparedness of the UN to establish an interpository force will be in inverse proportion to the imminence of the threat to peace, or the magnitude of the state alleged to be threatening it.

Such a force can make a useful or a valuable contribution, of a limited character, towards assisting quarrelsome neighbours to live in peace, particularly if that is the wish of both of them. Usually, however, when neighbours wish to live in peace, they do not require outside help to enable them to fulfil their mutual desire. But sometimes they may, especially where they are disengaging from a conflict, which has not settled the basic issue between them. And if the UN already has a hand in the dispute, then circumstances will perhaps be at their most propitious for the establishment of a border force. Then it will be open for the UN itself to take the initiative in suggesting this kind of help, and if there is a strong feeling that the fighting should be stopped, and the disputants prevented from getting at each other's throats again, the UN may even feel able to press strongly for such a course. For this to happen it is necessary that the states concerned should not be in the first rank of Powers, and preferably not in the second either. It is desirable, too, that they should not be well connected with any of the major Powers, or, if well connected, that they should have been behaving in a manner which is frowned upon by them. And it is very helpful indeed if the major Powers are in favour of a UN solution, or at least that none of them are strongly opposed to that course. In turn, this probably requires that the major Powers, or at least those of them who are in the UN, are not too deeply divided, and that the international climate at the time is relatively good. Possibly it ought not to be too euphoric if the UN is to appear on the scene, for in that event the Powers might organize an international force themselves. But, while this was possible at the end of the nineteenth century, it would seem to be excluded by the temper of mid-twentieth-century international politics.

Such a favourable conjunction of circumstances was provided by the Suez affair. However, it must be noted that even here the establishment of a border force was greatly facilitated by the fact that UNEF was already in Egypt to supervise the withdrawal of the invaders, a purpose which was supported by the host state. It was therefore not too difficult for her to agree to an alteration in UNEF's role which also served her purposes. But had the initial proposal been simply for a force to watch over the border, Egypt may well have felt it necessary to take a different view regarding its desirability. From the point of view of her dignity, it was fortunate that UNEF was on the spot. Thus the UN was able to take advantage of what Sir Leslie Munro of New Zealand called 'a golden opportunity which may never recur' to post an international force along the Israeli–Egyptian frontier.[20] Golden opportunities, however, are no more common in this context than in others, and so it is not surprising that there is only one other instance of the UN trying its hand at obstruction.

III

The UN's second interpository force was sent not to an international frontier but to an internal and unofficial dividing line, that between the Greeks and Turks in Cyprus.[21],[22] It was established in pursuance

[20] General Assembly, *Official Records*, 650th Plenary Meeting, para. 117.
[21] For the background to this dispute, the attempt at mediation, and an examination of the difficulties in the way of its settlement, see above, pp. 71–81.
[22] The classification of the Cyprus Force as an example of obstruction stems from the UN's immediate aim, its hope being that the establishment of a force between

of a Security Council resolution of 4 March 1964, the path to which was far from straight. Serious inter-communal violence had broken out in Cyprus on 21 December 1963, and the cease-fires which were arranged in the next few days proved extremely fragile. On 26 December, therefore, it had been agreed that the Greek and Turkish contingents in Cyprus should join with British troops from the Sovereign Base Areas[23] in an endeavour to maintain peace. The joint force was to be under British command, and an active peace-keeping role was to be confined to the British element. Within a few days agreement was reached on a line dividing the Greek and Turkish areas of Nicosia—the 'Green Line', so called because it was first mapped out with a pencil of that colour—and it was then policed by the force. Both here and elsewhere, violence subsided, a development which was matched by a corresponding reduction in Turkey's threat of invasion. In turn, however, this led to renewed tension. The Greeks began to conceive the 'Green Line' as the first step towards the Turkish solution of partition, and the British as the protectors of the Turks. An anti-British campaign was mounted, and early in February serious violence broke out once more, which the peace-keeping force felt itself unable to stem.

Britain had already made it clear that her ring-holding operation could not be continued indefinitely. She was prepared to maintain it while the parties, taking advantage of the lull in fighting, urgently sought a solution to the basic problem, and towards this end a conference met in London in mid-January 1964. But when it became evident that its prospects on the main issue were poor, Britain began to look around for helpers in the job of preventing a resumption of fighting, a search which was spurred by the deteriorating situation on the island. It was being realized that the force, the British element of which was now in the region of 5,000,[24] was too small and too restricted to do its job properly, and figures of between 10,000 and 15,000 were mentioned as the number of men which would be needed. This was a level to which Britain would have found it very difficult to go, especially at this time, for her military resources were stretched by the assistance she was giving to the three Commonwealth states in East Africa following the mutinies in their armed

---

[23] Two areas on the island of Cyprus which were not a part of the Republic of Cyprus, it having been agreed in the negotiations preceding independence that Britain should retain them.
[24] By mid-February it had been increased to about 7,000.

---

the Greeks and Turks in Cyprus would prevent inter-communal violence. However, inasmuch as this activity was also meant, at one stage removed, to keep Turkey, and therefore Greece, from intervening in Cyprus (which might have led to a wider war), the case could be regarded as an instance of refrigeration, of the UN maintaining order inside a state to keep outsiders out.

forces. She could have called out her reserves, but in the circumstances this would not have been well received at home. She might
also have been influenced by the argument that her efforts to obtain
a political settlement were not easily compatible with her role as the
only policeman. But a much more important reason for Britain's
desire to share the peace-keeping responsibility lay in the fact that
this task now looked like being long and difficult. It would probably
be dangerous for the troops who were involved, which would not
add to its domestic acceptability. Periodic brushes with all the
parties could be expected, and relations with the host state might
become difficult, which would be all the more embarrassing for
Britain on account of Cyprus being a member of the Commonwealth. And the possibility of a Turkish invasion could not be
excluded. Britain was therefore most anxious that she should not
continue to bear the peace-keeping burden alone. She could argue
that the situation concerned others besides herself, especially the
NATO countries, on account of the membership of both Greece
and Turkey. It was in this direction, therefore, that she turned for
relief.

Britain's first approach was to the United States, who received
the suggestion that she should send troops to Cyprus without much
warmth. This was an election year, and the Government was apprehensive lest such a commitment, however small and for however
short a period it was stated to be, might be very difficult to terminate
and lead to increasing demands. However, the prospect of a war
between two NATO allies was even more alarming, and she therefore agreed to go ahead with the idea. A scheme was evolved for
the Cyprus force to remain under British command but to be
supplemented by contingents from a number of NATO countries,
and to receive guidance from a committee of NATO ambassadors.
It also provided for an appointment of a neutral mediator. The
assent of Greece and Turkey was obtained, as was Italy's agreement
to participate in the force. France refused to contribute, but West
Germany was a probable starter if pressed. Thus the proposal
looked viable, provided Cyprus would accept it. But she would not,
and was supported by the Soviet Union, who issued a public warning
to the West against interference in the affairs of Cyprus. President
Johnson thereupon dispatched an emissary to Makarios and the plan
was amended to enable the mediator to report to the Secretary-
General of the UN, and to provide for the presence in Cyprus of a
representative of the Secretary-General. But to no avail.

President Makarios may well have felt that as Turkey was held in
higher esteem in NATO than Greece, a force drawn from the
NATO Powers might be more sympathetic to the arguments and

claims of the Turkish community, than those of the Cyprus Government. From his point of view the UN was a much more promising body. Not only had Cyprus identified herself with the non-aligned states of Africa and Asia, but she had also presented her case against the Turkish Cypriots in the context of the overriding importance of the doctrine of self-determination. Hence there were two grounds on which Cyprus might expect wide support among UN members. Moreover, she could assume that she would not be friendless in the Security Council, for the Soviet Union was more likely to back her case than that presented on behalf of the Turks. Thus the Secretary-General had been told before the end of January that Cyprus was prepared to accept a UN force in the island, provided its dispatch was authorized by the Security Council. And to those who were urging the desirability of a NATO force Makarios insisted that the UN must be brought into the picture in some substantial way.

This course was not much favoured by the Western Powers. There was some apprehension about the delay which it might involve before a force was organized, and much more about the opportunity it would give the Soviet Union to interfere in what was regarded as essentially a NATO problem. Moreover, it would mean that the matter would be placed in the hands of a body which might not feel great urgency about obtaining a settlement of the basic issue, and in particular, might be unwilling to press the Cyprus Government for concessions. However, in face of President Makarios's refusal to accept a NATO force Britain and the United States capitulated, hastening to take the matter to the Security Council before Cyprus could do so. This was on 15 February. There followed much discussion behind the scenes, accompanied by the postponement and cancellation of Security Council meetings, in an endeavour to obtain a resolution which could meet all requirements. Cyprus wanted her territorial integrity to be reaffirmed without reference to the right of Britain, Greece, and Turkey to intervene, for that would be a valuable step towards the scrapping of the treaties of alliance and guarantee, which were part of the package deal that had brought her to independence. Turkey, on the other hand, wanted the treaties and the constitution to be specifically approved. Besides this problem there were others connected with the composition, control, and financing of the UN force. Eventually a suitable formula was agreed and presented to the Council by five of its six non-permanent members. The sixth, Czechoslovakia, took exception to that part of the draft resolution which left the composition and size of the force to the Secretary-General (in consultation with the interested Powers) and also the appointment of its commander. So did the Soviet Union and France. The former complained that it embodied procedures which would circumvent the Security Council, and the latter said that the Council had gone too far in the direction of the delegation of powers to a single individual. In a separate vote on the paragraph all three abstained, but they joined with all the other Council members in voting for the resolution as a whole. It provided for the creation of a 'United Nations Peace-keeping Force in Cyprus', the function of which was, 'in the interest of preserving international peace and security, to use its best efforts to prevent a recurrence of fighting and, as necessary, to contribute to the maintenance and restoration of law and order and a return to normal conditions'.[25]

One reason for the Council's unanimity was that the host state itself was prepared to accept a UN force on the proposed terms. But another undoubtedly lay in the fact that several of those terms reflected Soviet and French ideas about the proper conduct of peace-keeping operations. They could not but have been pleased at the clause in the resolution which stated that the costs of the Force were to be met on a voluntary basis, so ensuring that there could be no subsequent argument as to their liability for its maintenance. An even more important aspect of the arrangement, from their point of view, was that the life of the Force was limited to three months. This meant that any question of its extension beyond this period would have to be considered and approved by the Security Council, so giving the permanent members of the Council a powerful lever over its control by the Secretary-General. It did not put him entirely in their hands, for it was always possible that a veto over the renewal of the Force might be evaded by recourse to the Assembly. But the emphasis on the Security Council's role could hardly fail to result in the Force being managed with a close eye to the attitudes of the permanent members. Over and above these considerations, however, a factor which caused the Soviet Union to welcome the establish-ment of a UN force was that it was an additional guarantee of the independence and non-alignment of Cyprus. A NATO force would have carried the possibility of pressure being brought in favour of a solution which satisfied Greece and Turkey at the expense of Cyprus. The UN's intervention, on the other hand, prevented the issue being dealt with as if it was essentially an intra-NATO affair.

At first the UN Secretariat had been most reluctant to become involved, the policy differences and financial fall-out of the Congo operation having had a marked effect on its willingness to see the Organization jump into a peace-keeping role. And in some respects the Cyprus situation looked all too like that of the Congo, inasmuch as it concerned the maintenance of civil order in a highly charged

[25] Security Council resolution 186 (1964).

political context. Thus, when early in January, Greece, Turkey,
Britain, and Cyprus all joined in asking the Secretary-General to
send a personal representative to observe what was going on in
Cyprus, he reacted ultra-cautiously. Evidently what the parties
wanted was a reporting presence, each of them being interested in
obtaining an impartial fifth party who could report on any of the
others' misdeeds, and on their own good faith. The Secretary-
General, however, offered no more than a preliminary mission to
report on how an observer could best function. No doubt he was
aware that one thing can lead to another, and was anxious to take
all precautions to guard against the UN getting accidentally
enmeshed in the situation. However, in response to further representations, he gave way, and agreed to send General Gyani, of
India, to observe the British-led peace-keeping operation—but only
until the end of February, and not for the three months which the
parties had requested. And this despite the fact that Cyprus had
offered to pay all the UN's costs for the longer period. At the end of
February, the Secretary-General agreed to extend General Gyani's
mission for one month. There was no need for a further extension as
by the end of March the UN Force was operational, and Gyani had
been appointed as its Commander.

Getting the UN Force into the field had proved to be a difficult
job. The presence of the British may have contributed to this, by
reducing the urgency of the operation. On the other hand the UN
might never have gone in had it not been for the British force. For
it was at least keeping things relatively quiet, and in its absence the
UN might have been faced with the prospect of having to fight its
way into the middle of a civil war, which would have made members
very reluctant to contribute contingents for the Force. As it was they
were hesitant enough. Even before the resolution of 4 March, a
number of states had been approached and had said that they were
unable to help.[26] To some of them the Secretary-General returned,
but he was unable to change Brazil's mind and was having considerable difficulty with Austria. Four members who seemed likely
suppliers of contingents—Canada, Sweden, Finland, and Ireland—
all required explanations or assurances of various kinds before they
would remove all doubt regarding their participation.

In part this was due to uncertainty as to the financing of the Force,
for the states providing contingents, together with the host, were
to be liable for all the costs which were not met by voluntary
contributions. However, much of this apprehension was removed
by a number of early financial offers, including those from Britain

[26] *The Times* of 24 February 1964 reported this of Australia, Brazil, India, and
Ireland.

and the United States. The major difficulty related to the circumstances under which the force would have to operate. A resumption
of fighting between the Greek and Turkish Cypriot communities
could not be ruled out, nor could the physical involvement of the
mainland Powers, which would mean danger for the UN troops
and perhaps international embarrassment for their Governments.
Moreover, quite apart from large-scale fighting, outbreaks of
sporadic shooting were very likely, for large numbers of the male
population on the island were armed. This could be even more
hazardous for the UN troops, who might both incur accidental
injuries and be used as targets by those who were frustrated by
the UN's interpository role. There was also the consideration that
the UN's difficult and unpleasant task, although it was only
scheduled for three months, might well last a good deal longer, in
which case there would be some pressure on contributory states not
to withdraw their troops. Additionally, some states had worries
which related to their own situation. Sweden was anxious not to be
the only neutral participant in the force, and Ireland wanted to be
sure that she would not be involved in an attempt to impose partition.
Nor did all the problems arise with the potential contributors. For
Cyprus, in order to obtain something of a balance between NATO
and non-NATO participation, prevented the inclusion of Dutch
and Norwegian contingents. And at the same time she made the
achievement of such a balance more difficult by refusing to have
coloured troops in the force—although she did not object to it being
commanded by an Indian.

On 13 March the Security Council urged the speedy implementation of its resolution of 4 March. It had met in response to a Turkish
ultimatum which, accusing the Greek Cypriots of attempting to
exterminate the Turks, threatened military intervention unless such
malpractices were brought to an immediate halt. U Thant assured
the Council that the UN Force was about to be established, and the
arrival of a Canadian advance party four days later enabled him to
declare it 'in being'.[27] But it was not until advance parties were due
to arrive from Finland on 26 March, and Sweden and Ireland on the
27th, that the Secretary-General was able to declare that, as from
the latter date, the UN Force in Cyprus (UNFICYP) would be
operational. By the end of April the main contingents from each
of these four countries had arrived, and were joined by a Danish
contingent in May. As troops from other countries arrived the
British element was reduced, making up a total force of something
in excess of 6,000 men. Austria contributed a medical unit, and the
Force included a small air component.

[27] UN Document S/5593, Add. 2.

The Force had no direct responsibility for the settlement of the problem which had led to its establishment. That lay with a UN mediator, provision for whom had also been made in the Council's resolution of 4 March. As had not been unexpected, he found that three months was not long enough to repair the situation that had led to the breakdown of the Cyprus Constitution and the violence of the previous December. This did not affect his own position, for his appointment was without a time limit. But the Force, which was designed to provide the required conditions for his work, had been set up for only three months. In June 1964, therefore, UNFICYP's life was extended for a further three months, and again in September, and in December. The process was repeated in March 1965, and in June the Security Council decided on a six-months extension. The Secretary-General thought this was a good idea, and at the end of the year recommended a further six months, but the Council thought otherwise and reverted to a three-monthly period. It did likewise in March 1966 and took the opportunity to state that it acted 'in the firm hope that by the end of this period substantial progress towards a solution will have been achieved'.[28] In June it granted UNFICYP a further six months of life, repeated its hope about a solution, and added the words, 'so as to render possible a withdrawal or substantial reduction of the Force'.[29] But neither this, nor the repetition of the formula in December 1966 and June 1967 was to any avail. Indeed, the serious incidents of November 1967 showed that the Cyprus problem was still as inflammable then as four years earlier. However, so as not to give the impression that it accepted this situation passively, the Council, in December 1967, renewed UNFICYP's mandate for three months only, and urged a 'new determined effort' towards a settlement.[30] It was renewed for a further three months in March 1968, 'in the expectation' that at the end of this period 'sufficient progress towards a final solution will make possible a withdrawal or substantial reduction of the Force'.[31] The same formula was used in June, but the fact that the life of the Force was then extended until December suggested that the Security Council was not too optimistic about the fulfilment of its formal expression of hope.

By this time UNFICYP had been reduced from its initial size of 6,000 men to 4,500. In July 1965 it had suffered the loss of an Irish infantry group (which cut the Irish contingent from 1,000 to 600), a move that reflected Ireland's concern over the financial arrangements for the Force and her firm opposition to their being on a

28 Security Council resolution 220 (1966).
29 *Ibid.*, 222 (1966).
30 *Ibid.*, 244 (1967).
31 *Ibid.*, 247 (1968).

voluntary basis.[32] The Secretariat was no happier about the system, for it was a constant problem, but there was nothing which could be done about it, except to economize. This need, together with Ireland's action, led to the reduction of UNFICYP by the end of 1965 to rather less than 5,500 men and to 4,500 by December 1966, at which figure it remained for the next eighteen months. By contrast, the group of civilian police which has formed a part of UNFICYP from the outset has remained at almost exactly the same level throughout. Drawn from Austria, Australia, Denmark, New Zealand, and Sweden, they numbered 173 in June 1964, and 175 in June 1968. Their task has been to maintain liaison with the local police authorities, accompany some Cypriot police patrols, man UN police posts in sensitive areas, observe searches by the local police, and investigate crimes which crossed communal boundaries. They are widely held to have been of considerable value, especially in the prevention of excessive and humiliating searches of Turkish Cypriots at Greek Cypriot roadblocks.[33]

The main work of the Force has varied very little throughout its stay in Cyprus. Following the disorders of December 1963 thousands of Turks uprooted themselves from mixed villages and the smaller Turkish hamlets to concentrate in larger groups. This led, in some parts of the island, to the establishment of what were in the nature of opposing frontlines. In such areas UNFICYP endeavoured to place itself between the Greek and Turkish military positions, and, where that was not possible, set up its own posts nearby. It has engaged in negotiations for its own occupation of disputed posts, and for the dismantling of fortifications and the demilitarization of some forward positions. It patrols main roads and also towns and villages in sensitive areas, and investigates incidents. In the event of shooting, UNFICYP tries to bring it to an end by negotiation and persuasion at the appropriate level, and where cease-fire lines have been agreed, it has demarcated them. In co-operation with the Red Cross, UNFICYP has sought the repatriation of prisoners.

These tasks have had to be attempted without recourse to force. UNFICYP personnel can use their arms to the minimum extent necessary in their own defence and that of their fellows, and also against an armed attack on UNFICYP's premises, posts, and vehicles. This general right has been interpreted to mean that they

---

[32] The withdrawal of the infantry group brought the Irish contingent down to its original size, an additional number of men having been supplied in August 1964.

[33] This was not the first occasion on which civilian police formed part of a UN operation. Nigeria contributed a police unit to the Congo Force, and their expertise in riot control proved very valuable. And the UN Temporary Executive Authority in West New Guinea had had the local Papuan police at its disposal.

are entitled to resist any attempt to make them withdraw from positions occupied under orders, or to prevent them from carrying out their responsibilities as ordered by their commanders. Attempts to disarm UNFICYP personnel by force may be met in a like manner.[34] However, this situation soon came to be regarded by the Secretary-General as insufficient in both precision and extent. He also had cause to complain regarding that part of the agreement between Cyprus and the UN regarding UNFICYP's status which guaranteed freedom of movement to the Force.[35]

In his report to the Security Council of 10 September 1964, therefore, he said that on the basis of 'certain assumptions'[36] he proposed to instruct UNFICYP's Commander that the Force must have complete freedom of movement and the right, in certain ominous circumstances, to remove positions and fortifications and to demand that opposing armed forces be separated by reasonable distances. This led to an attempt by the non-permanent members of the Council to obtain the agreement of the parties to a broadening of UNFICYP's mandate, but it was without success. Turkey would not agree to the UN Force having the right to remove fortifications, and Cyprus would only accept it if UNFICYP acted in agreement with the Government. Cyprus was also unwilling to give UNFICYP the right to demand the establishment of buffer zones. It may also be assumed that the Soviet Union and France would have had reservations on these matters. Hence, while the Security Council did not tell the Secretary-General that he must not act in the manner he had indicated, neither did it endorse his proposals. In fact, nothing further was heard of them in public, and it may be assumed that the Secretary-General concluded that the assumptions of which he had spoken were lacking. He may have instructed UNFICYP to act up to the limit of its moral authority and not to stop short of using bluff. But it would have been asking for trouble, both in the field and at UN headquarters, to have gone ahead on the basis of his report, and nothing has since happened in Cyprus to suggest that he did.

Thus UNFICYP operates under considerable handicaps, and as a result it has made little progress towards eliminating areas of armed confrontation and has failed to halt the extension, by both Greeks and Turks, of their military fortifications. It has no authority over either side and so, to stop fighting, has to rely on its persuasive powers and the general reluctance of the combatants to shoot at UN troops. The difficulties to which this situation gives rise were well illustrated by an incident which took place at the village of Arsos in

[34] See UN Document S/5653, paras 16–19.
[35] The agreement was signed on 31 March 1964.
[36] UN Document S/5950, para. 232.

September 1966. Here Greeks and Turks lived in almost equal numbers, and up till this time had done so in outward amity. However, without apparent reason, a Turk while cycling home was shot dead. Tension immediately rose and a small UNFICYP force moved in, getting there before the Greek National Guard. Two days later there was shooting, and a Greek was killed. It continued sporadically and both UNFICYP and innocent villagers were in danger. Therefore, under orders from the UN commander in the village, UNFICYP troops entered the houses from which the firing was coming and ordered the snipers to lay down their arms. They did so—but had they refused, the UN troops would have been unable to do anything about it. However, in the circumstances UNFICYP was able to ensure that in each house all the arms were placed in one central room and watched over by a UN sentry. UNFICYP was not allowed to confiscate them or withhold them from their owners, and thus its hope could only be that in time passions in the village would cool sufficiently to make the location of the arms a relatively unimportant matter. But, as it happened, less than a month elapsed before some Turks entered the rooms containing the arms and removed them, despite the verbal efforts of the UN soldiers to prevent this.

However, while displaying UNFICYP's limitations, the affair at Arsos also demonstrated the value of its presence. Had it not been on the island, or even had it got to the village after the Greek National Guard, the initial incident might well have flared up into something much bigger, and could even have spread beyond the confines of the immediate locality. In numerous situations of a similar character, UNFICYP has been able to lower tension, and prevent fighting from getting out of hand. It has also, in certain circumstances, been able to negotiate arrangements which decrease the likelihood of incidents. Two major examples of this are the reopening, under exclusive UNFICYP control, of the Nicosia–Kyrenia road, which took place in October 1964, and the de-fortification of the areas of direct confrontation in Famagusta, which was completed in January 1966. And in many smaller ways UNFICYP, providing the only machinery for cross-communal activity, has been able to mitigate the difficulties arising from the *de facto* division of the island. It has been called upon to deal with questions of food supply, relief and refugees, and inter-communal travel, and has encouraged the restoration, so far as possible, of normal conditions.

A major difficulty in Cyprus, however, has been the lack of agreement as to the norm in the light of which conditions should be regulated. In the economic sphere, it is not difficult to define, but this is not so in the political field. The Government of Cyprus thinks, firstly, in terms of the restoration of its authority over the whole of the island. In its eyes the Turks are rebels, and UNFI-CYP's refusal to act as the Government's handmaid and disarm them led to an early cooling of relationships between the formal host and the UN Force. And, secondly, it believes that the 1960 Constitution must be amended in favour of the centre. The Turks on the other hand, think that the first step must be to get back to the arrangements which were made for Cyprus's independence, and that there must be a move from that point towards a much more clear cut division between the two communities than that which was set out in the 1960 Constitution, and which, in their judgment, had by 1963 been shown to be insufficient. Until they can reach an agreement it is UNFICYP's task to keep the peace, and after four years in the field, it has an excellent record.

There seems virtually no doubt that, had it not been for UNFI-CYP's presence, the two Cypriot communities would have been at each other's throats. Even had their leaders wished it otherwise, conditions in Cyprus were such that, without the interposition of a third party, violence was just about unavoidable. The Greeks and Turks had become deeply suspicious of each other; the division between them was imperfect; and arms and ammunition were widely distributed. In these circumstances incidents were well-nigh inevitable, and their escalation hardly less so. Thus, the situation was tailor-made for, at the least, widespread disorder and very possibly civil war. Even the first outcome would probably have led to Turkey's intervention, and in the latter case it was little short of certain. Undoubtedly, there would have been urgent representations from her NATO allies advising against this course, but there is no reason to believe that this would have stopped her if she judged that the Cypriot minority was really in dire trouble. Moreover, if this was the position it was highly unlikely that the United States would have used her sea and air power to prevent Turkish intervention. In turn, this would almost surely have brought Greece into Cyprus, and a civil conflict would have quickly expanded into an international war. The condition for preventing this development was, and remains, the maintenance of relative quiet in Cyprus by an impartial third party. Despite its limitations, UNFICYP fulfils this role, and so makes a vital contribution to the maintenance of peace.

This is not to say that it is indispensable for the purpose. In its absence, or in the event of it being unable to control the situation, the job may be taken over by others, conceivably even without the consent of the Cyprus Government. The NATO Powers are the obvious, and only, candidates for this role, on account of their close interest in the prevention of a war between two of their fellows. They also have the resources which the task demands. But it would be a most unattractive course for them, particularly if it had to be done in the absence of the consent of the host state. Thus, from their point of view, and from that of all others who are interested in the maintenance of Middle Eastern stability, the UN is doing a very valuable job in Cyprus, and they are most anxious that it should be continued. By obstructing the outbreak or expansion of violence in Cyprus, UNFICYP stands in the way of a war which they would find most embarrassing.

UNFICYP's role is more crucial in Cyprus than was that of UNEF during its ten years on the Egyptian–Israeli border. For, while the absence of UNEF would undoubtedly have made the frontier more dangerous, it would probably have been within the power of the two states concerned to keep the dangers at a low level, had they made a determined effort to do so. However, in the case of Cyprus, the nature of the situation makes the prevention of incidents almost an impossibility, even if that is the wish of the community leaders on both sides, and encourages their expansion and imitation. Moreover, the internal character of the Cyprus conflict heightens the desire for revenge. It is one thing to be shot at across a recognized frontier by someone who represents the other state. That can be prevented as a normal hazard of life near a troubled frontier, and as an account which will one day receive an ample settlement. But to be shot at within the state, going about one's daily business, and by someone who is personally or vicariously vulnerable to similar treatment, is to invite the passionate planning of reprisals. Community leaders are powerless to prevent such action, and may find it necessary sometimes to espouse it if they are to maintain their positions. In Cyprus, therefore, there are far fewer control mechanisms than are available along a recognized frontier, which makes a body such as UNFICYP essential if tension is to be kept in check.

Nevertheless, its role, like UNEF's, is secondary, for the basic decisions regarding war and peace rest with the principal actors: the Cyprus Government and the Turkish community on the island, and Greece and Turkey beyond. If any of these four decided on a showdown, or on action so provocative as to precipitate one, UNFICYP would be unable to do anything about it. In practice, such a decision is unlikely to come from the Greek Government, on account of it being the weaker of the two outside protectors. Nor are the Turkish Cypriots likely to make serious trouble, for Turkey might arrive too late to help many of them. She would not be too late to take revenge on the Greek Cypriots, though, which encourages the Cyprus Government to stay its hand, despite being the stronger party on the island. And for as long as it makes no move against the Turkish Cypriots, Turkey herself has no desire to get involved in a costly and internationally unpopular invasion. Thus, all the parties have good reasons for avoiding a showdown, or provocative action so as to precipitate one, and for as long as they are of a cautious or conciliatory disposition UNFICYP can provide the parties with the help they need to maintain peace. But it is not a guarantee against inflammatory incidents, and there is always the possibility of one, or more, of the parties taking a deliberately belligerent line. In either event, UNFICYP alone would be unable to check the conflict which might well result. It can do a great deal to prevent an accidental war, and in a country so accident-prone as Cyprus such a role is essential if peace is to prevail. But in face of a calculated war the UN Force is powerless.

For as long as a settlement is beyond reach it is highly likely that the UN will strive to maintain its Force in Cyprus. And, although events can move with great rapidity and unexpectedness in politics, there is no immediate prospect of UNFICYP becoming superfluous. The crisis of November 1967[37], it is true, gave a new urgency to the search for a solution, and conditions on the island have since improved. But that is not to say that a settlement of the basic problem may soon be expected. What seems more probable is that Cyprus will remain in the uneasy condition which has been her lot since December 1963, with all parties wanting to avoid a major disturbance, and UNFICYP providing most valuable assistance towards that end.

IV

This, however, points to a criticism of UNFICYP which applies equally to UNEF and possibly also to much of the rest of the UN's prophylactic work. It appears in any of three closely associated forms. In the first place, complaints are sometimes made to the effect that bodies such as UNEF and UNFICYP do nothing to solve the problems which have given rise to their dispatch. This may be accepted as generally the case, but as a criticism it is out of order, for the reason that obstruction is not intended to have a direct bearing on problem-solving. It may be hoped that if it succeeds in preventing war, things will improve, but this is essentially a second-ary consideration—a subsidiary benefit. The main and immediate purpose of UNEF and UNFICYP was to prevent the situation from getting worse, which UNEF did for as long as it was permitted

[37] See above, pp. 264–268.

and which UNFICYP continues to do. They were not given any
responsibility for settling the underlying problems, and therefore
do not deserve criticism for their condition.

The UN itself has demonstrated this by charging others with the
improving task, the Palestine Conciliation Commission in the one
case, and the UN mediator in the other. This, however, points to
the second, and refined form of the criticism. It is that, by taking the
heat out of the situation, interpository presences also remove the
sense of urgency from the attempt at mediation. U Thant, for
example, has on several occasions warned that the success of
UNFICYP in maintaining quiet in Cyprus must not lead to the
failure of the effort to obtain a political solution, and he has made
similar comments regarding UNEF. This could be a fair criticism,
for it is almost a law of politics, that the degree of attention a problem
receives is in direct proportion to the immediate amount of trouble
which it threatens. However, it does not follow that it is always a fair
criticism, especially as it is often a reflection of the fallacy that
success in settling disputes is a function of the amount of effort and
attention given to them. And in the two questions mentioned above,
it is almost certainly not the case that their solution has been
retarded by the success of the UN's prophylactic measures. It may
be that a livelier sense of crisis might have resulted in more time,
and ingenuity, being given to the basic issues. But they are so deep-
rooted and intractable, that it seems unlikely in the extreme that
this would materially have advanced their settlement.

The third and final form of the criticism might be called, without
any pejorative implications, the brutal version. It allows that disputes
such as those between the Arabs and the Jews, and between the
Greek and Turkish Cypriots, are not likely to be solved by negotiations, however great the effort which is put into them. But it does not
conclude that by keeping them quiet the UN is performing a useful
service. Instead it argues that the UN is obstructing the only viable
form of settlement, one produced by force of arms, and that the
sooner this comes the sooner the area in question will be stabilized.

This argument rests on several assumptions, which can by no
means be taken as given in any particular case. They are that a
war will produce a clear cut decision; that the result will be accepted
by the defeated side, which will proceed to make a quick adjustment
to reality; and that the outcome will not be threatened by an alteration in the local balance of power, whether on account of a change
in the relative military strength of the erstwhile disputants, or of
diplomatic developments. Even, however, if all these conditions are
thought to hold, it does not follow that an armed conflict is the only
route to a settlement. Time, as has been noted, does not always have

a healing effect, but it may do so. Combined with persistent diplomatic pressure in favour of moderation, its healing potential may be improved.

Clearly, there is no sure way of assessing what might have happened if something else had not. But a result can be achieved in more than one way. The June 1967 war, for example, may prove to have put Arab-Israeli relations on a much more stable basis than those existing since 1948, inasmuch as the surrounding Arab states, or most of them, may now bow to the inevitable, and move towards a formal recognition of Israel's existence and the development of contacts with her. But it may be that had the war not occurred, and the 10-year calm along the Israeli–Egyptian border had continued for another 10 years, the parties might have found themselves moving towards the same position. Likewise in the case of Cyprus, there may seem much to commend in the idea that the best thing which could happen here would be a short sharp war followed by the partition of the island on Turkey's terms. Greece and Turkey could then repair their damaged relationship, and the rump Cypriot state, if any, would know to behave itself. But again it is not inconceivable that, under pressure both from the people below, and the interested outsiders above, and facilitated by the maintenance of quiet over a fairly long period, the leaders of the Greek and Turkish Cypriot communities may come to accept that they must jointly work out a way of living together in amity, within the confines of a single state.

Even, however, if these peaceful possibilities are rejected as too fanciful or uncertain, it still does not follow that the UN deserves criticism for attempting to provide the conditions which they require. At this level the matter reduces itself to a question of values, of the importance attached to the achievement of stability as against the preservation of peace. There are those who believe that a brief and limited war is justifiable if it serves likely to stabilize a difficult situation. Others assert that the maintenance of peace, even a tense and uneasy peace, is preferable to war, their claim sometimes resting on an absolute moral position but more commonly on the uncertainty which, in some measure, attaches to the course and consequences of any resort to arms. This is a dialogue which cannot be resolved, each participant having to come to his own conclusion on the basis of his personal prejudices and beliefs.

At the international level, however, the issue has to a large extent been prejudged, at least in theory. For the members of the UN have all renounced the threat or use of force against the territorial integrity or political independence of any state, except in individual or collective self-defence. Accordingly, a war for stability, even if it is only a little one, would seem to be impermissible, and contrariwise, the UN would appear to have a moral obligation to do what it can to stand in the way of such wars. Of course states, like individuals, do not always live up to their formal protestations, and are adept at stretching the letter of the law to cover desired action. But it is the case that the hostility of the Charter towards war, its elevation of peace over other desirable goals, does in many respects accord with the view which states generally take of the matter. It may therefore be expected that the UN will probably not reject opportunities to play a part in obstructing war on the ground that it would be better for events to take their 'natural' course. It is unlikely that such opportunities will be frequent. But when they do arise further UN forces may well take the field to assume a subordinate but valuable and perhaps vital role in the preservation of peace.

Chapter 9

Refrigeration

THE most far-reaching form of prophylaxis which is open to the UN consists of the exercise of governmental functions in an area which, on account of its ownership, use, or administration, has become a source of tension. A difficult territorial dispute, for example, may be held in check, and possibly eased, by the area in question being administered by the UN until a settlement can be reached. Or the Organization may take over some essential responsibilities from a state whose internal behaviour or incompetence bids fair to precipitate foreign intervention. In both cases the object is to stop the situation getting worse by introducing a neutral agent into a sensitive area, to prevent the generation of further heat by putting the relationship, as it were, on ice. No doubt it will be hoped that this process will also facilitate a settlement, or the adoption of less provocative policies, but the immediate aim is to bundle the issue into cold storage, and so avert an explosion. The actual refrigerative role is unlikely to be easy or straightforward, but if conditions are suitable, it can be a most effective way of keeping a problem under control.

Sometimes it may be possible for the UN to act in this way before a dispute has got to the festering stage, before, indeed, a dispute may be said to exist at all. There may merely be a question as to the best disposition of territory, or it may be apprehended that in the wrong hands a particular region could give rise to trouble. In respect of situations of this kind there is no reason, in principle, why immediate refrigerative measures should not be taken, perhaps on a permanent basis, in order to prevent subsequent contention. In practice even the discussion of such action is unlikely to be common, for states are even less minded than individuals to go out of their way to guard against theoretical difficulties. 'Sufficient unto the day is the evil thereof' is a popular maxim in both spheres. But events do occasionally take a turn which encourages states to consider the feasibility of an early prophylactic move.

I

An opportunity of this nature may arise at the end of a great war. In 1919 it had been accepted that defeat is a sign of a country's unfitness to rule dependent peoples, and victory no ground for their annexation. Accordingly, the mandates system was devised, under which the extra-metropolitan territories of the losers were divided up among the more prominent of the victors, who were to administer them as 'a sacred trust of civilisation'.[1] In some quarters, however, there was doubt as to whether this arrangement was much more than a façade: 'the old hag of colonization puts on a fig leaf and calls itself mandate' was how one observer put it.[2] Probably for this reason, the UN Charter provided that, as well as one or more states, the Organization itself could administer any of the territories which were placed under trusteeship—the name given to the revised mandates system.

There was no rush to take advantage of this possibility in the immediate post-World War II years. Some mandated territories had become or were in the process of becoming independent states. Of the others, all but one—South West Africa—were designated as trust territories, but with the exception of those which had been controlled by Japan, each of them stayed under the sole control of the old mandatory Power. Having been less successful in World War II than in World War I, Japan was to be deprived of her mandatory responsibilities in respect of the Marshall and Caroline Islands, but there was no question of handing them over to the UN. Instead they came under the authority of the United States who, although allowing them to be included in the trusteeship system, had them designated as a strategic area,[3] and so, in effect, completely removed them from the UN's supervision.

The United States had also made some other *de facto* acquisitions at Japan's expense: the Ryukyu and Bonin Islands. Strategic considerations led her to retain these areas, and she was no more willing to give the UN any responsibility for them, even of a minimal kind, than was the Soviet Union with regard to her territorial gains at Japan's expense, principally South Sakhalin and the Kurile Islands. But the United States did make a double gesture towards contemporary ideas about propriety in international relations. For, firstly, she recognized Japan's residual sovereignty. And, secondly, provision was made in the 1951 Peace Treaty between Japan and the Western Powers for the United States, if and when she wished, to place the Islands under the trusteeship system, with herself as the sole administering Power. Moreover, the lack of formal annexation did prove to be significant, for it helped to keep life in the question of

[1] League of Nations Covenant, Article 22.
[2] Salvador de Madariaga, quoted in Inis L. Claude Jr., *Swords into Plowshares* (New York: Random House, 2nd ed., 1959), p. 345.
[3] Taking advantage of Article 82 of the Charter, which had been included solely to cover American ambitions in respect of the Marshall and Caroline Islands.

the islands' eventual return to Japan. And in November 1967 it was announced that the Bonin Islands would soon be handed back, possibly within six months,[4] and that the United States and Japan would try to agree on the return of the Ryukyus within a few years. Subsequent events suggested that the price would be high, involving a bigger Japanese defence effort and the retention by the United States of her base on Okinawa, including its nuclear facilities. In the late 1940s, however, it appeared as if, for all practical purposes, the United States had annexed these two territories.

The post-war disposition of Italy's colonies—Eritrea, Libya and Somaliland—presented different problems. The United States did not have a compelling strategic or diplomatic interest in their annexation, and at the London Conference of Foreign Ministers held in September 1945 she urged an 'international' solution: that all three colonies should be placed under the UN's trusteeship system, with the Organization itself acting as the administering authority. This proposal had the merit that it held out the possibility of averting any argument as to the colonies' future and of helping the new institution to build up its strength. Accordingly, it could be presented as demanding the support of all well-intentioned states. Britain placed herself, more or less, into this category, for, apart from reservations regarding Eritrea, she supported the American plan. The Soviet Union, however, entered an immediate note of dissent.

What she favoured was individual trusteeship for each of the colonies, and she was clearly hoping to secure one of them for herself. Most of all she would have liked to act as trustee for Libya, for this would have given her a position on the Mediterranean, and in order to satisfy this aim she would have been prepared to rest content with one of Libya's three constituent parts. This, however, was not at all to the liking of Britain and France. It was, said Britain's Foreign Minister, Ernest Bevin, 'an effort to cut across the throat of the British Empire'.[5] Britain also became disenchanted with the idea of collective trusteeship. It was almost bound to involve all the permanent members of the Security Council in a position of some influence in the territories concerned, and therefore conflicted with her increasing anxiety to keep the Soviet Union out of any participation in African affairs, whether in the North or the East. For her part too, the Soviet Union was changing her position, for, encouraged by the showing of the Italian Communist Party, she began to take an interest in the idea that Italy should have her colonies back in the form of trusteeships. This also appealed to the

[4] They were returned to Japan on 26 June 1968.
[5] James N. Murray, Jr., *The United Nations Trusteeship System* (Urbana: University of Illinois, 1957), p. 81, n. 8.

United States, but was firmly opposed by Britain. However, the Italian elections of April 1948, in which the Christian Democrats did well and the Communists badly, induced further changes in the attitudes of the Powers, confirming the United States in the view that Italy could now be trusted with colonial responsibilities, converting Britain to it (except in relation to areas on which she had her strategic eye), and bringing the Soviet Union around to the original American idea of collective trusteeships for all the colonies.

As the Great Powers were unable to agree, the matter was transferred to the UN General Assembly in September 1948 for final decision, in accordance with the terms of the Italian Peace Treaty. The Western Powers had now lost interest in the idea of temporary international rule, but it might have been expected to have some appeal among other UN members. For, quite apart from the argument that it would benefit the UN, it offered everyone something of a finger in the pie. But advantage was not taken of this early opportunity to set the UN up as a governing body. In common with other such proposals, it would have caused less offence than some alternative schemes, but on the other hand it would have produced a generally low level of satisfaction. The only party who would have been reasonably content with the arrangement was the Soviet Union, which was enough to turn some against it. She could count on the support of her Communist allies, but apart from them was alone. The idea was espoused by some Asian states, but this was no help to the Soviet Union as they also proposed that the Great Powers should be excluded from an administrative role. Other members, more closely interested in the fate of the colonies, worked for a settlement which would meet their several concerns. Chiefly, these were the desire of the Arabs to revive an independent Libya, and the anxiety of the Latin Americans, a very powerful voting bloc, to ensure that Italy participated in at least one of the arrangements. As there were three colonies to dispose of, two of which could, if necessary, be subdivided, the broad lines of an acceptable compromise were not hard to discern, although the process by which it emerged was long and involved. Eventually it was decided that Libya should become independent not later than 1 January 1952, and that Somaliland, which, it was accepted on all sides, was not ready for independence, should become a trust territory for ten years with Italy as the administering Power. She was to be assisted by an advisory council of three small states, and at the end of the 10-year period Somaliland was to become independent. The decision on Eritrea was postponed.

Thus the United States' prophylactic proposal came to nought. As often happens, one party's long view ran counter to more

immediate and specific interests elsewhere, and here the proposer
also discovered that his idea was not such a good one after all. It
was taken up by another as a second best solution, but to no avail.
A seemingly innocuous suggestion had uncovered a latent dispute,
which in turn removed the issue from the stage at which it would
have been susceptible to precautionary measures, as well as making
such measures impossible to mount. As a result Italy, benefiting
from her ambiguous wartime record, the cold war, her cultural ties
with Latin America, and the absence of any other acceptable
candidate, found herself restored to one of her East African colonies,
albeit in a restricted context and for a limited time. And the Arabs,
taking advantage of the determination of East and West to keep each
other out of Libya and of the bargaining opportunities afforded by
the General Assembly, were able to secure independence for a
country which was desperately poor, had an illiteracy rate of 90
per cent, and could boast no more than 20 university graduates.[6]

Where there is no necessity to change a territory's status, thoughts
about the prophylactic value of doing so are unlikely to have any
practical results. For sitting tenants are almost invariably averse to
suggestions that they should vacate even the smallest or least
desirable part of their property, however probable it is that it will
subsequently be claimed by a Power who will be negotiating from
strength. It is, therefore, not to be expected that there will often be
withdrawals in favour of the UN while the going is good. But if an
incumbent is in any event planning to depart from territory to which
there is more than one claimant, or which otherwise might give rise
to trouble, he might well be sympathetic to the suggestion that it
should be placed in the UN's permanent keeping.

However, this circumstance does not leave the path to internationalization free of obstacles. The people whom it is proposed
to place under the UN's rule might well take a poor view of such an
eventuality. Should this not be an obstructive factor, the attitude
of the interested parties, in particular of the heir presumptive or
those who have constituted themselves as such, cannot be counted
upon to be positive. This would have the effect of producing an
immediate dispute without necessarily avoiding the one which is
thought to lie in the future. Which draws attention to the point
that even if the owner goes ahead with the idea, and offers the
territory to the UN, it is not certain that it would be gratefully
received, or received at all. It is one thing to act as a debating

[6] A UN Commissioner and a ten man council were appointed to assist in the
establishment of independence, which was proclaimed on 24 December 1951. Their
work is regarded by some as one of the UN's unsung success stories in the non-poli-
tical field.

depository for awkward issues. But to take over, for an indefinite period, an area which is only offered on account of the difficulties which are expected to arise regarding it, and the transfer of which to the UN might precipitate an immediate quarrel, is a different matter altogether. It invites problems of a vastly different scale, and in consequence some UN members, and also some members of the Secretariat, might well wish to look such a gift horse very closely in the mouth.

A case in point concerns the small island of Perim at the mouth of the Red Sea, the population of which has variously been given as in the region of 300 or 400. Until November 1967 it was a British possession, the Governor of Aden exercising legislative power over the island, and its future lay most obviously with the Federation of South Arabia, which was then due to achieve independence early in 1968. But Perim is strategically significant, at least in theory, for the island could control traffic passing between the Indian Ocean and the Gulfs of Aqaba and Suez. This consideration, together with the UAR's May 1967 attempt to blockade the Gulf of Aqaba, gave rise to the suggestion that Perim, instead of being handed over to the Federation, should be leased to the UN, provided that the consent of the inhabitants was forthcoming.

Part of the intention behind this proposal, made in June 1967, was to keep the island out of the hands of a state whose Government, at some future date, might wish to restrict freedom of passage through the Red Sea, possibly as part of a concerted endeavour to treat the Sea as a private Arab waterway. There did not seem to be much danger of this being the first move of an independent South Arabia, for it looked as if the new state was going to be heavily reliant for its security on Britain's support. But clearly the thought was that it might not be long before the South Arabian regime was replaced by one more in sympathy with the militant and 'progressive' forces of Arab nationalism, and, in particular, one responsive to the voice of Cairo. With large numbers of UAR troops already in the neighbouring Yemen, it was not difficult to imagine President Nasser's long arm stretching right down to the Indian Ocean.

In all probability this was the chief consideration which encouraged the British Government to endorse the proposal, and promise to do all things possible to ensure that Perim was transferred to the UN, although it would be surprising if domestic politics did not also play a part in this respect. For the prime movers behind the idea were a group of Conservatives, and the Labour Government could not afford to seem less zealous than the Opposition in a cause which, according to the folk-lore of British politics, is viewed much more sympathetically on the left than the right. One wonders,

however, how highly the Government rated its chances of implementation. It was supposed by its advocates that the Federation of
South Arabia would not object to their scheme, but in this they were
exceedingly optimistic. For, although the South Arabian Government viewed President Nasser with suspicion and distrust, this could
not be counted upon to secure its support for a plan which, while
reflecting the same feelings, also involved the loss of what it regarded
as part of its birthright. And, quite apart from straightforward
possessive grounds, South Arabia could hardly be expected to do
other than oppose an idea which clearly implied that she either
could not be trusted with Perim or would not long be in a position
to enjoy it. In the event it was only two days after Britain had
indicated her support for Perim's internationalization that word
came from Aden that the island was 'an inseparable part'[7] of South
Arabia, and, proof positive, had been so recognized by United
Nations resolutions. As well as the South Arabian Government, the
Yemen also objected to the scheme, no doubt in her capacity as
rightful ruler of 'occupied South Yemen'.

Not being a sovereign state, South Arabia was not, at that time,
in a strong position to pursue her objections. But, for this purpose,
and probably for this alone, she was not without friends at court.
For the other Arab states, while most of them would have welcomed
the overthrow of the South Arabian Government, quickly united
behind the principle of the integrity of Arab soil. This would have
been their reaction in any case, but the possibility of a change in the
South Arabian regime, and of the fact that Israel had something of
an interest in the success of the British proposal, made their opposition particularly keen. The Soviet Union and her friends, too, could
hardly be enthusiastic about a scheme which, essentially, reflected
a Western concern. Many of the Afro-Asian states were reluctant to
establish what could be, for some of them, a disturbing precedent.
And there must have been an awareness, especially in those states
who might be closely involved, of the cost and difficulty of trying
to hold the island in face of diplomatic and possibly physical harassment: Perim is, for example, only two miles or so from the Yemen
shore. Britain, for her part, made it quite clear that once South
Arabia was independent she had no intention of retaining responsibility for Perim. In the light of this it was not surprising that others,
who, in principle, were sympathetic to the idea of handing Perim
over to the UN, showed some reluctance even to share the necessary
burden.

For some members, an additional ground for encouraging the
Organization to take a negative attitude towards the scheme was

7 *The Times*, 1 July 1967.

to be found in the fact that it was linked with the suggestion that the island could, and should, provide a base for a permanent UN peace-keeping force, which, besides ensuring freedom of passage through the mouth of the Red Sea, would also enable the UN to act speedily and efficiently whenever a crisis arose. This was described as its chief aim, although whether it was the most immediate is perhaps questionable. Probably it was included, in part, in an effort to obtain wider support for the proposal, by making it look more than just an attempt, on the one hand, to safeguard the interests of the maritime nations, and, on the other, to check President Nasser's ambitions. But the use of Perim in this way would by no means be to everyone's liking, and the suggestion must have gone some way towards ensuring the opposition, among the Great Powers, of France as well as the Soviet Union. Nor is it likely that they would have been mollified by a preparedness on the part of the UN to disclaim, in advance, any intention of using the area under its government as a base for a standing force. For, once in possession, it would always be possible for the Organization to go back on its word, justifying itself with the popular assertion that the end justifies the means.

Thus it is not surprising that Britain's suggestion that Perim should be placed under UN administration was sharply rebuffed by the UN's Special Mission on Aden and found no support in the Assembly's Fourth Committee. Ten years earlier, with Britain still firmly in control of Aden and its hinterland, and less inclined to pay heed to the Assembly, which was also smaller and less extreme, the result might just possibly have been different. But in 1967 the proposal had come too late. In face of the opposition which it had aroused, Britain dropped the idea and, after consulting Perim's inhabitants, decided that it should form a part of the new People's Republic of Southern Yemen, which became independent on 30 November 1967.

The factors which resulted in the UN's failure to take advance prophylactic action in respect of Perim and the Italian colonies were not peculiar to those situations. The raising of a question as to the future of a piece of territory is calculated to produce a number of claimants, irrespective of whether they would otherwise have advanced their credentials, and also much general opposition to the idea that someone's territorial sovereignty should be curtailed. In consequence, while it will remain possible for the UN to snuff out trouble at its source by refrigerative action, it is highly unlikely that suggestions of this nature will often have positive results. If the Great Powers were united in a determination to use the UN for this purpose, the outcome would be very different, as, indeed, would the whole peace-keeping scene. But even a further blossoming of the growing *rapprochement* among the permanent members of the Security Council cannot be relied upon to have that result while, for reasons of propriety or prudence, they continue to defer, in non-vital matters of this kind, to the UN's numerical majority.

II

At the other extreme from situations which at the most call for precautionary measures are those where no settlement is in sight and where the only prospect is of continuing or increasing tension. Here, in theory, is a fruitful field for refrigerative activity on the part of the UN, and a large part of it consists of territorial issues. The question of whether the UN should intervene in such disputes may not be confined to the quarrels of established sovereign states, but may also arise in respect of internal conflicts which have acquired an international aspect. In the latter case the appropriate form of refrigeration would probably be for the UN to take over the maintenance of internal security in the disputed region. Where the conflict relates to an area which makes up only a part of one or both contestants, or is physically unconnected with either, the more obvious course would be for the UN to assume full governmental authority.

The circumstances in which the UN might be urged to play a refrigerative role with regard to territorial questions are twofold. In the first place, where fighting seems imminent or has actually begun, it might well be suggested that, as a means of checking the conflict, the UN should be allowed to take over essential governmental functions in the disputed area. Secondly, the same procedure might be advocated in respect of a situation which, although unlikely to precipitate an immediate war, has an ugly look. Where, for example, negotiations over a much-coveted piece of territory have collapsed, or where the attitude of the parties is such that there is no point in holding them, it may be that the dispute does not take an immediate turn for the worse. But although tempers may cool somewhat, this is by no means incompatible with a hardening of positions, which could result in an outwardly quiet but dangerously inflammable situation. In which case prophylactic action, such as the establishment of temporary international rule, might well be favoured by some.

While the immediate purpose of refrigerating territorial disputes is to stand in the way of an existing or threatening crisis, it is likely that the UN will agree to intervene only if it is given the right to remain until the parties have reached a settlement, for otherwise the whole issue would probably be reopened on its departure. And the UN would doubtless hope that its presence would assist the production of an agreement. The prospect of the UN being able to exert a positive influence, however, would not be good in respect of a territory which had been subject to internal disruption. The restoration of peaceful conditions might just possibly help rival factions to decide that they could live together safely within a single state. But in the absence of such a development the outlook would be bleak, for it is most unlikely that the stronger party, particularly if it was, in form, the government of the whole, would be prepared to make far-reaching concessions. The position would be rather more promising where the parties had retired from the disputed territory. For time might weaken the intensity of the absentee's claims, or at least the degree of their intransigence. And as a settlement would not now involve either disputant in a physical withdrawal, it would, perhaps, be easier to reach, especially if the splitting up of the territory held by the UN was not a political impossibility.

First of all, however, the UN has to take over the disputed territory, which implies not only a willingness to make way for the Organization but also a willingness on its part to play a refrigerative role. Even if both parties were agreed on the desirability of it doing so, the UN might be hesitant, thinking of the difficulty in which it would find itself if negotiations for an agreement broke down and the disputants prepared to settle the issue by force of arms. It would probably be even more reluctant if it was invited to take over some of a weaker state's territory in face of the opposition of the stronger. And, quite apart from other considerations, the UN might refuse to co-operate if an unpopular state might thereby be helped or a popular claim obstructed. But it is far from likely that the matter would get to the stage of the UN having to respond to an invitation. For it is only in very exceptional circumstances that a government faced by secessionist subjects would agree to the UN assuming responsibility for security throughout its domain, as that would be a tremendous blow to its prestige, both internally and internationally. And even in the case of a straightforward territorial dispute between countries the chances of the UN taking over the area in question are very slim.

Basically, this stems from the exceptional sensitivity of territorial issues, which makes states hostile to the suggestion that any part of their territory should be ruled, even on a temporary basis, by the UN. At the lowest level, there is the danger that some of the temporary administrators' policies may diverge from those which were previously followed: his hand, for example, might be thought to be insufficiently firm, or his attitude towards the expression of criticism too liberal. This could produce difficulties if and when the territory was returned. More serious would be the effect which the UN's role might have on the political allegiance of the inhabitants. For once a question has been raised as to an area's legitimate government, handing it over to an international body would seem to endorse the doubt, and would be a positive invitation to opportunist spirits to start a precautionary band-wagon in favour of the possible successor. Alternatively, it might encourage separatist tendencies. In consequence, the sovereign might have a hard job in reasserting his authority should the dispute end in his favour. And, to take the most obnoxious but very real possibility, allowing the UN to refrigerate one's territory pending an agreement regarding its future would carry the risk that it might not be returned at all. No government would normally be willing to do so much as contemplate such an eventuality, and any hint that it was doing so would bring it serious domestic trouble. If the plan was executed it could also lead to international difficulties, on account of others interpreting it as a sign of weakness and amending their policies accordingly.

In a very critical situation these considerations might be pushed on one side, where, for example, the loss of the disputed territory was virtually a foregone conclusion. But in that case the stronger party would only be likely to agree to the procedure if it was clearly understood that the UN's role was simply to pass the territory to him. If his terms were accepted, the dispute would have got beyond the stage of requiring prophylactic action, for it would to all intents and purposes have been patched-up, with the UN helping to save the face of the loser. Another set of circumstances in which a state might look favourably on the idea of temporary UN rule would be where it had already lost possession of some of its territory, with little chance of its immediate return. To have it placed in the UN's hands pending a final agreement would perhaps give the greatest hope of its recovery. This would be a genuine example of refrigeration, but it is most improbable that the victor would agree to it. For even if he was not averse to the idea of ultimate withdrawal, he would want to retain the territory in his own hands meanwhile in order not to lose an important negotiating asset. Nor is the UN likely to be allowed to play a refrigerative role at the point at which such action might be thought to be most necessary: where disputed ground is about to be or is being fought over. If the parties have reached this stage, it is improbable that this kind of UN intervention would appeal to them, certainly not to the contestant who is confident of success, of whom there may be more than one.

Left to themselves, therefore, the parties to a territorial dispute are unlikely to agree that the UN should play a refrigerative role in respect of the object of their contention. If, however, they are not of the very first rank, and if the UN is in a position to insist that their dispute be kept quiet, the position might be very different. For it to be so it is probably necessary that there be no deep divisions between the major Powers, no very close links between any of them and either party, and a keen interest on the part of all the Powers in the maintenance of stability in the area in question. Such conditions obtained at the end of the nineteenth century in respect of the Ottoman Empire, and permitted the dispatch of international forces to two of its crumbling parts. In 1897 the Powers prevented Greece from taking over Crete, an international military force being maintained on the island for the next 12 years as a sign of their determination to prevent the dispute giving rise to war. Macedonia too, at the same period, was occupied by a five-Power force in order to prevent Greece and Bulgaria from fighting over the succession. In neither case did the Powers formally assume governmental authority, although the status of Crete at this time was particularly obscure. But by checking internal dissidents and external claimants the Powers succeeded in freezing these two issues for the time being.

Since World War II, however, the relations of the Great Powers have not permitted a united front in favour of the refrigeration of territorial disputes, which helps to explain why the device has not been used. It has, however, occasionally been mooted. The first time was in 1948 in respect of Palestine, when the United States, realizing that the UN's partition plan[8] was not going to be peacefully implemented, proposed that upon Britain's withdrawal the country should be placed under UN trusteeship until its future had been agreed upon by the Arab and Jewish communities. If their representatives were unable to settle on a plan within three years, it was to be open to the Assembly to propose one and seek the approval of a majority of both groups. Authority was to be in the hands of a Governor-General, appointed by and responsible to the Trusteeship Council, and law and order was to be maintained by means of a volunteer force, supplemented, if necessary, by assistance from certain unspecified governments.

This refrigerative suggestion had first been raised in March. Its details were filled in a month later, on 20 April, and the United States now seemed to be taking it seriously. But it won no real support. The Arabs were only prepared to consider it if it was clearly associated with the subsequent establishment of a single Palestinian state, which was out of the question, and the Jews rejected it as an

[8] See above, pp. 170–171.

unwarranted retrogression from the Assembly's earlier espousal of partition. Thus if a UN trusteeship was to be established armed force would clearly be required. The United States professed herself willing to play her part in this activity, but her lead was not followed. She was hoping that Britain would halt the withdrawal of her armed forces so that they might help to fulfil this role, but although Britain did not reject the idea outright, it was exceedingly unlikely that she would agree to remain in Palestine, even on a joint basis. The embarrassing possibility that the Soviet Union might offer to help maintain law and order on the UN's behalf was removed when she condemned the American proposal. No doubt she realized that it was most unlikely that she would be allowed to play such a part, and therefore saw more profit in a reiteration of her earlier support for partition, which was a convenient vehicle for her desire to remove British influence from the Middle East and prevent its replacement by that of the United States.

The reactions of the other UN members did nothing to compensate for the lack of Great Power enthusiasm or unity. Those who wished to see the immediate emergence of a Jewish state were anxious only to defeat the American scheme, whether directly or by means of a filibuster.[9] Others, unhappy at the prospect of large-scale violence in Palestine, were even more unhappy at the thought of trying to impose peace on the disputants. And the United States was certainly not willing to attempt this on her own, even with the UN's moral support. Thus the debate meandered on, and eventually the trusteeship idea was quietly dropped. Instead the Assembly took thankful refuge in the infinitely less exacting proposal that a mediator should be appointed.[10] By the time this office was being established in New York the state of Israel had already been proclaimed in Tel Aviv,[11] and the United States made handsome amends for her trusteeship proposal by according the new state de facto recognition only 16 minutes after its proclamation.

The difficulty about this proposal for a temporary trusteeship was that the trustees would have had to fight their way in. As against this it could at least be argued that a crisis of the kind which hung over Palestine as Britain prepared to leave demanded far-reaching measures. Where, however, the international society is faced not with an imminent war but with a long drawn out and acrimonious territorial quarrel, the necessity for urgent and costly counteraction is less obvious, so that the state in possession is most unlikely to find

---

[9] On the possible use of the latter tactic in this debate see Jorge Garcia-Granados, *The Birth of Israel* (New York: Knopf, 1948), Chapter 26.
[10] See above, p. 60.
[11] Its proclamation had been brought forward from 15 to 14 May as the 15th fell on a Saturday, the Jewish Sabbath.

itself under such pressure as to lead or cause it to make way for an interim refrigerative regime.

A case in point concerns that part of the west bank of the River Jordan which had been seized first by Trans-Jordan (as she then was) in the 1948 war of Palestinian succession, and then by Israel in the war of June 1967. There was clearly no possibility, immediately following the latter conflict, of Israel giving up the Old City of Jerusalem, and it could also be assumed that she would insist on some other frontier modifications. But as regards much of the region she seemed to have far less reason for staying than in the Gaza Strip, which had given her a great deal of trouble up to 1956, and in the area above Lake Tiberias, which had been a thorn in her side throughout her existence. On the positive side, Israel's departure would relieve her of the very sizeable refugee problem with which she had saddled herself by occupying the west bank, for many of those who fled from Jewish-held Palestine in 1948 were, together with their descendants, still living in poverty there. Moreover she would partly have satisfied those who argued that all territory obtained during the war should be vacated. However, Israel insisted that the question of Jordan's claim to the west bank could only be discussed in direct negotiations and settled by way of a final agreement, a procedure which Jordan was almost certain to reject. This gave rise to the idea, in some unofficial quarters, that instead of becoming yet another piece of troublesome unfinished business, the west bank should be governed by the UN until its future was settled by a treaty of peace.

If such a scheme had been formally proposed it would no doubt have been loudly denounced by Jordan and the other Arab states, who would have refused to accept anything less than complete and immediate restitution. However, in reality their opposition might not have been as adamant as this, for temporary international government offered them several advantages. It would have achieved at least a partial Israeli withdrawal, and as this would have been secured without negotiations with the Arabs, there would have been no danger of their appearing to have condoned less than a complete evacuation. Additionally, Israel's departure could privately have been viewed as a necessary and possibly brief preliminary to the area's return to the Arab nation, and it is unlikely that this expectation would have been greatly disappointed. There was, therefore, something to commend the idea of a limited period of UN rule to both parties. Moreover, especially if it had been presented in conjunction with an international plan for the rehabilitation of the refugees it might also have won sufficient support among UN members to ensure the Organization's co-operation.

However, it also has to be noted that it was by no means clear that, on balance, the two states directly concerned would have thought that the benefits of this proposal outweighed its disadvantages. Jordan might well have had serious reservations about an arrangement which could revive the idea of a separate Palestinian Arab state, an idea which might well have received covert encouragement and support from her brother Arab states.[12] Thus the consequence of placing the west bank in the UN's temporary hands might be that it would not be returned. Faced with such a possibility, Jordan might have calculated that it would be better that the *status quo* should be maintained, for it at least enables her to appear as the victim of aggression, and therefore worthy of substantial economic assistance in order to compensate for the loss of a valuable area.

But far and away the most important factor affecting the idea of temporary international rule was the attitude of the occupant—Israel. Firmly in control of the disputed territory and with no expectation of finding herself in a position of weakness, the refrigeration of the west bank had, on balance, no appeal to her. For if she gave it up she would lose not only a defensible frontier but also, and very importantly, a most valuable bargaining counter in any subsequent negotiations with the Arabs. Moreover, as sentiment in the UN was strongly in favour of the return of occupied territory to its owner, the handing over of the west bank to the UN almost certainly meant that it would go back to the Arabs in time, quite possibly sooner rather than later. And there could be no guarantee that the new Arab regime would be less of a nuisance than the old. Such considerations as these must surely have been decisive, and as a result of Israel's negative attitude the question soon passed from public discussion.[13] It ought also to be noted, however, that even if

---

[12] On 27 October 1967 a group of leading Jordan Arabs called for the formation of a Palestinian Arab state, made up of the west bank of the Jordan (including the eastern sector of Jerusalem) and the Gaza Strip. They proposed that it should be under direct UN trusteeship for five years.

[13] Later, on 18 June 1968, it was reported by the *New York Times* that Israel was moving towards a plan for the west bank which would allow much of it either to be associated with Jordan or to become independent. In either event, the essential provision of the scheme was the establishment of a string of para-military Israeli settlements in the Jordan valley along the western edge of the river—a kind of Israeli corridor—through which the Arabs might have rights of passage. It was hoped that this would provide Israel with the strategic advantages which could otherwise only be obtained by annexation while avoiding all the disadvantages of that course. However, even if Jordan formally accepted an arrangement, it is difficult to see her resting content with it, any more than Germany reconciled herself to the indignity and inconvenience of the Polish corridor in the inter-war period. And if the plan was implemented in agreement only with the representatives of the west bank Arabs, it is virtually certain that Jordan would do her best to emphasize its illegitimacy.

the proposition had been viable from the point of view of the parties, the UN as a whole might not have been enthusiastic about a scheme which, failing to bring complete satisfaction and holding out the prospect of further change, might have helped to make the situation less rather than more settled.

A refrigerative suggestion which could find more favour at the UN was advanced by the Secretary-General late in 1967. It concerned Cyprus. On 3 December, in a formula which had been agreed with the parties, U Thant appealed to Greece and Turkey to end the crisis of the previous fortnight by withdrawing those of their forces which were in excess of the figures which had been laid down in 1960.[14] He then spoke of the possibility of a larger task for the UN force in Cyprus, 'including supervision of disarmament and the devising of practical arrangements to safeguard internal security, embracing the safety of all people of Cyprus'.[15] He may well have been hoping that if the UN Force was given the function of maintaining law and order throughout the island—upgraded from an obstructive to a refrigerative role—there would be very much less likelihood of incidents of the kind which had set off the crisis in the previous month, which in turn might increase the chances of a settlement.[16]

The extension of an existing force's mandate presents many fewer problems than the establishment of a new operation, and in the case of UNFICYP there are a number of other factors which favour this course. There is a widespread desire to prevent the Cyprus dispute from giving rise to war, especially among some influential Western Powers, and given the climate of her domestic opinion in the first half of 1968, Greece would probably accept a larger UN role. France and the Soviet Union could balk at the prospect of the UN carrying out the most basic of governmental tasks, but they might not deem it wise to press their opposition in face of general approval for the move. And it is conceivable that Turkey might be persuaded to accept U Thant's idea. She would certainly have some doubts about it, chiefly on the ground that if the UN was given responsibility for the island's internal security she would find it more difficult, in psychological and diplomatic terms, to intervene. But, under pressure, her hesitation might be outweighed by the consideration that as all illegal Greek units had left Cyprus by January 1968, the need for intervention should have been reduced. The

[14] See above, pp. 264–268.
[15] UN Information Centre, London: *Weekly Summary*, 5 December 1967.
[16] Equally, it would be possible for the UN Force to play a similar role after a settlement had been reached, and such a possibility could materially assist the conclusion of a settlement. See above, Chapter 5, especially at p. 146.

conciliatory gestures which President Makarios was making towards the Turkish Cypriots in the early months of that year might also have been thought to point towards the same conclusion.

The host state itself, however, although by far the smallest of all the interested parties, presents the biggest obstacle in the way of an expanded UN role. It is not that demilitarization would constitute a great loss for Cyprus, for her armed forces are insignificant. Nor is there any apparent or likely danger of the UN pressing for a settlement which the Government, composed of Greek Cypriots, would not like, for the UN does not show much sympathy towards partition. However, even the outside possibility that the UN might misbehave would be taken very seriously by the Government. And immediately and prominently linked with this consideration are questions of dignity and sovereign rights: Makarios would not want a force with general and far-reaching governmental responsibilities to be out of his control, yet the UN could not allow it to be a tool in his hands. The difficulty of resolving this problem greatly reduces the likelihood of the UN assuming the refrigerative role suggested by its Secretary-General, although its failure to do so does not necessarily stand in the way of the UN Force playing a bigger *de facto* part in the maintenance of order in Cyprus.

The failure of the two Cypriot communities to live together in peace has produced what amounts to an internal territorial conflict, the Government insisting that the authority runs throughout the island, and the Turkish Cypriot minority claiming that if it cannot be given satisfactory assurances as to its safety, Cyprus must be partitioned. Cyprus is by no means the only state to face such a problem, and more of a similar kind undoubtedly lie dormant. But the Cyprus dispute is rather unusual in that it impinges with clarity and force on the international political scene through each party's close affiliation with a nearby state. Where other internal quarrels do likewise, the possibility of using the UN as a refrigerative agent may also arise, and it may even do so in domestic disputes which have no specific international links but which arouse the concern of foreign states on more general grounds, perhaps of a humanitarian character.

The attempt of Eastern Nigeria to constitute itself as the independent state of Biafra is a possible case in point. There is no danger here of intervention on behalf of the secessionists, but the world shows increasing anxiety at the continuation of the war and particularly at the prospect of another mass slaughter of Ibos, which might well follow a Federal victory. One possible solution would be the UN's assumption of responsibility for law and order in Eastern Nigeria pending national reconciliation. However, even if this was practical from other points of view it is most unlikely to appeal to the Biafrans. It would necessitate the disbandment of their forces, and they might very well fear that a UN force would not provide an equal guarantee for their security. They might also worry lest the force be used to press them into an agreement which fell short of their requirements. And the Nigerian Government would almost certainly be extremely hostile to the UN's large-scale involvement in what it regards as a domestic problem. Its response would in no way be idiosyncratic, for the use of the UN in a refrigerative role is not at all a popular remedy for any kind of territorial conflict.

III

Many mid-twentieth-century disputes, however, are not territorial in character. What states often seek is not the formal enlargement of their domains at others' expense, but the establishment of the right kind of regime in foreign capitals. They have little hesitation about assisting this process, despite legal injunctions to the contrary, and it is commonly argued that such action is particularly likely and especially dangerous (on account of the possibility of counter-intervention) where law and order has broken down. This opens up a third refrigerative possibility for the UN: the holding together of a country's internal structure so as to discourage intervention. Invitations to do so are not likely to be freely forthcoming, if only because no state likes to admit that it is incapable of looking after its own affairs. But it is quite conceivable that an appeal of this nature may sometimes be made to the UN.

Such an event occurred in 1960, setting off the Organization's biggest and most controversial peace-keeping operation. It took place in the Congo, a country which was the second largest in Africa, had a population in the region of 14 million, and was rich in resources. It had been looked after relatively well by Belgium, but in a markedly paternalistic manner. Thus, right up to the end of the 1950s, independence had been thought of as a very long way away and no preparations had been made to enable the colony to stand on its own feet. Then, however, with the British and French retreat from Africa getting into top gear, and with Algeria providing an ominous example of what delay could mean, Belgium changed her tune in a manner which was abrupt, if not precipitous. In January 1960 she opened a conference with Congolese leaders with what was for her a dramatic proposal: independence in four years. She came out of the conference having agreed to independence in five months, on 30 June.

The deadline was met. However, not a week had elapsed before the Congo was displaying its deficiencies. On 5 July the soldiers of the National Army mutinied against their Belgian officers, and this was the beginning of a quickly spreading disorder. There were about 100,000 Belgians in the Congo at this time, and also two Belgian bases, which were being retained under a treaty of friendship with the new state. Belgium tried to persuade the Congo to allow her to use her troops to restore order, but without success. On 10 July, therefore, she took the matter into her own hands, and began a series of interventions in various parts of the country. Her troops had been reinforced for this purpose and by the middle of July, in both the Congo and neighbouring Ruanda-Urundi, numbered about 10,000.

In this deteriorating situation the Congolese Government sought international help. On 10 July it made an oral request to the UN for technical assistance referring particularly to its need for a reliable security force. Two days later, in the absence of the Prime Minister, Patrice Lumumba, three prominent Ministers appealed to the United States to restore order, but she, not wishing to become unilaterally embroiled, advised the Congo to look to the UN. The Prime Minister and President were already, on their own initiative, doing just that, but in terms very different from those of two days before. They complained of Belgian aggression and asked the UN to send troops for the Congo's protection. Their request was considered at an urgent meeting of the Security Council on 13–14 July, which, by eight votes to none with three abstentions (Britain, China, and France), called on Belgium to withdraw and authorized the Secretary-General to provide the Congo with 'such military assistance as may be necessary until . . . the national security force may be able, in the opinion of the Government, to meet fully their tasks'.[17] Mr Hammarskjöld quickly set to work, and the first contingents of UN troops arrived on 15 July. By 17 July approximately 3,500 troops from four African countries were in the Congo, having been flown in principally by the United States, the Soviet Union, and Britain. They formed the nucleus of the ONUC (*Organisation des Nations Unies au Congo*) Force, which by the end of the year was comprised of approximately 17,500 combat troops and 2,000 administrative and air personnel, the troops being drawn from nine African, two Asian and two European countries: Egypt, Ethiopia, Ghana, Guinea, Liberia, Morocco, Nigeria, Sudan and Tunisia; Indonesia and Malaya; and Ireland and Sweden.

From one point of view this Force could be seen as chiefly significant for its patching-up properties. It was common ground that the maintenance of law and order in the Congo required outside help;

[17] Security Council resolution 143 (1960).

as of the middle of July 1960 the function was being fulfilled by Belgian troops, but their presence was hotly opposed by the 'host' country; accordingly, their replacement by the UN force was to be the means of settling an international dispute in a manner which was agreeable to both parties. However, things were not quite as straightforward as this, for there was a sharp division of opinion in the Security Council as to the attitude it should take towards Belgium. The Soviet Union, and others, were anxious to brand her as an aggressor, and put prime emphasis on the need for her immediate withdrawal. Britain and France, on the other hand, wanted it to be recognized that Belgium was performing a valuable humanitarian task, and should not be called upon to withdraw 'on the off chance that the United Nations would be able to [establish law and order] all over the country'.[18] In their judgment the proper procedure would be for Belgium to withdraw in consequence of the arrival of UN troops, and they refused to vote for the Council's resolution of 14 July because it did not make this clear.[19] The United States said that she interpreted the resolution to mean just what Britain and France thought it should have stated. The Soviet Union, on the other hand, understood it to require an unconditional Belgium withdrawal.

Only eight days later, hardly a sufficient interval for the newly arrived UN troops to be in a position to assume the maintenance of law and order, Britain and France felt able, along with all the other Council members, to vote for a resolution which was no less peremptory in its demand for Belgium's withdrawal. How this was reconciled with their earlier abstention was not explained. The Soviet Union's production of a letter from the Congo threatening to ask for Soviet intervention in the event of the UN not taking sufficiently drastic action may have influenced their decision. It seems more likely, however, that they were anxious to avoid giving the impression of being unenthusiastic about the UN operation in support of a new African state. The Council's next resolution, passed on 9 August, was more difficult. It called on Belgium 'to withdraw immediately its troops from the Province of Katanga under speedy modalities determined by the Secretary-General',[20] which was too

---

[18] Mr Selwyn Lloyd, Foreign Secretary: House of Commons, *Debates*, Vol. 627, col. 1059.

[19] Explaining Britain's abstention in a House of Lords debate, Mr Lloyd's successor said that 'in the preamble there were all sorts of conditions attached to which we could not subscribe—namely, that all our Colonies should be independent within two years', House of Lords, *Debates*, vol., 234, col. 454. The Foreign Secretary was totally mistaken, for the resolution made no preambular, or substantive, reference of that kind. His error, however, was a graphic illustration of the impact of the UN's anti-colonial campaign on Britain's official mind.

[20] Security Council resolution 146 (1960).

much for a new West European combination, France and Italy. They abstained. Britain was very hesitant about voting for it, and only did so after receiving assurances from the Secretary-General that in arranging 'speedy modalities', a phrase which Britain's Sir Pierson Dixon found 'a little obscure to my ear',[21] account would be taken of the necessity for the maintenance of law and order.

In the event no serious difficulties arose over the withdrawal of the Belgian troops. All those who had been in her two bases at the time of the Congo's independence, together with the reinforcements which had been flown in to meet the subsequent crisis, had left the Congo by the first week of September, the bases being taken over by the UN pending a settlement between Belgium and her former colony. By the same date all the Belgian officers who had been attached to the Congolese Army had also been withdrawn, save for those who were now employed in the gendarmerie of the secessionist province of Katanga. They came to rather more than 100, together with about the same number of other ranks. A few dozen officers from Belgium's metropolitan forces also remained on loan to Mr Tshombe's Katangan Government. Their presence, together with the mercenary troops which Katanga recruited on an individual basis in Belgium and other countries, gave rise to an immense amount of trouble during the next year or so. This issue, however, was bound up with the whole question of Katangan secession.[22] It was quite distinct from the crisis which, arising in July over Belgium's unilateral attempt to restore order, was ended by the prompt provision of a form of foreign assistance which was acceptable to the Congo, and by Belgium's willingness to withdraw as soon as the UN Force was in a position to take over.

Securing Belgium's withdrawal, however, was not the only international purpose which the UN force was meant to serve. A number of Council members also saw it as having the prophylactic function of standing in the way of intervention by the Soviet Union, who, the United States told the Security Council in mid-July, was 'seeking to bring the cold war to the heart of Africa'.[23] For the United States this was probably the most valuable aspect of the UN's involvement. She had no desire to intervene herself: in neither colour nor experience were her forces best fitted for the task in hand, and it was not one which could be executed in a manner which would be equally pleasing to both the Afro-Asians and her NATO allies; moreover, sending troops abroad had little appeal to the administration with a presidential election only a few months

---

[21] Security Council, *Official Records*, 886th Meeting, para. 159.
[22] See below, pp. 411–423.
[23] Security Council, *Official Records*, 877th Meeting, para. 191.

away. But the United States was most anxious that order should be quickly restored, and in a manner which would prevent the Soviet Union from taking advantage of the situation. Failure in this respect would have been both a bad thing in itself and would have created some pressure for counter-measures. In these circumstances the introduction of the UN was an ideal solution, for it both removed an excuse for Soviet intervention and increased the physical and diplomatic hazards in the way of such a course.[24]

Quite apart from the *a priori* assumption that the Soviet Union would make what capital it could out of a dispute between a western colonial state and a recently emancipated colony, there was specific evidence of her close interest in the situation. On 13 July Lumumba and President Kasavubu had asked the Soviet Union to keep an hourly watch over their country, adding that they might find it necessary to call for Soviet assistance. The reply was appropriately sympathetic, alluding to the action which peace-loving states might have to take unless Belgian aggression was brought to an immediate halt. On 16 July Lumumba threatened to appeal to the Soviet Union unless Belgian troops were out of the country within 24 hours, and at the end of the month he received an offer of Soviet lorries and planes. By the middle of August Lumumba was completely disillusioned with the UN, on account of its refusal to subdue Katanga on his behalf, and as the Soviet Union joined him in denouncing the Organization it was quickly assumed in some Western quarters that they were hand in glove. This impression was reinforced when Lumumba, deciding that he would have to end Katangan secession by himself, asked the Soviet Union to implement her earlier offer of assistance with transport. As a result about 100 military trucks, intended for ONUC's use, and some[25] Ilyushin transport planes were put at Lumumba's disposal, together with the necessary technical staff of about 200.

These new resources were used to prepare an attack on Katanga. However, Lumumba's arrangements were hopelessly inadequate and his troops were involved in some ugly incidents, which served to increase the West's dissatisfaction with him and its apprehension that the Soviet Union might step-up its involvement in the Congo. Opinion among UN officials was also moving in the same direction, and both circles were probably not displeased, and also, perhaps,

[24] Inasmuch as the UN was performing the most basic of governmental tasks—the maintenance of law and order—and was also giving the Congo other essential assistance through its civilian operation, it could be said that, *de facto*, the UN was running the country. There were, in fact, suggestions from time to time that the UN should formally assume such powers, turning the Congo into a trust territory. But this would have been an extremely unpopular course, both within and outside the Congo, and it was never seriously considered.

[25] The figures given by different authors vary between 11 and 29.

not taken unawares when, on 5 September, Lumumba was deposed by Kasavubu. This brought an immediate counter-deposition of Kasavubu by Lumumba, the means adopted by both of them consisting of broadcasts over the radio. It seemed to Andrew Cordier, ONUC's temporary head, that the verbal conflict between the two men could easily become physical, and he was particularly worried about the possibility that Lumumba might use the Soviet planes to fly his soldiers into Leopoldville. Accordingly, early on 6 September, Cordier ordered that major airports throughout the Congo were to be closed to all traffic other than the UN's. Later in the day, following a number of pro-Lumumba broadcasts, Cordier also ordered UN troops to take control of Leopoldville's radio station, and closed it down.

These moves were justified on the ground that they were necessary for the maintenance of public order, and this was probably so. But whether they were within the terms of the UN's mandate, which laid it down that the Force 'will not be a party to or in any way intervene in or be used to influence the outcome of any internal conflict, constitutional or otherwise', is another question.[26] For the UN's action worked very much in Kasavubu's favour: in contrast to Lumumba he drew most of his support from the capital and its immediate environs, and he was also able to obtain publicity for his case over the radio of neighbouring Brazzaville, just across the Congo river. As might have been expected, the Soviet Union was furious, and if she was going to intervene this was clearly the opportune moment. However, she confined herself to a bitter attack on the Secretary-General and ONUC's activities, and soon was herself in the throes of a whole series of setbacks.

The Security Council met on 9 September, and proceeded to turn down a suggestion from Lumumba, endorsed by the Soviet Union, that the meeting should be transferred to Leopoldville. Then, on 14 September, it was announced by General Mobutu of the Congolese Army that he had decided to neutralize both Lumumba and Kasavubu. As with Kasavubu's earlier deposition of Lumumba, it was suggested by some that the hand of the West, including that of the American Central Intelligence Agency, was not uninvolved in this *coup*. It is also quite possible that Mobutu was encouraged by UN officials on the spot. Be that as it may, it was a serious blow to the Soviet Union, and as if that was not enough Mobutu took the opportunity to order the closing down of the Communist embassies in Leopoldville within 48 hours. Czechoslovakia was represented there as well as the Soviet Union, and all the diplomats of these two countries left on 17 September, an event

[26] Security Council resolution 146 (1960).

which also involved the departure of the Soviet planes and technicians. On the same day in the Security Council, the Soviet Union, isolated by her attack on Hammarskjöld, found herself in the position of having to veto a draft resolution in his support which was sponsored by Tunisia and Ceylon.

This led, against Soviet opposition, to the transfer of the Congo question to the General Assembly. Here the Afro-Asians put forward a more elaborate text which both dissociated the Assembly from Soviet criticism of the Secretary-General and yet made it clear that the recent turn of events in the Congo was by no means wholly pleasing. It might therefore have been expected that the Western countries would give it, as it stood, only qualified support. But this was not the case. The Assembly's endorsement of the draft resolution would cause the Soviet Union considerable embarrassment, whichever way she voted, and this made the West much more interested in emphasizing the extent of Soviet isolation than in introducing any reservations of its own. It was too good an opportunity to miss, and their tactics were successful. The Soviet attempt to amend the draft was a failure, and while she and her friends voted for the paragraph which condemned the provision of military assistance other than through the UN, they abstained on the resolution as a whole. The only other members to do so were France and South Africa, everyone else, except the absent Bolivia, voting in its favour. This was on 20 September, and was generally regarded as a diplomatic defeat of the first order for the Soviet Union. Meanwhile, in the Congo her protégé, although still living in the Prime Minister's residence, was without any effective power, and had it not been for his protection by the UN, a matter which contributed to the rapidly deteriorating relations between the Mobutu regime and ONUC's head, Mr R. Dayal, he would have been arrested.[27]

From this time onwards not much was heard about the likelihood of present or future Soviet intervention. There were, however, a number of Western references to the hazards which the Congo had undergone during the first few months of its life. Purportedly, the danger had not consisted simply of a heavier flow of Soviet material and technical assistance, nor even of an influx of avowedly political agents and advisers from the same source. What the Congo had faced, according to Britain, was an attempted 'Communist take-

---

[27] Congolese troops were posted beyond the UN troops outside Lumumba's house, but on 27 November he made a successful escape. He was caught four days later, and while under subsequent arrest received growing support. He was therefore transferred to Katanga on 17 January 1961. This move, as might have been and no doubt was anticipated, was fatal for him, although the manner in which he met his death, which was formally announced by the Katangan Minister of the Interior on 12 February, remains obscure.

over',[28] which, if successful, would have led to 'an East-West armed frontier in the Congo on the pattern of Korea'.[29] The fact that neither of these things happened was, by implication, attributed to the UN, which, by its own intervention, kept the Soviet Union out and so prevented the Congo from becoming an arena (a much-favoured metaphor) for the cold war.

This analysis cannot be accepted as it stands. At the outset of the crisis the Soviet Union gave every impression of not wanting to play a direct role in the Congo, not even by invitation, and keenly supported the dispatch of a UN force. Such a policy was quite consistent with the hope that a force would serve her own purposes, but much less so with the expectation that, if it did not, she would herself have to contemplate intervention. Had she thought that there was any chance of that, she would hardly have been so enthusiastic about the erection of what might prove to be an obstacle in her own way. Of course, when she realized that the UN was not going to take an aggressive line towards Belgium and appreciated the opportunities which were offered by Lumumba's dissatisfaction, she might have changed her mind about the desirability of her own involvement in the situation. This is what was quite widely apprehended towards the end of August, and the question therefore arises as to why the Soviet Union did not in fact markedly step up the level of her intervention. If she had come to the brink of doing so despite the presence of the UN Force, it was probably not the Force which caused her to reconsider the matter. A more plausible explanation would be that the UN's action in the first week of September not only had the effect of cutting the ground from under Lumumba's feet but also tipped the scales against large-scale Soviet intervention. It is doubtful, however, whether this was why the Soviet Union made no move.

If the Soviet Union had decided that Lumumba was worth supporting in a big way, it is quite probable that she would have begun moving into the Congo before he was deposed by Kasavubu. And, although his deposition made intervention more difficult, it is unlikely that she would have allowed herself to be checked by it, particularly as the UN's part in the matter provided an additional ground for action. And if she was going to intervene, she could hardly have expected to profit from waiting until the UN had debated the matter. All of which suggests that the premise is at fault, that the Soviet Union was not in fact planning massive intervention. There are a number of considerations which give weighty support to this view.

[28] House of Lords, *Debates*, Vol. 242, col. 1039.
[29] *Ibid.*, Vol. 228, col. 439.

The Congo was 5,000 miles away from the Soviet Union, had no sea coast or ports to speak of, and was surrounded by countries at least cool if not hostile to Communism. Thus even obtaining access to the Congo would not have been a straightforward task. Nor would the securing of effective control. The Congo was not much smaller than India and was in an exceedingly disordered condition. It had no Communist Party, and in view of the fact that the Congolese Senate had already stated its opposition to Soviet military intervention, the support of most of the politically conscious élite could by no means be counted upon. The Prime Minister's activities tended to take place around an axis which had a definite inclination to the left, but as the UN had already discovered, Lumumba's chameleon-like nature made him a very difficult person to work with. The prospect, therefore, was far from inviting.

Nor would the Soviet Union's problems have been at an end with the establishment of a satellite regime. Indeed, in many respects they would only have been beginning. Ensuring the Congo's continuing orthodoxy would in any event have been difficult enough, on account of Lumumba's personality and his country's distance from the Kremlin, but it might well have been exacerbated by tensions arising from the attempt of a white state to keep a black one in line. And the supply and defence of the Congo would not only have been costly but also precarious and unpopular. Substantial intervention may not have been easily sold at home, and probably would not have found a ready market among the uncommitted states of Asia and Africa. Soviet discomfort would be exploited by the West, and the possibility of some of its leading members responding in kind could not be ruled out—an activity for which they were in a much better position, both geographically and strategically, than the Soviet Union.

It is, therefore, most unlikely that massive intervention was seriously contemplated by the Soviet Union. She was very willing to provide diplomatic support for Lumumba's tirades against the West and the UN, and also to give him some material and technical help. No doubt the Soviet nationals in the Congo lost no opportunity to further their country's interests and damage those of Western states, and had Lumumba come out on top in the domestic struggle the Soviet Union would not have been at all displeased. But all this is a far cry from total commitment to his cause. That would have been to get out on a weak limb after an elusive prize of uncertain worth. Any state might have been reluctant to invest its resources and prestige in such an enterprise, however, well placed to do so in diplomatic and logistic terms. It would have been particularly out of keeping for the Soviet Union to undertake the risk, so cautious is she when it comes to the deployment of her forces beyond the secure lines of her own country and her East European supporters.

The UN operation in the Congo was not, therefore, of great importance so far as prevention of Soviet intervention was concerned. But this is not to say that it was without any prophylactic significance. It did provide an extra, albeit a relatively minor, obstacle in the Soviet Union's way in the event of her being disposed to underestimate the other factors which militated against her playing an active role on the Congolese scene. It furnished a convenient excuse for inaction on her part should she need one, though there is no evidence that she ever did. More important is the consideration that in the absence of ONUC there might well have been much greater pressure on the Soviet Union to intervene and she might have felt less well placed to resist it. From here it is easy to construct a scenario of catastrophe in three simple stages: Soviet intervention; Western counter intervention; world war. None of these possibilities is very convincing. Even if East and West had found themselves fighting in the Congo, there would have been strong incentives to localize the war. But it is not at all certain that armed intervention by the Soviet Union would have been imitated by the Western countries. The costs and risks might well have been too great, inclining them instead to leave the Soviet Union to get on as badly as she might while loudly drawing the appropriate moral, and perhaps stationing troops in adjacent countries. And the balance of probabilities suggests that the absence of the UN Force would not have resulted in large-scale Soviet intervention. Nevertheless, as an additional discouragement to dangerous behaviour its presence was of value, for amid the fluctuations and uncertainties of international politics no precaution is wholly superfluous.

The UN Force remained in the Congo until June 1964, and retained its refrigerative aspect throughout its life. However, it very soon became its lesser role. For by the end of 1960 large-scale Soviet intervention was no longer regarded as a present or anticipated danger, even by those who, in August, had thought it a real possibility. And for the next two years the UN was preoccupied with the Katangan question, the ONUC Force being the proselytizing instrument which was to bring Mr Tshombe's secession to an end.[30] By January 1963 this task had been completed. Thereafter the UN Force remained in being to assist the Congo with the maintenance of law and order, and the only international significance which could now be attributed to it was as a prophylactic agent, helping to keep the Congo out of high international politics. But at this stage none of the Powers had any desire at all to get physically

[30] See below, pp. 415–423.

entangled in the Congo, the UN having amply demonstrated the problems and pitfalls of such a course. During its last 18 months, therefore, the ONUC Force, was of little peace-keeping importance.

The UN's experiences in the Congo will probably result in future invitations of a similar nature being viewed with considerable caution. In 1960 it fairly leapt at its opportunity. The mounting of UNEF at the time of the Suez crisis had given a powerful impetus to the idea that, despite the breakdown of collective security, the UN could play a significant part in the maintenance of peace. The dispatch of the Observer Group to the Lebanon in 1958 had only whetted the Organization's appetite, so that the chance of playing an important role in the Congo was eagerly seized. Four years later the UN emerged wiser and poorer, acutely aware that there is no knowing what may be involved in the restoration and maintenance of law and order, or whither such an open-ended task may lead. In consequence, the suggestion that it should undertake a similar role even in what seems to be a straightforward situation may well be treated with some reserve. If the task of restoring order is clearly a formidable one, where, for example, a number of over-mighty and well-armed subjects are scattered about the country in question, the UN might take the view that the situation was beyond remedying with the capabilities it was able to command. It might also be given pause by the apparent imminence of substantial intervention from an extra-UN source. And besides all this, there is the further possibility that political considerations may dispose the UN to inactivity. Many members may be opposed to bolstering up the appellant, preferring to see it suffer some further disorder in the hope that the outcome might be its replacement by a more acceptable regime, perhaps assisted by some private meddling of their own. Should Cuba, for example, become disordered it is unlikely that the UN would speedily come to the aid of its present Government.

It is, however, unlikely that the UN will often be asked to give assistance in the kind of situation which arose in the Congo in July 1960, or feel able to take the initiative in offering such help. The fact that, as of the middle of 1968, it has received no further requests of this character is a significant pointer, and is not hard to explain. In the first place, the existence of anarchy within a state, meaning the complete lack of governmental authority, will probably be a relatively rare phenomenon. Governmental authority not infrequently breaks down, but the typical consequence is the quick appearance of one or more indigenous bodies claiming, with some show of effectiveness, the government's place. The armed forces are the obvious candidate for this role. Thus the result is either the speedy passage of authority from one source to another, or a clear-cut conflict, in the shape of civil war, as to its proper location or extent. Possibly the UN could assume a refrigerative role in respect of the latter type of situation,[31] but it would be rather different from the part it was called upon to play in the Congo following the disintegration of the armed forces and the collapse of the Government's authority.

Secondly, however, even if states find themselves in this kind of internal trouble, or something approaching it, they are not at all keen to turn to the UN for help. The idea may have some immediate appeal in respect of a troublesome dependent territory, but on further inspection it is unlikely to retain its attraction. At the Commonwealth Prime Ministers' Conference held in July 1964, for example, Dr Eric Williams of Trinidad is reported to have suggested a UN trusteeship for British Guiana. For the previous 12 months, this colony had been in a very uneasy condition, industrial disputes and racial conflict finding expression in arson and violence, and in one sense Britain would have been only too glad to hand her responsibilities over to the UN. But such a course would have created a very bad impression and, more importantly, a dangerous precedent. Accordingly, nothing came of it.

Where difficulties over the maintenance of order occur in the metropolitan territory, the state concerned is likely to be even less enthusiastic about seeking the UN's assistance. To do so would not only lead to international discussion regarding its domestic affairs, but would also involve a willingness to place them in the hands of a body which can by no means be relied upon not to misbehave, in the sense of being insufficiently responsive to the wishes of the host state. As Lumumba discovered to his cost, important differences may emerge between the UN and the host as to the nature or interpretation of the role of an international force. This can be bad enough if the force fails to execute a governmental request. It could be a good deal worse if the UN decided on action which the government considered to be contrary to its best interests. Nor is the problem in this respect confined to decisions emanating from UN headquarters, for some of the contingents making up the force may conceivably adopt an independent line. The host state may, initially, have approved the national composition of the UN force, but subsequent political changes, whether in the host or in the contributing country, may deprive this safety factor of much of its value. It would still be open to the host to press the UN to withdraw the offending contingent, and its efforts would probably be successful. But even if the

[31] See above, pp. 353–354. Also, p. 320, n. 22.

country in question agrees to go quietly, the damage may already have been done.

If, therefore, a state feels it essential to ask for help in the maintenance of law and order, it would much prefer to turn to a state with whom it is on good terms than to the UN. This does not eliminate all risk, for the presence of foreign troops on one's soil is always something of a hazard, and if they come from only one state their troublemaking potential is greater than that of a composite force, on account of their being under coherent and single-minded political control. But if a state is obtaining help from a trusted friend, the danger of this is minimal. Such a case occurred in January 1964 when there was a mutiny in the Tanganyikan Army, immediately followed by similar trouble in the two other East African countries which had until recently been under British control: Kenya and Uganda. All three states immediately asked Britain for assistance, and as a result the mutineers were quickly disarmed by British troops, who remained for two or three months. In the case of Tanganyika they were replaced by a Nigerian battalion which was sent following a Tanganyikan request to the Organization of African Unity. It stayed until September.

There was no evident danger, in these East African cases, of advantage being taken of the situation by an outside Power. But such a development could not be excluded, and clearly all three countries were in need of help. They disliked having to appeal to their former overlord—Tanganyika felt the indignity particularly keenly—but in the circumstances it was by far the best course from their point of view, for it ensured assistance which was both speedy and politically safe. The UN would not have been nearly so satisfactory on either ground. Similar considerations must have influenced the decision of the small Indian Ocean island of Mauritius to request that British forces remain following independence on 12 March 1968, in order to cope with the serious racial strife with which it was beset.

The political safety of a refrigerative operation may also be a matter of concern to states other than the potential host, which may provide a further reason for the bypassing of the UN. For if the disordered state is within the sphere of influence of a major Power, that Power may decide to intervene itself, irrespective of whether it has been asked to do so, in order to avoid the possibility of other states interfering in its preserve through the medium of a multinational force. It is difficult, for example, to see the Soviet Union or the United States allowing the UN to restore order in one of their East European or Central American friends.

However, states do not relish the idea of putting a disordered fellow to rights. It is likely to be a costly and troublesome business, and may prove unpopular at home and abroad. Thus, where the governmental apparatus collapses in a state in which none of the major Powers is vitally interested, and with whom none of them are bound by close ties, it may be generally agreed that the UN should assume the task of restoring order. Such a decision, assuming it was sought or accepted by the host, would at one and the same time increase the UN's chances of success as a refrigerative agent and make its services less important. For the very fact that the UN had been asked to intervene would be indicative of a reluctance on the part of individual members to do so; and, further, that reluctance would mean that the danger of the disordered state attracting unilateral intervention and so becoming a source of international tension, and perhaps worse, would be relatively minor. But in practice the situation is unlikely to be as clear cut as this, and the UN force, as well as reflecting might also encourage a disposition to stand off. Its contribution in this respect would probably be small, but that would not necessarily deprive it of marginal significance.

In theory, the employment of the UN as a refrigerative agent where law and order is in jeopardy has some marked advantages over its use for the same purpose in respect of a territorial conflict. For in the latter case the UN is unable to make a direct contribution towards the solution of the basic problem. By looking after the disputed area, the Organization may be able to keep the parties at arm's length, and in time a conciliatory frame of mind may emerge. But there is no guarantee that it will, and if it does not the UN can do nothing about it and may see no prospect of bringing its holding operation to an end. It is also quite conceivable that it will attract criticism on the ground that it is only postponing an inevitable war, and so stands in the way of ultimate stability.[32] By contrast, the situation is, on the face of it, much more promising where the UN endeavours to operate refrigeratively by way of the restoration of order. For inasmuch as such a task should be easily within the capabilities of an international force, the introduction of the UN should produce an immediate reduction in the danger of unilateral intervention. Moreover, through the training of indigenous forces, the UN should be able to remedy its host's defect before too long, and so permit its own departure.

In practice the situation may be a good deal less amenable to UN treatment. Order may be far from easy to restore, the conduct of the UN force may give rise to difficulties, and irrespective of its success in executing its immediate mandate, the presence of a UN force may not deter intervention. Quite apart from these matters, however,

[32] On this point, see further, above, pp. 333–336.

even the UN's departure may give rise to substantial problems of its own. There may be argument as to its timing, or, more importantly, dissension over the rightful heir to the better ordered state. Such disputes would involve, if they did not emanate from, the UN's political organs, illustrating the point that placing a matter in the UN's hands maximizes the opportunities for minor meddling. Further, the UN's withdrawal may promise to precipitate civil war, and a new threat of intervention may accompany such a prospect, or may exist independently of local disorder. Refrigerative activity, in short, of this no less than any other kind, may quieten one controversy but is not a form of political sterilization.

PART THREE

Proselytism

Chapter 10

Invalidation

ATTEMPTS to influence the ideological complexion of foreign regimes are not confined to times when a country's affairs are in the melting pot. In more normal conditions, too, ill-disposed Powers may try to foment opposition to the government, or to capitalize upon existing unrest. The choice of methods, however, will probably be governed by the consideration that there must be no public acknowledgement of responsibility for such acts. For, despite the practical inroads which it has suffered, international relations still proceed in the light of the theory that states do not interfere in each others' domestic concerns. The overt infringement of this rule would hardly be compatible with the continuation even of minimal contacts, including diplomatic links. This would probably be regretted on both sides, for the practical value of a means of official communication is considerable. Hence, even when a state is working for another's overthrow, it usually tries to do so without open provocation.

Where, however, relations are already bad, and the regime under attack is unpopular among its fellows, the prospect of its public denunciation at the international level may become more attractive. Such a course might pay dividends in terms of domestic politics, and could increase the extent and effectiveness of the campaign to paint the offending state in its true colours. But there may still be some hesitation about giving such blatant offence to the canons of diplomacy, not least because of a reluctance to do something which might encourage a lower standard. In these circumstances the possibility of turning the UN to a proselyitizing purpose holds out some marked advantages, chiefly inasmuch as, in the eyes of many, it would legitimize the whole process. To be one of a crowd is always comforting to those who are bent on some disturbing activity, and when that crowd has some claim to speak on behalf of the whole the action not only becomes psychologically easier but also gains in political strength. Moreover, by proceeding in this way, those who allege a government's unfitness to rule will have an opportunity to buttress their case. For, instead of just relying on their own evidence, they can try to persuade the UN to investigate the matter. Any such enquiry is unlikely to be exhaustive, for it will probably be some aspect of the government's internal conduct or policy with the UN wishes to place under scrutiny, and it is almost inconceivable that the subject of the investigation would facilitate the enterprise. But, quite apart from the fact that the UN can pursue its enquiries elsewhere, the frustration of its attempt to see for itself will not mean that the world will be left without guidance as to the conclusion to which it should come.[1]

Here, then, is another use to which international investigations may be put. As well as offering a means of settling disputes and of publicly revealing undesirable behaviour in the hope of curbing it, fact-finding, by showing that a regime has lost all moral right to continue its rule, may also be employed as a possible instrument of change. A government's espousal of an obnoxious ideology, its iniquitous domestic conduct, or its effective subordination to a foreign Power—any of these may be highlighted as a way of demonstrating its lack of validity. The implication of this conclusion is that the offending regime can no longer legitimately claim the obedience of its subjects, and that other states may feel free to encourage it, in one way and another, to reform or give way to a government which will know how to behave.

As with most instances of prophylactic enquiries, those who urge the UN to engage in fact gathering as a proselytizing device will be perfectly well aware of the facts which they want to be found. And, equally, they will want the investigating body to be composed in such a way that it can be relied upon to find them.[2] The use of the UN for the purpose of invalidation, however, is not simply the obverse of the accusatory procedure, for there are some important differences between the two activities. A typical case of defensive fact finding deals with action on the part of one state which is said to be detrimental to another. Thus it concentrates on an issue which is both specific and international, and, in principle, hopes for an immediate response, although in practice it is unlikely to achieve

[1] Where there is no possibility of a fact-finding body gaining admission to the state which has been judged worthy of examination, the information it is likely to procure by other field enquiries may not promise to be notably superior to that which it could obtain simply by holding meetings at New York. Such circumstances, however, have by no means always discouraged investigating missions from engaging in foreign travel. In part this may be due to the psychological value of peripatetic activity, for it highlights the suspect state's refusal to submit to investigation, and may add some credence to the investigator's conclusions. There are instances, however, of fact-finding bodies being proposed or established without any intention of their taking to the field. In such cases there is no question of the UN establishing a 'presence', but nevertheless, as their role is essentially similar to that of mobile proselytizing enquiries, they are included in this Chapter.

[2] On this point, see above, pp. 179 and 194, and also, more generally, the rest of the theoretical material relating to prophylactic enquiries, pp. 177–182 and 193–196. Much of it is equally relevant to the consideration of fact-finding as an invalidating mechanism.

more than a broad discrediting effect. Enquiries which are designed to induce change, on the other hand, usually emphasize matters which are less obviously international and more general in character. They may be pegged on a particular topic, but even so the object of the exercise goes beyond the disseminating of a judgment as to the government's behaviour in relation to that issue alone. Rather it hopes to discredit the regime in a more far reaching way, and, by so doing, to contribute to its downfall.

A UN investigation may achieve its more immediate, discrediting, aims, at least in the eyes of the already converted, but it cannot be assumed that this will bring the more ambitious goal any closer. It may do so in respect of dependent territories if the administering power is already willing to contemplate withdrawal. But it is hardly realistic to hope that the condemnation of the UN will in any way move a regime towards the abdication of its metropolitan responsibilities. This consideration, together with the difficulty of compiling a satisfactory report when access to the bulk of the evidence is denied, probably goes a considerable way towards accounting for the fact that during the UN's first decade it was only in unusual circumstances that the majority group pressed strongly for the use of this device against their arch rivals. And with the easing of the cold war and the admission of many states who are extremely sensitive about the private character of their domestic affairs, proselytizing enquiries in relation to metropolitan areas have not increased in popularity—except where the racial issue is involved.

I

An early example of fact-finding as a means of inducing change concerned Spain. The help which General Franco had received from Italy and Germany during the Spanish civil war, together with Spain's neutrality during World War II, meant that there was no question of her admission to the UN in 1945, not even if she had qualified as peace-loving by a late declaration of war on the Axis Powers. The widespread hostility to the Spanish Government was further exemplified in April 1946, when Poland asked the Security Council to declare that the existence and activities of the Franco regime had led to international friction and endangered peace and security. She would have had the Council call upon all members who maintained diplomatic relations with Spain to sever them immediately. Britain, however, felt that the premise of the argument went too far. To get around this difficulty, Australia proposed that the matter should be examined by a subcommittee, which was to make use of such statements and documents as were available or presented to it, and conduct such further enquiries as it might deem necessary. The Soviet Union abstained on the proposal, on the ground that it involved unnecessary delay, but all other Council members voted in favour.

The subcommittee, which was made up of the representatives of Australia, Brazil, China, France, and Poland, reported on 1 June 1946. Its unanimous conclusion was that Spain did not present an existing threat to peace, but that peace was likely to be endangered by the continuation of the Franco regime. It recommended that the General Assembly should urge all members to terminate diplomatic relations with Spain. This, however, was not enough for the Soviet Union, who, claiming that Franco already was a threat, and that he should be dealt with by the Council and not the Assembly, vetoed the subcommittee's recommendation. Nevertheless, in December 1946, two months after the Council had dropped the matter from its agenda, the Assembly made such a recommendation. However, it had little direct and no indirect effect, and in 1950 was revoked. Five years later Spain was admitted to the UN. Franco was still in control, but the fact that Spain was staunchly anti-Communist and occupied an important strategic position had caused her stock to rise in Western circles. European memories of the civil war prevented her admission to NATO, but through bilateral arrangements with the United States Spain was effectively brought into the Western defensive system.

It was the possibility of the West going on to the psychological offensive in the cold war which gave rise to the next few suggestions that the UN should engage in proselytizing enquiries. The first of these was in May 1948, following the Communist coup in Czechoslovakia. The question of whether that country's political independence had been violated by the threat of Soviet force came before the Security Council, and Chile proposed that a subcommittee of three should be appointed to receive evidence on the point. Through the use of her veto the Soviet Union carried her argument that this was not a procedural motion, and then went on to veto the substantive resolution.[3] As a counter-measure the United States declared that she would not allow the Soviet Union to obstruct a fair presentation of all aspects of the question, and, accordingly, would receive 'relevant'[4] statements from Czechoslovak refugees and make them available to the Council. She encouraged other members to do likewise.

---

[3] This was an instance of a 'double veto'. For further discussion, and an unsuccessful Soviet attempt to use the ploy, see above, pp. 203–204.
[4] Security Council, *Official Records*, 303rd Meeting, p. 31.

In 1950 there was some discussion in the General Assembly regarding the appointment of a fact-finding body to investigate the observance of human rights in three Soviet satellites: Bulgaria, Hungary, and Roumania. This arose out of the imprisonment, in the previous year, of church leaders in Hungary and Bulgaria, and of the failure of the three countries to implement those sections of the 1947 peace treaties which related to the settlement of disputes regarding human rights. However, it was recognized that there was no question of such a UN mission being admitted to the states concerned, and the Assembly therefore contented itself with an invitation to all members to let the Secretary-General have their evidence on the matter.

At the next session of the Assembly the question of an anti-Communist investigation arose in relation to a different issue: Germany. In November 1951, Britain, France, and the United States asked that an impartial international commission should be established under UN supervision to carry out a simultaneous investigation in East and West Germany, and Berlin, to determine whether conditions there permitted the holding of genuinely free and secret elections. As was to be expected, both East Germany and the Soviet Union indicated their opposition to the proposal, the latter claiming that it was an insult to the German people to suggest that they needed the help or supervision of the UN in organizing free elections. All that the Soviet Union was prepared to allow was that, if the Germans wanted it, the four occupying Powers should supervise an enquiry carried out by Germans representing the two zones. However, the Western Powers pressed their proposal, putting forward the names of Brazil, Iceland, the Netherlands, Pakistan, and Poland as potential members of the Commission, and the resolution was passed by a large majority. Poland had already made it clear that she would not serve, and so in practice the Commission was only four states strong.

The resolution provided that the Commission was to report to the Secretary-General on its efforts to make the arrangements which would enable it to carry out its task, and, if it was able to make such arrangements, to report its findings on the main issue. The Commission separated these two instructions, giving precedence to the first. In 1952 it reported that it had obtained very satisfactory assurances of co-operation in respect of West Germany and West Berlin, but that it had received no response at all from the authorities in the Soviet zone of Germany and East Berlin. Aware that in the Soviet Union's view the UN had no competence regarding Germany, the Commission concluded that it had little prospect of being able to execute its mandate, and, on 31 July 1952, adjourned *sine die.* The Western Powers having made their point, the matter was not pursued at the UN.

Communist activity in the Far East has also been the subject of a proposal for a UN enquiry. In September 1949 China had complained about threats to her integrity resulting, allegedly, from Soviet violations of the Sino-Soviet Treaty of Friendship and Alliance of 1945 and of the UN Charter, and in 1950 Chiang Kai-shek's Government, now based in Taiwan, asked the General Assembly to institute enquiries into its charges. Support for this suggestion came from the United States, who indicated her view of the UN's role by saying that the Organization must 'expose a master plan that had already resulted in the enslavement of one-third of the human race'.[5] But some of her friends, including Britain and France, were unenthusiastic, saying that the facts were already known, and on this last point the Soviet Union agreed, although she took a different view as to their nature. It was therefore proposed by Syria that the Assembly's Interim Committee, which had already discussed the question, should be instructed to continue its enquiry. China withdrew her draft resolution and nothing more was heard of her proposal, although in February 1952 she did obtain the satisfaction of an Assembly resolution supporting the opinion that the Soviet Union had violated her bilateral obligations towards China.

On the whole, however, the cold war has received very little of the UN's attention. The Great Powers have been anxious to keep it to themselves, and usually, therefore, the West has been willing to forgo such minor propaganda victories as it could have obtained from proselytizing enquiries. In this way it has lessened the risk of the UN deciding to give the whole issue more general consideration, or even just deciding that it should discuss the possibility of doing so. But to this generalization there are two major exceptions, one of which concerns Korea. Here the UN has been closely involved, and not just by way of providing a very acceptable name for the international force which was established immediately following North Korea's aggression in 1950. For the Korean problem was on the UN's agenda from the early post-war years, and resulted in the dispatch of a number of UN missions to the country. Formally, they were all designed to heal its division, but in practical terms they soon assumed an invalidating role, their intended victim being the Government of North Korea.

Before the end of World War II the United States had proposed that the surrender of Japanese forces in Korea north of the 38th parallel should be accepted by the Soviet Union, and south of that

[5] General Assembly, *Official Records*, First Committee, 400th Meeting, para. 56.

line by the United States. The Soviet Union agreed, and kept her part of the bargain by withdrawing from the areas south of the 38th parallel which she had occupied pending the arrival of American forces. Another aspect of their agreement, however, had a less harmonious conclusion. It was common ground that Korea, which had been under Japanese rule since 1910, should become free and independent in due course, and that meanwhile the Great Powers, acting jointly as trustees, should assume responsibility for it. But in the immediate post-war period the United States began to become disenchanted with the trusteeship idea. In part these doubts reflected a desire to deny the Soviet Union an opportunity to extend her influence in Korea beyond the Northern sector, where a 'reliable' regime was already being installed. Also, and quite separately, the United States was fast losing her willingness to extend her Korean responsibilities. Moreover, for as long as a Great Power trusteeship was formally pursued, the costly and troublesome occupation regime would have to continue, which was no more pleasing to the American armed services than it was to the South Koreans.

The abandonment of trusteeship was not a straightforward task for the United States, for she had committed herself to it and the Soviet Union remained greatly in its favour. However, one possible avenue of retreat lay via the General Assembly of the United Nations. The United States did not regard Korea as an area which was vital for her security, and so there was no objection to allowing the UN a voice in its future, particularly as at this time the Assembly could be relied upon to give the American case a favourable hearing. Further, as negotiations with the Soviet Union regarding the establishment of a provisional Korean Government had been proceeding fruitlessly for eighteen months, the United States was not without an excuse for turning to the UN. Accordingly, in September 1947 she asked that 'The Problem of the Independence of Korea' should be placed on the Assembly's agenda. The wording of the proposed item indicated that trusteeship had been put on one side and that an arrangement was to be sought which would permit the withdrawal of American forces: the multilateral process was to legitimize both departures. Quickly realizing the danger which this presented to her policy, the Soviet Union proposed, bilaterally, that all foreign forces should be withdrawn from Korea by the end of 1947 so that the Koreans could form their own government without outside interference. This embarrassed the United States, but not to such an extent as to prevent her from going ahead with her endeavour to obtain a UN solution for the Korean problem.

The United States may have hoped that the Soviet Union would accept a UN scheme for Korea's unification, but there was very little chance of such an outcome, whether under UN or any other auspices. North Korea was only half as populous as the South, so any all-Korean Government was likely to be dominated by the friends of the United States. Certainly, the Assembly would not knowingly open the way to office for the Soviet Union's Northern protégés and Southern sympathizers. Thus, by taking the question to the UN the United States accelerated the establishment of two independent governments in Korea, and it may well be that she recognized the risk of doing so from the outset. But such a result was probable in any event. As in the case of Germany, Korea's post-1945 political development was to be determined by the disposition of the victors' forces at the end of the war.

In the General Assembly the United States proposed that elections should be held throughout Korea under UN supervision with a view to the establishment of a national government and, subsequently, the withdrawal of foreign troops. The Soviet Union opposed this, arguing that the presence of foreign troops would not permit a free election, and that the UN commission would be an unjustified interference in the affairs of the Korean people. But the United States suggestion easily carried the day, and on 14 November 1947 the Assembly established the UN Temporary Commission on Korea (UNTCOK), composed of the representatives of Australia, Canada, China, El Salvador, France, India, Philippines, Syria, and the Ukraine. It was to have the right to travel freely throughout Korea in order to observe the preparations for and the conduct of an election, which was to be held not later than 31 March 1948.

UNTCOK soon ran into difficulties. The Ukraine refused to participate, and the Commission was unable to make contact with the Soviet military command in North Korea or to obtain access to that part of the country. The question therefore arose as to whether it should observe elections in the South alone. Not all of its members were in favour of this course, but the Interim Committee of the Assembly, strongly led by the United States, authorized the Commission to do so. With a maximum of 30 non-Korean personnel, therefore, UNTCOK supervised the Southern elections and concluded that they were fair. They led to the establishment of a right-wing regime under President Rhee, which, in August 1948, was recognized as the Government of Korea by the United States, who immediately put arrangements in hand for her withdrawal. They were temporarily halted so as to prevent their completion before the Assembly had had an opportunity to consider UNTCOK's report. But from the United States' point of view UNTCOK had clearly completed its task of legitimizing both her departure and the successor regime in South Korea.

It also, however, fulfilled another function, that of depriving the North Korean regime of legitimacy. For UNTCOK's inability to gain admission to the North allowed the General Assembly to declare, in December 1948, that the government which had emerged from the UN-supervised electoral process was the only lawful government in Korea. The opportunity of using the UN to underline this point was too good for the West to miss, and therefore a UN Commission on Korea (UNCOK) was established to replace UNTCOK, its membership consisting of all the states who had served on UNT-COK except for Canada and the Ukraine.[6] The new Commission's chief stated task was to lend its good offices towards obtaining a united Korea. However, there was no likelihood of this coming about by negotiation. Nor was there any chance of the North Korean Government standing down in consequence of the world being periodically reminded that, unlike the Southern Government, it had not received the stamp of international approval, and was demonstrating its iniquity by obstructing unification. Nevertheless, the West thought it valuable that the basis and nature of the Communist regime in the North should be highlighted from time to time, and the use of the UN for this purpose has continued ever since, although latterly with diminishing enthusiasm.

Besides working for unification, UNCOK was instructed to encourage the further development of representative government in South Korea. This made it less than wholly popular with President Rhee, who was unwilling to receive representations on the point and disapproved of the Commission playing any other part in South Korea's political affairs. In different circumstances this might have got him into trouble with UNCOK's sponsors, but the growing Communist ascendancy in China made the West increasingly unwilling to offend right-wing regimes in the area. And, as it happened, UNCOK's functions were now extended in a manner which was very acceptable to South Korea. In July 1949 UNTCOK had reported its failure to make any progress towards unification. It also said that it had been unable to verify the reported withdrawal of Soviet forces from North Korea by 1 January 1949, but was able to confirm that American forces had left the South by the end of June. By way of compensation for the latter event, UNCOK was asked to observe and report on developments which might lead to military conflict, an instruction which emphasized the impracticality of its major goal.

As a result of its wider mandate UNCOK was in a position to make an immediate report on the North Korean attack on the South which began on 25 June 1950. Led by the United States,

[6] In October 1949 Turkey took Syria's place on the Commission.

whose reaction seemed somewhat out of keeping with her previous anxiety to withdraw from Korea, a UN force quickly took the field to repel Communist aggression, and three months later the North Koreans were on the retreat. This produced a Soviet draft resolution which was in marked contrast with her previous view as to the proper way to handle the Korean problem. For she suggested that, following the cessation of hostilities and the withdrawal of foreign troops, elections should be held throughout Korea under the auspices of a joint North-South commission, in which each side would be equally represented. They were to be supervised by a UN committee which was to include states bordering on Korea, such as Communist China and herself. This was a big departure from the previous Soviet position, but it also contained much which was unsatisfactory from the Western point of view, and was rejected.

However, the advance of the UN force towards the internal Korean frontier also stimulated the Western camp into producing a proposal, for there was doubt as to whether the UN was entitled to pursue the North Korean forces into their sector of the country. It was therefore proposed that a UN Commission for the Unification and Rehabilitation of Korea (UNCURK) should be established, which, as well as taking over UNCOK's functions, was to represent the UN in bringing about a unified Korea. The new Commission was set up on 7 October, and, legally fortified, UN troops immediately crossed the border. But Korea was not to be united by arms. Within a matter of weeks the UN force was itself on the retreat, and the armistice line which was eventually agreed in 1953 ran more or less along the 38th parallel.

It proved, therefore, that the UN had built its new Commission unnecessarily, for UNCURK was confined, so far as North Korea was concerned, to the invalidating role which had earlier been played by UNCOK. And it soon found that for this purpose the full seven-member Commission was not required. Accordingly, in 1955, it reported to the General Assembly that Chile, the Netherlands, and Pakistan were now playing a less active role, as a committee of four—Australia, the Philippines, Thailand, and Turkey—had been set up to act on behalf of the Commission. The Assembly did not object to this nor, indeed, did it take much notice at all of UN-CURK's melancholy annual tale of its failure to move North Korea towards unification. Each year the Assembly simply repeated its commitment to this goal, urged UNCURK to continue its efforts, and placed North Korea's negative attitude on record. In its most recent resolution to this effect, for example, passed on 16 November 1967, the Assembly stated that the continued division of Korea did not correspond to the wishes of the Korean people and constituted a source of tension, and it therefore urged UNCURK to intensify its efforts to achieve a unified and democratic Korea through genuinely free elections. The resolution received 68 votes in its favour, with 23 members voting against it and 36 abstaining.

As these figures suggest, the UN, as now composed, cannot be described as enthusiastic in its efforts to undermine the legitimacy of the North Korean regime. However, the Organization has no compelling reason for withdrawing UNCURK, is still able to raise a fair head of steam on an anti-Communist issue, and on account of the war of 1950–53—one legacy of which is the continued existence of what is called a 'UN Command' in South Korea—it has its own stake in the Korean situation. UNCURK therefore remains in being as a symbol of the UN's formal commitment to change in this area. In practice, however, the heart has gone out even of the discrediting process. For many members, questions relating to North Korea's emergence as a separate entity lie sufficiently far into the past, in terms of both time and political development, as to be irrelevant. But as yet this view is not so widely held as to allow a different kind of change: the admission of the two Koreas to the UN.

The last instance of the UN using invalidation as a weapon in the cold war concerned Hungary. On 23 October 1956, immediately following Gomulka's overthrow of the Polish Stalinists, there was a mass demonstration in Budapest in support of the complaints of the students and factory workers. It straightaway brought Soviet tanks and troops to the city to restore order, with the consent of the Government. But, in keeping with its conciliatory attitude to the popular movement in Poland, the Soviet Union did not stand in the way of, and, indeed, encouraged changes in Hungary's leadership, Gerö being replaced as premier by Imre Nagy and as First Secretary of the Communist party by Janos Kadar. Soviet forces were then withdrawn. In this context, however, such moves were insufficient, being at once outdistanced by the revolution which had spread with great speed throughout the country.

At the twentieth congress of the Communist party of the Soviet Union, held in February 1956, Stalin had been denounced by Khrushchev, and the possibility of different roads to socialism had been admitted. In April the Cominform had been dissolved, which opened the way to a reconciliation with Yugoslavia. However, there were signs that the Soviet Union was already anxious to slow down the liberalization movement, and in any event it could scarcely go so far as to accept a change which would threaten its position not only in Hungary but also, and especially in view of its mild response to the Polish situation, throughout Eastern Europe. Nevertheless Nagy opted for the revolution. On 30 October the one-party system of government was abolished, and on 1 November the Warsaw Pact was repudiated and Hungary's neutrality proclaimed. At the same time Nagy asked the UN Secretary-General to put the question of Hungary's neutrality and its defence by the four Great Powers on the Assembly's agenda. He also complained about the entry of Soviet military units into Hungary, and on 2 November asked that the Security Council should instruct the Soviet Union and Hungary to begin immediate negotiations regarding a Soviet withdrawal. Kadar, however, went the other way, and by calling on the Soviet Union for help gave it a pretext for further intervention. Soviet troops and tanks returned to Budapest on 4 November, and in a much more efficient and brutal operation crushed the revolt, installing Kadar in Nagy's place.

Britain, France, and the United States had already, on 27 October, asked the Security Council to consider the situation in Hungary, but without any tangible profit, for on 4 November the Soviet Union vetoed a resolution calling for her withdrawal. She was unable, however, to prevent the question being immediately transferred to an Emergency Special Session of the Assembly, nor that body's passage, on the same day, of a resolution similar to that which had been defeated in the Council. Additionally, the Assembly asked the Secretary-General to investigate the situation, and called upon Hungary to submit to internal observation by his representatives. Five days later the Assembly repeated its call, now including the suggestion that as soon as circumstances permitted, free elections should be held in Hungary under UN auspices. No doubt it was India's fear of seeming to compromise herself over Kashmir which converted her abstention on the resolution of 4 November into a negative vote on that of the 9th.

The attempt to conduct an on the spot investigation in Hungary was a total failure. The Secretary-General appointed a group of three—an Indian, a Norwegian, and a Colombian—to act on his behalf, but Hungary would have nothing to do with them, claiming that their admission would violate both her sovereignty and the Charter. Nor was the Soviet Union, to whom Hammarskjöld had disingenuously turned for help, willing to support the Secretary-General's efforts. He therefore suggested that he should make a personal visit to Budapest, and in an effort to get his foot in the door was prepared to limit his public agenda to humanitarian matters. But Hungary, although not ruling out a visit at a later date, was unwilling to do more than have talks with the Secretary-General in Rome or New York. This led the Assembly on 4 December to authorize the dispatch of observers to countries other than Hungary, and then, on the 12th, to request the Secretary-General to take any initiative he deemed helpful.

In January 1957, however, Mr Hammarskjöld reported that there was little which he could do. His group of three had examined the evidence, but had concluded there was little purpose in trying to assess the situation without an on-the-spot investigation. And as only one of the countries surrounding Hungary—Austria—was prepared to admit observers, the Secretary-General suggested that the present attempt at investigation should be abandoned in favour of a new group with broader terms of reference. Accordingly, on 10 January a Special Committee, composed of the representatives of Australia, Ceylon, Denmark, Tunisia, and Uruguay, was appointed to establish and maintain direct observation in Hungary and elsewhere, observation being interpreted to include the receipt and collection of evidence. The formalities were observed, and Hungary was called upon to allow the Committee to enter and travel freely. This had no bearing on Hungary's attitude towards the UN's fact-finding activities, but the Special Committee was less inhibited than the individuals whom it had superseded, and reported in June that there had been a spontaneous national uprising followed by massive armed intervention.[7]

This conclusion was endorsed by the Assembly, which, while keeping the Special Committee in being, also appointed Prince Wan Waithayakon of Thailand as its special representative on the Hungarian problem. His mandate was to further the UN's objectives as set out in the Assembly's various resolutions, but his efforts to enter Hungary were no more successful than those of his predecessors. Accordingly, in December 1958 the Assembly deplored both Hungary's un-cooperative attitude and the internal situation which the UN was not allowed to observe at first-hand, and it now appointed Sir Leslie Munro of New Zealand to keep the implementation of the Assembly's will under review. He retained this position for four years until, in December 1962, the Assembly decided that the requirements of the situation would be met by a request that the Secretary-General should take any initiative which he deemed helpful. In effect the UN was saying that the events of six years before no longer demanded official remembrance.

It is thought by some that the UN might have been able to play a very different role in relation to Hungary had it moved with

[7] In an effort to rub the point home in graphic and familiar terms, Britain's representative at the UN had, in December 1956, described the Soviet Union's behaviour in Hungary as an instance of 'real colonialism', adding hastily that it was such as 'never in fact was pursued by the Western Powers': General Assembly, *Official Records*. 615th Plenary Meeting, para. 53.

greater speed and determination at the outset of the revolt. While Nagy was still in power there would probably not have been any formal difficulties in the way of the UN's admission to Hungary, and it has been suggested that the arrival of a planeload of observers before the second Soviet intervention might have caused the Soviet Union to have second thoughts. It is exceedingly doubtful, however, whether there was any practical possibility of the UN being able to act with prophylactic effect, even had it not been so deeply involved in the Suez crisis. Few UN members would have relished arranging an anti-Soviet intervention in a country which, since 1945, had been recognized as part of the Soviet Union's exclusive sphere of influence, and in which she had just given a clear, if less than whole-hearted, demonstration of the geopolitical basis of her overlordship. Even if such a move had been organized, it is most improbable that the Soviet Union would have been deterred by the presence of a team of UN reporters. The prospect of an on-the-spot verification of an act which would in any event be widely denounced was of relatively little account when weighed against what she had to lose in Hungary.

If the UN had little hope of being able to prevent the Soviet Union asserting herself in Hungary, it had still less of securing the resignation or drastic reform of the regime which was installed as the result of Soviet intervention. The Kadar Government and its sponsor were clearly not going to be moved to repentance by an authentic exposure of their sins, nor was such an exercise likely to induce the non-Communist countries to act in a way which would bring about change. Nothing short of armed force would have had a significant impact on Hungary, and there was no question of that, whether in the name or independently of the UN. However, this did not cause the Hungarian Government to take an indifferent attitude towards the question of whether UN observers should be admitted. It was evident that they would find little to commend, and their report would thus only add to the already numerous humiliations and embarrassments which Hungary was suffering in her international relations on account of recent events. In consequence, the door was firmly closed to the UN, and remained so.

There could never have been much expectation of it being otherwise. But this did not mean that the UN's attempt to obtain damning first hand evidence regarding the Hungarian regime was without effect. There was, in general terms, no doubt as to what had happened in Hungary in November 1956. But, nevertheless, by regularly asking for permission to make its own enquiries, the UN helped to keep before the public mind the fact that 'all is far from well in

Hungary, and that the Government has much to hide'.[8] There was no hope of toppling the Kadar regime, but it could at least be morally discredited, and in this way the West was able to turn the UN's proselytizing efforts to good account. However, after some years this gambit began to lose its attraction, not just through the passage of time but also because of the liberalizing measures which the Hungarian Government gradually began to introduce once it felt itself to be firmly in control of the country's internal situation. Moreover, the easing of the cold war which occurred as the 1960s progressed has resulted in there being no further effort, in this context, to utilize the UN as an invalidating agency.

II

Besides their use to undermine metropolitan regimes, UN invalidating missions may also be employed in the hope of loosening the hold of administering powers on their non-self-governing territories. Of this there have been a number of instances in the 1960s. During the first 15 years of the UN's life, however, such attempts were rare. At that time, while it was quite widely felt that independence was the proper destiny for colonies, members were either disinclined or not in a position to use the Organization to expedite the process in any far-reaching way. If a struggle for independence assumed significant proportions, or otherwise aroused keen international concern, it would probably be debated in the Assembly. But there was a marked reluctance to take the UN's involvement in colonial issues to the extent of dispatching missions to the field.

The colonial Powers claimed that such action would be a clear infringement of the legal rule prohibiting intervention in domestic affairs, and their arguments fell on receptive ears. Many UN members were anxious not to set what could be a very disturbing precedent. More immediately, there was no desire to offend the colonialists, who were, on the whole, still states to be reckoned with. And there was little hope of mollifying them by giving a mission apparently innocuous terms of reference, such as asking it to assist in the conduct of negotiations. For, in the context of a colonial insurgency, urging negotiations is tantamount to encouraging the administering Power to make an agreed withdrawal. It also carries the implication that the colonial Power should be thinking in those terms, and so provides a ground for later criticism should he fail to move in the favoured direction. Dressing a UN operation in a conciliatory garb, in short, is by no means incompatible with the

[8] Britain's representative to the UN: General Assembly, *Official Records*, 1087th Plenary Meeting, para. 179.

intention of assisting change. Hence, even the mildest attempt on the part of the UN to associate itself with the discussion of a territory's political future could be relied upon to meet with a stern rebuff, which, in a number of eyes, only underlined the futility and unwisdom of the Organization trying to assert itself in this field.

In 1952, for example, the Assembly's First Committee defeated an Arab-Asian draft resolution recommending the renewal of negotiations between France and the 'true representatives'[9] of the Tunisian people and proposing that the process should be assisted by a good offices commission. The most which the Committee and the Assembly was prepared to accept was a milder Latin American draft which omitted the good offices proposal altogether. Eight years later the composition and temper of the Assembly had undergone a considerable change, but not to such an extent that it was ready to pass a drastic proposal regarding Algeria, which was still formally in French hands. The First Committee endorsed a resolution which would have had the Assembly 'decide that a referendum should be conducted in Algeria, organized, controlled, and supervised by the United Nations',[10] but in the Assembly's plenary sessions this clause was struck out. Similarly, in 1958, when Cyprus was being discussed, a Greek proposal which would have set up a good offices committee to assist all concerned in bringing Cyprus to independence was not pressed to a vote. And a Colombian draft proposing that the Secretary-General should set up an observation group to promote negotiations towards the same end was not adopted.

At this period the UN was also unwilling to take a very aggressive line towards South Africa, despite the fact that her racial policy of apartheid, or separate development, was giving increasing offence to a number of countries.[11] The matter was raised in the Assembly in 1952 by 13 Arab-Asian states, who contended that the situation in South Africa was not just a flagrant violation of human rights but also a threat to peace. The response which they obtained was, by later standards, relatively mild, a three-man commission being appointed to study the situation. But it was too much for South Africa, who refused to co-operate in any way. Hence the commission was unable to make an on-the-spot examination of the problem. Nevertheless, it was able to find that South Africa's racial doctrines

[9] *Yearbook of the United Nations, 1952*, p. 272.
[10] *Yearbook of the United Nations, 1960*, p. 133.
[11] Two of the three forms in which this matter came before the UN could not be described as colonialism, in the usual sense of the word, and the third did not fall squarely into that category. However, in many minds the racial issue was closely linked with colonialism, inasmuch as both were held to involve the oppression of a subject people. Accordingly, the attempts at invalidation which concerned South Africa are considered here rather than in the first section of this Chapter.

endangered both internal peace and international relations. In 1954 it produced a similar report, but in 1955 noted that South Africa was showing more flexibility in its application of apartheid. It was also the case that at this point relations between the Union and the UN were better than they had been for some time, and, reflecting the more conciliatory atmosphere, the Assembly turned down the proposal of its *ad hoc* Political Committee that the commission's life should be extended. For the next seven years the UN restricted itself to strictly verbal activity.

An issue which, originally, was more firmly within the international province, concerned South Africa's treatment of those of her population who were of Indian origin. It was raised at the Assembly's first session, but then and thereafter South Africa denied that the UN had any standing in the matter. Various calls for discussions having failed to produce a positive result, the 1951 Assembly made provision for a special commission to assist the parties in carrying through negotiations. Nothing came of this, on account of South Africa's refusal to appoint her member, and therefore in the next year a Good Office Commission was appointed. South Africa having refused to recognize it, the Assembly, in 1954, went back to recommending direct negotiations, providing that if no progress was made within six months the Secretary-General should designate a person to assist the parties. The condition was satisfied, and a Brazilian—Mr. Luis de Faro, Jr.—was appointed, but to no avail.

The question of South West Africa gave rise to a similar story. Following World War I this former German colony was placed under the mandates system, South Africa being nominated in the administering Power. With the expiration of the League she suggested that the territory should be incorporated in the Union,[12] but the Assembly refused to agree. Instead it recommended trusteeship, which was unacceptable to South Africa. There the matter stood until 1950, when the International Court of Justice advised that, while South Africa had no legal obligation to place South West Africa under trusteeship, the mandate remained in force and South Africa was obliged to submit to supervision by the UN as the League's successor. As was her right, South Africa refused to accept this opinion. However, it was endorsed by the Assembly, and provided the basis for what was to be a series of attempts by the UN to secure a new international status for South West Africa.

Negotiations on this point were entrusted to an *ad hoc* committee, but it made no progress. It was also instructed to keep South Africa's

[12] Britain's post-war Labour Government supported South Africa's suggestion. In retrospect, this provides a startling indication of the extent to which attitudes on this and allied issues were to change during the next two decades.

administration of South West Africa under review, and, receiving no co-operation, was replaced in 1953 by a committee whose terms of reference allowed its reports on conditions in the territory to be based on wider sources of information. In 1957 the committee's efforts to open negotiations with South Africa were supplemented by a less offensive Good Offices Committee, which succeeded in establishing contact with South Africa. She confirmed her earlier willingness to enter into an agreement with Britain, France, and the United States regarding her position in South West Africa, and also expressed her preparedness to consider the possibility of placing the northern part of South West Africa under trusteeship if she was allowed to annex the rest. The Good Offices Committee hoped the Assembly would encourage this idea, but it refused to do so. Its attitude was hardening, as was indicated by a 1960 instruction to the Committee on South West Africa to investigate and make proposals regarding the territory's self-government and independence. In April 1961 the Committee was told that, if necessary, it should carry out its mission without South Africa's co-operation. Unable to gain access to South West Africa it held hearings in Ghana, Tanganyika, and the United Arab Republic, and was then replaced by a Special Committee on South West Africa, which was intended to approach the matter in an even more demanding way.[13]

The Assembly's tougher line was directly related to the fact that by the end of 1960 the balance of voting power was tipping heavily in the anti-colonialists' direction, 17 new states having been admitted to the UN in that year, all but one of them African. The most dramatic and far-reaching expression of this development was the passage, on 14 December 1960, of a 'Declaration on the Granting of Independence to Colonial Countries and Peoples'. By it the Assembly proclaimed that 'The subjection of peoples to alien subjugation, domination and exploitation constitutes a denial of fundamental human rights, is contrary to the Charter of the United Nations and is an impediment to the promotion of world peace and co-operation', and went on to state that 'Immediate steps shall be taken, in trust and non-self-governing territories . . . to transfer all powers to the people of those territories, without any conditions or reservations . . . in order to enable them to enjoy complete independence and freedom'.[14] No state felt able to vote against the Declaration, although nine abstained: Australia, Belgium, Britain, Dominica, France, Portugal, Spain, South Africa, and the United States.

The Declaration immediately became the anti-colonialists' touchstone. In effect the Assembly had declared that colonies, and, by

[13] The Special Committee did not live up to this expectation. See above, p. 257.
[14] General Assembly resolution 1514 (xv).

extension, racial policies, were an international offence and therefore could no longer be regarded as an essentially domestic preserve. Accordingly, they were now fair game for those of hostile intent, and the way was open for the UN to go about the business of their invalidation without restraint. To further this purpose the Assembly established a 17-member Special Committee in 1961, and in the following year increased its membership to 24. Also in 1962 the Special Committee on South West Africa was dissolved and its functions transferred to the Committee of 24. The same thing happened to a Special Committee on Portuguese Territories which had been set up in 1961, and, a year later, to the Assembly's Committee on Information from Non-Self-Governing Territories, which, in connection with Article 73(e) of the Charter, had been in existence in one form or another since 1947.

Thus the Assembly's anti-colonial activities, other than those relating to trust territories, were now centred in the Committee of 24. It has collected information regarding the territories under its purview, received and considered written petitions,[15] and has been prepared to hear petitioners. It has sent out visiting missions in respect of particular territories or situations, and has held meetings in the field in 1962 and annually since 1965. They have been justified on the ground that 'by reason of its proximity'[16] to territories to which it was denied access, the Committee 'would be in closer contact with the realities of the situation, and would be afforded more direct knowledge of the aspirations of the peoples'.[17] This was a reminder that in form the Committee existed to investigate and report on the facts, but there was no doubt about the invalidating purpose of its activities. In April 1967, for example, it was explained that the Committee's forthcoming journeys to Africa and the Middle East[18] would underline 'the active solidarity of the UN with the colonial peoples in their legitimate struggle' and increase the Organization's capacity 'to assist these peoples in realizing their aspirations'.[19]

There was little chance that these activities would have a direct or immediate bearing on the attitude of the colonial Powers towards

[15] But only those which were petitioning in the right direction. In March 1967 the Committee refused to circulate petitions from Aden which included allegations of interference in the territory's affairs by the United Arab Republic. It took a similar decision in October 1967 regarding petitions from Gibraltar which were critical of Spain.
[16] The Chairman of the Committee of 24, quoted in *International Conciliation*, No. 559 (September 1966), 'Issues before the 21st General Assembly', p. 57.
[17] *International Conciliation*, ibid.
[18] The Middle Eastern part of its itinerary was later postponed on account of the Arab–Israeli crisis.
[19] *International Conciliation*, No. 564 (September 1967), 'Issues before the 22nd General Assembly', p. 57.

the continuation of their rule. Nor has their reluctance to allow the UN to send investigation teams to their overseas territories been swept away. To extend such co-operation would generally be to ask for trouble, for a critical report can almost be relied upon. Hence, in 1963, when the internal situation in British Guiana was beginning to deteriorate, Britain would not allow the Special Committee of 24 to accept an (unauthorized) invitation which had been extended to it by the territory's Prime Minister, Dr Jagan. A year later the Committee itself decided to send a good offices subcommittee there, but to no avail, as Britain once again vetoed the visit. In 1967 Britain rebuffed an attempt by the Special Committee to send a mission to Fiji. And in the same year, when a controversial referendum was held in French Somaliland to find out whether it wished to remain a part of France, there was no question of the Assembly's call for the presence of UN observers being accepted.[20]

Undoubtedly, however, since 1960 there has been a marked change in the atmosphere which surrounds colonial issues. Now they are widely regarded as very much in the international domain, and the principle that all dependent territories should become independent at the earliest possible date is rarely questioned. It is not implausible to attribute this in large measure to the UN's persistent invalidating efforts. Moreover, the impact of the UN's campaign does not seem to have been confined to those without responsibility for non self-governing territories, for some of the colonial Powers have themselves made notable reassessments of the Organization's competence in this field. Even in the matter of the UN's attempt to get its foot, literally speaking, into the colonial door, there have been developments which would have been virtually inconceivable a decade earlier.

One case in which this occurred was that of Oman, an area which lies in the interior of the Sultanate of Muscat and Oman. The Sultanate is a sovereign state, but plays virtually no part in international affairs and enjoys a close treaty relationship with Britain. When, therefore, in 1957, there was a rebellion in favour of the Imam of Oman, backed, so it was said, from abroad, the Sultan was able to obtain help from Britain in putting it down. This led to the Arab states complaining to the Security Council about British aggression in Oman, but the Council defeated the attempt to have the matter put on its agenda. After an interval of three years, however, the question was raised in the Assembly, and a resolution was introduced recognizing the right of the people of Oman to self-

[20] The clause containing this proposal was voted on separately. Although 39 states abstained, only two voted against it. The number in favour was 72.

determination and independence, and calling for the withdrawal
of foreign forces. On account of a lack of time the matter was deferred, but this was not a sign that it was to be generally forgotten.
Indeed, it emerged that the issue was only now getting under way.
In 1961 the situation was pictured as a colonial war of aggression
inspired by a greed for oil, and a condemnatory resolution only
narrowly failed of adoption. In the following year it looked as
though such a resolution was going to get through, but Britain managed to avert it. Earlier in the debate reference had been made to
the lack of clear information, and before a vote was taken Britain
was able to announce that, while preserving his position, the Sultan
was prepared to invite, on a personal basis, a representative of the
Secretary-General to obtain first-hand information. Such an
arrangement was not a very promising one from the point of view
of those interested in invalidation, for it suggested that an individual,
non-partisan enquiry would find that the Sultan had little to hide.
And so it proved. A Swedish diplomat, Mr H. de Ribbing, was
appointed, and found no evidence of active warfare since 1959.
Moreover, he reported that many of those he interviewed did not
want the Imam to return, while others had no objection provided
he made his peace with the Sultan.

   This was not what the anti-colonialists had been wanting, and
accordingly they set about trying to rectify the record. An Afro-
Asian draft resolution proposed that the Committee of 24 be asked
to examine the situation, but this did not commend itself in all
quarters, and possibly the Afro-Asians had second thoughts about it.
Such action would imply that Oman was a colonial issue, which was
not only contrary to Britain's emphatic account of the case but might
also set a disturbing example of how to get a minority problem on the
UN's agenda. There was, however, a feeling that the UN could
do with a fuller account of the situation in Oman, linked in many
minds, no doubt, with the suspicion that Mr de Ribbing's report
was too good to be true. Thus there was very widespread support
for a Latin American suggestion that enquiries be made by an *ad hoc*
committee. The Afro-Asian draft was not proceeded with, and, in
December 1963, the Latin-American proposal was passed with 96
votes in its favour. Britain was in lone opposition, and there were just
four abstentions: Afghanistan, France, Portugal, and the United
States.

   The new body, made up of the representatives of Afghanistan,
Costa Rica, Nepal, Nigeria, and Senegal, could be relied upon not to
misconstrue the situation, and although it was not allowed into
Muscat and Oman it travelled widely in pursuit of truth. The Sultan
agreed to meet one of its members in London, and in Saudi Arabia

it met the Imam. It also worked in New York, Cairo, and Kuwait. Its conclusion was that there was an autonomous political entity in Oman, and that imperialistic policies and foreign intervention there had given rise to a serious international problem. It called for negotiations and proposed that they should be assisted by a UN good offices committee.

In, to use the official jargon, 'the special circumstances prevailing during the first part' of its 19th session, the Assembly was able to do no more than take note of this report. However, once the voting crisis had been solved, the Assembly, in December 1965, called on Britain to cease her oppressive action against the people of Oman and eliminate her domination. The question was now officially determined to be one of colonialism, and was therefore passed to the Committee of 24 for detailed examination. In December 1966 and again a year later Britain was condemned by the Assembly, and the inalienable right of the people of Oman to self-determination and independence was reaffirmed. By now it seemed that the 'people of Oman' included those of the coastal areas as well as the interior, for the Imam was claiming authority over the entire country of Muscat and Oman, as well as, for good measure, the adjoining Trucial States of the Persian Gulf. Possibly he could find some historical justification for these claims, for the history of the Imamate went back to the eighth century, while that of the Sultanate dated only from the last years of the eighteenth. In this light, it might have seemed strange that he should receive the support of the progressive forces of Arab nationalism. But the Imam is the best local challenger of Britain's position which the Arabs have. 'The enemy of my enemy is my friend.'

The willingness of the Sultan of Muscat and Oman to admit a UN representative to his country and then to discuss its affairs in London with a UN committee member was not calculated to provide the best ammunition for the Organization's invalidating designs. Nevertheless, the significance of these concessions was not inconsiderable, for they infringed the principle of not allowing the UN to pry into what the potential host regards as its private domain. Another instance of a move in the same direction concerns Southern Rhodesia. It had been internally self-governing since 1923, and Britain therefore maintained that she had no power to interfere in its domestic affairs. She also argued that the UN had no right to pass resolutions regarding the colony. Yet, in 1962, she decided to co-operate with the Assembly's enquiry into its status to the extent of holding discussions in London with a UN mission. On the basis of its report, the Assembly decided that Southern Rhodesia was a non-self-governing territory, and specified a number of far-reaching measures which it wanted Britain to take. Even this, however, did not stop Britain from agreeing to hold official talks in London with the representatives of the Committee of 24 in 1963 and again in 1964.[21]

The following year, 1965, saw the first occasion on which the UN was allowed to supervise a colony's decision regarding its future. The invitation to do so was issued by New Zealand in respect of the Cook Islands, which were widely scattered throughout an area of some 850,000 square miles in the South Pacific, and contained a population of about 20,000. The islanders were to vote for a new parliament, the first act of which would be to decide on a draft constitution which provided for full internal self-government and voluntary association with New Zealand. It also permitted the Cook Islanders to change their status at any time in whatever way they wanted. New Zealand suggested that the elections be supervised by the UN, and in February 1965 the Assembly authorized the appointment of a UN representative. Mr O. A. H. Adeel was named to fill the position, and he reported that the elections were properly and fairly conducted and with an awareness of the issue. The new Constitution came into force in August, and in December the Assembly gave the whole process its blessing, removing the Cook Islands from the category of territories on which it required periodic information. It affirmed, however, its responsibility and readiness to help the Cook Islands to amend its status in the direction of greater independence whenever it wished to do so.

Not everyone was entirely happy about the UN's part in this affair. In some quarters there was an apprehension that, in similar circumstances in the future other administering authorities would be under some pressure to follow New Zealand's example. Accordingly, Australia, Britain, France, and the United States all put on record their understanding that the UN's action was not to be regarded as a precedent. This, however, did not stop the UN from regarding it as such, and from now on the Organization's invalidating efforts included an insistence that it should supervise the various landmarks along a territory's path to independence. Thus, Spain, in 1966, earned a good mark by allowing a subcommittee of the Committee of 24 to visit Equatorial Guinea. Possibly the thought that this might help to win the Committee's support for her claims to Gibraltar was not entirely absent from her mind.

But the biggest turnabout regarding the UN's attempts to accelerate imperial disintegration concerned Aden and South Arabia. Britain's interest in having a secure port at the mouth of the Red Sea had led to the establishment of the colony of Aden in the

---

[21] For the UN's action after Rhodesia's unilateral declaration of independence in 1965, see below, pp. 406–410.

nineteenth century, and this was followed by treaties of protection
with the tribal rulers of the poor and sparsely populated areas to the
north and east. In 1959 six of the latter were persuaded to set up a
Federation of South Arabia; others joined later; and in January
1963 the urbanized and relatively prosperous colony of Aden
acceded. It was Britain's hope here, as in Central Africa and the
West Indies, that the federal device would lead to the establishment of a more or less viable unit, and so permit her eventual
withdrawal.

This series of events gave the UN's Special Committee of 24 a
double interest in the territory. Firstly, it was anxious to speed the
lifting of the colonial yoke. And, secondly, it wanted to ensure that
when South Arabia came to independence it did so with a more
satisfactory government than that which, dominated by the representatives of the feudal hinterland rather than the anti-British
nationalists of Aden, then spoke for the Federation. Thus in 1963 a
subcommittee was set up to engage in political investigation in the
territory, but, refused entry by Britain, had to content itself with
hearing petitioners in various Arab countries. This led to a General
Assembly resolution of 11 December 1963 calling for the establishment, prior to independence, of a representative government on the
basis of general elections, and requesting the Secretary-General to
arrange for an effective UN presence before and during the electoral
process. The Assembly also requested the repeal of certain laws,
the release of political prisoners and the return of political exiles,
the ending of all repressive action, and the removal of Britain's
military base. To these demands Britain and the Federal Government reacted very coolly. The nationalists, on the other hand, used
the resolution as a rallying cry, and the authorities failure to implement it set off sporadic acts of terrorism.

In 1964 a subcommittee of the Special Committee made another
unsuccessful attempt to visit South Arabia. Meanwhile, Britain had
set 1968 as the date for her withdrawal, but her subsequent failure
to bring the Federal and Aden representatives together in a constitutional conference, together with mounting terrorism, boded ill for
this goal. As a result she began to reconsider her view as to the
UN's proper role in respect of this case. To allow the Organization
into the Federation was offensive on general principles, and would
also increase the pressure for the giving up of her base at Aden. But
in the eyes of Britain's new Labour Government these arguments
were becoming overshadowed by the undesirability of having to
postpone her withdrawal or go in circumstances which threatened
the area's stability. Moreover her policy regarding the base was
being reviewed, and in February 1966 she announced that it would

not be retained after South Arabia had become independent. Thus the balance was tipping towards the involvement of the UN in the hope of achieving an orderly departure. Once Britain was moving in this direction the Federal Government was hardly in a position to do otherwise, for its local weakness did not permit it to incur Britain's grave displeasure. Accordingly, in May 1966, possibly stimulated by reports that a South Arabian government-in-Exile was about to be established, the Federation announced its acceptance of the UN's resolutions and its intention of discussing their implementation at an early conference with all interested parties. The Special Committee then recommended the appointment of a UN mission to Aden to recommend the steps which would be necessary in order to implement the Organization's will regarding the territory and to determine the UN's role in the preparation and supervision of elections. In August Britain agreed to invite a mission on these terms, subject to agreement regarding its composition, and on 12 December the Assembly authorized its establishment.[22]

However, contention regarding the UN's involvement was by no means over, and there was an immediate difficulty over the composition of the mission. Britain, strongly supported by the Federal Government, was opposed to it being wholly extremist in tone. As her representative put it, she did not wish to exclude those who had served on the Committee of 24, but thought the Secretary-General 'should not be restricted in any way in the selection of the strongest possible team'.[23] Eventually, on 23 February 1967, it was announced that the mission would be made up of Mr M. Perez-Guerrero of Venezuela, as Chairman, Mr A. S. Shalizi of Afghanistan, and Mr M. L. Keita of Mali. Its prospects, however, were not the brightest, for, after having urged UN intervention for several years, the nationalists had greeted the acceptance of their demand with derision. Doubtless they calculated that they now had Britain and the Federal Government on the run, and that a hard line was the most profitable for them. Thus they said they would have nothing to do with the mission, beyond acknowledging its arrival by demonstrations of strength. And the mission itself refused to have any contacts whatsoever with the Federal Government, which hardly facilitated its work.

The result was a fiasco. The mission arrived in Aden on 2 April for what was expected to be a visit of several weeks. Its hotel was surrounded by barbed wire, and its one significant excursion, to a

[22] The Assembly's resolution of the previous year, passed on 5 November 1965, had requested the Secretary-General to take such action as he deemed expedient to ensure its implementation. He subsequently appointed a personal representative on South Arabia, Mr S. O. Adeel.

[23] *UN Monthly Chronicle*, January 1967, p. 91.

camp for political detainees, was vastly less than successful: the prisoners would not talk, and on its return to Aden it came under fire. It then proposed to criticize its hosts on television, and on being refused permission by the Federal Government, flounced out of the territory after some improbable scenes at the airport. Alarmed by the incipient failure of the attempt to get the UN to facilitate his country's withdrawal, Britain's Foreign Secretary immediately invited the mission to meet him in London, and it did so. But by this point all the acknowledged parties were beginning to be outstripped by the passage of events.

The leading nationalist party in South Arabia was the Front for the Liberation of Occupied South Yemen (FLOSY). It had its headquarters in neighbouring Yemen, drew its inspiration from Cairo, and had the support of most Arab and several other states. But during 1967 a locally based movement, the National Liberation Front (NLF), which was critical of FLOSY's Egyptian connection, assumed a much more prominent role. The weakness of the Federal Government was emphasized by a mutiny in its army in June; FLOSY's prospects were to a considerable extent undermined by the UAR's renewed and much more credible commitment to withdraw from the Yemen; and by the end of August the NLF was claiming control of a majority of the states of the Federation. Talks between FLOSY and the NLF were subsequently held in Cairo, but broke down early in November just as the NLF was tightening its hold on South Arabia and Britain was announcing that instead of leaving on 9 January 1968 she would be gone before the end of the month. The South Arabian Army got on the NLF band-wagon, and on 30 November, only hours after Britain and the NLF had signed an agreement in Geneva regarding the transfer of power, the new People's Republic of the Southern Yemen came into being.

Thus, despite the fact that its efforts were invited by those whom it wished to overturn, the UN's attempt to play an important proselytizing role was frustrated. Nor was the outcome just as it would have liked, for FLOSY's international connections meant that the UN's sympathies were with it rather than the NLF. Hence the report of the UN mission to Aden, dated 10 November 1967, insisted that a representative South Arabian Government, while having nothing to do with the sultans of the hinterland, must include members of both the NLF and FLOSY. But the failure of events to produce such a result did not worry most UN members. The political tide had moved in the right direction, and the Organization therefore forgot its previous insistence that independence must be preceded by elections and admitted the new state to membership on 14 December 1967. It did so after having already affirmed the unity and integrity of the whole territory, a side swipe at Britain. For, although the islands of Kamaran and Perim[24] had been handed over to Southern Yemen, Britain had transferred the Kuria Muria Islands to the Sultan of Muscat after consulting their 78 inhabitants. This decision could be justified on two grounds other than that of self-determination, for the islands lay off shore from Muscat and not Southern Yemen, and had been owned by the Sultan until their cession to Britain in 1854. However, they had been administered from Aden as a matter of convenience and were therefore regarded by the NLF regime as part of its rightful inheritance.

The question of the Kuria Muria Islands will doubtless not be forgotten. Nevertheless, Britain could regard herself as relatively fortunate in the way in which Aden and the former Aden Protectorates were eventually disposed of. The invocation of the UN's help had been a failure, and this particular imperial withdrawal was neither smooth nor noticeable for its dignity. But, at least so far as its immediate aftermath was concerned, it could not be counted a disaster. Anything of the nature of a second Palestine, which was increasingly feared in many quarters as 1967 advanced, had been avoided, though more by luck than judgment.

Britain's willingness to admit a UN mission to South Arabia was to a large extent indicative of the extent of her predicament there. It may also, however, have partly reflected the consideration that, except for the special case of Rhodesia, it was the last of her major colonial responsibilities. As a precedent, therefore, Britain's concession was much less dangerous than it would have been some years earlier. Even, however, in 1961, when the Special Committee was established, by far the larger part of the British and most other colonial empires had already been liquidated. The Committee's creation, in fact, was in no small measure attributable to this development, the new states using their numerical strength in the Assembly to try to speed up the movement which was responsible for their birth. Thus for much of the time the Committee was pushing at what was perhaps a creaky but nevertheless an open door.

In this task the Committee was assiduous, compiling, in 1966, a list of 55 territories which required its attention. It was also usually reluctant to let a territory go unless it severed all ties with the metropolitan Power and expressed its decision to that effect in a manner which was wholly satisfactory to the Committee. In March 1967, for example, it refused to accept that the 'associated statehood' which Britain was granting to six Caribbean entities was sufficient to remove them from its purview. Britain had negotiated with the

[24] See above, pp. 342–345.

political leaders in each case, but this was not enough for the Committee, which emphasized the importance of holding referenda under UN supervision. As a result of this decision Britain has refused to take any substantive part in the Committee's subsequent consideration of the issue. In the case of Gibraltar, however, where it was clear that a majority favoured continued association with Britain, the Special Committee opposed Britain's intention to hold a referendum and called for the renewal of negotiations between Britain and Spain 'with a view to putting to an end the colonial situation in Gibraltar'.[25] The referendum having gone ahead under Commonwealth supervision and produced the expected result, the General Assembly, in December 1967, criticized Britain's contravention of the UN's will and repeated the Special Committee's call for negotiations and its description of their purpose.

These issues, however, like virtually all the others on the Committee's list, represented the crumbs in the colonial barrel, territories which, generally on account of their smallness, weakness, or isolation, could not or would not be brought into full membership of the international society. By the late 1960s, in fact, the only substantial targets for the UN's proselytizing activities were to be found in southern Africa: South Africa itself, and the associated problem of South West Africa, and the Portuguese possessions of Angola and Mozambique. Together with Portugal's other scattered overseas territories in Africa and the Far East, they became known, on account of the unyielding attitude of the states concerned, as the 'hard core' colonial (and racial) areas.

The first serious move against Portugal was made in March 1961, when the Security Council was asked to set up a subcommittee to examine the situation in Angola. The proposal received an insufficient number of votes, but in the following months its sponsors had no difficulty in persuading the Assembly to establish such a body. In December of the same year the Assembly decided to extend its enquiries to all Portugal's overseas territories, setting up a Special Committee for the purpose. Portugal would not allow it to make on-the-spot investigations, but at this time her attitude was not wholly negative. In 1961 the Chairman of the Angolan subcommittee had visited Lisbon, by invitation, and in 1962, as the result of high level negotiations with the United States, Portugal agreed to support a resolution requesting the President of the General Assembly to appoint two UN representatives, one for the purpose of gathering information on conditions in Angola and the other in Mozambique. The United States presented a resolution in these terms to the Assembly in December, but, in the light of the opposition of the anti-

[25] *UN Monthly Chronicle*, August–September 1967, p. 48.

colonialist group, did not press it to a vote. On behalf of the Afro-Asians it was argued that the resolution contained important omissions, which was another way of saying that an enquiry by an individual might come up with quite the wrong sort of result. Instead the Assembly passed two far-reaching and condemnatory resolutions which required Portugal's withdrawal from her colonies, and entrusted the UN's responsibility for securing this result to the Special Committee of 24.[26]

By means of accepting petitions, hearing petitioners, holding meetings in nearby territories, and filing critical reports, the Special Committee endeavoured to fulfil its mandate of bringing about Portugal's colonial downfall. The Security Council was also brought into the picture. In 1963 it determined that the situation in these areas was seriously disturbing peace and security in Africa and urged Portugal to do as she was told by the Assembly. It repeated this view in 1965, but both then and later the anti-colonialists failed to persuade the Council to impose sanctions on Portugal under Chapter VII of the Charter. All they could obtain were Assembly resolutions urging members to take various measures. However, Portugal would have nothing to do with the Special Committee, was unresponsive to the UN's calls, and if they led members to bring pressure on her, it had no obvious results. The UN's efforts with regard to Portugal were, in short, becoming a recipe for frustration.

The same might be said of the Organization's activities concerning South Africa. In 1962 the Assembly combined the two items of race conflict in South Africa and that country's treatment of people of Indian origin, and called on members to take various measures against South Africa. It also established a Special Committee to keep her racial policy under review and asked the Security Council to take measures, including sanctions, to secure South Africa's compliance with the UN's will. The Council, however, was not prepared to go this far, and the activities of the Special Committee and the UN's critical resolutions had no effect on the state they were intended to influence. In an endeavour to bring pressure on those UN members who were best placed to twist South Africa's arm, the Assembly decided in 1965 to enlarge the 11-member Special Committee so as to include the Great Powers and South Africa's major trading partners. The states concerned, however, were noticeably lacking in enthusiasm to join the Committee. Informal approaches having proved fruitless, 19 states were formally requested to consider membership, but this did not advance the matter. Of the 17 replies which were received, 14 were negative, including

[26] The Special Committee on Portuguese Territories was dissolved. The subcommittee on Angola adjourned *sine die*.

those from Britain, France, and the United States, and two conditional. The only state who was willing to live up to the majority's idea about the responsibilities of power was the Soviet Union. The Special Committee appealed for the reconsideration of these replies, but to no avail. The Assembly therefore had to return to passing resolutions, and supplemented this activity with a campaign to publicize the evils of apartheid through the holding of international 'seminars' and the establishment of a special unit within the Secretariat.

The UN was no more successful in its efforts to persuade or shame South Africa into giving up South West Africa. Its Chairman and Vice-Chairman having disgraced themselves,[27] the Special Committee for South West Africa which had been set up in 1961 was dissolved in the following year, and its functions transferred to the Special Committee of 24. While the International Court of Justice was hearing the South West Africa case, things were relatively quiet on this front. But following the Court's July 1966 refusal to rule on the applicant's claims, the question came to the forefront of the UN's deliberations. In October 1966 the Assembly declared that South Africa's mandate had come to an end and that henceforth South West Africa was the UN's direct responsibility. A committee was appointed to recommend a scheme for the territory's international administration, but was unable to agree. One group of members wanted to tell South Africa to leave and to impose sanctions if she didn't; another favoured the making of an agreement with South Africa regarding the transfer of authority; and a third urged the appointment of a special representative to gather information and make contacts. The Soviet Union was opposed to any transitional UN authority, wanting immediate independence for South West Africa. These alternatives were debated for three weeks at a Special Session of the Assembly before a compromise was worked out. It provided for the appointment of an 11-member Council for South West Africa which was to enter into contact with South Africa to lay down procedures for the territory's transfer to the UN. Until it became independent, and it was hoped that this would not be later than June 1968, the UN Council was to administer South West Africa, delegating such executive and administrative tasks as it thought fit to a UN Commissioner, who was to be elected by the Assembly on the Secretary-General's nomination. The compromise avoided any mention of sanctions.

The resolution to this effect was passed on 19 May 1967. Only two states voted against it, but the 30 abstainers included Britain, France, and the United States, as well as the Soviet Union. This in

[27] See above, p. 257.

itself suggested that the Assembly's decision might be difficult to implement, which proved to be the case. The Council for South West Africa was appointed, but the office of UN Commissioner was hard to fill. A willing candidate of the right standing not having been found, the head of the legal section of the UN Secretariat, Mr C. Stavroupoulos, was nominated to serve as Acting Commissioner, and in December 1967 the Assembly approved the continuation of this arrangement. At the same time South Africa was condemned for her refusal to comply with the Assembly's resolutions and called upon to withdraw from South West Africa unconditionally and without delay. The Security Council was asked to take measures which would allow the UN to play the role for which it had cast itself. The Great Powers failed to oblige the Assembly, but nevertheless it was announced on 1 April 1968 that the South West Africa Council would shortly take the first step towards fulfilling its mandate by travelling to Zambia and Tanzania. It got no further, and reported that force would be necessary to secure South Africa's withdrawal from South West Africa, warning that there was a threat of racial war in the territory unless the UN got in first with a war of liberation. Accordingly, it recommended that the General Assembly should reiterate its request to the Security Council 'to take effective measures to insure the immediate removal of South Africa's presence',[28] and the Assembly obliged on 12 June. The resolution received 96 votes in its favour, but as the 28 abstainers included Britain, France, and the United States, it was evident that the majority's wishes were still some considerable way from fulfilment.

The inability of the UN to make any impact on Portugal and South Africa is indicative of the limitations of invalidation as a means of change. It is easily embarked upon, and usually it is not difficult to add authority to the process by gathering evidence in the field, even if there is little chance of being able to make enquiries within the territories in question. But on the one hand, this will be a case of preaching to the converted, and on the other, those at whom the tactic is aimed are unlikely to be impressed by it. If they are in any event planning to leave, they may expedite their departure in order to avoid unnecessary trouble. But if they are not, there is little chance that they will change their minds on account of their position having been, in the eyes of the majority, morally undermined. Physically, it will remain intact. Accordingly, when invalidation has failed to produce results, those who are deeply committed to the cause have sometimes tried to secure the employment of a more promising proselytizing device: coercion.

28 UN Document A/7088, para. 63.

Chapter 11

Coercion

THE exercise of economic or, at the ultimate point, physical pressure appears to be an infinitely more effective way of undermining regimes than placing them in that moral obloquy which, hopefully, is associated with the process of invalidation. Accordingly, such sanctions have considerable appeal to those who are anxious to embark on a crusade. It might, however, be a matter for surprise that a question should be so much as raised as to the likelihood of such an activity being undertaken in the name of the UN, for the doctrine of the Charter sets its face firmly against the use of tangible proselytizing pressures.[1] Note is taken of the importance of change, but the prime ground rule of the post-1945 era is expressed in the obligation laid on all members 'to refrain in their international relations from the threat or use of force against the territorial integrity or political independence of any state'.[2] Force is, in fact, permissible only in individual or collective self-defence, and it has been influentially argued that this category does not even include the defence of legal rights if they do not relate to a state's existence or independence. Quite apart from the legal position, however, the UN, on first sight, seems an improbable exponent of coercive proselytism. It was, after all, its evident inability to fight against aggression which led to the collapse of its scheme for collective security, and to much closer attention being given to non-violent UN operations. If it was beyond the Organization's capacity to arrange for the deployment of armed force in response to an attack by one country on another, it might seem even less likely that it would take the initiative in an attempt to overthrow an obnoxious regime.

In principle, however, there was no reason why the UN should

[1] In an ideological context, the use of force for defensive purposes can easily acquire a proselytizing character, resulting from a desire not just to repulse aggression but also, at the least, to overthrow the aggressive regime. Such impulses were present during World War II, and may also be seen in the UN's crossing of the 38th parallel in Korea in the hope of unifying the country under a non-Communist regime. However, collective security is, in principle, a prophylactic exercise, being an attempt to deter aggression and, in the event of its failure to do so, to restore the *status quo ante*. The rationale of the imposition of economic sanctions on Italy in 1935–6 (although not the actual measures taken) is a good example of this.
[2] UN Charter, Article 2, para. 4.

not have served as a vehicle for collective security. Nor was its failure to do so a reflection of the view that it was improper to use force for defensive purposes. Rather, it was a particular case of the general proposition that the practical difficulties of arranging for mutual defence are in inverse proportion to the size of the group involved. Further, in this instance the position was aggravated by the tense political situation of the post-war period and the procedural character of the security plan which had been adopted in 1945. The organization of force for offensive purposes meets similar problems, usually in a heightened form. But there is no ground for supposing that, in political terms, the UN is inherently unsuitable for this purpose, and much interest is currently being taken in the possibility of its engaging in coercive proselytism.

I

This is due to three reasons. In the first place, the prevailing view regarding the legitimacy of force has, in one respect, undergone radical amendment since 1945. The Charter's elevation of order above change, or, to use a more exalted formulation, peace above justice, was perhaps somewhat ahead of its time, as is the manner of such documents. But it was in keeping with the trend of ideas about international behaviour, and subsequent events have substantially increased the esteem in which the principle is held. However, it has also received a major qualification in regard to those situations which are deemed to offend the 'right of self-determination', for it is now quite widely held that their rectification, by force if necessary, is the world community's business. This approach threatens stability less than it might, for there is general opposition to the raising of questions at the international level regarding the treatment meted out by independent states to their own minorities. The chief potential victims, therefore, are those non-self-governing territories which are refused sovereign statehood by their metropolitan superiors, and those countries where a coloured majority is denied power by a white minority, i.e. Portugal's colonies—principally Angola and Mozambique—and South Africa.

Secondly, these two countries have become increasingly isolated. Both have close associations with the West, but the argument for their condemnation has become so convincing, or popular, that there is now hardly a voice to be heard in the international society speaking up in their defence, not even on the procedural ground that a country's colonial or racial policies are its own affair. In political terms, they have become expendable. Thus the UN will not be prevented from moving against them on account of sympathy for their policies or the support they can muster, which makes it a promising body for those who do not rule out the use of force to secure change. But, in the third place, and very importantly, those in the proselytizing van have not turned to the UN just, or even chiefly, to legitimize their campaign. What they want from the world organization is power, the power which is held by its chief members. For one of the crucial controlling factors in the crusade against Portugal and South Africa is that the states who are most zealous in identifying and condemning sin do not possess the wherewithal for its eradication. Unlike those who felt themselves threatened in the post-1945 period, they are not in a position to satisfy their wants by private arrangements. Accordingly, the UN has become their best hope.

Before coercion can be channelled through the UN, however, it is politically necessary to show that the Organization is legally entitled to engage in such activity. In this connection the Charter's prohibition on the use of force for other than defensive purposes might have been thought a considerable obstacle. But it has not proved so. For it has been discovered that Portugal and South Africa, by their colonial and racial policies, are themselves presenting a threat to the peace, and are therefore liable to those pressures which, under Chapter VII, the Charter allows the UN to take in order to repel 'threats to the peace, breaches of the peace, and acts of aggression'. This was not at all the kind of danger which the Charter makers had in mind when they fashioned Chapter VII. Using the criteria of 1945, it is those states who wish to move against colonialism and racialism who stand in need of discipline. But, in accordance with contemporary thinking, on which it has itself had by far the greatest influence, the UN has stood the 1945 theory on its head, and the new orthodoxy has it that policies such as those of Portugal and South Africa represent 'permanent aggression'. To put it differently, justice, in some of its aspects, is now regarded as more important than peace. This is upsetting to those who lay stress on the importance of a strict interpretation of legal rights and duties. But, in the widest political terms, it can be argued that an institution must develop in accordance with its members' will if it is not to disintegrate. And there is a real sense in which Portugal and South Africa might threaten peace, by behaving in so abhorrent a manner as to provoke thoughts of violent and far-reaching intervention. In which case it is arguable that the cause of order is, on balance, best served by inducing them to reform, and, if necessary, using internationally organized pressures to force them to do so.

A difficulty about this latter argument, however, is that those who are most provoked are unable to present a serious threat to their provokers, so there is no question of others having to join their campaign in order to keep it under some control. Nor do the more powerful members of the international society show any sign of wanting, on their own initiative, to take any drastic action. And the weakness of the more militant also means that they are unable to induce a change of mind in their more powerful fellows. They have been able to secure general assent to the argument that unrepentant colonialism and apartheid present a threat to peace, but beyond that the crusaders have not made any headway. The result has been much talk but no effective action. Thus the General Assembly now makes an annual request to members to take various measures against Portugal, such as, to take an extract from the most recent example, to desist from supplying her with weapons and military equipment. This resolution was passed on 17 November 1967 by 82 votes to 7 with 21 abstentions. The numerical majority is impressive, but the Soviet Union and China were the only permanent members of the Council to vote for the resolution, and all efforts to get the Council to take mandatory action under Chapter VII have been unsuccessful. Likewise in respect of South Africa, the Assembly has appealed to members to cease economic and military collaboration with her, and, on 13 December 1967, by 89 votes to 2 with 12 states abstaining, asked the Security Council to take effective measures to secure the abandonment of apartheid. There is no indication, however, that the latest Assembly call for action will be any more successful than its earlier ones. Nor is it likely that the desired result will be achieved by the Assembly's June 1968 request that the Council remove South Africa from South West Africa.[3]

It is sometimes argued that these problems could be solved by universally applied economic sanctions, a view which was expressed by the Assembly in its South African resolution of December 1967. Even, however, if the assumption is granted, a total economic boycott would also require extra-economic measures to ensure its effectiveness. This, it would seem, is no obstacle at all to the Soviet Union, but her vociferousness has to be considered in the light of the doubt which exists as to her desire and suitability for a major economic or military role against the territories of southern Africa. Best fitted for it are two other permanent members of the Security Council, Britain and the United States. But the very considerable costs of putting South Africa, Angola, and Mozambique in complete economic isolation, let alone of more drastic measures, deprive the Western Powers of any enthusiasm for such enterprises. Doubtless they are also influenced in the same direction by certain emotional

[3] See above, pp. 400–401.

o

and political considerations. Conceivably, under continuing Afro-Asian pressure, Britain and the United States might alter their attitude, and the possibility that France might follow suit cannot be excluded, especially under a post de Gaulle regime. Or one or other of the beleaguered countries might find itself in serious internal trouble, or engage in some very provocative act, providing an opportunity or excuse for UN action which the Western members of the Council might find it embarrassing not to support and certainly to oppose. But such contingencies are less rather than more probable, making it unlikely that the despised and rejected states will soon have to reckon with a coercive UN crusade.[4]

Action of a related kind, however, has been taken by the UN in respect of Rhodesia. Political power in this British territory of about four and a half million people was firmly in the hands of its 250,000 whites, and on 11 November 1965 the minority regime, led by Prime Minister Ian Smith, declared it an independent sovereign state. Until this point Britain had maintained, more or less consistently, that as Rhodesia was internally self-governing it was no concern of the UN's. Now, however, she changed her line.

She still claimed final responsibility for the territory, but allowed that the UN had a legitimate interest in the new situation, a move which represented a concession to the almost inevitable, a bid to obtain support in her effort to restore Rhodesia to the fold, and an attempt to keep the anti-Rhodesian initiative in her own hands. The General Assembly had been very quick off the mark, condemning Rhodesia on the very day on which she announced her birth. On 12 November Britain herself took the matter to the Security Council, which immediately followed the Assembly's example. Then, on 20 November, the Council called on Britain to bring the secessionist regime to an immediate end and on all UN members to institute an embargo on the export of oil and petroleum products to Rhodesia. This important commodity normally reached the land-locked territory by way of a pipeline which ran from the port of Beira in the Portuguese territory of Mozambique. When, therefore, in the following April, two oil tankers with cargoes thought to be bound for Rhodesia appeared off Beira, there was international consternation. The UN's Special Committee on colonialism called on the Secretary-General to request the Security Council

---

[4] It is still possible that tough action might be taken against Portugal or South Africa outside the UN, although the obvious spearhead, the African subversive movement, does not seem at all in good shape. Nor can it be ruled out that under Salazar's successor Portugal might become less inflexible. There is not a scrap of evidence, however, which suggests that peaceful political developments will bring about a substantial modification of South Africa's position.

to take mandatory action, but Britain managed to get in first with a request for an urgent Council meeting. On 9 April 1966 the Council declared that the situation constituted a threat to peace, called on Portugal not to allow any oil to pass to Rhodesia, and on Britain to prevent, 'by the use of force if necessary' the arrival of vessels 'reasonably believed' to be transporting oil for Rhodesia.[5] Moreover, in respect of the tanker which had by now entered Beira, the *Joanna V*, Britain was empowered to arrest and detain it on leaving if its oil had been discharged. The resolution was passed without opposition, but five members abstained, including France and the Soviet Union.

Thus the Council authorized Britain to take action which would otherwise have been of very questionable legality.[6] It led to the establishment of a blockade off the East African coast, which was at first maintained by an aircraft carrier, and, subsequently, by two frigates supported by long-range aircraft based on Madagascar. For some time the operation was without incident. The second tanker which had been sighted near Beira in April 1966 did not attempt to put into port, and the *Joanna V* left with its cargo intact. During the next 18 months it was necessary to do no more than clear up some doubt about two Liberian-registered tankers. Then, however, in December 1967, shots were fired across the bows of a French ship in a vain endeavour to stop it proceeding to Beira. More drastic steps were withheld pending consultations with London, which was just as well, not least for the reason that the tanker's cargo was found to have a non-Rhodesian destination. Thus the blockade can, in itself, be counted a success. But its aim has been unfulfilled, for quite apart from the fact that Rhodesia has a large stockpile of oil she has been able to import considerable quantities of it by rail from Lourenço Marques, another Mozambique port, and by road from neighbouring South Africa.

This has caused great dissatisfaction among the Afro-Asians and Communists. However, the evidence of Rhodesia's continuing ability to import oil heightened rather than created their anger and impatience, which had already found expression in calls for a stronger policy. During the Council's April 1966 meetings some members proposed, unsuccessfully, that Britain be called upon to use force to end the illegal regime, and in the following month a draft resolution to this effect was pressed to a decision in the Council, falling three short of the nine votes which its adoption required. But the balance of opinion in the UN at large was clearly not as favourable to Britain as these figures suggested. Therefore, following

[5] Security Council resolution 221 (1966).
[6] Some have argued that not all legal doubts have been satisfied by the Council's resolution.

the breakdown of talks between the British and Rhodesian Prime Ministers on board H.M.S. *Tiger* in December 1966, Britain tried to keep control of the anti-Rhodesian movement by immediately asking the Security Council to order selective economic sanctions against Rhodesia. This was a more drastic proposal than that which had been adopted by the Council in November 1965, for that decision was a recommendation only. Now, by taking the initiative as regards mandatory sanctions, Britain hoped to stop the Council from pressing for too great an extension of the pressure on Rhodesia, either an extension in terms of area, to include South Africa, or in terms of methods, to include the direct use of armed force. She was compelled to make a number of concessions, but essentially won the day. The Council, again on the ground that the situation constituted a threat to peace, imposed a boycott on virtually all Rhodesian exports, forbade all UN members to assist in supplying it with oil, and called on all states not to give the illegal regime any financial or other economic aid. The resolution was passed on 16 December 1966 by 11 votes to none, with France, the Soviet Union, Bulgaria, and Mali abstaining.

But although the Council had moved from recommending economic sanctions to ordering them, this failed to produce any very obvious weakening of the Smith regime, which continued to receive quiet support from Portugal and South Africa. Accordingly, doubts grew as to the efficacy of the measures which the UN had so far adopted, and on 3 November 1967 the Assembly, repeating an earlier decision, called on Britain to take all necessary measures to topple the rebels, including armed force. This resolution was supported by 92 members, and in April 1968 the Afro-Asians tried to increase the authority behind it by putting a draft resolution in essentially similar terms to the Security Council.[7] As she had done before, Britain moved in to head off the ultras, proposing that the Council's sanctions decision of December 1966 should be strengthened, but not to the extent of advocating the use of force. A compromise was reached and passed unanimously by the Security Council on 29 May, but it was the British rather than the Afro-Asian approach which it expressed inasmuch as it made no mention of the use of force nor of sanctions against members who failed to comply with the resolution. However, it went appreciably further

---

[7] Even if the appropriate majority could be obtained for such a proposal, and neither Britain nor any of the other permanent members used their veto, the Council is not in a position to order the use of force against Rhodesia because no forces have been placed at its disposal. Under Article 43 of the Charter, agreements between members and the Council on this point are necessary before the Council can take armed action on its own initiative. The point is perhaps chiefly of academic interest, but is not wholly without practical importance.

than the previous resolution in that it established a full embargo on all trade and financial relations with Rhodesia except for those of a humanitarian character. A committee was set up to supervise the operation. The Council also ordered that all travel to Rhodesia should be prevented and that passports issued by the Smith regime should not be recognized, and recommended that withdrawal of all consular and trade representatives from Rhodesia. Additionally, it requested all states to take all possible further action under Article 41 of the Charter, which refers to the 'complete or partial interruption . . . of rail, sea, air, postal, telegraphic, radio, and other means of communication'. In theory, at least, the screws were being turned quite drastically.

Clearly, Britain is going to remain under considerable pressure to use force to bring the minority regime down. But it is unlikely that she will budge from her opposition to this course, and the advent of a Conservative government in London would hardly produce a more radical attitude. Moreover, on this point it is to be expected that she will continue, for all practical purposes, to call the tune at the UN. For, as with the same issue in the disputes regarding Portugal's colonies and South Africa, those (others) who can, won't, and those who would, can't. This is not going to satisfy the militants, not by a long way. But it is worth noting that by authorizing a blockade and deciding on mandatory economic sanctions, the UN has moved much further than it has on allied questions, even though, in comparison with South Africa, Rhodesia is of lesser importance by almost any standard.

One standard by which it is not, however, is that of British constitutional law, which has had a crucial bearing on the UN's role. For it was the illegitimate character of the situation which largely resulted in the Organization being invited to participate by the Power who was universally recognized as having international responsibility for Rhodesia. And as the Rhodesian oligarchy was white, and its subjects black, the situation was clearly distinguishable in the UN's eyes from a straightforward case of rebellion, and so justified international involvement. Hence there were no trying questions of competence here, or, rather, the UN, with Britain's encouragement, chose not to see any. The Organization could be and was given the green, or perhaps the amber, light in a way which could not arise, save through the establishment of governments-in-exile, in the case of the Portuguese colonies and South Africa. Moreover, in a manner which would be out of the question for governments-in-exile, the Power giving the UN the go-ahead in Rhodesia was also prepared to give a lead in the organization of pressure and able to play a major role in its implementation.

The rest of the UN was only too glad to give Britain's proposals encouragement and support, and will be sure to continue doing so, at least for as long as Britain keeps in the economic realm. Most members are not greatly inconvenienced by the present sanctions operation, and as a way of demonstrating their rectitude on racial questions it is cheap at the price. Certainly, not to have joined the band-wagon would have been very expensive, diplomatically speaking. Waging economic war on a state of South Africa's strength, by contrast, would present economic, and military, questions of a quite different order of magnitude. And the consideration of other, and possibly more drastic, infringements of human rights than those which were occurring in Rhodesia, such as the murder of Tutsis in Rwanda by the ten thousand and of Communists in Indonesia by the hundred thousand, would have raised embarrassing or divisive questions. Rhodesia, however, was small, without friends, and, according to UN dogma, threatened the peace. Accordingly, it was a highly appropriate subject for UN enthusiasm.

II

Secession is not normally a question with which the UN would wish to deal, if only on account of members' apprehension that the Organization's participation in one such issue might encourage it to take an unwelcome interest in their own internal problems. Secessionists, after all, can be upheld as well as harried. If, however, the situation can be shown to have a substantial international aspect, by raising the principle of self-determination (as internationally interpreted) for example, or through the interference of outside Powers, and if, too, it arouses strong feelings, there is likely to be a readiness in some quarters to involve the UN. Support for the move can be solicited by appealing to the principle of justice or constitutional government, as the case may be, or both in the event of an ideologically unpopular rebellion. If the lawful government is the favoured party, it may be glad to have international help, particularly if it contemplates the economic isolation of the rebels. For the assistance of an institution which is more or less universal in membership would be valuable and perhaps essential for the successful execution of such a plan. In the military field, rather different considerations may present themselves, for the use of an international force could cause the government to lose face as well as presenting it with the problem of keeping the force under satisfactory political control. Nevertheless, on balance a government might be very pleased at the prospect of such assistance.

The likelihood of the UN providing it, however, will usually be very small. As the cases of Portugal and South Africa have shown, UN members are, not surprisingly, most reluctant to make unnecessary difficulties for themselves, their fervour for coercive measures often being in inverse proportion to the sacrifices which would be required from them. There is, however, one set of circumstances in which the UN might be willing to upset an established situation by armed force, whether or not the question of constitutional legitimacy is at stake: where it already has a force in the area in question which seems to be capable of the proposed task.[8] (The existence of a standing UN force might have something of the same effect.) In that event there might be compelling temptations or pressures to extend the mandate of the force so as to give it an additional or new proselytizing role. Such occasions are likely to be very rare, making those concerned the recipients of quite exceptional good and ill luck—provided the UN is successful. Its abortive attempt to capitalize upon its temporary ascendancy in Korea by extending the authority of the South over the North highlighted the possible difficulties. This apart, there has only been one instance of the UN employing armed force in a direct endeavour to topple a regime. The scheduled and eventual victim was the province and aspirant sovereign state of Katanga, which suffered for its rightist attitudes and connections, and the beneficiary the moderate government which eventually came to power in the Congo (Leopoldville), its reward being due in no small measure to it being the alternative to a more radical regime.

Schemes for Katanga's secession were afoot immediately prior to 30 June 1960, when the Congo was to become independent, but in face of opposition from both the Belgian and the Congolese authorities, as well as the possibility of local trouble, they were put on one side. However, the issue was reopened by the disorder in which the new state soon found itself and the Government's refusal to use Belgian troops to deal with the situation, and on 11 July the province declared its independence. Neither then nor later was it formally recognized by any member of the international society, but at this time Belgium was very sympathetically inclined. Hence she allowed her intervening metropolitan forces to disband the Congolese army units in Katanga and prepare the way for the establishment of a gendarmerie which would be loyal to the head of the secessionist regime, Moise Tshombe.

In most left wing and African eyes, Tshombe's co-operation with

[8] In an emotional situation, a force's capability might assume subordinate importance in discussions regarding its use.

the former colonial Power compounded his already serious crime, and fed the ready suspicion that there was a good deal more to his behaviour than was apparent on the surface. Hence, many of these states supported the argument of Prime Minister Lumumba that the force which the UN was dispatching to the Congo[9] should take all necessary steps to re-establish the Central Government's authority in Katanga. In support of this case they could point to the fact that the Security Council had decided to give the Government 'military assistance' until its own forces were able 'to meet fully their tasks'.[10] Doubts regarding the propriety of UN participation in this particular task could be met by underlining Katanga's international connections. But most states on the Council were disposed to see the matter as essentially internal, and the Western members, particularly, did not want to jeopardize the calm which obtained in Katanga. Accordingly, they strongly supported the Secretary-General's insistence that there was no question of the UN Force being used to influence the course of Congolese politics, and the two (moderate) Afro-Asian members were prepared to go along with this view.

Nevertheless, there was a widespread feeling that UN troops ought to be deployed in all parts of the Congo. Tshombe, however, insisted that there was no need for them in Katanga, and showed every willingness to use force to keep the UN out. An authoritative ruling was therefore sought, and on 9 August the Council declared that the entry of the UN Force into Katanga was necessary. But, in order that there should be no misunderstanding about the implications of this, the Council also committed itself to the explicit statement that the Force 'will not be a party to or in any way intervene in or be used to influence the outcome of any internal conflict, constitutional or otherwise'.[11] The Secretary-General was able to satisfy Mr Tshombe as to the interpretation of the Council's resolution, and Belgium was ready to withdraw in the UN's favour. As a result, the UN took over the task of guaranteeing the maintenance of order in Katanga.

However, the UN's refusal to overturn Tshombe infuriated Lumumba, who immediately endeavoured to do the job on his own. He was wholly unsuccessful, but did have the indirect effect of stiffening the UN's attitude towards Katanga. For his ill-organized campaign sped his own downfall, and the UN's part in that event[12] attracted much criticism. By way of redressing the balance, therefore, the UN Secretary-General tried to persuade Belgium and Katanga

[9] See above, p. 355.
[10] Security Council resolution 143 (1960).
[11] Security Council resolution 146 (1960).
[12] See above, pp. 358–360.

to cut their links with each other.[13] He made no progress, but his efforts were significant as a concession to the increasing call for a more militant line against Katanga. As such, they were also the first instance of a pattern which was to be repeated on more than one occasion.

The dissatisfaction of some UN members regarding the Organization's Katanga policy was a mirror image of their attitude towards Lumumba. When, therefore, at the end of November 1960, he removed himself from the UN's custody and was captured a few days later by the regime which had deposed him, the issue was made the occasion for a vigorous attack on the UN's behaviour in the Congo. Already, early in August, Guinea had threatened that unless the UN took a stronger line towards Tshombe she would transfer her contingent in the UN Force to the control of the then Lumumba regime. Now, with Lumumba out of power, she had to content herself with urging the withdrawal of troops from the Force. In this she was joined by the other ex-French ultra, Mali, who had already recalled her contingent, although for reasons which were said to relate to the break-up of the Mali Federation. The leading ex-British radical, Ghana, had also threatened, before Lumumba's fall, to give him military support, but now she favoured staying in the UN Force and trying to get the Organization to adopt a tougher policy. Towards this end, a far-reaching resolution was put to the Assembly in December, including provision for the appointment of a standing Assembly delegation to act in the Congo with the head of the UN operation, but was rejected. This led to decisions by Guinea, the UAR, Indonesia, and Morocco to withdraw their troops, although Morocco's attitude was probably governed more by her desire to win support for her claim to Mauritania than by the course of events in the Congo. Yugoslavia was already in the process of withdrawing her small administrative group as a mark of her dissatisfaction with the UN's policy, and for other reasons the Burmese contingent was withdrawn in January 1961.[14]

---

[13] An important aspect of this problem was represented by about 250 Belgians who, until the mutiny of July 1960, had been members of the Congolese Army, and had thereafter been allowed to remain in or go to Katanga to help Tshombe build up his gendarmerie. Additionally, about three dozen officers of the Belgian metropolitan Army had been seconded to the secessionist regime, and there were getting on for twice that number of Belgian officers in the Katangan police. The mercenaries were in a different category, having been recruited to Katanga's gendarmerie on an individual basis. On the civilian side, there were a small but influential number of Belgian advisers.

[14] That unconnected events could cause a UN operation serious embarrassment was instanced in July and August 1961, when the Congolese National Assembly was meeting near Leopoldville. The UN had guaranteed the personal safety of the deputies and the atmosphere was tense. Just at this moment the Tunisian brigade in Leopoldville was recalled with immediate effect on account of the fighting between

Thus the UN operation was under considerable strain, and other Afro-Asians besides those on the extreme left wing were coming around to the view that a stronger mandate was needed. The new Kennedy administration in the United States was also thought to be sympathetic to such an approach, and the likelihood of its adoption was marginally increased by the fact that the number of Afro-Asian states on the Security Council had gone up from two to three, and now included the militant UAR. Negotiations were in progress, with the Afro-Asians pressing for more than the Western states and the Secretary-General were prepared to allow, when the news arrived, first, of Lumumba's death, and then of the murder of six of his supporters. This produced a very bitter Afro-Asian reaction against the conduct of the UN operation, and to a large extent swung the United States and the moderates behind their proposals. Thus although a Soviet draft resolution was soundly defeated, and an Afro-Asian draft just failed of adoption, another Afro-Asian proposal was passed on 21 February 1961 without any opposition, although France and the Soviet Union abstained.

The resolution 'Urge[d] that the United Nations take immediately all appropriate measures to prevent the occurrence of civil war in the Congo, including arrangements for cease-fires, the halting of all military operations, the prevention of clashes, and the use of force, if necessary, in the last resort'.[15] Thus for the first time the UN departed from the convention that its peace-keeping activities were to involve the use of force only in self-defence. Not everyone was happy about this. Britain, for example, although voting in its favour, made it clear in the preceding debate that she interpreted the resolution to mean that 'force will only be used by the United Nations to prevent a clash between hostile Congolese troops', her representative adding for good measure: 'There can be no question of empowering the United Nations to use its forces to impose a political settlement'.[16] The resolution also, in what was to prove a more potent clause, 'urge[d] that measures be taken for the immediate withdrawal and evacuation from the Congo of all Belgian and other foreign military and paramilitary personnel and political advisers not under the United Nations Command, and mercenaries'.[17]

For a while, however, the decision of 21 February had no impact on the situation in the Congo. It was not liked in Leopoldville, where

[15] Security Council resolution 161 (1961).
[16] Security Council, *Official Records*, 942nd Meeting, para. 21.
[17] Security Council resolution 161 (1961).

France and Tunisia at Bizerta. Also, the smaller Ghanaian contingent was withdrawn in August and September 1961, at an important stage of the operation, in connection with the reorganization of the Ghanaian Army. Both these withdrawals proved temporary.

the Government harboured suspicions that the UN might try to usurp its authority, and there were incidents between the UN troops and the Congolese Army. Relations between the UN and the Congo were also strained on account of the unpopularity of Mr Rajeshwar Dayal, the Indian head of the UN operation, who by this time had completely lost the confidence of most of the leading politicians in the capital. Moreover, there were signs of a reconciliation between Katanga and the Congolese Government. And in any event the UN was hardly in a position to take a strong line. Several contingents had already been withdrawn from the Force, and an appeal from the Secretary-General to Indonesia and Morocco not to go ahead with their plans to follow suit was without avail. Moreover, in April 1961, the Sudanese contingent was also withdrawn following fighting between it and the Congolese Army in which the Sudanese had, in effect, been defeated.

But the situation soon improved. India eventually agreed to the UN's request to provide 5,000 troops, making it publicly clear that she did so on the assumption that they would be used against Katanga. Dayal was recalled to New York for consultation early in March, and his temporary successor proved popular with the Congolese authorities. The announcement, two months later, of Dayal's impending return, provoked a crisis which was only solved by his own decision to resign. Even this, it was rumoured, had its price, in the shape of a promise exacted by India from Britain and the United States to withdraw their ambassadors from Leopoldville. Certainly the two ambassadors, both of whom had been hostile to Dayal, were replaced within a few months. Then, too, the agreement which had been reached between the central authorities and Katanga broke down, and the obstacles in the way of co-operation between the UN and the Congo against Tshombe's secessionist regime were finally removed on 2 August when, following a meeting of the Congolese Parliament, the country returned to constitutional rule under a Government led by the moderate Cyrille Adoula.

Meanwhile, pressure had been accumulating in New York for a stronger policy towards Katanga. In April 1961 a new Belgian Government had taken office under M. Spaak. It was prepared to co-operate with the UN, and as a result some Belgian political advisers had left Katanga with Tshombe's agreement. But this was not enough either for the Congo or the Afro-Asians, and the United States, too, was backing this camp now that the Congo was in 'responsible' hands. Towards this end a new UN representative in Katanga had been appointed in June, Mr Conor Cruise O'Brien, a former member of Ireland's delegation to the UN. And before long the Secretariat decided that if Tshombe refused to act more vigorously, the UN Force would itself arrest and expel his foreign officers. The resolution of 21 February had not authorized the use of force for this purpose, although it could perhaps be argued that the UN was covered by its right to use force to prevent civil war. But the argument that the presence of Belgian officers in Katanga was tantamount to the waging of civil war was very tenuous, and the UN did not rely on it. More promising, from its point of view, was an agreement of 17 April 1961 between the UN and President Kasavubu, under which the Congo accepted the 21 February resolution and the UN promised to help in its implementation. This was supplemented by an ordinance which the Government quietly enacted on 24 August at Hammarskjöld's suggestion. It provided for the expulsion of all non-Congolese officers and mercenaries serving with the Katangan forces who were not under contract with the Central Government, and Prime Minister Adoula formally asked for the UN's assistance in its execution.

This did not satisfy all doubts as to whether the UN had the right to use force against the foreign officers, but it was enough for the Secretariat to assume that it had. Accordingly, on 28 August, a number of them were arrested by the UN Force, without serious incident. However, following representations from the consular corps in Elisabethville, the UN agreed to halt its activities and allow the repatriation process to be continued voluntarily under the supervision of the Belgian consul. From the UN's point of view this proved to be a mistake, for the operation which it had begun lost its momentum and efficiency. Formally, the Europeans no longer held any positions in Katanga's gendarmerie, but an appreciable minority of them were still at large and thought to have a hand in the anti-UN demonstrations which were occurring in Katanga's capital. Thus O'Brien pressed for further and stronger action, and was aided and abetted by the Central Government who, through other UN hands, provided him with warrants for the arrest of the leading Katangan ministers, including Tshombe. The code-word for the new operation was 'Morthor,' a Hindi word meaning 'smash'.

Thus the action which was now envisaged went considerably beyond the removal of foreign officers from Katanga. By no stretch of the imagination could it be reconciled with that part of the Security Council's resolution of 9 August 1960 which prohibited interference in the Congo's internal affairs, and the argument that it was covered by the clause in the 21 February resolution which allowed the UN to use force as a means of preventing civil war was extremely thin. But legal doubts about a particular course generally present themselves most forcibly to those who, for one reason or another, are reluctant to follow it, and the UN officials who were involved did not fall into that category. O'Brien, for example, welcomed the opportunity, as he saw it, to end Katanga's secession, and claimed that his 'instructions taken as a whole, had [this] unmistakable meaning'.[18] A high Secretariat official has asserted that this is 'preposterous',[19] and certainly there is much obscurity as to whether the UN officer in local charge of the Congo operation, Sture Linner, and the Secretary-General himself, were fully aware of what was planned, or at least of the implications which were being put upon it. Be that as it may, even if the second UN action is regarded as no more than a continuation of the first, it is not thereby deprived of an anti-secessionist character. For it was the UN Secretariat's view that Tshombe would find it very difficult to maintain his position in the absence of foreign helpers. Hence, just the straightforward removal of the gendarmerie's European officers would have been a move against an independent Katanga. As such, it would undoubtedly have been in line with the numerical balance of opinion among UN members, who were increasingly in favour of a showdown with Tshombe.

As it happened, however, the UN's new operation misfired. It began on the morning of 13 September, but there was a failure to detain Tshombe and other key figures, and fighting broke out in Elisabethville. It met with strong criticism in a number of Western countries, which was not alleviated by O'Brien's reported statement that Katanga's secession was at an end. Britain, for example, who had already professed herself to be 'greatly disturbed'[20] by some aspects of the earlier move, now declared that she was 'shocked',[21] and the Government proceeded to use 'all their influence to urge a cease-fire and peaceful settlement'.[22] In face of these pressures, the Secretary-General, who had arrived in Leopoldville on 13 September, agreed to hold cease-fire talks with Tshombe, and a meeting was arranged at Ndola, in Northern Rhodesia. It was while he was on his way there that Hammarskjöld was killed in an aeroplane crash. A provisional cease-fire was signed on 20 September, and confirmed in October.

The Congolese Government had been strongly opposed to a cease-fire, and, as it had done a year earlier, tried to subdue Katanga on its own. But its efforts were unsuccessful, and only emphasized its dependence on the UN for the kind of co-operation which

[18] Conor Cruise O'Brien, *To Katanga and Back* (London: Hutchinson 1962), p. 266.
[19] In an anonymous review of O'Brien's book: *The Times Literary Suppement*, 16 November 1962.
[20] House of Commons, *Debates*, Vol. 646, col. 19.
[21] House of Lords, *Debates*, Vol. 234, col. 446.
[22] House of Commons, *Debates*, Vol. 646, col. 21.

Tshombe's removal required. And, from its point of view, the tide in the UN was continuing to move in the right direction. Early in November a Burmese, U Thant, was appointed as Acting Secretary-General, suggesting that the Afro-Asian attitude towards the Katanga problem would, at the least, not be less sympathetically viewed at the top of the UN Secretariat than formerly. Britain had come under strong criticism for the part she had played in September, and might therefore be expected to try to avoid giving unnecessary offence. And the United States' attitude was hardening against Tshombe. She was particularly worried, not for the first time, that a lack of success for the Central Government in this matter would redound to the advantage of the left wing secessionist regime in Stanleyville, which was led by Lumumba's follower, Gizenga. She therefore was in favour of supporting Adoula's moderate regime, and hoped that an anti-secessionist commitment on the part of the UN could also be used against Gizenga. The Afro-Asians were not at all keen on the latter aspect of the United States policy, but many of them, including some who were thought of as moderates, were growing ever more angry at the failure to topple Tshombe. In this mood they called for a meeting of the Security Council.

Now the pressure was building up, and on 24 November 1961, with Britain and France abstaining, the Council passed a very far-reaching resolution. It authorized the Secretary-General 'to take vigorous action, including the use of the requisite measure of force, if necessary, for the immediate apprehension, detention pending legal action and/or deportation of all foreign military and paramilitary personnel and political advisers not under the United Nations Command, and mercenaries'.[23] In this way the Council tried to clear all doubts about the legal propriety of an action such as that which had been taken in the previous August, although by now virtually all the Belgian regular army officers and political advisers had left. Beyond this, however, the Council condemned Katanga's secession and declared its full support, in accordance with UN decisions, for the Central Government's efforts to maintain the Congo's integrity. This was not quite the same thing as saying that the UN could now use force to end secession. But, short of that point, the Council had clearly gone as far as it could towards taking an anti-Tshombe stand.

The UN did not have to wait long to demonstrate that its approach to Tshombe would now be much tougher. It did not even have to seek out an opportunity to do so, for it was presented with one by provocative behaviour on the part of the Katangan gendarmerie. It seemed as if a campaign was afoot to isolate the UN's various camps, and therefore, early in December, the Secretary-General authorized

[23] Security Council resolution 169 (1961).

the Force to restore its freedom of movement. This was something to which even Britain could hardly object, and, under pressure, she went so far as to agree to provide the UN with two dozen 1,000 lb. bombs for British built bombers which were being operated by the Indian members of the Force. She did so on the understanding that they would only be used against Katangese aircraft and airstrips, but her decision provoked such a domestic outcry that within a few days she was seeking clarification of certain aspects of UN policy before releasing the bombs. Her doubts were increased by the fact that the UN action had led to general skirmishing in and around Elisabethville, which was accompanied by a considerable build up of UN forces in Katanga. Britain professed to find these developments 'difficult to reconcile with the aims of the operation as described at the moment by the Secretary-General',[24] and by way of providing authority for her position the Foreign Secretary observed in the House of Lords that, 'after all, we have had some experience of these kinds of colonial situations'.[25]

Accordingly, on 13 December, and supported by France, Britain made a formal request to the Secretary-General to secure an immediate cease-fire. However, by this time, almost all the necessary reinforcements had arrived in Katanga, and 'in defence of its communications' the UN Force was about to advance on Elisabethville. Thus Britain's initiative met with what amounted to a rebuff, accompanied by a withdrawal of the request for bombs, and the UN proceeded with its operation. It met with considerable resistance, but Tshombe's forces were clearly the weaker, and he therefore agreed to appeal to the United States for mediation. A meeting was quickly arranged with Adoula, which brought the fighting to a halt, and on 21 December Tshombe signed a declaration which, in effect, put a formal end to Katanga's secession.

The Secretary-General denied that it was the aim of the December operation to impose a political solution on the Congo. In a sense his denial was fair. The UN had always insisted on the principle of freedom of movement, and this had been allowed by the Congo in an agreement of July 1960. It could be reasonably argued that Tshombe's regime stood in the way of the implementation of that principle in Katanga, and that therefore by moving against the regime's principal city and installations the UN was doing no more than eliminating a real and persistent threat to its rights. But there was no doubt that such a tactic would have the effect at least of undermining the secessionist regime, nor that that consequence was heartily desired by a large majority of UN members. The most

[24] House of Commons, *Debates*, Vol. 651, col. 650.
[25] House of Lords, *Debates*, Vol. 236, col. 526.

important supporter of the UN's December activities was the United States, and she got her reward early in 1962 when the UN agreed to give the Central Government some help in bringing down the secessionist regime which was based on Stanleyville. This gave rise to little difficulty, and its leader, Gizenga, was arrested. The UN's part in the enterprise was justified by the Secretary-General on the ground that the UN was entitled to help the Central Government maintain law and order and prevent civil war. It had not, in fact, been clearly authorized to take action of the kind which felled Gizenga: the resolution of 21 February 1961 did not obviously imply that the right to prevent civil war by force was tantamount to giving the UN an equivalent right in respect of secession. But, although less so than in the case of the right-wing Tshombe, the consensus among UN members, especially among those who counted, was that the Congo's Central Government should receive full support in asserting its authority throughout the country, and therefore against the left-wing rebels. And on this, admittedly minor, case of UN participation in the Congo's political affairs, no condemnatory word was heard from London.

The Katanga story, however, was not yet over. As soon as Mr Tshombe got back there after apparently having capitulated to Adoula, he announced that the undertakings he had made were provisional until they had been ratified by the Katangan Parliament. This was the opening shot in a stalemate which lasted for a year. Numerous discussions were held, but no substantial progress was made in the direction of reintegrating the province with the rest of the Congo. In August U Thant put forward a plan for national reconciliation along federal lines, and tried to encourage its acceptance by providing for the imposition of sanctions against any defaulters —which, in isolation, would have been a remarkable step for the UN to take. But, in this context, it was but another move in what was now an established anti-Katangan policy, and, no substantial progress having been made, the Secretary-General announced in December that the sanctions would be applied against Tshombe's regime. Meanwhile, that a recalcitrant Katanga might have to face more than economic discomfort was being made plain by the gradual strengthening of the UN Force, the bulk of which was now deployed in the province. Moreover, its Indian members, who were important in terms of both numbers and influence, were said to be pressing for strong action to finish the problem off once and for all; their impatience may partly have stemmed from the possibility of their early recall on account of the recent hostilities between India and China.[26] Outside Katanga, the pressures were moving in the

[26] The Indian contingent was in fact withdrawn early in 1963.

same direction. The Afro-Asians were urging a further move against Tshombe. Even Belgium was prepared to see force being used as a last resort. And that the United States, worried about the weakening effect which the situation was having on Adoula's political position, also wanted to bring matters to a conclusion was evident from the fact that in December she sent a military mission to the Congo to consider 'what additional forms of assistance the United States could provide to ensure the ability of the United Nations to maintain peace in the Congo'.[27]

Thus things were looking black for Katanga. France was opposed to the imposition of economic sanctions, and Britain had expressed reservations about this aspect of the Thant plan. But they were now very much in a minority, and in any event Britain gave in to American pressure. Early in December, Tshombe agreed to implement the plan, which caused Britain to revert to her former position, but this had no more effect on the situation than Tshombe's own bid to avoid a complete disaster. Tension had been rising between the UN force and the Katangan gendarmerie, and after UN positions had been under sporadic fire from the gendarmerie for several days, the UN retaliated on 28 December with an operation which was given the codename 'Grandslam'. Britain pressed for a cease-fire and a resumption of negotiations, but in vain. First Elisabethville was taken over, and then, on the ground of establishing complete freedom of movement throughout Katanga, the surrounding area and other key points. In reply Tshombe could do little more than threaten a scorched-earth policy, but he soon capitulated, announcing on 14 January 1963, his willingness to allow freedom of movement to the UN and to implement the Thant plan. This time there was no mistake. Katanga was reintegrated into the Congo (on the Central Government's terms rather than those of the Thant plan) and the ministers of the former secessionist regime were deprived of all real power. In June Tshombe left the country. However, a year later, just a few days before the departure of the UN Force, he returned to the Congo at the invitation of its Government for what was to prove just one more stage in a fluctuating political career.

After two and a half years, the secessionist regime in Katanga had finally been brought down, and its fall was directly attributable to the use of force by the UN—the first occasion on which an established situation had been upset in this way. That it took so long was partly attributable to Tshombe's own skill, obstinacy, and not insignificant strength, which meant that the UN had to take time to build up its Force. It also reflected doubt regarding the propriety

[27] Quoted in Ernest W. Lefever; *Crisis in the Congo* (Washington, D.C.: Brookings Institute, 1965), p. 106.

P

of the UN's role, and the associated fact that, in formal terms, the Organization was at no time openly committed to destroying Tshombe's regime. Hence, even when that goal received over-whelming political support, the UN still wanted a suitable pretext for action. But it had grown increasingly apparent that Tshombe was living on borrowed time. The UN was clearly not going to be satisfied with anything less than the complete ending of secession, received two symbolically important extensions of its mandate, and was becoming ever more prepared to use force to achieve that result. That it had become just a question of time and means was evident from the fact that after the passage of the November 1961 resolution, the Security Council was never again called into session to discuss the activities of its Congo Force. The majority were satisfied with the way things were going, and those few who had doubts about the UN's policy knew better than to expose them at a Council meeting.

The whole Katanga question, in fact, provides eloquent testimony for the wedge-like possibilities of UN operations. In July and August 1960 suggestions that the UN should take positive and, if necessary, forceful action to undermine Katanga would have aroused great controversy, and some thought that the non-interven-tion clause of the Council's resolution of 9 August stood in the way of such developments. But only a year later action of that nature was taken twice, amid diminishing protests. And in 1962 the planning and execution of Tshombe's overthrow attracted relatively little critical comment. For this, circumstances were particularly propi-tious. Opinion within the UN was almost uniformly, although in varying degree, hostile to Tshombe. More importantly, the United States was an active and generous backer of the crusade, and the Soviet Union was unable to do other than assent to it. Hammar-skjöld was prepared to allow at least some anti-Tshombe measures, and his successor seemed to be an unambiguous supporter of the popular cause. It was also of the highest significance that the major contributors to the UN Force were among those who were very keen to see Katanga's secession brought to an end, and that the Force was in the field without a time limit.

It was not the first time that a UN operation, once under way, had assumed a larger or different role from that which was envisaged at the outset. It is open to question whether, at the time of its establishment in November 1956, it was generally expected that the UN Emergency Force would stay in the Middle East after the completion of the withdrawal which it was to supervise, encamping with what looked like semi-permanence at the Egyptian–Israeli border.[28] Likewise, in 1958, the Observation Group which was sent to

28 See above, pp. 100–103.

the Lebanon underwent a sudden and surprising enlargement before the end of the year.[29] But the way in which the task of the UN's Congo force gradually shifted was, in sum, by far the most dramatic and significant instance of this process. It can be attacked as subversive of confidence in the UN's readiness to adhere to initial guidelines, and therefore in the wisdom of entrusting it with substantial peace-keeping responsibilities. Or it can be defended as an example of that responsive sensitivity to changing needs and conditions which political bodies must display if they are not to suffer atrophy and rejection. Put rather differently, the argument can be phrased in terms of the traditional international principle of non-involvement in domestic issues as against the right of the majority to decide which matters require their concern. At another level, the UN's action in Katanga can be discussed simply on the basis of whether one's interests and prejudices indicated support for Tshombe or not, and undoubtedly considerations of this order must have presented themselves very forcibly to UN members. But it would be surprising if there were not at least some of them who appreciated that what the Organization was doing in Katanga might not be without significance for the future. And for those who felt that UN operations might conceivably hamper their own policies, the Katangan affair could not but have served as a warning.[30]

[29] See above, p. 225–229.

[30] It may well be that it was not just the financial problems to which the Congo operation gave rise which led the Security Council, in March 1964 and thereafter, to insist on the UN Force in Cyprus having a mandate which, in point of time, was strictly limited.

Chapter 12

The Powers and Peace-Keeping

As a peace-keeping agency, the UN is widely held to have gone into decline during the 1960s. The opening of the decade seemed to confirm and extend the promise of the Suez operation, as the Organization responded speedily and substantially to the Congo's appeal for help. But in a number of quarters optimism soon gave way to questioning and gloom as the UN's new mission led to controversy and mounting debt. The best legal advice—that of the International Court of Justice—confirmed, in 1962, that all members were liable for a proportionate share of the UN's peace-keeping expenses, but the defaulters, led by France and the Soviet Union, were unmoved. Nor did they give way under the threat to deprive them of their vote in the General Assembly under the mandatory provisions of Article 19 of the Charter. The crisis resulted in a lame-duck session of the Assembly (that of 1964–5) owing to the necessity of avoiding any votes, and a Special Committee of 33 which was appointed in February 1965 failed to resolve the issue.[1] Then, in August 1965, the United States, who had been leading the campaign to enforce Article 19 against the debtors, backed down. She had made many ringing statements on the theme of the need to uphold the integrity of the Charter, but now, in effect, agreed that Article 19 should be disregarded.

The immediate crisis was over, but not the disagreement as to the financing of future peace-keeping operations. Despite the efforts of the Committee of 33, and others, no progress was made in this direction during the next three years. Nor was it possible to arrive at an understanding on the associated disputes regarding the asserted right of the General Assembly to authorize peace-keeping missions in certain circumstances and the part which the Secretary-General should play in their control. This produced a marked despondency concerning the UN's peace-keeping capability, which was not relieved by what many regarded as the supine withdrawal of the UN Emergency Force from the Israel–UAR border in May 1967 at President Nasser's behest, and the Jarring mission's failure, as of

---

[1] The Committee was instructed to make 'a comprehensive review of the whole question of peace-keeping operations in all their aspects' (*Yearbook of the United Nations 1965*, p. 3). However, it was given no guidance on the ambit of the term 'peace-keeping', and was itself unable to agree on the matter.

mid-1968, to bring the contestants in the six-day war towards a final settlement.

There is a question, however, as to the ground for the view that the UN's peace-keeping fortunes are at a low ebb. To a large extent it is based on a supposed contrast with the latter part of the 1950s, which are held both to have been the UN's high noon and to have established the peace-keeping norm. However, although the UN Emergency Force was an organizational departure, it had basic functional similarities with some of the UN's previous operations. Essentially, it did not strike out in an entirely new direction but added a dimension to the Organization's prophylactic resources. Moreover, the Soviet Union and her friends made it clear in 1956 that they had reservations regarding the Assembly's role in UNEF's establishment and that they would not contribute to its cost, the last position being shared by Egypt and the other Arab states. Thus, even at this time the peace-keeping horizon was not unclouded. And the UN's activities in Lebanon and Jordan in 1958 were hardly sufficient to be regarded, in conjunction with UNEF, as establishing a trend towards a much more ambitious role for the Organization.

It is also the case that the period of the peace-keeping debate has by no means been accompanied by a failure on the part of the UN to respond to opportunities in this field. The Cyprus Force, which in many ways is comparable to UNEF, was established in March 1964 just when the financing problem was coming to a head. The UN's Dominican mission was set up in May 1965 at the height of the voting crisis. And hard on the heels of the American capitulation to the Soviet Union and France over Article 19 came the Indo-Pakistani war of September 1965, which not only caused the Security Council to react with a verbal strength almost without parallel in the UN's history but also led to the dispatch of an observer group to the sub-continent and the expansion of the mission already in Kashmir. The withdrawal of UNEF, it is true, cast a shadow over the scene. But there never could have been a realistic expectation that it would stay in its position contrary to the UAR's will. And a month after the end of the war which followed UNEF's withdrawal, the UN's Truce Supervision Organization was allowed to establish a watch along the Israel-UAR front which, while much less comprehensive than that which UNEF had maintained, was fuller than any of those which UNTSO had kept on the four Arab–Israeli borders during the previous 19 years. It could also be said that the lack of success attending Ambassador Jarring's mediatory efforts in the Middle East, far from being a new experience for the UN, was in keeping with a tradition which dated from the appointment of a

UN Mediator for Palestine at the time of Israel's birth in May 1948.

One major qualification which might be made to this line of argument is that while the central issues of authorization and finance are still unsettled, the outlook for peace-keeping is far from assured. On this view, the UN was lucky in that its third peace-keeping force, which kept order in West New Guinea in 1962–3, was non-controversial and paid for by the parties. The next major operation, however, can be put forward as an instance of the problems with which the UN is currently faced if it tries to take any substantial action. For the UN Force in Cyprus has had to be paid for voluntarily, and as a result has been, financially speaking, living from hand to mouth throughout its existence. And as it has never been given more than a six months mandate, it is subject to periodic extension by the Security Council. Clearly, this situation is highly unsatisfactory in several respects. But instead of being seen in terms of derogations from the norm, or just of straightforward disagreement, it could equally well be regarded as evidence of an emerging understanding that sizeable UN operations must be financed by those who are most interested in them and, as a general rule, must be kept under the clear and continued control of the Security Council. The mid and late-1960s, in fact, may be working out some implications of the UN's earlier activity which were not fully appreciated at the time. It may be, too, that this process is revealing that the Powers will tolerate a good deal, provided their view of their rights is respected and they are not asked to pay for measures which do not command their active support.

A development along these lines would still leave open the question of the General Assembly's peace-keeping role when the Security Council is blocked by a veto. The United States, supported by the vast majority of UN members, will not agree that the Council's competence is more or less exclusive; and the Soviet Union and France seem determined to insist that the Assembly should have no part in the conduct of operations of any size. Much the most likely outcome, therefore, is that the matter will be left on one side, so that when a problem arises those with the upper procedural hand will have to weigh the disadvantages of offending the objectors against the advantages of a UN operation. However, the necessity for such pragmatic calculations would no more seem to stand in the way of a peace-keeping role for the UN now and in the future than it has in the past. On a number of occasions the General Assembly has gone ahead with the establishment or continuation of operations in face of Great Power opposition, for example, in respect of the

Balkans, Korea, Hungary, and the Congo. There is no reason to suppose that it might not do so again, especially if no attempt is made to press the opponents for a share of the cost. Nor is there much evidence for the view that such action is likely to jeopardize the mounting of further peace-keeping operations by causing the dissenters to do everything they can to prevent them or to withdraw from the Organization. For, except in the very unlikely event of a state thinking that the UN or its peace-keeping operations could never be of benefit to itself, moves of that kind would be the international equivalent of cutting off one's nose to spite one's face—a luxury which states generally feel ill-able to afford.

There is, moreover, some ground for the opinion that the Powers may be quietly modifying their positions on the General Assembly's role. For most of the UN's life the United States has had no reason to fear that the Assembly might act contrary to her wishes. Accordingly, she has been an enthusiastic supporter of its right to act in place of a blocked Council. More recently, however, she has been given cause to reconsider this view. In December 1964 the African states reacted with great verbal violence against the American–Belgian intervention in the Congo to rescue the Europeans whose lives were endangered by rebel activity. Had the Dominican question gone to the Assembly in 1965, it is very probable that that body would have been no less ready than the Council to involve the UN in the affair despite American opposition. The role of the United States in Vietnam is very unpopular and could easily result in other American initiatives being regarded with considerable suspicion. And the majority in the Assembly want the UN to take much more drastic action against Portugal and South Africa than the United States is willing to support. All this is in addition to an existing American unease lest the Assembly should vote for ambitious economic aid programmes, the cost of which would in large measure fall on her. It would not be surprising, therefore, if these developments led the United States to think that there might possibly be some merit in the Soviet position regarding the General Assembly. This is certainly suggested by her reaction to her defeat in the voting dispute, for she took the opportunity to say that 'if any Member State could make an exception to the principle of collective financial responsibility with respect to certain UN activities, the United States reserved the same option to make exceptions if, in its view, there were compelling reasons to do so'.[2] It is very plausible to see here some concern about the temper of the Assembly. It could, as indicated, find expression in the United States following Soviet

[2] UN Document A/AC121/SR 15, p. 6.

financial practice,[3] which in all probability would be a crippling blow to the operation concerned. But it is at least, if not more, likely to result in the United States trying to keep a matter from the Assembly where there is a danger of unwise action. It may be, too, that the improving relationship between the two super-powers will in any event incline the United States to treat the Soviet view with more solicitude.

It is not all, however, a case of what Moscow thinks today Washington thinks tomorrow. For it is not inconceivable that the Soviet Union may not be so attached to her position as her public statements would suggest. In the first place, the residual role of the Assembly does allow her to make a public demonstration of her opposition to an operation (by obstructing it in the Council) while not preventing its conduct by the UN—which, after all, will often be better for her than having it conducted outside the UN. And, secondly, the possibility of her ideological brethren in Peking being given China's permanent seat on the Security Council might be encouraging second thoughts on the Assembly's role. For it is by no means impossible that China, on the Council, would adopt the attitude and tactics associated with the senior Communist member but which are now sometimes detrimental to its interests. In that event the Soviet Union may discover that in certain closely defined circumstances she is not totally opposed to using the Assembly.

It can, therefore, be argued that the UN's peace-keeping potential is not obviously much worse in mid 1968 than at most other times during its life. It is, however, very commonly claimed that the Organization is seriously deficient so far as the mounting and conduct of operations is concerned on account of its failure to prepare for them. On the face of it, this seems a fair criticism, for there would appear to be adequate scope for improvement in the efficiency

---

[3] In 1963 the Soviet Union announced that henceforth, as well as refusing to contribute to the cost of the Middle East and Congo operations (or towards the interest on the bonds which the UN issued to alleviate its financial crisis), it would also withhold that part of its annual assessment which related to the UN Commission for the Unification and Rehabilitation of Korea; the Memorial Cemetery in Korea; the UN Truce Supervision Organization in Palestine; and the UN Field Operations Service.

There was, however, an American precedent for this kind of action. In 1952 the Secretary-General, under pressure from the United States, discharged certain American members of the Secretariat. The United Nations Administrative Tribunal, supported by the International Court of Justice, subsequently ruled that the Secretary-General had acted unlawfully, and awarded compensation to the dismissed employees. The United States Congress replied by declaring that no American funds paid to the UN could be used for such compensation payments. In the event the problem was resolved without a showdown, as the Secretary-General, instead of drawing on the regular budget, made the necessary payments out of a staff fund which was independent of the contributions of member states.

with which the UN takes action. Calls for remedial measures have become one of the most popular—and also, one suspects, one of the easiest—ways of demonstrating support for UN peace-keeping. But so far as advance planning is concerned, the UN finds itself in some major difficulties, which stem from the nature of the Organization itself. Inasmuch as it can never have foreknowledge of the nature, quantity, and origin of the resources which will be made available for a hypothetical operation, contingency planning will be more than usually speculative, and perhaps just a waste of time. Additionally, the amount of detailed information which is available to the UN Secretariat regarding the areas in which the Organization might be asked to operate is very limited. The UN has no men on the spot from whom it can call for reports on political or physical conditions, its only local representatives being its information officers, who are neither trained nor equipped—nor, one might add, expected by their hosts—to act as would the staff of an embassy.

This draws attention to another point of importance: the political sensitivity of planning. Some very pertinent questions could be asked about the propriety of the UN's servants making plans for its possible activity without a mandate from its decision-making organs. And initiative is in any event discouraged by the need to satisfy 120 or so disunited masters. Indeed, there is some authority for the view that even two is one too many. More particularly, the states on whose territory the UN Secretariat appeared to be contemplating action might get very irate if, as is not unlikely, they discovered what was going on. A single state, if it apprehends that it might have to intervene abroad, can quietly make map studies, gather signals and transport equipment, alert its forces, and perhaps establish or build up an advance base near the likely scene of operations. All of which is entirely its own affair. None of these things are easily open to the UN Secretariat, however, if open to it at all. Even a blossoming of the Military Adviser's[4] interest in the terrain of a particular

[4] The Secretary-General appointed a Military Adviser in connection with the establishment of UNEF, and again when the Congo operation was launched. As from 1 January 1964 the post was made permanent as part of the Secretary-General's executive office. It has been held by General I. J. Rikhye of India since 1960.
It would probably be politically impossible, but a case can be made for treating the post of Military Adviser as one which, contrary to the practice regarding the office of Secretary-General, should be filled by a national of a Great Power. For the Secretary-General, ideally, enjoys the confidence of the major Powers, and must therefore, for as long as the Powers are suspicious of each other, come from a small, uncommitted state. However, these are the states who are most likely to be the scene of the UN's peace-keeping operations, which could give rise to a substantial difficulty if the Military Adviser was drawn from a party to a dispute in respect of which the UN was called upon to act. An instance of this occurred in 1965. At the outbreak of the Indo–Pakistan war and the subsequent establishment of a UN observation group to supervise the withdrawal of troops, General Rikhye was

area can lead to critical reactions, as happened in 1964 in respect of the Cambodian–South Vietnam border.

It is, however, frequently urged that the UN should at least engage in planning of a broader kind, and so put itself in a better position to act when the need arises. Popular suggestions here include the organization of courses for potential staff officers, the co-ordination of the training of those national units which have been earmarked for service with the UN[5] the gathering of information regarding possible logistical backing, the improvement of its field procedures, and the maintenance of a staff nucleus which could provide the backbone for the command of a UN force. Ideas such as these are usually linked, as are calls for more specific planning, with the proposal that the Military Adviser's office should be expanded.[6] Most of these schemes would require the co-operation of a number of members who, by definition, are among those who are best disposed towards an active peace-keeping role for the UN. Even so, not all of them might be keen to accommodate the UN to the extent which some of these proposals would require.

But by far the biggest obstacles would lie elsewhere. For, just as the states concerned may object to the UN making tentative arrangements concerning their territory, so more general planning will displease those, led by France and the Soviet Union, who take the view that the UN should not be encouraged to get big ideas about its role in the world and that the Secretariat should in any event be kept in a subordinate position. Both of them, therefore, want to avoid anything which might tempt the UN to act where it would not

---

[5] The following countries have said that they are holding part of their armed forces in readiness for inclusion in a UN force: Canada, Denmark, Finland, Iran, Italy, the Netherlands, Norway, and Sweden. In February 1965 Britain announced that she would provide logistic backing for a UN force of up to six infantry battalions. In all these cases, however, the offer has been subject to the proviso that national commitments permit the release of the earmarked forces when the UN asks for them. It may be supposed that each country's assessment of its commitments would be influenced by its view of the desirability of the operation in question.

The UN has never been authorized to enter into stand-by arrangements. It therefore treads very carefully when a member informs it of its intention to earmark a part of its forces, treating it as a gesture of goodwill which requires no more from the UN than an informal acknowledgement. Besides reflecting delicate political considerations, this course also avoids providing a basis for the suggestion that the UN might feel some obligation to assist in the financing of the earmarked contingents.

[6] During the Congo operation there were three Assistant Military Advisers, but with its winding up the number was reduced to one. It has remained at that figure since then, the post being held, as of mid-1968, by a Finnish colonel.

---

advising the small UN mission in Dominica. When, however, towards the end of the year, his services there became superfluous, it was hardly possible for him to go back to his permanent post on account of the access he would have to information regarding Pakistan's forces. He therefore went to Gaza as Commander of UNEF.

otherwise do so, wishing in particular not to make it easier for the General Assembly to institute peace-keeping operations of any magnitude. The French position reflects de Gaulle's distaste for the UN and his belief that international relations should be kept firmly in the hands of sovereign states. The Soviet Union, ironically, speaks less out of an ideological conviction than from an acute awareness of her minority position within the Organization.

The Soviet Union may not be alone in her attitude. In 1958 the Secretary-General presented a report setting out the experience which the UN had derived from the establishment and operation of UNEF, hoping that it might lead to the Assembly regularizing the Organization's peace-keeping procedures. The Middle East crisis of that year and the fact that President Eisenhower espoused the idea of a standby UN force—implying that the UN might have been able to do America's work in the Lebanon had it been better prepared—made a favourable reception for the Secretary-General's hope much less likely. But it emerged that, quite apart from the contemporary situation, a number of smaller Powers had reservations about equipping the UN to act more efficiently, fearing that they might be on the receiving end of such action. Nothing was done in this direction at the time, nor since, despite the Secretary-General's repeated angling for an invitation to make a study of the UN's peace-keeping capacity. In principle, the Afro-Asians should now have less to fear from an Assembly which is dominated by their own kind. But nevertheless, they can never be sure how it will act in particular cases, and the weak are bound to be especially aware that every member is a potential minority. Moreover, one of their leaders, India, is noted for her anxiety to discourage anything which might lead to her embarrassment in Kashmir. These factors, together with the touchiness of France and the Soviet Union, have led the other members to treat the matter of even general planning very cautiously. And in the absence of any instructions to engage in it, the Secretariat goes to great lengths not to cause offence, not least in the hope of minimizing the difficulties which could be put in the UN's way when the Organization is asked to undertake specific operations.

There may be something in the belief that the Secretariat's caution in this matter is partly a reflection of the prevailing attitude on the 38th floor—the Secretary-General's office in the Secretariat building. It is suggested that its members like to keep things to themselves, rather enjoy rising to a crisis, and are somewhat distrustful of soldiers. Be that as it may, the UN is in any event hardly in a position to make detailed or worthwhile plans for peace-keeping on account of the fact that it is an organization of sovereign states who are all, in degrees which vary with circumstances, jealous of their prerogatives. However, it is highly improbable that this is a handicap so far as an active peace-keeping role is concerned, and it may be that many of the comments as to the desirability of planning rest on a misconception regarding the part which the UN is able to play in the world, perhaps confusing its role with that of states. The latter need to be in a position to move with speed and efficiency, for such action, in self-defence, for example, or in bringing armed assistance to an ally, might literally be a matter of national life or death. The UN, however, does not carry similar responsibilities, and therefore is not under the same compulsion to be able to act with great competence at a moment's notice. For its purposes its present arrangements would not seem to be grossly inadequate. No case comes to mind where organizational insufficiencies were fatal either to the establishment or the success of an operation. And it is exceedingly unlikely that the UN's preparedness to act has any bearing on its being invited to do so.

It is sometimes argued that the UN's efficiency at peace-keeping is less than vitally relevant for a different reason: that the heyday of peace-keeping has passed. This claim often rests on the assumption that peace-keeping has been essentially a post-colonial phenomenon, which, in its major aspects, is disappearing with the final withdrawal of the colonial Powers. There is some apparent strength in this argument, inasmuch as many of the UN's field activities have had to do with or have followed from the winding up of a colonial relationship: Palestine, Kashmir, Indonesia (including the West New Guinea postscript), the Congo, and Cyprus are all cases in point. Even Suez could be seen to have a colonial aspect, through its relationship with the Palestine problem and inasmuch as it stemmed from a final fling by the two colonial Powers who had formerly dominated the Middle East. But Suez can be no more than a marginal case. And it becomes a bit unrealistic to talk of Palestine or Kashmir, or even Cyprus, as post-colonial problems so long after the departure of the metropolitan Powers. A much more basic inadequacy in this analysis, however, is its assumption that the disputes to which the ending of empire gave rise and in which the UN had a hand were typically and exclusively post-colonial. There would seem to be no ground for this view. Territorial claims, minority problems, and civil disorder are all the kind of matters which are not confined to the ending of colonial rule. They might well recur in a different context, particularly, maybe, between or in respect of new states. In which case the UN might be asked to assist in their resolution or dampening, just as in the past.

There is a second argument which throws doubt on the likelihood of the UN playing a significant peace-keeping role in the future. It suggests that the UN's activities in this field have, at least in their major aspects, been a function of the cold war, a reflection of the fact that the Powers have been unable to act jointly in the cause of international order and unwilling to act separately for fear of provoking a counter-intervention, and with it the danger of full-scale war. The UN has therefore been utilized as an acceptable third party, and by acting in place of the Powers has also served as an anti-escalation device. However, it is argued that the developing East–West *détente* will make UN operations superfluous, for the major Powers will be able and anxious to revert to their historic peace-keeping role.

For the frequency with which the anti-escalation side of this argument is heard, the evidence which can be adduced in its support is remarkably thin. Even on the very doubtful assumptions that armed intervention and counter-intervention in distant parts has been a hazard of the cold war, and that this would have presented a real risk of major war, the situations in which the adversaries might have intervened but for the presence of the UN are not easy to identify. Palestine, hardly; nor Kashmir. West New Guinea gave rise to no dangers of this kind, and the intervention problem in relation to Cyprus arose from within the Western alliance. There were vague threats of Soviet intervention over Suez, but it is unlikely in the extreme that there was any substance in them. The UN's observer mission in Greece had little bearing on the activities of her Communist neighbours, and in Korea the North invaded the South despite the presence of a UN commission. In the Lebanon it was the United States rather than the UN which stood in the way of an internal swing to the left. The Congo is the case where Soviet intervention was most talked about, but it does not seem that there was any real chance of troops with snow on their boots appearing in Central Africa.

There is, however, something in that part of the argument which suggests that many of the UN's operations have been of the type which, at an earlier date, and given reasonably satisfactory relations among the Powers, might have been conducted by one or more of them in what would have been accepted as the general good. The Congo and Cyprus are certainly cases where the dominant Power in each area might have taken it upon himself to restore and maintain order. The Suez and West New Guinea operations, insofar as they involved face-saving, might well have been conducted by a well disposed major Power. Nor is it difficult to see the Palestine and Kashmir problems being handled by a group of interested states.

But, on the by no means sure assumption that East–West relations will improve to a point which would permit the Powers to agree on their joint or several interventions in the cause of stability, it does not follow that they would always or even often take advantage of that opportunity, nor that they would be opposed to a continued peace-keeping role for the UN. For action by or on behalf of the Powers alone would meet with much greater opposition from the smaller states than in pre-UN days. And the Powers are not nearly so ready to ignore the lesser members of the international society as they once were. They have also got into the prevailing habit of thinking of the UN as the legitimate channel for collective action.

The argument that the UN's peace-keeping role will suffer a marked decline as the international climate improves is, therefore, not much more convincing than the claim that its activities in the field to date have been attempts to guard against escalation. Indeed, at first sight there would seem to be more strength in the opposite argument—that better relations between the Powers will lead to increased use of the UN's peace-keeping facilities. The Organization is, after all, predicated on the unity of the Great so far as the maintenance of peace is concerned. But although a good international atmosphere provides the most favourable context for UN peace-keeping, it is not a guarantee that it will flourish. The Powers may sometimes prefer to act outside the UN; their co-operation within the Organization may be prevented on particular issues by competing policies; or there may simply be a lack of crises. And past experience suggests that the corollary of this argument—that peace-keeping will be neglected in bad times—is insupportable. It could be said that the UN has developed its major peace-keeping capability in the post-Stalinist period. But as a substantiating assertion this tends to disintegrate upon closer examination. For Suez was contemporary with Hungary. The Congo operation was launched just a couple of months after the shooting down of the U2 led to the breakdown of the summit meeting at Paris. And the West New Guinea force was authorized just when the United States was getting suspicious about Soviet activities in Cuba. Moreover, the UN's cease-fire and truce observation machinery in both Palestine and Kashmir was being established at the time of the Berlin blockade.

In fact, one of the most striking things about the UN's peace-keeping operations is their *ad hoc* character, meaning not that each is mounted with such resources as can be quickly brought together (although this is so) but that they are not obviously related to any general international movements or developments, whether the atmosphere at the UN, the Organization's preparedness for action, the break-up of empire, the state of relations between the Great

Powers, or whatever. Rather, they are almost invariably a response to a crisis, whether mild or serious, local or far-reaching. And crises, especially those which are more likely to involve the UN because they do not involve a Great Power, tend to occur irrespective of the condition of the UN or, to a large extent, of the world. Thus, UN peace-keeping is unlikely to occur in cycles, or to be simply a reflection of international moods or trends. However, it is at the same time very arguable that, in its individual manifestations, peace-keeping is often deeply influenced by the Powers.

Universal or quasi-universal organizations such as the UN are often taken to be mechanisms for the more elevated conduct of international relations. In one sense they may serve this end, for action in the name of the whole is widely thought to gain considerably in legitimacy and propriety over the same action taken only by one or a number of interested states. But if, as sometimes seems to be the case, this view is based on the assumption that collective measures are in some way a-political, and, more particularly, get away from considerations of power, it is mistaken. Indeed, institutions may realistically be seen, so far as their effort to implement collective security is concerned, as attempts to organize power more efficiently. The hope is that they will ensure a permanent balance in favour of peace and against aggression. It might be thought that the UN's effective abandonment of this goal would have reduced the significance of the Powers, for the operations which are now the height of its ambitions in the field do not normally rely on armed force. Moreover, when troops are needed for peace-keeping, they are almost invariably drawn from states other than the permanent members of the Security Council. The exceptional circumstances of the only instance to the contrary—the use of British troops in Cyprus—amply prove this rule. Nevertheless, it is still the case that the Great frequently have a crucial bearing on peace-keeping, through their ability to speak persuasively to the parties, to grant or withhold essential logistics and money (the United States is particularly important here), and to influence UN decisions.

The attitudes and policies of the Powers towards proposals for UN action fall into six categories. In the first place, where all the Powers are opposed to the UN making a move there is very little likelihood of it doing so. A small Power revolt would be possible, and something of the kind occurred in respect of Albania in 1921. But the greater likelihood is that the view of the Powers would be shared by a sizeable proportion of the membership. None of the Powers, for example, showed any keenness to send observers to Goa in 1961 when India was preparing for a showdown, perhaps reflecting the fact that most states were even more hostile to Portugal's suggestion than themselves. Likewise, South Africa can expect no succour from the UN should she find herself in trouble, for although the permanent Council members are not prepared to move against her, they are also unwilling to give her any support—a position from which the Assembly certainly does not dissent.

The position is unlikely to be any more favourable for action where, secondly, only some of the Powers are opposed to it but where the others simply acquiesce. In these circumstances the compliant states might well be reluctant to go so far as to vote for the proposal for fear of giving unnecessary offence, and as a result it may well fail of adoption. The prospect for action is much brighter if, in the third place, all the Powers acquiesce, for then there would be no danger of any of them being regarded by its fellows as a trouble-maker. There might, though, be opposition among lesser states to the suggested operation, and if it included one of the parties, the Powers, being disinterested, might be reluctant to press the matter. More probably, however, the acquiescence of the major states would indicate that the proposed action was lacking in controversy, and so the way would be clear for its endorsement. Much of the UN's mediatory work would fall into this category. Alternatively, Great Power acquiescence might arise in connection with a course towards which they felt impelled by principle but for which they had no enthusiasm. Manchuria and Ethiopia are cases in point. The post-1945 period, significantly, provides none of this kind.

The fourth kind of situation is the most controversial: where some of the Powers favour the launching of a peace-keeping opera-tion and the others are opposed to it. Whether the UN takes action will depend on whether those who are better placed, procedurally, think it worth while offending the minority. On a number of occa-sions in the past they have thought that it is, and hence UN missions were established in respect of the Balkans, Korea, Hungary, and Laos, and the operation in the Congo was continued over Soviet protests. Clearly, however, unless relations are very bad, or the mission particularly important, there will probably be a limit to the extent to which the majority will think it wise to go. It may be that concern for the minority, at least for the Soviet-led minority, may be more evident in the future than in the past in order not to endanger the East–West détente.

The fifth Great Power constellation, and it is the one which has attended most UN operations, consists of the enthusiasm of some and the acquiescence of the others. On one occasion the United States was the compliant Power, the Dominican operation being estab-lished against her will but not her vote. Another case where the acquiescence of some of the Powers was obtained only with considerable difficulty was Suez, Britain and France being very doubtful about the desirability of the UN's intervention. Usually, however, it is the Soviet Union who has blown neither hot nor cold with regard to UN operations. In the cases of Lebanon and the Yemen she withheld her fire in order not to give offence to one of the parties. She may also have regarded UN action in both these countries as the least undesirable course. In other instances Soviet hesitation has been grounded in procedure rather than substance, in the sense that she does not oppose what is suggested but does not want to identify with the majority—as in the case of Indonesia, and also, perhaps, in respect of the Truce Supervision Organization in Palestine. Alternatively, she may refrain from giving a proposal active support in order not to jeopardize her stand on a constitutional matter: Suez is an example of this. Sometimes, too, Soviet acquiescence just reflects a willingness to let others use the Organization for their own purposes where her interests are not directly involved. West New Guinea was perhaps a case in point, and Cyprus certainly is. As the Soviet Union is supposed to have said when criticized for not making a voluntary payment towards the cost of the Cyprus Force, her contribution consists in allowing the West to use the UN in order to avoid a situation which would embarrass it greatly.[7]

Sixthly, and last, is the situation which is far the most advantageous for peace-keeping operations, where all the Powers are keen on their establishment. Even here, it does not follow that the UN will act, for the states concerned may be determined to resist the Organization, and the Powers may not be prepared to impose their will. Thus the arrangements which were made for the partition of Palestine in 1948 fell through on account of the attitude of the parties. It is not clear, 20 years later, that the agreement of the Powers on a Middle Eastern peace settlement would be sufficient to secure its acceptance. Rhodesia resisted UN observers in 1961, Cuba in 1962, and Cambodia in 1964. Nevertheless, these examples do not detract from the argument that the unity of the Powers is the most promising context for peace-keeping. The Greco-Bulgarian case of 1925 remains the classic example here, although it may be joined by the actions of the Powers in respect of the Indo-Pakistan war of 1965. The UN's role in Kashmir since 1949 may also reflect, in a lower key, the agreement of the Powers as to the undesirability of war on the sub-continent. Their basic unity in 1948 was very important in bringing the war of Palestinian succession to a halt, and their agree-

[7] Soviet restraint has also been notable in respect of the Secretary-General's decision, towards the end of the Congo operation, to transfer his Military Adviser to the UN's permanent staff.

ment greatly eased the re-establishment of the Truce Supervision
Organization on the Syrian and UAR fronts after the June 1967
war. The Congo operation, too, got under way on account of the
Powers being agreed regarding its necessity, although, in a manner
which clearly demonstrates the political character of peace-keeping,
it ran into serious trouble when the Soviet Union realized that the
UN was not going to act as Lumumba's agent.

It is unlikely that such peace-keeping proposals as are made during
the next decade or so will usually elicit the united support of the
Powers. Such a state of affairs would probably indicate the existence
of a nineteenth-century type Great Power concert, and the legacy of
past suspicion and the prospect of continuing conflicts of interest
would seem to stand in the way of an early development along those
lines. But it would be surprising if there were no instances of the
Powers agreeing on the desirability of UN action, and it might well
become more common for some of them to acquiesce in the UN's
conduct of operations which are keenly sought by the others. For
the improvement in East–West relations which has occurred in the
1960s both reflects and creates a growing Soviet interest in stability,
and it is to be expected that both sides will sometimes see the UN as
the best instrument for the achievement of that end. As in the past,
its use is most likely in areas where neither super-power holds or
claims dominance: the Middle East, South Asia, and Africa. But
it could be that the United States might agree to a UN operation
in respect of border conflicts or territorial wars in Central or South
America, which would be a means both of demonstrating her good
faith to the Latin Americans and of encouraging the Soviet Union
to assume wider responsibilities in the management of conflict. It
is even conceivable that an increasing tendency towards balkaniza-
tion in Eastern Europe might lead the Soviet Union to think in
terms of a quietening role for the UN in that part of the world also,
for her allies would find it infinitely more acceptable than her own
intervention. However, if the ideological inclination of a Latin
American or East European country was at stake, it seems certain
that the matter would still be regarded by the dominant Power as
wholly inappropriate for UN action. Instead, it would be thought to
require a degree of Soviet or American attention which, if not exclusive, was no more than formally diluted by a little regional participation in the interests of legitimacy.

A possible difficulty about the UN's future peace-keeping role lies
in the attitude of China. Her tirades against the United States seem
to represent genuine distrust and antagonism. She is increasingly
hostile to the Soviet Union (divided ideologists rarely got on well

'how these Communists love each other' may soon be the more apposite version of the maxim). And she is in any event ill-disposed towards the UN on account of her exclusion since 1949 and its 1951 finding that she had committed aggression in Korea. Further, she is generally supposed to have an interest in unrest and disorder. Thus there is ground for apprehension about the effect on Great Power co-operation within the UN of China's assumption of the permanent Security Council seat presently held by Chiang Kai-shek's Taiwan regime. She may not inherit it just yet, and in all probability not before the ending of the Vietnam war. But one day, presumably, China will take her rightful place at the UN. And it cannot be assumed that by then she will be in a less belligerent frame of mind.

However, it is unlikely that the sympathy which an obstructive China would receive will be any greater than that which the Soviet Union obtained at the heigh o' the cold war, and in that case it would, proportionately, be a good deal less on account of the increase in the Organization's size. Hence there would seem to be scope, as formerly, for the other Powers to resort to the Assembly when they were blocked in the Council. Procedurally, this would be more cumbersome, and it might also be more awkward in political terms. But there is little reason for supposing that the Assembly would not take the action which was sought by a majority of the Powers. There is, however, a further consideration which suggests that China's impact on the UN might not be so upsetting as is sometimes suggested. For it cannot be taken for granted that China within the UN would be the same as China without. This is not to imply that her present attitude is simply a reflection of her exclusion. But it may be that her membership would induce some changes in her approach to the Organization and the other Powers. For even if she still felt that she had little interest in the particular operations which the UN wished to mount, she might, in time, come to the view that those which did her no damage ought not to be opposed. In this way she would avoid giving needless offence to her fellow members, with whom she might occasionally wish to make common cause, whether inside or outside the Organization. It would not be the first example of a renegade choosing to clip his wings in consequence of being involved in the processes of society.

Certainly, UN peace-keeping seems to be firmly established as one of the processes to which states can resort for the furthering of their international purposes. Such a development was not envisaged in 1945, when thoughts regarding the maintenance of peace were concentrated on the threat or use of armed force. It may be that the UN will yet return to this matter, although it does not seem likely. But in any event, such a move would hardly be at the expense of those other devices through which the UN has, in a variety of forms been active in many parts of the world. Sometimes it has endeavoured to encourage change, and undoubtedly it will continue its efforts to eradicate the last remnants of colonialism. Much interest is also being taken in the possibility of the Organization using force in southern Africa. But for as long as the advocates of this course are chiefly those who are in a poor position to do anything about it themselves, it seems unlikely that the UN will depart from its generally pacific role. In any event, however, the bulk of its peace-keeping activity has been and will surely remain an expression of the desire for stability. Thus it has to do with securing or implementing agreements and the prevention of violence. Success here, as in so many other things, turns largely on the policies of the most powerful, although, short of their being willing to engage in coercion, it depends ultimately on the attitudes of the parties. The fact that this process is conducted through the UN does not deprive it of its political character—far from it. Nor does it necessarily add to its moral stature. Peace-keeping does, however, offer an additional channel for stabilizing action. In a world which does not get less turbulent and in which the potential for destruction is increasing on all sides, it is unlikely that such a facility will soon be regarded as superfluous.

Select Bibliography

ARMSTRONG, HAMILTON FISH: 'The UN Experience in Gaza', 35 *Foreign Affairs*, No. 4, July 1957.

AZCARATE, PABLO DE: *Mission in Palestine 1948–1952* (Washington: Middle East Institute, 1966).

BAR-YAACOV, N.: *The Israel-Syrian Armistice* (Jerusalem: Magnes Press, The Hebrew University, 1967).

BERNADOTTE, FOLKE: *To Jerusalem* (London: Hodder and Stoughton, 1951).

BLOOMFIELD, LINCOLN P., *et al.*: *International Military Forces* (Boston: Little, Brown, 1964).

——: 'Peacekeeping and Peacemaking'. 44 *Foreign Affairs*, No. 4, July 1966.

BOWETT, D. W.: *United Nations Forces. A Legal Study* (London: Stevens, 1964; New York: Praeger, 1965).

BOYD, JAMES M.: 'Cyprus: Episode in Peacekeeping' XX *International Organization*, No. 1, Winter 1966.

BRECHER, MICHAEL: *The Struggle for Kashmir* (New York: Oxford University Press, 1953).

BROOK, DAVID: *Preface to Peace. The United Nations and the Arab–Israel Armistice System* (Washington: Public Affairs Press, 1964).

BURNS, ARTHUR LEE, and HEATHCOTE, NINA: *Peace-keeping by UN Forces from Suez to the Congo* (London: Pall Mall; New York: Praeger, 1963).

BURNS, E. L. M.: *Between Arab and Israel* (London: Harrap, 1962; New York: Obolensky, 1963).

CALVOCORESSI, PETER: *World Order and New States* (London: Chatto and Windus; New York; Praeger, 1962).

CLAUDE, INIS L., JR.: 'The United Nations and the Use of Force'. *International Conciliation*, No. 532, March 1961.

——: 'The Political Framework of the United Nations' Financial Problems', XVII *International Organization*, No. 4, Autumn 1963.

——: 'The OAS, the UN, and the United States', *International Conciliation*, No. 547, March 1964.

——: 'Collective Legitimization as a Political Function of the United Nations', XX *International Organization*, No. 3, Summer 1966.

COLLINS, J. FOSTER: 'The United Nations and Indonesia', *International Conciliation*, No. 459, March 1950.

COMBS, JAMES JOSEPH: 'France and United Nations Peacekeeping', XXI *International Organization*, No. 2, Spring 1967.

COX, ARTHUR M.: *Prospects for Peacekeeping* (Washington: Brookings, 1967).

CURTIS, GERALD L.: 'The United Nations Observation Group in the Lebanon', XVIII *International Organization*, No. 4, Autumn 1964.

FRYDENBERG, PER, ed.: *Peace-keeping: Experience and Evaluation* (Oslo: Norwegian Institute of International Affairs, 1964).

FRYE, WILLIAM R.: *A United Nations Peace Force* (New York: Oceana; London: Stevens, 1957).

GAGNON, MONA HARRINGTON: 'Peace Forces and the Veto: The Relevance of Consent', XXI *International Organization*, No. 4, Autumn 1967.

GARCIA-GRANADOS, JORGE: *The Birth of Israel* (New York: Knopf, 1948).

GOODRICH, LELAND M.: *Korea: A Study of U.S. Policy in the United Nations* (New York: Council on Foreign Relations, 1956).

GOODRICH, LELAND M., and ROSNER, GABRIELLA E.: 'The United Nations Emergency Force', XI *International Organization*, No. 3, Summer 1957.

GORDENKER, LEON: *The United Nations and the Peaceful Unification of Korea* (The Hague: Nijhoff, 1959).

——: *The UN Secretary-General and the Maintenance of Peace* (New York and London: Columbia University Press, 1967).

HEATHCOTE, NINA: 'American Policy towards the U.N. Operation in the Congo', 18 *Australian Outlook*, No. 1, Autumn 1964.

HIGGINS, ROSALYN: 'United Nations Peace-keeping—Political and Financial Problems', 21 *The World Today*, No. 8, August 1965.

HOFFMAN, STANLEY: 'Sisyphus and the Avalanche: The United Nations, Egypt and Hungary', XI *International Organization*, No. 3, Summer 1957.

——: 'In Search of a Thread: The UN in the Congo Labyrinth', XVI *International Organization*, No. 2, Spring 1962.

——: 'Erewhon or Lilliput? A Critical View of the Problem', XVII *International Organization*, No. 2, Spring 1963.

HOLMES, JOHN W.: 'The Political and Philosophical Aspects of UN Security Forces', XIX *International Journal*, No. 3, Summer 1964.

HORN, CARL VON: *Soldiering for Peace* (London: Cassell; New York: McKay, 1966).

HOSKYNS, CATHERINE: *The Congo since Independence, January 1960–December 1961* (London and New York: Oxford University Press, 1965).

HUREWITZ, JACOB C.: 'The United Nations Conciliation Commission for Palestine', VII *International Organization*, No. 4, November 1953.

HUTCHISON, E. H.: *Violent Truce* (New York: Devin Adair, 1956).

JAMES, ALAN: 'UN Action for Peace, I. Barrier Forces, II. Law and Order Forces', 18 *The World Today*, Nos. 11 & 12, November and December 1962.

KAY, DAVID A.: 'The Politics of Decolonization: The New Nations and the United Nations' Political Process', XXI *International Organization*, No. 4 Autumn 1967.

LARUS, JOEL, ed.: *From Collective Security to Preventive Diplomacy* (New York: Wiley, 1965; London: Wiley).

LASH, JOSEPH P.: *Dag Hammarskjöld* (Garden City, N.Y.: Doubleday, 1961; London: Cassell, 1962).

LEFEVER, ERNEST W.: *Crisis in the Congo* (Washington: Brookings, London: Faber, 1965).

——: *Uncertain Mandate: Politics of the UN Congo Operation* (Baltimore: Johns Hopkins, 1967; London: Oxford U.P., 1968).

LEONARD, L. LARRY: 'The United Nations and Palestine', *International Conciliation*, No. 454, October 1949.

LIE, TRYGVE: *In the Cause of Peace* (London and New York: Macmillan, 1954).

LOURIE, SYLVAIN: 'The United Nations' Military Observer Group in India and Pakistan', IX *International Organization*, No. 1, February 1955.

MARTELLI, GEORGE: *Experiment in World Government, An Account of the United Nations' Operation in the Congo 1960–1964* (London: Johnson, 1966).

MOHN, PAUL: 'Problems of Truce Supervision', *International Conciliation*, No. 478, February 1952.

NICHOLAS, HERBERT: 'UN Peace Forces and the Changing Globe', XVII, *International Organization*, No. 2, Spring 1963.

——: 'The United Nations in Crisis', 41 *International Affairs*, No. 3, July 1965.

NOORANI, A. G.: *The Kashmir Question* (Bombay: Manaktalas, 1964).

O'BRIEN, CONOR CRUISE: *To Katanga and Back* (London: Hutchinson; New York: Grosset and Dunlop, 1962).

QUBAIN, FAHIM I.: *Crisis in Lebanon* (Washington: Middle East Institute, 1961).

RIKHYE, I. J.: *Preparation and Training of United Nations Peace-keeping Forces* (London: Institute for Strategic Studies, 1964).

ROSNER, GABRIELLA: *The United Nations Emergency Force* (New York and London: Columbia University Press, 1963).

RUSSELL, RUTH B.: *United Nations Experience with Military Forces* (Washington: Brookings, 1964).

——: 'Development by the United Nations of Rules Relating to Peace-keeping', *Proceedings*, American Society of International Law, 1965.

——: 'United Nations Financing and "The Law of the Charter"', (1966) *Columbia Journal of Transitional Law*, No. 1.

STEGENGA, JAMES A.: *The United Nations Force in Cyprus* (Columbus, Ohio: Ohio State University Press, 1968).

STEPHENS, ROBERT: *Cyprus: A Place of Arms* (London: Pall Mall Press, 1966).

TANDON, YASHPAL: 'Consensus and Authority Behind United Nations Peacekeeping Operations', XXI *International Organization*, No. 2, Spring 1967.

——: 'UNEF, The Secretary-General, and International Diplomacy in the Third Arab-Israeli War', XXII *International Organization*, No. 2, Spring 1968.

TAYLOR, ALASTAIR M.: *Indonesian Independence and the United Nations* (London: Stevens, 1960).

URQUHART, BRIAN E.: 'United Nations Peace Forces and the Changing United Nations: An Institutional Perspective', XVII *International Organization*, No. 2, Spring 1963.

VAN DER KROEF, JUSTUS M.: 'The West New Guinea Settlement: Its Origins and Implications', 7 *Orbis*, No. 1, Spring 1963.

VAN DER VEUR, PAUL W.: 'The United Nations in West Irian: A Critique', XVIII *International Organization*, No. 2, Winter 1964.

WAINHOUSE, DAVID W., *et al.*: *International Peace Observation* (Baltimore: Johns Hopkins; London: Oxford University Press, 1966).

WALTERS, F. P.: *A History of the League of Nations*, 2 vols. (London: Oxford University Press, 1952).

YOUNG, ORAN R.: *Trends in International Peacekeeping* (Princeton: Center of International Studies, 1966).

ZACHER, MARK W.: 'The Secretary-General and the United Nations' Function of Peaceful Settlement'; XX *International Organization*, No. 4, Autumn 1966.

ZIMMERN, ALFRED: *The League of Nations and the Rule of Law 1918–1935* (London: Macmillan [2nd edn.], 1939).

Index

Aaland Islands, 16
Abdoh, D., 163
Abu Dhabi, 69
Abyssinia, see Ethiopia
Adeel, O. A. H., 393
Adeel, S. O., 395 n
Aden: and Yemen, 110, 115–16; and South Arabia, 249; independence and UN mission, 393–7; and UAR, 115–16, 389 n.
Aduola, Cyrille, 416, 418–20
Afghanistan, 391
Africa, East, 321, 438
Africa, South, see South Africa
Africa, South West, see South West Africa
Afro-Asian bloc: and Suez war, 2; power in UN, 19, 156, 431; and Bizerta base, 58: and Congo, 67, 357, 360, 362; mutual help, 115; and W. New Guinea, 158; and S.W. Africa, 172, 406; and Portugal, 251, 253, 399, 406; and Cyprus, 323; and Perim, 343; and Oman, 391; and S. Africa, 406; and Rhodesia, 406–8; and Katanga secession, 412, 414–15, 418, 421
Albania, 18, 21, 182–4, 209–13, 435
Algeria, 57, 59, 88–9, 353, 386
Alva, M. de, 257
Alvim, Gen., 240
America, see Latin America; Organization of American States; United States of America
Anglo-Egyptian Treaty (1936), 278
Anglo-Persian Oil Company, 72 n.
Angola, 252–4, 398–9 n., 403, 405
Aqaba, Gulf of, 106, 297, 299, 300, 342
Arab League, 216–17, 313
Arabia, South, 8, 249–50, 342–3, 393–7
Arab States: and Israel, 29–30, 60–6, 127, 261–3, 272–90; Soviet support for, 66, 98, 284, 289, 296; and Jerusalem, 142–4; and Libya, 340–1; and Oman, 390; see also individual states
Arbenz, Col. J., 234, 236
Argentina, 25, 202, 237
Armas, Col. C., 234–6
Arsos incident (Cyprus), 329–30
Australia: and Palestine, 30; and Corfu channel, 21; and Indonesia, 43, 46–7, 50–1, 56; and Trieste, 136; and Cyprus, 325 n., 328; and Spain, 373–4; and Korea, 378, 380; and Hungary, 383; and colonialism, 388, 393
Austria, 139, 325–6, 328, 383

Baghdad Pact, 215
Balaguer, S., 246
Balkans, 137, 427; UN Special Commission on, 4, 11, 211–13, 436
Bandung Conference, 82
Bayar, President Celâl, 215
Beck-Friis, J., 84
Belgium: and Ruanda, 22; and Kashmir, 25; and Indonesia, 46, 51; and Congo

independence, 67, 354–8, 361, 413 n.; and Greece, 210 n.; and Palestine, 272, 274–5; and anti-colonialism, 388; and Katanga secession, 411–16, 420
Bennike, Gen. V., 283
Berlin, 59, 134, 146, 208, 375, 434
Bernades, C. A., 79, 80
Bernadotte, Count Folke, 60, 143 n., 273–5, 277, 279, 284
Bevin, Ernest, 339
Biafra, 89, 353–4
Bizerta, 57–60
Bolivia, 18, 41, 170, 360
Bonin Islands, 338–9
Borneo, North (Sabah), 10, 31–3, 127
Bosch, Juan, 238, 245–6
Botswana, 171, 172
Bourguiba, President Habib, 57–9
Brazil, 99, 150, 207, 211, 235–7, 245, 256, 325–6, 374–5
Briand-Kellogg Pact (1928), 186, 188
Britain: Suez war (1956), 2, 70, 95–9, 2 n.; Suez war (1956), 2, 70, 95–9, 102–5, 295, 304, 437; and Rhodesia, 4, 254, 392–3, 406–10; and Palestine, 7, 29–30, 142–3, 170, 262–3, 272, 274, 276, 278, 348–9; and League of Nations, 16, 40; and Corfu (1923), 18; and Saar, 18, 152; and Corfu channel (1946), 21; and Italian colonies, 23, 339–40; and Kashmir, 24, 290; and South Asia, 28; and anti-colonialism, 28, 251, 272, 290, 354, 356, 388, 390, 393; and Malaysia, 31–3; and Indonesia, 43, 45, 51, 55; and Bizerta, 58; and Congo, 68, 355–6; and Buraimi oasis, 69–70; relations with Egypt, 70; and Cyprus, 71–2, 321–3, 325, 435; and Yemen, 86, 110, 115, 249–50; use of veto, 99; and UNEF, 100–4, 304; and Aden, 110, 115–16, 344, 393–7 (see also and S. Arabia); and Indo-Pakistan war, 117; and Trieste, 136–9, 141; and S.W. Africa, 171–2, 256, 388, 400–1, 405–6; and Albania, 183–4; and Manchuria, 185–7, 194; and Ethiopia, 191; and Laos, 201–3; and Cambodia, 206; and post-war Greece, 209–12; and Turkish-Syrian dispute, 214; and Lebanon, 218; and Jordan, 221, 224–7, 229–33; and Dominica, 240, 243; and S. Arabia, 249–50, 393–7; and Goa, 251; and Angola, 254; and Isle of Man, 258; and Kuwait, 313; and Perim, 342–3; and British Guiana, 365, 390; and Kenya, Uganda and Tanganyika, 366; and Mauritius, 366; and Spain, 373; and German elections, 375; and Nationalist China, 376; and Hungarian revolution, 382–3 n.; and Oman, 390–2; and S. Africa, 400–1, 405–6; and Katanga secession, 415, 417–19, 421; support for UN force, 430 n.
British Guiana, 365, 390
Brosio, Manlio, 265

Brunei, 31–2
Bulgaria, 16–17, 209–13, 348, 375, 408, 437
Bull, Gen. Odd, 219, 284, 287–8
Bunche, Ralph, 60 n., 61, 87, 120, 273, 279
Bundy, McGeorge, 245
Bunker, Ellsworth, 57, 85, 87, 167
Buraimi oasis, 69–71
Burma, 24, 413
Burns, Gen. E. L. M., 108, 280, 284
Burundi, 71

Caamano, Col. F., 238–9, 241, 243–6
Cambodia, 80, 84–5, 128, 198–200, 203 n., 206–7, 430, 437
Cameroons, British, 22
Cameroun Republic, 22
Canada: and Palestine, 30, 289; and UNEF, 99, 100, 103, 300, 307; and Yemen, 111; and Indo-Pakistan war, 117; and Saar, 152; and W. New Guinea, 162; and Laos, 203; and Lebanon, 218; and Cyprus, 265, 325; and Kashmir, 290; and Korea, 378–9; and UN force, 430 n.
Caroline Islands, 338
Carpio, V., 257
Castro, President Fidel, 125–6
Central Intelligence Agency, 234, 359
Ceylon, 307, 360, 383
Chaco war (1933), 18, 41–2
Chamoun, Camille, 215, 217–21, 223–4, 228
Chehab, Gen. Fuad, 224, 226
Chiang Kai-shek, 224, 376, 439
Chile, 240, 374, 380
China (Communist): UN membership, 33, 428, 439; and India, 27, 118, 206, 251, 420; relations with Pakistan, 28, 118; and US airmen, 82; and International Control Commissions, 128; and Korea, 128, 197–8, 380, 439; and Laos, 201; hostility to UN, 207, 224, 317, 439; and the Powers, 438–9
China (Nationalist): 428, 439; and Manchuria, 18, 185–91; and Kashmir, 24; and Lebanon, 218, 224; and Guatemala, 236; and Congo, 355; and Spain, 374; Soviet violations, 376; and Korea, 378; and Portugal, 405
Chou En-lai, 83
Colombia, 21, 25, 99, 150–1, 212, 217, 219, 235–6, 300, 307, 386
Cominform, 140, 212, 381
Communist states and Communism: UN hostility, 9; US attitude to, 48, 55, 215; in Italy, 138–9, 339–40; in Greece, 139, 209, 211–13; in Indo-China, 198, 200; in Middle East, 215, 219, 263, 296; in UN, 233; and the Americas, 234, 237–9, 245, 248; and UNEF, 296; in Congo, 360–2; and Czechoslovakia, 374; in Far East, 376, 379–80; and Rhodesia, 407; Indonesian massacre of, 410
Congo: UN force (ONUC), 3, 9, 12, 161–2 n., 265 n., 267, 319, 324, 328 n., 354–64, 412–23, 427–8, 432–4, 438; UN mediation, 66–8, 71, 173;

Soviet intervention, 360–3, 433, 436; see also Katanga
Constantinople Convention (1888), 95
Cook Islands, 393
Cordier, Andrew, 26 n., 359
Corfu: 1923 incident, 17–18; 1946 channel dispute, 21
Costa Rica, 240, 391
Crete, 348
Cuba: 1962 missile crisis, 11, 86, 125–6, 244, 434; and Indonesia, 48; and Dominica, 239; and UN, 317, 364, 437
Cyprus: UN force in (UNFICYP), 3, 8, 9, 12, 73, 75–6, 79, 241, 320–34, 532, 423 n., 425–6, 432, 435, 437; intercommunal dispute, 71–81, 127; Cyprus National Guard, 74, 264–6, 330; non-alignment, 75; UN mediator in, 73, 76–80, 327; UN administration, 146; 1967 crisis, 264–7, 252–3; suggested NATO force, 322–6, 331; question of partition, 335; preindependence, 386; British troops in, 435
Czechoslovakia: and Kashmir, 25–6 n.; and Palestine, 30, 170; and Congo, 127; arms to Egypt, 263; and Congo, 359; and Cyprus, 323; 1948 coup, 374

Dahomey, 161
Danzig, 41
Dayal, Rajeshwar, 219, 360, 415
Delvoie, Gen., 290
Denktash, Rauf, 264
Denmark, 99, 300, 326, 328, 383, 430 n.
Dien Bien Phu, 199
Disarmament Commission, 198
Dixon, Sir Owen, 26
Dixon, Sir Pierson, 357
Dominica, 238–48, 388, 430 n., 436
Dorsinville, M., 71
Drummond, Sir Eric, 41
Dulles, John Foster, 234
Dutch East Indies, see Indonesia

Ecuador, 240
Eden, Sir Anthony, 95, 104
Egypt: Suez war (1956), 2, 95–9, 104; and Yemen, 4, 86–7, 110–11, 113, 115, 396; 6-day war (June 1967), 4, 64, 287, 309, 313, 335; and UNEF, 7, 9, 99–107, 121, 124–5, 281, 295–306, 320; 1967 request to withdraw UNEF, 306–13, 332, 422, 425; and armistice with Israel, 61, 106–8, 277–8, 282, 285; relations with Britain, 70; and Sinai, 145; and Pakistan, 162; and Lebanon, 215; forms UAR, 215; and Israel borders, 261, 281, 289, 295–306; Czech arms, 263; Guerrillas, 302; post-Suez policy, 305; and Congo force, 355; see also Suez War; United Arab Republic
Eisenhower, President Dwight D., 107, 215, 218, 224, 229, 431
El Salvador, 245, 378
Eritrea, 23–4, 339–40

Ethiopia, 23–4, 37 n., 171, 191–2, 258, 355, 436
Euratom, 129
Evans, Harold, 143 n.

Faro, Luis de, 387
Fiji, 258, 390
Finland, 16, 99, 300, 325, 430 n.
France: and Suez War (1956), 2, 95–9, 103–5, 215, 295, 304, 433; and League of Nations, 16; and Germany, 18, 151–4; and Togoland, 22; and Italian colonies, 23, 191, 339; and Indonesia, 44–5, 48, 51, 55, 233; use of veto, 44, 51, 99, 233; and Bizerta base, 57–60; attitude to UN, 60, 128, 431; and Palestine mediation, 61; and UNEF, 100–4, 304; and Israel, 107, 262, 289; and Unipom; and Trieste, 138; and Saar, 151–4; and W. New Guinea, 161; and S.W. Africa 171–2, 388, 400; and Manchuria, 186–7, 194; and Indo-China, 189–200, 202, 206; and Balkans, 212; and Lebanon, 214, 218; and Guatemala, 236; and Dominica, 240, 243; and colonies, 251, 354; and Goa, 251; and Palestine Truce, Commission, 272–5, 282; and Cyprus, 322–4, 329, 352; and Perim, 344; and Congo, 355–7, 360; and Spain, 374; and German elections, 375; and China, 376; and Korea, 378; and Hungary, 382; and Tunisia, 386, 414 n.; and anti-colonialism, 388, 390, 394; and Oman, 391; and S. Africa, 400–1; and Rhodesia, 407–8; and Katanga secession, 418–19, 421; and UN peace-keeping expenses, 424–6, 430–1
Franco, Gen. Francisco, 373

Gaulle, President Charles de, 58–9, 128, 431
Gaza Strip, 106–8, 124, 144–5, 162 n., 283, 295 n., 297–301
General Assembly: and Korea, 2, 198, 377–80; and Italian colonies, 23–4, 340–1; and Palestine, 29, 31, 61, 64, 107, 170–1, 273, 278, 349; and Malaysia, 31–2; and W. New Guinea, 56, 156–7, 160–1, 164; and Bizerta, 58–9; and Congo, 67–8, 360; and Cyprus, 80, 324; and China, 82; and Suez War, 99; and UNEF, 100–1 103–4, 296, 299, 300, 307–8, 310, 312; and Jerusalem, 142–3, 145 n.; and S.W. Africa, 171, 256–7, 399–401, 405; Peace Observation Commission, 199 n.–200, 212; and post-war Greece, 211–12, 233; and Lebanon, 216, 219, 224, 226, 228; and Dominica, 341; and Goa, 252; and Portuguese colonies, 252–3, 398–9, 405; and establishment of military forces, 317; and Spain, 374; and E. Europe, 375; and China, 376; and Hungary, 382–3; on colonialism, 386, 388–99; and S. Africa, 387–401, 405, 436; and Oman, 390–2; and Cook Islands, 393; and Rhodesia, 406, 408; and peace-keeping role, 424–7,

439; see also Security Council; United Nations
Geneva: China–US talks (1955), 83, 128; Conference on Indo-China and Korea (1954), 199–200, 203, 206; 1962 declaration on Laos, 205
Germany: and Memel, 16; and Saar, 18–19, 151–4; and Danzig, 41; and Upper Silesia, 127; and Balkans, 137; ambitions in 1930, 191; Lytton Commission, 194; division of 208; and Polish corridor, 351 n.; and Spanish civil war, 373
Germany, East, 208, 375
Germany, West, 146, 208, 322, 375
Gerö, E., 381
Ghana, 22, 253, 355, 413–14 n.
Gibraltar, 155, 389 n., 398
Gizenga, Antoine, 68, 418, 420
Glubb, Sir John, 262
Goa, 251–2, 254, 318, 435
Godoy, H. Garcia, 246
Gold Coast, see Ghana
Gomulka, Wladyslaw, 381
Graham, Frank P., 26
Greece: post-war regime and Special Committee on Balkans, 4, 209–13, 233; Bulgarian border, 16, 437; and Cyprus, 71–8, 80, 264–7, 322–5, 322, 335, 353, 386; and Communism, 139, 209; and Albania, 182–3; 1967 military government, 264–5; and Crete, 348; and Macedonia, 348
Greek Cypriots, 3, 71–2, 75–8, 81 n., 264, 320–1, 326, 328–30, 331, 334–5, 353, 386
Grivas, Gen. George, 264–5, 267
Guatemala, 24, 30; 1954 crisis, 234–7, 317
Guinea, 68, 158, 355, 393, 413
Guinea, Portuguese, 253
Gussing, N. S., 84–5
Gyani, Gen. Prem Singh, 325

Hague, The: Round Table Conference (1949), 48–9
Hammarskjöld, Dag: and Bizerta, 58–9; and US airmen in China, 82–3; and Thai–Cambodia dispute, 83–4; and UNEF, 99, 101; and Laos, 205; and Jordan, 232; and South Africa, 255; death of, 255, 417; and Israel borders, 262; and Congo, 360, 416–17, 422; and Hungary, 382–3
Hitler, Adolf, 152
Home, Earl of, 33
Honduras, 234–6, 240
Horn, Gen. Carl von, 111, 283–4
Hungary, 98, 316, 375, 381–5, 427, 434, 436
Hussein, King of Jordan, 221, 229, 288–9
Hutchison, Cdr. E. H., 280
Hutu people, 71

Ibn Saud, King of Saudi Arabia, 69
Ibos, 258, 353
Iceland, 375
Imbert, Gen. Antonio, 238, 242, 244–5
India: and Kashmir, 4, 24–8, 68, 117, 121–2, 290–3, 382, 431; and China, 27, 118, 206, 420; and Palestine, 30; and Indonesia, 43; and UNEF, 99, 300,

India—continued
307, 309; and war with Pakistan,
117–24; and the Powers, 118–19; and
UN, 120–1, 124–6; and attitude to
UNIPOM and withdrawal arrangements, 120–1, 123–4, 126; and W.
New Guinea, 158; and Korea, 197,
378; and Laos, 203; and Goa, 251–4,
318, 436; and Cyprus, 325; and Congo
force, 415, 420; see also Indo-Pakistan
War and Kashmir
Indo-China, 4, 8, 43–50
Indonesia: and W. New Guinea, 3, 49,
56–7, 85, 155–8, 160–9; independence,
4, 8, 43, 48–9; UN commissions to,
11, 46–52, 56, 95, 233, 432; hostility
to Malaysia, 10, 31–4, 43–57, 233; UN
mediation, 52–7, 60, 159, 432; and
UNEF, 99, 300, 309 n.; and Congo
force, 355, 413, 415
Indo-Pakistan war (1965), 4, 8, 117–24,
293, 437; UN observer missions, 117,
119–21, 123–4, 126, 290–3, 425, 429 n.
Inter-American Conference (10th, Cara-
cas, 1954), 234
Inter-American Peace Committee, 235–6
International Control Commission (Indo-
China), 128, 203, 206–7
International Court of Justice: and Corfu
channel case, 21; and W. New Guinea,
56; Thai-Cambodia dispute, 84; S.W.
Africa, 171, 258, 387, 400; and UN
expenses, 423
International Monetary Fund, 98
Iran, 30, 43, 430 n.
Iraq, 16, 116, 143, 218, 313; 1958 coup in,
220–2, 229, 313; UN presence proposed, 231
Ireland, 325–8, 355
Irian, West, see New Guinea, West
Israel: and Suez War (1956), 2, 3, 96–9,
105, 107, 215, 302; and UNEF, 3, 9,
11, 100–3, 295–312, 332, 422; and
6-day war (June 1967), 4, 64, 127,
287–9, 309, 313, 335; and UN
mediation, 60–6; and Arab refugees,
63, 350; and Suez Canal, 64–5, 106;
US support for, 66; post-Suez withdrawal, 106–7; and Jerusalem, 143–5 n.;
1956 border tension, 127, 261–2;
and 1948 armistice agreements, 61,
277–8, 280–8, 295–9; and UNTSO,
282–90; and Perim, 343; state proclaimed, 349; and W. bank of Jordan,
350; see also Palestine and individual
Arab states
Italy: colonies, 12, 23, 155, 339–41, 344;
and Corfu incident (1923), 18; and
Trieste, 136–41; and Communism,
138–9, 340; and Saar, 152; and
Albania, 182–4; attack on Ethiopia,
191–2; and Laos, 202; and San
Marino, 315–16; and Cyprus, 322;
and Congo, 357; and Spanish civil
war, 373; sanctions against, 402; and
UN forces, 430 n.
Ivory Coast, 207, 241

Jagan, Cheddi, 390

Japan: and Manchuria, 18, 185–90; and
India, 28; and Laos, 202; and
Lebanon, 217, 219, 222; and man-
dated territories, 338; and Ryukyu
and Bonin IS; and Korea, 376–7
Jarring, Gunnar, 64–6, 424–5
Jerusalem, 11, 30, 65–6, 141–5, 273, 350
Johnson, President Lyndon B., 238, 322
Jordan: and Israel, 65, 127, 277–8, 280,
283 n.–5, 288–9, 306, 350–2; and
Yemen, 109; and Jerusalem, 143–5 n.;
British troops in (1958), 221, 224–5,
227, 229–32; UN presence, 231–3,
425; and Dominica, 240; and west
bank of Jordan, 350–1

Kadar, Janos, 381–2, 384–5
Kamaran island, 397
Kasavubu, Joseph, 68, 358–9, 361, 416
Kashmir, 4, 8, 9, 10, 24–9, 68, 119, 122,
431–3, 437; and Indo-Pakistan war,
117, 119–22; UN Military Observer
Group (UNMOGIP), 4, 8, 290–3,
425
Katanga: secessionist regime, 4, 5, 9, 12,
67, 254, 356–8, 363, 411–23
Kennedy, President John F., 125, 146,
205
Kenya, 89, 366
Khan, Gen. Said Uddin, 162
Khrushchev, N. K., 118, 125–6, 146, 224,
381
Korea: war, 1, 2, 5, 197–8, 200, 376, 379,
402 n., 411; and China, 82, 197–8;
armistice agreements, 128, 198; UN
commissions in, 376–81, 428 n., 436
Krishna Menon, V. K., 293
Kuria Muria Islands, 397
Kurile Islands, 338
Kuwait, 313

Laos: International Control Commission
for, 128; and Viet Minh, 198–200,
204; appeal to UN, 200–6, 233, 316,
436
League of Nations, 10; investigatory role,
16–18, 20–1; territorial questions,
35; mediation, 39–42; and minorities,
127 n.; territorial administration, 150–
3; mandates system, 29, 338; see also
individual cases under names of
territories
Leary, Col. R., 284
Lebanon: UN   observer   group
(UNOGIL), 4, 10, 11, 216–17, 219–
20, 222–3, 225–30, 313, 364, 422–3,
425, 437; Palestine settlement, 61, 65,
143, 277–8; 1958 crisis, 214–29, 313;
US forces in, 220–8, 431, 433; and
Israel, 65, 281
Leopoldville, 68, 359, 411, 413 n.–14
Lesotho, 171–2
Leticia, 150–1
Liberia, 171, 258, 355
Libya, 23–4, 229 n., 339–41
Lie, Trygve, 37 n
Linner, Sture, 417
Lithuania, 16, 17
Lloyd, Selwyn, 356 n.
Lloyd George, David, 183

Locarno, Treaty of (1925), 17
Lodge, Henry Cabot, 222, 236
Lumumba, Patrice, 355, 358–62, 365, 412–13, 418, 438; death of, 360 n., 414
Lytton Commission, 187–9, 194

McCarthy, Joseph, 236
Macdonald, Gen. B. F., 119
Macedonia, 348
Makarios, President, 72, 75, 80, 127, 264–7, 322–3, 353
Malawi, 171
Malaya, 31–3, 48, 161, 355
Malaysia, Federation of, 10, 11, 31–4, 127–8, 165, 241
Mali, 68, 408, 413
Malik, A. (of Indonesia), 165
Malik, Charles (of Lebanon), 216
Man, Isle of, 258
Manchukuo, 188–9
Manchuria, 18, 185–91, 436
Marambio, Gen. Tulio, 124
Marshall Islands, 338
Mauritania, 413
Mauritius, 366
Mayobre, J. A., 242–3
Memel, 16
Mexico, 211, 237, 240, 290
Middle East, 4, 9; and Soviet interests, 61, 66; UN Special Representative to, 64–6; and the Powers, 66, 213, 221, 263, 275, 311, 438; and British, 69, 272, 296; Anglo-French dominance, 96; Eisenhower doctrine, 215, 218; see also individual countries
Mikoyan, A., 125
Mobutu, Gen. Joseph-Desiré, 359–60
Molucca Islands, 49
Montenegro, 182
'Morgan line' (Trieste), 136–8
Morocco, 88–9, 116, 207, 253, 355, 413, 415
Mosul, 16
Mozambique, 253, 398, 403, 405–6
Mukden, 185
Munro, Sir Leslie, 320, 383
Murphy, Robert, 223
Muscat and Oman, 69, 70, 390–2, 397
Mussolini, Benito, 18, 98

Nagas, 258
Nagy, Imre, 381–2, 384
Nasser, President Gamal and Lebanon, 215, 217, 219; and Israel, 65; and Yemen, 86, 109, 116; and Suez war (1956), 95–6, 105, 305; and Iraq coup, 221; and withdrawal of UNEF, 310–11; and Perim, 342–4
Nehru, Jawaharlal, 27, 251
Nepal, 391
Netherlands: and W. New Guinea, 3, 56–7, 85, 155–69; and Palestine, 30; and Indonesia dispute, 43–57, 233; and Greece, 211, and Cyprus, 326; and German elections, 375; and Korea, 380; and UN forces, 430 n.
Neuilly, Treaty of, 17
Neutral Nations Supervisory Commission (Korea), 128

New Guinea, West (later West Irian): UN in, 3, 8, 11, 95 n., 159–169, 319, 328 n., 426, 432–4, 437; and Indonesia, 3, 49, 56–7, 85–6, 164–6
New Zealand, 22, 99, 250, 328, 393
Nicaragua, 234–6
Nigeria: Brit. Cameroons 22; and Biafra, 89, 353–4; and Congo, 328 n., 355; and Tanganyika, 366; and Oman, 391
Nimmo, Gen. Robert H., 121, 291
North Atlantic Treaty Organization (NATO), 48, 75, 80, 322, 274
Norway, 24, 48, 99, 225, 291, 300, 307, 326, 430 n.
Nuclear test ban treaty, 129
Nuri-es-Said, 220–1
Nyasaland, 254

O'Brien, Conor Cruise, 415–17
Okinawa, 339
Oman, 390–2
Organisation des Nations Unies au Congo, see under Congo
Organization of African Unity, 88–9, 366
Organization of American States; and Guatemala, 234–8; and Dominica, 238–48
Osorio-Tafall, Bibiano F., 80
Ottoman Empire, 348

Pakistan: and Kashmir, 4, 24–8, 68, 117, 121–2, 290–3; and Eritrea, 24; relations with China, 28, 118; and UNEF, 99, 162, 307; and W. New Guinea force, 161–2; and the Powers, 118–19; and Greece, 211–12; in SEATO, 292; and German elections, 375; and Korea, 380; and war with India, 117–24
Palestine: dispute over, 7, 29–30, 60; UN Mediator for, 9, 60, 261, 273–8, 334, 426; UN Special Committee on (UNSCOP), 30, 141; Arab-Jewish war (1948), 60; Conciliation Commission, 60–3, 273, 278, 334; 1949 armistice, 61–2, 277–8; partition, 62, 143, 170, 348, 437; Arab refugees, 63–4, 106; UN commission for, 170–1; UN Truce Commission, 272–6, 278, 282; Truce Supervision Organization (UNTSO), 4, 12, 121, 219, 230, 278–90, 425, 428 n., 432–3, 437–8; Mixed Armistice Commission (MAC), 278, 280–2, 284–6, 297; trusteeship proposals, 171, 348–9; proposed Arab state, 351 n., Jarring mission, 64–6
Palmer, Gen., 240
Panama, 170, 217, 219
Paraguay, 18, 41–2, 246
Pathet Lao, 314
Peace Keeping: defined, 1, 3–5; general analysis of, 5–12, 333–6, 432–8; financing of, 424–6; advance planning for, 28–32; prospects for, 424–8, 438–40; see also United Nations
Pearson, Lester, 2, 100, 103
Perez-Guerrero, M., 395
Perim, 8, 12, 134, 342–4, 397
Persia, 72 n.

Persian Gulf, 69, 70, 224, 392
Peru, 30, 150–1, 170, 240
Philippines, 10, 31–2, 127, 170, 378, 380
Pipinelis, Panayotis, 265
Plaza, Galo, 73, 78–81, 219
Poland: and Memel, 16; and Vilna, 17; and Corfu channel, 21; and Danzig, 41; and Indonesia, 45–6, 233; and Palestine, 61; and Upper Silesia, 127; and Korea, 128; and Laos, 203; and Greece, 210–11; Polish corridor, 351 n.; hostility to Spain, 373–4; German elections, 375; Gomulka coup, 381
Pondicherry, 251
Portugal: colonies, 5, 9, 250–4, 389, 398–399, 409, 411; and S.W. Africa, 171–2; and Goa, 251–2, 318, 436; and UN anti-colonialism, 388, 391, 401–4, 399 n.; and Rhodesia, 406–8, 427

Rault, V., 152
Red Cross, International Committee of, 71, 126, 198, 254, 328
Rhee, Syngman, 378
Rhodesia, 4, 12, 254, 392–3, 406–10, 437
Ribbing, Herbert de, 70, 85, 391
Rikye, Gen. I. J., 161, 242, 306, 311, 429 n.
Riley, Gen. William Edward, 283
Rolz-Bennett, J., 73, 85, 163, 265, 267
Roosevelt, Franklin D., 238
Roumania, 375
Rwanda-Urundi, 22, 67, 355
Ruhr, 18
Russia, see Soviet Union
Ruanda, 71, 410
Ryukyu Islands, 338–9

Saar, 18–19, 151–4
Sabah, see Borneo, North
Sakhalin south, 338
Sallal, Abdullah al-, 116
Samoa, Western, 22
San Marino, 315–16
Santo Domingo, 239, 241, 243–4
Sarawak, 10, 31–3, 128
Sarmento, Gen. S., 123
Saudi Arabia: and Yemen, 4, 11, 86–7, 109–16; and Buraimi, 69–70; and Syria-Turkey dispute, 214
Security Council: and Korea, 1, 197; use of veto, 2, 44–5, 51, 67, 99, 198, 200–1, 203–4, 210, 217, 219, 222–3, 233, 236, 251, 317, 324, 360, 374, 382, 426; and Rhodesia, 4, 5, 406–9; and Lebanon, 10; and Corfu channel, 21; and Kashmir, 25–7, 290–1; and Palestine, 30, 60–1, 64–5, 272–9, 284; and mediation, 37; and Indonesia, 43–9, 51, 233; and Bizerta base, 57–8; and Congo, 67, 355–7, 359–60, 422–3 n., 433; and Buraimi, 69; and Cyprus, 72, 76–7, 265, 321–4, 326–7, 329; and Cuba, 86; and Yemen, 87, 109–10, 112; and Suez war (1956), 99; and Indo-Pakistan war, 117, 119–20, 122; and Secretary-General's powers, 120, 261, 308; and demili-

tarized zones, 127 n.; and international government, 134, 344–5; and Trieste, 136–7, 139; and W. New Guinea, 158, 165; and Thailand mission, 199 n.; and Laos appeal, 200, 202–5, 316; and Cambodia, 206–7; and Greece, 209–11, 233; and Middle East, 213; and Lebanon, 215–19, 221, 224–5, 228; and Jordan, 229–30; and Guatemala, 235–7; and Dominica, 240–1, 243–6, 248; and S. Arabia, 249–50; and Portugal, 251, 253, 398–9; 405; S. & S.W. Africa, 255, 399, 401, 405, 436; and Israel borders, 262, 272–9, 281–5, 289; and 6-day war (June 1967), 287; and Suez Canal (1967), 288; and the cold war, 295; and UNEF, 296, 308, 310; and requests for UN forces, 317; and Spain, 373–4; and Czech coup (1948), 374; and Hungary, 382; and Oman, 390; and economic sanctions, 405–6; and Katanga secession, 412, 414, 416, 418; and peace-keeping, 426–7, 435, 439; see also General Assembly; United Nations
Senegal, 161 n., 253
Serbia, 182
Shalizi, A. S., 395
Sharm-el-Sheikh, 106–8, 297–300
Siam, see Thailand
Sikkim, 118
Silesia, Upper, 127
Simon, Sir John, 73 n.
Sinai Peninsula, 105–6, 133, 145, 298–301, 307, 309, 311
Singapore, 11, 31
Smith, Ian, 406, 408
Somalia, 89
Somaliland, French, 390
Somaliland, Italian, 23–4, 37 n., 339–40
South Africa: UN attitude to, 5, 9, 254–9, 318, 386–8, 400–6 n., 409–11, 427, 436; on Eritrea, 24; and S.W. Africa, 166, 171–2, 256–8, 387–8, 400–1; and Congo, 360; and anti-colonialism, 388, 398–9; and Rhodesia, 407–8
South East Asia Treaty Organization (SEATO), 83, 292
South West Africa, 166, 171, 256–8, 338, 387–9, 398, 400, 405; UN commissions on, 171, 256, 388, 400–1
Soviet Union: and Security Council, 1, 2 n.; use of veto, 2, 44–5, 67, 198, 200–1, 204, 217, 219, 222–3, 236, 251, 360, 374, 382; and Suez war (1956), 2, 97–8, 305, 433; ideology, 21, 431; and Italian colonies, 23, 339–40; and Kashmir, 26–8; and Palestine, 30, 61, 63, 66, 272, 274–9, 842, 298, 296, 349; and Indonesia, 44–5, 48, 51, 54–5, 233; support for Arabs, 66, 98, 284, 289, 296; and Congo, 67, 355–63; and Saudi Arabia, 69–70; and Cyprus, 75, 322–4, 329, 352; and UNEF, 102, 300, 305, 310, 425; and Yemen, 110, 437; and Indo-Pakistan war, 117–18, 120, 122; and Cuba, 125–6, 434; and Trieste, 137, 139–40; in Austria, 139; and Yugoslavia, 140;

Soviet Union—continued
  and W. New Guinea, 160; and S. W.
  Africa, 172, 400; and Manchuria, 185,
  187, 190; and Korea, 197-8, 376-8,
  380; and Indo-China, 199, 202-5,
  207; and Berlin, 208; and Greece,
  209-11, 233; support for Syria, 214;
  and Lebanon, 216, 218-19, 222-3, 225,
  437; and Guatemala, 234, 236; and
  Latin America, 237-8; and Dominica,
  240, 243-4, 248; and S. Arabia, 249-
  50; and Goa, 251-2; and Suez Canal,
  288; and Hungary, 316, 381-4;
  and appeals for UN help, 317; and
  Japanese possessions, 338; and Perim,
  343-4; and E. Europe, 366, 438; and
  Spain, 374; and Czechoslovakia, 374;
  and German elections, 375; and
  Nationalist China, 376; and S.
  Africa, 400; and Portugal, 405; and
  Rhodesia, 407-8; and Katanga, 414;
  and UN expenses, 424-5, 427-8; and
  UN peace-keeping, 424-7, 430-1,
  437, 439
Spaak, Paul-Henri, 415
Spain, 4, 98, 373-4, 389 n., 393
Spinelli, P. P., 112, 232
Stavropoulos, C., 401
Stevenson, Adlai, 241, 243, 252
Sudan, 23, 116, 229 n., 241, 355, 415
Suez Canal: blocked, 64-5, 98, 103-4,
  106, 116; Company nationalized,
  95-7, 262; proposed international
  control, 146; UN observers, 288
Suez War (1956), 2, 64, 69-70, 95-9,
  102-5, 122, 146, 215, 222, 286, 295,
  304, 306, 432, 437
Sukarno, President I. H., 31, 158, 162, 165
Supreme Allied Council, 182-3
Sweden: and Aaland Is., 16; and Palestine, 30, 274-5; and UNEF, 99, 300;
  and Korea, 128, 197; and Balkans,
  212; and Lebanon, 217-19, 221-2,
  226-7; and Cyprus force, 325-6, 328;
  and Congo force, 355; and UN forces,
  430 n.
Syria, 143; and Lebanon, 4, 10, 216, 219-
  20; and Israel, 61, 261, 272, 274-5,
  278, 280-1, 283, 285-7, 289, 306,
  310-11, 438; and Suez Canal, 65;
  and Yemen, 116; and 1957 Turkish
  conflict, 214; part of UAR, 215,
  306 n.; and 6-day war (June 1967),
  287; and Nationalist China, 376; and
  Korea, 378; see also United Arab
  Republic

Taiwan, 82, 376
Tanganyika, 366
Tashkent, 28, 122, 124
Tassara-Gonzales, Gen. Luis, 291
Thailand (Siam), 83-5, 127-8, 199-200,
  314, 380
Thalmann, E. A., 145
Tiberias (Galilee), Lake, 283, 286, 350
Tiran, Straits of, 106-8, 299, 300, 310-11
Tito, President Josip Brod, 140
Togo, 22, 161
Transjordan, see Jordan

Trieste, 11, 136-42
Trujillo, Gen. Rafael L., 238, 242 n.
Truman doctrine, 210-11
Trusteeship Council, 142-3
Tshombe, Moise, 4, 67, 254, 357, 363,
  411-23
Tunisia: and Bizerta base, 57-60, 414 n.;
  and Laos, 202; and Congo force, 355,
  360, 413 n.; and Hungary, 383; 1952
  draft resolution on, 386
Tuomioja, S. S., 73, 205
Turkey: and Mosul, 16; and Palestine,
  61; and Cyprus, 72-5, 77-81, 264-5,
  267, 321-5, 329, 332-3, 335, 352; and
  Truman doctrine, 210; and Syria,
  214; and Guatemala, 236; and Goa,
  251; and Korea, 379 n.-80
Tutsi people, 71, 410

U Thant (Sec.-General), 418; and
  Malaysia, 31-3; and W. New Guinea,
  57, 159, 161; and Vietnam, 81; and
  Thai-Cambodia dispute, 85; and
  Cuba crisis, 86, 125; and Yemen, 87,
  109, 112; and Indo-Pakistan war, 117,
  120-4; powers of, 120; and Dominica,
  241, 247; and Portugal, 253-4; and
  Cyprus, 266, 326, 352; and Suez
  Canal, 288; and UNEF, 307-10; and
  Katanga, 418, 420
Uganda, 366
Ukraine, 43, 48, 209, 233, 279, 378-9
United Arab Republic: and Lebanon, 4,
  216-18, 225; and Yemen, 11, 86, 108-
  14; and Suez Canal, 65; and Congo,
  68, 413; and 6-day war (June 1967),
  116; and Indo-Pakistan war, 117; and
  W. New Guinea, 158; formed, 215,
  306 n.; proposed UN presence, 231;
  and S. Arabia, 250; and Israel, 289,
  438; and Aden, 389 n.; and UNEF,
  425; see also Egypt; Syria
United Nations: peace-keeping role, 1,
  3-5, 7-10, 424-40; Afro-Asian bloc,
  19-20, 431; and anti-colonialism, 22-4,
  45, 51, 154-5, 157, 248-52, 257, 259,
  356 n., 385, 388, 397-8, 404-5, 440;
  and arms control, 91-3, 129; trusteeship system, 155, 256, 338-41; and
  sanctions, 180, 402-5; and major
  powers, 182, 207, 270, 376, 434-6;
  and OAS 247; collective security,
  1-2, 5 n., 402 n; and Financing, 424-6,
  427-8, 435; Military Adviser, 429 n.,
  430 n., 437 n. See also General
  Assembly; Security Council.
    Factors affecting investigation, 15-
  16, 19-21, 34-5; affecting mediation,
  36-9, 42-3, 52-6, 68, 81-2, 87-8;
  affecting supervision, 90-5, 124, 126-9;
  affecting administration, 130-6, 147-9,
  154, 169-70, 173-4; affecting accusation, 177-82, 184-5, 193-6, 248,
  258-9; affecting sedation, 260-1,
  268-72; affecting obstruction, 294-5,
  313-15, 316-20; affecting refrigeration, 337, 341-2, 345-8, 354, 364-8;
  affecting invalidation, 371-3, 385, 390;
  affecting coercion, 402-6, 410-11

United Nations Commission for the
    Unification and Rehabilitation of
    Korea (UNCURK), *see* Korea
United Nations Commission on Korea
    (UNCOK), *see* Korea
United Nations Emergency Force
    (UNEF), 2, 3, 5, 9, 12, 98–108, 230,
    295–314, 318–20, 332–4, 364, 422,
    424–5, 431
United Nations Emergency Force, 2, 3, 5,
    9, 12, 98–108, 230, 295–314, 318–20,
    332–4, 364, 422, 424–5, 431
United Nations Force in Cyprus
    (UNFICYP), *see* Cyprus
United Nations India-Pakistan Observa-
    tion Mission (UNIPOM), *see* Indo-
    Pakistan War
United Nations Military Observer Group
    in India and Pakistan (UNMOGIP),
    see Kashmir
United Nations Observer Group in
    Lebanon (UNOGIL), *see* Lebanon
United Nations Security Force, *see*, New
    Guinea West
United Nations Special Mission on Aden,
    see Aden (and Arabia, South)
United Nations Special Committee on the
    Balkans (UNSCOB), *see* Balkans
United Nations Special Committee on
    Palestine, *see* Palestine
United Nations Temporary Commission
    on Korea (UNTCOK), *see* Korea
United Nations Temporary Executive
    Authority (UNTEA), *see* New Guinea,
    West
United Nations Truce Commission for
    Palestine, *see* Palestine
United Nations Truce Supervision Organ-
    ization (UNTSO), *see* Palestine
United Nations Yemen Observation
    Mission (UNYOM), *see* Yemen
United States: and Suez war (1956), 2,
    97–9; cold war, 21; and Italian
    colonies, 23, 339–40; and Kashmir,
    25–6 n., 28, 291; and Palestine, 30,
    61–3, 66, 272, 274–6, 278; and
    Indonesia, 45–8, 51, 54–5, 57;
    and defence of Europe, 46; 48, and
    Bizerta, 58; and Buraimi, 69–70; and
    Cyprus, 75, 267, 322–3, 325–6;
    and Mediterranean interests, 75; and
    Vietnam, 81, 206; airmen imprisoned
    by China, 82–3; S. and S. W. Africa,
    172, 400–1, 405–6; and Thailand, 83,
    313; and Cuba, 86, 125–6, 317, 434;
    and Aswan dam, 95; and UNEF,
    99–100, 104, 107, 262–3, 295, 305;
    and Yemen, 109, 112; and Indo-
    Pakistan war, 118–19; and Trieste,
    136–9, 141; and Leticia, 150; and W.

New Guinea, 157, 159, 162; and UN
    forces, 162; and Manchuria, 186–8,
    194; and Korea, 197–8, 376–9; and
    bacteriological warfare, 198; Indo-
    China and S. E. Asian security, 199–
    202; and Laos appeal, 200–5, 316;
    and Cambodia, 206–7; and Greece,
    209–13; Truman doctrine, 210–11;
    support for Turkey, 214; and
    Lebanon, 215–16, 218, 220–9, 433;
    and Guatemala, 234–7, 317; and
    OAS, 234–8, 243; and Dominican
    republic, 238–48, 436; and veto, 248;
    and S. Arabia, 249; and Goa, 251;
    and Portuguese colonies, 253, 398;
    and Israel borders, 262–3, 289, 305,
    348–9; and Japanese mandates, 338;
    and Ryukyu and Bonin Is., 9; and
    Congo, 355–8, 415, 421; and Latin
    America, 366, 438; and Spain,
    374; and 1948 Czech coup, 374; and
    German elections, 375; and Hungary,
    382; and UN anti-colonialism, 388,
    393; and Oman, 391; and Katanga,
    414, 418–22; and UN peace-keeping,
    426–8; and UN finances, 427–8 n.,
    435
Uruguay, 30, 240, 243, 383

Vance, Cyrus, 265–7
Vatican, 315
Venezuela, 240
Viet Cong, 173, 206–7
Vietnam, 81, 128, 173, 200–4, 206–7, 251,
    314, 316, 427, 430, 439
Vilna, 17–18

Waithayakon, Prince Wan, 383
Warsaw Pact, 382
Washington Treaty (1922), 188
Welensky, Sir Roy, 254
Wessin, Gen. Elias Wessin y, 238, 246
Western European Union, 129, 154
Williams, Eric, 365

Yalu river, 197
Yemen, 4, 11, 70, 86–7, 108–17, 342–4;
    UN Observation Mission, 110–15,
    437; and S. Arabian Federation, 249–
    50, 396
    People's Republic of Yemen, South-
    ern, 344, 396–7

Yugoslavia: and Palestine, 30; and
    UNEF, 99, 300, 309; and Yemen,
    111–12; and Indo-Pakistan war, 117;
    and Trieste, 136–41; and Cominform,
    140, 212–13, 381; and Albania, 182–4;
    and Greece, 209–12; and Congo, 413

Zellweger, E., 205